Stanley Gibbons

GREAT BRITAIN
CONCISE
STAMP CATALOGUE

2004 Edition

GW00361547

Stanley Gibbons Ltd
London and Ringwood

By Appointment to Her Majesty The Queen
Stanley Gibbons Ltd., London
Philatelists

Published by **Stanley Gibbons Publications**
Editorial, Sales Offices and Distribution Centre:
Parkside, Christchurch Road, Ringwood,
Hants BH24 3SH

First Edition — May 1986
Second Edition — May 1987
Third Edition — May 1988
Fourth Edition — May 1989
Fifth Edition — May 1990
Sixth Edition — May 1991
Seventh Edition — May 1992
Eighth Edition — April 1993
Ninth Edition — April 1994
Tenth Edition — April 1995
Eleventh Edition — April 1996
Twelfth Edition — April 1997
Thirteenth Edition — April 1998
Fourteenth Edition — April 1999
Fifteenth Edition — May 2000
Sixteenth Edition — April 2001
Seventeenth Edition — April 2002
Eighteenth Edition — April 2003
Nineteenth Edition — April 2004

© Stanley Gibbons Ltd. 2004

ISBN: 0–85259–562–X

Item No. 2887 (04)

Origination by Polestar Applied Solutions Ltd
Printed and bound by Polestar Wheatons Ltd, Exeter.

THE GREAT BRITAIN CONCISE CATALOGUE

2004 Edition

The *Concise Catalogue*, now in its 19th year of publication, has established itself as an essential guide for the "one-country" collector of Great Britain.

The popularity of Great Britain stamps continues to grow — the *Concise Catalogue* supplies the information to enhance your collection.

- All issues from the Penny Black of 1840 to 26 February 2004 including Regional, Postage Due, Official and Postal Fiscal stamps.
- All different stamp designs are illustrated.
- Every basic stamp listed, including those with different watermarks or perforations and those showing graphite lines or phosphor bands.
- Unmounted mint and mounted mint prices quoted for 1887 "Jubilee" series and all King Edward VII and King George V issues.
- Missing colours, missing embossing, watermark errors, imperforate errors and phosphor omitted varieties from those stamps normally issued with phosphor bands.
- Gutter Pairs and "Traffic light" Gutter Pairs listed in mint sets.
- First Day Covers for Special Issues from 1924 and for King Edward VIII and King George VI definitives. For the present reign the coverage also extends to Sponsored Booklet panes and Regionals. All British Post Office special First Day of Issue postmarks are illustrated and priced on cover.
- Post Office Picture Cards (PHQ cards) are priced as sets, both mint and used with First Day of Issue postmarks.
- Presentation, Collector and Gift Packs, including the scarce versions with foreign inscriptions.
- Quick-reference diagrams for listed Machin decimal booklet panes.
- Design Index for Commemorative and Special Stamps after the Philatelic Information Section.
- Machin and commemorative underprints given separate catalogue numbers.
- Post Office Yearbooks.
- Royal Mail Postage Labels priced in mint or used sets and on British Post Office First Day Covers.
- Notes on Postage Due bisects based on research by Mr. P. Frost.
- Wartime issues for the Channel Islands.
- Separate section for Post Office Stamp Booklets with dated editions of King George VI listed separately.
- New listing of Post Office Label Sheets, popularly known as 'Generic Smilers'.
- Helpful introductory section providing definitions and guidance for the collector and including all watermark illustrations shown together to assist identification.
- Separate section for Postmaster and U.P.U. Specimen overprints.
- Addresses for specialist philatelic societies covering Great Britain stamps.
- Recently discovered errors and varieties listed. See Nos. 254Ea, 2187aa, 187ba, 2337ab, 2348ab, 2424ab, O11b.
- We would like to thank all those who have assisted in the compilation of this catalogue. Special thanks for amendments to this edition are due to Messrs D. Allen, P. Mansfield, A. Musry and J. Townend.

Hugh Jefferies
Lesley Brine

Stanley Gibbons Holdings Plc.

STANLEY GIBBONS LTD, STANLEY GIBBONS AUCTIONS

399 STRAND, LONDON WC2R 0LX

Auction Room and Specialist Departments. Open Monday–Friday, 9.30 a.m. to 5.00 p.m.
Shop: Open Monday–Friday 9 a.m. to 5.30 p.m. and Saturday 9.30 a.m. to 5.30 p.m.
Telephone: 020 7836 8444, Fax: 020 7836 7342, E-mail: enquiries@stanleygibbons.co.uk and
Internet: www.stanleygibbons.com for all departments.

STANLEY GIBBONS PUBLICATIONS

PARKSIDE, CHRISTCHURCH ROAD, RINGWOOD, HANTS BH24 3SH

Telephone: 01425 472363 (24 hour answerphone service), **Fax: 01425 470247** and
E-mail: info@stanleygibbons.co.uk
Publications Mail Order, FREEPHONE **0800 611622.** Monday–Friday 8.30 a.m. to 5.00 p.m.

FRASER'S

399 STRAND, LONDON WC2R 0LX

Open Monday–Friday 9.00 a.m. to 5.30 p.m. and Saturday 10.00 a.m. to 4.00 p.m.
Telephone: 020 7836 8444, Fax: 020 7836 7342, E-mail: info@frasersautographs.co.uk and
Internet: www.frasersautographs.com

Great Britain Philatelic Societies

The Great Britain Philatelic Society. Hon. Membership Secretary: A. G. Lajer, The Old Post Office, Davis Way, Hurst, Berkshire, RG10 0TR.

The British Decimal Stamps Study Circle. The Secretary: Mr. D. Threadgold, 39 Scrub Rise, Billericay, CM12 9PG.

The Great Britain Decimal Stamp Book Study Circle. Hon. Membership Secretary: A. J. Wilkins, 3 Buttermere Close, Brierley Hill, West Midlands, DY5 3SD.

The Great Britain Collectors' Club. Secretary: Mr. Parker A. Bailey, 17 Greenwood Road, Merrimack, NH03054, U.S.A.

Contents

Queen Victoria Issue	1
Key to Line-engraved Issues	6
Key to Surface-printed Issues 1855–83	13
Key to Surface-printed Issues 1880–1900	18
King Edward VII Issues	23
King George V Issues	25
King Edward VIII Issues	34
King George VI Issues	34
Queen Elizabeth II Issues	39
Decimal Machin Index	79
Decimal Machin Multi-value Coil Index	84
Decimal Machin Booklet Pane Guide	85
Decimal Machin with Elliptical Perforations Index	189
Royal Mail Postage Labels	269
Regional Issues	269
Channel Islands: General Issue 1948	269
England	269
Northern Ireland	270
Scotland	274
Wales	278
Guernsey	282
Isle of Man	283
Jersey	283
Postage Due Stamps	284
Official Stamps	287
Postal Fiscal Stamps	289
Postmaster and U.P.U. Specimen Overprints	292
Post Office Stamp Booklets	294
King Edward VII	294
King George V	294
King Edward VIII	298
King George VI	298
Queen Elizabeth II	302
I. £.s.d. Booklets 1953–70	302
II. Decimal Booklets 1971 onwards	311
A. Stitched Booklets	311
B. Folded Booklets	319
Christmas Booklets 1978–86	334
Greetings Booklet 1989	336
III. Barcode Booklets	337
C. Machin Booklets 1987 onwards	337
D. Machin NVI Booklets 1989 onwards	341
E. Machin Penny Black Anniversary Booklet, 1990	348
F. Greetings Booklets 1990–98	349
G. Christmas Booklets 1990 onwards	351
H. Self-adhesive NVI Booklets 1993 onwards	354
I. Self-adhesive Booklets with face values 2002 onwards	356
J. Self-adhesive NVI Special and Machin Booklets 2001 onwards	357
Post Office Label Sheets	358

STANLEY GIBBONS PUBLICATIONS

OVERSEAS REPRESENTATION

Stanley Gibbons Publications are represented overseas by the following sole distributors (*), distributors (**) or licensees (***).

Australia
Lighthouse Philatelic (Aust.) Pty Ltd*
Locked Bag 5900
Botany DC
New South Wales 2019
Australia

Stanley Gibbons (Australia) Pty Ltd***
Level 6
36 Clarence Street
Sydney
New South Wales 2000
Australia

Belgium and Luxembourg**
Davo
c/o Philac
Rue du Midi 48
Bruxelles 1000
Belgium

Canada*
Lighthouse Publications (Canada) Ltd
255 Duke Street
Montreal
Quebec
Canada H3C 2M2

Denmark**
Samlerforum/Davo
Ostergade 3
DK7470 Karup
Denmark

Finland**
Davo
c/o Kapylan Merkkiky
Pohjolankatu 1
00610 Helsinki
Finland

France*
Davo France (Casteilla)
10 Rue Leon Foucault
78184 St. Quentin Yvelines Cesex
France

Hong Kong**
Po-on Stamp Service
GPO Box 2498
Hong Kong

Israel**
Capital Stamps
PO Box 3769
Jerusalem 91036
Israel

Italy*
Ernesto Marini Srl
Via Struppa 300
I-16165 Genova GE
Italy

Japan**
Japan Philatelic Co Ltd
PO Box 2
Suginami-Minami
Tokyo
Japan

Netherlands*
Davo Publications
PO Box 411
7400 AK Deventer
Netherlands

New Zealand***
Mowbray Collectables
PO Box 80
Wellington
New Zealand

Norway**
Davo Norge A/S
PO Box 738 Sentrum
N-01 05 Oslo
Norway

Singapore**
Stamp Inc Collectibles Pte Ltd
10 Ubi Crescent
01-43 Ubi Tech Park
Singapore 408564

Sweden*
Chr Winther Sorensen AB
Box 43
S-310 Knaered
Sweden

Switzerland**
Phila Service
Burgstrasse 160
CH4125 Riehen
Switzerland

PRICES

The prices quoted in this catalogue are the estimated selling prices of Stanley Gibbons Ltd at the time of publication. They are, *unless it is specifically stated otherwise*, for examples in fine condition for the issue concerned. Superb examples are worth more; those of a lower quality considerably less.

All prices are subject to change without prior notice and Stanley Gibbons Ltd may from time to time offer stamps below catalogue price. Individual low value stamps sold at 399, Strand are liable to an additional handling charge. Purchasers of new issues are asked to note that the prices charged for them contain an element for the service rendered and so may exceed the prices shown when the stamps are subsequently catalogued.

No guarantee is given to supply all stamps priced, since it is not possible to keep every catalogued item in stock.

Quotation of prices. The prices in the left-hand column are for unused stamps and those in the right-hand column are for used.

A dagger (†) denotes that the item listed does not exist in that condition and a blank, or dash, that it exists, or may exist, but no market price is known.

Prices are expressed in pounds and pence sterling. One pound comprises 100 pence (£1 = 100p).

The method of notation is as follows: pence in numerals (e.g. 5 denotes five pence); pounds and pence up to £100, in numerals (e.g. 4·25 denotes four pounds and twenty-five pence); prices above £100 expressed in whole pounds with the "£" sign shown.

Unused and Used stamps. The prices for unused stamps of Queen Victoria issued before 1887 are for lightly hinged examples. Unused stamps of the 1887 "Jubilee" issue and from the reigns of King Edward VII and King George V are priced in both unmounted and mounted condition. Unused prices for King Edward VIII to Queen Elizabeth II issues are for unmounted mint (though when not available, mounted mint stamps are often supplied at a lower price). Prices for used stamps are for postally used examples.

Prices quoted for bisects on cover or on large piece are for those dated during the period officially authorised.

Minimum price. The minimum price quoted is 10 pence. For individual stamps prices between 10 pence and 50 pence are provided as a guide for catalogue users. The lowest price *charged* for individual stamps or sets purchased from Stanley Gibbons Ltd is 50p.

Set prices. Set prices are generally for one of each value, excluding shades and varieties, but including major colour changes. Where there are alternative shades, etc., the cheapest is usually included. The number of stamps in the set is always stated for clarity.

The mint prices for sets containing *se-tenant* pieces are based on the prices quoted for such combinations, and not on those for individual stamps. The used set price is for single stamps.

Used sets containing *se-tenant* combinations are usually worth the same as the prices quoted for the cheapest First Day Cover.

Gutter Pairs. These, and traffic light gutter pairs, are priced as complete sets.

Used on Cover prices. To assist collectors, cover prices are quoted in a third column for postage and Official stamps issued in the reign of Queen Victoria and in boxed notes for the 1887 "Jubilee" issue and for King Edward VII and King George V stamps.

The cover should be of non-philatelic origin, bearing the correct postal rate for the period and distance involved and cancelled with the markings normal to the offices concerned. Purely philatelic items have a cover value only slightly greater than the catalogue value for the corresponding used stamps. This applies generally to those high-value stamps used philatelically rather than in the normal course of commerce.

Oversized covers, difficult to accommodate on an album page, should be reckoned as worth little more than the corresponding value of the used stamps. The condition of a cover affects its value. Except for "wreck covers", serious damage or soiling reduce the value where the postal markings and stamps are ordinary ones. Conversely, visual appeal adds to the value and this can include freshness of appearance, important addresses, old-fashioned but legible handwriting, historic town-names, etc. The prices quoted are a base on which further value would be added to take account of the cover's postal historical importance in demonstrating such things as unusual, scarce or emergency cancels, interesting routes, significant postal markings, combination usage, the development of postal rates, and so on.

First Day Cover prices. Prices are quoted for commemorative first day covers from 1924 British Empire Exhibition pair onwards. These prices are for special covers (from 1937) franked with complete sets and cancelled by ordinary operational postmarks to the end of 1962 or the various standard "First Day of Issue" markings from 1963.

Prices are provided for King Edward VIII and King George VI definitives on plain covers with operational postmarks of the first day of issue. For some values special covers also exist and these are worth more than the prices quoted.

The Philatelic Bureau and other special "First Day of Issue" postmarks provided by the Post Office since 1963 are listed under each issue. Prices quoted are for these postmarks used on illustrated covers (from 1964 those produced by the Post Office), franked with complete sets.

The British Post Office did not introduce special First Day of Issue postmarks for definitive issues until the first instalment of the Machin £sd series, issued 5 June 1967, although "First Day" treatment had been provided for some Regional stamps from 8 June 1964 onwards. Prices for the First Day Covers from 1952 to 1966, showing definitive stamps as indicated, used on illustrated envelopes and postmarked with operational cancellations.

From 1967 onwards the prices quoted are for stamps as indicated, used on illustrated envelopes and postmarked with special First Day of Issue handstamps. Other definitives issued during this period were not accepted for "First Day" treatment by the British Post Office.

Guarantee

All stamps are guaranteed genuine originals in the following terms:

If not as described, and returned by the purchaser, we undertake to refund the price paid to us in the original transaction. If any stamp is certified as genuine by the Expert Committee of the Royal Philatelic Society, London, or by B.P.A. Expertising Ltd, the purchaser shall not be entitled to make any claim against us for any error, omission or mistake in such certificate.

Consumers' statutory rights are not affected by the above guarantee.

The recognised Expert Committees in this country are those of the Royal Philatelic Society, 41 Devonshire Place, London W1G 6JY, and B.P.A. Expertising Ltd, P.O. Box 137, Leatherhead, Surrey KT22 0RG. They do not undertake valuations under any circumstances and fees are payable for their services.

CONTACTING THE CATALOGUE EDITOR

The Editor is always interested in hearing from people who have new information which will improve or correct the Catalogue. As a general rule he must see and examine the actual stamps before they can be considered for listing; photographs or photocopies are insufficent evidence.

Submissions should be made in writing to the Catalogue Editor, Stanley Gibbons Publications. The cost of return postage for items submitted is appreciated, and this should include the registration fee if required.

Where information is solicited purely for the benefit of the enquirer, the editor cannot undertake to reply if the answer is already contained in these published notes or if return postage is omitted. Written communications are greatly preferred to enquiries by telephone and the editor regrets that he or his staff cannot see personal callers without a prior appointment being made. Correspondence may be subject to delay during the production period of each new edition.

Please note that the following classes of material are outside the scope of this Catalogue:

(a) Non-postal revenue or fiscal stamps.
(b) Postage stamps used fiscally.
(c) Local carriage labels and private local issues.
(d) Punctured postage stamps (perfins).
(e) Telegraph stamps.
(f) Bogus or phantom stamps.
(g) Railway or airline letter fee stamps, bus or road transport company labels.
(h) Postal stationery cut-outs.
(i) All types of non-postal labels and souvenirs.
(j) Documentary labels for the postal service, e.g. registration, recorded delivery, airmail etiquettes, etc.
(k) Privately applied embellishments to official issues and privately commissioned items generally.
(l) Stamps for training postal staff.

> We regret we do not give opinions as to the genuineness of stamps, nor do we identify stamps or number them by our Catalogue.

GENERAL ABBREVIATIONS

Alph	Alphabet
Anniv	Anniversary
Brt	Bright (colour)
C,c	Chalky paper
C.	Overprinted in carmine
Des	Designer; designed
Dp	Deep (colour)
Eng	Engraver; engraved
Horiz	Horizontal; horizontally
Imp, Imperf	Imperforate
Inscr	Inscribed
L	Left
Litho	Lithographed
Lt	Light (colour)
mm	Millimetres
MS	Miniature sheet
O,o	Ordinary paper
Opt(d)	Overprint(ed)
P, Perf	Perforated
Photo	Photogravure
Pl	Plate
Pr	Pair
Ptd	Printed
Ptg	Printing
PVA	Polyvinyl alcohol (gum)
R	Right
R.	Row
Recess	Recess-printed
T	Type
Typo	Typographed
Un	Unused
Us	Used
Vert	Vertical; vertically
W or wmk	Watermark
Wmk s	Watermark sideways

(†) = Does not exist.

(—) (or blank price column) = Exists, or may exist, but no market price is known.

/ between colours means "on" and the colour following is that of the paper on which the stamp is printed.

PRINTERS

B.W.	Bradbury Wilkinson & Co, Ltd.
D.L.R.	De La Rue & Co, Ltd, London, and (from 1961) Bogota, Colombia. De La Rue Security Print (formerly Harrison & Sons Ltd) from 8 September 1997.
Enschedé	Joh. Enschedé en Zonen, Haarlem, Netherlands.
Harrison	Harrison & Sons, Ltd, High Wycombe.
J.W.	John Waddington Security Print, Ltd, Leeds.
P.B.	Perkins Bacon Ltd, London.
Questa	Questa Colour Security Printers, Ltd.
Waterlow	Waterlow & Sons, Ltd, London.
Walsall	Walsall Security Printers, Ltd.

PHILATELIC INFORMATION

Catalogue Numbers

The catalogue number appears in the extreme left column. The boldface Type numbers in the next column are merely cross-reference to illustrations. Catalogue numbers in the *Gibbons Stamp Monthly* Supplements are provisional only and may need to be altered when the lists are consolidated.

Our Catalogue numbers are universally recognised in specifying stamps and as a hallmark of status.

Inverted and other watermark varieties incorporate "Wi", etc., within the number. Other items which appear in this Catalogue but not *Part 1 (British Commonwealth) Catalogue*, incorporate "Ea", etc.

Catalogue Illustrations

Stamps and first day postmarks are illustrated at three-quarters linear size. Stamps not illustrated are the same size and format as the value shown, unless otherwise indicated. Overprints, surcharges and watermarks are normally actual size. Illustrations of varieties are often enlarged to show the detail. Illustrations of miniature sheets are half linear size and their dimensions, in millimetres, are stated with the width given first.

Designers

Designers' names are quoted where known, though space precludes naming every individual concerned in the production of a set. In particular, photographers supplying material are usually named only when they also make an active contribution in the design stage; posed photographs of reigning monarchs are, however, an exception to this rule.

Printing Errors

Errors in printing are of major interest to this Catalogue. Authenticated items meriting consideration would include: background, centre or frame inverted or omitted; centre or subject transposed; error of colour; error or omission of value; double prints and impressions; printed both sides; and so on. Designs *tête-bêche*, whether intentionally or by accident, are listable. Colours only partially omitted are not listed. However, stamps with embossing, phosphor or both omitted and stamps printed on the gummed side are included.

Printing technology has radically improved over the years, during which time photogravure and lithography have become predominant. Varieties nowadays are more in the nature of flaws which are almost always outside the scope of this book.

In no catalogue, however, do we list such items as: dry prints, kiss prints, doctor-blade flaws, colour shifts or registration flaws (unless they lead to the complete omission of a colour from an individual stamp), lithographic ring flaws, and so on. Neither do we recognise fortuitous happenings like paper creases or confetti flaws.

Paper Types

All stamps listed are deemed to be on "ordinary" paper of the wove type and white in colour; only departures from this are normally mentioned.

A coloured paper is one that is coloured right through (front and back of the stamp). In the Catalogue the colour of the paper is given in *italics*, thus:

purple/*yellow* = purple design on yellow paper.

Papers have been made specially white in recent years by, for example, a very heavy coating of chalk. We do not classify shades of whiteness of paper as distinct varieties.

The availability of many postage stamps for revenue purposes made necessary some safeguard against the illegitimate re-use of stamps with removable cancellations. This was at first secured by using fugitive inks and later by printing on chalky (chalk-surfaced) paper, both of which made it difficult to remove any form of obliteration without also damaging the stamp design. We have indicated the existence of the papers by the letters "O" (ordinary) and "C" (chalky) after the description of all stamps where the chalky paper may be found. Where no indication is given the paper is "ordinary".

Our chalky paper is specifically one which shows a black mark when touched with a silver wire. Stamps on chalk-surfaced paper can easily lose this coating through immersion in water.

Perforation Measurement

The gauge of a perforation is the number of holes in a length of 2 cm.

The Gibbons *Instanta* gauge is the standard for measuring perforations. The stamp is viewed against a dark background with the transparent gauge put on top of it. Though the gauge measures to decimal accuracy, perforations read from it are generally quoted in the Catalogue to the nearest half. For example:

Just over perf $12\frac{3}{4}$ to just under $13\frac{1}{4}$	= perf 13
Perf $13\frac{1}{4}$ exactly, rounded up	= perf $13\frac{1}{2}$
Just over perf $13\frac{1}{4}$ to just under $13\frac{3}{4}$	= perf $13\frac{1}{2}$
Perf $13\frac{3}{4}$ exactly, rounded up	= perf 14

However, where classification depends on it, actual quarter-perforations are quoted. Perforations are usually abbreviated (and spoken) as follows, though sometimes they may be spelt out for clarity.

P 14: perforated alike on all sides (read: "perf 14").

P 14 x 15: the first figure refers to top and bottom, the second to left and right sides (read: "perf 14 by 15"). This is a compound perforation.

Such headings as "*P* 13 x 14 (*vert*) and *P* 14 x 13 (*horiz*)" indicate which perforations apply to which stamp format—vertical or horizontal.

From 1992 onwards most definitive and greetings stamps from both sheets and booklets occur with a large elliptical (oval) hole inserted in each line of vertical perforations as a security measure. The £10 definitive, No. 1658, is unique in having two such holes in the horizontal perforations.

Elliptical Perforations

Perforation Errors

Authenticated errors, where a stamp normally perforated is accidentally issued imperforate, are listed provided no traces of perforations (blind holes or indentations) remain. They must be provided as pairs, both stamps wholly imperforate, and are only priced in that form.

Numerous part-perforated stamps have arisen from the introduction of the Jumelle Press. This has a rotary perforator with rows of pins on one drum engaging with holes on another. Engagement is only gradual when the perforating unit is started up or stopped, giving rise to perforations "fading out", a variety mentioned above as not listed.

Stamps from the Jumelle printings sometimes occur imperforate between stamp and sheet margin. Such errors are not listed in this catalogue, but are covered by the volumes of the *Great Britain Specialised Catalogue*.

Pairs described as "imperforate between" have the line of perforations between the two stamps omitted.

Imperf between (*horiz pair*): a horizontal pair of stamps with perfs all around the edges but none between the stamps.

Imperf between (*vert pair*): a vertical pair of stamps with perfs all around the edges but none between the stamps.

Imperf between   Imperf horizontally
(vertical pair)   (vertical pair)

Where several of the rows have escaped perforation the resulting varieties are listable. Thus:

Imperf vert (horiz pair): a horizontal pair of stamps perforated at top and bottom; all three vertical directions are imperf—the two outer edges and between the stamps.

Imperf horiz (vert pair): a vertical pair perforated at left and right edges; all three horizontal directions are imperf—the top, bottom and between the stamps.

Varieties of double, misplaced or partial perforation caused by error or machine malfunction are not listable, neither are freaks, such as perforations placed diagonally from paper folds, nor missing holes caused by broken pins.

Phosphor Issues

Machines which sort mail electronically have been introduced progressively and the British Post Office issued the first stamps specially marked for electronic sorting in 1957. This first issue had easily visible graphite lines printed on the back beneath the gum (see Nos. 561/6). They were issued in the Southampton area where the experiment was carried out.

The graphite lines were replaced by phosphor bands, activated by ultra-violet light. The bands are printed on the front of the stamps and show as a matt surface against the usual smooth or shiny appearance of the untreated surface of the paper. The bands show clearly in the top or bottom horizontal margins of the sheet.

The first phosphor issues appeared in 1959 (see Nos. 599/609) and these stamps also had graphite lines on the back. Further details will be found in the listings above No. 599 and 619. From 1962 onwards most commemoratives were issued in versions with or without bands. From 1967 all commemorative stamps had phosphor bands, but from 1972 they were replaced by "all-over" phosphor covering the entire area of the stamp.

After a considerable period of development a special paper was produced in which the phosphor had been incorporated into the coating. From 15 August 1979 to April 1996 phosphorised paper was accepted for use generally, replacing phosphor bands on most issues for all values except the second class letter rate. Phosphorised paper can only be identified by ultra-violet light. The Stanley Gibbons Uvitec Micro ultra-violet lamp is firmly recommended for use in identifying the phosphor stamps listed in this Catalogue. *Warning.* Never stare at the lighted lamp but follow the manufacturer's instructions. Phosphor bands were re-introduced for all issues from April 1996.

During the years 1967 to 1972, when all issues, except the high values, should have shown phosphor bands, a number of stamps appeared with them omitted in error. These varieties are listed in this Catalogue. Stamps with "all-over" phosphor omitted can only be detected by the use of an ultra-violet lamp and these varieties are listed in the Stanley Gibbons *Great Britain Specialised Catalogue*. Note that prices are for unmounted mint examples only. Varieties such as double bands, misplaced or printed on the back are not listed in this Catalogue.

Gum Description

All stamps listed are assumed to have gum of some kind and original gum (o.g.) means that which was present on the stamp as issued to the public. Deleterious climates and the presence of certain chemicals can cause gum to crack and, with early stamps, even make the paper deteriorate. Unscrupulous fakers are adept in removing it and regumming the stamp to meet the unreasoning demand often made for "full o.g." in cases where such a thing is virtually impossible.

The gum normally used on stamps has been gum arabic until the late 1960's when synthetic adhesives were introduced. Harrison and Sons Ltd for instance use *polyvinyl alcohol*, known to philatelists as PVA (see note above SG723).

Colour Identification

The 200 colours most used for stamp identification are given in the Stanley Gibbons Stamp Colour Key. The Catalogue has used the Colour Key as a standard for describing new issues for some years. The names are also introduced as lists are rewritten, though exceptions are made for those early issues where traditional names have become universally established.

In compound colour names the second is the predominant one, thus:

orange-red = a red tending towards orange.

red-orange = an orange containing more red than usual.

When comparing actual stamps with colour samples in the Colour Key, view in a good north daylight (or its best substitute: fluorescent "colour-matching" light). Sunshine is not recommended. Choose a solid portion of the stamp design; if available, marginal markings such as solid bars of colour or colour check dots are helpful. Shading lines in the design can be misleading as they appear lighter than solid colour. Furthermore, the listings refer to colours as issued: they may deteriorate into something different through the passage of time.

Shades are particularly significant when they can be linked to specific printings. In general, shades need to be quite marked to fall within the scope of this Catalogue.

Modern colour printing by lithography is prone to marked differences of shade, even within a single run, and variations can occur within the same sheet. Such shades are not listed.

Errors of Colour

Major colour errors in stamps or overprints which qualify for listing are: wrong colours; albinos (colourless impressions), where these have Expert Committee certificates; colours completely omitted, but only on unused stamps (if found on used stamps the information is usually footnoted) and with good credentials, missing colours being frequently faked.

Colours only partially omitted are not recognised. Colour shifts, however spectacular, are not listed.

Booklet Stamps

Single stamps from booklets are listed if they are distinguishable in some way (such as watermark or phosphor bands) from similar sheet stamps.

Booklet Pane with Printed Labels

Se-tenant Pane of Four

Booklet panes are listed where they contain stamps of different denominations *se-tenant*, where stamp-size printed labels are included, or where such panes are otherwise identifiable. Booklet panes are placed in the listing under the lowest denomination present.

In the listing of complete booklets the numbers and prefix letters are the same as used in the Stanley Gibbons *Great Britain Specialised Catalogue.*

Coil Stamps

Stamps only issued in coil form are given full listing. If stamps are issued in both sheets and coils, the coil stamps are listed separately only where there is some feature (e.g. watermark sideways or gum change) by which single stamps can be distinguished. Coil strips containing different values *se-tenant* are also listed.

Multi-value Coil Strip

Coil join pairs are generally too random and easily faked to permit listing; similarly ignored are coil stamps which have accidentally suffered an extra row of perforations from the claw mechanism in a malfunctioning vending machine.

Gutter Pairs

In 1988 the recess-printed Castle high value definitives were issued in sheets containing four panes separated by a gutter margin. All modern Great Britain commemoratives and special stamps are produced in sheets containing two panes separated by a blank horizontal or vertical margin known as a gutter. This feature first made its appearance on some supplies of the 1972 Royal Silver Wedding 3p and marked the introduction of Harrison & Sons' new "Jumelle" stamp-printing press. There are advantages for both the printer and the Post Office in such a layout which has been used for most commemorative issues since 1974.

The term "gutter pair" is used for a pair of stamps separated by part of the blank gutter margin as illustrated below.

Most printers include some form of colour check device on the sheet margins, in addition to the cylinder or plate numbers. Harrison & Sons use round "dabs", or spots of colour, resembling traffic lights. For the period from the 1972 Royal Silver Wedding until the end of 1979 these colour dabs appeared in the gutter margin. There was always one example to every double pane sheet of stamps. They can also be found in the high value Machin issue printed in photogravure. Gutter pairs showing these "traffic lights" are worth considerably more than the normal version.

Gutter Pair   Traffic Light Gutter Pair

Miniature Sheets

A miniature sheet contains a single stamp or set with wide inscribed or decorated margins. The stamps usually also exist in normal sheet format. This Catalogue lists, with **MS** prefix, complete miniature sheets which have been issued by the Post Office and which are valid for postal purposes.

Miniature Sheet containing a set of stamps

Se-tenant Combinations

Se-tenant means "joined together". Some sets include stamps of different design arranged *se-tenant* as blocks or strips and, in mint condition, these are usually collected unsevered as issued. Such *se-tenant* combinations are supplied in used condition at a premium over the used prices of the individual stamps. See also the note on Set Prices.

Specimen Stamps

Stamps of Great Britain overprinted "SPECIMEN" for circulation to postmasters and the Universal Postal Union are listed in a special section following the Postal Fiscal stamps. For other "SPECIMEN" overprints see Stanley Gibbons *Great Britain Specialised Catalogue*.

Presentation and Souvenir Packs

Special Packs comprising slip-in cards with printed commemorative inscriptions and notes on the back and with protective covering, were introduced in 1964 for the Shakespeare issue. Definitive issues first appeared in Presentation Packs in 1960. Notes will be found in the listings to describe souvenir books issued on special occasions.

Issues of 1968–1969 (British Paintings to the Prince of Wales Investiture) were also issued in packs with text in German for sale through the Post Office's German Agency and these are also included.

13 August 1975 Public Railways Presentation Pack

Collectors packs, first called gift packs, containing commemoratives issued in the preceding twelve months, first appeared in 1967. These are listed and priced.

Yearbooks

Special Post Office Yearbooks were first available in 1984. They contain all of the commemorative issues for one year in a hardbound book, illustrated in colour complete with slip case. These are listed and priced.

Commemorative First Day Covers

Until 1963 the Post Office did not provide any special first day of issue postmark facilities for collectors. Several philatelic organisations and stamp dealers did produce pictorial covers for the various commemorative issues and collectors serviced these to receive ordinary operational postmarks. Occasionally a special handstamp was produced which coincided with a new stamp issue, or relevant slogan postmarks, like the 1953 "Long Live the Queen" type, were in general use at the time.

On 21 March 1963 the Post Office installed special posting boxes at eleven main post offices so that collectors could obtain "uniformly high standard" impressions, from normal operational postmarks, for their first day covers. From 7 May 1963 special "First Day of Issue" slogans (Type A) were applied to mail posted in these special boxes, whose number had, by then, risen to thirty. The Philatelic Bureau accepted orders by post for such covers from the issue of 16 May 1963 onwards.

The slogan type was replaced on 23 April 1964 by "First Day of Issue" handstamps (Type B). These were, initially, of considerable size, but were later replaced by smaller versions (Type C) which remained in use at nearly 200 principal offices until the Christmas issue of 2 November 1998. From 1970 the Bureau postmarks as Type C were inscribed "British Philatelic Bureau".

Since 1972 the Post Office has provided for virtually all issues an additional "alternative" pictorial "First Day of Issue" cancellation, at a location connected with the issue. Being available from the Bureau, these cancellations are illustrated and listed in this catalogue.

From 12 January 1999 (Millennium Inventors' Tale issue) the "alternative" pictorial postmark has been applied to all covers posted in special first day boxes throughout the country, replacing the local, non-pictorial, cancels. A bilingual version is used when the "alternative" office is in Wales. For collectors who prefer plain postmarks a non-pictorial version of the "alternative" postmark is available from Royal Mail Special Handstamp Centres.

"First Day of Issue" postmarks of standard or pictorial type have occasionally been provided on a "one-off" basis for places linked to particular stamp issues, eg Weymouth for the 1975 Sailing set. Such postmarks, which are not available from the Bureau, are footnoted only.

Royal Mail established Special Handstamp Centres in 1990 where all sponsored special handstamps and many "First Day of Issue" postmarks are now applied.

Pictorial local "First Day of Issue" postmarks were in use between 1988 and 1998 applied to covers posted in first day boxes and sent to main offices or Special Handstamp Centres. These included Birmingham (1993–98), Durham (1988–98), City of London (1989–98), London (1993–98), Newcastle upon Tyne (1992–94), and St Albans (1995–98). Different designs were used at the Glasgow Handstamp Centre for various places, 1993–98. As these postmarks were not available from the Bureau they are not included in this catalogue.

Type A. First Day of Issue Slogan   **Type B.** Large Handstamp   **Type C.** Small Handstamp

Type D. Maltese Cross   **Type E**   **Type F.** £ Sign   **Type G.** Three Lions

Type H. Four Castles   **Type I.** Windsor Keep   **Type J.** Millennium (2000 issues are inscr "Beyond 2000")   **Type K.** Arms of Post Office

No Value Indicated Stamps

From 22 August 1989 various definitive and special stamps appeared inscribed "2nd", "1st" or "E" instead of a face value. These were sold at the current minimum rates for these services which were as follows:

Inland Postage Rate	2nd Class	Ist Class	European Airmail Rate	
5 September 1988	14p.	19p.	26 April 1999	30p.
2 October 1989	15p.	20p.	25 October 1999	34p.
17 September 1990	17p.	22p.	27 April 2000	36p.
16 September 1991	18p.	24p.	2 July 2001	37p.
1 November 1993	19p.	25p.	27 March 2003	38p.
8 July 1996	20p.	26p.	1 April 2004	40p.
26 April 1999	19p.	26p.		
17 April 2000	19p.	27p.		
8 May 2003	20p.	28p.		
1 April 2004	21p.	28p.		

PHQ Cards

From 1973 the Post Office produced sets of picture cards to accompany commemorative issues which can be sent through the post as postcards. Each card shows an enlarged colour reproduction of one stamp, initially of a single value from one set and subsequently of all values. The Post Office gives each card a "PHQ" serial number, hence the term. The cards are usually on sale shortly before the date of issue of the stamps, but there is no officially designated "first day".

PHQ Card cancelled on First Day of Issue

Cards are priced in fine mint condition for complete sets as issued. Used prices are for cards franked with the stamp affixed, on the obverse, as illustrated above, or reverse; the stamp being cancelled with an official postmark for first day of issue.

Watermark Types

Stamps are on unwatermarked paper except where the heading to the set states otherwise.

Watermarks are detected for Catalogue description by one of four methods: (1) holding stamps to the light; (2) laying stamps face down on a dark background; (3) by use of the Morley-Bright Detector, which works by revealing the thinning of the paper at the watermark; or (4) by the more complex electric watermark detectors such as the Signoscope.

The diagram below shows how watermark position is described in the Catalogue. Watermarks are usually impressed so that they read normally when looked through from the printed side. However, since philatelists customarily detect watermarks by looking at the back of the stamp, the watermark diagram also makes clear what is actually seen. Note that "G v R" is only an example and illustrations of the different watermarks employed are shown in the listings. The illustrations are actual size and shown in normal positions (from the front of the stamps).

AS DESCRIBED (Read through front of stamp)		AS SEEN DURING WATERMARK DETECTION (Stamp face down and back examined)
GvR	Normal	ЯvƆ
ЯʌƆ	Inverted	ϾʌЯ
ЯvƆ	Reversed	GvR
ϾʌЯ	Reversed and inverted	ЯʌƆ
GvR (sideways)	Sideways	ϾʌЯ (sideways)
GvR (sideways)	Sideways inverted	ЯʌƆ (sideways)

General Types of watermark as seen through the front side of the stamp.

2 Small Crown

4 Large Crown

9 (Extends over three stamps)

13 V R

15 Small Garter

16 Medium Garter

17 Large Garter

20 Emblems

33 Spray of Rose

39 Maltese Cross

40 Large Anchor

47 Small Anchor

48 Orb

49 Imperial Crown

100 Simple Cypher

103 Multiple Cypher

110 Single Cypher   **111** Block Cypher   **117** PUC £1

125 E8R   **127**   **133**   **153** Tudor Crown

Postal Fiscals

165 St. Edward's Crown   **179** Multiple Crowns   **F5** Double-lined Anchor   **F6** Single-lined Anchor

Watermark Errors and Varieties

Watermark errors are recognised as of major importance. They comprise stamps showing the wrong watermark devices or stamps printed on paper with the wrong watermark. Stamps printed on paper showing broken or deformed bits on the dandy roll, are not listable.

Underprints

From 1982 various values appeared with underprints, printed on the reverse, in blue, over the gum. These were usually from special stamp booklets, sold at a discount by the Post Office, but in 1985 surplus stocks of such underprinted paper were used for other purposes.

In this Catalogue stamps showing underprints are priced mint only. Used examples can be obtained, but care has to be taken in floating the stamps since the ink employed to print the device is solvent in water.

Underprint Types

1 Star with central dot

2 Double-lined Star

3 Double-lined "D"

4 Multiple double-lined Stars

5 Multiple double-lined "D"

(Types **4/5** are shown $\frac{3}{4}$ actual size)

Note: Types **4/5** are arranged in a random pattern so that the stamps from the same sheet or booklet pane will show the underprint in a slightly different position to the above. Stamps, when inspected, should be placed the correct way up, face down, when comparing with the illustrations.

COMMEMORATIVE DESIGN INDEX

This index gives an easy reference to the inscriptions and designs of the Special Stamps 1953 to April 2000. Where a complete set shares an inscription or type of design, then only the catalogue number of the first stamp is given in addition to separate entries for stamps depicting popular thematic subjects. Paintings, inventions, etc., are indexed under the name of the artist or inventor, where this is shown on the stamp.

1. £.s.d. ISSUES 1953–70

Aberfeldy Bridge	764
Alcock, John (aviator)	791
Antrim	690
Arbroath Declaration, 650th Anniversary	819
Architecture: Cathedrals	796
Rural	815
Atlantic Flight, 50th Anniversary	791
Automatic Sorting	811
Battle of Britain, 25th Anniversary	671
Battle of Hastings, 900th Anniversary	705
Blackbird	699
Black Headed Gull	696
Blue Tit	697
Bridges	763
Brown, Arthur (aviator)	791
Burns, Robert	685
Cairngorms	692
Canterbury Cathedral	799
C.E.P.T.	621, 626
Christmas 1966, Children's Paintings (3d., 1s. 6d.)	713
1967, Paintings (3d., 4d., 1s. 6d.)	756
1968, Children's Toys (4d., 9d., 1s. 6d.)	775
1969, Traditional Religious Themes (4d., 5d., 1s. 6d.)	812
1970, Lisle Psalter (4d., 5d., 1s. 6d.)	838
Churchill, Winston	661
Commonwealth Arts Festival	669
Commonwealth Cable	645
Commonwealth Games (1958)	567
Commonwealth Games (1970)	832
Commonwealth Parliamentary Conference	629
Concorde	784
Constable, John (artist)	774
Cook's First Voyage of Discovery, 200th Anniversary	770
Co-operative Alliance, 75th Anniversary	821
Coronation	532
Cotswold Limestone	816
Cutty Sark	781
Dickens, Charles, Death Centenary	824
Durham Cathedral	796
East Indiaman	780
E.F.T.A.	715
Elizabethan Galleon	779
"Elizabeth I"	771
England Winners World Cup Football Championships, 1966	700
Europa, C.E.P.T., 1st Anniversary	621
Europa, C.E.P.T., 10th Anniversary	792
Fife Harling	815
First England-Australia Flight, 50th Anniversary	795
Flowers	717
Forth Road Bridge	659
Freedom from Hunger	634
Gandhi, Mahatma, Birth Centenary	807
General Letter Office, Tercentenary	619
Gipsy Moth IV	751
Great Britain	782
Harlech Castle	691
Hovercraft	703

International Botanical Congress	655
International Geographical Congress	651
International Labour Organisation, 50th Anniversary	793
International Lifeboat Conference	639
International Telecommunications Union, Centenary	683
Jet Engine	754
Jubilee Jamboree (1957)	557
Landscapes	689
Lawrence, Thomas (artist)	748, 772
Le Nain, Louis (artist)	758
Lister, Joseph	667
Liverpool Metropolitan Cathedral	801
Lowry, L.S. (artist)	750
Mauritania	783
Mayflower, 350th Anniversary of Voyage	822
Menai Bridge	765
Montfort's Parliament, 700th Anniversary	663
Motor Cars	702
Murillo (artist)	757
M4 Viaduct	766
National Giro	808
National Nature Week	637
National Productivity Year	631
Nightingale, Florence, 150th Birth Anniversary	820
North Atlantic Treaty Organisation (NATO), 20th Anniversary	794
Nuclear Power	704
Paris Postal Conference, Centenary	636
Parliamentary Conference	560
Parliament, 700th Anniversary	663
Penicillin	753
Philympia 1970	835
Piper, John (artist)	773
Post Office Savings Bank, Centenary	623
Post Office Tower	679
Prince of Wales, Investiture	802
Queen Elizabeth 2	778
Radar	752
Radio Telescope	701
Red Cross Centenary Congress	642
Robin	698
Royal Air Force, 50th Anniversary	769
Royal Astronomical Society, 150th Anniversary	823
St. Giles' Edinburgh	798
St. Paul's Cathedral	800
Salvation Army Centenary	665
Seville School	756
Shakespeare Festival	646
Stubbs, George (artist)	749
Sussex	689
Tarr Steps	763
Telecommunications	809
Television	755
Trades Union Congress, Centenary	767
Ulster Thatch	818
United Nations, 20th Anniversary	681

Commemorative Design Index

Votes for Women, 50th Anniversary 768

Welsh Stucco. 817
Westminster Abbey, 900th Anniversary 687
World Cup Football Championships, 1966. 693
Wordsworth, William, 200th Birth Anniversary 828

York Minster. 797

2. DECIMAL CURRENCY 1971-2004

Abbotsbury Swannery 1639
Aberystwyth University College. 890
Accession, 40th Anniversary 1602
"Acid Rain Kills". 1629
Age of Steam. 1795
Airbus A340-600 2284
Aircraft Designers 1984
Airliners 2284
Airmail, blue van and postbox 1930. 956
Alexander the Great. 2405
Alexandra Palace. 1493
Alice's Adventures in Wonderland 1094
American Independence Bicentennial 1005
Amser Haf/Summertime 1834
Animals, Species at Risk 1320
Anne of Cleves 1969
Apple 2350
Architecture: Modern University Buildings. 890
                Village Churches 904
                Historic Buildings. 1054
Armada, 400th Anniversary 1400
Armagh Observatory 1522
Arthurian Legends. 1294
Astronomy 1522
Athletics. 1134, 1328
Aubergine. 2357
Austen, Jane, Birth Centenary 989
Austin (cars) 1198
Austin-Healey (cars) 1947
Australian Bicentenary 1396
Autumn 1779
Avocet (bird). 1420
Avro Lancaster Mk 1 1985

Babbage-Computer. 1547
Badger 1043
Ballyroney, County Down. 2000
Bannockburn 2111
Barbirolli, Sir John (conductor) 1133
Barn Owl. 2125, 2327
Bath Spa 2168
Bawden, Edward 1768
BBC, 50th Anniversary 909
Beacons across the Land. 2129
Beddgelert, Gwynedd. 1999
Beecham, Sir Thomas (conductor). 1131
Beetle 1280
Bell, Alexander Graham, First Telephone Call Cen-
    tenary. 997
Ben Arkle. 1811
Ben More, Isle of Mull 2386
Biddulph Grange 1224
"Bird of Hope". 1632
Birds 1109, 1915, 2087, 2103, 2125, 2128, 2238
Bishop, Ronald. 1986
Blackfriars Bridge. 2312
Black Prince 961
"Black Swan" 2393
Blake, Admiral and Triumph. 1188
Blanchflower, Danny. 1929
Blenheim Palace. 1225

Blues and Royals Drum Horse 1991
Blyton, Enid (authoress). 2001
Body/The Dome. 2166
Boleyn, Anne. 1967
Boxing. 1136
BR Standard Class (railway loco) 2422
Braemar (highland games) 1833
Bridges of London 2309
British Architects in Europe. 1355
British Army Uniforms 1218
British Composers 1282
British Council 1263
British Horse Society 1989
British Legion, 50th Anniversary 887
British Museum, 250th Anniversary. 2404
British Philatelic Bureau, Edinburgh 1495
British Rail Inter-City Service HST 987
British Textiles 1192
Broadstairs, Kent. 2269
Brontë, Charlotte (authoress). 1125
Brontë, Emily (authoress) 1127
Brown Hare 1040
Brussells Sprout 2356
Buckingham Palace. 1120
Bumble Bee 1277
Burns, Robert (poet). 1901
Buses. 2210
Bush-cricket. 1279
Bush House, Bristol 1247
Butterflies. 1151

Caernarvon Castle. 1056
Caerphilly Castle (railway loco) 986
Camm, Sir Sidney 1988
Campbell, Donald 2063
Campbell, Sir Malcolm 2059
Canals. 1775
Canolfan Mileniwm/Cardiff 2176
Carnival 2055
Carnoustie: "Luckyslap" (golf). 1831
Carriage Horse 1989
Carroll, Lewis. 1094, 2054
Carter, George 1987
Castell Y Waun 1810
Catherine of Aragon. 1966
Cats. 1848, 2187
Cattle 1240
Caxton, William 1014
Centre for Life/Newcastle 2169
CERAMICA/Stoke-on-Trent 2142
Chadwick, Roy. 1985
Channel Tunnel, Opening of 1820
Chaplin, Charlie 1300, 2095
Charity 970
Charlotte Square, Edinburgh. 975
Chequered Skipper (butterfly). 1154
Chichester, Francis 2364
Children 2178
Children's Television, 50th Anniversary 1940
Children's Toys and Board Games. 1436
Chillingham Wild Bull. 1241
Chirk Castle 1810
Christmas:
    1971. Stained Glass Windows (2$\frac{1}{2}$p., 3p., 7$\frac{1}{2}$p.) 894
    1972. Angels (2$\frac{1}{2}$p., 3p., 7$\frac{1}{2}$p.). 913
    1973. Scenes depicting carol "Good King Wence-
          slas" (3p. × 5, 3$\frac{1}{2}$p.). 943
    1974. Roof Bosses (3$\frac{1}{2}$p., 4$\frac{1}{2}$p., 8p., 10p.) 966
    1975. Angels (6$\frac{1}{2}$p., 8$\frac{1}{2}$p., 11p., 13p.). 993
    1976. Embroideries (6$\frac{1}{2}$p., 8$\frac{1}{2}$p., 11p., 13p.) 1018
    1977. The Twelve Days of Christmas (7p. × 5, 9p.) 1044
    1978. Carol Singers (7p., 9p., 11p., 13p.) 1071

1979. Scenes depicting the Nativity (8p., 10p., 11½p., 13p., 15p.) 1104
1980. Christmas Decorations (10p., 12p., 13½p., 15p., 17½p.) 1138
1981. Children's Paintings (11½p., 14p., 18p., 22p., 25p.) 1170
1982. Carols (12½p., 15½p., 19½p., 26p., 29p.) 1202
1983. Birds (12½p., 16p., 20½p., 28p., 31p.) 1231
1984. Scenes depicting the Nativity (13p., 17p., 22p., 31p., 34p.) 1267
1985. Pantomime (12p., 17p., 22p., 31p., 34p.) 1303
1986. Christmas Legends (12p., 13p., 18p., 22p., 31p., 34p.) 1341
1987. A Child's Christmas Day (13p., 18p., 26p., 31p., 34p.) 1375
1988. Christmas Cards (14p., 19p., 27p., 32p., 35p.) 1414
1989. 800th Anniversary of Ely Cathedral (15p., 15p. + 1p., 20p + 1p., 34p. + 1p., 37p. + 1p.) 1462
1990. Christmas Scenes (17p., 22p., 26p., 31p., 37p.) 1526
1991. Illuminated Manuscripts from the Bodleian Library, Oxford (18p., 24p., 28p., 33p., 39p.).. 1582
1992. Stained Glass Windows (18p., 24p., 28p., 33p., 39p.) 1634
1993. 150th Anniv of A Christmas Carol by Charles Dickens (19p., 25p., 30p., 35p., 41p.,) 1790
1994. Children's Nativity Plays (19p., 25p., 30p., 35p., 41p.,) 1843
1995. Christmas Robins (19p., 25p., 30p., 41p., 60p.). 1896
1996. Biblical Scenes (2nd, 1st, 31p., 43p., 63p.) 1950
1997. 150th Anniv of the Christmas Cracker (2nd, 1st, 31p., 43p., 63p.) 2006
1998. Angels (20p., 26p., 30p., 43p., 63p.) 2064
1999. Christians' Tale (19p., 26p., 44p., 64p.) 2115
2000. Spirit and Faith (2nd, 1st, 45p., 65p.) 2170
2001. Robins (2nd, 1st, E, 45p., 65p.) 2238
2002. Christmas Plants (2nd, 1st, E, 47p., 68p.).... 2321
2004. Christmas Ice Sculptures (2nd, 1st, E, 53p., 68p., £1.12). 2410
Churches 904
Church Floodlighting 2171
Churchill, Winston, Birth Centenary.............. 962
Cinema Centenary 1920
Circus 2275
City Finance 2091
Civil War 1620, 2112
Classic Sports Cars 1945
Coal 1051
Coastguard, 150th Anniversary 902
Coastlines 2265
Cobb, John R................................... 2062
Coffin of Denytenamun.......................... 2404
Colchicum (flower) 1350
Columbus, 500th Anniversary of Discovery of America...................................... 1617
Comedians 2041
Comet (airliner) 2288
Commercial St. Development, Perth 1248
Common Dormouse.............................. 2015
Commonwealth Day 1211
Commonwealth Games, Edinburgh, 1986........... 1328
Commonwealth Games, Manchester, 2002 2299
Commonwealth Heads of Government Meeting, 1977 1038
Commonwealth Parliamentary Conf................ 939, 1335
Computed Tomography 1842
Computer 1547, 2072
Concorde 2285
Contemporary Art............................... 1767
Conwy (sand-spit) 2274
Cook, Capt James............................... 2076
Cook, Peter.................................... 2045
Cooper, Tommy................................. 2041

Coronation, 25th Anniversary.................... 1059
Coronation 50th Anniversary 2368
County Cricket, Centenary....................... 928
Court Masque Costumes.......................... 935
Court Masque Stage Scene....................... 938
Cowes (sailing) 1836
CR Class 439 (railway loco) 2418
Cricket 1137
Cultural Traditions.............................. 1010
Cunningham, Viscount and H.M.S. Warspite 1191
Cycle Network Artworks 2144
Cycling 1878-1978.............................. 1067

Dalek.. 2094
Dalveen Pass, Lowther Hills...................... 2388
Dangermouse 1944
Darwin, Charles 1175
Darwin's Theory................................ 2103
Dawson, Les 2044
D-Day, 50th Anniversary......................... 1824
Dean, Dixie 1925
Decoding DNA.................................. 2102
Deer 1587
De Havilland Mosquito B Mk XVI 1986
Derby Bicentenary............................... 1087
Dersingham 1813
Derwentwater, England 1156
Destination Australia............................ 2086
Devil's Bolete 2020
Diana, Princess of Wales........................ 2021
Dickens, Charles 1790
Dinky Toys 2400
Dinosaurs...................................... 1573
Dipper... 1110
Doctor Who 2094
Dogs 1075, 1531, 2187
Dolgoch (railway loco) 2417
Dolwyddelan................................... 1814
Domesday Book................................. 1324
Dover, Kent (cliffs)............................. 2267
Dowding, Lord and Hawker Hurricane.............. 1336
Dracula.. 1980
Dragonfly...................................... 1281
Drake, Francis (explorer)........................ 925
Dr. Jekyll and Mr. Hyde 1982
Duckling....................................... 1481
Duke of Edinburgh Award Scheme................ 1162
Duke of Edinburgh's Horse 1992
Du Maurier 1938
Dunster Beach, Somerset........................ 2271
Dynamic Earth/Edinburgh 2131

Earls Barton, Northants.......................... 905
Earth Centre, Doncaster......................... 2140
Echeveria (flower) 1349
Echinops (flower) 1348
Eclipse... MS2106
ECOS/Ballymena 2138
Eden Project/St Austell.......................... 2157
Edwards, Duncan................................ 1927
Eisteddfod of Wales 1010
Electricity 1053, 1546
Eliot, George (authoress)........................ 1126
"Elizabeth of Glamis" (rose)...................... 1006
Endangered Species............................. 2015
Energy... 1050
Engineering Achievements....................... 1215
"Ensure Children's Freedom" 2181
Environment 1629
Equestrienne 2279
"Europa" (showing symbol):
  1982. British Theatre (15½p., 19½p., 26p., 29p.) 1183/6

Commemorative Design Index

1983. Engineering Achievements (16p., 20½p., 28p.) 1215/17
1984. 25th Anniversary (16p., 20½p.) 1249, 1251
1985. European Music Year. British Composers (17p., 22p., 31p., 34p.) 1282/5
1986. Nature Conservation–Endangered Species (17p., 22p., 31p., 34p.) 1320/3
1987. British Architects in Europe (18p., 22p., 31p., 34p.) 1355/8
1988. Transport and Mail Services in the 1930s (18p., 26p., 31p., 34p.) 1392/5
1989. Games and Toys (19p., 27p., 32p., 35p.) 1436/9
1990. "Stamp World London 90"/Philatelic Bureau (20p., 29p.) 1493, 1495
1991. Europe in Space (22p., 37p., each × 2) 1560/3
1992. International Events (24p., 39p.) 1617/18
1993. Contemporary Art (24p., 28p., 33p., 39p.) 1767/70
1994. Medical Discoveries (25p., 30p., 35p., 41p.) . . . 1839/42
1995. Peace and Freedom (25p., 30p.) 1876/7
1996. Famous Women (26p., 31p.) 1936/7
1997. Tales and Legends. Horror Stories (26p., 31p.) . . 1980/1
1998. Festivals. Notting Hill Carnival (20p., 26p.) 2055/6
1999. The Farmers' Tale (19p.) 2107
2001. Pond Life (1st, E) 2220/1
2002. Circus (1st, E) 2276/7
Equal Rights 2098
European Architectural Heritage Year 975
European Assembly Elections 1083
European Communities 919
European Football Championship 1925
European Parliament, Third Direct Elections 1433
Europe in Space 1560
Everest, British Team 2361
Explorers 923, 2360
Expo '92, Seville 1619

Face Paintings 2178
"FAIR" 2198
Faisrs 1227
Famous Five 2002
Famous Women 1935
Faraday-Electricity 1546, 2104
Faraway Tree 2004
Films 1227
Fire Engines 950
First Christmas 2118
First official airmail Coronation 1911 955
First Rights 2101
Fisher, Lord and H.M.S. Dreadnought 1190
Fishes 1207
Fishing 1166
Flags and Ensigns MS2206, 2208
Fleming's Penicillin 2083
Flower Paintings 1955
Flowers 1347
Fonteyn, Margot 1936
Food and Farming Year 1989 1428
Food from Afar 2109
Football 1391, 2093
Ford (cars) 1199
"Forest for Scotland" 2159
Four Seasons:
  Spring 1853
  Summer 1834
  Autumn 1779
  Winter 1587
Fox 1587
Frankenstein 1981
Franklin, Benjamin 1005
Frink, Elizabeth 1937
Frobisher, Martin (explorer) 898
Fruit and Vegetables 2348

Fruits and Leaves 1779
Fry, Elizabeth 1004

Gaillardia (flowers) 1347
Gallantry Awards 1517
Gannets 2128
Gaskell, Mrs. (authoress) 1128
Gateshead Millennium Bridge 2149
GCR Class 8K (railway loco) 2419
General Post, c. 1839 1096
Genome 2343
Giant's Causeway, N. Ireland 1158
Gilbert and Sullivan Operas 1624
Glasgow, School of Art 1494
Glenfinnan, Scotland 1155
Glenfinnan Viaduct, Lochaber 2389
Globe Theatre 1882
Gloster Meteor F Mk 8 1987
Glyndwr, Owain 959
Golden Jubilee 2253
Golden Wedding 2011
Golf, Scottish Courses 1829
Grahame, Kenneth 1092
"Grandpa Dickson" (rose) 1007
Gray, Thomas, Death Bicentenary 885
Great Britons 958
Great Western Railway Castle Class 986
"Greenhouse Effect" 1631
Greensted-juxta-Ongar, Essex 904
Greenwich Meridian 1254
Grenfell, Joyce 2043
Groundwork's Changing Places 2155
GWR Manor Class Bradley Manor (railway loco) 2420
Gymnastics 1388

Halley's Comet 1312
Hampden Park/Glasgow 2167
Hampton Court Palace 1057, 1123
Hardy, Thomas, 150th Birth Anniversary 1506
Hare 1587
"Hark the Herald Angels Sing" (carol) 2115
Haroldswick, Shetland 1997
Harris, Sir Arthur and Avro Lancaster 1339
Harrison, John, 300th Birth Anniversary 1654
Hartman, Marea 1939
Hats, Fashion 2216
Hawker Hunter FGA Mk 9 1998
"Health and Handicap" Charities 970
Hedgehog 1039
Helpringham, Lincolnshire 907
Henry V 960
Henry VIII 1187, 1965
Henry VIII, 450th Death Anniversary 1965
Hepburn, Thomas 1001
Heraldry 1236, 1363, 2026
Hereford Bull 1242
Highland Cow 1240
Highland Gathering 1012
High-Speed Train 987
Hill, Rowland 1095, 1887
Hitchcock, Alfred 1302
Hoa Hakananai'a 2409
Hockey Cup 1332
Hodgkin, Dorothy 1935
Holmes, Sherlock 1784
Holyroodhouse 1055
Hornby 2399
Horror 1980
Horse Chestnut 949
Horse racing paintings 1087
Horses 1063
Hound of the Baskervilles 1983

Howard, Catherine 1970
Hudson, Henry (explorer).......................... 899
Huish Episcopi, Somerset......................... 908
Humber Bridge.................................. 1215
Hummingbird................................... 2087

Imperial Airways Flying Boat 1937 957
Industry Year 1986 1308
Information Technology.......................... 1196
Inland Waterways.............................. 1775
Insects 1277
International Stamp Exhibition.................... 1118
International Year of Disabled People 1147
Inter-Parliamentary Union Conference............. 988, 1435
Iolair (oilfield support vessel).................... 1217
Irish Moiled Cow 1244
Irish Setter.................................... 1078
Ironbridge, Shropshire 1440

Jaguar (cars) 1200, 1948
Jenner's Vaccination............................ 2080
Jet Engine-Whittle.............................. 1549
Jet Travel..................................... 2073
Johnson, Amy.................................. 2360
Jones, Inigo, 400th Birth Anniversary 935

Keats, John, 150th Death Anniversary 884
Kemp Experiment 1897 912
Kensington Palace.............................. 1124
Kestrel 2332
Kew Gardens 1840-1990 1502
Kingdom of Fife Cycle Ways 2154
Kingfisher..................................... 1109
King James Bible 2116
Kipling's *Just So Stories*......................... 2243
Kitten 1479
Krazy Kar..................................... 2278

Ladybird...................................... 1278
Lady's Slipper Orchid........................... 2016
Lammastide................................... 1145
Lancaster House 1253
Land Speed Record Holders 2059
Large Blue (butterfly)........................... 1152
Leaf Sculptures................................ 1853
Lear, Edward.................................. 1405
Leigh, Vivien.............................. 1301, 1921
Lemon.. 2355
Letheringsett, Norfolk........................... 906
Lewis, C. S.................................... 2051
Liberation by Bike.............................. 2074
Lifeguards' Horse............................... 1990
Lighthouses................................... 2034
Lighting Croydon's Skyline 2132
Linking the Nation.............................. 2075
Linnean Society 1788/1988 1380
Lion Tamer.................................... 2276
"Listen to Children" 2179
Liverpool and Manchester Railway 1830........... 1113
Liverpool, Garden Festival Hall................... 1245
Livingstone, David (explorer)...................... 923
Llanelwedd, Royal Welsh Show................... 1834
Loch Assynt, Sutherland 2385
London 1980.................................. 1118
London Bridge................................. 2313
London Post, c. 1839 1097
Lord Mayor's Show, London...................... 1457
Lord's (cricket)................................ 1832
Luskentyre, South Harris 2266

Magna Carta.................................. 2101
Magnetic Resonance Imaging...................... 1841
Malory Towers 2005

Marconi Experiment 1897 912
Marconi First Wireless Message 1895.............. 1889
Mask of Xiuhtecuhtli............................ 2408
Meccano...................................... 2397
Marine Timekeeper No.4 1654
Maritime Heritage 1187
Mary Rose 1187
Mechanical Farming 2108
Medals and Decorations 1517
Medical Discoveries 1839
Medieval Mummers............................. 1146
Mercury, Freddie 2092
Mettoy 2401
MG (cars) 1946
Migration to Scotland........................... 2084
Migration to U.K............................... 2087
Milburngate Centre, Durham 1246
Mile End Park/London........................... 2150
Millennium Bridge 2309
Millennium definitive........................... 2124
"Millennium Greens"............................ 2148
Millennium Point, Birmingham 2164
Millennium Projects Series
  "Above and Beyond" 2000/Nos. 1 to 4 2125
  "Fire and Light" 2000/Nos. 5 to 8 2129
  "Water and Coast" 2000/Nos. 9 to 12............ 2134
  "Life and Earth" 2000/Nos. 13 to 16 2138
  "Art and Craft" 2000/Nos. 17 to 20 2142
  "People and Places" 2000/Nos. 21 to 24 2148
  "Stone and Soil" 2000/Nos. 25 to 28 2152
  'Tree and Leaf" 2000/Nos. 29 to 32 2156
  "Mind and Matter" 2000/Nos. 33 to 36........... 2162
  "Body and Bone" 2000/Nos. 37 to 40............ 2166
  "Spirit and Faith" 2000/Nos. 41 to 44........... 2170
  "Sound and Vision" 2000/Nos. 45 to 48 2174
Millennium Seed Bank/Ardingly 2158
Millennium Series
  The Inventors' Tale 1999/Nos. 48 to 45 2069
  The Travellers' Tale 1999/Nos. 44 to 41 2073
  The Patients' Tale 1999/Nos. 40 to 37 2080
  The Settlers' Tale 1999/Nos. 36 to 33............ 2084
  The Workers' Tale 1999/Nos. 32 to 29............ 2088
  The Entertainers' Tale 1999/Nos. 28 to 25 2092
  The Citizens' Tale 1999/Nos. 24 to 21 2098
  The Scientists' Tale 1999/Nos. 20 to 17 2102
  The Farmers' Tale 1999/Nos. 16 to 13 2107
  The Soldiers' Tale 1999/Nos. 12 to 9............. 2111
  The Christians' Tale 1999/Nos. 8 to 5............ 2115
  The Artists' Tale 1999/Nos. 4 to 1 2119
  "Millennium Timekeeper" **MS**2123
Millennium 2001............................... 2178
Mills, New Lanark, Strathclyde 1442
Mill Towns.................................... 2089
Milne, A. A................................... 1093
Mitchell, Reginald.............................. 1984
Mole Cricket.................................. 2019
Moore, Bobby............................. 1926, 2093
Moore, Henry 1767
Moorhen 1111
Morecambe, Eric 2042
Morgan (cars) 1949
Morris Dancing........................... 1011, 1144
Motor Car Industry 1198
Mourne Mountains 1812
Muffin the Mule 1940
Muirfield: 18th Hole (golf)....................... 1830
Music 1282
Mystery Plays/York Minster...................... 2173

National Health Service 2046
National Pondlife/Merseyside 2135
National Space Centre/Leicester 2126

Commemorative Design Index

National Theatre, London 979
National Trust. 1155, 1868
Natural Gas. 1052
Nature Conservation 1320
Nelson, Lord and H.M.S. *Victory* 1189
Nesbit, E. 2052
Newquay, Cornwall (beach) 2272
Newton, Sir Isaac. 1351
Newton/Hubble Telescope 2105, **MS**2106
New Worlds 2122
NHS. 2046
Nicholson, Ben. 1770
Niven, David. 1299
Nobel Prizes 2232
Noddy. 2001
Norfolk and Norwich Project 2163
North British Railway Drummond (railway loco) 985
Norton, Mary 2053
Nursing Care. 2081
"Nurture Children" 2178

Oak. 922
Odeon, Harrogate. 1920
Oil. 1050
Old English Sheepdog 1075
Olivier, Laurence. 1921
Olympic and Paralympic Games, Atlanta. 1930
Olympic Games, Barcelona 1615
"On the Line" 2151
Operation Raleigh. 1618
Orange. 2353
Orchids 1659
Order of the Garter 2026
Ordnance Survey (maps). 1578
Otter 1042
Owen, Robert. 1002
Oystercatcher (bird) 1421
"Ozone Layer". 1630

Padstow, Cornwall. 2268
Painswick, Gloucestershire 1998
P & O packet steamer *Peninsular* 1888. 954
Papa Little, Shetland Islands 2390
Paralympics, Barcelona. 1616
Parc Arfordirol/Llanelli Coast 2136
Parr, Catherine. 1971
Pathé 1923
Peace and Freedom 1873
Peace Keeping 2114
Peacock (butterfly) 1153
Pear. 2352
Penny Black, 150th Anniversary 1467, **MS**1501
Perch 1210
Peter Pan. 2304
Philatelic Bureau, Edinburgh 1495
Photography 2071
Pictorial Postcards 1894-1994. 1815
Pike. 1208
Pilgrim Fathers 2085
Pillar Boxes 2316
Pioneers of Communications 1887
Pitmedden, Scotland. 1226
Planetary Nebula **MS**2315
Polar Explorers 897
Police 1100
Pond Life. 2220
Pontcysyllte Aqueduct, Clwyd. 1443
Portal, Lord and Mosquito 1340
Portrush, County Antrim. 2273
Portsmouth Harbour. 2137
Postal Telegraph & Telephone, Int. World Congress . . 1434
Potato. 2349

Potter, Beatrix. 1091
Pottery 1371
Prince of Wales Investiture Anniversary 1810
Prince's Lodging, Newmarket 937
Prince William 2381
Project SUZY/Teeside 2141
Public Education. 150th Anniversary. 1432
Puffin (bird) 1419
Punch and Judy Puppets 2224
Puppy 1482

Queen Elizabeth II Accession 40th Anniversary. 1602
Queen Elizabeth II 60th Birthday 1316
Queen Mother Commemoration. 2280
Queen Mother's 80th Birthday. 1129
Queen Mother's 90th Birthday. 1507
Queen Mother's 100th Birthday. 2160
Queen's Award to Industry. 1497
Queen's Beasts. 2026

Rabbit 1480
Racket Sports 1022
Radar-Watson Watt 1548
Raeburn, Sir Henry, 150th Death Anniversary 932
Railway Locomotives. 984, 1113, 1272, 1795, 2417
"RAIN" 2197
Raleigh, Walter (explorer). 926
Red Cross. 1874
Red Pepper 2351
Red Squirrel. 1041
Redwing 1587
Reynolds, Sir Joshua, 250th Birth Anniversary 931
Rheilffordd Eryri/Snowdonia 2130
Right to Health. 2099
Right to Learn. 2100
Ringing in the Millennium 2174
Robert the Bruce 958, 2111
Robin. 1896, 2238
Rolls-Royce (cars) 1201
Roman Britain 1771
"Rosa Mundi" (rose) 1008
Roses. 1006, 1568
Ross, James Clark (explorer). 897
Rothiemurchus, Cairngorms 2387
Rowing. 1329
Royal Air Force. 1336
Royal Institute of Chemistry 1029
Royal Mail Coach, 200th Anniversary. 1258
Royal Mail, 350 Years Service. 1290
Royal Microscopical Society, 150th Anniversary 1453
Royal Navy Submarine Service. 2202, 2207
Royal Observatory, Greenwich. 977, 1524
Royal Opera House. 1122
Royal Troon: The Postage Stamp (golf). 1832
Royal Wedding. 941, 1160, 1333, 2096
RSPB 1889-1989 (birds) 1419
RSPCA 1840-1990 (animals) 1479
Rugby Football Union, 100th Anniversary 889
Rugby League, Centenary 1891
Rugby Union 1135
Rugby World Champions, 2003 . . . . **MS**2416
Rugby World Cup 1991 1567

Safety at Sea. 1286
Sailing 980
St. Abb's Head, Scottish Borders 2270
St. Andrews Pilgrimage. 2117
St. Andrews, The Old Course (golf). 1829
St. Augustine. 1974
St. Columba 1972
St. Edmundsbury Cathedral. 2170
St. George's Chapel, Windsor. 978

St. John Ambulance 1887–1987	1359
St. Kilda, Scotland	1159
St. Patrick Centre/Downpatrick	2172
St. Paul's, Covent Garden	936
St. Valentine's Day	1143
Salmon	1207
Saturn	2105, **MS**2106
Sargent, Sir Malcolm (conductor)	1132
Satellite Agriculture	2110
Scanning Electron Microscopy	1840
Science Fiction	1878
Scientific Achievements	1546
Scott, Robert Falcon (explorer)	900, 2365
Scott, Sir Walter, Birth Bicentenary	886
Scottish Heraldry	1363
SCRAN/Internet	2165
Sculpture of Parvati	2407
Seabird Centre/North Berwick	2128
Secret Seven	2003
Segrave, Sir Henry	2060
Sellers, Peter	1298
Seyfest 2 Galaxy	**MS**2315
Seymour, Jane	1968
Shackleton, Ernest	2363
Shaftesbury, Lord	1003
Shakespeare's Globe Theatre	1882
Sheep	1587
Shetland Pony	1064
Shining Ram's-horn Snail	2018
Shipbuilding	2090
Shire Horse	1063
Shooting	1331
Silver Jubilee	1033
Silver Wedding	916
Single European Market	1633
Sissinghurst, Kent	1223
Skiing	1389
Slack Wire Act	2275
Small Tortoiseshell (butterfly)	1151
Social Reformers	1001
Song Thrush	2017
Sooty	1941
Spencer, Stanley	1769
Spring Flowers	1079
Springtime	1853
SR West Country Class Blackmoor Vale (railway loco)	2421
Stackpole Head, Wales	1157
Stanley, Henry (explorer)	924
Stark, Freya	2362
Steam Power	2070
Steam Train	2130
Stephenson's *Locomotion*	984
Stingray	1942
Stockton and Darlington Railway	984
Stonehenge	1525
"STORMY"	2199
Strangford Stone/Killyleagh	2152
Strawberry	2348
Strip Farming	2107
Stubbs, George (artist)	1531
Studland Bay, Dorset	2265
Sturt, Charles (explorer)	927
Submarines	2202, 2207
Sub Post Offices	1997
Summertime	1834
Supermarine Spitfire MkIIA	1984
Sutton Hoo Helmet	2406
Swans	1639
"Sweet Briar" (rose)	1009
Tate Modern/London	2143
"Teach Children"	2180

Tedder, Lord and Hawker Typhoon	1337
Telephone, First call by Alexander Graham Bell, Centenary	997
Templeton Carpet Factory, Glasgow	1496
Tennis	1390
Tennyson	1607
Test-tube Baby	2082
Textiles	1192
Thames Flood Barrier	1216
The Albert Memorial	1121
Theatre	1183
"The Barley Sheaf"	2396
The Clangers	1943
"The Cross Keys"	2394
The Lowry/Salford	2145
"The Mayflower"	2395
The Rows, Chester	976
"The Stamp Show 2000", Earls Court, London	**MS**2146, **MS**2147
"The Station"	2392
The Tale of Peter Rabbit	1091
The Wind in the Willows	1092
Third Millennum/Muncaster	2125
Thomas, John G. Parry	2061
Thoroughbred	1066
Timekeeping	2069
Tin Mine, St. Agnes, Cornwall	1441
Titanic (liner)	1890
Tolkien, J. R. R.	2050, 2429
Tomato	2354
Torrs Walkway/New Mills	2127
Tower Bridge	2310
Tower of London	1054
Toys and Games	1436, 2397
Trains	1272
Trans Pennine Trail	2153
Transport	1392
Trees	922, 949
Trenchard, Lord and De Havilland DH9A	1338
Trick Tricyclists	2277
Trident	2286
Triumph (cars)	1945
Trout	1209
TS²K Talent & Skills 2000	2177
Tunnicliffe	1915
Turnberry, 9th Hole (golf)	1833
Turner, Joseph, Birth Bicentenary	971
Turning the Tide/Durham Coast	2134
Tutankhamun Discovery, 50th Anniversary	901
"Ulster '71" Paintings	881
Ultrasonic Imaging	1839
Uniform Postage, 1840	1098
United Nations	1876
Universal Postal Union Centenary	954
University of Essex	893
University of Leicester	892
University of Southampton	891
Urban Renewal	1245
Vaughan Williams, Ralph, Birth Centenary	903
VC10	2287
VE Day	1873, 1875
"VERY DRY"	2200
Victoria	1367
Victorian Britain	1367
Votes for Women	2098
War Cemetery	2113
Waverley Class (railway loco)	985
Weather	2197
Weaver's Craft	2088
Web of Life/London Zoo	2139

Commemorative Design Index

Weightlifting	1330	Wood, Sir Henry (conductor)	1130
Wells-Brimtoy	2398	World Cup (football)	2093, 2291
Wells, H.G.	1878	World of Literature	2121
Welsh Bible	1384	World of Music	2120
Welsh Black Bull	1243	World of the Stage	2119
Welsh Pony	1065	World Student Games 1991	1564
Welsh Springer Spaniel	1076	World Wars	2113
Wesley	2115	Wright, Billy	1928
West Highland Terrier	1077		
Westminster Bridge	2311	Yachts	980
Westminster Palace	988	Year of the Artist	2175
Wildfowl and Wetlands Trust	1915	Year of the Child	1091
Wildscreen-at-Bristol	2162	Yellow Wagtail	1112
Wimbledon (tennis)	1835	"Yews For The Millennium"	2156
Winnie-the-Pooh	1093	York, 1900th Anniversary	888
Wintertime	1587	Youth Organisations	1179
Wireless First Message 1895	1889		

UNITED KINGDOM OF GREAT BRITAIN AND IRELAND

QUEEN VICTORIA

20 June 1837-22 January 1901

MULREADY ENVELOPES AND LETTER SHEETS, so called from the name of the designer, William Mulready, were issued concurrently with the first British adhesive stamps.

1d. black

Envelopes: ...... £250 *unused*; £325 *used*.
Letter Sheets: ... £225 *unused*; £300 *used*.

2d. blue

Envelopes: ...... £325 *unused*; £900 *used*.
Letter Sheets: ... £300 *unused*; £850 *used*.

LINE-ENGRAVED ISSUES

GENERAL NOTES

Brief notes on some aspects of the line-engraved stamps follow, but for further information and a full specialist treatment of these issues collectors are recommended to consult Volume 1 of the Stanley Gibbons *Great Britain Specialised Catalogue*.

Alphabet I   Alphabet II

Alphabet III   Alphabet IV

Typical Corner Letters of the four Alphabets

Alphabets. Four different styles were used for the corner letters on stamps prior to the issue with letters in all four corners, these being known to collectors as:
Alphabet I. Used for all plates made from 1840 to the end of 1851. Letters small.
Alphabet II. Plates from 1852 to mid-1855. Letters larger, heavier and broader.
Alphabet III. Plates from mid-1855 to end of period. Letters tall and more slender.
Alphabet IV. 1861. 1d. Die II, Plates 50 and 51 only. Letters were hand-engraved instead of being punched on the plate. They are therefore inconsistent in shape and size but generally larger and outstanding.
While the general descriptions and the illustrations of typical letters given above may be of some assistance, only long experience and published aids can enable every stamp to be allocated to its particular Alphabet without hesitation, as certain letters in each are similar to those in one of the others.

Blued Paper. The blueing of the paper of the earlier issues is believed to be due to the presence of prussiate of potash in the printing ink, or in the paper, which, under certain conditions, tended to colour the paper when the sheets were damped for printing. An alternative term is bleuté paper.

Corner Letters. The corner letters on the early British stamps were intended as a safeguard against forgery, each stamp in the sheet having a different combination of letters. Taking the first 1d. stamp, printed in 20 horizontal rows of 12, as an example, the lettering is as follows:

Row 1.   A A, A B, A C, etc. to A L.

Row 2.   B A, B B, B C, etc. to B L.

and so on to

Row 20.   T A, T B, T C, etc. to T L.

On the stamps with four corner letters, those in the upper corners are in the reverse positions to those in the lower corners. Thus in a sheet of 240 (12 × 20) the sequence is:

Row 1.   A A A B A C etc. to   L A
           A A A A B A C   A L

Row 2.   A B B B C B etc. to   L B
           B A B B B C   B L

and so on to

Row 20.   A T B T C T etc. to   L T
          T A T B T C   T L

Placing letters in all four corners was not only an added precaution against forgery but was meant to deter unmarked parts of used stamps being pieced together and passed off as an unused whole.

Dies. The first die of the 1d. was used for making the original die of the 2d., both the No Lines and White Lines issues. In 1855 the 1d. Die I was amended by retouching the head and deepening the lines on a transferred impression of the original. This later version, known to collectors as Die II, was used for making the dies for the 1d. and 2d. with letters in all four corners and also for the 1½d.

The two dies are illustrated above No. 17 in the catalogue.

Double letter   Guide line in corner

Guide line through value

Double Corner Letters. These are due to the workman placing his letter-punch in the wrong position at the first attempt, when lettering the plate, and then correcting the mistake; or to a slight shifting of the punch when struck. If a wrong letter was struck in the first instance, traces of a wrong letter may appear in a corner in addition to the correct one. A typical example is illustrated.

Guide Lines and Dots. When laying down the impressions of the design on the early plates, fine vertical and horizontal guide lines were marked on the plates to assist the operative. These were usually removed from the gutter margins, but could not be removed from the stamp impression without damage to the plate, so that in such cases they appear on the printed stamps, sometimes in the corners, sometimes through "POSTAGE" or the value. Typical examples are illustrated.

Guide dots or cuts were similarly made to indicate the spacing of the guide lines. These too sometimes appear on the stamps.

Ivory Head

"Ivory Head". The so-called "ivory head" variety is one in which the Queen's Head shows white on the back of the stamp. It arises from the comparative absence of ink in the head portion of the design, with consequent absence of blueing. (*See* "Blued Paper", on page 1).

Line-engraving. In this context "line-engraved" is synonymous with recess-printing, in which the engraver cuts recesses in a plate and printing (the coloured areas) is from these recesses. "Line-engraved" is the traditional philatelic description for these stamps; other equivalent terms found are "engraving in *taille-douce*" (French) or "in *intaglio*" (Italian).

Plates. Until the introduction of the stamps with letters in all four corners, the number of the plate was not indicated in the design of the stamp, but was printed on the sheet margin. By long study of identifiable blocks and the minor variation in the design, coupled with the position of the corner letters, philatelists are now able to allot many of these stamps to their respective plates. Specialist collectors often endeavour to obtain examples of a given stamp printed from its different plates and our catalogue accordingly reflects this depth of detail.

Maltese Cross   Type of Town postmark

Type of Penny Post cancellation

Example of 1844 type postmark

Postmarks. The so-called "Maltese Cross" design was the first employed for obliterating British postage stamps and was in use from 1840 to 1844. Being hand-cut, the obliterating stamps varied greatly in detail and some distinctive types can be allotted to particular towns or offices. Local types, such as those used at Manchester, Norwich, Leeds, etc., are keenly sought. A red ink was first employed, but was superseded by black, after some earlier experiments, in February 1841. Maltese Cross obliterations in other colours are rare.

Obliterations of this type, numbered 1 to 12 in the centre, were used at the London Chief Office in 1843 and 1844.

Some straight-line cancellations were in use in 1840 at the Penny Post receiving offices, normally applied on the envelope, the adhesives then being obliterated at the Head Office. They are nevertheless known, with or without Maltese Cross, on the early postage stamps.

In 1842 some offices in S.W. England used dated postmarks in place of the Maltese Cross, usually on the back of the letter since they were not originally intended as obliterators. These town postmarks have likewise been found on adhesives.

In 1844 the Maltese Cross design was superseded by numbered obliterators of varied type, one of which is illustrated. They are naturally comparatively scarce on the first 1d. and 2d. stamps. Like the Maltese Cross they are found in various colours, some of which are rare.

Re-entry

"Union Jack" re-entry

Re-entries. Re-entries on the plate show as a doubling of part of the design of the stamp generally at top or bottom. Many re-entries are very slight while others are most marked. A typical one is illustrated.

The *"Union Jack" re-entry*, so-called owing to the effect of the re-entry on the appearance of the corner stars (*see illustration*) occurs on stamp L K of Plate 75 of the 1d. red, Die I.

T A (T L)   M A (M L)
Varieties of Large Crown Watermark

I   Two states of Large Crown Watermark   II

Watermarks. Two watermark varieties, as illustrated, consisting of crowns of entirely different shape, are found in sheets of the Large Crown paper and fall on stamps lettered M A and T A (or M L and T L when the paper is printed on the wrong side). Both varieties are found on the 1d. rose-red of 1857, while the M A (M L) variety comes also on some plates of the 1d. of 1864 (Nos. 43, 44) up to about Plate 96. On the 2d. the T A (T L) variety is known on plates 8 and 9, and the M A (M L) on later prints of plate 9. These varieties may exist inverted, or inverted reversed on stamps lettered A A and A L and H A and H L, and some are known.

In 1861 a minor alteration was made in the Large Crown watermark by the removal of the two vertical strokes, representing *fleurs-de-lis*, which projected upwards from the uppermost of the three horizontal curves at the base of the Crown. Hence two states are distinguishable, as illustrated.

CONDITION—IMPERFORATE LINE-ENGRAVED ISSUES

The prices quoted for the 1840 and 1841 imperforate Line-engraved issues are for "fine" examples. As condition is most important in assessing the value of a stamp, the following definitions will assist collectors in the evaluation of individual examples.

Four main factors are relevant when considering quality.

(a) **Impression.** This should be clean and the surface free of any rubbing or unnatural blurring which would detract from the appearance.

(b) **Margins.** This is perhaps the most difficult factor to evaluate. Stamps described as "fine", the standard adopted in this catalogue for pricing purposes, should have margins of the recognised width, defined as approximately one half of the distance between two adjoining unsevered stamps. Stamps described as "very fine" or "superb" should have margins which are proportionately larger than those of a "fine" stamp. Examples with close margins should not, generally, be classified as "fine".

(c) **Cancellation.** On a "fine" stamp this should be reasonably clear and not noticeably smudged. A stamp described as "superb" should have a neat cancellation, preferably centrally placed or to the right.

(d) **Appearance.** Stamps, at the prices quoted, should always be without any tears, creases, bends or thins and should not be toned on either the front or back. Stamps with such defects are worth only a proportion of the catalogue price.

Good

Fine

Very Fine

Superb

The actual size illustrations of 1840 1d. blacks show the various grades of quality. When comparing these illustrations it should be assumed that they are all from the same plate and that they are free of any hidden defects.

PRINTERS. Nos. 1/53a were recess-printed by Perkins, Bacon & Petch, known from 1852 as Perkins, Bacon & Co.

STAMPS ON COVER. Prices are quoted, for those Victorian and Edwardian issues usually found used on cover. In general these prices refer to the cheapest versions of each basic stamp with other shades, plates or varieties, together with unusual frankings and postmarks, being worth more.

1

1a

2 Small Crown

(Eng Charles and Frederick Heath)

1840 (6 May). *Letters in lower corners. Wmk Small Crown, W **2**. Imperf.*

				Un	Used	Used on cover
1	**1**	1d.	intense black	£5500	£300	
2		1d.	black	£4500	£225	£400
	Wi.		Watermark inverted	£7500	£1000	
3		1d.	grey-black (worn plate)	£5250	£325	
4	**1a**	2d.	dp full blue	£13000	£650	
5		2d.	blue	£10000	£500	£1100
	Wi.		Watermark inverted	£18000	£2500	
6		2d.	pale blue	£13000	£550	

The 1d. stamp in black was printed from Plates 1 to 11. Plate 1 exists in two states (known to collectors as 1a and 1b), the latter being the result of extensive repairs.

Repairs were also made to plates 2, 5, 6, 8, 9, 10 and 11, and certain impressions exist in two or more states.

The so-called "Royal reprint" of the 1d. black was made in 1864, from Plate 66, Die II, on paper with Large Crown watermark, inverted. A printing was also made in carmine, on paper with the same watermark, normal.

For 1d. black with "VR" in upper corners *see* No. V1 under Official Stamps.

The 2d. stamps were printed from Plates 1 and 2.

Plates of 1d. black

Plate	Un	Used	Used on cover
1a	£6000	£250	£475
1b	£4500	£225	£400
2	£4500	£225	£400
3	£5750	£275	£500
4	£4500	£250	£425
5	£4500	£225	£425
6	£4500	£225	£425
7	£4750	£250	£500
8	£5250	£300	£550
9	£6250	£350	£650
10	£7750	£500	£1100
11	£8500	£3000	£6000

Varieties of 1d. black

			Un	Used
a.	On *bleuté* paper (Plates 1 to 8) .... from		—	£350
b.	Double letter in corner .... from		£4750	£250
bb.	Re-entry .... from		£5000	£275
bc.	"PB" re-entry (Plate 5, 3rd state)		—	£4500
c.	Guide line in corner .... from		£4750	£250
cc.	Large letters in each corner (E J, I L, J C and P A) (Plate 1*b*) .... from		£4750	£375
d.	Guide line through value		£4750	£275
g.	Obliterated by Maltese Cross			
		In red	—	£250
		In black	—	£225
		In blue	—	£3750
		In magenta	—	£1250
		In yellow	—	—
h.	Obliterated by Maltese Cross with number in centre .... from			
		No. 1	—	£3500
		No. 2	—	£3500
		No. 3	—	£3500
		No. 4	—	£3500
		No. 5	—	£3500
		No. 6	—	£3500
		No. 7	—	£3500
		No. 8	—	£3500
		No. 9	—	£3500
		No. 10	—	£3500
		No. 11	—	£3500
		No. 12	—	£3500
i.	Obliterated "Penny Post" in black (without Maltese Cross) .... from		—	£1900
j.	Obliterated by town postmark (without Maltese Cross)			
		In black .... from	—	£2500
		In yellow .... from	—	£15000
		In red .... from	—	£2500
k.	Obliterated by 1844 type postmark in black from		—	£650

Plates of 2d. blue

Plate		Un	Used	Used on cover
1	...............Shades from	£10000	£500	£1250
2	...............Shades from	£12000	£550	£1100

Varieties of 2d. blue

			Un	Used
a.	Double letter in corner		—	£550
aa.	Re-entry		—	£600
b.	Guide line in corner		—	£525
c.	Guide line through value		—	£525
e.	Obliterated by Maltese Cross			
		In red	—	£550
		In black	—	£500
		In blue	—	£4750
		In magenta	—	£4000
f.	Obliterated by Maltese Cross with number in centre .... from			
		No. 1	—	£4000
		No. 2	—	£4000
		No. 3	—	£4250
		No. 4	—	£4000
		No. 5	—	£4000
		No. 6	—	£4250
		No. 7	—	£4250
		No. 8	—	£4750
		No. 9	—	£4750
		No. 10	—	£4250
		No. 11	—	£4250
		No. 12	—	£3750

			Un	Used
g.	Obliterated "Penny Post" in black (without Maltese Cross) ....from		—	£2250
h.	Obliterated by town postmark (without Maltese Cross) in black		—	£2500
i.	Obliterated by 1844 type postmark			
		In black ....from	—	£1250
		In blue ....from	—	£5250

1841 (10 Feb). *Printed from "black" plates. Wmk W* **2***. Paper more or less blued. Imperf.*

			Un	Used	Used on cover
7	**1**	1d. red-brown (*shades*)	£950	75·00	£175
		a. "PB" re-entry (Plate 5, 3rd state)	—	£1500	
		Wi. Watermark inverted (Plates 1*b*, 8 and 10) .... from	—	£1250	

The first printings of the 1d. in red-brown were made from Plates 1*b*, 2, 5 and 8 to 11 used for the 1d. black.

1d. red-brown from "black" plates

Plate	Un	Used	Used on cover
1*b*	£4000	£250	£425
2	£2750	£200	£275
5	£950	£110	£220
8	£950	90·00	£180
9	£950	90·00	£180
10	£950	90·00	£200
11	£700	75·00	£200

1841 (late Feb). *Plate 12 onwards. Wmk W* **2***. Paper more or less blued. Imperf.*

			Un	Used	Used on cover
8	**1**	1d. red-brown	£250	15·00	25·00
		Wi. Watermark inverted	£950	£175	
8a		1d. red-brown on very blue paper	£300	15·00	
9		1d. pale red-brown (worn plates)	£350	25·00	
10		1d. deep red-brown	£400	30·00	
11		1d. lake-red	£2000	£425	
12		1d. orange-brown	£750	£125	

Error. No letter "A" in right lower corner (Stamp B (A), Plate 77)

			Un	Used
12a	**1**	1d. red-brown	—	£7500

The error "No letter A in right corner" was due to the omission to insert this letter on stamp B A of Plate 77. The error was discovered some months after the plate was registered and was then corrected.

There are innumerable variations in the colour shade of the 1d. "red" and those given in the above list represent colour groups each covering a wide range.

Varieties of 1d. red-brown, etc.

			Un	Used
b.	Re-entry ....from		—	50·00
c.	Double letter in corner .... from		—	25·00
d.	Double Star (Plate 75) "Union Jack" re-entry £10000		£1500	
e.	Guide line in corner		—	18·00
f.	Guide line through value		—	22·00
g.	Thick outer frame to stamp		—	22·00
h.	Ivory head	£275	22·00
j.	Left corner letter "S" inverted (Plates 78, 105, 107) from		—	£100
k.	P converted to R (Plates 30/1, 33, 83, 86) ... from		—	60·00
l.	Obliterated by Maltese Cross			
		In red	—	£2500
		In black	—	40·00
		In blue	—	£350
m.	Obliterated by Maltese Cross with number in centre			
		No. 1	—	£100
		No. 2	—	£100
		No. 3	—	£125
		No. 4	—	£300

No. 5	—	£100
No. 6	—	80·00
No. 7	—	80·00
No. 8	—	80·00
No. 9	—	£100
No. 10	—	£150
No. 11	—	£175
No. 12	—	£200

n. Obliterated "Penny Post" in black (without
Maltese Cross) .... — £400
o. Obliterated by town postmark (without Maltese
Cross)

In black ....from	—	£350
In blue ....from	—	£800
In green ....from	—	£1200
In yellow ....from	—	—
In red ....from	—	£4500

p. Obliterated by 1844 type postmark

In blue ....from	—	£150
In red ....from	—	£3000
In green ....from	—	£750
In violet ....from	—	£1400
In black ....from	—	15·00

Stamps with thick outer frame to the design are from plates on
which the frame-lines have been straightened or recut, particularly
Plates 76 and 90.

For "Union Jack" re-entry *see* General Notes to Line-engraved
Issues.

In "P converted to R" the corner letter "R" is formed from the "P",
the distinctive long tail having been hand-cut.

KEY TO LINE-ENGRAVED ISSUES

S.G. Nos.

Nos.	Description	Date	Wmk	Perf	Die	Alpha-bet
THE IMPERFORATE ISSUES						
1/3	1d. black	6.5.40	SC	Imp	I	I
4/6	2d. no lines	8.5.40	SC	Imp	I	I
PAPER MORE OR LESS BLUED						
7	1d. red-brown	Feb 1841	SC	Imp	I	I
8/12	1d. red-brown	Feb 1841	SC	Imp	I	I
8/12	1d. red-brown	6.2.52	SC	Imp	I	II
13/15	2d. white lines	13.3.41	SC	Imp	I	I
THE PERFORATED ISSUES						
ONE PENNY VALUE						
16a	1d. red-brown	1848	SC	Roul	I	I
16b	1d. red-brown	1850	SC	16	I	I
16c	1d. red-brown	1853	SC	16	I	II
17/18	1d. red-brown	Feb 1854	SC	16	I	II
22	1d. red-brown	Jan 1855	SC	14	I	II
24/5	1d. red-brown	28.2.55	SC	14	II	II
21	1d. red-brown	1.3.55	SC	16	II	II
26	1d. red-brown	15.5.55	LC	16	II	II
29/33	1d. red-brown	Aug 1855	LC	14	II	III
NEW COLOURS ON WHITE PAPER						
37/41	1d. rose-red	Nov 1856	LC	14	II	III
36	1d. rose-red	26.12.57	LC	16	II	III
42	1d. rose-red	1861	LC	14	II	IV
TWO PENCE VALUE						
19, 20	2d. blue	1.3.54	SC	16	I	I
23	2d. blue	22.2.55	SC	14	I	I
23a	2d. blue	5.7.55	SC	14	I	II
20a	2d. blue	18.8.55	SC	16	I	II
27	2d. blue	20.7.55	LC	16	I	II
34	2d. blue	20.7.55	LC	14	I	II
35	2d. blue	2.7.57	LC	14	I	III
36a	2d. blue	1.2.58	LC	16	I	III

LETTERS IN ALL FOUR CORNERS

48/9	½d. rose-red	1.10.70	W **9**	14	—	
43/4	1d. rose-red	1.4.64	LC	14	II	
53a	1½d. rosy mauve	1860	LC	14	II	
51/3	1½d.rose-red	1.10.70	LC	14	II	
45	2d. blue	July 1858	LC	14	II	
46/7	2d. thinner lines	7.7.69	LC	14	II	

Watermarks: SC = Small Crown, T **2**. LC = Large Crown, T **4**.
Dies: See notes above No. 17 in the catalogue.
Alphabets: See General Notes to this section.

3 White lines added

1841 (13 Mar)–**51**. *White lines added. Wmk W **2**. Paper more or less
blued. Imperf.*

				Un	Used	Used on cover
13	**3**	2d. pale blue		£2500	80·00	
14		2d. blue		£2250	70·00	£225
		Wi. Watermark inverted		£4000	£400	
15		2d. dp full blue		£2500	80·00	
15aa		2d. violet-blue (1851) £12000	£800			

The 2d. stamp with white lines was printed from Plates 3 and 4.
No. 15aa came from Plate 4 and the quoted price is for examples on
thicker, lavender tinted paper.

Plates of 2d. blue

Plate		Un	Used
3	...............Shades from	£2250	80·00
4	...............Shades from	£2250	70·00

Varieties of 2d. blue

		Un	Used
a.	Guide line in corner	—	85·00
b.	Guide line through value	£2500	85·00
bb.	Double letter in corner	—	90·00
be.	Re-entry	£3000	£110
c.	Ivory head	£2500	80·00
e.	Obliterated by Maltese Cross		
	In red	—£11000	
	In black	—	£150
	In blue	—	£2250
f.	Obliterated by Maltese Cross with number in centre		
	No. 1	—	£350
	No. 2	—	£350
	No. 3	—	£350
	No. 4	—	£325
	No. 5	—	£475
	No. 6	—	£350
	No. 7	—	£650
	No. 8	—	£500
	No. 9	—	£650
	No. 10	—	£700
	No. 11	—	£475
	No. 12	—	£275
g.	Obliterated by town postmark (without Maltese Cross)		
	In black ....from	—	£750
	In blue ....from	—	£1250

h.	Obliterated by 1844 type postmark				
	In black .... *from*	—	70·00		
	In blue .... *from*	—	£500		
	In red .... *from*	—	£8500		
	In green .... *from*	—	£1500		

1841 (Apr). *Trial printing (unissued) on Dickinson silk-thread paper. No wmk. Imperf.*

16	**1**	1d. red-brown (Plate 11)	£3000		

Eight sheets were printed on this paper, six being gummed, two ungummed, but we have only seen examples without gum.

1848. *Wmk W* **2**. *Rouletted approx 11½ by Henry Archer.*

16a	**1**	1d. red-brown (Plates 70, 71)	£6500		

1850. *Wmk W* **2**. *P 16 by Henry Archer.*

16b	**1**	1d. red-brown (Alph 1) (from Plates 90–101)			
		from	£1000	£350	£850
	*b*Wi.	Watermark inverted	—	£1100	

1853. *Wmk W* **2**. *Government Trial Perforation.*

16c	**1**	1d. red-brown (p 16) (Alph II) (on cover)	†	£9000	

SEPARATION TRIALS. Although the various trials of machines for rouletting and perforating were unofficial, Archer had the consent of the authorities in making his experiments, and sheets so experimented upon were afterwards used by the Post Office.

As Archer ended his experiments in 1850 and plates with corner letters of Alphabet II did not come into issue until 1852, perforated stamps with corner letters of Alphabet I may safely be assumed to be Archer productions, if genuine.

The Government trial perforation is believed to have been done on Archer's machines after they had been purchased in 1853. As Alphabet II was by that time in use, the trials can be distinguished from the perforated stamps listed below by being dated prior to 24 February 1854, the date when the perforated stamps were officially issued.

Die I, Alphabet I, stamps from plates 74 and 113 perforated 14 have been recorded for many years, but it is now generally recognised that the type of comb machine used, producing one extension hole in the side margins, cannot be contemporary with other trials of this period.

Die I   Die II   **4** Large Crown

Die I: The features of the portrait are lightly shaded and consequently lack emphasis.

Die II (Die I retouched): The lines of the features have been deepened and appear stronger.

The eye is deeply shaded and made more lifelike. The nostril and lips are more clearly defined, the latter appearing much thicker. A strong downward stroke of colour marks the corner of the mouth. There is a deep indentation of colour between lower lip and chin. The band running from the back of the ear to the chignon has a bolder horizontal line below it than in Die I.

1854–57. *Paper more or less blued.* (a) *Wmk Small Crown, W* **2**.

			Un	★ Used on Used cover

17	**1**	1d. red-brown (Die I) (24.2.54)	£250	18·00	40·00
	a.	Imperf three sides (horiz pair)	†	—	
	Wi.	Watermark inverted	—	£150	

18	**1**	1d. yellow-brown (Die I)	£300	40·00	
19	**3**	2d. dp blue (Plate 4) (12.3.54)	£2500	85·00	£130
	a.	Imperf three sides (horiz pair)	†		
	Wi.	Watermark inverted		£210	
20		2d. pale blue (Plate 4)	£2500	90·00	
20a		2d. blue (Plate 5) (18.8.55)	£4500	£250	£400
	aWi.	Watermark inverted	—	£550	
21	**1**	1d. red-brown (Die II) (22.2.55)	£275	50·00	90·00
	a.	Imperf (Plates 2, 14)			
	Wi.	Watermark inverted	£600	£150	

(b) Wmk Small Crown, W **2**. *P* 14

22	**1**	1d. red-brown (Die I) (1.55)	£450	60·00	£110
	Wi.	Watermark inverted	—	£200	
23	**3**	2d. blue (Plate 4) (22.2.55)	£4500	£180	£275
	Wi.	Watermark inverted	—	£400	
23a		2d. blue (Plate 5) (4.7.55)	£5500	£250	£350
	b.	Imperf (Plate 5)			
	aWi.	Watermark inverted	—	£450	
24	**1**	1d. red-brown (Die II) (27.2.55)	£400	45·00	75·00
	Wi.	Watermark inverted	£1000	£150	
24a		1d. dp red-brown (very blue paper) (Die II)	£475	70·00	
25		1d. orange-brown (Die II)	£1200	£125	

(c) Wmk Large Crown, W **4**. *P* 16

26	**1**	1d. red-brown (Die II) (15.5.55)	£700	80·00	£150
	a.	Imperf (Plate 7)	—		
	Wi.	Watermark inverted	—	£200	
27	**3**	2d. blue (Plate 5) (20.7.55)	£6000	£325	£400
	a.	Imperf	—	£4000	
	Wi.	Watermark inverted	—	£550	

(d) Wmk Large Crown, W **4**. *P* 14.

29	**1**	1d. red-brown (Die II) (6.55)	£180	15·00	30·00
	a.	Imperf (*shades*) (Plates 22, 24, 25, 32, 43)	£1500	£1200	
	Wi.	Watermark inverted	£650	80·00	
30		1d. brick-red (Die II)	£250	35·00	
31		1d. plum (Die II) (2.56)	£1500	£500	
32		1d. brown-rose (Die II)	£250	35·00	
33		1d. orange-brown (Die II) (3.57)	£375	40·00	
34	**3**	2d. blue (Plate 5) (20.7.55)	£1750	50·00	£130
	Wi.	Watermark inverted	—	£200	
35		2d. blue (Plate 6) (2.7.57)	£2000	50·00	£130
	a.	Imperf	—	£4000	
	b.	Imperf horiz (vert pair)	†	—	
	Wi.	Watermark inverted	—	£200	
★17/35a		**For well-centred, lightly used**	+125%		

1856–58. *Wmk Large Crown, W* **4**. *Paper no longer blued.* (a) *P* 16.

36	**1**	1d. rose-red (Die II) (26.12.57)	£1250	60·00	£130
	Wi.	Watermark inverted	—	£225	
36a	**3**	2d. blue (Plate 6) (1.2.58)	£6000	£300	£400
	aWi.	Watermark inverted	—	£500	

(b) Die II. P 14

37	**1**	1d. red-brown (11.56)	£700	£175	£450
38		1d. pale red (9.4.57)	75·00	15·00	
	a.	Imperf	£1200	£850	
39		1d. pale rose (3.57)	75·00	25·00	
40		1d. rose-red (9.57)	40·00	9·00	20·00
	a.	Imperf	£1200	£850	
	b.	Imperf vert (horiz pair)	†	—	
	Wi.	Watermark inverted	£100	50·00	
41		1d. dp rose-red (7.57)	90·00	12·00	

1861. *Letters engraved on plate instead of punched (Alphabet IV).*

42	**1**	1d. rose-red (Die II) (Plates 50 & 51)	£200	30·00	50·00
	a.	Imperf	—	£2250	
	Wi.	Watermark inverted	£325	70·00	
★36/42a		**For well-centred, lightly used**	+125%		

The original die (Die I) was used to provide roller dies for the laying down of all the line-engraved stamps from 1840 to 1855. In that year a

Andrew Claridge

Specialist in the Postage Stamps
of Great Britain

Buying or Selling Great Britain?

With wide experience of the market in British philately, in the United
Kingdom and Overseas, both as an auctioneer and a dealer, I am ideally placed
to assist the discerning collector

Collection building can be a time consuming pastime and
professional assistance can make all the difference. When it comes to selling it
is also important to make the correct choice, whether private treaty, auction,
or direct sale

Consultancy and Advice

I am keen to help you find the items you are looking for, or achieve the best
possible realisation for your collection. I offer considered and practical advice on
the best method of disposal. Colour illustrated lists available on request.

Please contact me for further information

P.O. Box 1999 Witham Essex CM8 1RZ
Telephone/Fax 01376 584412 Fax 01376 585388
E-mail Andrew.Claridge@btinternet.com

new master die was laid down (by means of a Die I roller die) and the impression was retouched by hand engraving by William Humphrys. This retouched die, always known to philatelists as Die II, was from that time used for preparing all new roller dies.

One Penny. The numbering of the 1d. plates recommenced at 1 on the introduction of Die II. Plates 1 to 21 were Alphabet II from which a scarce plum shade exists. Corner letters of Alphabet III appear on Plate 22 and onwards.

As an experiment, the corner letters were engraved by hand on Plates 50 and 51 in 1856, instead of being punched (Alphabet IV), but punching was again resorted to from Plate 52 onwards. Plates 50 and 51 were not put into use until 1861.

Two Pence. Unlike the 1d. the old sequence of plate numbers continued. Plates 3 and 4 of the 2d. had corner letters of Alphabet I, Plate 5 Alphabet II and Plate 6 Alphabet III. In Plate 6 the white lines are thinner than before.

In both values, varieties may be found as described in the preceding issues—ivory heads, inverted watermarks, re-entries, and double letters in corners.

The change of perforation from 16 to 14 was decided upon late in 1854 since the closer holes of the former gauge tended to cause the sheets of stamps to break up when handled, but for a time both gauges were in concurrent use. Owing to faulty alignment of the impressions on the plates and to shrinkage of the paper when dampened, badly perforated stamps are plentiful in the line-engraved issues.

5

6

Showing position of the plate number on the 1d. and 2d. values. (Plate 170 shown)

1858–79. *Letters in all four corners. Wmk Large Crown, W **4**. Die II (1d. and 2d.). P 14.*

			Un	Used	★ Used on cover
43	5	1d. rose-red (1.4.64)	15·00	2·00	6·00
44		1d. lake-red	15·00	2·00	
	a.	Imperf	*from* £1600	£1250	
	Wi.	Watermark inverted	*from* 60·00	20·00	
★43/4a		**For well-centred, lightly used**		+ **125%**	

Plate	Un	Used		Plate	Un	Used
71	35·00	3·00		88	£130	8·00
72	40·00	4·00		89	40·00	2·00
73	40·00	3·00		90	40·00	2·00
74	40·00	2·00		91	55·00	6·00
76	35·00	2·00		92	35·00	2·00
77	—	£120000		93	50·00	2·00
78	90·00	2·00		94	45·00	5·00
79	30·00	2·00		95	40·00	2·00
80	45·00	2·00		96	45·00	4·00
81	45·00	2·25		97	40·00	3·50
82	90·00	4·00		98	50·00	6·00
83	£110	7·00		99	55·00	5·00
84	60·00	2·25		100	60·00	2·25
85	40·00	2·25		101	60·00	9·00
86	50·00	4·00		102	45·00	2·00
87	30·00	2·00		103	50·00	3·50

Plate	Un	Used
104	75·00	5·00
105	90·00	7·00
106	55·00	2·00
107	60·00	7·00
108	80·00	2·25
109	85·00	3·50
110	60·00	9·00
111	50·00	2·25
112	70·00	2·25
113	50·00	12·00
114	£250	12·00
115	90·00	2·25
116	75·00	9·00
117	45·00	2·00
118	50·00	2·00
119	45·00	2·00
120	15·00	2·00
121	40·00	9·50
122	15·00	2·00
123	40·00	2·00
124	28·00	2·00
125	40·00	2·00
127	55·00	2·25
129	40·00	8·00
130	55·00	2·25
131	65·00	16·00
132	£130	22·00
133	£110	9·00
134	15·00	2·00
135	95·00	26·00
136	90·00	20·00
137	28·00	2·25
138	18·00	2·00
139	60·00	16·00
140	18·00	2·00
141	£110	9·00
142	70·00	24·00
143	60·00	15·00
144	95·00	20·00
145	30·00	2·25
146	40·00	6·00
147	50·00	3·00
148	40·00	3·00
149	40·00	6·00
150	15·00	2·00
151	60·00	9·00
152	60·00	5·50
153	£100	9·00
154	50·00	2·00
155	50·00	2·25
156	45·00	2·00
157	50·00	2·00
158	30·00	2·00
159	30·00	2·00
160	30·00	2·00
161	60·00	7·00
162	50·00	7·00
163	50·00	3·00
164	50·00	3·00
165	45·00	2·00

Plate	Un	Used
166	45·00	6·00
167	45·00	2·00
168	50·00	8·00
169	60·00	7·00
170	35·00	2·00
171	15·00	2·00
172	30·00	2·00
173	70·00	9·00
174	30·00	2·00
175	60·00	3·50
176	60·00	2·25
177	40·00	2·00
178	60·00	3·50
179	50·00	2·25
180	60·00	5·00
181	45·00	2·00
182	90·00	5·00
183	55·00	3·00
184	30·00	2·25
185	50·00	3·00
186	65·00	2·25
187	50·00	2·00
188	70·00	10·00
189	70·00	7·00
190	50·00	6·00
191	30·00	7·00
192	50·00	2·00
193	30·00	2·00
194	50·00	8·00
195	50·00	8·00
196	50·00	5·00
197	55·00	9·00
198	40·00	6·00
199	55·00	6·00
200	60·00	2·00
201	30·00	5·00
202	60·00	8·00
203	30·00	16·00
204	55·00	2·25
205	55·00	3·00
206	55·00	9·00
207	60·00	9·00
208	55·00	16·00
209	50·00	9·00
210	65·00	12·00
211	70·00	20·00
212	60·00	11·00
213	60·00	11·00
214	65·00	18·00
215	65·00	18·00
216	70·00	18·00
217	70·00	7·00
218	65·00	8·00
219	90·00	70·00
220	40·00	7·00
221	70·00	16·00
222	80·00	40·00
223	90·00	60·00
224	£100	50·00
225	£1750	£650

Error. Imperf. Issued at Cardiff (Plate 116)

			Un	Used
44b	5	1d. rose-red (18.1.70)	£4000	£2000

The following plate numbers are also known imperf and used (No. 44a); 72, 79, 80, 81, 82, 83, 84, 85, 86, 87, 88, 90, 91, 92, 93, 96, 97, 98, 100, 101, 102, 103, 104, 105, 107, 108, 109, 112, 113, 114, 116, 117, 120, 121, 122, 136, 137, 142, 146, 148, 158, 162, 164, 166, 171, 174, 191 and 202.

The numbering of this series of 1d. red plates follows after that of the previous 1d. stamp, last printed from Plate 68.

Plates 69, 70, 75, 126 and 128 were prepared for this issue but rejected owing to defects, and stamps from these plates do not exist, so that specimens which appear to be from these plates (like many of those which optimistic collectors believe to be from Plate 77) bear other plate numbers. Owing to faulty engraving or printing it is not always easy to identify the plate number. Plate 77 was also rejected but some stamps printed from it were used. One specimen is in the Tapling Collection and six or seven others are known. Plates 226 to 228 were made but not used.

Specimens from most of the plates are known with inverted watermark. The variety of watermark described in the General Notes to this section occurs on stamp M A (or M L) on plates up to about 96 (*Prices from* £110 *used*).

Re-entries in this issue are few, the best being on stamps M K and T K of Plate 71 and on S L and T L, Plate 83.

			Un	★ Used on Used	cover
45	**6**	2d. blue (thick lines) (7.58)	£275	10·00	35·00
		a. Imperf (Plate 9)	—	£3750	
		Wi. Watermark inverted	£425	£150	
		Plate			
		7	£1000	45·00	
		8	£900	32·00	
		9	£275	10·00	
		12	£1500	£110	
46		2d. blue (thin lines) (1.7.69)	£300	20·00	50·00
		Wi. Watermark inverted	£750	£150	
47		2d. dp blue (thin lines)	£300	20·00	
		a. Imperf (Plate 13)	£4500		
		Plate			
		13	£300	20·00	
		14	£375	25·00	
		15	£350	25·00	
★45/7		**For well-centred, lightly used**		+**125**%	

Plates 10 and 11 of the 2d. were prepared but rejected. Plates 13 to 15 were laid down from a new roller impression on which the white lines were thinner.

There are some marked re-entries and repairs, particularly on Plates 7, 8, 9 and 12.

Stamps with inverted watermark may be found and also the T A (T L) and M A (M L) watermark varieties (see General Notes to this section).

Though the paper is normally white, some printings showed blueing and stamps showing the "ivory head" may therefore be found.

7 Showing the plate number (9)

9

1870 (1 Oct). *Wmk W* **9**, *extending over three stamps. P* 14.

			Un	★ Used on Used	cover
48	**7**	½d. rose-red	85·00	15·00	55·00
49		½d. rose	85·00	15·00	
		a. Imperf (Plates 1, 4, 5, 6, 8, 14) *from*	£1500	£1000	
		Wi. Watermark inverted	—	£100	
		Wj. Watermark reversed	—	£100	

(49)	Wk. Watermark inverted & reversed ..	£180	70·00
	Plate		
	1	£180	70·00
	3	£140	35·00
	4	£120	25·00
	5	85·00	15·00
	6	90·00	15·00
	8	£225	90·00
	9	£3250	£600
	10	£100	15·00
	11	90·00	15·00
	12	90·00	15·00
	13	90·00	15·00
	14	90·00	15·00
	15	£140	35·00
	19	£160	50·00
	20	£190	70·00
★48/9a	**For well-centred, lightly used**		+**200**%

The ½d. was printed in sheets of 480 (24 × 20) so that the check letters run from AA AA to XT TX

Plates 2, 7, 16, 17 and 18 were not completed while Plates 21 and 22, though made, were not used.

Owing to the method of perforating, the outer side of stamps in either the A or X row (ie the left or right side of the sheet) is imperf.

Stamps may be found with watermark inverted or reversed, or without watermark, the latter due to misplacement of the paper when printing.

8 Position of plate number

1870 (1 Oct). *Wmk W* **4**. *P* 14.

			Un	★ Used on Used	cover
51	**8**	1½d. rose-red	£350	45·00	£200
52		1½d. lake-red	£350	45·00	
		a. Imperf (Plates 1 & 3) ....*from*	£3000	†	
		Wi. Watermark inverted	—	£250	
		Plate			
		(1)	£500	65·00	
		3	£350	40·00	

Error of lettering. OP–PC *for* CP–PC (*Plate* 1)

| 53 | **8** | 1½d. rose-red .... | £8000 | £900 |

Prepared for use in 1860, but not issued; blued paper.

53a	**8**	1½d. rosy mauve (Plate 1)	£3500	
		b. Error of lettering, OP–PC for CP–PC	—	†
★51/3		**For well-centred, lightly used**	+**125**%	

Owing to a proposed change in the postal rates, 1½d. stamps were first printed in 1860, in rosy mauve, No. 53a, but the change was not approved and the greater part of the stock was destroyed, although three or four postally used examples have been recorded.

In 1870 a 1½d. stamp was required and was issued in rose-red.

Plate 1 did not have the plate number in the design of the stamps, but on stamps from Plate 3 the number will be found in the frame as shown above.

Plate 2 was defective and was not used.

The error of lettering OP–PC on Plate 1 was apparently not noticed by the printer, and therefore not corrected.

EMBOSSED ISSUES

Volume 1 of the Stanley Gibbons *Great Britain Specialised Catalogue* gives further detailed information on the embossed issues.

PRICES. The prices quoted are for cut-square stamps with average to fine embossing. Stamps with exceptionally clear embossing are worth more.

| 10 | 11 | 12 |

13 Position of die number

(Primary die engraved at the Royal Mint by William Wyon. Stamps printed at Somerset House)

1847–54. *Imperf* (For paper and wmk see footnote).

				Un	Used	Used on cover
54	**10**	1s. pale green (11.9.47)		£7000	£500	£800
55		1s. green		£7000	£550	
56		1s. dp green		£7500	£550	
		Die 1 (1847)		£7000	£500	
		Die 2 (1854)		£7500	£575	
57	**11**	10d. brown (6.11.48)		£4500	£900	£1500
		Die 1 (1848)		£5000	£900	
		Die 2 (1850)		£4500	£900	
		Die 3 (1853)		£4500	£900	
		Die 4 (1854)		£5000	£900	
		Die 5				
58	**12**	6d. mauve (1.3.54)		£5250	£675	
59		6d. dull lilac		£5250	£675	£900
60		6d. purple		£5250	£675	
		Wi. Watermark upright		—	£675	
		Wj. Watermark inverted		—	£675	
		Wk. Watermark inverted & reversed		£5250	£675	
61		6d. violet		£6500	£1750	

The 1s. and 10d. are on "Dickinson" paper with "silk" threads. The 6d. is on paper watermarked V R in single-lined letters, W **13**, which may be found in four ways—upright, inverted, upright reversed, and inverted reversed.

The die numbers are indicated on the base of the bust. Only Die 1 (1 W W) of the 6d. was used for the adhesive stamps. The 10d. is from Die 1 (W.W.1 on stamps), and Dies 2 to 5 (2.W.W., 3.W.W., 4.W.W. and 5.W.W.) but the number and letters on stamps from Die 1 are seldom clear and many specimens are known without any trace of them. Because of this stamp we previously listed as "No die number" has been deleted. That they are from Die 1 is proved by the existence of blocks showing stamps with and without the die number. The 1s. is from Dies 1 and 2 (W.W.1, W.W.2).

The normal arrangement of the "silk" threads in the paper was in pairs running down each vertical row of the sheets, the space between the threads of each pair being approximately 5 mm and between pairs of threads 20 mm. Varieties due to misplacement of the paper in printing show a single thread on the first stamp from the sheet margin and two threads 20 mm apart on the other stamps of the row. Faulty manufacture is the cause of stamps with a single thread in the middle.

Through bad spacing of the impressions, which were handstruck, all values may be found with two impressions more or less overlapping. Owing to the small margin allowed for variation of spacing, specimens with good margins on all sides are not common.

Double impressions are known of all values.

Later printings of the 6d. had the gum tinted green to enable the printer to distinguish the gummed side of the paper.

SURFACE-PRINTED ISSUES

GENERAL NOTES

Volume 1 of the Stanley Gibbons *Great Britain Specialised Catalogue* gives further detailed information on the surface-printed issues.

"Abnormals". The majority of the great rarities in the surface-printed group of issues are the so-called "abnormals", whose existence is due to the practice of printing six sheets from every plate as soon as made, one of which was kept for record purposes at Somerset House, while the others were perforated and usually issued. If such plates were not used for general production or if, before they came into full use, a change of watermark or colour took place, the six sheets originally printed would differ from the main issue in plate, colour or watermark and, if issued would be extremely rare.

The abnormal stamps of this class listed in this Catalogue and distinguished, where not priced, by an asterisk (*) are:

No.	
78	3d. Plate 3 (with white dots)
152	4d. vermilion, Plate 16
153	4d. sage-green, Plate 17
109	6d. mauve, Plate 10
124/a	6d. pale chestnut & 6d. chestnut, Plate 12
145	6d. pale buff, Plate 13
88	9d. Plate 3 (hair lines)
98	9d. Plate 5 (see footnote to No. 98)
113	10d. Plate 2
91	1s. Plate 3 ("Plate 2")
148/50	1s. green, Plate 14
120	2s. blue, Plate 3

Those which may have been issued, but of which no specimens are known, are 2½d. wmk Anchor, Plates 4 and 5; 3d. wmk Emblems, Plate 5; 3d. wmk Spray, Plate 21, 6d. grey, wmk Spray, Plate 18; 8d. orange, Plate 2; 1s. wmk Emblems, Plate 5; 5s. wmk Maltese Cross, Plate 4.

The 10d. Plate 1, wmk Emblems (No. 99), is sometimes reckoned among the abnormals, but was an error, due to the use of the wrong paper.

Corner Letters. With the exception of the 4d., 6d. and 1s. of 1855–57, the ½d., 1½d., 2d. and 5d. of 1880, the 1d. lilac of 1881 and the £5 (which had letters in lower corners only, and in the reverse order to the normal), all the surface-printed stamps issued prior to 1887 had letters in all four corners, as in the later line-engraved stamps. The arrangement is the same, the letters running in sequence right across and down the sheets, whether these were divided into panes or not. The corner letters existing naturally depend on the number of stamps in the sheet and their arrangement.

Imprimaturs and Imperforate Stamps. The Post Office retained in their records (now in the National Postal Museum) one imperforate sheet from each plate, known as the Imprimatur (or officially approved) sheet. Some stamps were removed from time to time for presentation purposes and have come on to the market, but these imperforates are not listed as they were not issued. Full details can be found in Volume 1 of the *Great Britain Specialised Catalogue*.

However, other imperforate stamps are known to have been issued and these are listed where it has been possible to prove that they do not come from the Imprimatur sheets. It is therefore advisable to purchase these only when accompanied by an Expert Committee certificate of genuineness.

Plate Numbers. All stamps from No. 75 to No. 163 bear in their designs either the plate number or, in one or two earlier instances, some other indication by which one plate can be distinguished from another. With the aid of these and of the corner letters it is thus possible to "reconstruct" a sheet of stamps from any plate of any issue or denomination.

Surface-printing. In this context the traditional designation "surface-printing" is synonymous with typo(graphy)—a philatelic term—or letterpress—the printers' term—as meaning printing from (the surface of) raised type. It is also called relief-printing, as the image is in relief (in French, *en épargne*), unwanted parts of the design having been cut away. Duplicate impressions can be electrotyped or stereotyped from an original die, the resulting *clichés* being locked together to form the printing plate.

Wing Margins. As the vertical gutters (spaces) between the panes, into which sheets of stamps of most values were divided until the introduction of the Imperial Crown watermark, were perforated through the centre with a single row of holes, instead of each vertical row of stamps on the inner side of the panes having its own line of perforation as is now usual, a proportion of the stamps in each sheet have what is called a "wing margin" about 5 mm wide on one or other side.

The stamps with "wing margins" are the watermark Emblems and Spray of Rose series (3d., 6d., 9d., 10d., 1s. and 2s.) with letters D, E, H or I in S.E. corner, and the watermark Garter series (4d. and 8d.) with letters F or G in S.E. corner. Knowledge of this lettering will enable collectors to guard against stamps with wing margin cut down and re-perforated, but note that wing margin stamps of Nos. 62 to 73 are also to be found re-perforated.

PRINTERS. The issues of Queen Victoria, Nos. 62/214, were typo by Thomas De La Rue & Co.

PERFORATIONS. All the surface-printed issues of Queen Victoria are perf 14, with the exception of Nos. 126/9.

1855–57. *No corner letters.*
(a) *Wmk Small Garter, W* **15**. *Highly glazed, deeply blued paper* (31 July 1855)

				Un	Used	★ Used on cover
62	**14**	4d.	carmine (*shades*)	£4000	£325	£500
		a.	Paper slightly blued	£4250	£325	
		b.	White paper	—	£600	
		Wi.	Watermark inverted	—	£700	

(b) *Wmk Medium Garter, W* **16**

(i) *Thick, blued highly glazed paper* (25 February 1856)

63	**14**	4d.	carmine (*shades*)	£4750	£375	£500
		a.	White paper	£3750		
		Wi.	Watermark inverted	—	£750	

(ii) *Ordinary thin white paper* (September 1856)

64	**14**	4d.	pale carmine	£3500	£300	£375
		a.	Stamp printed double	†	—	
		Wi.	Watermark inverted	—	£550	

(iii) *Ordinary white paper, specially prepared ink* (1 November 1856)

65	**14**	4d.	rose or dp rose	£3750	£325	£425

(c) *Wmk Large Garter, W* **17**. *Ordinary white paper* (January 1857)

66	**14**	4d.	rose-carmine	£1100	90·00	£150
		a.	Rose	£1000	90·00	
		aWi.	Watermark inverted	—	£250	
		aWj.	Watermark inverted & reversed			
		b.	Thick glazed paper	£2500	£225	
		bWi.	Watermark inverted			

★62/6b **For well-centred, lightly used** .... +**125**%

18

19

20 Emblems wmk (normal)

14   15 Small Garter

16 Medium Garter

17 Large Garter

20a Watermark error, three roses and shamrock

20b Watermark error, three roses and thistle

(d) *Wmk Emblems, W* **20**

				Un	Used	★ Used on cover
69	**18**	6d.	dp lilac (21.10.56)	£1000	£110	
70		6d.	pale lilac	£800	85·00	£150
		a.	Azure paper	£3250	£500	
		b.	Thick paper	£2000	£275	
		c.	Error. Watermark W **20a**			
		Wi.	Watermark inverted	—	£225	
		Wj.	Watermark reversed			
		Wk.	Watermark inverted & reversed			
71	**19**	1s.	dp green (1.11.56)	£2000	£275	

72 **19**	1s. green	....	£1000	£250	£300
73	1s. pale green	....	£1000	£250	
	a. Azure paper	....	—	£900	
	b. Thick paper	....	—	£275	
	c. Imperf	....	†	—	
	Wi. Watermark inverted	....		£375	
	Wj. Watermark reversed	....	—	£900	
	Wk. Watermark inverted and reversed .				
★69/73b	**For well-centred, lightly used**			+125%	

KEY TO SURFACE-PRINTED ISSUES 1855–83

S.G. Nos.	Description	Watermark	Date of Issue

NO CORNER LETTERS

62	4d. carmine	Small Garter	31.7.55
63/5	4d. carmine	Medium Garter	25.2.56
66/a	4d. carmine	Large Garter	Jan 1857
69/70	6d. lilac	Emblems	21.10.56
71/3	1s. green	Emblems	1.11.56

SMALL WHITE CORNER LETTERS

75/7	3d. carmine	Emblems	1.5.62
78	3d. carmine (dots)	Emblems	Aug 1862
79/82	4d. red	Large Garter	15.1.62
83/5	6d. lilac	Emblems	1.12.62
86/8	9d. bistre	Emblems	15.1.62
89/91	1s. green	Emblems	1.12.62

LARGE WHITE CORNER LETTERS

92	3d. rose	Emblems	1.3.65
102/3	3d. rose	Spray	July 1867
93/4	4d. vermilion	Large Garter	4.7.65
96/7	6d. lilac	Emblems	7.3.65
104/7	6d. lilac	Spray	21.6.67
108/9	6d. lilac	Spray	8.3.69
122/4	6d. chestnut	Spray	12.4.72
125	6d. grey	Spray	24.4.73
98	9d. straw	Emblems	30.10.65
110/11	9d. straw	Spray	3.10.67
99	10d. brown	Emblems	11.11.67
112/14	10d. brown	Spray	1.7.67
101	1s. green	Emblems	19.1.65
115/17	1s. green	Spray	13.7.67
118/20b	2s. blue	Spray	1.7.67
121	2s. brown	Spray	27.2.80
126/7	5s. rose	Cross	1.7.67
128	10s. grey	Cross	26.9.78
129	£1 brown-lilac	Cross	26.9.78
130, 134	5s. rose	Anchor	25.11.82
131, 135	10s. grey-green	Anchor	Feb 1883
132, 136	£1 brown-lilac	Anchor	Dec 1882
133, 137	£5 orange	Anchor	21.3.82

LARGE COLOURED CORNER LETTERS

138/9	2½d. rosy mauve	Anchor	1.7.75
141	2½d. rosy mauve	Orb	1.5.76
142	2½d. blue	Orb	5.2.80
157	2½d. blue	Crown	23.3.81
143/4	3d. rose	Spray	5.7.73
158	3d. rose	Crown	Jan 1881
159	3d. on 3d. lilac	Crown	1.1.83
152	4d. vermilion	Large Garter	1.3.76
153	4d. sage-green	Large Garter	12.3.77
154	4d. brown	Large Garter	15.8.80
160	4d. brown	Crown	9.12.80

145	6d. buff	Spray	15.3.73
146/7	6d. grey	Spray	20.3.74
161	6d. grey	Crown	1.1.81
162	6d. on 6d. lilac	Crown	1.1.83
156a	8d. purple-brown	Large Garter	July 1876
156	8d. orange	Large Garter	11.9.76
148/50	1s. green	Spray	1.9.73
151	1s. brown	Spray	14.10.80
163	1s. brown	Crown	24.5.81

Watermarks:	Anchor	W **40, 47**
	Cross	W **39**
	Crown	W **49**
	Emblems	W **20**
	Large Garter	W **17**
	Medium Garter	W **16**
	Orb	W **48**
	Small Garter	W **15**
	Spray	W **33**

21   **22**

23   **24**   **25** Plate 2

A. White dots added

B. Hair lines

1862–64. *A small uncoloured letter in each corner, the 4d. wmk Large Garter, W* **17**, *the others Emblems, W* **20.**

				★ Used on	
			Un	Used	cover
75 **21**	3d. dp carmine-rose (Plate 2) (1.5.62) ..	£2500	£325		
76	3d. brt carmine-rose	£1400	£225	£400	
	Wi. Watermark inverted	—	£450		
77	3d. pale carmine-rose	£1400	£225		
	b. Thick paper	—	£325		
	Wj. Watermark reversed				
78	3d. rose (with white dots, Type A, Plate 3) (8.62) £17500	£6000			
	a. Imperf (Plate 3)	£3250			
79 **22**	4d. brt red (Plate 3) (15.1.62)	£1200	£100		
80	4d. pale red	£1000	80·00	£175	
	Wi. Watermark inverted	—	£225		

13

				Un	Used	Used on cover
81	**22**	4d. brt red (Hair lines, Type B, Plate 4) (16.10.63)	£1250	90·00		
82		4d. pale red (Hair lines, Type B, Plate 4)	£1100	80·00	£180	
		a. Imperf (Plate 4)	£3000			
		Wi. Watermark inverted	—	£200		
83	**23**	6d. dp lilac (Plate 3) (1.12.62)	£1300	£100		
84		6d. lilac	£1250	80·00	£150	
		a. Azure paper	—	£700		
		b. Thick paper	—	£200		
		c. Error. Shamrock missing from wmk (stamp TF)				
		d. Error. Watermark W **20**b (stamp TF)	—	£5750		
		Wi. Watermark inverted	—	£250		
		Wj. Watermark reversed				
		Wk. Watermark inverted and reversed				
85		6d. lilac (Hair lines, Plate 4) (20.4.64)	£1600	£160	£250	
		a. Imperf (watermark inverted)	£2750			
		Eb. Imperf and watermark upright				
		c. Thick paper	£2000	£200		
		d. Error. Watermark W **20**b (stamp TF)				
		Wi. Watermark inverted	—	£300		
		Wj. Watermark inverted and reversed				
86	**24**	9d. bistre (Plate 2) (15.1.62)	£2500	£300	£425	
		Wi. Watermark inverted	—	£425		
		Wj. Watermark reversed	—	£475		
		Wk. Watermark inverted and reversed				
87		9d. straw	£2500	£275		
		a. On azure paper				
		b. Thick paper	£3250	£350		
		c. Error. Watermark W **20**b (stamp TF)	†	—		
88		9d. bistre (Hair lines, Plate 3) (5.62)	£10000	£6500		
89	**25**	1s. dp green (Plate No. 1 = Plate 2) (1.12.62)	£2250	£300		
90		1s. green (Plate No. 1 = Plate 2)	£1500	£150	£225	
		a. "K" in lower left corner in white circle (stamp KD)	£5000	£800		
		aa. "K" normal (stamp KD)	—	£1100		
		b. On azure paper				
		c. Thick paper	—	£250		
		ca. Thick paper, "K" in circle as No. 90a	—	£1900		
		Wi. Watermark inverted	—	£250		
		Wj. Watermark reversed				
		Wk. Watermark inverted and reversed	—	£250		
91		1s. dp green (Plate No. 2 = Plate 3)	£17500			
		a. Imperf	£3000			
		aWi. Watermark inverted	£2000			
★75/91		**For well-centred, lightly used**		**+125**%		

The 3d. as Type **21**, but with network background in the spandrels
which is found overprinted SPECIMEN, was never issued.

The plates of this issue may be distinguished as follows:

3d.	Plate 2	No white dots.
	Plate 3	White dots as Illustration A.
4d.	Plate 3	No hair lines. Roman I next to lower corner letters.
	Plate 4	Hair lines in corners. (Illustration B.). Roman II.
6d.	Plate 3	No hair lines.
	Plate 4	Hair lines in corners.
9d.	Plate 2	No hair lines.
	Plate 3	Hair lines in corners. Beware of faked lines.
1s.	Plate 2	Numbered 1 on stamps.
	Plate 3	Numbered 2 on stamps & with hair lines.

The 9d. on azure paper (No. 87a) is very rare, only one confirmed
example being known.

The variety "K" in circle, No. 90a, is believed to be due to a damaged
letter having been cut out and replaced. It is probable that the punch
was driven in too deeply, causing the flange to penetrate the surface,
producing an indentation showing as an uncoloured circle.

The watermark variety "three roses and a shamrock" illustrated in
W **20**a was evidently due to the substitution of an extra rose for the
thistle in a faulty watermark bit. It is found on stamp TA of Plate 4 of
the 3d., Plates 1 (No. 70c), 3, 5 and 6 of the 6d., Plate 4 of the 9d. and
Plate 4 of the 1s.

Similar problems occurred on stamp TF of the 6d. and 9d. Here the
shamrock emblem became detached and a used example of the 6d.
(No. 84) is known showing it omitted. It was replaced by a third rose (W
20b) and this variety exists on the 6d. (Nos. 84/5 and 97) and 9d. (Nos.
87 and 98).

26	27

28 (with hyphen)	28a (without hyphen)

29	30	31

1865–67. *Large uncoloured corner letters. Wmk Large Garter (4d.);
others Emblems.*

				Un	Used	★ Used on cover
92	**26**	3d. rose (Plate 4) (1.3.65)	£1000	£100	£175	
		a. Error. Watermark W **20**a	£1950	£650		
		b. Thick paper	£900	£125		
		Wi. Watermark inverted	—	£225		
		Wj. Watermark reversed				
		Wk. Watermark inverted and reversed				
93	**27**	4d. dull vermilion (4.7.65)	£500	80·00		
94		4d. vermilion	£425	50·00	£125	
		a. Imperf (Plates 11, 12)	£1300			
		Wi. Watermark inverted	£425	50·00		
		Plate				
		7 (1865)	£500	80·00		
		8 (1866)	£450	50·00		
		9 (1867)	£450	50·00		
		10 (1868)	£500	90·00		
		11 (1869)	£450	50·00		
		12 (1870)	£425	50·00		
		13 (1872)	£450	50·00		
		14 (1873)	£500	80·00		
96	**28**	6d. dp lilac (with hyphen) (7.3.65)	£750	90·00		
97		6d. lilac (with hyphen)	£650	75·00	£110	
		a. Thick paper	£750	£100		
		b. Stamp doubly printed (Plate 6)	—	£10000		
		c. Error. Watermark W **20**a (Pl 5, 6) from	—	£700		
		d. Error. Watermark W **20**b (Plate 5)				
		Wi. Watermark inverted	—	£150		
		Wj. Watermark reversed				
		Wk. Watermark inverted and reversed	†	—		
		Plate				
		5 (1865)	£650	75·00		
		6 (1867)	£2000	£140		

			Un	Used	cover
98	**29**	9d. straw (Plate 4) (30.10.65)	£1800	£375	£500
		a. Thick paper	£2000	£500	
		b. Error. Watermark W **20**a	—	£700	
		c. Error. Watermark W **20**b (stamp TF)		*£25000	
		Wi. Watermark inverted	—	£475	
99	**30**	10d. red-brown (Plate 1) (11.11.67)		*£25000	
101	**31**	1s. green (Plate 4) (19.1.65)	£1200	£150	£200
		a. Error. Watermark W **20**a	—	£750	
		b. Thick paper	£1300	£240	
		c. Imperf between (vert pair)	—	£7000	
		Wi. Watermark inverted	—	£350	
		Wj. Imperf watermark inverted			

★92/101c **For well-centred, lightly used** .... + **100**%

From mid-1866 to about the end of 1871 4d. stamps of this issue appeared generally with watermark inverted.

Unused examples of No. 98 from Plate 5 exist, but this was never put to press and all evidence points to such stamps originating from a portion of the Imprimatur sheet which was perforated by De La Rue in 1887 for insertion in albums to be presented to members of the Stamp Committee (*Price £14000 un*).

The 10d. stamps, No. 99, were printed in *error* on paper watermarked "Emblems" instead of on "Spray of Rose".

32   **33** Spray of Rose   **34**

1867–80. *Wmk Spray of Rose.* W **33**.

				★ Used on	
			Un	Used	cover
102	**26**	3d. dp rose (12.7.67)	£700	£150	
103		3d. rose	£350	45·00	75·00
		a. Imperf (Plates 5, 6, 8) .....*from*	£1900		
		Wi. Watermark inverted	£525	£125	
		Plate			
		4 (1867)	£700	£150	
		5 (1868)	£350	45·00	
		6 (1870)	£375	45·00	
		7 (1871)	£450	50·00	
		8 (1872)	£425	45·00	
		9 (1872)	£425	50·00	
		10 (1873)	£450	90·00	
104	**28**	6d. lilac (with hyphen) (Plate 6) (21.6.67)	£850	75·00	£140
		a. Imperf			
		Wi. Watermark inverted	—	£175	
105		6d. dp lilac (with hyphen) (Plate 6) .	£850	75·00	
106		6d. purple (with hyphen) (Plate 6) ..	£850	£100	
107		6d. brt violet (with hyphen) (Plate 6) (22.7.68)	£850	80·00	
108	**28**a	6d. dull violet (without hyphen) (Plate 8) (8.3.69)	£500	75·00	
		Wi. Watermark inverted	—	£160	
109		6d. mauve (without hyphen)	£450	75·00	£100
		a. Imperf (Plate Nos. 8 & 9)	£3500	£2500	
		Wi. Watermark inverted	—	£160	
		Plate			
		8 (1869, mauve)	£450	75·00	
		9 (1870, mauve)	£450	75·00	
		10 (1869, mauve)		*£17500	
110	**29**	9d. straw (Plate No. 4) (3.10.67)	£1250	£200	£325
		Wi. Watermark inverted	—	£375	

			Un	Used	cover
111	**29**	9d. pale straw (Plate No. 4)	£1100	£200	
		a. Imperf (Plate 4)	£3800		
112	**30**	10d. red-brown (1.7.67)	£1850	£275	£650
		Wi. Watermark inverted		£550	
113		10d. pale red-brown	£1850	£300	
114		10d. dp red-brown	£2500	£400	
		a. Imperf (Plate 1)	£4500		
		Plate			
		1 (1867)	£1850	£275	
		2 (1867)	£17500	£6000	
115	**31**	1s. dp green (13.7.67)	£650	35·00	
117		1s. green	£550	32·00	50·00
		a. Imperf between (horiz pair) (Pl 7)			
		b. Imperf (Plate 4)	£2250	£1300	
		Wi. Watermark inverted	£1000	£125	
		Plate			
		4 (1867)	£650	35·00	
		5 (1871)	£625	35·00	
		6 (1871)	£950	35·00	
		7 (1873)	£900	60·00	
118	**32**	2s. dull blue (1.7.67)	£1800	£125	£600
		Wi. Watermark inverted	—	£400	
119		2s. dp blue	£1800	£125	
120		2s. pale blue	£2500	£180	
		a. Imperf (Plate 1)	£5000		
120a		2s. cobalt	£10000	£2000	
120b		2s. milky blue	£8500	£1200	
		Plate			
		1 (1867)	£1800	£125	
		3 (1868)		*£6000	
121		2s. brown (Plate No. 1) (27.2.80) ...	£12000	£2500	
		a. Imperf	£10000		
		b. No watermark	†	—	
		Wi. Watermark inverted	—	£3500	

★102/21 **For well-centred, lightly used** ... + **75**%

Examples of the 1s. from Plates 5 and 6 *without* watermark are postal forgeries used at the Stock Exchange Post Office in the early 1870s.

1872–73. *Uncoloured letters in corners. Wmk Spray,* W **33**.

				★ Used on	
			Un	Used	cover
122	**34**	6d. dp chestnut (Plate 11) (12.4.72) .	£700	70·00	90·00
122a		6d. chestnut (Plate 11) (22.5.72)	£600	45·00	
		Wi. Watermark inverted	—	£180	
122b		6d. pale chestnut (Plate 11) (1872) ..	£500	45·00	
123		6d. pale buff (19.10.72)	£550	75·00	£200
		Wi. Watermark inverted	—	£180	
		Plate			
		11 (1872, pale buff)	£550	75·00	
		12 (1872, pale buff)	£1500	£200	
124		6d. chestnut (Plate 12) (1872)	*	£2500	
124a		6d. pale chestnut (Plate 12) (1872) ..	*	£2500	
125		6d. grey (Plate No. 12) (24.4.73)	£1250	£200	£240
		a. Imperf	£3000		
		Wi. Watermark inverted	£2750	£375	

★122/5 **For well-centred, lightly used** ... + **50**%

35   **36**

37

38

41

42

43

44

45

46

39 Maltese Cross   **40** Large Anchor

47 Small Anchor

48 Orb

1873–80. *Large coloured letters in the corners.*

(a) Wmk Anchor, W **47**

				Un	Used	★ Used on cover
138	**41**	2½d. rosy mauve (*blued paper*) (1.7.75)		£625	£110	
		a. Imperf				
		Wi. Watermark inverted		£1100	£225	
		Plate				
		1 (*blued paper*) (1875)		£625	£110	
		2 (*blued paper*) (1875)		£4500	£950	
		3 (*blued paper*) (1875)		—	£4000	
139		2½d. rosy mauve (*white paper*)		£450	75·00	£125
		Wi. Watermark inverted		£750	£160	
		Plate				
		1 (*white paper*) (1875)		£450	75·00	
		2 (*white paper*) (1875)		£450	75·00	
		3 (*white paper*) (1875)		£700	£110	

Error of Lettering L H—F L *for* L H—H L (*Plate* 2)

140	**41**	2½d. rosy mauve		£12500	£1700

(b) Wmk Orb, W **48**

141	**41**	2½d. rosy mauve (1.5.76)		£380	45·00	70·00
		Wi. Watermark inverted		£550	90·00	
		Plate				
		3 (1876)		£850	90·00	
		4 (1876)		£380	45·00	
		5 (1876)		£380	45·00	
		6 (1876)		£380	45·00	
		7 (1877)		£380	45·00	
		8 (1877)		£380	45·00	
		9 (1877)		£380	45·00	
		10 (1878)		£420	60·00	
		11 (1878)		£380	45·00	
		12 (1878)		£380	45·00	
		13 (1878)		£380	45·00	
		14 (1879)		£380	45·00	
		15 (1879)		£380	45·00	
		16 (1879)		£380	45·00	
		17 (1880)		£1100	£220	

1867–83. *Uncoloured letters in corners.*

(a) Wmk Maltese Cross, W **39**. P $15\frac{1}{2} \times 15$

				Un	★ Used
126	**35**	5s. rose (1.7.67)		£4500	£550
127		5s. pale rose		£4500	£550
		a. Imperf (Plate 1)		£7000	
		Plate			
		1 (1867)		£4500	£550
		2 (1874)		£6500	£850
128	**36**	10s. greenish grey (Plate 1) (26.9.78)		£35000	£2000
129	**37**	£1 brown-lilac (Plate 1) (26.9.78)		£42000	£3000

(b) Wmk Anchor, W **40**. P 14. (i) *Blued paper*

130	**35**	5s. rose (Plate 4) (25.11.82)		£12000	£3000
		Wi. Watermark inverted		—	£6000
131	**36**	10s. grey-green (Plate 1) (2.83)		£50000	£3500
132	**37**	£1 brown-lilac (Plate 1) (12.82)		£65000	£7000
133	**38**	£5 orange (Plate 1) (21.3.82)		£30000	£9000

(ii) *White paper*

134	**35**	5s. rose (Plate 4)		£10000	£2400
135	**36**	10s. greenish grey (Plate 1)		£50000	£2800
136	**37**	£1 brown-lilac (Plate 1)		£70000	£5500
137	**38**	£5 orange (Plate 1)		£7000	£3500
★126/37		**For well-centred, lightly used**			+75%

WHEN YOU BUY AN ALBUM LOOK FOR THE NAME 'STANLEY GIBBONS'
It means Quality combined with Value for Money.

142	**41**	2½d. blue (5.2.80)	£350	50·00	70·00
		Wi. Watermark inverted	£450	£125	
		Plate			
		17 (1880)	£350	50·00	
		18 (1880)	£375	35·00	
		19 (1880)	£350	35·00	
		20 (1880)	£350	35·00	

*(c) Wmk Spray, W **33***

143	**42**	3d. rose (5.7.73)	£325	35·00	50·00
		Wi. Watermark inverted	£600	£175	
144		3d. pale rose	£400	35·00	
		Plate			
		11 (1873)	£325	35·00	
		12 (1873)	£380	35·00	
		14 (1874)	£400	35·00	
		15 (1874)	£325	35·00	
		16 (1875)	£325	35·00	
		17 (1875)	£380	35·00	
		18 (1875)	£380	35·00	
		19 (1876)	£325	35·00	
		20 (1879)	£380	60·00	
145	**43**	6d. pale buff (Plate 13) (15.3.73)		*£12000	
146		6d. dp grey (20.3.74)	£350	50·00	80·00
147		6d. grey	£350	50·00	
		Wi. Watermark inverted	£600	£175	
		Plate			
		13 (1874)	£350	50·00	
		14 (1875)	£350	50·00	
		15 (1876)	£350	50·00	
		16 (1878)	£350	50·00	
		17 (1878)	£500	£100	
148	**44**	1s. dp green (1.9.73)	£500	85·00	
150		1s. green	£425	70·00	£140
		Wi. Watermark inverted	£750	£150	
		Plate			
		8 (1873)	£500	85·00	
		9 (1874)	£500	85·00	
		10 (1874)	£500	90·00	
		11 (1875)	£500	90·00	
		12 (1875)	£425	70·00	
		13 (1876)	£425	70·00	
		14 (—)		*£20000	
151		1s. orange-brown (Plate 13)			
		(14.10.80)	£2850	£475	£650
		Wi. Watermark inverted	£4000	£650	

*(d) Wmk Large Garter, W **17***

152	**45**	4d. vermilion (1.3.76)	£1400	£325	£500
		Wi. Watermark inverted	—	£475	
		Plate			
		15 (1876)	£1400	£325	
		16 (1877)		*£18500	
153		4d. sage-green (12.3.77)	£800	£225	£350
		Wi. Watermark inverted	—	£350	
		Plate			
		15 (1877)	£800	£225	
		16 (1877)	£700	£200	
		17 (1877)		*£12500	
154		4d. grey-brown (Plate 17) (15.8.80) ..	£1250	£325	£600
		a. Imperf	£5250		
		Wi. Watermark inverted	—	£700	
156	**46**	8d. orange (Plate 1) (11.9.76)	£900	£250	£300
		Wi. Watermark inverted	—	£500	
★138/56		**For well-centred, lightly used**		+ **100%**	

1876 (July). *Prepared for use but not issued.*

156a	**46**	8d. purple-brown (Plate 1)	£5500	

49 Imperial Crown   **(50)**

1880–83. *Wmk Imperial Crown, W **49**.*

					★ *Used on*
			Un	*Used*	*cover*
157	**41**	2½d. blue (23.3.81)	£325	25·00	40·00
		Wi. Watermark inverted	—	£300	
		Plate			
		21 (1881)	£375	30·00	
		22 (1881)	£325	30·00	
		23 (1881)	£325	25·00	
158	**42**	3d. rose (3.81)	£375	70·00	£125
		Wi. Watermark inverted	—	£300	
		Plate			
		20 (1881)	£425	£110	
		21 (1881)	£375	70·00	
159	**50**	3d. on 3d. lilac (C.) (Plate 21) (1.1.83) .	£375	£125	£325
		Wi. Watermark inverted			
160	**45**	4d. grey-brown (8.12.80)	£300	50·00	£120
		Wi. Watermark inverted	—	£400	
		Plate			
		17 (1880)	£300	50·00	
		18 (1882)	£300	50·00	
161	**43**	6d. grey (1.1.81)	£300	55·00	80·00
		Wi. Watermark inverted	—	£450	
		Plate			
		17 (1881)	£350	55·00	
		18 (1882)	£300	55·00	
162	**50**	6d. on 6d. lilac (C.) (Plate 18) (1.1.83)	£400	£120	£300
		a. Slanting dots (various) ......*from*	£600	£250	
		b. Opt double	—	£8000	
		Wi. Watermark inverted	£900	£450	
163	**44**	1s. orange-brown (24.5.81)	£400	£110	£300
		Wi. Watermark inverted	£950	£450	
		Plate			
		13 (1881)	£475	£110	
		14 (1881)	£400	£110	
★157/63		**For well-centred, lightly used**		+ **75%**	

The 1s. plate 14 (line perf 14) exists in purple but was not issued in this shade (*Price £4500 unused*). Examples were included in a few of the Souvenir Albums prepared for members of the "Stamp Committee of 1884".

52   **53**

54	55	56

1880–81. *Wmk Imperial Crown, W* **49.**

				★ *Used on*
			Un	*Used cover*
164	52	½d. dp green (14.10.80)	40·00	10·00 20·00
		a. Imperf	£1200	
		b. No watermark	£5000	
		Wi. Watermark inverted	—	£200
165		½d. pale green	40·00	15·00
166	53	1d. Venetian red (1.1.80)	20·00	10·00 18·00
		a. Imperf	£1300	
		Wi. Watermark inverted	—	£175
167	54	1½d. Venetian red (14.10.80)	£150	40·00 £120
168	55	2d. pale rose (8.12.80)	£200	80·00 £150
		Wi. Watermark inverted	£750	£400
168a		2d. dp rose	£225	80·00
169	56	5d. indigo (15.3.81)	£575	£100 £200
		a. Imperf	£2500	£2000
		Wi. Watermark inverted	—	£2500

★164/9   **For well-centred, lightly used** ....   **+75%**

Two used examples of the 1d. value have been reported on the Orb (fiscal) watermark.

57	Die I	Die II

1881. *Wmk Imperial Crown, W* **49.** (a) 14 *dots in each corner, Die I* (12 July).

				★ *Used on*
			Un	*Used cover*
170	57	1d. lilac	£175	28·00 45·00
		Wi. Watermark inverted	—	£400
171		1d. pale lilac	£175	28·00
		(b) 16 *dots in each corner, Die II* (13 December)		
172	57	1d. lilac	2·50	2·00 3·00
		Wi. Watermark inverted	35·00	25·00
172a		1d. bluish lilac	£250	85·00
173		1d. dp purple	2·50	2·00
		a. Printed both sides	£700	†
		b. Frame broken at bottom	£750	£275
		c. Printed on gummed side	£650	†
		d. Imperf three sides (pair)	£4500	†
		e. Printed both sides but impression		
		on back inverted	£750	†
		f. No watermark	£2500	†
		g. Blued paper	£3250	
174		1d. mauve	2·50	1·50
		a. Imperf (pair)	£2200	

★170/4   **For well-centred, lightly used** ....   **+50%**

1d. stamps with the words "PEARS SOAP" printed on the back in *orange*, *blue* or *mauve* price *from* £500, *unused*.

The variety "frame broken at bottom" (No. 173b) shows a white space just inside the bottom frame-line from between the "N" and "E" of "ONE" to below the first "N" of "PENNY", breaking the pearls and cutting into the lower part of the oval below "PEN".

KEY TO SURFACE-PRINTED ISSUES
1880–1900

S.G. Nos.	Description	Date of Issue
164/5	½d. green	14.10.80
187	½d. slate-blue	1.4.84
197/e	½d. vermilion	1.1.87
213	½d. blue-green	17.4.1900
166	1d. Venetian red	1.1.80
170/1	1d. lilac, Die I	12.7.81
172/4	1d. lilac, Die II	12.12.81
167	1½d. Venetian red	14.10.80
188	1½d. lilac	1.4.84
198	1½d. purple & green	1.1.87
168/a	2d. rose	8.12.80
189	2d. lilac	1.4.84
199/200	2d. green & red	1.1.87
190	2½d. lilac	1.4.84
201	2½d. purple on blue paper	1.1.87
191	3d. lilac	1.4.84
202/4	3d. purple on yellow paper	1.1.87
192	4d. dull green	1.4.84
205/a	4d. green & brown	1.1.87
206	4½d. green and carmine	15.9.92
169	5d. indigo	15.3.81
193	5d. dull green	1.4.84
207	5d. purple & blue, Die I	1.1.87
207a	5d. purple & blue, Die II	1888
194	6d. dull green	1.4.84
208/a	6d. purple on rose-red paper	1.1.87
195	9d. dull green	1.8.83
209	9d. purple & blue	1.1.87
210/b	10d. purple & carmine	24.2.90
196	1s. dull green	1.4.84
211	1s. green	1.1.87
214	1s. green & carmine	11.7.1900
175	2s. 6d. lilac on blued paper	2.7.83
178/9	2s. 6d. lilac	1884
176	5s. rose on blued paper	1.4.84
180/1	5s. rose	1884
177/a	10s. ultramarine on blued paper	1.4.84
182/3a	10s. ultramarine	1884
185	£1 brown-lilac, wmk Crowns	1.4.84
186	£1 brown-lilac, wmk Orbs	6.1.88
212	£1 green	28.1.91

Note that the £5 value used with the above series is listed as Nos. 133 and 137.

58	59

60

62   **63**   **64**

65   **66**

1883–84. *Coloured letters in the corners. Wmk Anchor, W* **40**.

(a) *Blued paper*

				★
			Un	*Used*
175	**58**	2s. 6d. lilac (2.7.83)	£3750	£950
176	**59**	5s. rose (1.4.84)	£7500	£2500
177	**60**	10s. ultramarine (1.4.84)	£26000	£6000
177a		10s. cobalt (5.84)	£32000	£9000

(b) *White paper*

178	**58**	2s. 6d. lilac	£400	£125
179		2s. 6d. dp lilac	£400	£125
		a. Error. On blued paper	£5000	£2000
		Wi. Watermark inverted	—	£5000
180	**59**	5s. rose	£800	£180
		Wi. Watermark inverted	†	£6000
181		5s. crimson	£700	£180
182	**60**	10s. cobalt	£20000	£6000
183		10s. ultramarine	£1500	£450
183a		10s. pale ultramarine	£1700	£450
★175/83a		**For well-centred, lightly used**		+50%

For No. 180 perf 12 *see second note below No. 196.*

61

Broken frames, Plate 2

1884 (1 Apr). *Wmk Three Imperial Crowns, W* **49**.

				★
			Un	*Used*
185	**61**	£1 brown-lilac	£20000	£2000
		a. Frame broken	£28000	£3250
		Wi. Watermark inverted	—	£6500

1888 (Feb). *Watermark Three Orbs, W* **48**.

186	**61**	£1 brown-lilac	£45000	£3250
		a. Frame broken	£48000	£5000
★185/6a		**For well-centred, lightly used**		+50%

The broken-frame varieties, Nos. 185a and 186a, are on Plate 2 stamps JC and TA, as illustrated. *See also No. 212a.*

1883 (1 Aug) (9d.) *or* **1884** (1 Apr) (*others*). *Wmk Imperial Crown, W* **49** *(sideways on horiz designs).*

				★	*Used on*
			Un	*Used*	*cover*
187	**52**	½d. slate-blue	20·00	7·00	12·00
		a. Imperf	£1250		
		Wi. Watermark inverted	—	£175	
188	**62**	1½d. lilac	90·00	35·00	£100
		a. Imperf	£1250		
		Wi. Watermark inverted	—	£180	
189	**63**	2d. lilac	£150	65·00	£110
		a. Imperf	£1500		
		Wi. Watermark sideways-inverted			
190	**64**	2½d. lilac	70·00	12·00	24·00
		a. Imperf	£1500		
		Wi. Watermark sideways-inverted	£375		
191	**65**	3d. lilac	£180	85·00	£125
		a. Imperf	£1500		
		Wi. Watermark inverted	†	£750	
192	**66**	4d. dull green	£400	£175	£250
		a. Imperf	£1800		
193	**62**	5d. dull green	£400	£175	£250
		a. Imperf	£1800		
194	**63**	6d. dull green	£425	£200	£275
		a. Imperf	£1800		
		Wi. Watermark sideways-inverted	£650		
195	**64**	9d. dull green (1.8.83)	£800	£375	£1500
		Wi. Watermark sideways-inverted	£1250	£600	
196	**65**	1s. dull green	£750	£200	£450
		a. Imperf	£3000		
		Wi. Watermark-inverted			
★187/96		**For well-centred, lightly used**			+100%

The above prices are for stamps in the true dull green colour. Stamps which have been soaked, causing the colour to run, are virtually worthless.

Stamps of the above set and No. 180 are also found perf 12; these are official perforations, but were never issued. A second variety of the 5d. is known with a line instead of a stop under the "d" in the value; this was never issued and is therefore only known *unused* (Price £12000).

71   **72**   **73**

74   75   76

77   78   79

80   81   82

Die I   Die II

Die I: Square dots to right of "d".
Die II: Thin vertical lines to right of "d".

1887 (1 Jan)–**92**. *"Jubilee" issue. New types. The bicoloured stamps have the value tablets, or the frames including the value tablets, in the second colour. Wmk Imperial Crown, W* **49** *(Three Crowns on £1).*

			Unmtd Mint	Mtd Mint	Used
197	71	½d. vermilion	2·25	1·50	1·00
		a. Printed on gummed side	£1700	£1300	†
		b. Printed both sides			
		c. Doubly printed	—	£9000	
		d. Imperf	—	£1600	
		Wi. Watermark inverted	40·00	30·00	25·00
197e		½d. orange-vermilion	2·25	1·50	1·00
198	72	1½d. dull purple & pale green	22·00	15·00	7·00
		a. Purple part of design double	—	—	£6000
		Wi. Watermark inverted	£700	£550	£275
199	73	2d. green & scarlet	£425	£350	£225
200		2d. grey-green & carmine	40·00	28·00	12·00
		Wi. Watermark inverted	£700	£575	£300
201	74	2½d. purple/blue	35·00	22·00	3·00
		a. Printed on gummed side	£4000	£3500	†
		b. Imperf three sides	—	£2750	
		c. Imperf	—	£3000	
		Ed. Missing "d" in value	†	†	£5000
		Wi. Watermark inverted	£950	£600	£400

202	75	3d. purple/yellow	35·00	22·00	3·25
		a. Imperf (wmk inverted)	—	£4500	
		Wi. Watermark inverted	—	—	£375
203		3d. dp purple/yellow	35·00	22·00	3·25
204		3d. purple/orange (1890)	£750	£475	
205	76	4d. green & purple-brown	45·00	30·00	13·00
		aa. Imperf	—	£5000	
		Wi. Watermark inverted	£750	£500	£275
205a		4d. green & dp brown	45·00	30·00	13·00
206	77	4½d. green & carmine (15.9.92)	15·00	10·00	40·00
		Wi. Watermark inverted			
206a		4½d. green & dp brt carmine	£650	£475	£400
207	78	5d. dull purple & blue (Die I)	£600	£475	75·00
207a		5d. dull purple & blue (Die II) (1888)	50·00	35·00	11·00
		Wi. Watermark inverted	—	—	£325
208	79	6d. purple/rose-red	50·00	30·00	10·00
		Wi. Watermark inverted	£1500	£100	£500
208a		6d. dp purple/rose-red	50·00	30·00	11·00
209	80	9d. dull purple & blue	90·00	60·00	40·00
		Wi. Watermark inverted	£1000	£1000	£500
210	81	10d. dull purple & carmine (shades) (24.2.90)	70·00	45·00	38·00
		aa. Imperf	—	£6000	
		Wi. Watermark inverted	£1800	£1000	£600
210a		10d. dull purple & dp dull carmine	£550	£400	£200
210b		10d. dull purple & scarlet	£110	60·00	45·00
211	82	1s. dull green	£275	£200	60·00
		Wi. Watermark inverted	£650	£475	£300
212	61	£1 green (28.1.91)	£4000	£2500	£600
		a. Frame broken	£7000	£5500	£1600
		Wi. Watermark inverted	—	£40000	£4000

★197/212a   **For well-centred, lightly used**   **+50%**

The broken-frame varieties, No. 212a, are on Plate 2 stamps JC or TA, as illustrated above No. 185.

½d. stamps with "PEARS SOAP" printed on the back in *orange, blue* or *mauve*, price *from* £475 each.

No used price is quoted for No. 204 as it is not possible to authenticate the paper colour on stamps in used condition.

1900. *Colours changed. Wmk Imperial Crown, W* **49**.

213	71	½d. blue-green (17.4)	2·25	1·75	2·00
		a. Printed on gummed side	—	—	†
		b. Imperf	—	£3000	
		Wi. Watermark inverted	40·00	30·00	30·00
214	82	1s. green & carmine (11.7)	80·00	50·00	£125
		Wi. Watermark inverted	£1000	£750	£400
		Set of 14	£750	£500	£325

★213/14   **For well-centred, lightly used**   **+50%**

The ½d. No. 213, in bright blue, is a colour changeling caused by a constituent of the ink used for some months in 1900.

USED ON COVER PRICES					
No. 197	£6	No. 205	£35	No. 209	£200
No. 198	£22	No. 206	£75	No. 210	£225
No. 200	£24	No. 207	£150	No. 211	£125
No. 201	£6	No. 207a	£40	No. 213	£6
No. 202	£30	No. 208	£75	No. 214	£750

For full information on all future British issues, collectors should write to the British Post Office Philatelic Bureau, 21 South Gyle Crescent, Edinburgh EH12 9PB

21

KING EDWARD VII

22 January 1901–6 May 1910

PRINTINGS. Distinguishing De La Rue printings from the provisional printings of the same values made by Harrison & Sons Ltd. or at Somerset House may prove difficult in some cases. For very full guidance Volume 2 of the Stanley Gibbons *Great Britain Specialised Catalogue* should prove helpful.

Note that stamps perforated 15 × 14 must be Harrison; the 2½d., 3d. and 4d. in this perforation are useful reference material, their shades and appearance in most cases matching the Harrison perf 14 printings.

Except for the 6d. value, all stamps on chalk-surfaced paper were printed by De La Rue.

Of the stamps on ordinary paper, the De La Rue impressions are usually clearer and of a higher finish than those of the other printers. The shades are markedly different except in some printings of the 4d., 6d. and 7d. and in the 5s., 10s. and £1.

Used stamps in good, clean, unrubbed condition and with dated postmarks can form the basis of a useful reference collection, the dates often assisting in the assignment to the printers.

PRICES. For Nos. 215/456a prices are quoted for unmounted mint, mounted mint and used stamps.

USED STAMPS. For well-centred, lightly used examples of King Edward VII stamps, add the following percentages to the used prices quoted below:

De La Rue printings (Nos. 215/66)—3d. values + 35%, 4d. orange + 100%, 6d. + 75%, 7d. & 1s. + 25%, all other values + 50%.
Harrison printings (Nos 267/86)—all values and perforations + 75%.
Somerset House printings (Nos. 287/320)—1s. values + 25%, all other values + 50%.

89   90   91

92   93

94   95   96

97

(Des E. Fuchs)

1902 (1 Jan)–**10**. *Printed by De La Rue & Co. Wmk Imperial Crown W 49 (½d. to 1s. Three Crowns on £1); Anchor, W 40 (2s. 6d. to 10s.). Ordinary paper. P 14.*

			Unmtd mint	Mtd mint	Used
215	83	½d. dull blue-green (1.1.02)	2·50	2·00	1·50
		Wi. Watermark inverted	£2000	£1400	£750
216		½d. blue-green	2·50	2·00	1·50
217		½d. pale yellowish green (26.11.04) ..	2·50	2·00	1·50
218		½d. yellowish green	2·50	2·00	1·50
		a. Booklet pane. Five stamps plus St. Andrew's Cross label (6.06)	£500	£350	
		b. Doubly printed (bottom row on one pane) (Control H9) £25000	£17500		
		Wi. Watermark inverted	18·00	12·00	9·00
219		1d. scarlet (1.1.02)	2·50	2·00	1·50
220		1d. brt scarlet	2·50	2·00	1·50
		a. Imperf (pair)	—£12000		
		Wi. Watermark inverted	5·00	4·00	3·00
221	84	1½d. dull purple & green (21.3.02)	70·00	35·00	18·00
222		1½d. slate-purple & green	85·00	38·00	18·00
		Wi. Watermark inverted	—	—	£550
223		1½d. pale dull purple & green (chalk-surfaced paper) (8.05)	65·00	40·00	18·00
224		1½d. slate-purple & bluish green (chalk-surfaced paper)	65·00	40·00	15·00
225	85	2d. yellowish green & carmine-red (25.3.02)	70·00	45·00	18·00
		Wi. Watermark inverted £16000			

83   84   85

86   87   88

226	**85**	2d. grey-green & carmine-red (1904)	80·00	45·00	20·00
227		2d. pale grey-green & carmine-red (*chalk-surfaced paper*) (4.06)	70·00	40·00	24·00
		Wi. Watermark inverted			
228		2d. pale grey-green & scarlet (*chalk-surfaced paper*) (1909)	70·00	40·00	24·00
229		2d. dull blue-green & carmine (*chalk-surfaced paper*) (1907)	£140	70·00	45·00
230	**86**	2½d. ultramarine (1.1.02)	30·00	20·00	10·00
231		2½d. pale ultramarine	30·00	20·00	10·00
		Wi. Watermark inverted	—	—	£1100
232	**87**	3d. dull purple/orange-yellow (20.3.02)	70·00	40·00	12·00
		Wi. Watermark inverted			
		a. Chalk-surfaced paper (3.06)	£260	£150	70·00
232b		3d. dp purple/orange-yellow	70·00	40·00	12·00
232c		3d. pale reddish purple/orange-yellow (*chalk-surfaced paper*) (3.06)	£260	£150	60·00
233		3d. dull reddish purple/yellow (*lemon back*) (*chalk-surfaced paper*)	£260	£150	75·00
233b		3d. pale purple/lemon (*chalk-surfaced paper*)	60·00	35·00	15·00
234		3d. purple/lemon (*chalk-surfaced paper*)	60·00	35·00	15·00
235	**88**	4d. green & grey-brown (27.3.02)	£110	50·00	30·00
		Wi. Watermark inverted			
236		4d. green & chocolate-brown	£110	50·00	30·00
		a. Chalk-surfaced paper (1.06)	65·00	40·00	18·00
238		4d. dp green & chocolate-brown (*chalk-surfaced paper*) (1.06)	65·00	40·00	18·00
239		4d. brown-orange (1.11.09)	£240	£150	£130
240		4d. pale orange (12.09)	40·00	20·00	15·00
241		4d. orange-red (12.09)	40·00	20·00	15·00
242	**89**	5d. dull purple & ultramarine (14.5.02)	£125	55·00	20·00
		a. Chalk-surfaced paper (5.06)	£100	50·00	20·00
244		5d. slate-purple & ultramarine (*chalk-surfaced paper*) (5.06)	£100	50·00	20·00
		Wi. Watermark inverted	£5000	£3000	
245	**83**	6d. pale dull purple (1.1.02)	70·00	35·00	18·00
		a. Chalk-surfaced paper (1.06)	70·00	35·00	18·00
246		6d. slate-purple	70·00	35·00	18·00
248		6d. dull purple (*chalk-surfaced paper*) (1.06)	70·00	35·00	18·00
		Wi. Watermark inverted	—	—	£1300
249	**90**	7d. grey-black (4.5.10)	20·00	10·00	18·00
249a		7d. dp grey-black	£140	£110	£100
250	**91**	9d. dull purple & ultramarine (7.4.02)	£160	80·00	60·00
		a. Chalk-surfaced paper (6.05)	£190	80·00	60·00
		aWi. Watermark inverted	—	—	£1100
251		9d. slate-purple & ultramarine	£175	80·00	60·00
		a. Chalk-surfaced paper (6.05)	£175	80·00	60·00
254	**92**	10d. dull purple & carmine (3.7.02)	£175	80·00	60·00
		a. No cross on crown	£500	£300	£200
		b. Chalk-surfaced paper (9.06)	£175	80·00	60·00
255		10d. slate-purple & carmine (*chalk-surfaced paper*) (9.06)	£175	80·00	60·00
		a. No cross on crown	£500	£300	£200
256		10d. dull purple & scarlet (*chalk-surfaced paper*) (9.10)	£175	80·00	60·00
		a. No cross on crown	£500	£300	£200
257	**93**	1s. dull green & carmine (24.3.02)	£175	80·00	35·00
		a. Chalk-surfaced paper (9.05)	£175	80·00	35·00
259		1s. dull green & scarlet (*chalk-surfaced paper*) (9.10)	£175	80·00	50·00
260	**94**	2s. 6d. lilac (5.4.02)	£400	£220	£120
		Wi. Watermark inverted	£3000	£2000	£1200
261		2s. 6d. pale dull purple (*chalk-surfaced paper*) (7.10.05)	£450	£225	£150
		Wi. Watermark inverted	£3000	£2000	£1250

262	**94**	2s. 6d. dull purple (*chalk-surfaced paper*)	£450	£225	£150
263	**95**	5s. brt carmine (5.4.02)	£600	£350	£200
		Wi. Watermark inverted	—	—	£2500
264		5s. dp brt carmine	£600	£350	£200
265	**96**	10s. ultramarine (5.4.02)	£1200	£600	£450
266	**97**	£1 dull blue-green (16.6.02)	£2200	£1500	£650
		Wi. Watermark inverted	—	£25000	£8000

USED ON COVER PRICES

No. 215	£2·50	No. 217	£2·50	No. 219	£2·50
No. 222	£28	No. 225	£30	No. 230	£20
No. 232	£30	No. 236a	£40	No. 240	£35
No. 242	£50	No. 245	£45	No. 249	£175
No. 250	£175	No. 254	£190	No. 257	£120
No. 260	£600	No. 263	£700		

97a

1910 (May). *Prepared for use, by De La Rue but not issued. Wmk Imperial Crown, W 49. P 14.*

266a **97a** 2d. Tyrian plum .... — £40000

One example of this stamp is known used, but it was never issued to the public.

1911. *Printed by Harrison & Sons. Ordinary paper. Wmk Imperial Crown, W 49.* (a) *P 14.*

			Unmtd mint	Mtd mint	Used
267	**83**	½d. dull yellow-green (3.5.11)	3·00	2·50	1·50
		Wi. Watermark inverted	30·00	15·00	8·00
268		½d. dull green	3·50	2·75	1·50
269		½d. dp dull green	15·00	11·00	4·00
270		½d. pale bluish green	70·00	40·00	40·00
		a. Booklet pane. Five stamps plus St. Andrew's Cross label	£750	£500	
		b. Watermark sideways	†		†£15000
		c. Imperf (pair)	—	£17000	†
271		½d. brt green (fine impression) (6.11)	£300	£225	£140
272		1d. rose-red (3.5.11)	12·00	8·00	12·00
		Wi. Watermark inverted	30·00	15·00	12·00
		a. No wmk	50·00	40·00	40·00
273		1d. dp rose-red	12·00	8·00	12·00
274		1d. rose-carmine	80·00	55·00	30·00
275		1d. aniline pink (5.11)	£850	£550	£300
275a		1d. aniline rose	£275	£180	£140
276	**86**	2½d. brt blue (10.7.11)	85·00	45·00	30·00
		Wi. Watermark inverted	£900	£700	
277	**87**	3d. purple/lemon (12.9.11)	£125	65·00	£180
277a		3d. grey/lemon	£4000	£3000	
278	**88**	4d. brt orange (12.7.11)	£140	65·00	50·00

(b) *P 15 × 14*

279	**83**	½d. dull green (30.10.11)	65·00	40·00	45·00
279a		½d. dp dull green	75·00	40·00	45·00
280		1d. rose-red (4.10.11)	65·00	38·00	25·00
281		1d. rose-carmine	35·00	15·00	15·00
282		1d. pale rose-carmine	40·00	22·00	15·00
283	**86**	2½d. brt blue (14.10.11)	50·00	22·00	15·00
284		2½d. dull blue	50·00	22·00	15·00
		Wi. Watermark inverted	—	—	£400
285	**87**	3d. purple/lemon (22.9.11)	70·00	45·00	15·00
285a		3d. grey/lemon	£3000	£2250	
286	**88**	4d. brt orange (11.11.11)	60·00	30·00	15·00
		Set of 5	£250	£130	90·00

USED ON COVER PRICES					
No. 267	£4	No. 272	£15	No. 276	£50
No. 277	£500	No. 278	£175	No. 279	£100
No. 281	£30	No. 283	£30	No. 285	£40
No. 286	£65				

1911–13. *Printed at Somerset House. Ordinary paper. Wmk as 1902–10. P 14.*

287	**84**	1½d. reddish purple & brt green (13.7.11)	85·00	40·00	35·00
288		1½d. dull purple & green	50·00	25·00	28·00
289		1½d. slate-purple & green (9.12)	55·00	28·00	28·00
290	**85**	2d. dp dull green & red (8.8.11)	50·00	25·00	20·00
291		2d. dp dull green & carmine	50·00	25·00	20·00
292		2d. grey-green & brt carmine (carmine shows clearly on back) (11.3.12)	50·00	25·00	25·00
293	**89**	5d. dull reddish purple & brt blue (7.8.11)	55·00	30·00	20·00
294		5d. dp dull reddish purple & brt blue	50·00	28·00	20·00
295	**83**	6d. royal purple (31.10.11)	85·00	50·00	85·00
296		6d. brt magenta (*chalk-surfaced paper*) (31.10.11)	£7500	£4500	
297		6d. dull purple	50·00	30·00	20·00
298		6d. reddish purple (11.11)	50·00	30·00	25·00
		a. No cross on crown (*various shades*)	£700	£500	
299		6d. very deep reddish purple (11.11)	85·00	40·00	40·00
300		6d. dark purple (3.12)	50·00	30·00	35·00
301		6d. dull purple "Dickinson" coated paper* (3.13)	£240	£140	£140
303		6d. dp plum (*chalk-surfaced paper*) (7.13)	50·00	28·00	70·00
		a. No cross on crown	£850	£575	
305	**90**	7d. slate-grey (1.8.12)	25·00	15·00	22·00
306	**91**	9d. reddish purple & lt blue (24.7.11)	£150	80·00	75·00
306a		9d. dp dull reddish purple & dp brt blue (9.11)	£150	80·00	75·00
307		9d. dull reddish purple & blue (10.11)	£110	60·00	60·00
307a		9d. dp plum & blue (7.13)	£110	60·00	60·00
308		9d. slate-purple & cobalt-blue (3.12)	£150	95·00	£100
309	**92**	10d. dull purple & scarlet (9.10.11)	£130	80·00	75·00
310		10d. dull reddish purple & aniline pink	£400	£250	£225
311		10d. dull reddish purple & carmine (5.12)	£110	60·00	60·00
		a. No cross on crown	£1200	£750	
312	**93**	1s. dark green & scarlet (13.7.11)	£175	90·00	60·00
313		1s. dp green & scarlet (9.10.11)	£130	60·00	35·00
		Wi. Wmk inverted	£160	£110	†
314		1s. green & carmine (15.4.12)	£125	50·00	35·00
315	**94**	2s. 6d. dull greyish purple (15.9.11)	£750	£550	£350
316		2s. 6d. dull reddish purple	£400	£200	£140
		Wi. Watermark inverted	†	†	—
317		2s. 6d. dark purple	£425	£200	£140
318	**95**	5s. carmine (29.2.12)	£600	£250	£175
319	**96**	10s. blue (14.1.12)	£1350	£700	£500
320	**97**	£1 dp green (3.9.11)	£2200	£1500	£700

*No. 301 was on an experimental coated paper which does not respond to the silver test.

USED ON COVER PRICES					
No. 288	£50	No. 290	£40	No. 293	£65
No. 297	£70	No. 305	£175	No. 307	£175
No. 311	£225	No. 314	£125	No. 316	£750
No. 318	£625				

KING GEORGE V

6 May 1910–20 January 1936

Further detailed information on the issues of King George V will be found in Volume 2 of the Stanley Gibbons *Great Britain Specialised Catalogue.*

PRINTERS. Types **98** to **102** were typographed by Harrison & Sons Ltd, with the exception of certain preliminary printings made at Somerset House and distinguishable by the controls "A.11", "B.11" or "B.12" (the Harrison printings do not have a full stop after the letter). The booklet stamps, Nos. 334/7, and 344/5 were printed by Harrison only.

WATERMARK VARIETIES. Many British stamps to 1967 exist without watermark owing to misplacement of the paper, and with either inverted, reversed, or inverted and reversed watermarks. A proportion of the low-value stamps issued in booklets have the watermark inverted in the normal course of printing.

Low values with *watermark sideways* are normally from stamp rolls used on machines with sideways delivery or, from June 1940, certain booklets.

STAMPS WITHOUT WATERMARK. Stamps found without watermark, due to misplacement of the sheet in relation to the paper, are not listed here but will be found in the *Great Britain Specialised Catalogue.*

The 1½d. and 5d. 1912–22, and 2d. and 2½d., 1924–26, listed here, are from *whole* sheets completely without watermark.

| **98** | **99** | **100** Simple Cypher |

For type difference with T **101/2** *see notes below the latter.*

Die A   Die B

Dies of Halfpenny

Die A. The three upper scales on the body of the right hand dolphin form a triangle; the centre jewel of the cross inside the crown is suggested by a comma.

Die B. The three upper scales are incomplete; the centre jewel is suggested by a crescent.

Die A   Die B

1840–1951

All Aspects and Periods of Great Britain

For your **free** list of Great Britain 1840–1951 please call, write, fax or email

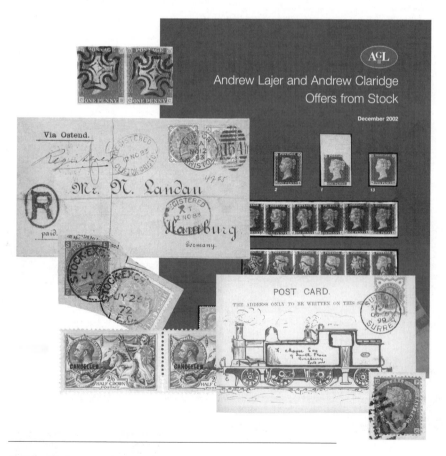

Andrew G Lajer

The Old Post Office   Davis Way   Hurst   Berkshire RG10 0TR   United Kingdom

T: +44 (0)1189 344151   F: +44 (0)1189 344947   E: Andrew.Lajer@btinternet.com

Dies of One Penny

Die A. The second line of shading on the ribbon to the right of the crown extends right across the wreath; the line nearest to the crown on the right hand ribbon shows as a short line at the bottom of the ribbon.

Die B. The second line of shading is broken in the middle; the first line is little more than a dot.

(Des Bertram Mackennal and G. W. Eve. Head from photograph by W. and D. Downey. Die eng J.A.C. Harrison)

1911–12. *Wmk Imperial Crown, W* **49**. *P* 15 × 14.

			Unmtd mint	Mtd mint	Used
321	98	½d. pale green (Die A) (22.6.11)	10·00	5·00	4·00
322		½d. green (Die A) (22.6.11)	10·00	5·00	4·00
		a. Error. Perf 14 (8.11)	—	£11000	£600
		Wi. Watermark inverted £16000		—	£1000
323		½d. bluish green (Die A)	£400	£300	£180
324		½d. yellow-green (Die B)	15·00	8·00	1·50
325		½d. brt green (Die B)	10·00	4·50	1·50
		a. Watermark sideways	—	—	£3500
		Wi. Watermark inverted	20·00	10·00	4·50
326		½d. bluish green (Die B)	£250	£160	£100
327	99	1d. carmine-red (Die A) (22.6.11) ..	10·00	4·50	2·50
		c. Watermark sideways	†	†	—
		Wi. Watermark inverted	£1300	£800	£700
328		1d. pale carmine (Die A) (22.6.11)	22·00	14·00	3·00
		a. No cross on crown	£550	£400	£275
329		1d. carmine (Die B)	15·00	7·00	3·00
		Wi. Watermark inverted	22·00	12·00	4·00
330		1d. pale carmine (Die B)	15·00	10·00	4·00
		a. No cross on crown	£750	£500	£350
331		1d. rose-pink (Die B)	£160	£100	40·00
332		1d. scarlet (Die B) (6.12)	50·00	25·00	18·00
		Wi. Watermark inverted	50·00	25·00	18·00
333		1d. aniline scarlet (Die B)	£275	£175	£100

For note on the aniline scarlet No. 333 *see* below No. 343.

1912 (Aug). *Booklet stamps. Wmk Royal Cypher ("Simple"), W* **100**. *P* 15 × 14.

334	98	½d. pale green (Die B)	60·00	40·00	40·00
335		½d. green (Die B)	60·00	40·00	40·00
		Wi. Watermark inverted	60·00	40·00	40·00
		Wj. Watermark reversed	£700	£600	£300
		Wk. Watermark inverted and reversed	£700	£600	£300
336	99	1d. scarlet (Die B)	40·00	30·00	30·00
		Wi. Watermark inverted	40·00	30·00	30·00
		Wj. Watermark reversed	£850	£650	
		Wk. Watermark inverted and reversed	—	—	£200
337		1d. brt scarlet (Die B)	40·00	30·00	30·00

1912 (1 Jan). *Wmk Imperial Crown, W* **49**. *P* 15 × 14.

338	101	½d. dp green	28·00	15·00	8·00
339		½d. green	15·00	8·00	4·00
340		½d. yellow-green	15·00	8·00	4·00
		a. No cross on crown	£150	£100	50·00
		Wi. Watermark inverted	£750	£550	£350
341	102	1d. brt scarlet	10·00	5·00	2·00
		a. No cross on crown	£120	80·00	50·00
		b. Printed double, one albino	£275	£180	
		Wi. Watermark inverted	£400	£275	£200
342		1d. scarlet	10·00	5·00	2·00
343		1d. aniline scarlet*	£250	£175	£100
		a. No cross on crown	£1400	£1000	

*Our prices for the aniline scarlet 1d. stamps, Nos. 333 and 343, are for the specimens in which the colour is suffused on the surface of the stamp and shows through clearly on the back. Specimens without these characteristics but which show "aniline" reactions under the quartz lamp are relatively common.

1912 (Aug). *Wmk Royal Cypher ("Simple"), W* **100**. *P* 15 × 14.

344	101	½d. green	14·00	7·00	3·00
		a. No cross on crown	£160	£100	50·00
		Wi. Watermark inverted	£200	£140	60·00
		Wj. Watermark reversed	£160	£100	50·00
		Wk. Watermark inverted and reversed	15·00	8·00	4·50
345	102	1d. scarlet	15·00	8·00	3·00
		a. No cross on crown	£140	£100	50·00
		Wi. Watermark inverted	20·00	13·00	15·00
		Wj. Watermark reversed	30·00	20·00	13·00
		Wk. Watermark inverted and reversed	16·00	9·00	9·00

1912 (Sept–Oct). *Wmk Royal Cypher ("Multiple"), W* **103**. *P* 15 × 14.

346	101	½d. green (Oct)	20·00	12·00	8·00
		a. No cross on crown	£140	£100	60·00
		b. Imperf	£200	£130	
		c. Watermark sideways	†	†	£2200
		d. Printed on gummed side	—	—	†
		Wi. Watermark inverted	20·00	12·00	15·00
		Wj. Watermark reversed	20·00	12·00	9·00
		Wk. Watermark inverted and reversed	30·00	20·00	
347		½d. yellow-green	20·00	15·00	8·00
348		½d. pale green	25·00	15·00	8·00
349	102	1d. brt scarlet	25·00	18·00	10·00
350		1d. scarlet	25·00	18·00	10·00
		a. No cross on crown	£180	£120	50·00
		b. Imperf	£200	£130	
		c. Watermark sideways	£225	£130	£150
		d. Watermark sideways. No cross on crown	£1000	£750	
		Wi. Watermark inverted	25·00	15·00	15·00
		Wj. Watermark reversed	25·00	15·00	15·00
		Wk. Watermark inverted and reversed	£1000	£750	£350

101

102

103 Multiple Cypher

104

105

106

107

108

Type differences

½d. In T **98** the ornament above "P" of "HALFPENNY" has two thin lines of colour and the beard is undefined. In T **101** the ornament has one thick line and the beard is well defined.

1d. In T **99** the body of the lion is unshaded and in T **102** it is shaded.

No. 357ab

No. 357ac

No. 357a

Die I

Die II

Two Dies of the 2d.

Die I.— Inner frame-line at top and sides close to solid of background. *Four* complete lines of shading between top of head and oval frame-line. These four lines do *not* extend to the oval itself. White line round "TWOPENCE" thin.

Die II.—Inner frame-line further from solid of background. *Three* lines between top of head and extending to the oval. White line round "TWOPENCE" thicker.

(Des Bertram Mackennal (heads) and G.W. Eve (frames). Coinage head ($\frac{1}{2}$, $1\frac{1}{2}$, 2, 3 and 4d.); large medal head (1d., $2\frac{1}{2}$d.); intermediate medal head (5d. to 1s.); small medal head used for fiscal stamps. Dies eng J. A. C. Harrison)

(Typo by Harrison & Sons Ltd., except the 6d. printed by the Stamping Department of the Board of Inland Revenue, Somerset House. The latter also made printings of the following which can only be distinguished by the controls: $\frac{1}{2}$d. B.13; $1\frac{1}{2}$d. A.12; 2d. C.13; $2\frac{1}{2}$d. A.12; 3d. A12, B.13, C.13; 4d. B.13; 5d. B.13; 7d. C.13; 8d. C.13; 9d. agate B.13; 10d. C.13; 1s. C.13)

1912–24. *Wmk Royal Cypher, W* **100**. *Chalk-surfaced paper* (6d.). P 15 × 14.

351	**105**	$\frac{1}{2}$d. green (1.13)	3·00	1·00	1·00
		a. Partial double print (half of bottom row) (Control G15)	— £16000		†
		b. Gummed both sides			
		Wi. Watermark inverted	4·00	3·00	1·50
		Wj. Watermark reversed	25·00	15·00	7·00
		Wk. Watermark inverted and reversed	6·00	4·00	3·00
352		$\frac{1}{2}$d. brt green	3·00	1·00	1·00
353		$\frac{1}{2}$d. dp green	8·00	4·00	2·00
354		$\frac{1}{2}$d. yellow-green	9·00	5·00	3·00
355		$\frac{1}{2}$d. very yellow (Cyprus) green (1914)	£6000	£4000	†
356		$\frac{1}{2}$d. blue-green	60·00	40·00	25·00

357	**104**	1d. brt scarlet (8.10.12)	3·00	1·00	1·00
		a. "Q" for "O" (R.1/4) (Control E14)	£200	£150	£140
		ab. "Q" for "O" (R.4/11) (Control T22)	£400	£350	£175
		ac. Reversed "Q" for "O" (R.15/9) (Control T22)	£375	£300	£225
		ad. Inverted "Q" for "O" (R.20/3) ..	£450	£375	£225
		b. Tête-bêche (pair)	— £50000		†
		Wi. Watermark inverted	4·00	2·00	1·00
		Wj. Watermark reversed	25·00	15·00	8·00
		Wk. Watermark inverted and reversed	6·00	3·00	2·50
358		1d. vermilion	9·00	5·00	2·50
359		1d. pale rose-red	22·00	15·00	2·50
360		1d. carmine-red	20·00	11·00	5·00
361		1d. scarlet-vermilion	£175	£125	50·00
		a. Printed on back†	£350	£275	†
362	**105**	$1\frac{1}{2}$d. red-brown (15.10.12)	6·00	4·00	1·50
		a. "PENCF" (R.15/12)	£225	£180	£150
		b. Booklet pane. Four stamps plus two printed labels (2.24)	£550	£450	
		Wi. Watermark inverted	9·00	5·00	2·00
		Wj. Watermark reversed	35·00	25·00	6·00
		Wk. Watermark inverted and reversed	15·00	8·00	6·00
363		$1\frac{1}{2}$d. chocolate-brown	15·00	9·00	2·00
		a. No watermark	£250	£175	£110
364		$1\frac{1}{2}$d. chestnut	9·00	5·00	1·00
		a. "PENCF" (R.15/12)	£140	£100	80·00
365		$1\frac{1}{2}$d. yellow-brown	30·00	20·00	16·00
366	**106**	2d. orange-yellow (Die I) (20.8.12)	12·00	7·00	3·00
367		2d. reddish orange (Die I) (11.13) ...	10·00	6·00	3·00
368		2d. orange (Die I)	10·00	6·00	3·00
		Wi. Watermark inverted	18·00	10·00	10·00
		Wj. Watermark reversed	18·00	10·00	10·00
		Wk. Watermark inverted and reversed	15·00	8·00	8·00
369		2d. brt orange (Die I)	8·00	5·00	3·00
370		2d. orange (Die II) (9.21)	8·00	5·00	3·50
		Wi. Watermark inverted	25·00	16·00	16·00
		Wk. Watermark inverted and reversed	40·00	30·00	30·00
371	**104**	$2\frac{1}{2}$d. cobalt-blue (18.10.12)	22·00	12·00	4·00
371a		$2\frac{1}{2}$d. brt blue (1914)	22·00	12·00	4·00
372		$2\frac{1}{2}$d. blue	22·00	12·00	4·00
		Wi. Watermark inverted	75·00	50·00	50·00
		Wj. Watermark reversed	30·00	18·00	18·00
		Wk. Watermark inverted and reversed	30·00	18·00	18·00
373		$2\frac{1}{2}$d. indigo-blue* (1920)	£2500	£1700	£1000
373a		$2\frac{1}{2}$d. dull Prussian blue* (1921)	£1000	£700	£600
374	**106**	3d. dull reddish violet (9.10.12) ..	22·00	12·00	2·00
375		3d. violet	12·00	7·00	3·00
		Wi. Watermark inverted	£100	75·00	75·00
		Wj. Watermark reversed	£175	£110	£110
		Wk. Watermark inverted and reversed	30·00	20·00	20·00
376		3d. bluish violet (11.13)	12·00	7·00	2·00
377		3d. pale violet	12·00	7·00	2·00
378		4d. dp grey-green (15.1.13)	55·00	35·00	10·00
379		4d. grey-green	25·00	15·00	2·00
		Wi. Watermark inverted	40·00	25·00	25·00
		Wj. Watermark reversed	80·00	45·00	45·00
		Wk. Watermark inverted and reversed	50·00	30·00	30·00
380		4d. pale grey-green	40·00	25·00	5·00
381	**107**	5d. brown (30.6.13)	25·00	15·00	5·00
		Wi. Watermark inverted	£500	£350	£350
		Wj. Watermark reversed	†	†	—
		Wk. Watermark inverted and reversed	£250	£175	£175

382	**107**	5d. yellow-brown	25·00	15·00	5·00
		a. No watermark	£800	£500	
383		5d. bistre-brown	£175	£100	50·00
384		6d. dull purple (1.8.13)	40·00	25·00	10·00
385		6d. reddish purple (8.13)	30·00	15·00	7·00
		a. Perf 14 (9.20)	£125	90·00	£110
		Wi. Watermark inverted	50·00	35·00	35·00
		Wj. Watermark reversed	£850	£650	
		Wk. Watermark inverted and reversed	40·00	20·00	20·00
386		6d. dp reddish purple	40·00	20·00	5·00
387		7d. olive (1.8.13)	35·00	20·00	10·00
		Wi. Watermark inverted	60·00	35·00	35·00
		Wj. Watermark reversed	†	†	—
		Wk. Watermark inverted and reversed	£1600	£1000	
388		7d. bronze-green (1915)	90·00	60·00	25·00
389		7d. sage-green (1917)	90·00	60·00	15·00
390		8d. black/*yellow* (1.8.13)	55·00	32·00	11·00
		Wi. Watermark inverted	£125	80·00	80·00
		Wj. Watermark reversed	£175	£125	£125
		Wk. Watermark inverted and reversed	£1800	£1400	
391		8d. black/*yellow-buff* (granite) (5.17) .	60·00	40·00	15·00
392	**108**	9d. agate (30.6.13)	40·00	20·00	6·00
		a. Printed double, one albino			
		Wi. Watermark inverted	£125	75·00	75·00
		Wk. Watermark inverted and reversed	80·00	55·00	55·00
393		9d. dp agate	45·00	25·00	6·00
393*a*		9d. olive-green (9.22)	£200	£100	30·00
		aWi. Watermark inverted	£700	£500	£500
		aWk. Watermark inverted and reversed	£600	£400	£400
393*b*		9d. pale olive-green	£225	£100	40·00
394		10d. turquoise-blue (1.8.13)	40·00	22·00	20·00
		Wi. Watermark inverted	£2500	£1600	£800
		Wk. Watermark inverted and reversed	£225	£175	£120
394*a*		10d. dp turquoise-blue	£100	70·00	25·00
395		1s. bistre (1.8.13)	35·00	20·00	4·00
		Wi. Watermark inverted	£200	£150	£100
		Wk. Watermark inverted and reversed	85·00	50·00	50·00
396		1s. bistre-brown	55·00	35·00	12·00
		Set of 15	£475	£260	95·00

Imperf stamps of this issue exist but may be war-time colour trials.
† The impression of No. 361a is set sideways and is very pale.
Nos. 362a and 364a occur on Plates 12 and 29 and are known from Controls L18, M18, M19, O19 and Q21. The flaws were corrected by 1921.
*No. 373 comes from Control O20 and also exists on toned paper.
No. 373a comes from Control R21 and also exists on toned paper, but both are unlike the rare Prussian blue shade of the 1935 2½d. Jubilee issue.
Examples of the 2d., T **106** which were in the hands of philatelists, are known bisected in Guernsey from 27 December 1940 to February 1941.
See also Nos. 418/29.

1913 (Aug). *Wmk Royal Cypher ("Multiple"), W* **103**. *P* 15 × 14.

397	**105**	½d. brt green	£250	£150	£180
		a. Watermark sideways	†	†	£18000
		Wi. Watermark inverted	£600	£450	
⁰398	**104**	1d. dull scarlet	£350	£225	£225
		Wi. Watermark inverted	£750	£550	

Both these stamps were originally issued in rolls only. Subsequently sheets were found, so that horizontal pairs and blocks are known but are of considerable rarity.

109

A

110 Single Cypher

Major Re-entries on 2s. 6d.

Nos. 400a and 408a

No. 415b

(Des Bertram Mackennal. Dies eng J.A.C. Harrison. Recess)

High values, so-called "Sea Horses" design: T **109**. Background around portrait consists of horizontal lines, Type A. Wmk Single Cypher, W **110**. P 11 × 12.

1913 (30 June–Aug). *Printed by Waterlow Bros & Layton.*

399	**109**	2s. 6d. dp sepia-brown	£500	£240	£160
400		2s. 6d. sepia-brown	£425	£225	£140
		a. Re-entry (R.2/1)	£1600	£800	£525
401		5s. rose-carmine	£850	£325	£275
402		10s. indigo-blue (1 Aug)	£1400	£550	£375
403		£1 green (1 Aug)	£3000	£1500	£950
404		£1 dull blue-green (1 Aug)	£3000	£1500	£1000
★399/404		**For well-centred, lightly used**			+**35%**

1915 (Oct–Dec). *Printed by De la Rue & Co.*

405	**109**	2s. 6d. dp yellow-brown	£475	£250	£190
		Wi. Watermark inverted	£1200	£750	

SELLING YOUR COLLECTION?

Warwick and Warwick have an expanding requirement for world collections, single country collections, single items, covers, proof material and specialised collections, especially G.B. Our customer base is increasing dramatically and we need an ever larger supply of quality material to keep pace with demand. The market for quality material has never been stronger and if you are considering the sale of your collection, now is the time to act.

FREE VALUATIONS

We will provide a free professional and without obligation valuation of your collection. Either we will make you a fair, binding private treaty offer, or we will recommend inclusion of your property in our next public auction.

FREE TRANSPORTATION

We can arrange insured transportation of your collection to our Warwick offices completely free of charge. If you decline our offer we ask you to cover the return carriage costs only.

FREE VISITS

Visits by our valuers are possible anywhere in the country or abroad, usually within 48 hours, in order to value larger collections. Please phone for details.

EXCELLENT PRICES

Because of the strength of our customer base we are in a position to offer prices that we feel sure will exceed your expectations.

ACT NOW

Telephone today with details of your property. E-mail or fax us if you prefer.

Get the experts on your side.

Warwick & Warwick

www.warwickandwarwick.com

 Warwick & Warwick Ltd., Chalon House, Scar Bank, Millers Rd, Warwick CV34 5DB
Tel: 01926-499031 Fax: 01926-491906 E-mail: info@warwickandwarwick.com

406	**109**	2s. 6d. yellow-brown	£450	£225	£190
		a. Re-entry (R.2/1)			
		Wi. Watermark inverted	£1000	£650	
		Wj. Watermark reversed	£1000	£650	
		Wk. Watermark inverted and reversed	£2250	£1400	
407		2s. 6d. pale brown	£450	£225	£190
		a. Re-entry (R.2/1)	£1600	£900	£550
		Wi. Watermark inverted	£1000	£650	
		Wj. Watermark reversed	£1200	£700	
408		2s. 6d. sepia (seal-brown)	£375	£225	£190
		Wi. Watermark inverted	£1000	£650	
		Wj. Watermark reversed	£1000	£650	
409		5s. brt carmine	£750	£375	£300
		Wi. Watermark inverted	£2500	£1600	
		Wj. Watermark reversed	£2200	£1500	
		Wk. Watermark inverted and reversed	—	£5000	†
410		5s. pale carmine	£800	£450	£280
411		10s. dp blue (Dec)	£3000	£1900	£875
412		10s. blue	£2200	£1500	£700
		Wi. Watermark inverted and reversed	—		†
413		10s. pale blue	£2400	£1600	£700
★405/13		**For well-centred, lightly used**			**+45%**

No. 406/7 were produced from the original Waterlow plates as were all De La Rue 5s and 10s printings. Examples of No. 406/7, 410 and 411 occur showing degrees of plate wear.

1918 (Dec)–**19.** *Printed by Bradbury, Wilkinson & Co, Ltd.*

413a	**109**	2s. 6d. olive-brown	£190	£100	65·00
414		2s. 6d. chocolate-brown	£240	£125	70·00
415		2s. 6d. reddish brown	£240	£125	70·00
415a		2s. 6d. pale brown	£200	£110	65·00
		b. Major re-entry (R.1/2)	£900	£650	£400
416		5s. rose-red (1.19)	£380	£250	£110
417		10s. dull grey-blue (1.19)	£650	£350	£160
		Set of 4 (inc. no. 403)	£3800	£2100	£1200
★413a/17		**For well-centred, lightly used**			**+35%**

DISTINGUISHING PRINTINGS. Note that the £1 value was only printed by Waterlow.

Waterlow and De La Rue stamps measure exactly 22 mm vertically. In the De La Rue printings the gum is usually patchy and yellowish, and the colour of the stamp, particularly in the 5s., tends to show through the back. The holes of the perforation are smaller than those of the other two printers, but there is a thick perforation tooth at the top of each vertical side.

In the Bradbury Wilkinson printings the height of the stamp is 22¼ or 23 mm due to the use of curved plates. On most of the 22¼ mm high stamps a minute coloured guide dot appears in the margin just above the middle of the upper frame-line.

For (1934) re-engraved Waterlow printings *see* Nos. 450/2.

UNITED KINGDOM OF GREAT BRITAIN AND NORTHERN IRELAND

111	Block Cypher	**111a**

The watermark Type **111a**, as compared with Type **111**, differs as follows: Closer spacing of horizontal rows (12½ mm instead of 14½ mm). Letters shorter and rounder. Watermark thicker.

The dandy roll to produce watermark Type **111a** was provided by Somerset House in connection with experiments in paper composition undertaken during 1924–25. These resulted in a change from rag only paper to that made from a mixture including esparto and sulphite.

(Typo by Waterlow & Sons, Ltd (all values except 6d.) and later, 1934–35, by Harrison & Sons, Ltd (all values). Until 1934 the 6d. was printed at Somerset House where a printing of the 1½d. was also made in 1926 (identifiable only by control E.26). Printings by Harrisons in 1934–35 can be identified, when in mint condition, by the fact that the gum shows a streaky appearance vertically, the Waterlow gum being uniformly applied, but Harrisons also used up the balance of the Waterlow "smooth gum" paper)

1924 (Feb)–**26.** *Wmk Block Cypher, W* **111**. P 15 × 14.

418	**105**	½d. green	2·00	1·00	1·00
		a. Watermark sideways (5.24)	10·00	6·00	3·25
		aWi. Watermark sideways-inverted ..	£450	£350	
		b. Doubly printed £10000	£7500		†
		Wi. Watermark inverted	4·00	2·00	1·00
419	**104**	1d. scarlet	2·00	1·00	1·00
		a. Watermark sideways	25·00	15·00	15·00
		b. Experimental paper, W **111a**			
		(10.24)	40·00	22·00	
		c. Partial double print, one			
		inverted	—	£6500	
		d. Inverted "Q" for "O" (R.20/3) ..	£550	£375	
		Wi. Watermark inverted	5·00	3·00	1·50
420	**105**	1½d. red-brown	2·00	1·00	1·00
		a. Tête-bêche (pair)	£550	£375	£750
		b. Watermark sideways (8.24)	13·00	7·00	3·50
		bWi. Watermark sideways-inverted ..	—	£600	
		c. Printed on the gummed side	£600	£400	†
		d. Booklet pane. Four stamps plus			
		two printed labels (3.24)	£175	£125	
		e. Ditto. Watermark sideways	£6000	£5000	
		f. Experimental paper, W **111a**			
		(10.24)	90·00	60·00	70·00
		g. Double impression	—	£10000	†
		Wi. Watermark inverted	1·50	1·00	50
421	**106**	2d. orange (Die II) (7.24)	4·00	2·50	2·50
		a. No watermark	£1200	£675	
		b. Watermark sideways (7.26)	£125	70·00	80·00
		c. Partial double print	—	£14000	
		Wi. Watermark inverted	35·00	20·00	20·00
422	**104**	2½d. blue (10.24)	10·00	5·00	3·00
		a. No watermark	£1800	£1100	
		b. Watermark sideways	†	†	£5500
		Wi. Watermark inverted	45·00	30·00	30·00
423	**106**	3d. violet (10.24)	20·00	10·00	2·50
		Wi. Watermark inverted	50·00	30·00	30·00
424		4d. grey-green (11.24)	28·00	12·00	2·50
		a. Printed on the gummed side ..	£2400	£1750	†
		Wi. Watermark inverted	£125	75·00	60·00
425	**107**	5d. brown (11.24)	40·00	20·00	3·00
		Wi. Watermark inverted	80·00	50·00	50·00
426		6d. reddish purple (*chalk-surfaced*			
		paper) (9.24)	20·00	12·00	2·50
		Wi. Watermark inverted	55·00	35·00	35·00
		Wk. Watermark inverted and			
		reversed	£350	£225	£125
426a		6d. purple (6.26)	6·00	3·00	1·50
		aWi. Watermark inverted	50·00	30·00	30·00
427	**108**	9d. olive-green (12.24)	40·00	12·00	3·50
		Wi. Watermark inverted	£100	60·00	60·00
428		10d. turquoise-blue (11.24)	70·00	35·00	40·00
		Wi. Watermark inverted	£2500	£1500	£1000
429		1s. bistre-brown (10.24)	50·00	22·00	3·00
		Wi. Watermark inverted	£450	£325	£300
		Set of 12	£250	£110	60·00

There are numerous shades in this issue.

The 6d. on chalk-surfaced and ordinary papers was printed by both Somerset House and Harrisons. The Harrison printings have streaky gum, differ slightly in shade, and that on chalk-surfaced paper is printed in a highly fugitive ink. The prices quoted are for the commonest (Harrison) printing in each case.

112

(Des H. Nelson. Eng J. A. C. Harrison. Recess Waterlow)

1924–25. British Empire Exhibition. W 111. P 14.

(a) Dated "1924" (23.4.24)

430	112	1d. scarlet	12·00	10·00	11·00
431		1½d. brown	18·00	15·00	15·00
		Set of 2	30·00	25·00	26·00
		First Day Cover			£375

(b) Dated "1925" (9.5.25)

432	112	1d. scarlet	20·00	15·00	30·00
433		1½d. brown	55·00	40·00	70·00
		Set of 2	75·00	55·00	£100
		First Day Cover			£1300

113

114

115

116 St. George and the Dragon

117

(Des J. Farleigh (T **113** and **115**), E. Linzell (T **114**) and H. Nelson (T **116**). Eng C. G. Lewis (T **113**), T.E. Storey (T **115**), both at the Royal Mint; J. A. C. Harrison, of Waterlow (T **114** & **116**). Typo by Waterlow from plates made at the Royal Mint, except T **116**, recess by Bradbury, Wilkinson from die and plate of their own manufacture)

1929 (10 May). **Ninth U.P.U. Congress, London.**

*(a) W **111**. P 15 × 14*

434	113	½d. green	3·00	2·25	2·25
		a. Watermark sideways	55·00	35·00	35·00
		Wi. Watermark inverted	25·00	12·00	10·00
435	114	1d. scarlet	3·00	2·25	2·25
		a. Watermark sideways	£100	60·00	60·00
		Wi. Watermark inverted	25·00	12·00	10·00
436		1½d. purple-brown	3·00	2·25	1·75
		a. Watermark sideways	55·00	35·00	35·00
		b. Booklet pane. Four stamps plus two printed labels	£275	£225	
		Wi. Watermark inverted	10·00	5·00	6·00
437	115	2½d. blue	18·00	10·00	10·00
		Wi. Watermark inverted	£2500	£1500	£800

*(b) W **117**. P 12*

438	116	£1 black	£1000	£750	£550
		Set of 4 (to 2½d.)	24·00	15·00	14·50
		First Day Cover (4 vals.)			£500
		First Day Cover (5 vals.)			£7000

PRINTERS. All subsequent issues were printed in photogravure by Harrison & Sons Ltd *except where otherwise stated*.

118

119

120

121

122

1934–36. W **111**. P 15 × 14.

439	118	½d. green (19.11.34)	1·00	50	50
		a. Watermark sideways	15·00	7·00	3·50
		aWi. Watermark sideways-inverted ...	£375	£275	75·00
		b. Imperf three sides	£2500	£1800	
		Wi. Watermark inverted	15·00	4·50	1·25
440	119	1d. scarlet (24.9.34)	1·00	50	50
		a. Imperf (pair)	£2000	£1500	
		b. Printed on gummed side	£650	£500	†
		c. Watermark sideways	25·00	12·00	6·00
		cWi. Watermark sideways-inverted ...	£125	75·00	
		d. Double impression	†		† £15000
		e. Imperf between (pair)	£4000	£2500	
		f. Imperf (three sides) (pair)	£2500	£1700	
		Wi. Watermark inverted	15·00	7·00	3·00
441	118	1½d. red-brown (20.8.34)	1·00	50	50
		a. Imperf (pair)	£700	£550	
		b. Imperf (three sides) (lower stamp in vert pair)	£1500	£1000	
		c. Imperf between (horiz pair)			
		d. Watermark sideways	10·00	6·00	4·00
		dWi. Watermark sideways-inverted ...			
		e. Booklet pane. Four stamps plus two printed labels (1.35)	£150	£100	
		Wi. Watermark inverted	5·00	2·00	1·00

442	**120**	2d. orange (21.1.35)	1·50	75	75
		a. Imperf (pair)	£2500	£2000	
		b. Watermark sideways	£160	90·00	60·00
443	**119**	2½d. ultramarine (18.3.35)	2·50	1·50	1·25
444	**120**	3d. violet (18.3.35)	2·50	1·50	1·25
		Wi. Watermark inverted	—	—	£800
445		4d. dp grey-green (2.12.35)	4·00	2·00	1·25
		Wi. Watermark inverted	†	†	£750
446	**121**	5d. yellow-brown (17.2.36)	12·00	6·00	2·75
447	**122**	9d. dp olive-green (2.12.35)	20·00	12·00	2·25
448		10d. turquoise-blue (24.2.36)	28·00	15·00	10·00
449		1s. bistre-brown (24.2.36)	35·00	15·00	1·25
		a. Double impression	—	—	†
		Set of 11	95·00	50·00	20·00

Owing to the need for wider space for the perforations the size of the designs of the ½d. and 2d. were once, and the 1d. and 1½d. twice reduced from that of the first printings.

The format description, size in millimetres and S.G. catalogue number are given but further details will be found in the *Great Britain Specialised Catalogue, Volume 2.*

Description	Size	S.G. Nos.	Date of Issue
½d. intermediate format	18.4 × 22.2	—	19.11.34
½d. small format	17.9 × 21.7	439	1935
1d. large format	18.7 × 22.5	—	24.9.34
1d. intermediate format	18.4 × 22.2	—	1934
1d. small format	17.9 × 21.7	440	1935
1¼d. large format	18.7 × 22.5	—	20.8.34
1¼d. intermediate format	18.4 × 22.2	—	1934
1½d. small format	17.9 × 21.7	441	1935
2d. intermediate format	18.4 × 22.2	—	21.1.35
2d. small format	18.15 × 21.7	442	1935

There are also numerous minor variations, due to the photographic element in the process.

The ½d. imperf three sides, No. 439b, is known in a block of four, from a sheet, in which the bottom pair is imperf at top and sides.

Examples of 2d., T **120**, which were in the hands of philatelists are known bisected in Guernsey from 27 December 1940 to February 1941.

B   **123**

(Eng J .A .C. Harrison. Recess Waterlow)

1934 (16 Oct). T **109** (re-engraved). *Background around portrait consists of horizontal and diagonal lines, Type B, W* **110**. *P* 11 × 12.

450	**109**	2s. 6d. chocolate-brown	£100	70·00	40·00
451		5s. brt rose-red	£260	£160	85·00
452		10s. indigo	£425	£340	80·00
		Set of 3	£700	£525	£190

There are numerous other minor differences in the design of this issue.

(Des B. Freedman)

1935 (7 May). **Silver Jubilee**. W **111**. *P* 15 × 14.

453	**123**	½d. green	75	75	50
		Wi. Watermark inverted	12·00	6·00	3·00
454		1d. scarlet	2·00	1·25	1·50
		Wi. Watermark inverted	12·00	6·00	4·00
455		1½d. red-brown	75	75	50
		Wi. Watermark inverted	4·00	3·00	1·50
456		2½d. blue	5·00	4·50	5·50
456a		2½d. Prussian blue	£7500	£6000	£6000
		Set of 4	7·00	6·00	7·00
		First Day Cover			£600

The 1d., 1½d. and 2½d. values differ from T **123** in the emblem in the panel at right.

Four sheets of No. 456a, printed in the wrong shade, were issued in error by the Post Office Stores Department on 25 June 1935. It is known that three from the sheets were sold from the sub-office at 134 Fore Street, Upper Edmonton, London, between that date and 4 July.

KING EDWARD VIII
20 January–10 December 1936

Further detailed information on the stamps of King Edward VIII will be found in Volume 2 of the Stanley Gibbons *Great Britain Specialised Catalogue.*

PRICES. From S.G. 457 prices quoted in the first column are for stamps in unmounted mint condition.

---

124   125

(Des H. Brown, adapted Harrison using a photo by Hugh Cecil)

1936. W **125**. *P* 15 × 14.

457	**124**	½d. green (1.9.36)		30	30
		a. Double impression			
		Wi. Watermark inverted		10·00	5·00
458		1d. scarlet (14.9.36)		60	50
		Wi. Watermark inverted		8·50	5·00
459		1½d. red-brown (1.9.36)		30	30
		a. Booklet pane. Four stamps plus two printed labels (10.36)		60·00	
		Wi. Watermark inverted		1·00	1·00
460		2½d. brt blue (1.9.36)		30	85
		Set of 4		1·25	1·75

First Day Covers

1.9.36	½d., 1½d., 2½d. (457, 459/60)		£150
14.9.36	1d. (458)		£170

KING GEORGE VI
11 December 1936–6 February 1952

Further detailed information on the stamps of King George VI will be found in Volume 2 of the Stanley Gibbons *Great Britain Specialised Catalogue.*

126 King George VI and Queen Elizabeth   **127**

(Des E. Dulac)

1937 (13 May). **Coronation.** W **127**. P 15 × 14.
461 **126** 1½d. maroon 30 30
          First Day Cover .... 35·00

128   **129**   **130**

King George VI and National Emblems

(Des T **128**/9, E. Dulac (head) and E. Gill (frames). T **130**, E. Dulac (whole stamp))

1937–47. W **127**. P 15 × 14.
462 **128** ½d. green (10.5.37) 30 25
          a. Watermark sideways (1.38) 50 50
          ab. Booklet pane of 4 (6.40) .... 38·00
          Wi. Watermark inverted .... 10·00 60
463   1d. scarlet (10.5.37) 30 25
          a. Watermark sideways (2.38) .... 20·00 9·00
          ab. Booklet pane of 4 (6.40) .... 95·00
          Wi. Watermark inverted .... 38·00 3·00
464   1½d. red-brown (30.7.37) 20 25
          a. Watermark sideways (2.38) .... 1·00 1·25
          b. Booklet pane. Four stamps plus two printed labels (8.37) .... 55·00
          c. Imperf three sides (pair) ....
          Wi. Watermark inverted .... 15·00 1·25
465   2d. orange (31.1.38) 75 50
          a. Watermark sideways (2.38) .... 70·00 38·00
          b. Bisected (on cover) .... † 40·00
          Wi. Watermark inverted .... 55·00 18·00
466   2½d. ultramarine (10.5.37) 30 25
          a. Watermark sideways (6.40) .... 70·00 32·00
          b. *Tête-bêche* (horiz pair) £12000
          Wi. Watermark inverted .... 50·00 18·00
467   3d. violet (31.1.38) .... 3·75 1·00
468 **129** 4d. grey-green (21.11.38) 60 75
          a. Imperf (pair) £4500
          b. Imperf three sides (horiz pair) £5250
469   5d. brown (21.11.38) .... 2·50 85
          a. Imperf (pair) £5500
          b. Imperf three sides (horiz pair) £4750
470   6d. purple (30.1.39) .... 1·25 60
471 **130** 7d. emerald-green (27.2.39) .... 4·50 60
          a. Imperf three sides (horiz pair) £5000
472   8d. brt carmine (27.2.39) .... 4·00 80
473   9d. dp olive-green (1.5.39) .... 5·75 80
474   10d. turquoise-blue (1.5.39) .... 6·00 80
          aa. Imperf (pair) £6000
474a   11d. plum (29.12.47) .... 2·00 2·75
475   1s. bistre-brown (1.5.39) .... 7·00 75
          Set of 15 .... 35·00 10·00

For later printings of the lower values in apparently lighter shades and different colours, see Nos. 485/90 and 503/8.

No. 465b was authorised for use in Guernsey from 27 December 1940 until February 1941.

Nos. 468b and 469b are perforated at foot only and each occurs in the same sheet as Nos. 468a and 469a.

No. 471a is also perforated at foot only, but occurs on the top row of a sheet.

First Day Covers
10.5.37   ½d., 1d., 2½d. (462/3, 466) .... 35·00
30.7.37   1½d. (464) .... 35·00
31.1.38   2d., 3d. (465, 467) .... 80·00
21.11.38 4d., 5d. (468/9) .... 50·00
30.1.39   6d. (470) .... 50·00
27.2.39   7d., 8d. (471/2) .... 75·00
1.5.39   9d., 10d., 1s. (473/4, 475) £450
29.12.47 11d. (474a) .... 45·00

131   **132**

133

(Des E. Dulac (T **131**) and Hon. G. R. Bellew (T **132**). Eng J. A. C. Harrison. Recess Waterlow)

1939–48. W **133**. P 14.
476 **131** 2s. 6d. brown (4.9.39) .... 35·00 6·00
476a   2s. 6d. yellow-green (9.3.42) ...... 4·50 1·50
477   5s. red (21.8.39) .... 9·00 2·00
478 **132** 10s. dark blue (30.10.39) .... £225 20·00
478a   10s. ultramarine (30.11.42) .... 20·00 5·00
478b   £1 brown (1.10.48) .... 7·00 26·00
             Set of 6 .... £275 55·00

First Day Covers
21.8.39   5s. (477) £700
4.9.39   2s. 6d. brown (476) £1250
30.10.39 10s. dark blue (478) £2200
9.3.42   2s. 6d. yellow-green (476a) £1250
30.11.42 10s. ultramarine (478a) £2750
1.10.48   £1 (478b) £250

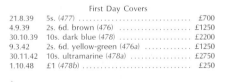

134 Queen Victoria and King George VI

(Des H. L. Palmer)

1940 (6 May). **Centenary of First Adhesive Postage Stamps.** W **127**. P 14½ × 14.

479	**134**	½d. green		30	30
480		1d. scarlet		1·00	40
481		1½d. red-brown		50	75
482		2d. orange		1·00	40
		a. Bisected (on cover)		†	30·00
483		2½d. ultramarine		2·25	50
484		3d. violet		3·00	3·50
		Set of 6		7·00	5·25
		First Day Cover			55·00

No. 482a was authorised for use on Guernsey from 27 December 1940 until February 1941.

1941–42. *Head as Nos. 462/7, but with lighter background to provide a more economic use of the printing ink.* W **127**. P 15 × 14.

485	**128**	½d. pale green (1.9.41)		30	30
		a. Tête-bêche (horiz pair)	£10000		
		b. Imperf (pair)	£4500		
		Wi. Watermark inverted		4·00	50
486		1d. pale scarlet (11.8.41)		30	30
		a. Watermark sideways (10.42)		4·00	4·50
		b. Imperf (pair)	£6000		
		c. Imperf three sides (horiz pair)	£6000		
487		1½d. pale red-brown (28.9.42)		50	80
488		2d. pale orange (6.10.41)		50	50
		a. Watermark sideways (6.42)		28·00	19·00
		b. Tête-bêche (horiz pair)	£10000		
		c. Imperf (pair)	£5000		
		d. Imperf pane*	£15000		
		Wi. Watermark inverted		4·00	1·00
489		2½d. light ultramarine (21.7.41)		30	30
		a. Watermark sideways (8.42)		15·00	12·00
		b. Tête-bêche (horiz pair)	£10000		
		c. Imperf (pair)	£4000		
		d. Imperf pane*	£10000		
		e. Imperf three sides (horiz pair)	£6000		
		Wi. Watermark inverted		1·50	1·00
490		3d. pale violet (3.11.41)		2·00	1·00
		Set of 6		3·50	2·75

The *tête-bêche* varieties are from defectively made-up stamp booklets.

Nos. 486c and 489e are perforated at foot only and occur in the same sheets as Nos. 486b and 489c.

*BOOKLET ERRORS. Those listed as "imperf panes" show one row of perforations either at the top or at the bottom of the pane of 6.

First Day Covers

21.7.41	2½d. (489)	45·00
11.8.41	1d. (486)	20·00
1.9.41	½d. (485)	20·00
6.10.41	2d. (488)	60·00
3.11.41	3d. (490)	£110
28.9.42	1½d. (487)	55·00

135

136

(Des H. L. Palmer (T **135**) and R. Stone (T **136**))

1946 (11 June). **Victory.** W **127**. P 15 × 14.

491	**135**	2½d. ultramarine		20	15
492	**136**	3d. violet		20	40
		Set of 2		40	50
		First Day Cover			65·00

137   **138**

King George VI and Queen Elizabeth

(Des G. Knipe and Joan Hassall from photographs by Dorothy Wilding)

1948 (26 Apr). **Royal Silver Wedding.** W **127**. P 15 × 14 (2½d.) or 14 × 15 (£1).

493	**137**	2½d. ultramarine		35	20
494	**138**	£1 blue		40·00	40·00
		Set of 2		40·00	40·00
		First Day Cover			£425

1948 (10 May). Stamps of 1d. and 2½d. showing seaweed-gathering were on sale at eight Head Post Offices in Great Britain, but were primarily for use in the Channel Islands and are listed there (see Nos. C1/2, after Royal Mail Postage Labels).

139 Globe and Laurel Wreath   **140** "Speed"

141 Olympic Symbol   **142** Winged Victory

(Des P. Metcalfe (T **139**), A. Games (T **140**), S. D. Scott (T **141**) and E. Dulac (T **142**))

1948 (29 July). **Olympic Games.** W **127**. P 15 × 14.

495	**139**	2½d. ultramarine		35	10
496	**140**	3d. violet		35	55
497	**141**	6d. brt purple		75	40
498	**142**	1s. brown		1·40	1·60
		Set of 4		2·50	2·40
		First Day Cover			42·00

143 Two Hemispheres

144 U.P.U. Monument, Berne

145 Goddess Concordia, Globe and Points of Compass

146 Posthorn and Globe

147 H.M.S. *Victory*

148 White Cliffs of Dover

149 St. George and the Dragon

150 Royal Coat of Arms

(Des Mary Adshead (T **143**), P. Metcalfe (T **144**), H. Fleury (T **145**) and Hon. G. R. Bellew (T **146**))

1949 (10 Oct). **75th Anniv of Universal Postal Union.** *W* **127.** *P* 15 × 14.

499	**143**	2½d. ultramarine	15	10
500	**144**	3d. violet	15	50
501	**145**	6d. brt purple	25	50
502	**146**	1s. brown	60	1·25
		Set of 4	1·00	2·10
		First Day Cover		70·00

1950–52. *4d. as No. 468 and others as Nos. 485/9, but colours changed.* W **127.** P 15 × 14.

503	**128**	½d. pale orange (3.5.51)	30	30
		a. Imperf (pair)	£4000	
		b. Tête-bêche (horiz pair) £10000		
		c. Imperf pane* £12000		
		Wi. Watermark inverted	50	50
504		1d. lt ultramarine (3.5.51)	30	30
		a. Watermark sideways (5.51)	1·10	1·25
		b. Imperf (pair)	£3000	
		c. Imperf three sides (horiz pair)	£4000	
		d. Booklet pane. Three stamps plus three printed labels (3.52)	18·00	
		e. Ditto. Partial tête-bêche pane	£6000	
		Wi. Watermark inverted	4·50	2·50
505		1½d. pale green (3.5.51)	65	60
		a. Watermark sideways (9.51)	3·25	5·00
		Wi. Watermark inverted	3·00	1·00
506		2d. pale red-brown (3.5.51)	75	40
		a. Watermark sideways (5.51)	1·75	2·00
		b. Tête-bêche (horiz pair) £10000		
		c. Imperf three sides (horiz pair)	£4000	
		Wi. Watermark inverted	4·25	6·50
507		2½d. pale scarlet (3.5.51)	60	40
		a. Watermark sideways (5.51)	1·75	1·75
		b. Tête-bêche (horiz pair)		
		Wi. Watermark inverted	1·10	1·25
508	**129**	4d. lt ultramarine (2.10.50)	2·00	1·75
		a. Double impression	†	£7000
		Set of 6	4·00	3·25

*BOOKLET ERRORS. Those listed as "imperf panes" show one row of perforations either at the top or at the bottom of the pane of 6.

No. 504c is perforated at foot only and occurs in the same sheet as No. 504b.

No. 506c is also perforated at foot only.

First Day Covers

2.10.50	4d. *(508)*	£120
3.5.51	½d., 1d., 1½d., 2d., 2½d. *(503/7)*	55·00

(Des Mary Adshead (T **147/8**), P. Metcalfe (T **149/50**). Recess Waterlow)

1951 (3 May). W **133.** P 11 × 12.

509	**147**	2s. 6d. yellow-green	2·00	1·00
510	**148**	5s. red	40·00	1·50
511	**149**	10s. ultramarine	10·00	8·50
512	**150**	£1 brown	48·00	20·00
		Set of 4	90·00	27·00
		First Day Cover		£900

151 "Commerce and Prosperity"

152 Festival Symbol

(Des E. Dulac (T **151**), A. Games (T **152**))

1951 (3 May). **Festival of Britain.** W **127.** P 15 × 14.

513	**151**	2½d. scarlet	15	20
514	**152**	4d. ultramarine	30	65
		Set of 2	40	80
		First Day Cover		35·00

QUEEN ELIZABETH II
6 February 1952

Further detailed information on the stamps of Queen Elizabeth II will be found in Volumes 3, 4 and 5 of the Stanley Gibbons *Great Britain Specialised Catalogue*.

153 Tudor Crown   **154**

155   **156**   **157**

158   **159**   **160**

Queen Elizabeth II and National Emblems

I   II

Two types of the 2½d.

Type I:—In the frontal cross of the diadem, the top line is only half the width of the cross.

Type II:—The top line extends to the full width of the cross and there are signs of strengthening in other parts of the diadem.

(Des Enid Marx (T **154**), M. Farrar-Bell (T **155/6**), G. Knipe (T **157**), Mary Adshead (T **158**), E. Dulac (T **159/60**). Portrait by Dorothy Wilding)

1952–54. *W* **153**. *P* 15 × 14.

515	**154**	½d. orange-red (31.8.53)	10	15
		Wi. Watermark inverted (3.54)	60	60
516		1d. ultramarine (31.8.53)	20	20
		a. Booklet pane. Three stamps plus three printed labels	28·00	
		Wi. Watermark inverted (3.54)	4·50	2·75
517		1½d. green (5.12.52)	10	20
		a. Watermark sideways (15.10.54)	50	70
		b. Imperf pane*		
		Wi. Watermark inverted (5.53)	60	70
518		2d. red-brown (31.8.53)	20	20
		a. Watermark sideways (8.10.54)	1·00	2·00
		Wi. Watermark inverted (3.54)	25·00	18·00
519	**155**	2½d. carmine-red (Type I) (5.12.52)	15	15
		a. Watermark sideways (15.11.54)	7·00	8·00
		b. Type II (booklets) (5.53)	1·25	1·25
		bWi. Watermark inverted (5.53)	30	75

520	**155**	3d. dp lilac (18.1.54)	75	55
521	**156**	4d. ultramarine (2.11.53)	3·25	1·25
522	**157**	5d. brown (6.7.53)	75	3·50
523		6d. reddish purple (18.1.54)	4·00	1·00
		a. Imperf three sides (pair)		
524		7d. brt green (18.1.54)	9·50	5·50
525	**158**	8d. magenta (6.7.53)	75	85
526		9d. bronze-green (8.2.54)	23·00	4·75
527		10d. Prussian blue (8.2.54)	18·00	4·75
528		11d. brown-purple (8.2.54)	30·00	15·00
529	**160**	1s. bistre-brown (6.7.53)	80	50
530	**159**	1s. 3d. green (2.11.53)	4·50	3·75
531	**160**	1s. 6d. grey-blue (2.11.53)	14·00	3·75
		Set of 17	£100	40·00

See also Nos. 540/56, 561/6, 570/94 and 599/618a.

*BOOKLET ERRORS.—This pane of 6 stamps is *completely* imperf (see No. 540a, etc).

Stamps with *sideways watermark* come from left-side delivery coils and stamps with *inverted watermark* are from booklets.

For stamps as Types **154/5** and **157/60** with face values in decimal currency see Nos. 2031/3, 2258/9 and **MS**2326.

First Day Covers

5.12.52	1½d., 2½d. (517, 519)	15·00
6.7.53	5d., 8d., 1s. (522, 525, 529)	45·00
31.8.53	½d., 1d., 2d. (515/16, 518)	45·00
2.11.53	4d., 1s. 3d., 1s. 6d. (521, 530/1)	£170
18.1.54	3d., 6d., 7d. (520, 523/4)	£110
8.2.54	9d., 10d., 11d. (526/8)	£225

161   **162**

163   **164**

(Des E. Fuller (2½d.), M. Goaman (4d.), E. Dulac (1s. 3d.), M. Farrar-Bell (1s. 6d.). Portrait (except 1s. 3d.) by Dorothy Wilding)

1953 (3 June). **Coronation**. *W* **153**. *P* 15 × 14.

532	**161**	2½d. carmine-red	20	25
533	**162**	4d. ultramarine	1·10	1·90
534	**163**	1s. 3d. dp yellow-green	4·25	3·00
535	**164**	1s. 6d. dp grey-blue	8·00	4·75
		Set of 4	12·00	9·00
		First Day Cover		75·00

For a £1 value as Type **163** see No. **MS**2147.

165 St. Edward's Crown

166 Carrickfergus Castle

167 Caernarvon Castle

168 Edinburgh Castle

169 Windsor Castle

(Des L. Lamb. Portait by Dorothy Wilding. Recess Waterlow (until 31.12.57) and De La Rue (subsequently))

1955–58. W **165**. P 11 × 12.

536	**166**	2s. 6d. black-brown (23.9.55)	9·00	2·00
		a. De La Rue printing (17.7.58)	30·00	2·50
		Wi. Watermark inverted	†	£2000
537	**167**	5s. rose-carmine (23.9.55)	35·00	4·00
		a. De La Rue printing (30.4.58)	80·00	10·00
538	**168**	10s. ultramarine (1.9.55)	85·00	14·00
		a. De La Rue printing. *Dull ultramarine* (25.4.58)	£200	22·00
539	**169**	£1 black (1.9.55)	£130	35·00
		a. De La Rue printing (28.4.58)	£325	65·00
		Set of 4 (Nos. 536/9)	£225	50·00
		Set of 4 (Nos 536a/9a)	£550	90·00
		First Day Cover (538/9)		£800
		First Day Cover (536/7)		£600

See also Nos. 595/8a & 759/62.

On 1 January 1958, the contract for printing the high values, T **166** to **169**, was transferred to De La Rue & Co. Ltd.

The work of the two printers is very similar, but the following notes will be helpful to those attempting to identify Waterlow and De La Rue stamps of the W **165** issue.

The De La Rue sheets are printed in pairs and have a −| or |− shaped guide-mark at the centre of one side-margin, opposite the middle row of perforations, indicating left and right-hand sheets respectively.

The Waterlow sheets have a small circle (sometimes crossed) instead of a "|−" and this is present in both side-margins opposite the 6th row of stamps, though one is sometimes trimmed off. Short dashes are also present in the perforation gutter between the marginal stamps marking the middle of the four sides and a cross is at the centre of the sheet. The four corners of the sheet have two lines forming a right-angle as trimming marks, but some are usually trimmed off. All these gutter marks and sheet-trimming marks are absent in the De La Rue printings.

De La Rue used the Waterlow die and no alterations were made to it, so that no difference exists in the design or its size, but the making of new plates at first resulted in slight but measurable variations in the width of the gutters between stamps, particularly the horizontal, as follows:

	Waterlow	De La Rue
Horiz gutters, mm	3.8 to 4.0	3.4 to 3.8

Later D.L.R. plates are however less distinguishable in this respect.

For a short time in 1959 the D.L.R. 2s. 6d. appeared with one dot in the bottom margin below the first stamp.

It is possible to sort singles with reasonable certainty by general characteristics. The individual lines of the D.L.R. impression are cleaner and devoid of the whiskers of colour of Waterlow's, and the whole impression lighter and softer.

Owing to the closer setting of the horizontal rows the strokes of the perforating comb are closer; this results in the topmost tooth on each side of De La Rue stamps being narrower than the corresponding teeth in Waterlow's which were more than normally broad.

Shades also help. The 2s. 6d. D.L.R. is a warmer, more chocolate shade than the blackish brown of Waterlow; the 5s. a lighter red with less carmine than Waterlow's; the 10s. more blue and less ultramarine; the £1 less intense black.

The paper of D.L.R. printings is uniformly white, identical with that of Waterlow printings from February 1957 onwards, but earlier Waterlow printings are on paper which is creamy by comparison.

In this and later issues of T **166/9** the dates of issue given for changes of watermark or paper are those on which supplies were first sent by the Supplies Department to Postmasters.

1955–58. W **165**. P 15 × 14.

540	**154**	½d. orange-red (booklets 8.55, sheets 12.12.55)	15	15
		a. Part perf pane*	£3500	
		Wi. Watermark inverted (9.55)	20	30
541		1d. ultramarine (19.9.55)	30	15
		a. Booklet pane. Three stamps plus three printed labels	16·00	
		b. *Tête-bêche* (horiz pair)		
		Wi. Watermark inverted (9.55)	65	55
542		1½d. green (booklet 8.55, sheets 11.10.55)	25	30
		a. Watermark sideways (7.3.56)	35	70
		b. *Tête-bêche* (horiz pair)	£2250	
		Wi. Watermark inverted (8.55)	30	60
543		2d. red-brown (6.9.55)	25	35
		aa. Imperf between (vert pair)	£2500	
		a. Watermark sideways (31.7.56)	55	70
		ab. Imperf between (horiz pair)	£2500	
		Wi. Watermark inverted (9.55)	11·00	9·00
543b		2d. light red-brown (17.10.56)	20	20
		ba. *Tête-bêche* (horiz pair)	£1500	
		bb. Imperf pane*		
		bc. Part perf pane*	£3500	
		bWi. Watermark inverted (1.57)	7·00	6·00
		d. Watermark sideways (5.3.57)	8·00	8·00
544	**155**	2½d. carmine-red (Type I) (28.9.55)	20	25
		a. Watermark sideways (Type I) (23.3.56)	1·50	1·75
		b. Type II (booklets 9.55, sheets 1957)	45	45
		ba. *Tête-bêche* (horiz pair)	£1500	
		bb. Imperf pane*	£2500	
		bc. Part perf pane*	£2500	
		bWi. Watermark inverted (9.55)	25	70
545		3d. dp lilac (17.7.56)	25	25
		aa. *Tête-bêche* (horiz pair)	£1500	
		a. Imperf three sides (pair)	£1300	
		b. Watermark sideways (22.11.57)	18·00	17·00
		Wi. Watermark inverted (1.10.57)	70	1·00
546	**156**	4d. ultramarine (14.11.55)	1·25	45
547	**157**	5d. brown (21.9.55)	5·50	5·75
548		6d. reddish purple (20.12.55)	4·00	1·25
		aa. Imperf three sides (pair)	£2000	
		a. *Deep claret* (8.5.58)	4·00	1·40
		ab. Imperf three sides (pair)	£2000	
549		7d. brt green (23.4.56)	42·00	9·50
550	**158**	8d. magenta (21.12.55)	7·00	1·25
551		9d. bronze-green (15.12.55)	20·00	2·75
552		10d. Prussian blue (22.9.55)	20·00	2·75
553		11d. brown-purple (28.10.55)	50	1·10
554	**160**	1s. bistre-brown (3.11.55)	22·00	65
555	**159**	1s. 3d. green (27.3.56)	30·00	1·60
556	**160**	1s. 6d. grey-blue (27.3.56)	23·00	1·60
		Set of 18	£160	27·00

The dates given for Nos. 540/556 are those on which they were first issued by the Supplies Dept to postmasters.

In December 1956 a completely imperforate sheet of No. 543b was noticed by clerks in a Kent post office, one of whom purchased it against P.O. regulations. In view of this irregularity we do not consider it properly issued.

Types of 2½d. In this issue, in 1957, Type II formerly only found in stamps from booklets, began to replace Type I on sheet stamps.

*BOOKLET ERRORS. Those listed as "imperf panes" show one row of perforations either at top or bottom of the booklet pane; those as "part perf panes" have one row of 3 stamps imperf on three sides.

For Nos. 542 and 553 in Presentation Pack, see after No. 586.

170 Scout Badge and "Rolling Hitch" **171** "Scouts coming to Britain"

172 Globe within a Compass

(Des Mary Adshead (2½d.), P. Keely (4d.), W. H. Brown (1s. 3d.))

1957 (1 Aug). **World Scout Jubilee Jamboree.** W **165.** P 15 × 14.
557	**170**	2½d.	carmine-red	15	20
558	**171**	4d.	ultramarine	35	80
559	**172**	1s.	3d. green	3·50	3·50
			Set of 3	3·50	4·00
			First Day Cover		25·00

173 ½d. to 1½d., 2½d., 3d.   2d.
Graphite-line arrangements
(Stamps viewed from back)

(Adapted F. Langfield)

1957 (12 Sept). **46th Inter-Parliamentary Union Conference.** W **165.** P 15 × 14.
560	**173**	4d.	ultramarine	1·00	1·00
			First Day Cover		£120

WHEN YOU BUY AN ALBUM LOOK FOR THE NAME 'STANLEY GIBBONS'
It means Quality combined with Value for Money.

GRAPHITE-LINED ISSUES. These were used in connection with automatic sorting machinery, first introduced experimentally at Southampton.

The graphite lines were printed in black on the back, beneath the gum; two lines per stamp, except for the 2d.

In November 1959 phosphor bands were introduced (see notes after No. 598).

1957 (19 Nov). *Graphite-lined issue. Two graphite lines on the back, except 2d. value, which has one line.* W **165.** P 15 × 14.
561	**154**	½d.	orange-red	25	25
562		1d.	ultramarine	25	30
563		1½d.	green	1·00	1·40
		a.	Both lines at left	£800	£400
564		2d.	light red-brown	1·40	2·25
		a.	Line at left	£500	£180
565	**155**	2½d.	carmine-red (Type II)	7·50	6·75
566		3d.	dp lilac	60	50
			Set of 6	10·00	10·50
			First Day Cover		85·00

No. 564a results from a misplacement of the line and horizontal pairs exist showing one stamp without line. No. 563a results from a similar misplacement.

See also Nos. 587/94.

176 Welsh Dragon **177** Flag and Games Emblem

178 Welsh Dragon

(Des R. Stone (3d.), W. H. Brown (6d.), P. Keely (1s. 3d.))

1958 (18 July). **Sixth British Empire and Commonwealth Games, Cardiff.** W **165.** P 15 × 14.
567	**176**	3d.	dp lilac	20	20
568	**177**	6d.	reddish purple	40	45
569	**178**	1s.	3d. green	2·25	2·40
			Set of 3	2·50	2·75
			First Day Cover		75·00

179 Multiple Crowns

1958–65. W **179.** P 15 × 14.
570	**154**	½d.	orange-red (25.11.58)	10	10
		a.	Watermark sideways (26.5.61)	30	40

(570)	c.	Part perf pane*	£2500		
	Wi.	Watermark inverted (11.58)		30	25
	k.	Chalk-surfaced paper (15.7.63)	2·50	2·75
	kWi.	Watermark inverted	2·75	3·00
	l.	Booklet pane. No. 570a × 4	3·50	
	m.	Booklet pane. No. 570k × 3 se-tenant with 574k	9·00	
	n.	Booklet pane. No. 570a × 2 se-tenant with 574l × 2 (1.7.64)	2·25	
571 **154**		1d. ultramarine (booklets 11.58, sheets 24.3.59)		10	10
	aa.	Imperf (vert pair from coil)		
	a.	Watermark sideways (26.5.61)	1·50	1·25
	b.	Part perf pane*	£3000	
	c.	Imperf pane		
	Wi.	Watermark inverted (11.58)		15	20
	l.	Booklet pane. No. 571a × 4	4·50	
	m.	Booklet pane. No. 571a × 2 se-tenant with 575a × 2 (1d. values at left) (16.8.65)	10·00	
	ma.	Ditto. 1d. values at right	11·00	
572		1½d. green (booklets 12.58, sheets 30.8.60)		10	15
	a.	Imperf three sides (horiz strip of 3)		
	b.	Watermark sideways (26.5.61)	9·00	5·00
	Wi.	Watermark inverted (12.58)	1·50	80
	l.	Booklet pane. No. 572b × 4	35·00	
573		2d. light red-brown (4.12.58)		10	10
	a.	Watermark sideways (3.4.59)	50	1·00
	Wi.	Watermark inverted (10.4.61)	£130	70·00
574 **155**		2½d. carmine-red (Type II) (booklets 11.58, sheets 15.9.59)		10	20
	a.	Imperf strip of 3		
	b.	Téte-bêche (horiz pair)		
	c.	Imperf pane*	£3000	
	Wi.	Watermark inverted (Type II) (11.58)	4·50	3·00
	d.	Watermark sideways (Type I) (10.11.60)	25	40
	da.	Imperf strip of 6		
	e.	Type I (wmk upright) (4.10.61)	70	70
	k.	Chalk-surfaced paper (Type II) (15.7.63)	50	80
	kWi.	Do. Watermark inverted (15.7.63)	75	1·25
	l.	Watermark sideways (Type II) (1.7.64)	70	1·25
575		3d. dp lilac (booklets 11.58, sheets 8.12.58)		10	20
	a.	Watermark sideways (24.10.58)	25	35
	b.	Imperf pane*	£2750	
	c.	Part perf pane*	£2500	
	d.	Phantom "R" (Cyl 41 no dot)	£325	
	Eda.	Do. First retouch	20·00	
	Edb.	Do. Second retouch	20·00	
	e.	Phantom "R" (Cyl 37 no dot)	45·00	
	Eea.	Do. Retouch	12·00	
	Wi.	Watermark inverted (11.58)	25	40
	l.	Booklet pane. No. 575a × 4 (26.5.61)	3·25	
576 **156**		4d. ultramarine (29.10.58)	45	35
	a.	Dp ultramarine†† (28.4.65)	15	15
	ab.	Watermark sideways (31.5.65)	70	55
	ac.	Imperf pane*	£3250	
	ad.	Part perf pane*	£2750	
	al.	Booklet pane. No. 576ab × 4 (16.8.65)	3·25	
	aWi.	Watermark inverted (21.6.65)	60	50
577		4½d. chestnut (9.2.59)	10	25
	Ea.	Phantom frame	7·50	
578 **157**		5d. brown (10.11.58)	30	40
579		6d. dp claret (23.12.58)	30	25
	a.	Imperf three sides (pair)	£725	
	b.	Imperf (pair)	£825	
580		7d. brt green (26.11.58)	50	45
581 **158**		8d. magenta (24.2.60)	60	40
582		9d. bronze-green (24.3.59)	60	40
583		10d. Prussian blue (18.11.58)	90	50
584 **160**		1s. bistre-brown (30.10.58)	45	30
585 **159**		1s. 3d. green (17.6.59)	45	30

586 **160**		1s. 6d. grey-blue (16.12.58)		4·00	60
		Set of 17 (one of each value)	8·00	4·25
		First Day Cover (577)		£250
		Presentation Pack**		£150

*BOOKLET ERROR. See note after No. 556.

**This was issued in 1960 and comprises Nos. 542, 553, 570/1 and 573/86. It exists in two forms: (a) inscribed "10s 6d" for sale in the U.K.; and (b) inscribed "$1.80" for sale in the U.S.A.

††This "shade" was brought about by making more deeply etched cylinders, resulting in apparent depth of colour in parts of the design. There is no difference in the colour of the ink.

Sideways watermark. The 2d., 2½d., 3d. and 4d. come from coils and the ½d., 1d., 1½d., 2½d., 3d. and 4d. come from booklets. In coil stamps the sideways watermark shows the top of the watermark to the left as seen from the front of the stamp. In the booklet stamps it comes equally to the left or right.

Nos. 570k and 574k only come from 2s. "Holiday Resort" experimental undated booklets issued in 1963, in which one page contained 1 × 2½d. se-tenant with 3 × ½d. (See No. 570l).

No. 574l comes from coils, and the "Holiday Resort" experimental booklets dated "1964" comprising four panes each containing two of these 2½d. stamps se-tenant vertically with two ½d. No. 570a. (See No. 570m).

2½d. imperf. No. 574a comes from a booklet with watermark upright. No. 574da is from a coil with sideways watermark.

No. 574e comes from sheets bearing cylinder number 42 and is also known on vertical delivery coils.

In 1964 No. 575 was printed from cylinder number 70 no dot and dot on an experimental paper which is distinguishable by an additional watermark letter "T" lying on its side, which occurs about four times in the sheet, usually in the side margins, 48,000 sheets were issued.

Phantom "R" varieties

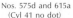

Nos. 575d and 615a (Cyl 41 no dot)	No. 575Eda

No. 575e (Cyl 37 no dot)

3d. An incomplete marginal rule revealed an "R" on cyls 37 and 41 no dot below R.20/12. It is more noticeable on cyl 41 because of the wider marginal rule. The "R" on cyl 41 was twice retouched, the first being as illustrated here (No. 575Eda) and traces of the "R" can still be seen in the second retouch.

No. 575d is best collected in a block of 4 or 6 with full margins in order to be sure that it is not 615a with phosphor lines removed.

The retouch on cyl 37 is not easily identified: there is no trace of the "R" but the general appearance of that part of the marginal rule is uneven.

Phantom Frame variety

Nos. 577Ea and 616Eba

4½d. An incomplete marginal rule revealed a right-angled shaped frame-line on cyl 8 no dot below R.20/12. It occurs on ordinary and phosphor.

WHITER PAPER. On 18 May 1962 the Post Office announced that a whiter paper was being used for the current issue (including Nos. 595/8). This is beyond the scope of this catalogue, but the whiter papers are listed in Vol. 3 of the Stanley Gibbons *Great Britain Specialised Catalogue.*

1958 (24 Nov)–**61.** *Graphite-lined issue. Two graphite lines on the back, except 2d. value, which has one line.* W **179.** P 15 × 14.

587	**154**	½d. orange-red (15.6.59)		9·00	9·00
		Wi. Watermark inverted (4.8.59)		3·25	3·75
588		1d. ultramarine (18.12.58)		1·25	1·50
		a. Misplaced graphite lines (7.61)*		80	1·25
		Wi. Watermark inverted (4.8.59)		1·25	2·00
589		1½d. green (4.8.59)		90·00	80·00
		Wi. Watermark inverted (4.8.59)		50·00	48·00
590		2d. lt red-brown (24.11.58)		7·00	3·50
591	**155**	2½d. carmine-red (Type II) (9.6.59)		9·00	10·00
		Wi. Watermark inverted (21.8.59)		65·00	50·00
592		3d. dp lilac (24.11.58)		50	65
		a. Misplaced graphite lines (5.61)*		£450	£380
		Wi. Watermark inverted (4.8.59)		45	75
593	**156**	4d. ultramarine (29.4.59)		4·50	5·00
		a. Misplaced graphite lines (1961)*		£1800	
594		4½d. chestnut (3.6.59)		6·50	5·00
		Set of 8 (cheapest)		80·00	60·00

Nos. 587/9 were only issued in booklets or coils (587/8).

*No. 588a (in coils), and Nos. 592a and 593a (both in sheets) result from the use of a residual stock of graphite-lined paper. As the use of graphite lines had ceased, the register of the lines in relation to the stamps was of no importance and numerous misplacements occurred —two lines close together, one line only, etc. No. 588a refers to two lines at left or right; No. 592a refers to stamps with two lines only at left and both clear of the perforations and No. 593a to stamps with two lines at left (with left line down perforations) and traces of a third line down the opposite perforations.

(Recess D.L.R. (until 31.12.62), then B.W.)

1959–68. W **179.** P 11 × 12.

595	**166**	2s. 6d. black-brown (22.7.59)		8·00	75
		Wi. Watermark inverted			
		a. B.W. printing (1.7.63)		35	40
		aWi. Watermark inverted		£1000	75·00
		k. Chalk-surfaced paper (30.5.68)		25	1·50

596	**167**	5s. scarlet-vermilion (15.6.59)		65·00	2·00
		Wi. Watermark inverted		—	£275
		a. B.W. ptg. Red (shades) (3.9.63)		90	50
		ab. Printed on the gummed side		£800	
		aWi. Watermark inverted		£275	60·00
597	**168**	10s. blue (21.7.59)		50·00	5·00
		a. B.W. ptg. Bright ultramarine (16.10.63)		4·00	4·50
		aWi. Watermark inverted		—	£650
598	**169**	£1 black (23.6.59)		£100	12·00
		Wi. Watermark inverted		—	£1750
		a. B.W. printing (14.11.63)		11·00	7·00
		aWi. Watermark inverted		£7000	£2500
		Set of 4 (Nos. 595/8)		£195	17·00
		Set of 4 (Nos. 595a/8a)		15·00	11·00
		Presentation Pack (1960)*		£875	

The B.W. printings have a marginal Plate Number. They are generally more deeply engraved than the D.L.R. showing more of the Diadem detail and heavier lines on Her Majesty's face. The vertical perf is 11.9 to 12 against D.L.R. 11.8.

*This exists in three forms: (a) inscribed "$6.50" for sale in the U.S.A.; (b) without price for sale in the U.K.; (c) inscribed "£1 18s" for sale in the U.K.

See also Nos. 759/62.

PHOSPHOR BAND ISSUES. These are printed on the front and are wider than graphite lines. They are not easy to see but show as broad vertical bands at certain angles to the light.

Values representing the rate for printed papers (and when this was abolished in 1968 for second issue class mail) have one band and others two, three or four bands as stated, according to the size and format.

In the small size stamps the bands are on each side with the single band at left (*except where otherwise stated*). In the large-size commemorative stamps the single band may be at left, centre or right, varying in different designs. The bands are vertical on both horizontal and vertical designs *except where otherwise stated.*

The phosphor was originally applied typographically but later usually by photogravure and sometimes using flexography, a typographical process using rubber cylinders.

Three different types of phosphor have been used, distinguishable by the colour emitted under an ultra-violet lamp, the first being green, then blue and now violet. Different sized bands are also known. All these are fully listed in Vol. 3 of the Stanley Gibbons *Great Britain Specialised Catalogue.*

Varieties. Misplaced and missing phosphor bands are known but such varieties are beyond the scope of this Catalogue.

1959 (18 Nov). *Phosphor-Graphite issue. Two phosphor bands on front and two graphite lines on back, except 2d. value, which has one band on front and one line on back.* P 15 × 14. (a) W **165.**

599	**154**	½d. orange-red		3·25	3·50
600		1d. ultramarine		8·25	9·00
601		1½d. green		3·25	3·25

(b) W **179**

605	**154**	2d. lt red-brown (1 band)		4·25	4·25
		a. Error. W **165**		£180	£150
606	**155**	2½d. carmine-red (Type II)		17·00	15·00
607		3d. dp lilac		8·50	7·00
608	**156**	4d. ultramarine		15·00	16·00
609		4½d. chestnut		24·00	20·00
		Set of 8		75·00	70·00
		Presentation Pack		£285	

Examples of the 2½d., No. 606, exist showing watermark W **165** in error. It is believed that phosphor-graphite stamps of this value with this watermark were not used by the public for postal purposes.

The Presentation Pack was issued in 1960 and comprises two each of Nos. 599/609. It exists in two forms: (a) inscribed "3s 8d" for sale in the U.K. and (b) inscribed "50 c" for sale in the U.S.A.

1960 (22 June)–**67**. *Phosphor issue. Two phosphor bands on front, except where otherwise stated.* W **179**. *P* 15 × 14.

610	**154**	½d. orange-red	10	15
		a. Watermark sideways (14.7.61)	10·00	10·00
		Wi. Watermark inverted (14.8.60)	60	60
		l. Booklet pane. No. 610a × 4	40·00	
611		1d. ultramarine	10	10
		a. Watermark sideways (14.7.61)	35	40
		Wi. Watermark inverted (14.8.60)	20	30
		l. Booklet pane. No. 611a × 4	9·00	
		m. Booklet pane. No. 611a × 2 *se-tenant* with 615d × 2† (16.8.65)	14·00	
		ma. Booklet pane. No. 611a × 2 *se-tenant* with 615dEa × 2 (16.8.65)	14·00	
		n. Booklet pane. No. 611a × 2 *se-tenant* with 615b × 2†† (11.67)	8·00	
612		1½d. green	10	15
		a. Watermark sideways (14.7.61)	9·00	9·00
		Wi. Watermark inverted (14.8.60)	8·00	8·50
		l. Booklet pane. No. 612a × 4	40·00	
613		2d. lt red-brown (1 band)	16·00	18·00
613a		2d. lt red-brown (2 bands) (4.10.61)	10	15
		aa. Imperf three sides***		
		ab. Watermark sideways (6.4.67)	25	25
614	**155**	2½d. carmine-red (Type II) (2 bands)*	20	30
		Wi. Watermark inverted (14.8.60)	£170	90·00
614a		2½d. carmine-red (Type II) (1 band) (4.10.61) .	50	75
		aWi. Watermark inverted (3.62)	30·00	32·00
614b		2½d. carmine-red (Type I) (1 band) (4.10.61) ...	40·00	40·00
615		3d. dp lilac (2 bands)	60	55
		a. Phantom "R" (Cyl 41 no dot)	40·00	
		Wi. Watermark inverted (14.8.60)	45	70
		b. Watermark sideways (14.7.61)	1·75	1·75
		l. Booklet pane. No. 615b × 4	7·50	
615c		3d. dp lilac (1 band at right) (29.4.65)	60	55
		cEa. Band at left	60	70
		cWi. Watermark inverted (band at right) (2.67)	2·75	2·75
		cWia. Watermark inverted (band at left) (2.67)	45·00	40·00
		d. Watermark sideways (band at right) (16.8.65)	5·50	5·00
		dEa. Watermark sideways (band at left)	5·50	5·00
		e. One centre band (8.12.66)	40	45
		eWi. Watermark inverted (8.67)	3·00	3·00
		ea. Wmk sideways (19.6.67)	70	50
616	**156**	4d. ultramarine	3·00	3·00
		a. Dp ultramarine (28.4.65)	25	25
		aa. Part perf pane		
		ab. Watermark sideways (16.8.65)	35	50
		aWi. Watermark inverted (21.6.65)	40	40
		l. Booklet pane. No. 616ab × 4	2·50	
616b		4½d. chestnut (13.9.61)	20	30
		Eba. Phantom frame	15·00	
616c	**157**	5d. brown (9.6.67)	25	35
617		6d. dp claret (27.6.60)	30	30
617a		7d. brt green (15.2.67)	55	50
617b	**158**	8d. magenta (28.6.67)	40	45
617c		9d. bronze-green (29.12.66)	55	55
617d		10d. Prussian blue (30.12.66)	70	60
617e	**160**	1s. bistre-brown (28.6.67)	35	35
618	**159**	1s. 3d. green	1·90	2·50
618a	**160**	1s. 6d. grey-blue (12.12.66)	2·00	1·60
		Set of 17 (one of each value)	7·50	8·00

The automatic facing equipment was brought into use on 6 July 1960 but the phosphor stamps may have been released a few days earlier.

The stamps with watermark sideways are from booklets except Nos. 613ab and 615ea which are from coils. No. 616ab comes from both booklets and coils.

No. 615a. See footnote after No. 586.

*No. 614 with two bands on the creamy paper was originally from cylinder 50 dot and no dot. When the change in postal rates took place in 1965 it was reissued from cylinder 57 dot and no dot on the whiter paper. Some of these latter were also released in error in districts of S.E. London in September 1964. The shade of the reissue is slightly more carmine.

***This comes from the bottom row of a sheet which is imperf at bottom and both sides.

†Booklet pane No. 611m shows the 1d. stamps at left and No. 611ma the 1d. stamps at right.

††Booklet pane No. 611n comes from 2s. booklets of January and March 1968. The two bands on the 3d. stamp were intentional because of the technical difficulties in producing one band and two band stamps *se-tenant*.

The Phosphor-Graphite stamps had the phosphor applied by typography but the Phosphor issue can be divided into those with the phosphor applied typographically and others where it was applied by photogravure. Moreover the photogravure form can be further divided into those which phosphoresce green and others which phosphoresce blue under ultra-violet light. From 1965 violet phosphorescence was introduced in place of the blue. All these are fully listed in Vol. 3 of the Stanley Gibbons *Great Britain Specialised Catalogue.*

Unlike previous one-banded phosphor stamps, No. 615c has a broad band extending over two stamps so that alternate stamps have the band at left or right (same prices either way). No. 615cWi comes from the 10s phosphor booklet of February 1967 and No. 615eWi comes from the 10s. phosphor booklets of August 1967 and February 1968.

Nos. 615a (Phantom "R") and 615Eba (Phantom frame), *see* illustrations following No. 586.

180 Postboy of 1660   **181** Posthorn of 1660

(Des R. Stone (3d.), Faith Jaques (1s. 3d.))

1960 (7 July).   **Tercentenary of Establishment of General Letter Office.** W **179** (*sideways on* 1s. 3d.). P 15 × 14 (3d.) *or* 14 × 15 (1s. 3d.).

619	**180**	3d. dp lilac	20	20
620	**181**	1s. 3d. green	2·75	3·50
		Set of 2	2·75	3·50
		First Day Cover		40·00

182 Conference Emblem

(Des R. Stone (emblem, P. Rahikainen))

1960 (19 Sept).   **First Anniversary of European Postal and Telecommunications Conference.** *Chalk-surfaced paper.* W **179**. P 15 × 14.

621	**182**	6d. bronze-green & purple	50	50
622		1s. 6d. brown & blue	6·50	5·00
		Set of 2	7·00	5·50
		First Day Cover		38·00

SCREENS. Up to this point all photogravure stamps were printed in a 200 screen (200 dots per linear inch), but all later commemorative stamps are a finer 250 screen. Exceptionally No. 622 has a 200 screen for the portrait and a 250 screen for the background.

184 "Growth of Savings"

183 Thrift Plant   **185** Thrift Plant

(Des P. Gauld (2½d.), M. Goaman (others))

1961 (28 Aug). **Centenary of Post Office Savings Bank.** *Chalk-surfaced paper.* W **179** (*sideways on* 2½d.) P 14 × 15 (2½d.) *or* 15 × 14 (*others*).

A. *"Timson" Machine*
623A	**183**	2½d. black & red	25	25
		a. Black omitted	£6500	
624A	**184**	3d. orange-brown & violet	20	20
		a. Orange-brown omitted	£140	
		Eb. Perf through side sheet margin	25·00	30·00
625A	**185**	1s. 6d. red & blue	2·25	2·25
		Set of 3	2·50	2·50
		First Day Cover		60·00

B. *"Thrissell" Machine*
623B	**183**	2½d. black & red	2·25	2·25
624B	**184**	3d. orange-brown & violet	40	40
		a. Orange-brown omitted	£650	

2½d. TIMSON. Cyls 1E–1F. Deeply shaded portrait (brownish black).

2½d. THRISSELL. Cyls 1D–1B or 1D (dot)–1B (dot). Lighter portrait (grey-black).

3d. TIMSON. Cyls 3D–3E. Clear, well-defined portrait with deep shadows and bright highlights.

3d. THRISSELL. Cyls 3C–3B or 3C (dot)–3B (dot). Dull portrait, lacking in contrast.

Sheet marginal examples *without* single extension perf hole on the short side of the stamp are always "Timson", as are those with large punch-hole *not* coincident with printed three-sided box guide mark.

The 3d. "Timson" perforated completely through the right-hand side margin comes from a relatively small part of the printing perforated on a sheet-fed machine.

Normally the "Timsons" were perforated in the reel, with three large punch-holes in both long margins and the perforations completely through both short margins. Only one punch-hole coincides with the guide-mark.

The "Thrissells" have one large punch-hole in one long margin, coinciding with guide-mark and one short margin imperf (except sometimes for encroachments).

186 C.E.P.T. Emblem   **187** Doves and Emblem

188 Doves and Emblem

(Des M. Goaman (doves T. Kurpershoek))

1961 (18 Sept). **European Postal and Telecommunications (C.E.P.T.) Conference, Torquay.** *Chalk-surfaced paper.* W **179**. P 15 × 14.
626	**186**	2d. orange, pink & brown	15	20
		a. Orange omitted £10000		
627	**187**	4d. buff, mauve & ultramarine	15	25
628	**188**	10d. turquoise, pale green & Prussian blue ...	15	80
		a. Pale green omitted £4750		
		b. Turquoise omitted £2750		
		Set of 3	40	1·10
		First Day Cover		6·00

189 Hammer Beam   **190** Palace of
Roof, Westminster Hall   Westminster

(Des Faith Jaques)

1961 (25 Sept). **Seventh Commonwealth Parliamentary Conference.** *Chalk-surfaced paper.* W **179** (*sideways on* 1s. 3d.). P 15 × 14 (6d.) *or* 14 × 15 (1s. 3d.).
629	**189**	6d. purple & gold	25	25
		a. Gold omitted	£700	
630	**190**	1s. 3d. green & blue	2·50	2·75
		a. Blue (Queen's head) omitted	£6500	
		Set of 2	2·75	3·00
		First Day Cover		30·00

191 "Units of Productivity"   **192** "National Productivity"

193 "Unified Productivity"

(Des D. Gentleman)

1962 (14 Nov). **National Productivity Year.** *Chalk-surfaced paper.*
W **179** *(inverted on* 2½d. *and* 3d.*). P* 15 × 14.

631	**191**	2½d. myrtle-green & carmine-red *(shades)*	20	15
		Ea. *Blackish olive & carmine-red*	25	15
		p. One phosphor band. *Blackish olive &*		
		carmine-red	60	50
632	**192**	3d. light blue & violet *(shades)*	25	15
		a. Lt blue (Queen's head) omitted	£1000	
		p. Three phosphor bands	1·50	80
633	**193**	1s. 3d. carmine, lt blue & dp green	1·50	1·75
		a. Lt blue (Queen's head) omitted	£4250	
		p. Three phosphor bands	35·00	22·00
		Set of 3 (Ordinary)	1·75	1·90
		Set of 3 (Phosphor)	35·00	22·00
		First Day Cover (Ordinary)	48·00	
		First Day Cover (Phosphor)	£120	

194 Campaign Emblem and Family   **195** Children of Three Races

(Des M. Goaman)

1963 (21 Mar). **Freedom from Hunger.** *Chalk-surfaced paper. W* **179**
(inverted). P 15 × 14.

634	**194**	2½d. crimson & pink	10	10
		p. One phosphor band	3·00	1·25
635	**195**	1s. 3d. bistre-brown & yellow	1·60	1·90
		p. Three phosphor bands	30·00	23·00
		Set of 2 (Ordinary)	1·60	2·00
		Set of 2 (Phosphor)	32·00	24·00
		First Day Cover (Ordinary)		32·00
		First Day Cover (Phosphor)		40·00

196 "Paris Conference"

(Des R. Stone)

1963 (7 May). **Paris Postal Conference Centenary.** *Chalk-surfaced
paper. W* **179** *(inverted). P* 15 × 14.

636	**196**	6d. green & mauve	30	40
		a. Green omitted	£1600	
		p. Three phosphor bands	6·00	6·00
		First Day Cover (Ordinary)		14·00
		First Day Cover (Phosphor)		27·00

197 Posy of Flowers   **198** Woodland Life

(Des S. Scott (3d.), M. Goaman (4½d.))

1963 (16 May). **National Nature Week.** *Chalk-surfaced paper. W* **179**.
P 15 × 14.

637	**197**	3d. yellow, green, brown & black	15	15
		p. Three phosphor bands	55	60
638	**198**	4½d. black, blue, yellow, magenta & brown-		
		red	20	35
		p. Three phosphor bands	2·75	3·00
		Set of 2 (Ordinary)	35	50
		Set of 2 (Phosphor)	3·25	3·50
		First Day Cover (Ordinary)		18·00
		First Day Cover (Phosphor)		32·00

Special First Day of Issue Postmark

	Ordin-	Phos-
	ary	phor
London E.C. (Type A)	24·00	30·00

This postmark was used on first day covers serviced by the Philatelic
Bureau.

199 Rescue at Sea   **200** 19th-century Lifeboat

201 Lifeboatmen

(Des D. Gentleman)

1963 (31 May). **Ninth International Lifeboat Conference, Edinburgh.**
Chalk-surfaced paper. W **179**. *P* 15 × 14.

639	**199**	2½d. blue, black & red	15	20
		p. One phosphor band	50	60
640	**200**	4d. red, yellow, brown, black & blue	40	40
		p. Three phosphor bands	50	60
641	**201**	1s. 6d. sepia, yellow & grey-blue	2·40	2·50
		p. Three phosphor bands	48·00	28·00
		Set of 3 (Ordinary)	2·75	2·75
		Set of 3 (Phosphor)	48·00	28·00
		First Day Cover (Ordinary)		35·00
		First Day Cover (Phosphor)		45·00

Special First Day of Issue Postmark

	Ordin-	Phos-
	ary	phor
London	65·00	80·00

This postmark was used on first day covers serviced by the Philatelic
Bureau.

202 Red Cross   **203**

204

(Des H. Bartram)

1963 (15 Aug). **Red Cross Centenary Congress.** *Chalk-surfaced paper.*
W **179**. P 15 × 14.

642	**202**	3d. red & dp lilac		15	15
		a. Red omitted		£3000	
		p. Three phosphor bands		1·10	85
		pa. Red omitted		£6000	
643	**203**	1s. 3d. red, blue & grey		2·50	2·50
		p. Three phosphor bands		38·00	30·00
644	**204**	1s. 6d. red, blue & bistre		2·50	2·50
		p. Three phosphor bands		35·00	25·00
		Set of 3 (Ordinary)		4·75	4·75
		Set of 3 (Phosphor)		65·00	50·00
		First Day Cover (Ordinary)			40·00
		First Day Cover (Phosphor)			60·00

Special First Day of Issue Postmark

1863 RED CROSS
CENTENARY
A CENTURY
OF SERVICE 1963

	Ordin-	Phos-
	ary	phor
London E.C.	75·00	£100

This postmark was used on first day covers serviced by the Philatelic
Bureau.

205 Commonwealth Cable

(Des P. Gauld)

1963 (3 Dec). **Opening of COMPAC (Trans-Pacific Telephone Cable).**
Chalk-surfaced paper. W **179**. P 15 × 14.

645	**205**	1s. 6d. blue & black		2·00	2·25
		a. Black omitted		£3000	
		p. Three phosphor bands		16·00	15·00
		First Day Cover (Ordinary)			24·00
		First Day Cover (Phosphor)			30·00

Special First Day of Issue Postmark

	Ordin-	Phos-
	ary	phor
Philatelic Bureau, London E.C.1 (Type A)	45·00	50·00

PRESENTATION PACKS. Special Packs comprising slip-in cards with
printed commemorative inscriptions and descriptive notes on the back
and with protective covering, were introduced in 1964 with the
Shakespeare issue. These are listed and priced.

Issues of 1968–69 (British Paintings to the Prince of Wales
Investiture) were also issued in packs with text in German for sale
through the Post Office's German Agency and these are also quoted.
Subsequently, however, the packs sold in Germany were identical to
the normal English version with the addition of a separate printed
insert card with German text. These, as also English packs with
Japanese and Dutch printed cards for sale in Japan and the
Netherlands respectively, are listed in Vols. 3 and 5 of the Stanley
Gibbons *Great Britain Specialised Catalogue.*

206 Puck and Bottom   **207** Feste (*Twelfth Night*)
(*A Midsummer Night's Dream*)

208 Balcony Scene (*Romeo and*   **209** ''Eve of Agincourt'' (*Henry V*)
Juliet)

210 Hamlet contemplating Yorick's Skull (*Hamlet*)
and Queen Elizabeth II

(Des D. Gentleman. Photo Harrison & Sons (3d., 6d., 1s. 3d., 1s. 6d.). Des
C. and R. Ironside. Recess B.W. (2s. 6d.))

1964 (23 Apr). **Shakespeare Festival.** *Chalk-surfaced paper.* W **179**.
P 11 × 12 (2s. 6d.) or 15 × 14 (*others*).

646	**206**	3d. yellow-bistre, black & dp violet-blue			
		(shades)		15	15
		p. Three phosphor bands		25	30
647	**207**	6d. yellow, orange, black & yellow-olive			
		(shades)		30	30
		p. Three phosphor bands		75	1·00
648	**208**	1s. 3d. cerise, blue-green, black & sepia			
		(shades)		70	90
		Wi. Watermark inverted			
		p. Three phosphor bands		4·00	6·50
		pWi. Watermark inverted		£125	
649	**209**	1s. 6d. violet, turquoise, black & blue			
		(shades)		1·00	85
		Wi. Watermark inverted			
		p. Three phosphor bands		8·00	8·00
650	**210**	2s. 6d. dp slate-purple (shades)		2·75	2·75
		Wi. Watermark inverted		£350	
		Set of 5 (Ordinary)		4·50	4·50
		Set of 4 (Phosphor)		12·00	14·00
		First Day Cover (Ordinary)			10·00
		First Day Cover (Phosphor)			17·00
		Presentation Pack (Ordinary)		12·50	

The 3d. is known with yellow-bistre missing in the top two-thirds of the figures of Puck and Bottom. This occured in the top row only of a sheet.

Special First Day of Issue Postmark

	Ordin-ary	Phos-phor
Stratford-upon-Avon, Warwicks	15·00	22·00

This postmark was used on first day covers serviced by the Philatelic Bureau, as well as on covers posted at Stratford P.O.

211 Flats near Richmond Park ("Urban Development") **212** Shipbuilding Yards, Belfast ("Industrial Activity")

213 Beddgelert Forest Park, Snowdonia ("Forestry") **214** Nuclear Reactor, Dounreay ("Technological Development")

(Des D. Bailey)

1964 (1 July). **20th International Geographical Congress, London.**
Chalk-surfaced paper. W **179**. P 15 × 14.

651	**211**	2½d. black, olive-yellow, olive-grey & turquoise-blue	10	10
		p. One phosphor band	40	50
652	**212**	4d. orange-brown, red-brown, rose, black & violet	30	30
		a. Violet (face value) omitted	£180	
		c. Violet and red-brown (dock walls) omitted	£275	
		Wi. Watermark inverted	£500	
		p. Three phosphor bands	1·25	1·25
653	**213**	8d. yellow-brown, emerald, green & black ..	65	75
		a. Green (lawn) omitted	£7000	
		Wi. Watermark inverted	£300	
		p. Three phosphor bands	2·50	2·75
654	**214**	1s. 6d. yellow-brown, pale pink, black, & brown	2·75	3·00
		Wi. Watermark inverted	22·00	
		p. Three phosphor bands	28·00	22·00
		Set of 4 (Ordinary)	3·50	3·75
		Set of 4 (Phosphor)	30·00	24·00
		First Day Cover (Ordinary)		22·00
		First Day Cover (Phosphor)		35·00
		Presentation Pack (Ordinary)	£120	

A used example of the 4d. is known with the red-brown omitted.

Special First Day of Issue Postmark

	Ordin-ary	Phos-phor
G.P.O. Philatelic Bureau, London E.C.1 (Type B)	27·00	35·00

215 Spring Gentian **216** Dog Rose

217 Honeysuckle **218** Fringed Water Lily

(Des M. and Sylvia Goaman)

1964 (5 Aug). **Tenth International Botanical Congress, Edinburgh.**
Chalk-surfaced paper. W **179**. P 15 × 14.

655	**215**	3d. violet, blue & sage-green	10	10
		a. Blue omitted	£4250	
		b. Sage-green omitted	£6500	
		p. Three phosphor bands	40	40
656	**216**	6d. apple-green, rose, scarlet & green	30	35
		Wi. Watermark inverted		
		p. Three phosphor bands	2·50	2·75
657	**217**	9d. lemon, green, lake & rose-red	1·60	2·25
		a. Green (leaves) omitted	£6500	
		Wi. Watermark inverted	37·00	
		p. Three phosphor bands	4·50	4·00
658	**218**	1s. 3d. yellow, emerald, reddish violet & grey-green	2·25	2·50
		a. Yellow (flowers) omitted £10000		
		Wi. Watermark inverted	£250	
		p. Three phosphor bands	25·00	20·00
		Set of 4 (Ordinary)	3·75	4·75
		Set of 4 (Phosphor)	30·00	24·00
		First Day Cover (Ordinary)		25·00
		First Day Cover (Phosphor)		35·00
		Presentation Pack (Ordinary)	£120	

Special First Day of Issue Postmark

	Ordin-ary	Phos-phor
G.P.O. Philatelic Bureau, London E.C.1 (Type B)	28·00	45·00

219 Forth Road Bridge **220** Forth Road and Railway Bridges

(Des A. Restall)

1964 (4 Sept). **Opening of Forth Road Bridge.** *Chalk-surfaced paper.*
W **179**. P 15 × 14.

659	**219**	3d. black, blue & reddish violet	10	10
		p. Three phosphor bands	50	50
660	**220**	6d. blackish lilac, lt blue & carmine-red	40	40
		a. Lt blue omitted	£1750	
		Wi. Watermark inverted	2·00	
		p. Three phosphor bands	3·75	3·75
		pWi. Watermark inverted	£1500	
		Set of 2 (Ordinary)	50	50
		Set of 2 (Phosphor)	4·25	4·25
		First Day Cover (Ordinary)		7·00
		First Day Cover (Phosphor)		18·00
		Presentation Pack (Ordinary)	£350	

Special First Day of Issue Postmarks

	Ordin-ary	Phos-phor
G.P.O. Philatelic Bureau, London E.C.1 (Type B)	20·00	28·00
North Queensferry, Fife	40·00	£130
South Queensferry, West Lothian	32·00	95·00

The Queensferry postmarks were applied to first day covers sent to a temporary Philatelic Bureau at Edinburgh.

221 Sir Winston Churchill

(Des D. Gentleman and Rosalind Dease, from photograph by Karsh)

1965 (8 July). **Churchill Commemoration.** *Chalk-surfaced paper.*
W **179**. P 15 × 14.

I. "REMBRANDT" Machine

661	**221**	4d. black & olive-brown	10	10
		Wi. Watermark inverted	2·25	
		p. Three phosphor bands	25	25

II. "TIMSON" Machine

661a	**221**	4d. black & olive-brown	35	35

III. "L. & M. 4" Machine

662	—	1s. 3d. black & grey	30	40
		Wi. Watermark inverted	75·00	
		p. Three phosphor bands	2·50	3·00
		Set of 2 (Ordinary)	40	50
		Set of 2 (Phosphor)	2·75	3·25
		First Day Cover (Ordinary)		8·00
		First Day Cover (Phosphor)		9·00
		Presentation Pack (Ordinary)	24·00	

The 1s. 3d. shows a closer view of Churchill's head.

Two examples of the 4d. value exist with the Queen's head omitted, one due to something adhering to the cylinder and the other due to a paper fold. The stamp also exists with Churchill's head omitted, also due to a paper fold.

4d. REMBRANDT, Cyls 1A-1B dot and no dot. Lack of shading detail on Churchill's portrait. Queen's portrait appears dull and coarse. This is a rotary machine which is sheet-fed.

4d. TIMSON. Cyls 5A-6B no dot. More detail on Churchill's portrait—furrow on forehead, his left eyebrow fully drawn and more shading on cheek. Queen's portrait lighter and sharper. This is a reel-fed two-colour 12-in. wide rotary machine and the differences in impressions are due to the greater pressure applied by this machine.

1s. 3d. Cyls 1A-1B no dot. The "Linotype and Machinery No. 4" machine is an ordinary sheet-fed rotary press machine. Besides being used for printing the 1s. 3d. stamps it was also employed for overprinting the phosphor bands on both values.

Special First Day of Issue Postmark

	Ordin-ary	Phos-phor
G.P.O. Philatelic Bureau, London E.C.1 (Type B)	10·00	16·00

A First Day of Issue handstamp was provided at Bladon, Oxford, for this issue.

222 Simon de Montfort's Seal

223 Parliament Buildings
(after engraving by Hollar, 1647)

(Des S. Black (6d.), R. Guyatt (2s. 6d.))

1965 (19 July). **700th Anniversary of Simon de Montfort's Parliament.** *Chalk-surfaced paper.* W **179**. P 15 × 14.

663	**222**	6d. olive-green	20	20
		p. Three phosphor bands	60	75
664	**223**	2s. 6d. black, grey & pale drab	80	1·00
		Wi. Watermark inverted	20·00	
		Set of 2 (Ordinary)	1·00	1·10
		First Day Cover (Ordinary)		12·00
		First Day Cover (Phosphor)		20·00
		Presentation Pack (Ordinary)	45·00	

Special First Day of Issue Postmark

	Ordin-ary
G.P.O. Philatelic Bureau, London E.C.1 (Type B)	15·00

A First Day of Issue handstamp was provided at Evesham, Worcs, for this issue.

224 Bandsmen and Banner   **225** Three Salvationists

(Des M. Farrar-Bell (3d.), G. Trenaman (1s. 6d.))

1965 (9 Aug). **Salvation Army Centenary.** *Chalk-surfaced paper.*
W **179**. *P* 15 × 14.

665	**224**	3d. indigo, grey-blue, cerise, yellow & brown	10	15
		p. One phosphor band	30	40
666	**225**	1s. 6d. red, blue, yellow & brown	65	1·00
		p. Three phosphor bands	2·50	2·75
		Set of 2 (Ordinary)	75	1·10
		Set of 2 (Phosphor)	2·75	3·00
		First Day Cover (Ordinary)		22·00
		First Day Cover (Phosphor)		30·00

The Philatelic Bureau did not provide first day cover services for Nos.
665/70.

226 Lister's Carbolic Spray

227 Lister and Chemical Symbols

(Des P. Gauld (4d.), F. Ariss (1s.))

1965 (1 Sept). **Centenary of Joseph Lister's Discovery of Antiseptic
Surgery.** *Chalk-surfaced paper.* W **179**. *P* 15 × 14.

667	**226**	4d. indigo, brown-red & grey-black	10	15
		a. Brown-red (tube) omitted	£300	
		b. Indigo omitted	£2800	
		p. Three phosphor bands	25	25
		pa. Brown-red (tube) omitted	£2000	
668	**227**	1s. black, purple & new blue	70	1·10
		Wi. Watermark inverted	£190	
		p. Three phosphor bands	2·00	2·10
		pWi. Watermark inverted	£190	
		Set of 2 (Ordinary)	80	1·25
		Set of 2 (Phosphor)	2·25	2·25
		First Day Cover (Ordinary)		12·00
		First Day Cover (Phosphor)		14·00

228 Trinidad Carnival Dancers

229 Canadian Folk-dancers

(Des D. Gentleman and Rosalind Dease)

1965 (1 Sept). **Commonwealth Arts Festival.** *Chalk-surfaced paper.*
W **179**. *P* 15 × 14.

669	**228**	6d. black & orange	20	20
		p. Three phosphor bands	30	40
670	**229**	1s. 6d. black & lt reddish violet	80	1·10
		p. Three phosphor bands	2·50	2·50
		Set of 2 (Ordinary)	1·00	1·25
		Set of 2 (Phosphor)	2·75	2·75
		First Day Cover (Ordinary)		14·00
		First Day Cover (Phosphor)		18·00

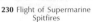
230 Flight of Supermarine
Spitfires

231 Pilot in Hawker
Hurricane Mk I

232 Wing-tips of Supermarine
Spitfire and Messerschmitt Bf 109

233 Supermarine Spitfires
attacking Heinkel HE-111H
Bomber

234 Supermarine Spitfire attacking
Junkers Ju 87B "Stuka"
Dive-bomber

235 Hawker Hurricanes Mk I
over Wreck of Dornier
Do-17Z Bomber

236 Anti-aircraft Artillery in Action

237 Air-battle over St. Paul's
Cathedral

(Des D. Gentleman and Rosalind Dease (4d. × 6 and 1s. 3d.), A. Restall
(9d.))

1965 (13 Sept). **25th Anniv of Battle of Britain.** *Chalk-surfaced paper.*
W **179**. *P* 15 × 14.

671	**230**	4d. yellow-olive & black	50	70
		a. Block of 6. Nos. 671/6	6·00	10·00
		p. Three phosphor bands	90	1·00
		pa. Block of 6. Nos. 671p/6p	10·00	15·00
672	**231**	4d. yellow-olive, olive-grey & black	50	70
		p. Three phosphor bands	90	1·00
673	**232**	4d. red, new blue, yellow-olive, olive-grey &		
		black	50	70
		p. Three phosphor bands	90	1·00
674	**233**	4d. olive-grey, yellow-olive & black	50	70
		p. Three phosphor bands	90	1·00
675	**234**	4d. olive-grey, yellow-olive & black	50	70
		p. Three phosphor bands	90	1·00
676	**235**	4d. olive-grey, yellow-olive, new blue &		
		black	50	70
		a. New blue omitted	† £3500	
		p. Three phosphor bands	90	1·00
677	**236**	9d. bluish violet, orange & slate-purple	1·25	1·50
		Wi. Watermark inverted	28·00	
		p. Three phosphor bands	1·25	1·50
678	**237**	1s. 3d. lt grey, dp grey, black, lt blue & brt		
		blue	1·25	1·50
		Wi. Watermark inverted	24·00	
		p. Three phosphor bands	1·25	1·50
		pWi. Watermark inverted	3·00	
		Set of 8 (Ordinary)	7·75	6·50
		Set of 8 (Phosphor)	11·50	8·00
		First Day Cover (Ordinary)		25·00
		First Day Cover (Phosphor)		28·00
		Presentation Pack (Ordinary)	45·00	

Nos. 671/6 were issued together *se-tenant* in blocks of 6 (3 × 2)
within the sheet.

No. 676a is only known commercially used on cover from Truro.

Special First Day of Issue Postmark

	Ordinary	Phosphor
G.P.O. Philatelic Bureau, London E.C.1 (Type C)	25·00	28·00

238 Tower and Georgian Buildings

239 Tower and "Nash" Terrace, Regent's Park

(Des C. Abbott)

1965 (8 Oct). **Opening of Post Office Tower.** *Chalk-surfaced paper.* W **179** (*sideways on* 3d.). P 14 × 15 (3d.) *or* 15 × 14 (1s. 3d.).

679	238	3d. olive-yellow, new blue & bronze-green .	10	15
		a. Olive-yellow (Tower) omitted	£1000	
		p. One phosphor band at right	15	15
		pEa. Band at left	15	10
		pEb. Horiz pair. Nos. 679p/pEa	30	20
680	239	1s. 3d. bronze-green, yellow-green & blue ..	30	45
		Wi. Watermark inverted	45·00	
		p. Three phosphor bands	30	50
		pWi. Watermark inverted	50·00	
		Set of 2 (Ordinary)	40	60
		Set of 2 (Phosphor)	45	65
		First Day Cover (Ordinary)	6·00	
		First Day Cover (Phosphor)	7·00	
		Presentation Pack (Ordinary)	4·00	
		Presentation Pack (Phosphor)	4·00	

The one phosphor band on No. 679p was produced by printing broad phosphor bands across alternate vertical perforations. Individual stamps show the band at right or left.

Special First Day of Issue Postmark

	Ordinary	Phosphor
G.P.O. Philatelic Bureau, London E.C.1 (Type C)	10·00	12·00

The Philatelic Bureau did not provide first day cover services for Nos. 681/4.

240 U.N. Emblem

241 I.C.Y. Emblem

(Des J. Matthews)

1965 (25 Oct). **20th Anniv of U.N.O. and International Co-operation Year.** *Chalk-surfaced paper.* W **179**. P 15 × 14.

681	240	3d. black, yellow-orange & lt blue	15	20
		p. One phosphor band	25	30
682	241	1s. 6d. black, brt purple & lt blue	75	80
		Wi. Watermark inverted		
		p. Three phosphor bands	2·75	3·00
		Set of 2 (Ordinary)	90	1·00
		Set of 2 (Phosphor)	3·00	3·25
		First Day Cover (Ordinary)	10·00	
		First Day Cover (Phosphor)	12·00	

242 Telecommunications Network

243 Radio Waves and Switchboard

(Des A. Restall)

1965 (15 Nov). **I.T.U. Centenary.** *Chalk-surfaced paper.* W **179**. P 15 × 14.

683	242	9d. red, ultramarine, dp slate, violet, black & pink	30	40
		Wi. Watermark inverted	14·00	
		p. Three phosphor bands	60	75
		pWi. Watermark inverted	70·00	
684	243	1s. 6d. red, greenish blue, indigo, black & lt pink	1·00	1·25
		a. Lt pink omitted	£1100	
		Wi. Watermark inverted	55·00	
		p. Three phosphor bands	4·25	5·25
		Set of 2 (Ordinary)	1·25	1·60
		Set of 2 (Phosphor)	4·75	6·00
		First Day Cover (Ordinary)	17·00	
		First Day Cover (Phosphor)	20·00	

Originally scheduled for issue on 17 May 1965, supplies from the Philatelic Bureau were sent in error to reach a dealer on that date and another dealer received his supply on 27 May.

244 Robert Burns (after Skirving chalk drawing)

245 Robert Burns (after Nasmyth portrait)

(Des G. Huntly)

1966 (25 Jan). **Burns Commemoration.** *Chalk-surfaced paper.* W **179**. P 15 × 14.

685	244	4d. black, dp violet-blue & new blue	15	15
		p. Three phosphor bands	25	40
686	245	1s. 3d. black, slate-blue & yellow-orange.. .	40	70
		p. Three phosphor bands	2·25	1·75
		Set of 2 (Ordinary)	55	85
		Set of 2 (Phosphor)	2·50	2·10
		First Day Cover (Ordinary)	6·00	
		First Day Cover (Phosphor)	7·00	
		Presentation Pack (Ordinary)	40·00	

Special First Day of Issue Postmarks
(35 mm diameter)

	Ordin-ary	Phos-phor
Alloway, Ayrshire	12·00	12·00
Ayr	12·00	12·00
Dumfries	15·00	15·00
Edinburgh	15·00	15·00
Glasgow	15·00	15·00
Kilmarnock, Ayrshire	15·00	15·00

A special Philatelic Bureau was set up in Edinburgh to deal with first day covers of this issue. The Bureau serviced covers to receive the above postmarks, and other versions were applied locally. The locally applied handstamps were 38–39mm in diameter, the Bureau postmarks, applied by machine, 35mm. The Ayr, Edinburgh, Glasgow and Kilmarnock postmarks are similar in design to that for Alloway. Similar handstamps were also provided at Greenock and Mauchline, but the Bureau did not provide a service for these.

246 Westminster Abbey   **247** Fan Vaulting, Henry VII Chapel

(Des Sheila Robinson. Photo Harrison (3d.). Des and eng Bradbury, Wilkinson. Recess (2s. 6d.))

1966 (28 Feb). **900th Anniversary of Westminster Abbey.** *Chalk-surfaced paper* (3d.). W **179**. *P* 15 × 14 (3d.) or 11 × 12 (2s. 6d.).

687	246	3d. black, red-brown & new blue	15	20
		p. One phosphor band	20	25
688	247	2s. 6d. black	55	80
		Set of 2	70	1·00
		First Day Cover (Ordinary)		8·00
		First Day Cover (Phosphor)		14·00
		Presentation Pack (Ordinary)	20·00	

Special First Day of Issue Postmark

	Ordin-ary
G.P.O. Philatelic Bureau, London E.C.1 (Type B)	15·00

The Bureau did not provide a first day cover service for the 3d. phosphor stamp.

248 View near Hassocks, Sussex   **249** Antrim, Northern Ireland

250 Harlech Castle, Wales   **251** Cairngorm Mountains, Scotland

(Des L. Rosoman. Queen's portrait, adapted by D. Gentleman from coinage)

1966 (2 May). **Landscapes.** *Chalk-surfaced paper.* W **179**. *P* 15 × 14.

689	248	4d. black, yellow-green & new blue	10	15
		p. Three phosphor bands	10	15
690	249	6d. black, emerald & new blue	15	20
		Wi. Watermark inverted	6·00	
		p. Three phosphor bands	15	20
		pWi. Watermark inverted	30·00	
691	250	1s. 3d. black, greenish yellow & greenish blue	25	35
		p. Three phosphor bands	25	35
692	251	1s. 6d. black, orange & Prussian blue	40	35
		Wi. Watermark inverted	15·00	
		p. Three phosphor bands	40	40
		Set of 4 (Ordinary)	80	95
		Set of 4 (Phosphor)	80	1·00
		First Day Cover (Ordinary)		7·00
		First Day Cover (Phosphor)		8·00

A block of four of No. 689 is known with the top right stamp showing the face value and the bottom right the Queen's head and the face value both omitted due to a paper fold.

Special First Day of Issue Postmark

	Ordin-ary	Phos-phor
G.P.O. Philatelic Bureau, London E.C.1 (Type B)	12·00	12·00

First Day of Issue handstamps were provided at Lewes, Sussex; Coleraine, Co. Londonderry; Harlech, Merioneth and Grantown-on-Spey, Morayshire, for this issue.

252 Players with Ball   **253** Goalmouth Mêlée

254 Goalkeeper saving Goal

(Des D. Gentleman (4d.), W. Kempster (6d.), D. Caplan (1s. 3d.). Queen's portrait adapted by D. Gentleman from coinage)

1966 (1 June). **World Cup Football Championship.** *Chalk-surfaced paper.* W **179** (*sideways on* 4d.). *P* 14 × 15 (4d.) or 15 × 14 (*others*).

693	252	4d. red, reddish purple, brt blue, flesh & black	10	10
		p. Two phosphor bands	10	10
694	253	6d. black, sepia, red, apple-green & blue ...	15	25
		a. Black omitted	£110	
		b. Apple-green omitted	£2400	
		c. Red omitted	£3000	
		Wi. Watermark inverted	2·00	
		p. Three phosphor bands	15	25
		pa. Black omitted	£575	

695	254	1s.	3d. black, blue, yellow, red & lt yellow-olive	50	70
		a.	Blue omitted	£175	
		Wi.	Watermark inverted	90·00	
		p.	Three phosphor bands	50	70
		pWi.	Watermark inverted	1·25	
			Set of 3 (Ordinary)	70	95
			Set of 3 (Phosphor)	70	95
			First Day Cover (Ordinary)		15·00
			First Day Cover (Phosphor)		20·00
			Presentation Pack (Ordinary)		15·00

Special First Day of Issue Postmark

	Ordinary	Phosphor
G.P.O. Philatelic Bureau, London E.C.1 (Type C)	20·00	25·00

A First Day of Issue handstamp was provided at Wembley, Middx, for this issue.

255 Black-headed Gull

256 Blue Tit

257 European Robin

258 Blackbird

(Des J. Norris Wood)

1966 (8 Aug). **British Birds.** *Chalk-surfaced paper.* W **179**. P 15 × 14.

696	255	4d.	grey, black, red, emerald-green, brt blue, greenish yellow & bistre	10	20
		Wi.	Watermark inverted	4·00	
		a.	Block of 4. Nos. 696/9	80	2·00
		ab.	Black (value), etc. omitted * *(block of four)*	£6000	
		ac.	Black only omitted*	—	
		aWi.	Watermark inverted *(block of four)*	17·00	
		p.	Three phosphor bands	10	20
		pWi.	Watermark inverted	18·00	
		pa.	Block of 4. Nos. 696p/9p	75	2·00
		paWi.	Watermark inverted *(block of four)*	75·00	
697	256	4d.	black, greenish yellow, grey, emerald-green, brt blue & bistre	10	20
		Wi.	Watermark inverted	4·00	
		p.	Three phosphor bands	10	20
		pWi.	Watermark inverted	18·00	
698	257	4d.	red, greenish yellow, black, grey, bistre, reddish brown & emerald-green	10	20
		Wi.	Watermark inverted	4·00	
		p.	Three phosphor bands	10	20
		pWi.	Watermark inverted	18·00	

699	258	4d.	black, reddish brown, greenish yellow, grey & bistre**	10	20
		Wi.	Watermark inverted	4·00	
		p.	Three phosphor bands	10	20
		pWi.	Watermark inverted	16·00	
			Set of 4 (Ordinary)	80	70
			Set of 4 (Phosphor)	75	70
			First Day Cover (Ordinary)		10·00
			First Day Cover (Phosphor)		10·00
			Presentation Pack (Ordinary)		9·00

Nos. 696/9 were issued together *se-tenant* in blocks of four within the sheet.

*In No. 696ab the blue, bistre and reddish brown are also omitted but in No. 696ac only the black is omitted.

**In No. 699 the black was printed over the bistre.

Other colours omitted, and the stamps affected:

d.	Greenish yellow (Nos. 696/9)	£450
pd.	Greenish yellow (Nos. 696p/9p)	£2500
e.	Red (Nos. 696 and 698)	£450
f.	Emerald-green (Nos. 696/8)	90·00
pf.	Emerald-green (Nos. 696p/8p)	90·00
g.	Brt blue (Nos. 696/7)	£350
pg.	Brt blue (Nos. 696p and 697p)	£3500
h.	Bistre (Nos. 696/9)	90·00
ph.	Bistre (Nos. 696p/9p)	£2000
j.	Reddish brown (Nos. 698/9)	90·00
pj.	Reddish brown (Nos. 698p and 699p)	90·00

The prices quoted are for each stamp.

Special First Day of Issue Postmark

	Ordinary	Phosphor
G.P.O. Philatelic Bureau, London E.C.1 (Type C)	22·00	22·00

259 Cup Winners

1966 (18 Aug). **England's World Cup Football Victory.** *Chalk-surfaced paper.* W **179** *(sideways).* P 14 × 15.

700	259	4d.	red, reddish purple, brt blue, flesh & black	30	30
			First Day Cover		10·00

These stamps were only put on sale at post offices in England, the Channel Islands and the Isle of Man, and at the Philatelic Bureau in London and also, on 22 August, in Edinburgh on the occasion of the opening of the Edinburgh Festival as well as at Army post offices at home and abroad.

The Philatelic Bureau did not service first day covers for this stamp, but a First Day of Issue handstamp was provided inscribed "Harrow & Wembley" to replace the "Wembley, Middx", postmark of the initial issue.

For full information on all future British issues, collectors should write to the British Post Office Philatelic Bureau, 21 South Gyle Crescent, Edinburgh EH12 9PB

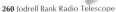

260 Jodrell Bank Radio Telescope

261 British Motor-cars

262 "SRN 6" Hovercraft

263 Windscale Reactor

(Des D. and A. Gillespie (4d., 6d.), A. Restall (others))

1966 (19 Sept). **British Technology.** *Chalk-surfaced paper. W* **179**.
P 15 × 14.

701	**260**	4d. black & lemon	10	10
		p. Three phosphor bands	10	10
702	**261**	6d. red, dp blue & orange	15	20
		a. Red (Mini-cars) omitted	£5000	
		b. Dp blue (Jaguar & inscr) omitted	£3500	
		p. Three phosphor bands	15	25
703	**262**	1s. 3d. black, orange-red, slate & lt greenish blue	25	40
		p. Three phosphor bands	35	40
704	**263**	1s. 6d. black, yellow-green, bronze-green, lilac & dp blue	40	60
		p. Three phosphor bands	50	60
		Set of 4 (Ordinary)	80	1·10
		Set of 4 (Phosphor)	1·00	1·10
		First Day Cover (Ordinary)		8·00
		First Day Cover (Phosphor)		8·00
		Presentation Pack (Ordinary)	9·00	

Special First Day of Issue Postmark

	Ordinary	Phosphor
G.P.O. Philatelic Bureau, Edinburgh 1 (Type C)	12·00	12·00

264

265

266

267

268

269

All the above show battle scenes and they were issued together *se-tenant* in horizontal strips of six within the sheet.

270 Norman Ship

271 Norman Horsemen attacking Harold's Troops

(All the above are scenes from the Bayeux Tapestry)

(Des D. Gentleman. Photo. Queen's head die-stamped (6d., 1s. 3d.))

1966 (14 Oct). **900th Anniv of Battle of Hastings.** *Chalk-surfaced paper. W* **179** (*sideways on* 1s. 3d.). *P* 15 × 14.

705	**264**	4d. black, olive-green, bistre, dp blue, orange, magenta, green, blue & grey	10	20
		a. Strip of 6. Nos. 705/10	1·90	6·00
		aWi. Strip of 6. Watermark inverted	45·00	
		Wi. Watermark inverted	7·00	
		p. Three phosphor bands	10	25
		pa. Strip of 6. Nos. 705p/10p	1·90	6·00
		paWi. Strip of 6. Watermark inverted	20·00	
		pWi. Watermark inverted	3·00	
706	**265**	4d. black, olive-green, bistre, dp blue, orange, magenta, green, blue & grey	10	20
		Wi. Watermark inverted	7·00	
		p. Three phosphor bands	10	25
		pWi. Watermark inverted	2·00	
707	**266**	4d. black, olive-green, bistre, dp blue, orange, magenta, green, blue & grey	10	20
		Wi. Watermark inverted	7·00	
		p. Three phosphor bands	10	25
		pWi. Watermark inverted	3·00	
708	**267**	4d. black, olive-green, bistre, dp blue, magenta, green, blue & grey	10	20
		Wi. Watermark inverted	7·00	
		p. Three phosphor bands	10	25
		pWi. Watermark inverted	3·00	
709	**268**	4d. black, olive-green, bistre, dp blue, orange, magenta, green, blue & grey	10	20
		Wi. Watermark inverted	7·00	
		p. Three phosphor bands	10	25
		pWi. Watermark inverted	3·00	
710	**269**	4d. black, olive-green, bistre, dp blue, orange, magenta, green, blue & grey	10	20
		Wi. Watermark inverted	7·00	
		p. Three phosphor bands	10	25
		pWi. Watermark inverted	3·00	

711 **270** 6d. black, olive-green, violet, blue, green &
gold 10 20
Wi. Watermark inverted .... 38·00
p. Three phosphor bands 10 20
pWi. Watermark inverted .... 50·00
712 **271** 1s. 3d. black, lilac, bronze-green, rosine
bistre-brown & gold 20 40
a. Lilac omitted £600
Wi. Watermark sideways inverted (top of
crown pointing to right)* .... 35·00
p. Four phosphor bands 20 50
pa. Lilac omitted £650
pWi. Watermark sideways inverted (top of
crown pointing to right)* .... 14·00
Set of 8 (Ordinary) .... 2·00 1·60
Set of 8 (Phosphor) .... 2·00 2·00
First Day Cover (Ordinary) .... 8·00
First Day Cover (Phosphor) .... 9·00
Presentation Pack (Ordinary) .... 9·00

*The normal sideways watermark shows the tops of the Crowns pointing to the left, *as seen from the back of the stamp*.
Other colours omitted in the 4d. values and the stamps affected:

b. Olive-green (Nos. 705/10) .... 55·00
pb. Olive-green (Nos. 705p/10p) .... 55·00
c. Bistre (Nos. 705/10) .... 55·00
pc. Bistre (Nos. 705p/10p) .... 55·00
d. Dp blue (Nos. 705/10) .... 65·00
pd. Dp blue (Nos. 705p/10p) .... 65·00
e. Orange (Nos. 705/7 and 709/10) .... 55·00
pe. Orange (Nos. 705p/7p and 709p/10p) .... 55·00
f. Magenta (Nos. 705/10) .... 55·00
pf. Magenta (Nos. 705p/10p) .... 55·00
g. Green (Nos. 705/10) .... 55·00
pg. Green (Nos. 705p/10p) .... 55·00
h. Blue (Nos. 705/10) .... 55·00
ph. Blue (Nos. 705p/10p) .... 55·00
j. Grey (Nos. 705/10) .... 55·00
pj. Grey (Nos. 705p/10p) .... 55·00
pk. Magenta & green (Nos. 705p/10p) ....

The prices quoted are for each stamp.
Nos. 705 and 709, with grey and blue omitted, have been seen commercially used, posted from Middleton-in-Teesdale.
The 6d. phosphor is known in a yellowish gold as well as the reddish gold as used in the 1s. 3d.
Three examples of No. 712 in a right-hand top corner block of 10 (2 × 5) are known with the Queen's head omitted as a result of a double paper fold prior to die-stamping. The perforation is normal. Of the other seven stamps, four have the Queen's head misplaced and three are normal.

MISSING GOLD HEADS. The 6d. and 1s. 3d. were also issued with the die-stamped gold head omitted but as these can also be removed by chemical means we are not prepared to list them unless a way is found of distinguishing the genuine stamps from the fakes which will satisfy the Expert Committees.
The same remarks apply to Nos. 713/14.

Special First Day of Issue Postmark
Ordin- Phos-
ary phor
G.P.O. Philatelic Bureau, Edinburgh 1
(Type C) .... 10·00 12·00
A First Day of Issue handstamp was provided at Battle, Sussex, for this issue.

For full information on all future British issues, collectors should write to the British Post Office Philatelic Bureau, 21 South Gyle Crescent, Edinburgh EH12 9PB

272 King of the Orient **273** Snowman
(Des Tasveer Shemza (3d.), J. Berry (1s. 6d.) (winners of children's design competition). Photo, Queen's head die-stamped)

1966 (1 Dec). **Christmas.** *Chalk-surfaced paper.* W 179 (*sideways on 3d.*). *P* 14 × 15.
713 **272** 3d. black, blue, green, yellow, red & gold ... 10 10
a. Queen's head double .... † —
ab. Queen's head double, one albino £550
b. Green omitted £5500
p. One phosphor band at right 10 10
pEa. Band at left 10 10
pEb. Horiz pair. Nos. 713p/pEa 20 20
714 **273** 1s. 6d. blue, red, pink, black & gold 30 30
a. Pink (hat) omitted £1000
Wi. Watermark inverted .... 13·00
p. Two phosphor bands 30 35
pWi. Watermark inverted .... 42·00
Set of 2 (Ordinary) 40 40
Set of 2 (Phosphor) 40 45
First Day Cover (Ordinary) .... 4·00
First Day Cover (Phosphor) .... 4·00
Presentation Pack (Ordinary) .... 8·00
Special First Day of Issue Postmarks
Ordin- Phos-
ary phor
G.P.O. Philatelic Bureau, Edinburgh 1
(Type C) .... 10·00 10·00
Bethlehem, Llandeilo, Carms (Type C) .... 10·00 10·00

274 Sea Freight **275** Air Freight
(Des C. Abbott)

1967 (20 Feb). **European Free Trade Association (EFTA).** *Chalk-surfaced paper.* W 179. *P* 15 × 14.
715 **274** 9d. dp blue, red, lilac, green, brown, new
blue, yellow & black 15 20
a. Black (Queen's head, etc.), brown, new
blue & yellow omitted £750
b. Lilac omitted .... 60·00
c. Green omitted .... 60·00
d. Brown (rail trucks) omitted .... 45·00
e. New blue omitted .... 60·00
f. Yellow omitted .... 60·00
Wi. Watermark inverted .... 24·00
p. Three phosphor bands 15 20
pb. Lilac omitted £125
pc. Green omitted .... 60·00
pd. Brown omitted .... 45·00
pe. New blue omitted .... 60·00
pf. Yellow omitted £100
pWi. Watermark inverted .... 12·00

716 **275** 1s. 6d. violet, red, dp blue, brown, green, blue-grey, new blue, yellow & black 30 45
  a. Red omitted ....
  b. Dp blue omitted £375
  c. Brown omitted .... 60·00
  d. Blue-grey omitted .... 60·00
  e. New blue omitted .... 60·00
  f. Yellow omitted .... 60·00
  p. Three phosphor bands 25 40
  pa. Red omitted ....
  pb. Dp blue omitted £375
  pc. Brown omitted .... 45·00
  pd. Blue-grey omitted .... 60·00
  pf. New blue omitted .... 60·00
  pWi. Watermark inverted .... 25·00
    Set of 2 (Ordinary) 45 65
    Set of 2 (Phosphor) 40 60
    First Day Cover (Ordinary) .... 4·00
    First Day Cover (Phosphor) .... 4·00
    Presentation Pack (Ordinary) .... 3·50

Special First Day of Issue Postmark

	Ordinary	Phosphor
G.P.O. Philatelic Bureau, Edinburgh 1 (Type C)	6·00	6·00

276 Hawthorn and Bramble

277 Larger Bindweed and Viper's Bugloss

278 Ox-eye Daisy, Coltsfoot and Buttercup

279 Bluebell, Red Campion and Wood Anemone

T **276/9** were issued together *se-tenant* in blocks of four within the sheet.

(Des Rev. W. Keble Martin (T **276/9**), Mary Grierson (others))

1967 (24 Apr). **British Wild Flowers.** *Chalk-surfaced paper.* W **179.** P 15 × 14.

717 **276** 4d. grey, lemon, myrtle-green, red, agate & slate-purple 20 20
  a. Block of 4. Nos. 717/20 .... 80 3·00
  aWi. Block of 4. Watermark inverted .... 9·00
  b. Grey double* £1500
  c. Red omitted £2250
  f. Slate-purple omitted £4000
  Wi. Watermark inverted .... 2·00
  p. Three phosphor bands 10 15
  pa. Block of 4. Nos. 717p/20p .... 50 2·75
  paWi. Block of 4. Watermark inverted .... 9·00
  pd. Agate omitted £2500
  pf. Slate-purple omitted £200
  pWi. Watermark inverted .... 2·00
718 **277** 4d. grey, lemon, myrtle-green, red, agate & violet 20 20
  b. Grey double* £1500
  Wi. Watermark inverted .... 2·00
  p. Three phosphor bands 10 15
  pd. Agate omitted £2500
  pe. Violet omitted £4000
  pWi. Watermark inverted .... 2·00
719 **278** 4d. grey, lemon, myrtle-green, red & agate . 20 20
  b. Grey double* £1500
  Wi. Watermark inverted .... 2·00
  p. Three phosphor bands 10 15
  pd. Agate omitted £2500
  pWi. Watermark inverted .... 2·00
720 **279** 4d. grey, lemon, myrtle-green, reddish pur-ple, agate & violet 20 20
  b. Grey double* £1500
  c. Reddish purple omitted £1000
  d. Value omitted† ....
  Wi. Watermark inverted .... 2·00
  p. Three phosphor bands 10 15
  pd. Agate omitted £2500
  pe. Violet omitted £4000
  pWi. Watermark inverted .... 2·00
721 **280** 9d. lavender-grey, green, reddish violet & orange-yellow 20 25
  Wi. Watermark inverted .... 1·25
  p. Three phosphor bands 15 25
722 **281** 1s. 9d. lavender-grey, green, greenish yellow & orange 25 35
  p. Three phosphor bands 20 30
    Set of 6 (Ordinary) .... 1·10 1·25
    Set of 6 (Phosphor) .... 75 1·00
    First Day Cover (Ordinary) .... 5·50
    First Day Cover (Phosphor) .... 7·00
    Presentation Pack (Ordinary) .... 5·25
    Presentation Pack (Phosphor) .... 5·25

*The double impression of the grey printing affects the Queen's head, value and inscription.

†No. 720d was caused by something obscuring the face value on R14/6 during the printing of one sheet.

Special First Day of Issue Postmark

	Ordinary	Phosphor
G.P.O. Philatelic Bureau, Edinburgh 1 (Type C)	10·00	12·00

PHOSPHOR BANDS. Issues from No. 723 are normally with phosphor bands only, except for the high values but most stamps have appeared with the phosphor bands omitted in error. Such varieties are listed under "Ey" numbers and are priced unused only. See also further notes after 1971–95 Decimal Machin issue.

280 Dog Violet

281 Primroses

PHOSPHORISED PAPER. Following the adoption of phosphor bands the Post Office started a series of experiments involving the addition of the phosphor to the paper coating before the stamps were printed. No. 743c was the first of these experiments to be issued for normal postal use. See also notes after 1971–96 Decimal Machin issue.

PVA GUM. Polyvinyl alcohol was introduced by Harrisons in place of gum arabic in 1968. As it is almost invisible a small amount of pale yellowish colouring was introduced to make it possible to check that the stamps had been gummed. Although this can be distinguished from gum arabic in unused stamps there is, of course, no means of detecting it in used examples. Where the two forms of gum exist on the same stamps, the PVA type are listed under "Ev" numbers, except in the case of the 1d. and 4d. (vermilion), both one centre band, which later appeared with gum arabic and these have "Eg" numbers. "Ev" and "Eg" numbers are priced unused only. All stamps printed from No. 763 onwards were issued with PVA gum only *except where otherwise stated.*

It should be further noted that gum arabic is shiny in appearance, and that, normally, PVA gum has a matt appearance. However, depending upon the qualities of the paper ingredients and the resultant absorption of the gum, occasionally, PVA gum has a shiny appearance. In such cases, especially in stamps from booklets, it is sometimes impossible to be absolutely sure which gum has been used except by testing the stamps chemically which destroys them. Therefore, whilst all gum arabic is shiny it does not follow that all shiny gum is gum arabic.

282   **282a**

I   II

Two types of the 2d.

I. Value spaced away from left side of stamp (cylinders 1 no dot and dot).

II. Value close to left side from new multipositive used for cylinders 5 no dot and dot onwards. The portrait appears in the centre, thus conforming to the other values.

Three types of the Machin head, known as Head A, B or C, are distinguished by specialists. These are illustrated in Vol. 3 of the *Great Britain Specialised Catalogue.*

(Des after plaster cast by Arnold Machin)

1967 (5 June)–**70**. *Chalk-surfaced paper. Two phosphor bands except where otherwise stated. No wmk. PVA gum except Nos. 725m, 728, 729, 731, 731Ea, 740, 742/Ea, 743/a and 744/Ea.*

723	**282**	½d. orange-brown (5.2.68)	10	20
		Ey. Phosphor omitted	30·00	
724		1d. lt olive (*shades*) (2 bands) (5.2.68)	10	10
		a. Imperf (coil strip)†	£1500	
		b. Part perf pane*		
		c. Imperf pane*	£4000	
		d. Uncoated paper (1970)**	70·00	
		Ey. Phosphor omitted	1·00	
		I. Booklet pane. No. 724 × 2 *se-tenant* with 730 × 2 (6.4.68)	3·00	
(724)	**282**	IEy. Booklet pane. Phosphor omitted	75·00	
		m. Booklet pane. No. 724 × 4 *se-tenant* with 734 × 2 (6.1.69)	3·50	
		mEy. Booklet pane. Phosphor omitted	£160	
		n. Booklet pane. No. 724 × 6, 734 × 3, 734Eb × 3 & 735 × 3 *se-tenant* (1.12.69) .	8·50	
		na. Booklet pane. Uncoated paper**	£900	
		nEy. Booklet pane. Phosphor omitted	£150	
725		1d. yellowish olive (1 centre band) (16.9.68)	30	35
		Eg. Gum arabic (27.8.69)	30	
		I. Booklet pane. No. 725 × 4 *se-tenant* with 732 × 2	4·00	
		IEy. Booklet pane. Phosphor omitted	30·00	
		m. Coil strip. No. 728 × 2 *se-tenant* with 729, 725Eg & 733Eg (27.8.69)	1·25	
726		2d. lake-brown (Type I) (2 bands) (5.2.68) ...	10	15
		Ey. Phosphor omitted	30·00	
727		2d. lake-brown (Type II) (2 bands) (1969) ...	15	20
		Ey. Phosphor omitted	1·00	
728		2d. lake-brown (Type II) (1 centre band) (27.8.69)	70	90
729		3d. violet (*shades*) (1 centre band) (8.8.67) ..	15	10
		a. Imperf (pair)	£700	
		Ey. Phosphor omitted	1·25	
		Ev. PVA gum (*shades*) (12.3.68)	15	
		Evy. Phosphor omitted	2·00	
730		3d. violet (2 bands) (6.4.68)	30	35
		a. Uncoated paper**	£2000	
731		4d. dp sepia (*shades*) (2 bands)	10	10
		Ey. Phosphor omitted	1·00	
		Ea. *Dp olive-brown*	10	15
		Eay. Phosphor omitted	2·00	
		b. Part perf pane*	£1750	
		Ev. PVA gum (*shades*) (22.1.68)	10	
		Evy. Phosphor omitted	2·00	
732		4d. dp olive-brown (*shades*) (1 centre band) (16.9.68)	10	10
		a. Part perf pane*	£1750	
		I. Booklet pane. Two stamps plus two printed labels	1·00	
		IEy. Booklet pane. Phosphor omitted	60·00	
733		4d. brt vermilion (1 centre band) (6.1.69) ...	10	10
		a. *Tête-bêche* (horiz pair)	£2500	
		b. Uncoated paper**	6·00	
		Ey. Phosphor omitted	1·25	
		Eg. Gum arabic (27.8.69)	10	
		Egy. Phosphor omitted	£1200	
		I. Booklet pane. Two stamps plus two printed labels (3.3.69)	1·00	
		IEy. Booklet pane. Phosphor omitted	70·00	
734		4d. brt vermilion (1 band at left) (6.1.69) ...	1·50	1·90
		a. Uncoated paper**	£180	
		Eb. One band at right (1.12.69)	1·75	2·50
		Eba. Ditto. Uncoated paper**	£180	
735		5d. royal blue (*shades*) (1.7.68)	10	10
		a. Imperf pane*	£1800	
		b. Part perf pane*	£1000	
		c. Imperf (pair)††	£200	
		d. Uncoated paper**	15·00	
		Ey. Phosphor omitted	2·00	
		Ee. *Dp blue*	10	15
		Eey. Phosphor omitted	3·00	
736		6d. brt reddish purple (*shades*) (5.2.68)	20	25
		Ey. Phosphor omitted	6·50	
		Ea. *Brt magenta*	3·00	50
		Eb. *Claret*	50	45
		Eby. Phosphor omitted	10·00	
737	**282a**	7d. brt emerald (1.7.68)	40	35
		Ey. Phosphor omitted	55·00	

738	**282**a	8d. brt vermilion (1.7.68)		20	45
		Ey. Phosphor omitted		£400	
739		8d. lt turquoise-blue (6.1.69)		50	60
		Ey. Phosphor omitted		60·00	
740		9d. myrtle-green (8.8.67)		40	25
		Ey. Phosphor omitted		20·00	
		Ev. PVA gum (29.11.68)		50	
		Evy. Phosphor omitted		25·00	
741	**282**	10d. drab (1.7.68)		50	50
		a. Uncoated paper**		23·00	
		Ey. Phosphor omitted		40·00	
742		1s. lt bluish violet (shades)		45	25
		Ey. Phosphor omitted		75·00	
		Ea. Pale bluish violet		1·25	30
		Ev. Ditto. PVA gum (26.4.68)		45	
		Evy. Phosphor omitted		3·50	
743		1s. 6d. greenish blue & deep blue (shades)			
		(8.8.67)		50	50
		a. Greenish blue omitted		80·00	
		Ey. Phosphor omitted		6·00	
		Ev. PVA gum (28.8.68)		60	
		Eva. Greenish blue omitted		80·00	
		Evy. Phosphor omitted		14·00	
		Evb. Prussian blue & indigo		2·25	75
		Evby. Phosphor omitted		11·00	
		c. Phosphorised paper (Prussian blue &			
		indigo) (10.12.69)		80	80
		ca. Prussian blue omitted		£400	
744		1s. 9d. dull orange & black (shades)		50	45
		Ey. Phosphor omitted		30·00	
		Ea. Brt orange & black		1·50	70
		Ev. PVA gum (brt orange & black) (16.11.70)		50	
		Set of 16 (one of each value & colour) ..		4·00	4·00
		Presentation Pack (one of each value)			
		(1968)		7·00	
		Presentation Pack (German) (1969)		45·00	

*BOOKLET ERRORS. See note after No. 556.

** Uncoated paper. This does not respond to the chalky test, and may be further distinguished from the normal chalk-surfaced paper by the fibres which clearly show on the surface, resulting in the printing impression being rougher, and by the screening dots which are not so evident. The 1d., 4d. and 5d. come from the £1 "Stamps for Cooks" Booklet (1970); the 3d. and 10d. from sheets (1969). The 20p. and 50p. high values (Nos. 830/1) exist with similar errors.

†No. 724a occurs in a vertical strip of four, top stamp perforated on three sides, bottom stamp imperf three sides and the two middle stamps completely imperf.

††No. 735c comes from the original state of cylinder 15 which is identifiable by the screening dots which extend through the gutters of the stamps and into the margins of the sheet. This must not be confused with imperforate stamps from cylinder 10, a large quantity of which was stolen from the printers early in 1970.

The 1d. with centre band and PVA gum (725) only came in the September 1968 10s. booklet (No. XP6). The 1d., 2d. and 4d. with centre band and gum arabic (725Eg, 728 and 733Eg respectively) only came in the coil strip (725m). The 3d. (No. 730) appeared in booklets on 6.4.68, from coils during Dec 68 and from sheets in Jan 1969. The 4d. with one side band at left (734) came from 10s. (band at left) and £1 (band at left or right) booklet se-tenant panes, and the 4d. with one side band at right (734Eb) came from the £1 booklet se-tenant panes only.

The 4d. (731) in shades of washed-out grey are colour changelings which we understand are caused by the concentrated solvents used in modern dry cleaning methods.

For decimal issue, see Nos. X841, etc.

First Day Covers

5.6.67	4d., 1s., 1s. 9d.	(731, 742, 744)	3·00
8.8.67	3d., 9d., 1s. 6d.	(729, 740, 743)	3·00
5.2.68	½d., 1d., 2d., 6d.	(723/4, 726, 736)	3·00
1.7.68	5d., 7d., 8d., 10d.	(735, 737/8, 741)	3·00

283 "Master Lambton" **284** "Mares and Foals in a Landscape"
(Sir Thomas Lawrence) (George Stubbs)

285 "Children Coming Out of School"
(L. S. Lowry)

(Des S. Rose)

1967 (10 July). **British Paintings.** Chalk-surfaced paper. Two phosphor bands. No wmk. P 14 × 15 (4d.) or 15 × 14 (others).

748	**283**	4d. rose-red, lemon, brown, black, new blue			
		& gold		10	10
		a. Gold (value & Queen's head) omitted ...		£200	
		b. New blue omitted		£3750	
		Ey. Phosphor omitted		7·00	
749	**284**	9d. Venetian red, ochre, grey-black, new			
		blue, greenish yellow & black		15	15
		a. Black (Queen's head & value) omitted ..		£400	
		ab. Black (Queen's head only) omitted		£750	
		b. Greenish yellow omitted		£1500	
		Ey. Phosphor omitted		£450	
750	**285**	1s. 6d. greenish yellow, grey, rose, new blue,			
		grey-black & gold		25	35
		a. Gold (Queen's head) omitted		£2750	
		b. New blue omitted		£180	
		c. Grey (clouds and shading) omitted ...		95·00	
		Ey. Phosphor omitted		£300	
		Set of 3		45	50
		First Day Cover			3·00
		Presentation Pack		6·00	

Special First Day of Issue Postmark

G.P.O. Philatelic Bureau, Edinburgh 1 (Type C)....... 7·00

A First Day of Issue handstamp was provided at Bishop Auckland, Co. Durham, for this issue.

286 Gypsy Moth IV

(Des M. and Sylvia Goaman)

1967 (24 July). **Sir Francis Chichester's World Voyage.** Chalk-surfaced paper. Three phosphor bands. No wmk. P 15 × 14.

751	**286**	1s. 9d. black, brown-red, lt emerald & blue		20	20
		First Day Cover			1·75

Special First Day of Issue Postmarks

G.P.O. Philatelic Bureau, Edinburgh 1 .... 7·00
Greenwich, London SE10 .... 7·00
Plymouth, Devon .... 7·00
The Philatelic Bureau and Greenwich postmarks are similar in design to that for Plymouth. A First Day of Issue handstamp was provided at Chichester, Sussex for this issue.

287 Radar Screen

288 *Penicillium notatum*

289 Vickers VC-10 Jet Engines   **290** Television Equipment

(Des C. Abbott (4d., 1s.), Negus-Sharland team (others))

1967 (19 Sept). **British Discovery and Invention.** *Chalk-surfaced paper. Three phosphor bands (4d.) or two phosphor bands (others). W 179 (sideways on 1s. 9d.). P 14 × 15 (1s. 9d.) or 15 × 14 (others).*

752	**287**	4d.	greenish yellow, black & vermilion	10	10
			Ey. Phosphor omitted	2·00	
753	**288**	1s.	blue-green, lt greenish blue, slate-purple & bluish violet	10	20
			Wi. Watermark inverted	12·00	
			Ey. Phosphor omitted	9·00	
754	**289**	1s.	6d. black, grey, royal blue, ochre & turquoise-blue	20	25
			Wi. Watermark inverted	33·00	
			Ey. Phosphor omitted	£500	
755	**290**	1s.	9d. black, grey-blue, pale olive-grey, violet & orange	20	30
			a. Grey-blue omitted	£500	
			Ey. Phosphor omitted	£500	
			Set of 4	50	75
			First Day Cover		3·00
			Presentation Pack	2·75	

Special First of Issue Postmark
G.P.O. Philatelic Bureau, Edinburgh (Type C)......... 4·00

WATERMARK. All issues from this date are on unwatermarked paper.

291 "The Adoration of the Shepherds" (School of Seville)

292 "Madonna and Child" (Murillo)

293 "The Adoration of the Shepherds" (Louis le Nain)

(Des S. Rose)

1967. Christmas. *Chalk-surfaced paper. One phosphor band (3d.) or two phosphor bands (others). P 15 × 14 (1s. 6d.) or 14 × 15 (others).*

756	**291**	3d.	olive-yellow, rose, blue, black & gold (27.11)	10	10
			a. Gold (value & Queen's head) omitted ...	75·00	
			b. Printed on the gummed side	£400	
			c. Rose omitted	£2500	
			Ey. Phosphor omitted	1·00	
757	**292**	4d.	brt purple, greenish yellow, new blue, grey-black & gold (18.10)	10	10
			a. Gold (value & Queen's head) omitted ...	60·00	
			b. Gold ("4D" only) omitted	£1500	
			c. Greenish yellow (Child, robe & Madonna's face) omitted	£6000	
			Ey. Phosphor omitted	£125	
758	**293**	1s.	6d. brt purple, bistre, lemon, black, orange-red, ultramarine & gold (27.11) ..	15	30
			a. Gold (value & Queen's head) omitted ...	£4000	
			ab. Gold (Queen's head only) omitted	£1500	
			b. Ultramarine omitted	£375	
			c. Lemon omitted £10000	
			Ey. Phosphor omitted	12·00	
			Set of 3	30	45
			First Day Covers (2)		3·50

Distinct shades exist of the 3d. and 4d. values but are not listable as there are intermediate shades. For the 4d., stamps from one machine show a darker background and give the appearance of the yellow colour being omitted, but this is not so and these should not be confused with the true missing yellow No. 757c.

No. 757b comes from stamps in the first vertical row of a sheet.

Special First Day of Issue Postmarks
G.P.O. Philatelic Bureau, Edinburgh 1 (4d.) (18 Oct.) (Type C) .... 3·00
G.P.O. Philatelic Bureau, Edinburgh 1 (3d., 1s. 6d.) (27 Nov.) (Type C) .... 3·00
Bethlehem, Llandeilo, Carms (4d.) (18 Oct.) (Type C) .. 4·50
Bethlehem, Llandeilo, Carms (3d., 1s. 6d.) (27 Nov.) (Type C) .... 5·00

Gift Pack 1967

1967 (27 Nov). *Comprises Nos. 715p/22p and 748/58.*
GP758c   Gift Pack . . . .   2·75

(Recess Bradbury, Wilkinson)

1967–68. *No wmk. White paper. P 11 × 12.*
759 **166**   2s. 6d. black-brown (1.7.68)   30   45
760 **167**   5s. red (10.4.68)   70   75
761 **168**   10s. brt ultramarine (10.4.68) . . . .   4·75   6·25
762 **169**   £1 black (4.12.67) . . . .   4·50   6·00
            Set of 4 . . . .   9·25   12·00

PVA GUM. All the following issues from this date have PVA gum *except where footnotes state otherwise.*

294 Tarr Steps, Exmoor

295 Aberfeldy Bridge

296 Menai Bridge

297 M4 Viaduct

(Des A. Restall (9d.), L. Rosoman (1s. 6d.), J. Matthews (others))

1968 (29 Apr).   **British Bridges.** *Chalk-surfaced paper. Two phosphor bands. P 15 × 14.*
763 **294**   4d. black, bluish violet, turquoise-blue &
            gold   10   10
        a. Printed on gummed side . . . .   25·00
        Ey. Phosphor omitted . . . .   5·00
764 **295**   9d. red-brown, myrtle-green, ultramarine,
            olive-brown, black & gold   10   15
        a. Gold (Queen's head) omitted £150
        b. Ultramarine omitted . . . .   †   £4250
        Ey. Phosphor omitted . . . .   15·00
765 **296**   1s. 6d. olive-brown, red-orange, brt green,
            turquoise-green & gold   15   25
        a. Gold (Queen's head) omitted £180
        b. Red-orange (rooftops) omitted £180
        Ey. Phosphor omitted . . . .   50·00
766 **297**   1s. 9d. olive-brown, greenish yellow, dull
            green, dp ultramarine & gold   20   30
        a. Gold (Queen's head) omitted £180
        Ey. Phosphor omitted . . . .   10·00
            Set of 4   50   70
            First Day Cover . . . .   3·00
            Presentation Pack . . . .   2·25
No 764b is only known on first day covers posted from Canterbury, Kent, or the Philatelic Bureau, Edinburgh.
Used examples of the 1s. 6d. and 1s. 9d. are known with both the gold and the phosphor omitted.

Special First Day of Issue Postmarks

G.P.O. Philatelic Bureau, Edinburgh 1 . . . .   6·00
Bridge, Canterbury, Kent . . . .   7·00
Aberfeldy, Perthshire (Type A) (9d. value only) . . . .   10·00
Menai Bridge, Anglesey (Type A) (1s. 6d. value only)   .   10·00
The Bridge, Canterbury, postmark is similar in design to that for the Philatelic Bureau.

298 "TUC" and Trades Unionists

299 Mrs. Emmeline Pankhurst (statue)

300 Sopwith Camel and English Electric Lightning Fighters

301 Captain Cook's *Endeavour* and Signature

(Des D. Gentleman (4d.), C. Abbott (others))

1968 (29 May).   **British Anniversaries.** *Events described on stamps. Chalk-surfaced paper. Two phosphor bands. P 15 × 14.*
767 **298**   4d. emerald, olive, blue & black   10   10
        Ey. Phosphor omitted . . . .   12·00
768 **299**   9d. reddish violet, bluish grey & black   10   15
        Ey. Phosphor omitted . . . .   7·00
769 **300**   1s. olive-brown, blue, red, slate-blue & black   15   25
        Ey. Phosphor omitted . . . .   10·00
770 **301**   1s. 9d. yellow-ochre & blackish brown   35   40
        Ey. Phosphor omitted £150
            Set of 4   60   80
            First Day Cover . . . .   5·50
            Presentation Pack . . . .   2·50

WHEN YOU BUY AN ALBUM LOOK
FOR THE NAME 'STANLEY GIBBONS'
It means Quality combined with Value for Money.

Special First Day of Issue Postmarks

G.P.O. Philatelic Bureau, Edinburgh 1 (Type C) .... 10·00
Manchester (4d. value only) .... 3·50
Aldeburgh, Suffolk (9d. value only) .... 4·00
Hendon, London NW4 (1s. value only) .... 4·00
Whitby, Yorkshire (1s. 9d. value only) .... 4·00
The Philatelic Bureau postmark was used on sets of four, but the other postmarks were only available on single stamps.

302 "Queen Elizabeth I" (unknown artist)   **303** "Pinkie" (Lawrence)

304 "Ruins of St. Mary Le Port" (Piper)   **305** "The Hay Wain" (Constable)

(Des S. Rose)

1968 (12 Aug). **British Paintings.** *Queen's head embossed. Chalk-surfaced paper. Two phosphor bands.* P 15 × 14 (1s. 9d.) or 14 × 15 (*others*).

771	**302**	4d. black, vermilion, greenish yellow, grey & gold	10	10
		a. Gold (value & Queen's head) omitted ...	£150	
		b. Vermilion omitted*	£350	
		Ec. Embossing omitted	80·00	
		Ey. Phosphor omitted	1·50	
		Eya. Gold (value & Queen's head) & phosphor omitted	£180	

772	**303**	1s. mauve, new blue, greenish yellow, black, magenta & gold	10	20
		a. Gold (value & Queen's head) omitted ...	£3000	
		Eb. Gold (value & Queen's head), embossing & phosphor omitted	£250	
		Ec. Embossing omitted		
		Ey. Phosphor omitted	7·00	
773	**304**	1s. 6d. slate, orange, black, mauve, greenish yellow, ultramarine & gold	20	25
		a. Gold (value & Queen's head) omitted ...	£100	
		Eb. Embossing omitted		
		Ey. Phosphor omitted	10·00	
774	**305**	1s. 9d. greenish yellow, black, new blue, red & gold	25	40
		a. Gold (value & Queen's head) & embossing omitted	£500	
		b. Red omitted £10000		
		Ec. Embossing omitted		
		Ey. Phosphor omitted	20·00	
		Set of 4	50	85
		First Day Cover		3·00
		Presentation Pack	2·50	
		Presentation Pack (German)	7·00	

No. 774a is only known with the phosphor also omitted.
*The effect of this is to leave the face and hands white and there is more yellow and olive in the costume.
The 4d. also exists with the value only omitted resulting from a colour shift.

Special First Day of Issue Postmark
G.P.O. Philatelic Bureau, Edinburgh 1 (Type C) .... 7·00

Gift Pack 1968

1968 (16 Sept). *Comprises Nos. 763/74.*
GP774c   Gift Pack .... 8·00
GP774d   Gift Pack (German) .... 22·00

Collectors Pack 1968

1968 (16 Sept). *Comprises Nos. 752/8 and 763/74.*
CP774e   Collectors Pack .... 9·00

306 Boy and Girl with Rocking Horse

307 Girl with Doll's House   **308** Boy with Train Set

(Des Rosalind Dease. Head printed in gold and then embossed)

1968 (25 Nov). **Christmas.** *Chalk-surfaced paper. One centre phosphor band (4d.) or two phosphor bands (others). P 15 × 14 (4d.) or 14 × 15 (others).*

775	**306**	4d. black, orange, vermilion, ultramarine, bistre & gold	10	10
		a. Gold omitted	£3500	
		b. Vermilion omitted*	£300	
		c. Ultramarine omitted	£180	
		Ed. Embossing omitted	6·00	
		Ey. Phosphor omitted	5·00	
776	**307**	9d. yellow-olive, black, brown, yellow, magenta, orange, turquoise-green & gold ..	15	15
		a. Yellow omitted	65·00	
		b. Turquoise-green (dress) omitted	£8500	
		Ec. Embossing omitted	6·00	
		Ey. Phosphor omitted	10·00	
		Eya. Embossing & phosphor omitted	10·00	
777	**308**	1s. 6d. ultramarine, yellow-orange, brt purple, blue-green, black & gold	15	30
		Ea. Embossing omitted		
		Ey. Phosphor omitted	15·00	
		Set of 3	35	45
		First Day Cover		2·50
		Presentation Pack	3·00	
		Presentation Pack (German)	7·00	

*The effect of the missing vermilion is shown on the rocking horse, saddle and faces which appear orange instead of red.

A single used example of the 4d. exists with the bistre omitted.

No. 775c is only known with phosphor also omitted.

Two machines were used for printing for the 4d. value:

Stamps from cylinders 1A–1B–2C–1D–1E in combination with 1F, 2F or 3F (gold) were printed entirely on the Rembrandt sheet-fed machine. They invariably have the Queen's head level with the top of the boy's head and the sheets are perforated through the left side margin.

Stamps from cylinders 2A–2B–3C–2D–2E in combination with 1F, 2F, 3F or 4F (gold) were printed on the reel-fed Thrissell machine in five colours (its maximum colour capacity) and subsequently sheet-fed on the Rembrandt machine for the Queen's head and the embossing. The position of the Queen's head is generally lower than on the stamps printed at one operation but it varies in different parts of the sheet and is not, therefore, a sure indication for identifying single stamps. Another small difference is that the boy's grey pullover is noticeably "moth-eaten" in the Thrissell printings and is normal on the Rembrandt. The Thrissell printings are perforated through the top margin.

Special First Day of Issue Postmarks
G.P.O. Philatelic Bureau, Edinburgh 1 (Type C) .... 4·00
Bethlehem, Llandeilo, Carms (Type C) .... 7·00

309 *Queen Elizabeth 2*

310 Elizabethan Galleon

311 East Indiaman

312 *Cutty Sark*

313 *Great Britain*

314 *Mauretania I*

(Des D. Gentleman)

1969 (15 Jan). **British Ships.** *Chalk-surfaced paper. Two vertical phosphor bands at right (1s.), one horizontal phosphor band (5d.) or two phosphor bands (9d.). P 15 × 14.*

778	**309**	5d. black, grey, red & turquoise	10	15
		a. Black (Queen's head, value, hull and inscr) omitted	£750	
		b. Grey (decks, etc.) omitted	90·00	
		c. Red (inscription) omitted	50·00	
		Ey. Phosphor omitted	5·00	
		Eya. Red & phosphor omitted	90·00	
779	**310**	9d. red, blue, ochre, brown, black & grey ..	10	25
		a. Strip of 3. Nos. 779/81	1·50	3·00
		ab. Red & blue omitted	£1600	
		ac. Blue omitted	£1600	
		Ey. Phosphor omitted	12·00	
		Eya. Strip of 3. Nos. 779/81. Phosphor omitted	40·00	
780	**311**	9d. ochre, brown, black & grey	10	25
		Ey. Phosphor omitted	12·00	
781	**312**	9d. ochre, brown, black & grey	10	25
		Ey. Phosphor omitted	12·00	
782	**313**	1s. brown, black, grey, green & greenish yellow	40	35
		a. Pair. Nos. 782/3	1·25	2·50
		ab. Greenish yellow omitted	£2500	
		Ey. Phosphor omitted	28·00	
		Eya. Pair. Nos. 782/3. Phosphor omitted	65·00	
783	**314**	1s. red, black, brown, carmine & grey	40	35
		a. Carmine (hull overlay) omitted £12500		
		b. Red (funnels) omitted £10000		
		c. Carmine and red omitted £11000		
		Ey. Phosphor omitted	30·00	
		Set of 6	2·50	1·40
		First Day Cover		7·00
		Presentation Pack	4·00	
		Presentation Pack (German)	22·00	

The 9d. and 1s. values were arranged in horizontal strips of three and pairs respectively throughout the sheet.

No. 779ab is known only with the phosphor also omitted.

Special First Day of Issue Postmark
G.P.O. Philatelic Bureau, Edinburgh 1 (Type C) .... 15·00

315 Concorde in Flight   316 Plan and Elevation Views

317 Concorde's Nose and Tail

(Des M. and Sylvia Goaman (4d.), D. Gentleman (9d., 1s. 6d.))

1969 (3 Mar). **First Flight of Concorde.** *Chalk-surfaced paper. Two phosphor bands.* P 15 × 14.

784	315	4d. yellow-orange, violet, greenish blue, blue-green & pale green		25	25
		a. Violet (value etc.) omitted		£225	
		b. Yellow-orange omitted		£225	
		Ey. Phosphor omitted		1·00	
		Eya. Yellow-orange & phosphor omitted		£225	
785	316	9d. ultramarine, emerald, red & grey-blue		55	80
		a. Face value and inscr omitted		†	£1500
		Ey. Phosphor omitted		£100	
786	317	1s. 6d. deep blue, silver-grey & lt blue		85	1·10
		a. Silver-grey omitted		£275	
		Ey. Phosphor omitted		9·00	
		Set of 3		1·50	2·00
		First Day Cover			6·00
		Presentation Pack		9·50	
		Presentation Pack (German)		20·00	

No. 785a is caused by a colour shift of the grey-blue. On the only known example the top of the Queen's head appears across the perforations at foot.

No. 786a affects the Queen's head which appears in the light blue colour.

Special First Day of Issue Postmarks
G.P.O. Philatelic Bureau, Edinburgh (Type C) .... 4·00
Filton, Bristol (Type C) .... 12·00

318 Queen Elizabeth II. (See also Type *357*)

(Des after plaster cast by Arnold Machin. Recess Bradbury, Wilkinson)

1969 (5 Mar). P 12.

787	318	2s. 6d. brown		35	30
788		5s. crimson-lake		1·75	60
789		10s. dp ultramarine		6·00	7·00
790		£1 bluish black		3·25	1·50
		Set of 4		10·00	8·50
		First Day Cover			9·50
		Presentation Pack		16·00	
		Presentation Pack (German)		42·00	

Special First Day of Issue Postmarks
G.P.O. Philatelic Bureau (Type C) .... 12·00
Windsor, Berks (Type C) .... 18·00
For decimal issue, see Nos. 829/31b and notes after No. 831b.

319 Page from *Daily Mail*, and   320 Europa and CEPT Emblems
Vickers FB-27 Vimy Aircraft

321 ILO Emblem   322 Flags of NATO Countries

323 Vickers FB-27 Vimy Aircraft and Globe
showing Flight

(Des P. Sharland (5d., 1s., 1s. 6d.), M. and Sylvia Goaman (9d., 1s. 9d.))

1969 (2 Apr). **Anniversaries.** *Events described on stamps. Chalk-surfaced paper. Two phosphor bands.* P 15 × 14.

791	319	5d. black, pale sage-green, chestnut & new blue		10	10
		Ey. Phosphor omitted			
792	320	9d. pale turquoise, dp blue, lt emerald-green & black		15	20
		a. Uncoated paper*		£1500	
		Ey. Phosphor omitted		18·00	
793	321	1s. brt purple, dp blue & lilac		15	20
		Ey. Phosphor omitted		10·00	
794	322	1s. 6d. red, royal blue, yellow-green, black, lemon & new blue		15	25
		e. Black omitted		60·00	
		f. Yellow-green (from flags) omitted		50·00	
		g. Lemon (from flags) omitted		†	£3500
		Ey. Phosphor omitted		9·00	
		Eya. Yellow-green & phosphor omitted		55·00	
795	323	1s. 9d. yellow-olive, greenish yellow & pale turquoise-green		20	35
		a. Uncoated paper*		£200	
		Ey. Phosphor omitted		6·00	
		Set of 5		65	95
		First Day Cover			5·00
		Presentation Pack		3·50	
		Presentation Pack (German)		42·00	

*Uncoated paper. The second note after No. 744 also applies here.
No. 794g is only known used on first day cover from Liverpool.

Special First Day of Issue Postmark
G.P.O. Philatelic Bureau, Edinburgh (Type C) .... 6·50

324 Durham Cathedral

325 York Minster

330 The King's Gate,
Caernarvon Castle

331 The Eagle Tower,
Caernarvon Castle

326 St. Giles' Cathedral, Edinburgh

327 Canterbury Cathedral

328 St. Paul's Cathedral

329 Liverpool Metropolitan Cathedral

332 Queen Eleanor's Gate,
Caernarvon Castle

333 Celtic Cross,
Margam Abbey

(Des P. Gauld)

1969 (28 May).   **British Architecture. Cathedrals.** *Chalk-surfaced paper. Two phosphor bands. P* 15 × 14.

796	**324**	5d. grey-black, orange, pale bluish violet & black	10	20
		a. Block of 4. Nos. 796/9	75	2·50
		ab. Block of 4. Uncoated paper†		
		b. Pale bluish violet omitted	£3500	
797	**325**	5d. grey-black, pale bluish violet, new blue & black	10	20
		b. Pale bluish violet omitted	£3500	
798	**326**	5d. grey-black, purple, green & black	10	20
		c. Green omitted*	50·00	
799	**327**	5d. grey-black, green, new blue & black	10	20
800	**328**	9d. grey-black, ochre, pale drab, violet & black	15	25
		a. Black (value) omitted	£100	
		Ey. Phosphor omitted	45·00	
		Eya. Black and phosphor omitted	£150	
801	**329**	1s. 6d. grey-black, pale turquoise, pale reddish violet, pale yellow-olive & black	15	25
		a. Black (value) omitted	£1800	
		b. Black (value) double		
		Ey. Phosphor omitted	20·00	
		Set of 6	95	1·10
		First Day Cover		5·00
		Presentation Pack	3·25	
		Presentation Pack (German)	21·00	

*The missing green on the roof top is known on R.2/5, R.8/5 and R.10/5 but all are from different sheets and it only occured in part of the printing, being "probably caused by a batter on the impression cylinder". Examples are also known with the green partly omitted.

†Uncoated paper. The second note after No. 744 also applies here. The 5d. values were issued together *se-tenant* in blocks of four throughout the sheet.

Special First Day of Issue Postmark
G.P.O. Philatelic Bureau, Edinburgh (Type C) .... 6·00

334 H.R.H. The Prince of Wales
(after photo by G. Argent)

(Des D. Gentleman)

1969 (1 July).   **Investiture of H.R.H. The Prince of Wales.** *Chalk-surfaced paper. Two phosphor bands. P* 14 × 15.

802	**330**	5d. dp olive-grey, lt olive-grey, dp grey, lt grey, red, pale turquoise-green, black & silver	10	15
		a. Strip of 3. Nos. 802/4	30	1·50
		b. Black (value & inscr) omitted	£225	
		c. Red omitted*	£375	
		d. Dp grey omitted**	£160	
		e. Pale turquoise-green omitted	£375	
		Ey. Phosphor omitted	5·00	
		Eya. Strip of 3. Nos. 802/4. Phosphor omitted	15·00	
803	**331**	5d. dp olive-grey, lt olive-grey, dp grey, lt grey, red, pale turquoise-green, black & silver	10	15
		b. Black (value and inscr) omitted	£225	
		c. Red omitted*	£375	
		d. Dp grey omitted**	£160	
		e. Pale turquoise-green omitted	£375	
		f. Light grey (marks on walls, window frames, etc) omitted	† £7500	
		Ey. Phosphor omitted	5·00	

804 **332** 5d. dp olive-grey, lt olive-grey, dp grey, lt
grey, red, pale turquoise-green, black &
silver 10   15
     b. Black (value & inscr) omitted £225
     c. Red omitted* £375
     d. Dp grey omitted** £160
     e. Pale turquoise-green omitted £375
     Ey. Phosphor omitted . . . . 5·00
805 **333** 9d. dp grey, lt grey, black & gold 15   20
     Ey. Phosphor omitted . . . . 22·00
806 **334** 1s. blackish yellow-olive & gold 15   20
     Ey. Phosphor omitted . . . . 15·00
     Set of 5 50   60
     First Day Cover . . . .   2·50
     Presentation Pack† . . . . 2·50
     Presentation Pack (German) . . . . 20·00

The 5d. values were issued together *se-tenant* in strips of three
throughout the sheet.

*The 5d. value is also known with the red misplaced downwards and
where this occurs the red printing does not take very well on the silver
background and in some cases is so faint it could be mistaken for a
missing red. However, the red can be seen under a magnifying glass
and caution should therefore be exercised when purchasing copies of
Nos. 802/4c.

**The deep grey affects the dark portions of the windows and doors.

†In addition to the generally issued Presentation Pack a further pack
in different colours and with all texts printed in both English and Welsh
was made available exclusively through Education Authorities for free
distribution to all schoolchildren in Wales and Monmouthshire (*Price*
£6).

No. 803f is only known commercially used on cover.

Special First Day of Issue Postmarks

G.P.O. Philatelic Bureau, Edinburgh 1 (Type C) . . . . 5·00
Day of Investiture, Caernarvon . . . . 5·00

335 Mahatma Gandhi

(Des B. Mullick)

1969 (13 Aug). **Gandhi Centenary Year.** *Chalk-surfaced paper. Two
phosphor bands.* P 15 × 14.
807 **335** 1s. 6d. black, green, red-orange & grey 20   20
     a. Printed on the gummed side £350
     Ey. Phosphor omitted . . . . 4·00
     First Day Cover . . . .   2·00

Special First Day of Issue Postmark
G.P.O. Philatelic Bureau, Edinburgh (Type C) . . . . 2·50

Collectors Pack 1969

1969 (15 Sept). *Comprises Nos. 775/86 and 791/807.*
CP807*b*   Collectors Pack . . . . 20·00

336 National Giro "G" Symbol

337 Telecommunications—
International Subscriber Dialling

338 Telecommunications—
Pulse Code Modulation

339 Postal Mechanisation—
Automatic Sorting

(Des D. Gentleman. Litho De La Rue)

1969 (1 Oct). **Post Office Technology Commemoration.** *Chalk-
surfaced paper. Two phosphor bands.* P 13½ × 14.
808 **336** 5d. new blue, greenish blue, lavender &
black 10   10
     Ey. Phosphor omitted . . . . 5·00
809 **337** 9d. emerald, violet-red & black 15   20
810 **338** 1s. emerald, lavender & black 15   20
     Ey. Phosphor omitted £300
811 **339** 1s. 6d. brt purple, lt blue, grey-blue & black 15   35
     Set of 4 50   75
     First Day Cover . . . .   2·50
     Presentation Pack . . . . 2·50

Special First Day of Issue Postmark
G.P.O. Philatelic Bureau, Edinburgh (Type C) . . . . 3·00

340 Herald Angel

341 The Three Shepherds

342 The Three Kings

(Des F. Wegner. Queen's head (and stars 4d., 5d. and scroll-work
1s. 6d.) printed in gold and then embossed)

1969 (26 Nov). **Christmas.** *Chalk-surfaced paper. Two phosphor bands
(5d., 1s. 6d.) or one centre band (4d.).* P 15 × 14.
812 **340** 4d. vermilion, new blue, orange, brt purple, lt
green, bluish violet, blackish brown &
gold 10   10
     a. Gold (Queen's head etc.) omitted £3500
     Eb. Centre band 3½ mm 30   20

813 **341** 5d. magenta, lt blue, royal blue, olive-brown,
    green, greenish yellow, red & gold   15   15
    a. Lt blue (sheep, etc.) omitted . . . . 60·00
    b. Red omitted* £600
    c. Gold (Queen's head) omitted £450
    d. Green omitted £200
    e. Olive-brown, red & gold omitted £8000
    Ef. Embossing omitted . . . . 22·00
    Ey. Phosphor omitted . . . . 5·00
814 **342** 1s. 6d. greenish yellow, brt purple, bluish
    violet, dp slate, orange, green, new blue
    & gold   20   30
    a. Gold (Queen's head etc.) omitted . . . . . . 90·00
    b. Dp slate (value) omitted £250
    c. Greenish yellow omitted £250
    e. New blue omitted . . . . 60·00
    Ef. Embossing omitted . . . . 10·00
    Ey. Phosphor omitted . . . . 6·00
    Eya. Embossing and phosphor omitted . . . . . . 10·00
    Set of 3   40   50
    First Day Cover . . . .   1·75
    Presentation Pack . . . . 2·50

*The effect of the missing red is shown on the hat, leggings and purse which appear as dull orange.

No. 812 has one centre band 8 mm. wide but this was of no practical use in the automatic facing machines and after about three-quarters of the stamps had been printed the remainder were printed with a 3½mm. band (No. 812Eb).

No. 813e was caused by a paper fold and also shows the phosphor omitted.

Used copies of the 5d. have been seen with the olive-brown or greenish yellow (tunic at left) omitted.

Special First Day of Issue Postmarks

P.O. Philatelic Bureau, Edinburgh (Type C) . . . . 3·00
Bethlehem, Llandeilo, Carms (Type C) . . . . 3·00

343 Fife Harling

344 Cotswold Limestone

345 Welsh Stucco

346 Ulster Thatch

(Des D. Gentleman (5d., 9d.), Sheila Robinson (1s., 1s. 6d.))

1970 (11 Feb). **British Rural Architecture.** *Chalk-surfaced paper. Two phosphor bands.* P 15 × 14.

815 **343** 5d. grey, grey-black, black, lemon, greenish
    blue, orange-brown, ultramarine & green   10   10
    a. Lemon omitted . . . . 80·00
    b. Grey (Queen's head & cottage shading)
    omitted £5000
    c. Greenish blue (door) omitted . . . .   † £3500
    Ey. Phosphor omitted . . . . 2·00

816 **344** 9d. orange-brown, olive-yellow, brt green,
    black, grey-black & grey   10   20
    Ey. Phosphor omitted . . . . 10·00
817 **345** 1s. dp blue, reddish lilac, drab & new blue .   15   20
    a. New blue omitted . . . . 80·00
    Ey. Phosphor omitted . . . . 15·00
818 **346** 1s. 6d. greenish yellow, black, turquoise-
    blue & lilac   20   30
    a. Turquoise-blue omitted £5000
    Ey. Phosphor omitted . . . . 5·00
    Set of 4   50   70
    First Day Cover . . . .   2·25
    Presentation Pack . . . . 3·25

Used examples of the 5d. exist, one of which is on piece, with the greenish blue colour omitted.

Special First Day of Issue Postmark

British Philatelic Bureau, Edinburgh (Type C) . . . . 3·00

347 Signing the Declaration of Arbroath

348 Florence Nightingale attending Patients

349 Signing of International Co-operative Alliance

350 Pilgrims and *Mayflower*

351 Sir William Herschel, Francis Baily, Sir John Herschel and Telescope

(Des F. Wegner (5d., 9d., and 1s. 6d.), Marjorie Saynor (1s., 1s. 9d.). Queen's head printed in gold and then embossed)

1970 (1 Apr). **Anniversaries.** *Events described on stamps. Chalk-surfaced paper. Two phosphor bands.* P 15 × 14.

819 **347** 5d. black, yellow-olive, blue, emerald, green-
    ish yellow, rose-red, gold & orange-red .   10   10
    a. Gold (Queen's head) omitted £700
    b. Emerald omitted £180
    Ey. Phosphor omitted £300
820 **348** 9d. ochre, dp blue, carmine, black, blue-
    green, yellow-olive, gold & blue   15   15
    a. Ochre omitted £180
    Eb. Embossing omitted . . . . 15·00
    Ey. Phosphor omitted . . . . 5·00
821 **349** 1s. green, greenish yellow, brown, black,
    cerise, gold & lt blue   20   25
    a. Gold (Queen's head) omitted . . . . 50·00
    Eb. Green & embossing omitted . . . . 80·00
    c. Green omitted . . . . 80·00
    d. Brown omitted £125
    Ee. Embossing omitted . . . . 12·00

(821)	Ey. Phosphor omitted	5·00		
	Eya. Brown & phosphor omitted	£125		
	Eyb. Embossing & phosphor omitted	22·00		
822 **350**	1s. 6d. greenish yellow, carmine, dp yellow-			
	olive, emerald, black, blue, gold & sage-			
	green	20	30	
	a. Gold (Queen's head) omitted	£130		
	b. Emerald omitted	65·00		
	Ec. Embossing omitted	6·00		
	Ey. Phosphor omitted	5·00		
823 **351**	1s. 9d. black, slate, lemon, gold & brt purple	25	30	
	a. Lemon (trousers and document) omitted	£7500		
	Eb. Embossing omitted	75·00		
	Ey. Phosphor omitted	5·00		
	Set of 5	80	1·00	
	First Day Cover		3·00	
	Presentation Pack	3·00		

No. 823a is known mint, or used on first day cover postmarked London WC.

Special First Day of Issue Postmark
British Philatelic Bureau, Edinburgh (Type C) .... 3·50
First Day of Issue handstamps were provided at Arbroath, Angus, Billericay, Essex; Boston, Lincs and Rochdale, Lancs for this issue.

352 "Mr. Pickwick and Sam"   **353** "Mr. and Mrs. Micawber"
(Pickwick Papers)   *(David Copperfield)*

354 "David   **355** "Oliver asking for   **356** "Grasmere" (from
Copperfield and Betsy   more" (*Oliver Twist*)   engraving by
Trotwood" (*David   J. Farrington, R.A.)
Copperfield*)

T **352/5** were issued together *se-tenant* in blocks of four throughout the sheet.

(Des Rosalind Dease. Queen's head printed in gold and then embossed)

1970 (3 June). **Literary Anniversaries. Death Centenary of Charles Dickens** (novelist) (5d. × 4) **and Birth Bicentenary of William Wordsworth** (poet) (1s. 6d.). *Chalk-surfaced paper. Two phosphor bands.* P 14 × 15.

824 **352**	5d. black, orange, silver, gold & magenta ...	10	15	
	a. Block of 4. Nos. 824/7	75	2·00	
	ab. Imperf (block of four)	£750		
	ac. Silver (inscr) omitted			

825 **353**	5d. black, magenta, silver, gold & orange ...	10	15
826 **354**	5d. black, lt greenish blue, silver, gold &		
	yellow-bistre	10	15
	b. Yellow-bistre (value) omitted	£1600	
827 **355**	5d. black, yellow-bistre, silver, gold & lt		
	greenish blue	10	15
	b. Yellow-bistre (background) omitted	£3500	
	c. Lt greenish blue (value) omitted*	£400	
	d. Lt greenish blue and silver (inscr at foot)		
	omitted	£7500	
828 **356**	1s. 6d. yellow-olive, black, silver, gold &		
	bright blue	20	35
	a. Gold (Queen's head) omitted	£2000	
	b. Silver ("Grasmere") omitted	£110	
	c. Bright blue (face value) omitted	£7500	
	Ed. Embossing omitted	6·00	
	Ey. Phosphor omitted	5·00	
	Eya. Embossing & phosphor omitted	22·00	
	Set of 5	85	85
	First Day Cover		3·75
	Presentation Pack	3·00	

*No. 827c (unlike No. 826b) comes from a sheet on which the colour was only partially omitted so that, although No. 827 was completely without the light greenish blue colour, it was still partially present on No. 826.

Essays exist of Nos. 824/7 showing the Queen's head in silver and with different inscriptions.

Special First Day of Issue Postmarks
British Philatelic Bureau, Edinburgh (Type C) .... 5·00
Cockermouth, Cumberland (Type C) (No. 828 only) .. 7·00
Rochester, Kent (Type C) (Nos. 824/7) .... 6·00
A First Day of Issue handstamp was provided at Broadstairs, Kent, for this issue.

356a   **357** (Value redrawn)

(Des after plaster cast by Arnold Machin. Recess B.W.)

1970 (17 June)–**72**. *Decimal Currency. Chalk-surfaced paper or phosphorised paper* (10p.). P 12.

829 **356a**	10p. cerise	50	75
830	20p. olive-green	60	25
	Ea. Thinner uncoated paper*		
831	50p. dp ultramarine	1·25	40
	Ea. Thinner uncoated paper*	45·00	
831b **357**	£1 bluish black (6.12.72)	3·50	80
	Set of 4	5·25	2·00
	First Day Cover (829/31)		2·75
	First Day Cover (831b)		3·00
	Presentation Pack No. 18 (829/31)	9·00	
	Presentation Pack No. 38 (790 (or 831b),		
	830/1)	10·00	

*These are not as apparent as uncoated photogravure issues where there is normally a higher degree of chalk-surfacing. The 20p. is known only as a block of four with Plate No. 5. The 50p. comes from Plate No. 9.

The 10p. on phosphorised paper continued the experiments which started with the Machin 1s. 6d. When the experiment had ended a quantity of the 50p. value was printed on the phosphorised paper to use up the stock. These stamps were issued on 1 February 1973, but they cannot be distinguished from No. 831 by the naked eye. (*Price £2*).

A £1 was also issued in 1970, but it is difficult to distinguish it from the earlier No. 790. In common with the other 1970 values it was issued in sheets of 100.

A whiter paper was introduced in 1973. The £1 appeared on 27 Sept. 1973, the 20p. on 30 Nov. 1973 and the 50p. on 20 Feb. 1974.

Imperforate examples of No. 831*b* are believed to be printer's waste.

361 1d. Black (1840)	**362** 1s. Green (1847)

Special First Day of Issue Postmarks
British Philatelic Bureau, Edinburgh (Type C) (Nos. 829/
31) . . . . 6·00
Windsor, Berks (Type C) (Nos. 829/31) . . . . 12·00
Philatelic Bureau, Edinburgh (Type E) (No. 831*b*) . . . . . . 6·00
Windsor, Berks (Type E) (No 831*b*) . . . . 9·00

363 4d. Carmine (1855)

358 Runners	**359** Swimmers

360 Cyclists

(Des A. Restall. Litho D.L.R.)

1970 (15 July).   **Ninth British Commonwealth Games.** *Chalk-surfaced paper. Two phosphor bands.* P 13½ × 14.

832	**358**	5d.	pink, emerald, greenish yellow & dp yellow-green	10	10
		a.	Greenish yellow omitted	£6000	
		Ey.	Phosphor omitted	£200	
833	**359**	1s.	6d. lt greenish blue, lilac, bistre-brown & Prussian blue	25	35
		Ey.	Phosphor omitted	60·00	
834	**360**	1s.	9d. yellow-orange, lilac, salmon & dp red-brown	30	35
			Set of 3	60	70
			First Day Cover		1·50
			Presentation Pack	3·00	

Special First Day of Issue Postmark
British Philatelic Bureau, Edinburgh (Type C) . . . . 8·00

Collectors Pack 1970

1970 (14 Sept). *Comprises Nos. 808/28 and 832/4.*
CP834*a*   Collectors Pack . . . . 20·00

(Des D. Gentleman)

1970 (18 Sept).   **"Philympia 70" Stamp Exhibition.** *Chalk-surfaced paper. Two phosphor bands.* P 14 × 14½.

835	**361**	5d.	grey-black, brownish bistre, black & dull purple	10	10
		a.	Grey-black (Queen's head) omitted	£10000	
		Ey.	Phosphor omitted	5·00	
836	**362**	9d.	lt drab, bluish green, stone, black & dull purple	20	30
		Ey.	Phosphor omitted	11·00	
837	**363**	1s.	6d. carmine, lt drab, black & dull purple	20	45
		Ey.	Phosphor omitted	4·00	
			Set of 3	45	80
			First Day Cover		2·00
			Presentation Pack	2·75	

Special First Day of Issue Postmark
British Post Office Philatelic Bureau, Edinburgh
(Type D) . . . . 3·50

364 Shepherds and Apparition of the Angel	**365** Mary, Joseph, and Christ in the Manger

366 The Wise Men bearing gifts

(Des Sally Stiff after De Lisle Psalter. Queen's head printed in gold and
then embossed)

1970 (25 Nov). **Christmas.** *Chalk-surfaced paper. One centre phosphor
band (4d.) or two phosphor bands (others). P* 14 × 15.

838	**364**	4d. brown-red, turquoise-green, pale chest-		
		nut, brown, grey-black, gold & vermilion	10	10
		Ea. Embossing omitted	50·00	
		Ey. Phosphor omitted	60·00	
839	**365**	5d. emerald, gold, blue, brown-red, ochre,		
		grey-black & violet	10	15
		a. Gold (Queen's head) omitted	†	£3500
		b. Emerald omitted	60·00	
		c. Imperf (pair)	£275	
		Ed. Embossing omitted	15·00	
		Ey. Phosphor omitted	5·00	
840	**366**	1s. 6d. gold, grey-black, pale turquoise-		
		green, salmon, ultramarine, ochre &		
		yellow-green	20	30
		a. Salmon omitted	80·00	
		b. Ochre omitted	50·00	
		Ec. Embossing omitted	35·00	
		Ey. Phosphor omitted	5·00	
		Eya. Embossing and phosphor omitted		
		Set of 3	35	50
		First Day Cover		2·25
		Presentation Pack	2·75	

Special First Day of Issue Postmarks

First Day of Issue 25 Nov 70

Bethlehem
Llandeilo
Carms

British Post Office Philatelic Bureau, Edinburgh
(Type D) .... 3·00
Bethlehem, Llandeilo, Carms .... 4·50

(New Currency. 100 new pence = £1)

"X" NUMBERS. The following definitive series has been allocated "X" prefixes to the catalogue numbers to avoid re-numbering all subsequent issues.

NO VALUE INDICATED. Stamps as Types 367/a inscribed "2nd" or "1st" are listed as Nos. 1445/52, 1511/16, 1663a/6, 1979 and 2039/40.

ELLIPTICAL PERFORATIONS. These were introduced in 1993 and stamps showing them will be found listed as Nos. Y1667 etc.

367   367a

Printing differences

Litho   **Photo**
(Illustrations enlarged × 6)

Litho. Clear outlines to value and frame of stamp.
Photo. Uneven lines to value and frame formed by edges of screen.

Two types of the 3p, 10p and 26p (Nos. X930/c, X886/b and X971/b)

Figures of face value as I (all ptgs of 3p. brt magenta except the multi-value coil No. 930cl and sheets from 21.1.92 onwards, 10p. orange-brown except 1984 "Christmas Heritage" £4 booklet and 26p rosine except 1987 £1.04 barcode booklet.

Figures of face value narrower as II (from coil No. X930cl and in sheets from 21.1.92 (3p.), 1984 "Christian Heritage" £4 booklet (10p.) or 1987 £1.04 barcode booklet (26p.).

This catalogue includes changes of figure styles on these stamps where there is no other listable difference. Similar changes have also taken place on other values, but only in conjuction with listed colour, paper or perforation changes.

1971 (15 Feb)–**96.** *Decimal Currency. T 367. Chalk-surfaced paper.*

(a) Photo Harrison (except for some printings of Nos. X879 and X913 in sheets produced by Enschedé and issued on 12 Dec 1979 (8p.) and 19 Nov 1991 (18p.)). With phosphor bands. P 15 × 14.

X841	½p. turquoise-blue (2 bands)		10	10
	a. Imperf (pair)†	£1200		
	l. Booklet pane. No. X841 × 2 se-tenant vert with X849 × 2	6·00		
	lEy. Booklet pane. Phosphor omitted	£200		
	la. Booklet pane. No. X841 × 2 se-tenant horiz with X849 × 2 (14.7.71)	1·00		
	laEy. Booklet pane. Phosphor omitted	£350		
	m. Booklet pane. No. X841 × 5 plus label	2·75		
	mEy. Booklet pane. Phosphor omitted	£110		
	n. Coil strip. No. X849Eg, X841Eg × 2 and X844Eg × 2	1·75		
	nEy. Coil strip. Phosphor omitted	40·00		
	nEv. Coil strip. PVA gum. No. X849, X841 × 2 and X844 × 2 (4.74)	45		
	nEvy. Coil strip. Phosphor omitted	15·00		
	o. Booklet pane. No. X841, X851, X852, X852Ea, each × 3 (24.5.72)	10·50		
	oEy. Booklet pane. Phosphor omitted	£1500		
	p. Booklet pane. No. X841 × 3, X842 and X852 × 2 (24.5.72)	55·00		
	pEy. Booklet pane. Phosphor omitted			
	q. Coil strip. No. X870, X849, X844 and X841 × 2 (3.12.75)	1·00		
	r. Booklet pane. No. X841 × 2, X844 × 3 and X870 (10.3.76)	75		
	s. Booklet pane. No. X841 × 2, X844 × 2, X873 × 2 and X881 × 4 (8½p. values at right) (26.1.77)	2·00		
	sa. Ditto, but No. X873Ea and 8½p. values at left	2·00		
	t. Booklet pane. No. X841, X844, X894 × 3 and X902 (14p. value at right) (26.1.81)	2·00		
	tEy. Booklet pane. Phosphor omitted	60·00		
	ta. Booklet pane. No. X841, X844, X894Ea × 3 and X902 (14p. value at left)	1·90		
	taEy. Booklet pane. Phosphor omitted	60·00		
	u. Booklet pane. No. X841, X857 × 4 and X899 × 3 (12½p. values at left) (1.2.82)	3·00		
	ua. Ditto, but No. X899Ea and 12½p. values at right	3·00		
	Eg. Gum arabic (from coil strip, and on 22.9.72 from sheets)	40		
	Egy. Phosphor omitted	45·00		
X842	½p. turquoise-blue (1 side band at left) (24.5.72)		48·00	30·00
X843	½p. turquoise-blue (1 centre band) (14.12.77)		40	25
	l. Coil strip. No. X843 × 2, X875 and X845 × 2 (14.12.77)	85		
	m. Booklet pane. No. X843 × 2, X845 × 2 and X875 plus label (8.2.78)	60		
	mEy. Booklet pane. Phosphor omitted	40·00		
X844	1p. crimson (2 bands)		10	15
	a. Imperf (vert coil)			
	b. Pair, one imperf 3 sides (vert coil)			
	c. Imperf (pair)	£1000		
	l. Booklet pane. No. X844 × 2 se-tenant vert with X848 × 2	6·00		
	m. Ditto, but se-tenant horiz (14.7.71)	1·00		
	mEy. Booklet pane. Phosphor omitted	£150		
	n. Booklet pane. No. X844 × 2, X876 × 3 and X883 × 3 (9p. values at right) (13.6.77)	4·75		
	na. Ditto, but No. X876Ea and 9p. values at left	2·75		
	Eg. Gum arabic (from coil strip)	50		
	Egy. Phosphor omitted	45·00		

X845	1p. crimson (1 centre band) (14.12.77)	25	20
	l. Booklet pane. No. X879 and X845 × 2 plus label (17.10.79)	60	
	m. Coil strip. No. X879 and X845 × 2 plus 2 labels (16.1.80)	85	
	n. Booklet pane. No. X845 × 2, X860 and X898 each × 3 (5.4.83)	4·00	
	nEy. Booklet pane. Phosphor omitted	20·00	
	p. Booklet pane. No. X845 × 3, X863 × 2 and X900 × 3 (3.9.84)	4·00	
	pEy. Booklet pane. Phosphor omitted	£225	
	q. Booklet pane. No. X845 × 2 and X896 × 4 (29.7.86)	9·00	
	s. Booklet pane. No. X845, X867 × 2 and X900 × 3 (20.10.86)	4·00	
	sa. Ditto, but with vertical edges of pane imperf (29.9.87)	3·00	
	saEy. Booklet pane. Phosphor omitted	£200	
X846	1p. crimson ("all-over") (10.10.79)	15	25
X847	1p. crimson (1 side band at left) (20.10.86) ..	80	1·25
	Ea. Band at right (3.3.87)	2·50	2·75
	l. Booklet pane. No. X847, X901 and X912 × 2 (20.10.86)	2·75	
	lEy. Booklet pane. Phosphor omitted	£100	
	m. Booklet pane. No. X847Ea, X901 × 2, X912 × 5 and X918 with margins all round (3.3.87)	14·00	
X848	1½p. black (2 bands)	15	25
	a. Uncoated paper*	£130	
	b. Imperf (pair)		
	c. Imperf 3 sides (horiz pair)		
	Ey. Phosphor omitted	15·00	
X849	2p. myrtle-green (2 bands)	15	20
	a. Imperf (horiz pair)	£1400	
	l. Booklet pane. No. X849 × 2, X880 × 2 and X886 × 3 plus label (10p. values at right) (28.8.79)	2·50	
	la. Ditto, but No. X880Ea and 10p. values at left	2·50	
	m. Booklet pane. No. X849 × 3, X889 × 2 and X895 × 2 plus label (12p. values at right) (4.2.80)	2·50	
	mEy. Booklet pane. Phosphor omitted	50·00	
	ma. Booklet pane. No. X849 × 3, X889Ea × 2 and X895 × 2 plus label (12p. values at left)	2·50	
	maEy. Booklet pane. Phosphor omitted	50·00	
	n. Booklet pane. No. X849, X888 × 3, X889Ea and X895 × 4 with margins all round (16.4.80)	4·25	
	nEy. Booklet pane. Phosphor omitted	50·00	
	o. Booklet pane. No. X849 × 6 with margins all round (16.4.80)	1·40	
	oEy. Booklet pane. Phosphor omitted	55·00	
	p. Booklet pane. No. X849, X857, X898, X899 × 3 and X899Ea × 3 with margins all round (19.5.82)	6·00	
	pEy. Booklet pane. Phosphor omitted	£150	
	Eg. Gum arabic (from coil strip)	2·25	
	Ey. Phosphor omitted	£200	
X850	2p. myrtle-green ("all-over") (10.10.79)	25	30
X851	2½p. magenta (1 centre band)	20	15
	a. Imperf (pair)†	£275	
	Ey. Phosphor omitted	10·00	
	l. Booklet pane. No. X851 × 5 plus label ...	4·50	
	lEy. Booklet pane. Phosphor omitted	35·00	
	m. Booklet pane. No. X851 × 4 plus two labels	5·00	
	mEy. Booklet pane. Phosphor omitted	£150	
(X851)	n. Booklet pane. No. X851 × 3, X852Ea × 3 and X855 × 6 (24.5.72)	8·00	
	nEy. Booklet pane. Phosphor omitted		
	Eg. Gum arabic (13.9.72)	30	
X852	2½p. magenta (1 band at left)	90	1·75
	l. Booklet pane. No. X852 × 2 and X855 × 4	6·00	
	lEy. Booklet pane. Phosphor omitted	£150	
	Ea. Band at right (24.5.72)	1·00	1·75
X853	2½p. magenta (2 bands) (21.5.75)	25	50
X854	2½p. rose-red (2 bands) (26.8.81)	40	60
	l. Booklet pane. No. X854 × 3, X862 × 2 and X894 × 3, (11½p. values at left)	5·25	
	la. Ditto, but No. X894Ea and 11½p. values at right	7·00	
X855	3p. ultramarine (2 bands)	20	25
	a. Imperf (coil strip of 5)	£1750	
	b. Imperf (pair)†	£275	
	c. Uncoated paper*	45·00	
	Ey. Phosphor omitted	2·00	
	l. Booklet pane. No. X855 × 5 plus label ...	2·50	
	lEy. Booklet pane. Phosphor omitted	£375	
	n. Booklet pane. No. X855 × 12 (24.5.72) ...	5·00	
	nEy. Booklet pane. Phosphor omitted	£250	
	Eg. Gum arabic (23.8.72)	50	
	Egy. Phosphor omitted	10·00	
X856	3p. ultramarine (1 centre band) (10.9.73)	15	20
	a. Imperf (pair)†	£275	
	b. Imperf between (vert pair)†	£375	
	c. Imperf horiz (vert pair)†	£225	
	Eg. Gum arabic	50	
X857	3p. brt magenta (Type I) (2 bands) (1.2.82) ...	35	35
X858	3½p. olive-grey (2 bands) (shades)	25	30
	a. Imperf (pair)	£400	
	Ey. Phosphor omitted	10·00	
	Eb. Bronze-green (18.7.73)	25	30
	Eby. Phosphor omitted	10·00	
X859	3½p. olive-grey (1 centre band) (24.6.74)	30	35
X860	3½p. purple-brown (1 centre band) (5.4.83) ...	1·10	1·25
X861	4p. ochre-brown (2 bands)	20	25
	a. Imperf (pair)†	£1100	
	Ey. Phosphor omitted	35·00	
	Eg. Gum arabic (1.11.72)	40	
X862	4p. greenish blue (2 bands) (26.8.81)	1·75	2·00
X863	4p. greenish blue (1 centre band) (3.9.84) ...	1·50	1·90
X864	4p. greenish blue (1 band at right) (8.1.85) ..	1·75	1·75
	Ea. Band at left	1·60	1·75
	l. Booklet pane. No. X864, X864Ea, X901 × 2, X901Ea × 2, X909 × 2 and X920 with margins all round (8.1.85)	14·00	
	lEy. Booklet pane. Phosphor omitted	£1400	
X865	4½p. grey-blue (2 bands) (24.10.73)	25	30
	a. Imperf (pair)	£325	
	Ey. Phosphor omitted	8·00	
X866	5p. pale violet (2 bands)	20	20
X867	5p. claret (1 centre band) (20.10.86)	1·75	2·25
	Ey. Phosphor omitted	80·00	
X868	5½p. violet (2 bands) (24.10.73)	25	30
X869	5½p. violet (1 centre band) (17.3.75)	25	30
	a. Uncoated paper*	£400	
	Ey. Phosphor omitted	18·00	
X870	6p. lt emerald (2 bands)	25	20
	a. Uncoated paper*	20·00	
	Ey. Phosphor omitted	70·00	
	Eg. Gum arabic (6.6.73)	2·50	
X871	6½p. greenish blue (2 bands) (4.9.74)	30	35
X872	6½p. greenish blue (1 centre band) (24.9.75) ..	25	20
	a. Imperf (vert pair)	£325	
	b. Uncoated paper*	£175	
	Ey. Phosphor omitted	13·00	

X873	6½p. greenish blue (1 band at right) (26.1.77) .	70	75
	Ea. Band at left	55	55
X874	7p. purple-brown (2 bands) (15.1.75)	30	35
	a. Imperf (pair)	£500	
	Ey. Phosphor omitted	1·50	
X875	7p. purple-brown (1 centre band) (13.6.77) ..	25	30
	a. Imperf (pair)	£140	
	l. Booklet pane. No. X875 and X883, each × 10 (15.11.78)	4·50	
X876	7p. purple-brown (1 band at right) (13.6.77) ..	50	50
	Ea. Band at left	45	50
X877	7½p. pale chestnut (2 bands)	25	35
	Ey. Phosphor omitted	16·00	
X878	8p. rosine (2 bands) (24.10.73)	25	30
	a. Uncoated paper*	15·00	
X879	8p. rosine (1 centre band) (20.8.79)	25	30
	a. Uncoated paper*	£750	
	b. Imperf (pair)	£650	
	Ey. Phosphor omitted	£275	
	l. Booklet pane. No. X879 and X886, each × 10 (14.11.79)	5·00	
X880	8p. rosine (1 band at right) (28.8.79)	60	75
	Ea. Band at left	60	75
X881	8½p. lt yellowish green (2 bands) (shades) (24.9.75)	30	25
	a. Imperf (pair)	£1000	
	Eb. Yellowish green (24.3.76)	35	35
X882	9p. yellow-orange and black (2 bands)	45	55
	Ey. Phosphor omitted	£100	
X883	9p. dp violet (2 bands) (25.2.76)	35	25
	a. Imperf (pair)	£275	
	Ey. Phosphor omitted	4·00	
X884	9½p. purple (2 bands) (25.2.76)	35	45
	Ey. Phosphor omitted	20·00	
X885	10p. orange-brown & chestnut (2 bands) (11.8.71)	35	30
	a. Orange-brown omitted	£160	
	b. Imperf (horiz pair)	£1500	
	Ey. Phosphor omitted	10·00	
X886	10p. orange-brown (Type I) (2 bands) (25.2.76)	35	25
	a. Imperf (pair)	£275	
	b. Type II (4.9.84)	22·00	22·00
	bl. Booklet pane. No. X886b, X901Ea and X909 × 7 with margins all round	32·00	
	blEy. Booklet pane. Phosphor omitted	£2000	
X887	10p. orange-brown (Type I) ("all-over") (3.10.79)	35	45
X888	10p. orange-brown (Type I) (1 centre band) (4.2.80)	35	25
	a. Imperf (pair)	£300	
	l. Booklet pane. No. X888 × 9 with margins all round (16.4.80)	3·75	
	lEy. Booklet pane. Phosphor omitted	50·00	
	m. Booklet pane. No. X888 and X895, each × 10 (12.11.80)	5·50	
X889	10p. orange-brown (Type I) (1 band at right) (4.2.80)	70	80
	Ea. Band at left	70	80
X890	10½p. yellow (2 bands) (25.2.76)	40	45
X891	10½p. dp dull blue (2 bands) (26.4.78)	45	50
X892	11p. brown-red (2 bands) (25.2.76)	40	30
	a. Imperf (pair)	£2250	
X893	11½p. drab (1 centre band) (14.1.81)	40	35
	a. Imperf (pair)	£300	
	Ey. Phosphor omitted	6·00	
	l. Booklet pane. No. X893 and X902, each × 10 (11.11.81)	8·50	
X894	11½p. drab (1 band at right) (26.1.81)	55	70
	Ea. Band at left	55	70

(X894)	l. Booklet pane. No. X894/Ea, each × 2 & X902 × 6 (6.5.81)	6·50	
X895	12p. yellowish green (2 bands) (4.2.80)	45	45
	l. Booklet pane. No. X895 × 9 with margins all round (16.4.80)	4·00	
	lEy. Booklet pane. Phosphor omitted	40·00	
X896	12p. brt emerald (1 centre band) (29.10.85) ...	45	45
	a. Imperf (pair)		
	Eu. Underprint Type 4 (29.10.85)	55	
	Ey. Phosphor omitted	10·00	
	l. Booklet pane. No. X896 × 9 with margins all round (18.3.86)	4·75	
	lEy. Booklet pane. Phosphor omitted	£200	
X897	12p. brt emerald (1 band at right) (14.1.86) ...	80	85
	Ea. Band at left	80	85
	l. Booklet pane. No. X897/Ea, each × 2 and X909 × 6 (12p. values at left) (14.1.86) ...	6·00	
	la. Ditto, but 12p. values at right	6·00	
	m. Booklet pane. No. X897/Ea, each × 3, X909 × 2 and X919 with margins all round (18.3.86)	17·00	
	mEy. Booklet pane. Phosphor omitted	£1250	
X898	12½p. lt emerald (1 centre band) (27.1.82) ...	45	40
	a. Imperf (pair)	£100	
	Eu. Underprint Type 1 (10.11.82)	60	
	Euy. Phosphor omitted	70·00	
	Ev. Underprint Type 2 (9.11.83)	60	
	Ey. Phosphor omitted	5·50	
	l. Booklet pane. No. X898Eu and X907Eu, each × 10 (10.11.82)	8·50	
X899	12½p. lt emerald (1 band at right) (1.2.82)	70	75
	Ea. Band at left	70	75
	l. Booklet pane. No. X899/Ea, each × 2 and X907 × 6 (1.2.82)††	5·00	
	lEy. Booklet pane. Phosphor omitted		
	m. Booklet pane. No. X899/Ea, each × 3 with margins all round (19.5.82)	3·25	
	mEy. Booklet pane. Phosphor omitted	40·00	
	n. Booklet pane. No. X899/Ea, each × 2, and X908 × 6 (12½p. values at left) (5.4.83)	8·50	
	na. Ditto, but 12½p. values at right	8·00	
X900	13p. pale chestnut (1 centre band) (28.8.84) ..	40	40
	a. Imperf (pair)	£550	
	Eu. Underprint Type 2 (2.12.86)	90	
	Ey. Phosphor omitted	5·50	
	l. Booklet pane. No. X900 × 9 with margins all round (8.1.85)	4·50	
	lEy. Booklet pane. Phosphor omitted	£400	
	m. Booklet pane. No. X900 × 6 with margins all round (3.3.87)	3·75	
	n. Booklet pane. No. X900 × 4 with margins all round (4.8.87)	3·00	
	o. Booklet pane. No. X900 × 10 with margins all round (4.8.87)	5·00	
X901	13p. pale chestnut (1 band at right) (3.9.84) ..	50	60
	Ea. Band at left	50	60
	l. Booklet pane. No. X901/Ea, each × 2, and X909 × 6 (13p. values at left)††	5·00	
	la. Ditto, but 13p. values at right	5·00	
	m. Booklet pane. No. X901/Ea, each × 3 with margins all round (4.9.84)	4·50	
	mEy. Booklet pane. Phosphor omitted	£300	
	n. Booklet pane. No. X901Ea and X912 × 5 (20.10.86)	4·50	
	na. Ditto, but with vertical edges of pane imperf (29.9.87)	4·75	
X902	14p. grey-blue (2 bands) (26.1.81)	75	80
X903	14p. dp blue (1 centre band) (23.8.88)	40	50
	a. Imperf (pair)	£300	
	Ey. Phosphor omitted	7·00	

(X903)	l. Booklet pane. No. X903 × 4 with margins all round	6·00		
	lEy. Booklet pane. Phosphor omitted	£100		
	m. Booklet pane. No. X903 × 10 with margins all round	9·50		
	n. Booklet pane. No. X903 × 4 with horizontal edges of pane imperf (11.10.88)	6·50		
	p. Booklet pane. No. X903 × 10 with horizontal edges of pane imperf (11.10.88)	9·00		
	pEy. Booklet pane. Phosphor omitted	£150		
	q. Booklet pane. No. X903 × 4 with three edges of pane imperf (24.1.89)	32·00		
	qEy. Booklet pane. Phosphor omitted	35·00		
X904	14p. dp blue (1 band at right) (5.9.88)	4·00	4·00	
	l. Booklet pane. No. X904 and X914 × 2 plus label	5·00		
	lEy. Booklet pane. Phosphor omitted	12·00		
	m. Booklet pane. No. X904 × 2 and X914 × 4 with vertical edges of pane imperf	6·50		
	mEy. Booklet pane. Phosphor omitted	£800		
X905	15p. brt blue (1 centre band) (26.9.89)	65	65	
	a. Imperf (pair)	£475		
	Ey. Phosphor omitted	10·00		
X906	15p. brt blue (1 band at left) (2.10.89)	3·00	3·00	
	Ea. Band at right (20.3.90)	2·50	2·50	
	l. Booklet pane. No. X906 × 2 and X916 plus label	8·50		
	lEy. Booklet pane. Phosphor omitted	£500		
	m. Booklet pane. No. X906Ea, X916, X922, 1446, 1448, 1468Ea, 1470 and 1472 plus label with margins all round (20.3.90)	20·00		
X907	15½p. pale violet (2 bands) (1.2.82)	60	65	
	Eu. Underprint Type 1 (10.11.82)	60		
	l. Booklet pane. No. X907 × 6 with margins all round (19.5.82)	4·00		
	lEy. Booklet pane. Phosphor omitted	80·00		
	m. Booklet pane. No. X907 × 9 with margins all round (19.5.82)	5·25		
	mEy. Booklet pane. Phosphor omitted	45·00		
X908	16p. olive-drab (5.4.83)	1·25	1·40	
X909	17p. grey-blue (2 bands) (3.9.84)	60	60	
	Eu. Underprint Type 4 (4.11.85)	70		
	l. Booklet pane. No. X909Eu × 3 plus label (4.11.85)	2·50		
	lEy. Booklet pane. Phosphor omitted	60·00		
	Ela. Booklet pane. No. X909 × 3 plus label (12.8.86)	3·00		
X910	17p. dp blue (1 centre band) (4.9.90)	80	85	
	a. Imperf (pair)			
	Ey. Phosphor omitted	8·00		
X911	17p. dp blue (1 band at right) (4.9.90)	2·50	2·75	
	Ea. Band at left	1·25	1·25	
	l. Booklet pane. No. X911 and X911Ea × 2 plus label	4·75		
	lEy. Booklet pane. Phosphor omitted	60·00		
	m. Booklet pane. No. X911 × 2 and X917 × 3 plus three labels with vertical edges of pane imperf	4·25		
	mEy. Booklet pane. Phosphor omitted	70·00		
X912	18p. dp olive-grey (2 bands) (20.10.86)	70	80	
X913	18p. brt green (1 centre band) (10.9.91)	60	50	
	a. Imperf (pair)	£425		
	Ey. Phosphor omitted	20·00		
X914	19p. brt orange-red (2 bands) (5.9.88)	1·40	1·50	
X915	20p. dull purple (2 bands) (25.2.76)	75	35	
X916	20p. brownish black (2 bands) (2.10.89)	1·40	1·60	
X917	22p. brt orange-red (2 bands) (4.9.90)	1·50	1·25	
X917a	25p. rose-red (2 bands) (6.2.96)	5·50	6·00	
X918	26p. rosine (Type I) (2 bands) (3.3.87)	7·00	7·50	
X919	31p. purple (2 bands) (18.3.86)	14·00	14·00	

X920	34p. ochre-brown (2 bands) (8.1.85)	7·00	7·50	
X921	50p. ochre-brown (2 bands) (2.2.77)	2·00	60	
X922	50p. ochre (2 bands) (20.3.90)	4·50	4·50	

(b) Photo Harrison. On phosphorised paper. P 15 × 14

X924	½p. turquoise-blue (10.12.80)	10	15	
	a. Imperf (pair)	£130		
	l. Coil strip. No. X924 and X932 × 3 (30.12.81)	75		
X925	1p. crimson (12.12.79)	10	15	
	a. Imperf (pair)	£1000		
	l. Coil strip. No. X925 and X932Ea × 3 (14.8.84)	90		
	m. Booklet pane. No. X925 and X969, each × 2 (10.9.91)	1·75		
X926	2p. myrtle-green (face value as T 367) (12.12.79)	15	20	
	a. Imperf (pair)	£1200		
X927	2p. dp green (face value as T 367a) (26.7.88)	15	20	
	a. Imperf (pair)			
	l. Booklet pane. No. X927 × 2 and X969 × 4 plus 2 labels with vert edges of pane imperf (10.9.91)	3·25		
X928	2p. myrtle-green (face value as T 367a) (5.9.88)	2·75	2·75	
	l. Coil strip. No. X928 and X932Ea × 3	3·50		
X929	2½p. rose-red (14.1.81)	15	20	
	l. Coil strip. No. X929 and X930 × 3 (6.81)	1·00		
X930	3p. brt magenta (Type I) (22.10.80)	20	25	
	a. Imperf (horiz pair)	£1000		
	b. Booklet pane. No. X930, X931 × 2 and X949 × 6 with margins all round (14.9.83)	6·50		
	c. Type II (10.10.89)	90	70	
	cl. Coil strip. No. X930c and X933 × 3	2·25		
X931	3½p. purple-brown (30.3.83)	50	60	
X932	4p. greenish blue (30.12.81)	25	40	
	Ea. Pale greenish blue (14.8.84)	25	40	
X933	4p. new blue (26.7.88)	20	25	
	a. Imperf (pair)	£1500		
	l. Coil strip. No. X933 × 3 and X935 (27.11.90)	1·40		
	m. Coil strip. No. X933 and X935, each × 2 (1.10.91)	1·00		
	n. Coil strip. No. X933 and X935 × 3 (31.1.95)	1·00		
X934	5p. pale violet (10.10.79)	30	35	
X935	5p. dull red-brown (26.7.88)	25	30	
	a. Imperf (pair)	£2000		
X936	6p. yellow-olive (10.9.91)	30	30	
X937	7p. brownish red (29.10.85)	1·10	1·25	
X938	8½p. yellowish green (24.3.76)	40	50	
X939	10p. orange-brown (Type I) (11.79)	35	35	
X940	10p. dull orange (Type II) (4.9.90)	40	35	
X941	11p. brown-red (27.8.80)	70	80	
X942	11½p. ochre-brown (15.8.79)	55	55	
X943	12p. yellowish green (30.1.80)	45	45	
X944	13p. olive-grey (15.8.79)	45	50	
X945	13½p. purple-brown (30.1.80)	60	60	
X946	14p. grey-blue (14.1.81)	50	50	
X947	15p. ultramarine (15.8.79)	60	60	
X948	15½p. pale violet (14.1.81)	60	50	
	a. Imperf (pair)	£250		
X949	16p. olive-drab (30.3.83)	55	55	
	a. Imperf (pair)	£180		
	Eu. Underprint Type 3 (10.8.83)	80		
	l. Booklet pane. No. X949 × 9 with margins all round (14.9.83)	5·00		
X950	16½p. pale chestnut (27.1.82)	80	75	
X951	17p. lt emerald (30.1.80)	60	60	

X952	17p. grey-blue (30.3.83)	60	60
	a. Imperf (pair)	£300	
	Eu. Underprint Type 3 (5.3.85)	80	
	l. Booklet pane. No. X952 × 6 with margins all round (4.9.84)	4·50	
	m. Booklet pane. No. X952 × 9 with margins all round (8.1.85)	6·00	
X953	17½p. pale chestnut (30.1.80)	70	75
X954	18p. dp violet (14.1.81)	70	70
X955	18p. dp olive-grey (28.8.84)	75	60
	a. Imperf (pair)	£150	
	l. Booklet pane. No. X955 × 9 with margins all round (3.3.87)	6·00	
	m. Booklet pane. No. X955 × 4 with margins all round (4.8.87)	3·50	
	n. Booklet pane. No. X955 × 10 with margins all round (4.8.87)	7·50	
X956	19p. brt orange-red (23.8.88)	80	60
	a. Imperf (pair)	£400	
	l. Booklet pane. No. X956 × 4 with margins all round	7·00	
	m. Booklet pane. No. X956 × 10 with margins all round	12·00	
	n. Booklet pane. No. X956 × 4 with horizontal edges of pane imperf (11.10.88)	8·50	
	o. Booklet pane. No. X956 × 10 with horizontal edges of pane imperf (11.10.88)	12·00	
	q. Booklet pane. No. X956 × 4 with three edges of pane imperf (24.1.89)	32·00	
X957	19½p. olive-grey (27.1.82)	1·50	1·50
X958	20p. dull purple (10.10.79)	75	50
X959	20p. turquoise-green (23.8.88)	75	70
X960	20p. brownish black (26.9.89)	1·00	1·00
	a. Imperf (pair)	£800	
	l. Booklet pane. No. X960 × 5 plus label with vertical edges of pane imperf (2.10.89) ..	6·25	
X961	20½p. ultramarine (30.3.83)	1·00	1·00
	a. Imperf (pair)	£850	
X962	22p. blue (22.10.80)	90	75
	a. Imperf (pair)	£250	
X963	22p. yellow-green (28.8.84)	90	80
	a. Imperf (horiz pair)	£1400	
X964	22p. brt orange-red (4.9.90)	90	80
	a. Imperf (pair)		
X965	23p. brown-red (30.3.83)	1·25	85
	a. Imperf (horiz pair)	£1100	
X966	23p. brt green (23.8.88)	90	90
X967	24p. violet (28.8.84)	1·40	1·50
X968	24p. Indian red (26.9.89)	2·00	1·60
	a. Imperf (horiz pair)	£2250	
X969	24p. chestnut (10.9.91)	75	80
	a. Imperf (pair)	£225	
X970	25p. purple (14.1.81)	90	1·00
X971	26p. rosine (Type I) (27.1.82)	1·10	60
	a. Imperf (horiz pair)		
	b. Type II (4.8.87)	3·50	4·00
	bl. Booklet pane. No. X971b × 4 with margins all round	17·00	
X972	26p. drab (Type II) (4.9.90)	1·50	1·25
X973	27p. chestnut (23.8.88)	1·25	1·25
	l. Booklet pane. No. X973 × 4 with margins all round	12·50	
	m. Booklet pane. No. X973 × 4 with horizontal edges of pane imperf (11.10.88)	30·00	
X974	27p. violet (4.9.90)	1·50	1·25
X975	28p. dp violet (30.3.83)	1·25	1·25
	a. Imperf (pair)	£1200	
X976	28p. ochre (23.8.88)	1·40	1·25

X977	28p. dp bluish grey (10.9.91)	1·40	1·25
	a. Imperf (pair)	£1600	
X978	29p. ochre-brown (27.1.82)	1·75	1·75
X979	29p. dp mauve (26.9.89)	1·75	1·75
X980	30p. dp olive-grey (26.9.89)	1·25	1·25
X981	31p. purple (30.3.83)	1·25	1·25
	a. Imperf (pair)	£1100	
X982	31p. ultramarine (4.9.90)	1·60	1·50
X983	32p. greenish blue (23.8.88)	1·90	1·75
	a. Imperf (pair)	£1200	
X984	33p. lt emerald (4.9.90)	1·75	1·60
X985	34p. ochre-brown (28.8.84)	1·75	1·75
X986	34p. dp bluish grey (26.9.89)	2·00	1·90
X987	34p. dp mauve (10.9.91)	1·75	1·75
X988	35p. sepia (23.8.88)	1·60	1·60
	a. Imperf (pair)	£1100	
X989	35p. yellow (10.9.91)	1·75	1·60
X990	37p. rosine (26.9.89)	2·00	1·75
X991	39p. bright mauve (10.9.91)	1·60	1·50

(c) *Photo Harrison. On ordinary paper. P* 15 × 14

X992	50p. ochre-brown (21.5.80)	1·60	70
	a. Imperf (pair)	£600	
X993	75p. grey-black (face value as T **367**a) (26.7.88)	2·50	1·50

(d) *Photo Harrison. On ordinary or phosphorised paper. P* 15 × 14

X994	50p. ochre (13.3.90)	1·75	70
	a. Imperf (pair)	£1000	

(e) *Litho J.W. P* 14

X996	4p. greenish blue (2 bands) (30.1.80)	25	35
X997	4p. greenish blue (phosphorised paper) (11.81)	35	40
X998	20p. dull purple (2 bands) (21.5.80)	1·25	1·00
X999	20p. dull purple (phosphorised paper) (11.81) .	1·75	1·10

(f) *Litho Questa. P* 14 (*Nos.* X1000, X1003/4 *and* X1023) *or* 15 × 14 (*others*)

X1000	2p. emerald-green (face value as T **367**) (phosphorised paper) (21.5.80)	20	25
	a. Perf 15 × 14 (10.7.84)	35	35
X1001	2p. brt green and dp green (face value as T **367**a) (phosphorised paper) (23.2.88)	75	70
X1002	4p. greenish blue (phosphorised paper) (13.5.86)	70	75
X1003	5p. lt violet (phosphorised paper) (21.5.80) ..	40	40
X1004	5p. claret (phosphorised paper) (27.1.82)	50	50
	a. Perf 15 × 14 (21.2.84)	65	60
X1005	13p. pale chestnut (1 centre band) (9.2.88) ...	70	75
	l. Booklet pane. No. X1005 × 6 with margins all round	4·75	
X1006	13p. pale chestnut (1 side band at right) (9.2.88)	75	75
	Ea. Band at left	75	75
	l. Booklet pane. No. X1006/Ea each × 3, X1010, X1015 and X1021 with margins all round	20·00	
	lEa. Grey-green (on 18p.) ptg double	£1200	
X1007	14p. dp blue (1 centre band) (11.10.88)	1·75	1·75
X1008	17p. dp blue (1 centre band) (19.3.91)	80	80
	Ey. Phosphor omitted	£180	
	l. Booklet pane. No. X1008 × 6 with margins all round	4·00	
	lEy. Booklet pane. Phosphor omitted	£750	
X1009	18p. dp olive-grey (phosphorised paper) (9.2.88)	90	95
	l. Booklet pane. No. X1009 × 9 with margins all round	6·00	
	m. Booklet pane. No. X1009 × 6 with margins all round	5·00	

X1010	18p. dp olive-grey (2 bands) (9.2.88)	7·00	7·00
X1011	18p. brt green (1 centre band) (27.10.92)	75	75
	l. Booklet pane. No. X1011 × 6 with margins all round	5·00	
X1012	18p. brt green (1 side band at right) (27.10.92)	1·25	1·40
	Ea. Band at left (10.8.93)	1·75	2·00
	l. Booklet pane. No. X1012 × 2, X1018 × 2, X1022 × 2, 1451a, 1514a and centre label with margins all round	12·00	
	lEa. Bright blue (on 2nd) ptg treble		
	m. Booklet pane. No. X1012Ea, X1020, X1022 and 1451aEb, each × 2, with centre label and margins all round (10.8.93)	13·00	
	mEy. Booklet pane. Phosphor omitted	£1600	
X1013	19p. brt orange-red (phosphorised paper) (11.10.88)	1·90	2·00
X1014	20p. dull purple (phosphorised paper) (13.5.86)	1·40	1·40
X1015	22p. yellow-green (2 bands) (9.2.88)	9·00	9·00
X1016	22p. brt orange-red (phosphorised paper) (19.3.91)	80	90
	l. Booklet pane. No. X1016 × 9 with margins all round	7·25	
	m. Booklet pane. No. X1016 × 6, X1019 × 2 and centre label with margins all round .	9·00	
X1017	24p. chestnut (phosphorised paper) (27.10.92)	90	1·10
	l. Booklet pane. No. X1017 × 6 with margins all round	4·50	
X1018	24p. chestnut (2 bands) (27.10.92)	1·25	1·40
X1019	33p. lt emerald (phosphorised paper) (19.3.91)	2·50	2·50
X1020	33p. lt emerald (2 bands) (25.2.92)	1·25	1·50
X1021	34p. bistre-brown (2 bands) (9.2.88)	7·50	7·50
X1022	39p. brt mauve (2 bands) (27.10.92)	1·50	1·60
X1023	75p. black (face value as T **367**) (ordinary paper) (30.1.80)	2·75	95
	a. Perf 15 × 14 (21.2.84)	3·25	1·60
X1024	75p. brownish grey and black (face value as T **367**a) (ordinary paper) (23.2.88)	9·00	8·50

(g) Litho Walsall. P 14

X1050	2p. dp green (phosphorised paper) (9.2.93) ..	1·00	1·10
	l. Booklet pane. No. X1050 × 2 and X1053 × 4 plus 2 labels with vert edges of pane imperf	6·75	
X1051	14p. dp blue (1 side band at right) (25.4.89) ..	4·50	4·50
	Ey. Phosphor omitted	£275	
	l. Booklet pane. No. X1051 × 2 and X1052 × 4 with vertical edges of pane imperf	10·00	
	lEy. Booklet pane. Phosphor omitted	£950	
X1052	19p. brt orange-red (2 bands) (25.4.89)	3·00	3·00
	Ey. Phosphor omitted	£225	
X1053	24p. chestnut (phosphorised paper) (9.2.93) ..	1·10	1·25
X1054	29p. dp mauve (2 bands) (2.10.89)	2·75	3·00
	l. Booklet pane. No. X1054 × 4 with three edges of pane imperf	15·00	
X1055	29p. dp mauve (phosphorised paper) (17.4.90)	4·50	4·50
	l. Booklet pane. No. X1055 × 4 with three edges of pane imperf	17·00	
X1056	31p. ultramarine (phosphorised paper) (17.9.90)	1·40	1·40
	l. Booklet pane. No. X1056 × 4 with horizontal edges of pane imperf	6·00	
X1057	33p. light emerald (phosphorised paper) (16.9.91)	1·25	1·25
	l. Booklet pane. No. X1057 × 4 with horiz edges of pane imperf	5·00	
X1058	39p. brt mauve (phosphorised paper) (16.9.91)	1·60	1·60
	l. Booklet pane. No. X1058 × 4 with horiz edges of pane imperf	6·00	

*See footnote after No. 744.

†These come from sheets with gum arabic.

††Examples of Booklet panes Nos. X899l, X901l and X901la are known on which the phosphor bands were printed on the wrong values in error with the result that the side bands appear on the 15½p. or 17p. and the two bands on the 12½p. or 13p. Similarly examples of the 1p. with phosphor band at right instead of left and of the 13p. with band at left instead of right, exist from 50p. booklet pane No. X847l.

Nos. X844a/b come from a strip of eight of the vertical coil. It comprises two normals, one imperforate at sides and bottom, one completely imperforate, one imperforate at top, left and bottom and partly perforated at right due to the bottom three stamps being perforated twice. No. X844b is also known from another strip having one stamp imperforate at sides and bottom.

Nos. X848b/c come from the same sheet, the latter having perforations at the foot of the stamps only.

Multi-value coil strips Nos. X924l, X925l, X928l, X929l, X930cl and X933l/n were produced by the Post Office for use by a large direct mail marketing firm. From 2 September 1981 No. X929l was available from the Philatelic Bureau, Edinburgh, and, subsequently from a number of other Post Office counters. Later multi-value coil strips were sold at the Philatelic Bureau and Post Office philatelic counters.

In addition to booklet pane No. X1012m No. X1020 also comes from the *se-tenant* pane in the Wales £6 booklet. This pane is listed under No. W49a in the Wales Regional section.

PANES OF SIX FROM STITCHED BOOKLETS. Nos. X841m, X851l/m and X855l include one or two printed labels showing commercial advertisements. These were originally perforated on all four sides, but from the August 1971 editions of the 25p. and 30p. booklets (Nos. DH42, DQ59) and December 1971 edition of the 50p. (No. DT4) the line of perforations between the label and the binding margin was omitted. Similar panes, with the line of perforations omitted, exist for the 3p., 3½p. and 4½p. values (Nos. X856, X858 and X865), but these are outside the scope of this listing as the labels are blank.

PART-PERFORATED SHEETS. Since the introduction of the "Jumelle" press in 1972 a number of part perforated sheets, both definitives and commemoratives, have been discovered. It is believed that these occur when the operation of the press in interrupted. Such sheets invariably show a number of "blind" perforations, where the pins have failed to cut the paper. Our listings of imperforate errors from these sheets are for pairs showing no traces whatsoever of the perforations. Examples showing "blind" perforations are outside the scope of this catalogue.

In cases where perforation varieties affect *se-tenant* stamps, fuller descriptions will be found in Vols. 4 and 5 of the *G.B. Specialised Catalogue.*

WHITE PAPER. From 1972 printings appeared on fluorescent white paper giving a stronger chalk reaction than the original ordinary cream paper.

PHOSPHOR OMITTED ERRORS. These are listed for those stamps or booklet panes which were not subsequently issued on phosphorised paper. The following phosphor omitted errors also exist, but can only be identified by the use of an ultra-violet lamp. Prices quoted are for mint examples:

½p. X841 (£1)	8½p. X881 (£1·75)	18p. X912 (£27)
1p. X844 (£3)	10p. X886 (£1)	19p. X914 (£4)
2p. X849 (£5)	11p. X892 (£4)	20p. X916 (£425)
3p. X857 (£100)	12p. X895 (£6)	22p. X917 (£20)
3½p. X860 (£5·50)	14p. X902 (£28)	31p. X919 (£650)
4p. X863 (£85)	15½p. X907 (£4)	33p. X1020 (£375)
4p. X996	16p. X908 (£100)	34p. X920 (£750)
5p. X866 (£225)	17p. X909 (£150)	

No. X909Eu with underprint Type 4 also exists without phosphor (*price* £10).

"ALL-OVER" PHOSPHOR. To improve mechanised handling most commemoratives from the 1972 Royal Silver Wedding 3p. value to the 1979 Rowland Hill Death Centenary set had the phosphor applied by printing cylinder across the entire surface of the stamp, giving a matt effect. Printings of the 1, 2 and 10p. definitives, released in October 1979, also had "all-over" phosphor, but these were purely a temporary expedient pending the adoption of phosphorised paper. Nos. X883, X890 and X921 have been discovered with "all-over" phosphor in addition to the normal phosphor bands. These errors are outside the scope of this catalogue.

PHOSPHORISED PAPER. Following the experiments on Nos. 743c and 829 a printing of the $4\frac{1}{2}$p. definitive was issued on 13 November 1974, which had, in addition to the normal phosphor bands, phosphor included in the paper coating. Because of difficulties in identifying this phosphorised paper with the naked eye this printing is not listed separately in this catalogue.

No. X938 was the first value printed on phosphorised paper without phosphor bands and was a further experimental issue to test the efficacy of this system. From 15 August 1979 phosphorised paper was accepted for use generally, this paper replacing phosphor bands on values other than those required for the second-class rate.

Stamps on phosphorised paper show a shiny surface instead of the matt areas of those printed with phosphor bands.

DEXTRIN GUM. From 1973 printings in photogravure appeared with PVA gum to which dextrin had been added. Because this is virtually colourless a bluish green colouring matter was added to distinguish it from the earlier pure PVA.

The 4p., 5p. (light violet), 20p. and 75p. printed in lithography exist with PVA and PVAD gum. From 1988 Questa printings were with PVAD gum, but did not show the bluish green additive.

VARNISH COATING. Nos. X841 and X883 exist with and without a varnish coating. This cannot easily be detected without the use of an ultra-violet lamp as it merely reduces the fluorescent paper reaction.

POSTAL FORGERIES. In mid-1993 a number of postal forgeries of the 24p. chestnut were detected in the London area. These forgeries, produced by lithography, can be identified by the lack of phosphor in the paper, screening dots across the face value and by the perforations which were applied by a line machine gauging 11.

First Day Covers

15.2.71	$\frac{1}{2}$p., 1p., $1\frac{1}{2}$p., 2p., $2\frac{1}{2}$p., 3p., $3\frac{1}{2}$p., 4p., 5p., 6p., $7\frac{1}{2}$p., 9p. (X841, X844, X848/9, X851, X855, X858, X861, X866, X870, X877, X882) (Covers carry "POSTING DELAYED BY THE POST OFFICE STRIKE 1971" cachet) .	3·50
11.8.71	10p. (X885)	2·25
24.5.72	Wedgwood *se-tenant* pane $\frac{1}{2}$p., $2\frac{1}{2}$p. (X841p)	25·00
24.10.73	$4\frac{1}{2}$p., $5\frac{1}{2}$p., 8p. (X865, X868, X878)	2·00
4.9.74	$6\frac{1}{2}$p. (X871)	3·00
15.1.75	7p. (X874)	2·00
24.9.75	$8\frac{1}{2}$p. (X881)	2·00
25.2.76	9p., $9\frac{1}{2}$p., 10p., $10\frac{1}{2}$p., 11p., 20p. (X883/4, X886, X890, X892, X915)	3·00
2.2.77	50p. (X921)	2·00
26.4.78	$10\frac{1}{2}$p. (X891)	2·00
15.8.79	$11\frac{1}{2}$p., 13p., 15p. (X942, X944, X947)	2·25
30.1.80	4p., 12p., $13\frac{1}{2}$p., 17p., $17\frac{1}{2}$p., 75p. (X996, X943, X945, X951, X953, X1023)	3·25
16.4.80	Wedgwood *se-tenant* pane 2p., 10p., 12p. (X849n)	2·25
22.10.80	3p., 22p. (X930, X962)	2·00
14.1.81	$2\frac{1}{2}$p., $11\frac{1}{2}$p., 14p., $15\frac{1}{2}$p., 18p., 25p. (X929, X893, X946, X948, X954, X970)	2·25
27.1.82	5p., $12\frac{1}{2}$p., $16\frac{1}{2}$p., $19\frac{1}{2}$p., 26p., 29p. (X1004, X898, X950, X957, X971, X978)	4·00
19.5.82	Stanley Gibbons *se-tenant* pane 2p., 3p., $12\frac{1}{2}$p. (X849p)	3·00
30.3.83	$3\frac{1}{2}$p., 16p., 17p., $20\frac{1}{2}$p., 23p., 28p., 31p. (X931, X949, X952, X961, X965, X975, X981)	5·00
14.9.83	Royal Mint *se-tenant* pane 3p., $3\frac{1}{2}$p., 16p. (X930b)	4·00
28.8.84	13p., 18p., 22p., 24p., 34p. (X900, X955, X963, X967, X985)	3·00
4.9.84	Christian Heritage *se-tenant* pane 10p., 13p., 17p. (X886bl)	28·00
8.1.85	*The Times se-tenant* pane 4p., 13p., 17p., 34p. (X864l)	8·50
29.10.85	7p., 12p. (X937, X896)	7·00
18.3.86	British Rail *se-tenant* pane 12p., 17p., 31p. (X897m)	9·00
3.3.87	P & O *se-tenant* pane 1p., 13p., 18p., 26p. (X847m)	7·50
9.2.88	*Financial Times se-tenant* pane 13p., 18p., 22p., 34p. (X1006l)	8·00
23.8.88	14p., 19p., 20p., 23p., 27p., 28p., 32p., 35p. (X903, X956, X959, X966, X973, X976 X983, X988)	6·00
26.9.89	15p., 20p., 24p., 29p., 30p., 34p., 37p. (X905, X960, X968, X979/80, X986, X990) .	5·50
20.3.90	London Life *se-tenant* pane 15p., (2nd), 20p., (1st); 15p., 20p., 29p. (X906m)	7·50
4.9.90	10p., 17p., 22p., 26p., 27p., 31p., 33p. (X910, X940, X964, X972, X974, X982, X984)	5·50
19.3.91	Alias Agatha Christie *se-tenant* pane 22p., 33p. (X1016m)	8·00
10.9.91	6p., 18p., 24p., 28p., 34p., 35p., 39p. (X936, X913, X969, X977, X987, X989, X991)	6·00
27.10.92	Tolkien *se-tenant* pane. 18p., (2nd), 24p., (1st), 39p. (X1012l)	4·25
10.8.93	Beatrix Potter *se-tenant* pane 18p., (2nd), 33p., 39p. (X1012m)	10·00

Post Office Presentation Packs

15.2.71	P.O. Pack No. 26. $\frac{1}{2}$p. (2 bands), 1p. (2 bands), $1\frac{1}{2}$p. (2 bands), $2\frac{1}{2}$p. magenta (1 centre band), 3p. ultramarine (2 bands), $3\frac{1}{2}$p. olive-grey (2 bands), 4p. ochre-brown (2 bands), 5p. pale violet (2 bands), 6p. light emerald (2 bands), $7\frac{1}{2}$p. (2 bands), 9p. yellow-orange and black (2 bands). (Nos. X841, X844, X848/9, X851, X855, X858, X861, X866, X870, X877, X882)	5·00
15.4.71**	"Scandinavia 71". Contents as above ...	30·00
25.11.71	P.O. Pack No. 37. $\frac{1}{2}$p. (2 bands), 1p. (2 bands), $1\frac{1}{2}$p., (2 bands), 2p. (2 bands), $2\frac{1}{2}$p. magenta (1 centre band), 3p. ultramarine (2 bands) or (1 centre band), $3\frac{1}{2}$p. olive-grey (2 bands) or (1 centre band). 4p. ochre-brown (2 bands), $4\frac{1}{2}$p. (2 bands), 5p. pale violet (2 bands), $5\frac{1}{2}$p. (2 bands) or (1 centre band), 6p. (2 bands), $6\frac{1}{2}$p. (2 bands) or (1 centre band), 7p. (2 bands), $7\frac{1}{2}$p. (2 bands), 8p. (2 bands), 9p. yellow-orange and black (2 bands), 10p. orange-brown and chestnut (2 bands). (Nos. X841, X844, X848/9, X851, X855 or X856, X858 or X859, X861, X865/6, X868 or X869, X870, X871 or X872, X874, X877/8, X885). Later issues of this Pack contained the alternatives	5·00

2.2.77 P.O. Pack No. 90. $\frac{1}{2}$p. (2 bands), 1p. (2 bands), 1$\frac{1}{2}$p. (2 bands), 2p. (2 bands), 2$\frac{1}{2}$p. magenta (1 centre band), 3p. ultramarine (1 centre band), 5p. pale violet (2 bands), 6$\frac{3}{4}$p. (1 centre band), 7p. (2 bands) or (1 centre band), 7$\frac{1}{2}$p. (2 bands), 8p. (2 bands), 8$\frac{1}{2}$p. (2 bands), 9p. deep violet (2 bands), 9$\frac{1}{2}$p. (2 bands), 10p. orange-brown (2 bands), 10$\frac{1}{2}$p. yellow (2 bands), 11p. (2 bands), 20p. dull purple (2 bands), 50p. ochre-brown (2 bands). (Nos. X841, X844, X848/9, X851, X856, X866, X872, X874 or X875, X877/8, X881, X883/4, X886, X890, X892, X915, X921) .... 6·00

28.10.81 P.O. Pack No. 129a. 10$\frac{1}{2}$p. deep dull blue (2 bands), 11$\frac{1}{2}$p. (1 centre band), 2$\frac{1}{2}$p. (phos paper), 3p. (phos paper), 11$\frac{1}{2}$p. (phos paper), 12p. (phos paper), 13p. (phos paper), 13$\frac{1}{2}$p. (phos paper), 14p. (phos paper), 15p. (phos paper), 15$\frac{1}{2}$p. (phos paper), 17p. light emerald (phos paper), 17$\frac{1}{2}$p. (phos paper), 18p. deep violet (phos paper), 22p. blue (phos paper), 25p. (phos paper), 4p. greenish blue (litho, 2 bands), 75p. (litho). (Nos. X891, X893, X929/30, X942/8, X951, X953/4, X962, X970, X996, X1023) .... 18·00

3.8.83 P.O. Pack No. 1. 10p. orange-brown (1 centre band), 12$\frac{1}{2}$p. (1 centre band), $\frac{1}{2}$p. (phos paper), 1p. (phos paper), 3p. (phos paper), 3$\frac{1}{2}$p. (phos paper), 16p. (phos paper), 16$\frac{1}{2}$p. (phos paper), 17p. grey-blue (phos paper), 20$\frac{1}{2}$p. (phos paper), 23p. brown-red (phos paper), 26p. rosine (phos paper), 28p. deep violet (phos paper), 31p. purple (phos paper), 50p. (ord paper), 2p. (litho phos paper), 4p. (litho phos paper), 5p. claret (litho phos paper), 20p. (litho phos paper), 75p. (litho). (Nos. X888, X898, X924/5, X930/1, X949/50, X952, X961, X965, X971, X975, X981, X992, X997, X999, X1000, X1004, X1023) .... 30·00

23.10.84 P.O. Pack No. 5. 13p. (1 centre band), $\frac{1}{2}$p. (phos paper), 1p. (phos paper), 3p. (phos paper), 10p. orange-brown (phos paper), 16p. (phos paper), 17p. grey-blue (phos paper), 18p. dp olive-grey (phos paper), 22p. yellow-green (phos paper), 24p. violet (phos paper), 26p. rosine (phos paper), 28p. deep violet (phos paper), 31p. purple (phos paper), 34p. ochre-brown (phos paper), 50p. (ord paper), 2p. (litho phos paper), 4p. (litho phos paper), 5p. claret (litho phos paper), 20p. (litho phos paper), 75p. (litho). (Nos. X900, X924/5, X930, X939, X949, X952, X955, X963, X967, X971, X975, X981, X985, X992, X1000a, X997, X1004a, X999, X1023a) .... 28·00

3.3.87 P.O. Pack No. 9. 12p. (1 centre band), 13p. (1 centre band), 1p. (phos paper), 3p. (phos paper), 7p. (phos paper), 10p. orange-brown (phos paper), 17p. grey-blue (phos paper), 18p. dp olive-grey (phos paper), 22p. yellow-green (phos paper), 24p. violet (phos paper), 26p. rosine (phos paper), 28p. deep violet (phos paper), 31p. purple (phos paper),

34p. ochre-brown (phos paper), 50p. (ord paper), 2p. (litho phos paper), 4p. (litho phos paper), 5p. claret (litho phos paper), 20p. (litho phos paper), 75p. (litho). (Nos. X896, X900, X925, X930, X937, X939, X952, X955, X963, X967, X971, X975, X981, X985, X992, X1000a, X997, X1004a, X999, X1023a) .... 26·00

23.8.88 P.O. Pack No. 15. 14p. (1 centre band), 19p. (phos paper), 20p. turquoise-green (phos paper), 23p. bright green (phos paper), 27p. chestnut (phos paper), 28p. ochre (phos paper), 32p. (phos paper), 35p. sepia (phos paper). (Nos. X903, X956, X959, X966, X973, X976, X983, X988) .... 11·00

26.9.89 P.O. Pack No. 19. 15p. (centre band), 20p. brownish black (phos paper), 24p. Indian red (phos paper), 29p. deep mauve (phos paper), 30p. (phos paper), 34p. deep bluish grey (phos paper), 37p. (phos paper). (Nos. X905, X960, X968, X979/80, X986, X990) .... 10·00

4.9.90 P.O. Pack No. 22. 10p. dull orange (phos paper), 17p. (centre band), 22p. bright orange-red (phos paper), 26p. drab (phos paper), 27p. violet (phos paper), 31p. ultramarine (phos paper), 33p. (phos paper). (Nos. X940, X910, X964, X972, X974, X982, X984) .... 9·00

14.5.91 P.O. Pack No. 24. 1p. (phos paper), 2p. (phos paper), 3p. (phos paper), 4p. new blue (phos paper), 5p. dull red-brown (phos paper), 10p. dull orange (phos paper), 17p. (centre band), 20p. turquoise-green (phos paper), 22p. bright orange-red (phos paper), 26p. drab (phos paper), 27p. violet (phos paper), 30p. (phos paper), 31p. ultramarine (phos paper), 32p. (phos paper), 33p. (phos paper), 37p. (phos paper), 50p. (ord paper), 75p. (ord paper). (Nos. X925, X927, X930, X933, X935, X940, X910, X959, X964, X972, X974, X980, X982/4, X990, X994, X993) .... 21·00

10.9.91 P.O. Pack No. 25. 6p. (phos paper), 18p. (centre band), 24p. chestnut (phos paper), 28p. deep bluish grey (phos paper), 34p. deep mauve (phos paper), 35p. yellow (phos paper), 39p. (phos paper). (Nos. X913, X936, X969, X977, X987, X989, X991) 9·00

**The "Scandinavia 71" was a special pack produced for sale during a visit to six cities in Denmark, Sweden and Norway by a mobile display unit between 15 April and 20 May 1971. The pack gives details of this tour and also lists the other stamps which were due to be issued in 1971, the text being in English. A separate insert gives translations in Danish, Swedish and Norwegian. The pack was also available at the Philatelic Bureau, Edinburgh.

DECIMAL MACHIN INDEX

Those booklet stamps shown below with an * after the catalogue number do not exist with perforations on all four sides, but show one or two sides imperforate.

Val.	Process	Colour	Phosphor	Cat. No.	Source
$\frac{1}{2}$p.	photo	turquoise-blue	2 bands	X841/Eg	(a) with P.V.A. gum—sheets, 5p. m/v coil (X841nEv), 10p. m/v coil (X841q), 10p. booklets FA1/3), 25p. booklets (DH39/52), 50p. booklets (DT1/12, FB1, FB14/16, FB19/23), £1 Wedgwood booklet (DX1) (b) with gum arabic—sheets, 5p. m/v coil (X841n)
$\frac{1}{2}$p.	photo	turquoise-blue	1 band at left	X842	£1 Wedgwood booklet (DX1)
$\frac{1}{2}$p.	photo	turquoise-blue	1 centre band	X843	10p. m/v coil (X843l), 10p. booklets (FA4/9)
$\frac{1}{2}$p.	photo	turquoise-blue	phos paper	X924	sheets, 12$\frac{1}{2}$p. m/v coil (X924l)
1p.	photo	crimson	2 bands	X844/Eg	(a) with P.V.A. gum—sheets, vertical coils, 5p. m/v coil (X841nEv), 10p. m/v coil (X841q), 10p. booklets (DN46/75, FA1/3), 50p. booklets (FB1/8, FB14/16) (b) with gum arabic—vertical coils, 5p. m/v coil (X841n)
1p.	photo	crimson	1 centre band	X845	10p. m/v coils (X843l, X845m), 10p. booklets (FA4/11), 50p. booklets (FB24/30, 34/36, 43/6, 48, 50)
1p.	photo	crimson	"all-over"	X846	sheets
1p.	photo	crimson	phos paper	X925	sheets, horizontal and vertical coils, 13p. m/v coil (X925l), 50p. booklet (FB59/66)
1p.	photo	crimson	1 band at left	X847	50p. booklets (FB37/42, 47, 49)
1p.	photo	crimson	1 band at right	X847Ea	£5 P. & O. booklet (DX8)
1$\frac{1}{2}$p.	photo	black	2 bands	X848	sheets, 10p. booklets (DN46/75)
2p.	photo	myrtle-green	2 bands	X849/Eg	(a) with P.V.A. gum—sheets, 5p. m/v coil (X841nEv), 10p. m/v coil (X841q), 10p. booklets (DN46/75), 50p. booklets (FB9/13), £3 Wedgwood booklet (DX2), £4 SG booklet (DX3) (b) with gum arabic—5p. m/v coil (X841n)
2p.	photo	myrtle-green	"all-over"	X850	sheets
2p.	photo	myrtle-green	phos paper	X926	sheets
2p.	photo	myrtle-green	phos paper	X928	14p. m/v coil (X928l)
2p.	litho	emerald-green	phos paper	X1000/a	sheets
2p.	litho	brt grn & dp grn	phos paper	X1001	sheets
2p.	photo	dp green	phos paper	X927	sheets, £1 booklets (FH23/7)
2p.	litho	dp green	phos paper	X1050*	£1 booklets (FH28/30)
2$\frac{1}{2}$p.	photo	magenta	1 centre band	X851/Eg	(a) with P.V.A. gum—sheets, horizontal and vertical coils, 25p. booklets (DH39/52), 50p. booklets (DT1/12), £1 Wedgwood booklet (DX1) (b) with gum arabic—sheets, horizontal coils
2$\frac{1}{2}$p.	photo	magenta	1 side band	X852/Ea	(a) band at left—50p. booklets (DT1/12), £1 Wedgwood booklet (DX1) (b) band at right—£1 Wedgwood booklet (DX1)
2$\frac{1}{2}$p.	photo	magenta	2 bands	X853	sheets
2$\frac{1}{2}$p.	photo	rose-red	phos paper	X929	sheets, 11$\frac{1}{2}$p. m/v coil (X929l)
2$\frac{1}{2}$p.	photo	rose-red	2 bands	X854	50p. booklets (FB17/18)
3p.	photo	ultramarine	2 bands	X855/Eg	(a) with P.V.A. gum—sheets, horizontal and vertical coils, 30p. booklets (DQ56/72), 50p. booklets (DT1/12), £1 Wedgwood booklet (DX1) (b) with gum arabic—sheets, horizontal coils
3p.	photo	ultramarine	1 centre band	X856/Eg	(a) with P.V.A. gum—sheets, horizontal and vertical coils, 30p. booklets (DQ73/4), 50p. booklets (DT13/14) (b) with gum arabic—sheets
3p.	photo	brt magenta	phos paper	X930	Type I. sheets, 11$\frac{1}{2}$p. m/v coil (X929l), £4 Royal Mint booklet (DX4)
3p.	photo	brt magenta	phos paper	X930c	Type II. sheets (from 21.1.92), 15p. m/v coil (X930cl)
3p.	photo	brt magenta	2 bands	X857	Type I. 50p. booklets (FB19/23), £4 SG booklet (DX3)
3$\frac{1}{2}$p.	photo	olive-grey	2 bands	X858/Eb	sheets, coils, 35p. booklets (DP1/3), 50p. booklets (DT13/14)
3$\frac{1}{2}$p.	photo	olive-grey	1 centre band	X859	sheets, coils, 35p. booklet (DP4), 85p. booklet (DW1)
3$\frac{1}{2}$p.	photo	purple-brown	phos paper	X931	sheets, £4 Royal Mint booklet (DX4)
3$\frac{1}{2}$p.	photo	purple-brown	1 centre band	X860	50p. booklets (FB24/6)

Val.	Process	Colour	Phosphor	Cat. No.	Source
4p.	photo	ochre-brown	2 bands	X861/Eg	(a) with P.V.A. gum—sheets. (b) with gum arabic—sheets
4p.	litho	greenish blue	2 bands	X996	sheets
4p.	photo	greenish blue	2 bands	X862	50p. booklets (FB17/18)
4p.	litho	greenish blue	phos paper	X997 X1002	sheets J.W. ptg. sheets Questa ptg.
4p.	photo	greenish blue	phos paper	X932 X932Ea	$12\frac{1}{2}$p. m/v coil (X924l) 13p. m/v coil (X925l), 14p. m/v coil (X928l)
4p.	photo	greenish blue	1 centre band	X863	50p. booklets (FB27/30)
4p.	photo	greenish blue	1 side band	X864/Ea	(a) band at right—£5 Times booklet (DX6) (b) band at left—£5 Times booklet (DX6)
4p.	photo	new blue	phos paper	X933	sheets, 15p. m/v coil (X930cl), 17p. m/v coil (X933l), 18p. m/v coil (X933m), 19p m/v coil (X933n)
$4\frac{1}{2}$p.	photo	grey-blue	2 bands	X865	sheets, horizontal coils, 45p. booklets (DS1/2), 85p. booklet (DW1)
5p.	photo	pale violet	2 bands	X866	sheets
5p.	photo	pale violet	phos paper	X934	sheets
5p.	litho	lt violet	phos paper	X1003	sheets
5p.	litho	claret	phos paper	X1004/a	sheets
5p.	photo	claret	1 centre band	X867	50p. booklets (FB35/36, 43/6, 48, 50)
5p.	photo	dull red-brown	phos paper	X935	sheets, 17p. m/v coil (X933l), 18p. m/v coil (X933m), 19p m/v coil (X933n)
$5\frac{1}{2}$p.	photo	violet	2 bands	X868	sheets
$5\frac{1}{2}$p.	photo	violet	1 centre band	X869	sheets
6p.	photo	lt emerald	2 bands	X870/Eg	(a) with P.V.A. gum—sheets, 10p. m/v coil (X841q), 10p. booklets (FA1/3) (b) with gum arabic—sheets
6p.	photo	yellow-olive	phos paper	X936	sheets
$6\frac{1}{2}$p.	photo	greenish blue	2 bands	X871	sheets
$6\frac{1}{2}$p.	photo	greenish blue	1 centre band	X872	sheets, horizontal and vertical coils, 65p. booklet (FC1)
$6\frac{1}{2}$p.	photo	greenish blue	1 side band	X873/Ea	(a) band at right—50p. booklet (FB1A). (b) band at left—50p. booklet (FB1B)
7p.	photo	purple-brown	2 bands	X874	sheets
7p.	photo	purple-brown	1 centre band	X875	sheets, horizontal and vertical coils, 10p. m/v coil (X843l), 10p. booklets (FA4/9), 70p. booklets (FD1/7), £1.60 Christmas booklet (FX1)
7p.	photo	purple-brown	1 side band	X876/Ea	(a) band at right—50p. booklets (FB2A/8A) (b) band at left—50p. booklets (FB2B/8B)
7p.	photo	brownish red	phos paper	X937	sheets
$7\frac{1}{2}$p.	photo	pale chestnut	2 bands	X877	sheets
8p.	photo	rosine	2 bands	X878	sheets
8p.	photo	rosine	1 centre band	X879	sheets, vertical coils, 10p. m/v coil (X845m), 10p. booklets (FA10/11), 80p. booklet (FE1), £1.80 Christmas booklet (FX2)
8p.	photo	rosine	1 side band	X880/Ea	(a) band at right—50p. booklets (FB9A/10A) (b) band at left—50p. booklets (FB9B/10B)
$8\frac{1}{2}$p.	photo	lt yellowish green	2 bands	X881	sheets, horizontal and vertical coils, 50p. booklet (FB1), 85p. booklet (FF1)
$8\frac{1}{2}$p.	photo	yellowish green	phos paper	X938	sheets
9p.	photo	yellow-orange & black	2 bands	X882	sheets
9p.	photo	dp violet	2 bands	X883	sheets, horizontal and vertical coils, 50p. booklet (FB2/8), 90p. booklets (FG1/8), £1.60 Christmas booklet (FX1)
$9\frac{1}{2}$p.	photo	purple	2 bands	X884	sheets
10p.	recess	cerise	phos paper	829	sheets
10p.	photo	orange-brown & chestnut	2 bands	X885	sheets
10p.	photo	orange-brown	2 bands	X886	Type I. sheets, 50p. booklets (FB9/10), £1.80 Christmas booklet (FX2)
10p.	photo	orange-brown	2 bands	X886b	Type II. £4 Christian Heritage booklet (DX5)
10p.	photo	orange-brown	"all-over"	X887	Type I. sheets, vertical coils, £1 booklet (FH1)
10p.	photo	orange-brown	phos paper	X939	Type I. sheets

Val.	Process	Colour	Phosphor	Cat. No.	Source
10p.	photo	orange-brown	1 centre band	X888	Type I. sheets, vertical coils, £1 booklets (FH2/4), £2.20 Christmas booklet (FX3), £3 Wedgwood booklet (DX2)
10p.	photo	orange-brown	1 side band	X889/Ea	Type I. (a) band at right—50p. booklets (FB11A/13A) (b) band at left—50p. booklets (FB11B/13B), £3 Wedgwood booklet (DX2)
10p.	photo	dull orange	phos paper	X940	sheets
$10\frac{1}{2}$p.	photo	yellow	2 bands	X890	sheets
$10\frac{1}{2}$p.	photo	dp dull blue	2 bands	X891	sheets
11p.	photo	brown-red	2 bands	X892	sheets
11p.	photo	brown-red	phos paper	X941	sheets
$11\frac{1}{2}$p.	photo	ochre-brown	phos paper	X942	sheets
$11\frac{1}{2}$p.	photo	drab	1 centre band	X893	sheets, vertical coils, £1.15 booklets (FI/4), £2.55 Christmas booklet (FX4)
$11\frac{1}{2}$p.	photo	drab	1 side band	X894/Ea	(a) band at right—50p. booklets (FB14A/18A), £1.30 booklets (FL1/2) (b) band at left—50p. booklets FB14B/18B), £1.30 booklets (FL1/2)
12p.	photo	yellowish green	phos paper	X943	sheets, vertical coils, £1.20 booklets (FJ1/3)
12p.	photo	yellowish green	2 bands	X895	50p. booklets (FB11/13), £2.20 Christmas booklet (FX3), £3 Wedgwood booklet (DX2)
12p.	photo	brt emerald	1 centre band	X896	sheets, horizontal and vertical coils, 50p. booklet (FB34), £1.20 booklets (FJ4/6), £5 British Rail booklet (DX7)
12p.	photo	brt emerald	1 side band	X897/Ea	(a) band at right—£1.50 booklets (FP1/2), £5 British Rail booklet (DX7) (b) band at left—£1.50 booklets (FP1/2), £5 British Rail booklet (DX7)
12p.	photo	brt emerald	1 centre band Underprint T.4	X896Eu	sheets
$12\frac{1}{2}$p.	photo	lt emerald	1 centre band	X898	sheets, vertical coils, 50p. booklets (FB24/6), £1.25 booklets (FK1/8), £4 SG booklet (DX3)
$12\frac{1}{2}$p.	photo	lt emerald	1 centre band Underprint T.1	X898Eu	£2.80 Christmas booklet (FX5)
$12\frac{1}{2}$p.	photo	lt emerald	1 centre band Underprint T.2	X898Ev	£2.50 Christmas booklet (FX6)
$12\frac{1}{2}$p.	photo	lt emerald	1 side band	X899/Ea	(a) band at right—50p. booklets (FB19A/23A), £1.43 booklets (FN1/6), £1.46 booklets (FO1/3), £4 SG booklet (DX3), £4 Royal Mint booklet (DX4) (b) band at left—50p. booklets (FB19B/23B), £1.43 booklets (FN1/6), £1.46 booklets (FO1/3), £4 SG booklet (DX3), £4 Royal Mint booklet (DX4)
13p.	photo	olive-grey	phos paper	X944	sheets
13p.	photo	pale chestnut	1 centre band	X900	sheets, horizontal and vertical coils, 50p. booklets (FB27/30, 35/6, 43/6, 48, 50), 52p. booklet (GA1), £1.30 booklets (FL3/14, GI1), £5 Times booklet (DX6), £5 P & O booklet (DX8)
13p.	photo	pale chestnut	1 centre band Underprint T.2	X900Eu	£1.30 Christmas booklet (FX9)
13p.	photo	pale chestnut	1 side band	X901/Ea	(a) band at right—50p. booklets (FB37/42, 47, 49), £1.54 booklets (FQ1/4), £4 Christian Heritage booklet (DX5), £5 Times booklet (DX6), £5 P & O booklet (DX8) (b) band at left—£1 booklets (FH6/13), £1.54 booklets (FQ1/4), £4 Christian Heritage booklet (DX5), £5 Times booklet (DX6)
13p.	litho	pale chestnut	1 centre band	X1005	£5 Financial Times booklet (DX9)
13p.	litho	pale chestnut	1 side band	X1006/Ea	£5 Financial Times booklet (DX9)
$13\frac{1}{2}$p.	photo	purple-brown	phos paper	X945	sheets
14p.	photo	grey-blue	phos paper	X946	sheets, vertical coils, £1.40 booklets (FM1/4)
14p.	photo	grey-blue	2 bands	X902	50p. booklets (FB14/16), £1.30 booklets (FL1/2), £2.55 Christmas booklet (FX4)
14p.	photo	dp blue	1 centre band	X903	sheets, horizontal and vertical coils, 56p. booklets (GB1/4), £1.40 booklets (FM5/6, GK1, 3)
14p.	photo	dp blue	1 band at right	X904	50p. booklets (FB51/4), £1 booklets (FH14/15)
14p.	litho	dp blue	1 centre band	X1007	£1.40 booklets (GK2, 4)
14p.	litho	dp blue	1 band at right	X1051*	£1 booklet (FH16)
15p.	photo	ultramarine	phos paper	X947	sheets

Decimal Machin Index (continued)

Val.	Process	Colour	Phosphor	Cat. No.	Source
15p.	photo	brt blue	1 centre band	X905	sheets, horizontal and vertical coils
15p.	photo	brt blue	1 side band	X906/Ea	(a) band at left—50p. booklet (FB55) (b) band at right—£5 London Life booklet (DX11)
15½p.	photo	pale violet	phos paper	X948	sheets, vertical coils, £1.55 booklets (FR1/6)
15½p.	photo	pale violet	2 bands	X907	£1.43 booklets (FN1/6), £4 SG booklet (DX3)
15½p.	photo	pale violet	2 bands Underprint T.1	X907Eu	£2.80 Christmas booklet (FX5)
16p.	photo	olive-drab	phos paper	X949	sheets, vertical coils, £1.60 booklets (FS1, 3/4), £4 Royal Mint booklet (DX4)
16p.	photo	olive-drab	phos paper Underprint T.3	X949Eu	£1.60 booklet (FS2)
16p.	photo	olive-drab	2 bands	X908	£1.46 booklets (FO1/3)
16½p.	photo	pale chestnut	phos paper	X950	sheets
17p.	photo	lt emerald	phos paper	X951	sheets
17p.	photo	grey-blue	phos paper	X952	sheets, vertical coils, £1 booklet (FH5), £1.70 booklets (FT1, 3 & 5/7), £4 Christian Heritage booklet (DX5), £5 Times booklet (DX6), £5 British Rail booklet (DX7)
17p.	photo	grey-blue	phos paper Underprint T.3	X952Eu	£1.70 booklet (FT2)
17p.	photo	grey-blue	2 bands	X909	50p. booklet (FB33), £1.50 booklets (FP1/3), £1.54 booklets (FQ1/4), £4 Christian Heritage booklet (DX5), £5 Times booklet (DX6), £5 British Rail booklet (DX7)
17p.	photo	grey-blue	2 bands Underprint T.4	X909Eu	50p. booklets (FB31/3)
17p.	photo	dp blue	1 centre band	X910	sheets, vertical coils
17p.	photo	dp blue	1 side band	X911/Ea	(a) band at right—50p. booklet (FB57/8), £1 booklet (FH21/2) (b) band at left—50p. booklet (FB57/8)
17p.	litho	dp blue	1 centre band	X1008	£6 Alias Agatha Christie booklet (DX12)
17½p.	photo	pale chestnut	phos paper	X953	sheets
18p.	photo	dp violet	phos paper	X954	sheets
18p.	photo	dp olive-grey	phos paper	X955	sheets, vertical coils, 72p. booklet (GC1), £1.80 booklets (FU1/8, GO1), £5 P & O booklet (DX8)
18p.	photo	dp olive-grey	2 bands	X912	50p. booklets (FB37/42, 47, 49), £1 booklet (FH6/13), £5 P & O booklet (DX8)
18p.	litho	dp olive-grey	phos paper	X1009	£5 Financial Times booklet (DX9)
18p.	litho	dp olive-grey	2 bands	X1010	£5 Financial Times booklet (DX9)
18p.	photo	brt green	1 centre band	X913	sheets, vertical coils
18p.	litho	brt green	1 centre band	X1011	£6 Tolkien booklet (DX14)
18p.	litho	brt green	1 side band	X1012/Ea	(a) band at right—£6 Tolkien booklet (DX14). (b) band at left—£6 (£5.64) Beatrix Potter booklet (DX15)).
19p.	photo	brt orange-red	phos paper	X956	sheets, vertical coils, 76p. booklets (GD1/4), £1.90 booklets (FV1/2, GP1, 3)
19p.	photo	brt orange-red	2 bands	X914	50p. booklets (FB51/4), £1 booklets (FH14/15, 17)
19p.	litho	brt orange-red	phos paper	X1013	£1.90 booklets (GP2, 4)
19p.	litho	brt orange-red	2 bands	X1052*	£1 booklet (FH16)
19½p.	photo	olive-grey	phos paper	X957	sheets
20p.	recess	olive-green	none	830	sheets
20p.	photo	dull purple	2 bands	X915	sheets
20p.	photo	dull purple	phos paper	X958	sheets
20p.	litho	dull purple	2 bands	X998	sheets
20p.	litho	dull purple	phos paper	X999 X1014	sheets J.W. ptg. sheets Questa ptg.
20p.	photo	turquoise-green	phos paper	X959	sheets
20p.	photo	brownish black	phos paper	X960	sheets, horizontal and vertical coils, £1 booklet (FH18)
20p.	photo	brownish black	2 bands	X916	50p. booklet (FB55), £5 London Life booklet (DX11)
20½p.	photo	ultramarine	phos paper	X961	sheets
22p.	photo	blue	phos paper	X962	sheets
22p.	photo	yellow-green	phos paper	X963	sheets

Val.	Process	Colour	Phosphor	Cat. No.	Source
22p.	litho	yellow-green	2 bands	X1015	£5 Financial Times booklet (DX9)
22p.	photo	brt orange-red	2 bands	X917*	£1 booklet (FH21/2)
22p.	photo	brt orange-red	phos paper	X964	sheets, vertical coils
22p.	litho	brt orange-red	phos paper	X1016	£6 Alias Agatha Christie booklet (DX12)
23p.	photo	brown-red	phos paper	X965	sheets
23p.	photo	brt green	phos paper	X966	sheets
24p.	photo	violet	phos paper	X967	sheets
24p.	photo	Indian red	phos paper	X968	sheets
24p.	photo	chestnut	phos paper	X969	sheets, vertical coils, 50p. booklets (FB59/66), £1 booklets (FH23/7)
24p.	litho	chestnut	phos paper	X1017 X1053*	£6 Tolkien booklet (DX14) (Questa ptg) £1 booklet (FH28/30) Walsall ptg
24p.	litho	chestnut	2 bands	X1018	£6 Tolkien booklet (DX14)
25p.	photo	purple	phos paper	X970	sheets
25p.	photo	rose-red	2 bands	X917a	horizontal coils
26p.	photo	rosine	phos paper	X971	Type I. sheets
26p.	photo	rosine	2 bands	X918	Type I. £5 P & O booklet (DX8)
26p.	photo	rosine	phos paper	X971b	Type II. £1.04 booklet (GE1)
26p.	photo	drab	phos paper	X972	sheets
27p.	photo	chestnut	phos paper	X973	sheets, £1.08 booklets (GF1/2)
27p.	photo	violet	phos paper	X974	sheets
28p.	photo	dp violet	phos paper	X975	sheets
28p.	photo	ochre	phos paper	X976	sheets
28p.	photo	dp bluish grey	phos paper	X977	sheets
29p.	photo	ochre-brown	phos paper	X978	sheets
29p.	photo	dp mauve	phos paper	X979	sheets
29p.	litho	dp mauve	2 bands	X1054*	£1.16 booklet (GG1)
29p.	litho	dp mauve	phos paper	X1055*	£1.16 booklet (GG2)
30p.	photo	dp olive-grey	phos paper	X980	sheets
31p.	photo	purple	phos paper	X981	sheets
31p.	photo	purple	2 bands	X919	£5 British Rail booklet (DX7)
31p.	photo	ultramarine	phos paper	X982	sheets
31p.	litho	ultramarine	phos paper	X1056*	£1.24 booklet (GH1)
32p.	photo	greenish blue	phos paper	X983	sheets
33p.	photo	lt emerald	phos paper	X984	sheets, vertical coils
33p.	litho	lt emerald	phos paper	X1019	£6 Alias Agatha Christie booklet (DX12)
33p.	litho	lt emerald	phos paper	X1057*	£1.32 booklet (GJ1)
33p.	litho	lt emerald	2 bands	X1020	£6 Wales booklet (DX13), £6 (£5.64) Beatrix Potter booklet (DX15)
34p.	photo	ochre-brown	phos paper	X985	sheets
34p.	photo	ochre-brown	2 bands	X920	£5 Times booklet (DX6)
34p.	litho	bistre-brown	2 bands	X1021	£5 Financial Times booklet (DX9)
34p.	photo	dp bluish grey	phos paper	X986	sheets
34p.	photo	dp mauve	phos paper	X987	sheets
35p.	photo	sepia	phos paper	X988	sheets
35p.	photo	yellow	phos paper	X989	sheets
37p.	photo	rosine	phos paper	X990	sheets
39p.	photo	brt mauve	phos paper	X991	sheets, vertical coils
39p.	litho	brt mauve	phos paper	X1058*	78p. booklet (GD4a), £1.56 booklet (GM1)
39p.	litho	brt mauve	2 bands	X1022	£6 Tolkien booklet (DX14), £6 (£5.64) Beatrix Potter booklet (DX15)
50p.	recess	dp ultramarine	none or phos paper	831/Ea	sheets

Val.	Process	Colour	Phosphor	Cat. No.	Source
50p.	photo	ochre-brown	2 bands	X921	sheets
50p.	photo	ochre-brown	none	X992	sheets
50p.	photo	ochre	2 bands	X922	£5 London Life (DX11)
50p.	photo	ochre	none or phos paper	X994	sheets
75p.	litho	black	none	X1023/a	sheets
75p.	litho	brownish grey & black	none	X1024	sheets
75p.	photo	grey-black	none	X993	sheets
£1	recess	bluish black	none	831b	sheets
£1	photo	brt yellow-green & blackish olive	none	1026	sheets
£1.30	photo	drab & dp greenish blue	none	1026b	sheets
£1.33	photo	pale mauve & grey-black	none	1026c	sheets
£1.41	photo	drab & dp greenish blue	none	1026d	sheets
£1.50	photo	pale mauve & grey-black	none	1026e	sheets
£1.60	photo	pale drab & dp greenish blue	none	1026f	sheets
£2	photo	lt emerald & purple-brown	none	1027	sheets
£5	photo	salmon & chalky blue	none	1028	sheets

For 1st and 2nd class no value indicated (NVI) stamps, see Nos. 1445/52, 1511/16 and 1663a/6.
For table covering Machin stamps with elliptical perforations see after Nos. Y1667, etc, in 1993.

DECIMAL MACHIN MULTI-VALUE COIL INDEX

The following is a simplified checklist of horizontal multi-value coils, to be used in conjunction with the main listing as details of stamps listed there are not repeated.

Strip Value	Date	Contents	Cat No.
5p.	15.2.71	$\frac{1}{2}$p. × 2, 1p. × 2, 2p.	X841n
10p.	3.12.75	$\frac{1}{2}$p. × 2, 1p., 2p., 6p.	X841q
10p.	14.12.77	$\frac{1}{2}$p. × 2, 1p. × 2, 7p.	X843l
10p.	16.1.80	1p. × 2, 8p. plus 2 labels	X845m
11$\frac{1}{2}$p.	6.81	2$\frac{1}{2}$p., 3p. × 3	X929l
12$\frac{1}{2}$p.	30.12.81	$\frac{1}{2}$p., 4p. × 3	X924l
13p.	14.8.84	1p., 4p. × 3	X925l
14p.	5.9.88	2p., 4p. × 3	X928l
15p.	10.10.89	3p., 4p. × 3	X930cl
17p.	27.11.90	4p. × 3, 5p.	X933l
18p.	1.10.91	4p. × 2, 5p. × 2	X933m
19p.	31.1.95	4p., 5p. × 3	X933n

Abbreviations used in the diagrams: 2B = 2 bands, CB = centre band, LB = left band and RB = right band. The shaded squares represent printed labels. Panes completed by unprinted white labels are outside the scope of this catalogue.

Unless otherwise stated the panes were printed in photogravure. Some panes exist in photogravure and lithography and these are separately identified and listed. **Imperforate or straight edges.** These are described under the appropriate illustration and listed as complete panes.

X841l (2 bands)

2	2
½	½

X841la (2 bands)

2	½
2	½

X841m (2 bands)

½	½	½
[label]	½	½

X841o — £1 Wedgwood

2½ RB	½ 2B	2½ LB	2½ CB
2½ RB	½ 2B	2½ LB	2½ CB
2½ RB	½ 2B	2½ LB	2½ CB

X841p — £1 Wedgwood

½ 2B	2½ LB
½ 2B	2½ LB
½ 2B	2½ LB

X841r (2 bands)

½	½
6	1
1	1

X841s

½ 2B	½ 2B
1 2B	8½ 2B
1 2B	8½ 2B
6½ RB	8½ 2B
6½ RB	8½ 2B

X841sa

½ 2B	½ 2B
8½ 2B	1 2B
8½ 2B	1 2B
8½ 2B	6½ LB
8½ 2B	6½ LB

X841t

11½ RB	½ 2B
11½ RB	1 2B
11½ RB	14 2B

X841ta

½ 2B	11½ LB
1 2B	11½ LB
14 2B	11½ LB

X841u

½ 2B	3 2B
12½ RB	3 2B
12½ RB	3 2B
12½ RB	3 2B

X841ua

3 2B	½ 2B
3 2B	12½ LB
3 2B	12½ LB
3 2B	12½ LB

X843m (centre band)

½	[label]
½	1
7	1

X844l (2 bands)

1	1
1½	1½

X844m (2 bands)

1½	1
1½	1

X844n

1 2B	1 2B
7 RB	9 2B
7 RB	9 2B
7 RB	9 2B

X844na

1 2B	1 2B
9 2B	7 LB
9 2B	7 LB
9 2B	7 LB

X845l (centre band)

[label]	1
8	1

X845n (centre band)

3½	12½
3½	12½
3½	12½

X845p (centre band)

1	13
4	13
4	13

X845q (centre band)

1	1
12	12
12	12

X845s/sa (centre band)
X845sa imperf at left and right

1	13
5	13
5	13

X847l

1 LB	13 RB
18 2B	18 2B

X847m — £5 P & O

13 RB	18 2B	18 2B
1 RB	18 2B	26 2B
13 RB	18 2B	18 2B

X849l

[label]	2 2B
2 2B	10 2B
8 RB	10 2B
8 RB	10 2B

X849la

2 2B	[label]
10 2B	2 2B
10 2B	8 LB
10 2B	8 LB

X849m

[label]	2 RB
2 2B	2 2B
10 RB	2 2B
10 RB	12 2B

X849ma

2 2B	[label]
2 2B	2 2B
12 2B	10 LB
12 2B	10 LB

X849n
£3 Wedgwood

X849o
(2 bands)
£3 Wedgwood

X849p
£4 Stanley Gibbons

X851l
(centre band)

X851m
(centre band)

X851n
£1 Wedgwood

X852l

X854l

X854la

X855l
(2 bands)

X864l
£5 The Times

X875l
Christmas 1978

X879l
Christmas 1979

X886bl
£4 Christian Heritage

X888l
(centre band)
£3 Wedgwood

X888m
Christmas 1980

X893l
Christmas 1981

X894l
Margin at left or right

X895l
(2 bands)
£3 Wedgwood

X896l
(centre band)
£5 British Rail

X897l

X897la

X897m
£5 British Rail

X898l
Christmas 1982

X899l
Margin at left or right

X899m
£4 Stanley Gibbons
£4 Royal Mint

X899n

X899na

X900l
(centre band)
£5 The Times
£5 P & O

X900m, (photo), X1005l (litho)
(centre band)
£5 P & O (X900m)
£5 Financial Times (X1005l)

X900n
(centre band)
52p. Barcode Booklet

X900o
(centre band)
£1.30 Barcode Booklet

X901l

X901la

X901m
£4 Christian Heritage

X901n/na
X901na imperf at
left and right

X903l
(centre band)
56p. Barcode Booklet

Decimal Machin Booklet Pane Guide (continued)

14	14	14	14	14
14	14	14	14	14

X903m)
(centre band)
£1.40 Barcode Booklet

14	14
14	14

X903n, X903q
(centre band)
56p. Barcode Booklet
X903n imperf at top
and bottom
X903q imperf 3 sides

14	14	14	14	14
14	14	14	14	14

X903p
(centre band)
£1.40 Barcode Booklet
Imperf at top
and bottom

	19 2B
14 RB	19 2B

X904l

14 RB	19 2B
14 RB	19 2B
19 2B	19 2B

X904m, (photo)
X1051l (litho)
imperf at left
and right

---

	15 LB
20 2B	15 LB

X906l

2ND RB	50 2B	1ST 2B
15 RB		20 2B
15 RB	29 2B	20 2B

X906m
£5 London Life
The stamps in the bottom row are
Penny Black Anniversary definitives
(Nos. 1468Ea, 1470 and 1472)

$15\frac{1}{2}$	$15\frac{1}{2}$
$15\frac{1}{2}$	$15\frac{1}{2}$
$15\frac{1}{2}$	$15\frac{1}{2}$

X907l
(2 bands)
£4 Stanley Gibbons

$15\frac{1}{2}$	$15\frac{1}{2}$	$15\frac{1}{2}$
$15\frac{1}{2}$	$15\frac{1}{2}$	$15\frac{1}{2}$
$15\frac{1}{2}$	$15\frac{1}{2}$	$15\frac{1}{2}$

X907m
(2 bands)
£4 Stanley Gibbons

	17
17	17

X909l
(2 bands)
and underprint
X909 Ela (as X909l
but without
underprint)

	17 LB
17 RB	17 LB

X911l

	22 2B
17 RB	22 2B
17 RB	22 2B

X911m
Imperf at left
and right

1	1
24	24

X925m
(phosphorised paper)

2	2
24	24
24	24

X927l (photo)
X1050l (litho)
(phosphorised paper)
Imperf at left and
right

16	16	16
$3\frac{1}{2}$	3	$3\frac{1}{2}$
16	16	16

X930b
(phosphorised paper)
£4 Royal Mint

16	16	16
16	16	16
16	16	16

X949l
(phosphorised paper)
£4 Royal Mint

17	17
17	17
17	17

X952l
(phosphorised paper)
£4 Christian Heritage
£5 The Times
£5 British Rail
X1008l
(centre band)
£6 Agatha Christie

17	17	17
17	17	17
17	17	17

X952m
(phosphorised paper)
£5 The Times
£5 British Rail

18	18	18
18	18	18
18	18	18

X955l (photo), X1009l (litho)
(phosphorised paper)
£5 P & O (X955l)
£5 Financial Times (X1009l)

368 "A Mountain Road"
(T. P. Flanagan)

369 "Deer's Meadow"
(Tom Carr)

371 John Keats
(150th Death Anniv)

372 Thomas Gray
(Death Bicentenary)

370 "Slieve na brock"
(Colin Middleton)

373 Sir Walter Scott (Birth Bicentenary)

(Des Rosalind Dease. Queen's head printed in gold and then embossed)

1971 (28 July). **Literary Anniversaries.** *Chalk-surfaced paper. Two phosphor bands. P 15 × 14.*

884	371	3p. black, gold & greyish blue	10	10
		a. Gold (Queen's head) omitted	£100	
		Ey. Phosphor omitted	5·00	
885	372	5p. black, gold & yellow-olive	40	45
		a. Gold (Queen's head) omitted	£300	
		Ey. Phosphor omitted	32·00	
886	373	7½p. black, gold & yellow-brown	40	50
		Eb. Embossing omitted	40·00	
		Ey. Phosphor omitted	22·00	
		Set of 3	80	90
		First Day Cover		3·25
		Presentation Pack	5·00	

Special First Day of Issue Postmarks

1971 (16 June). **"Ulster 1971" Paintings.** *Chalk-surfaced paper. Two phosphor bands. P 15 × 14.*

881	368	3p. yellow-buff, pale yellow, Venetian red, black, blue & drab	10	10
		Ey. Phosphor omitted	6·00	
882	369	7½p. olive-brown, brownish grey, pale olive-grey, dp blue, cobalt & grey-blue	40	45
		a. Pale olive-grey omitted*	90·00	
		Ey. Phosphor omitted	22·00	
883	370	9p. greenish yellow, orange, grey, lavender-grey, bistre, black, pale ochre-brown & ochre-brown	45	45
		a. Orange (flowers) omitted	£1700	
		Ey. Phosphor omitted	22·00	
		Set of 3	80	90
		First Day Cover		2·50
		Presentation Pack	5·00	

A used example of the 3p. has been seen with the Venetian red omitted.

*This only affects the boulder in the foreground, which appears whitish and it only applied to some stamps in the sheet.

Special First Day of Issue Postmarks

FIRST DAY OF ISSUE
16 JUNE 1971
BELFAST

British Post Office Philatelic Bureau, Edinburgh
(Type D, see Introduction) .... 3·50
Belfast .... 8·00

First Day of Issue handstamps, in the same design as that for Belfast, were provided at Armagh, Ballymena, Coleraine, Cookstown, Enniskillen, Londonderry, Newry, Omagh and Portadown for this issue.

British Post Office Philatelic Bureau, Edinburgh
(Type D, see Introduction) .... 5·00
London EC .... 8·00

HAVE YOU READ THE NOTES AT THE BEGINNING OF THIS CATALOGUE?

These often provide answers to the enquiries we receive.

374 Servicemen and Nurse of 1921

375 Roman Centurion

376 Rugby Football, 1871

(Des F. Wegner)

1971 (25 Aug). **British Anniversaries.** *Events described on stamps. Chalk-surfaced paper. Two phosphor bands.* P 15 × 14.

887	374	3p. red-orange, grey, dp blue, olive-green, olive-brown, black, rosine & violet-blue .		10	10
		a. Dp blue omitted*		£650	
		b. Red-orange (nurse's cloak) omitted		£300	
		c. Olive-brown (faces, etc.) omitted		£250	
		d. Black omitted		£12000	
		Ey. Phosphor omitted		3·00	
888	375	7½p. grey, yellow-brown, vermilion, mauve, grey-black, black, silver, gold & ochre ..		40	45
		a. Grey omitted		90·00	
		Ey. Phosphor omitted		15·00	
889	376	9p. new blue, myrtle-green, grey-black, lemon, olive-brown, magenta & yellow-olive		40	45
		a. Olive-brown omitted		£130	
		b. New blue omitted		£3750	
		c. Myrtle-green omitted		£7500	
		Ey. Phosphor omitted		£400	
		Set of 3		80	90
		First Day Cover			2·50
		Presentation Pack		5·00	

*The effect of the missing deep blue is shown on the sailor's uniform, which appears as grey.

Used examples have been seen of the 3p. with grey omitted and of the 9p. with the lemon (jerseys) omitted.

Special First Day of Issue Postmarks

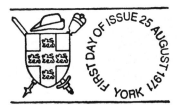

British Post Office Philatelic Bureau, Edinburgh (Type D, see Introduction)		3·50
Maidstone		16·00
Twickenham		16·00
York		16·00

377 Physical Sciences Building, University College of Wales, Aberystwyth

378 Faraday Building, Southampton University

379 Engineering Department, Leicester University

380 Hexagon Restaurant, Essex University

(Des N. Jenkins)

1971 (22 Sept). **British Architecture. Modern University Buildings.** *Chalk-surfaced paper. Two phosphor bands.* P 15 × 14.

890	377	3p. olive-brown, ochre, lemon, black & yellow-olive		10	10
		a. Lemon omitted		†	£5000
		b. Black (windows) omitted		£10000	
		Ey. Phosphor omitted		8·00	
891	378	5p. rose, black, chestnut & lilac		25	20
		Ey. Phosphor omitted		70·00	
892	379	7½p. ochre, black & purple-brown		45	55
		Ey. Phosphor omitted		12·00	
893	380	9p. pale lilac, black, sepia-brown & dp blue		75	80
		a. Pale lilac omitted		£2750	
		Ey. Phosphor omitted		18·00	
		Set of 4		1·40	1·50
		First Day Cover			2·75
		Presentation Pack		5·50	

Mint examples of the 5p. exist with a larger "P" following the face value

No. 890a is only known used on commercial cover from Wantage.

British Post Office Philatelic Bureau, Edinburgh
    (Type D, see Introduction) .... 4·00
Aberystwyth .... 14·00
Colchester .... 14·00
Leicester .... 14·00
Southampton .... 14·00

Collectors Pack 1971

1971 (29 Sept). *Comprises Nos. 835/40 and 881/93.*
CP893a   Collectors Pack .... 27·00

381 "Dream of the Wise Men"

382 "Adoration of the Magi"

383 "Ride of the Magi"

HAVE YOU READ THE NOTES AT THE BEGINNING OF THIS CATALOGUE?
These often provide answers to the enquiries we receive.

(Des Clarke-Clements-Hughes design team, from stained-glass windows, Canterbury Cathedral. Queen's head printed in gold and then embossed)

1971 (13 Oct).   **Christmas.** *Ordinary paper. One centre phosphor band* ($2\frac{1}{2}$p.) *or two phosphor bands (others). P 15 × 14.*

894	381	$2\frac{1}{2}$p.	new blue, black, lemon, emerald, reddish violet, carmine-red, carmine-rose & gold	10	10
		a.	Imperf (pair)	£450	
		Eb.	Embossing omitted		
895	382	3p.	black, reddish violet, lemon, new blue, carmine-rose, emerald, ultramarine & gold	10	10
		a.	Gold (Queen's head) omitted	£550	
		b.	Carmine-rose omitted	£3000	
		c.	Lemon (window panels) omitted	£120	
		d.	New blue omitted	†	£7000
		e.	Reddish violet (tunics etc) omitted	£3250	
		Ef.	Embossing omitted	15·00	
		Ey.	Phosphor omitted	5·00	
		Eya.	Embossing and phosphor omitted	£100	
896	383	$7\frac{1}{2}$p.	black, lilac, lemon, emerald, new blue, rose, green & gold	55	75
		a.	Gold (Queen's head) omitted	£110	
		b.	Lilac omitted	£550	
		c.	Emerald omitted	£275	
		Ed.	Embossing omitted	50·00	
		Ee.	Embossing double	50·00	
		Ey.	Phosphor omitted	12·00	
		Eya.	Embossing and phosphor omitted	32·00	
			Set of 3	65	85
			First Day Cover		2·75
			Presentation Pack	4·50	

The 3p. is known with reddish violet and embossing omitted, used in Llandudno and with lemon and carmine-rose both omitted used in Falkirk. The $7\frac{1}{2}$p. is known in used condition showing the lemon omitted.

British Post Office Philatelic Bureau, Edinburgh
    (Type D, see Introduction) .... 4·50
Bethlehem, Llandeilo, Carms .... 10·00
Canterbury .... 10·00

WHITE CHALK-SURFACED PAPER. From No. 897 all issues, with the exception of Nos. 940/8, were printed on fluorescent white paper, giving a stronger chalk reaction than the original cream paper.

384 Sir James Clark Ross

385 Sir Martin Frobisher

386 Henry Hudson

387 Capt. Scott

(Des Marjorie Saynor. Queen's head printed in gold and then embossed)

1972 (16 Feb). **British Polar Explorers.** *Two phosphor bands.* P 14 × 15.

897	**384**	3p. yellow-brown, indigo, slate-black, flesh, lemon, rose, brt blue & gold	10	10
		a. Gold (Queen's head) omitted	80·00	
		b. Slate-black (hair, etc.) omitted	£3000	
		c. Lemon omitted	£6500	
		Ed. Embossing omitted	45·00	
		Ee. Gold (Queen's head) & embossing omitted	£110	
		Ey. Phosphor omitted	5·00	
		Eya. Embossing and phosphor omitted	35·00	
898	**385**	5p. salmon, flesh, purple-brown, ochre, black & gold	15	15
		a. Gold (Queen's head) omitted	£100	
		Eb. Embossing omitted	25·00	
		Ey. Phosphor omitted	12·00	
		Eya. Gold and phosphor omitted	£130	
		Eyb. Embossing and phosphor omitted		
899	**386**	7½p. reddish violet, blue, dp slate, yellow-brown, buff, black & gold	45	40
		a. Gold (Queen's head) omitted	£275	
		Ey. Phosphor omitted	20·00	
900	**387**	9p. dull blue, ultramarine, black, greenish yellow, pale pink, rose-red & gold	70	75
		Ey. Phosphor omitted	£325	
		Set of 4	1·25	1·25
		First Day Cover		3·50
		Presentation Pack	4·75	

An example of the 3p. is known used on piece with the flesh colour omitted.

Philatelic Bureau, Edinburgh .... 10·00
London WC .... 15·00

388 Statuette of Tutankhamun

389 19th-century Coastguard

390 Ralph Vaughan Williams and Score

(Des Rosalind Dease (3p.), F. Wegner (7½p.), C. Abbott (9p.). Queen's head printed in gold and then embossed (7½p., 9p.))

1972 (26 Apr). **General Anniversaries.** *Events described on stamps. Two phosphor bands.* P 15 × 14.

901	**388**	3p. black, grey, gold, dull bistre-brown, blackish brown, pale stone & lt brown ..	15	10
902	**389**	7½p. pale yellow, new blue, slate-blue, violet-blue, slate & gold	30	45
		Ea. Embossing omitted	£200	
		Ey. Phosphor omitted	£250	
903	**390**	9p. bistre-brown, black, sage-green, dp slate, yellow-ochre, brown & gold	40	50
		a. Gold (Queen's head) omitted	£2750	
		b. Brown (facial features) omitted	£950	
		c. Deep slate omitted		
		Ed. Embossing omitted		
		Ey. Phosphor omitted	32·00	
		Set of 3	80	90
		First Day Cover		2·75
		Presentation Pack	4·25	

Philatelic Bureau, Edinburgh .... 4·00
London EC .... 7·00

391 St. Andrew's, Greensted-juxta-Ongar, Essex

392 All Saints, Earls Barton, Northants

393 St. Andrew's, Letheringsett, Norfolk

394 St. Andrew's, Helpringham, Lincs

395 St. Mary the Virgin, Huish Episcopi, Somerset

(Des R. Maddox. Queen's head printed in gold and then embossed)

1972 (21 June). **British Architecture. Village Churches.** *Ordinary paper. Two phosphor bands. P* 14 × 15.

904	**391**	3p. violet-blue, black, lt yellow-olive, emerald-green, orange-vermilion & gold	10	10
		a. Gold (Queen's head) omitted	80·00	
		Eb. Embossing omitted	35·00	
		Ey. Phosphor omitted	6·00	
		Eya. Gold (Queen's head) & phosphor omitted	£130	
		Eyb. Embossing & phosphor omitted	20·00	
905	**392**	4p. dp yellow-olive, black, emerald, violet-blue, orange-vermilion and gold	10	20
		a. Gold (Queen's head) omitted	£4250	
		b. Violet-blue omitted	£130	
		Ec. Embossing omitted	12·00	
		Ey. Phosphor omitted	18·00	
906	**393**	5p. dp emerald, black, royal blue, lt yellow-olive, orange-vermilion & gold	15	20
		a. Gold (Queen's head) omitted	£160	
		Eb. Embossing omitted	50·00	
		Ey. Phosphor omitted	25·00	
907	**394**	7½p. orange-red, black, dp yellow-olive, royal blue, lt emerald & gold	60	75
		Ey. Phosphor omitted	18·00	
		Eya. Embossing and phosphor omitted	45·00	
908	**395**	9p. new blue, black, emerald-green, dp yellow-olive, orange-vermilion & gold . . .	60	80
		Ea. Embossing omitted	20·00	
		Ey. Phosphor omitted	22·00	
		Set of 5	1·40	1·90
		First Day Cover		3·75
		Presentation Pack		6·00

Nos. 905a and 906a only exist with the phosphor omitted.

An example of the 3p. is known used on piece with the orange-vermilion omitted.

Special First Day of Issue Postmarks

Philatelic Bureau, Edinburgh	6·00
Canterbury	8·00

"Belgica '72" Souvenir Pack

1972 (24 June). *Comprises Nos. 894/6 and 904/8.*

CP908*b* Souvenir Pack . . . . 12·00

This pack was specially produced for sale at the "Belgica '72" Stamp Exhibition, held in Brussels between 24 June and 9 July. It contains information on British stamps with a religious theme with text in English, French and Flemish, and was put on sale at Philatelic Bureaux in Britain on 26 June.

396 Microphones, 1924–69

397 Horn Loudspeaker

398 T.V. Camera, 1972

399 Oscillator and Spark Transmitter, 1897

(Des D. Gentleman)

1972 (13 Sept). **Broadcasting Anniversaries. 75th Anniv of Marconi and Kemp's Radio Experiments** (9p.), **and 50th Anniv of Daily Broadcasting by the B.B.C.** (others). *Two phosphor bands. P* 15 × 14.

909	**396**	3p. pale brown, black, grey, greenish yellow & brownish slate	10	10
		a. Greenish yellow (terminals) omitted	£4000	

910	**397**	5p. brownish slate, lake-brown, salmon, lt brown, black & red-brown	10	20
		Ey. Phosphor omitted	6·00	
		Eya. Phosphor on back but omitted on front	45·00	
911	**398**	7½p. lt grey, slate, brownish slate, magenta & black	45	55
		a. Brownish slate (Queen's head) omitted .	† £2750	
		Ey. Phosphor omitted	12·00	
912	**399**	9p. lemon, brown, brownish slate, dp brownish slate, bluish slate & black	50	65
		a. Brownish slate (Queen's head) omitted .	£2750	
		Ey. Phosphor omitted	13·00	
		Set of 4	1·00	1·40
		First Day Cover		3·75
		Presentation Pack	3·75	

In addition to the generally issued Presentation Pack a further pack exists inscribed "1922–1972". This pack of stamps commemorating the 50th Anniversary of the B.B.C. was specially produced as a memento of the occasion for the B.B.C. staff. It was sent with the good wishes of the Chairman and Board of Governors, the Director-General and Board of Management. The pack contains Nos. 909/11 only (*Price* £35).

No. 911a is only found in first day covers posted from the Philatelic Bureau in Edinburgh.

Special First Day of Issue Postmarks

Philatelic Bureau, Edinburgh	5·50	
London W1	12·00	

400 Angel holding Trumpet

401 Angel playing Lute

402 Angel playing Harp

(Des Sally Stiff. Photo and embossing)

1972 (18 Oct). **Christmas.** *One centre phosphor band (2½p.) or two phosphor bands (others). P* 14 × 15.

913	**400**	2½p. cerise, pale reddish brown, yellow-orange, orange-vermilion, lilac, gold, red-brown & dp grey	10	10
		a. Gold omitted	£325	
		Eb. Embossing omitted	15·00	
		c. Dp grey omitted	£1800	
		Ey. Phosphor omitted	12·00	
914	**401**	3p. ultramarine, lavender, lt turquoise-blue, brt green, gold, red-brown & bluish violet	10	10
		a. Red-brown omitted	£550	
		b. Brt green omitted	£110	
		c. Bluish violet omitted	£110	
		Ed. Embossing omitted	9·00	
		Ey. Phosphor omitted	6·00	
		Eya. Embossing and phosphor omitted	15·00	
915	**402**	7½p. dp brown, pale lilac, lt cinnamon, ochre, gold, red-brown & blackish violet	50	70
		a. Ochre omitted	80·00	
		b. Blackish violet (shadow) omitted	£6500	
		Ec. Embossing omitted	18·00	
		Ey. Phosphor omitted	12·00	
		Eya. Embossing and phosphor omitted	30·00	
		Set of 3	60	80
		First Day Cover		2·50
		Presentation Pack	3·00	

The gold printing on the 3p. is from two cylinders: 1E and 1F. Examples have been seen with the gold of the 1F cylinder omitted, but these are difficult to detect on single stamps.

Special First Day of Issue Postmarks

Philatelic Bureau, Edinburgh	5·00	
Bethlehem, Llandeilo, Carms	7·50	

403 Queen Elizabeth and Duke of Edinburgh

404 "Europe"

(Des J. Matthews from photo by N. Parkinson)

1972 (20 Nov). **Royal Silver Wedding.** *"All-over" phosphor (3p.) or without phosphor (20p.)* P 14 × 15.

I. *"Rembrandt" Machine*

916	**403**	3p. brownish black, dp blue & silver	20	15
		a. Silver omitted	£375	
917		20p. brownish black, reddish purple & silver .	75	70

II. *"Jumelle" Machine*

918	**403**	3p. brownish black, dp blue & silver	40	10
		Set of 2	90	80
		Gutter Pair (No. 918)	80	
		Traffic Light Gutter Pair	14·00	
		First Day Cover		2·00
		Presentation Pack	3·00	
		Presentation Pack (Japanese)	7·00	
		Souvenir Book	6·00	

The souvenir book is a twelve-page booklet containing photographs of the Royal Wedding and other historic events of the royal family and accompanying information.

The 3p. "JUMELLE" has a lighter shade of the brownish black than the 3p. "REMBRANDT". It also has the brown cylinders less deeply etched, which can be distinguished in the Duke's face which is slightly lighter, and in the Queen's hair where the highlights are sharper.

3p. "REMBRANDT". Cyls. 3A–1B–11C no dot. Sheets of 100 (10 x 10).
3p. "JUMELLE". Cyls. 1A–1B–3C dot and no dot. Sheets of 100 (two panes 5 x 10, separated by gutter margin).

Special First Day of Issue Postmarks

Philatelic Bureau, Edinburgh	. . . .	4·00
Windsor, Berks	. . . .	8·00

Collectors Pack 1972

1972 (20 Nov). *Comprises Nos. 897/918.*

CP918a	Collectors Pack	27·00

(Des P. Murdoch)

1973 (3 Jan). **Britain's Entry into European Communities.** *Two phosphor bands.* P 14 × 15.

919	**404**	3p. dull orange, brt rose-red, ultramarine, lt lilac & black	10	15
920		5p. new blue, brt rose-red, ultramarine, cobalt-blue & black	25	40
		a. Pair. Nos. 920/1	80	1·40
921		5p. lt emerald-green, brt rose-red, ultramarine, cobalt-blue & black	25	40
		Set of 3	80	90
		First Day Cover		2·00
		Presentation Pack	2·75	

Nos. 920/1 were printed horizontally *se-tenant* throughout the sheet.

Special First Day of Issue Postmark

Philatelic Bureau, Edinburgh	4·50

405 Oak Tree

(Des D. Gentleman)

1973 (28 Feb). **Tree Planting Year. British Trees (1st issue).** *Two phosphor bands.* P 15 × 14.

922	**405**	9p. brownish black, apple-green, dp olive, sepia, blackish green & brownish grey . .	35	40
		a. Brownish black (value & inscr) omitted .	£425	
		b. Brownish grey (Queen's head) omitted . .	£300	
		Ey. Phosphor omitted	90·00	
		First Day Cover		2·25
		Presentation Pack	2·25	

See also No. 949.

Special First Day of Issue Postmark

Philatelic Bureau, Edinburgh	5·50

CHALK-SURFACED PAPER. The following issues are printed on chalk-surfaced paper but where "all-over" phosphor has been applied there is no chalk reaction except in the sheet margins outside the phosphor area.

406 David Livingstone

407 H. M. Stanley

T **406/7** were printed together, horizontally *se-tenant* within the sheet

408 Sir Francis Drake

409 Walter Raleigh

410 Charles Sturt

(Des Marjorie Saynor. Queen's head printed in gold and then embossed)

1973 (18 Apr). **British Explorers.** *"All-over"* phosphor. P 14 × 15.

923	406	3p. orange-yellow, lt orange-brown, grey-black, lt turquoise-blue, turquoise-blue & gold		20	15
		a. Pair. Nos. 923/4		80	1·00
		b. Gold (Queen's head) omitted		55·00	
		c. Turquoise-blue (background & inscr) omitted		£400	
		d. Lt orange-brown omitted		£375	
		Ee. Embossing omitted		35·00	
924	407	3p. orange-yellow, lt orange-brown, grey-black, lt turquoise-blue, turquoise-blue & gold		20	15
		b. Gold (Queen's head) omitted		55·00	
		c. Turquoise-blue (background & inscr) omitted		£400	
		d. Lt orange-brown omitted		£375	
		Ee. Embossing omitted		35·00	
925	408	5p. lt flesh, chrome-yellow, orange-yellow, sepia, brownish grey, grey-black, violet-blue & gold		20	35
		a. Gold (Queen's head) omitted		£120	
		b. Grey-black omitted		£600	
		c. Sepia omitted		£550	
		Ed. Embossing omitted		9·00	
926	409	7½p. lt flesh, reddish brown, sepia, ultramarine, grey-black, brt lilac & gold		20	45
		a. Gold (Queen's head) omitted		£2500	
		b. Ultramarine (eyes) omitted		£3000	
927	410	9p. flesh, pale stone, grey-blue, grey-black, brown-grey, Venetian red, brown-red & gold		20	50
		a. Gold (Queen's head) omitted		£110	
		b. Brown-grey printing double	from	£850	
		c. Grey-black omitted		£1200	
		d. Brown-red (rivers on map) omitted		£500	
		Ee. Embossing omitted		40·00	
		Set of 5		1·25	1·50
		First Day Cover			3·25
		Presentation Pack		3·50	

Caution is needed when buying missing gold heads in this issue as they can be removed by using a hard eraser, etc., but this invariably affects the "all-over" phosphor. Genuine examples have the phosphor intact. Used examples off cover cannot be distinguished as much of the phosphor is lost in the course of floating.

In the 5p. value the missing grey-black affects the doublet, which appears as brownish grey, and the face ruff, which is entirely missing. The missing sepia affects only Drake's hair, which appears much lighter.

The double printing of the brown-grey (cylinder 1F) on the 9p., is a most unusual type of error to occur in a multicoloured photogravure issue. Two sheets are known and it is believed that they stuck to the cylinder and went through a second time. This would result in the following two sheets missing the colour but at the time of going to press this error has not been reported. The second print is slightly askew and more prominent in the top half of the sheets. Examples from the upper part of the sheet showing a clear double impression of the facial features are worth a substantial premium over the price quoted.

Special First Day of Issue Postmark

Philatelic Bureau, Edinburgh .... 10·00

First Day of Issue handstamps were provided at Blantyre, Glasgow, and Denbigh for this issue.

411

412

413

(T **411/13** show sketches of W.G. Grace by Harry Furniss)

(Des E. Ripley. Queen's head printed in gold and then embossed)

1973 (16 May). **County Cricket 1873–1973.** *"All-over" phosphor.* P 14 × 15.
928	**411**	3p. black, ochre & gold	10	10
		a. Gold (Queen's head) omitted	£2000	
		Eb. Embossing omitted	20·00	
929	**412**	7½p. black, light sage-green & gold	65	75
		Eb. Embossing omitted	30·00	
930	**413**	9p. black, cobalt & gold	80	90
		Eb. Embossing omitted	80·00	
		Set of 3	1·50	1·60
		First Day Cover		3·50
		Presentation Pack	3·50	
		Souvenir Book	10·00	
		P.H.Q. Card (No. 928)	65·00	£225

The souvenir book is a 24-page illustrated booklet containing a history of County Cricket with text by John Arlott.

The P.H.Q. card did not become available until mid-July. The used price quoted is for an example used in July or August 1973.

Special First Day of Issue Postmarks

Philatelic Bureau, Edinburgh .... 6·00
Lords, London NW .... 9·00

414 "Self-portrait"
(Reynolds)

415 "Self-portrait"
(Raeburn)

416 "Nelly O'Brien"
(Reynolds)

417 "Rev. R. Walker
(The Skater)" (Raeburn)

(Des S. Rose. Queen's head printed in gold and then embossed)

1973 (4 July). **British Paintings. 250th Birth Anniv of Sir Joshua Reynolds and 150th Death Anniv of Sir Henry Raeburn.** *"All-over" phosphor.* P 14 × 15.
931	**414**	3p. rose, new blue, jet-black, magenta, greenish yellow, black, ochre & gold ...	10	10
		a. Gold (Queen's head) omitted	65·00	
		Ec. Gold (Queen's head) & embossing omitted	70·00	
932	**415**	5p. cinnamon, greenish yellow, new blue, lt magenta, black, yellow-olive & gold	15	20
		a. Gold (Queen's head) omitted	80·00	
		b. Greenish yellow omitted	£450	
		Ec. Embossing omitted	30·00	
933	**416**	7½p. greenish yellow, new blue, lt magenta, black, cinnamon & gold	50	45
		a. Gold (Queen's head) omitted	£120	
		b. Cinnamon omitted	£5500	
		Ec. Embossing omitted	25·00	
934	**417**	9p. brownish rose, black, dull rose, pale yellow, brownish grey, pale blue & gold ...	60	55
		b. Brownish rose omitted	50·00	
		Ec. Embossing omitted	£120	
		Set of 4	1·25	1·25
		First Day Cover		2·25
		Presentation Pack	3·25	

Special First Day of Issue Postmark

Philatelic Bureau, Edinburgh .... 5·50

418 Court Masque Costumes

419 St. Paul's Church, Covent Garden

420 Prince's Lodging, Newmarket   **421** Court Masque Stage Scene

T **418/19** and T **420/1** were printed horizontally *se-tenant* within the sheet.

(Des Rosalind Dease. Litho and typo B.W.)

1973 (15 Aug).   **400th Birth Anniv of Inigo Jones (architect and designer).** *"All-over" phosphor.* P 15 × 14.

935	418	3p. dp mauve, black & gold	10	10
		a. Pair. Nos. 935/6	30	40
		ab. Face values omitted		
		Eac. Dp mauve ptg double (pair)	£5000	
		Ec. 9 mm. phosphor band*	15·00	
936	419	3p. dp brown, black & gold	10	10
937	420	5p. blue, black & gold	35	45
		a. Pair. Nos. 937/8	1·00	1·25
		Ec. 9 mm. phosphor band*	18·00	
938	421	5p. grey-olive, black & gold	35	45
		Set of 4	1·25	1·00
		First Day Cover		2·25
		Presentation Pack	3·50	
		P.H.Q. Card (No. 936)	£150	£150

No. 935ab is caused by the omission of virtually all the black printing from one horizontal row.

*On part of the printings for both values the "all-over" phosphor band missed the first vertical row and a 9 mm. phosphor band was applied to correct this.

Special First Day of Issue Postmark

Philatelic Bureau, Edinburgh .... 5·00

422 Palace of Westminster   **423** Palace of Westminster
seen from Whitehall   seen from Millbank

(Des R. Downer. Recess and typo B.W.)

1973 (12 Sept).   **19th Commonwealth Parliamentary Conference.** *"All-over" phosphor.* P 15 × 14.

939	422	8p. black, brownish grey & stone	45	50
940	423	10p. gold & black	45	40
		Set of 2	90	90
		First Day Cover		2·00
		Presentation Pack	3·00	
		Souvenir Book	6·00	
		P.H.Q. Card (No. 939)	40·00	£150

The souvenir book is a twelve-page booklet containing a history of the Palace of Westminster.

Special First Day of Issue Postmark

Philatelic Bureau, Edinburgh .... 4·00

424 Princess Anne and Capt. Mark Phillips

(Des C. Clements and E. Hughes from photo by Lord Litchfield)

1973 (14 Nov).   **Royal Wedding.** *"All-over" phosphor.* P 15 × 14.

941	424	3½p. dull violet & silver	15	10
		a. Imperf (horiz pair)	£1900	
942		20p. dp brown & silver	60	75
		a. Silver omitted	£1800	
		Set of 2	75	85
		Set of 2 Gutter Pairs	2·75	
		Set of 2 Traffic Light Gutter Pairs	75·00	
		First Day Cover		2·00
		Presentation Pack	2·25	
		P.H.Q. Card (No. 941)	8·00	40·00

Special First Day of Issue Postmarks

Philatelic Bureau, Edinburgh .... 4·00
Westminster Abbey, London SW1 .... 7·00
Windsor, Berks .... 7·00

425   426

427   428

429

T **425/9** depict the carol "Good King Wenceslas" and were printed horizontally *se-tenant* within the sheet.

430 Good King Wenceslas, the Page and Peasant

(Des D. Gentleman)

1973 (28 Nov). **Christmas.** *One centre phosphor band* (3p.) *or "all-over" phosphor* ($3\frac{1}{2}$p.). P 15 × 14.

943	**425**	3p. grey-black, violet-blue, slate, brown, rose-red, rosy mauve, turquoise-green, salmon-pink & gold		20	25
		a. Strip of 5. Nos. 943/7		2·25	3·25
		b. Imperf (horiz strip of 5)		£1500	
		Eg. Gum arabic		25	
		Ega. Strip of 5. Nos. 943Eg/7Eg		3·00	
		Egb. Imperf (strip of 5. Nos. 943Eg/7Eg)			
944	**426**	3p. grey-black, violet-blue, slate, brown, rose-red, rosy mauve, turquoise-green, salmon-pink & gold		20	25
		a. Rosy mauve omitted		£1750	
		Eg. Gum arabic		25	
945	**427**	3p. grey-black, violet-blue, slate, brown, rose-red, rosy mauve, turquoise-green, salmon-pink & gold		20	25
		a. Rosy mauve omitted		£1750	
		Eg. Gum arabic		25	

946	**428**	3p. grey-black, violet-blue, slate, brown, rose-red, rosy mauve, turquoise-green, salmon-pink & gold		20	25
		a. Rosy mauve omitted		£1750	
		Eg. Gum arabic		25	
947	**429**	3p. grey-black, violet-blue, slate, brown, rose-red, rosy mauve, turquoise-green, salmon-pink & gold		20	25
		a. Rosy mauve omitted		£1750	
		Eg. Gum arabic		25	
948	**430**	$3\frac{1}{2}$p. salmon-pink, grey-black, red-brown, blue, turquoise-green, brt rose-red, rosy mauve, lavender-grey & gold		20	25
		a. Imperf (pair)		£425	
		b. Grey-black (value, inscr, etc.) omitted		80·00	
		c. Salmon-pink omitted		75·00	
		d. Blue (leg, robes) omitted		£140	
		e. Rosy mauve (robe at right) omitted		85·00	
		f. Blue and rosy mauve omitted		£375	
		g. Brt rose-red (King's robe) omitted		80·00	
		h. Red-brown (logs, basket, etc.) omitted			
		i. Turquoise-green (leg, robe, etc.) omitted		£2500	
		j. Gold (background) omitted		†	£750
		Set of 6		2·25	2·00
		First Day Cover			3·25
		Presentation Pack		4·00	

Examples of No. 948j are only known used on covers from Gloucester. The $3\frac{1}{2}$p. has also been seen with the lavender-grey omitted used on piece.

The 3p. and $3\frac{1}{2}$p. are normally with PVA gum with added dextrin, but the $3\frac{1}{2}$p. also exists with normal PVA gum.

Special First Day of Issue Postmarks

Philatelic Bureau, Edinburgh		4·00
Bethlehem, Llandeilo, Carms		8·00

Collectors Pack 1973

1973 (28 Nov). *Comprises Nos. 919/48.*
CP948*k* Collectors Pack .... 27·00

431 Horse Chestnut

(Des D. Gentleman)

1974 (27 Feb). **British Trees (2nd issue).** *"All-over"* phosphor. P 15 × 14.
949 **431** 10p. lt emerald, brt green, greenish yellow,
brown-olive, black & brownish grey 35   35
Gutter Pair .... 2·00
Traffic Light Gutter Pair .... 42·00
First Day Cover ....   2·00
Presentation Pack .... 2·50
P.H.Q. Card £120 £140

Special First Day of Issue Postmark

Philatelic Bureau, Edinburgh .... 5·00

432 First Motor Fire-engine, 1904   **433** Prize-winning Fire-engine, 1863

434 First Steam Fire-engine, 1830   **435** Fire-engine, 1766

(Des D. Gentleman)

1974 (24 Apr). **Bicentenary of the Fire Prevention (Metropolis) Act.**
"All-over" phosphor. P 15 × 14.
950 **432** 3½p. grey-black, orange-yellow, greenish yellow,
dull rose, ochre & grey 10   10
   a. Imperf (pair) £825
951 **433** 5½p. greenish yellow, dp rosy magenta, orange-
yellow, lt emerald, grey-black & grey 25   30
952 **434** 8p. greenish yellow, lt blue-green, lt greenish
blue, lt chestnut, grey-black & grey 45   50
953 **435** 10p. grey-black, pale reddish brown, lt brown,
orange-yellow & grey 45   50
Set of 4 .... 1·10 1·25
Set of 4 Gutter Pairs .... 3·50
Set of 4 Traffic Light Gutter Pairs .... 42·00
First Day Cover ....   3·25
Presentation Pack .... 2·75
P.H.Q. Card (No. 950) £120 £140
The 3½p. exists with ordinary PVA gum.

Special First Day of Issue Postmark

Philatelic Bureau, Edinburgh .... 5·00

436 P & O Packet, *Peninsular,*   **437** Farman H.F. III Biplane,
1888   1911

438 Airmail-blue Van and   **439** Imperial Airways Short S.21
Postbox, 1930   Flying Boat *Maia,* 1937

(Des Rosalind Dease)

1974 (12 June). **Centenary of Universal Postal Union.** *"All-over"*
phosphor. P 15 × 14.
954 **436** 3½p. dp brownish grey, brt mauve, grey-black
& gold 10   10
955 **437** 5½p. pale orange, lt emerald, grey-black &
gold 25   30
956 **438** 8p. cobalt, brown, grey-black & gold 25   35
957 **439** 10p. dp brownish grey, orange, grey-black &
gold 35   40
Set of 4 .... 85 1·00
Set of 4 Gutter Pairs .... 2·75
Set of 4 Traffic Light Gutter Pairs .... 35·00
First Day Cover ....   3·00
Presentation Pack .... 2·75

Special First Day of Issue Postmark

Philatelic Bureau, Edinburgh .... 5·00

440 Robert the Bruce

441 Owain Glyndwr

442 Henry the Fifth

443 The Black Prince

(Des F. Wegner)

1974 (10 July). **Medieval Warriors.** *"All-over"* phosphor. P 15 × 14.

958	**440**	4½p. greenish yellow, vermilion, slate-blue, red-brown, reddish brown, lilac-grey & gold	10	10
959	**441**	5½p. lemon, vermilion, slate-blue, red-brown, reddish brown, olive-drab & gold	20	35
960	**442**	8p. dp grey, vermilion, greenish yellow, new blue, red-brown, dp cinnamon & gold	45	50
961	**443**	10p. vermilion, greenish yellow, new blue, red-brown, reddish brown, lt blue & gold	50	50
		Set of 4	1·10	1·25
		Set of 4 Gutter Pairs	4·00	
		Set of 4 Traffic Light Gutter Pairs	48·00	
		First Day Cover		3·25
		Presentation Pack	3·50	
		P.H.Q. Cards (set of 4)	28·00	60·00

Special First Day of Issue Postmark

Philatelic Bureau, Edinburgh .... 6·00

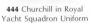

444 Churchill in Royal Yacht Squadron Uniform

445 Prime Minister, 1940

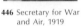

446 Secretary for War and Air, 1919

447 War Correspondent, South Africa, 1899

(Des C. Clements and E. Hughes)

1974 (9 Oct). **Birth Centenary of Sir Winston Churchill.** *"All-over"* phosphor. P 14 × 15.

962	**444**	4½p. Prussian blue, pale turquoise-green & silver	20	15
963	**445**	5½p. sepia, brownish grey & silver	35	35
964	**446**	8p. crimson, lt claret & silver	60	55
965	**447**	10p. lt brown, stone & silver	60	50
		Set of 4	1·60	1·40
		Set of 4 Gutter Pairs	4·00	
		Set of 4 Traffic Light Gutter Pairs	32·00	
		First Day Cover		2·50
		Presentation Pack	2·50	
		Souvenir Book	4·00	
		P.H.Q. Card (No. 963)	6·00	22·00

The souvenir book consists of an illustrated folder containing a biography of Sir Winston.

Nos. 962/5 come with PVA gum containing added dextrin, but the 8p. also exists with normal PVA.

Special First Day of Issue Postmarks

Philatelic Bureau, Edinburgh .... 6·50
Blenheim, Woodstock, Oxford .... 10·00
House of Commons, London SW .... 10·00

ALBUM LISTS
Write for our latest list of albums and accessories.
These will be sent on request.

448 "Adoration of the Magi"
(York Minster, *circa* 1355)

449 "The Nativity" (St. Helen's
Church, Norwich, *circa* 1480)

450 "Virgin and Child" (Ottery
St. Mary Church, *circa* 1350)

451 "Virgin and Child"
(Worcester Cathedral, *circa* 1224)

(Des Peter Hatch Partnership)

1974 (27 Nov). **Christmas. Church Roof Bosses.** *One phosphor band* (3½p.) *or* "all-over" *phosphor* (others). *P* 15 × 14.

966	**448**	3½p. gold, lt new blue, lt brown, grey-black & lt stone	10	10
		a. Lt stone (background shading) omitted .. £10000		
		Ey. Phosphor omitted	12·00	
967	**449**	4½p. gold, yellow-orange, rose-red, lt brown, grey-black & lt new blue	10	10
968	**450**	8p. blue, gold, lt brown, rose-red, dull green & grey-black	30	35
969	**451**	10p. gold, dull rose, grey-black, lt new blue, pale cinnamon & lt brown	40	45
		Set of 4	80	90
		Set of 4 Gutter Pairs	2·50	
		Set of 4 Traffic Light Gutter Pairs	38·00	
		First Day Cover	3·00	
		Presentation Pack	2·25	

The phosphor band on the 3½p. was first applied down the centre of the stamp but during the printing this was deliberately placed to the right between the roof boss and the value; however, intermediate positions, due to shifts, are known.

Two used examples of the 3½p. have been reported with the light brown colour omitted.

Special First Day of Issue Postmarks

Philatelic Bureau, Edinburgh	4·50
Bethlehem, Llandeilo, Carms	7·00

Collectors Pack 1974

1974 (27 Nov). *Comprises Nos.* 949/69.
CP969a Collectors Pack .... 12·00

452 Invalid in Wheelchair

(Des P. Sharland)

1975 (22 Jan). **Health and Handicap Funds.** "All-over" *phosphor. P* 15 × 14.

970	**452**	4½p. + 1½p. azure & grey-blue	25	25
		Gutter Pair	60	
		Traffic Light Gutter Pair	1·25	
		First Day Cover		1·75

Special First Day of Issue Postmark

Philatelic Bureau, Edinburgh .... 3·00

453 "Peace—Burial at Sea"

454 "Snowstorm—Steamer off a
Harbour's Mouth"

455 "The Arsenal, Venice"

456 "St. Laurent"

(Des S. Rose)

1975 (19 Feb). **Birth Bicentenary of J. M. W. Turner (painter).** "All-over" *phosphor. P* 15 × 14.

971	**453**	4½p. grey-black, salmon, stone, blue & grey	10	10
972	**454**	5½p. cobalt, greenish yellow, lt yellow-brown, grey-black & rose	15	20
973	**455**	8p. pale yellow-orange, greenish yellow, rose, cobalt & grey-black	25	35

974 **456** 10p. dp blue, lt yellow-ochre, lt brown, dp
cobalt & grey-black 40 40
Set of 4 .... 80 95
Set of 4 Gutter Pairs .... 2·25
Set of 4 Traffic Light Gutter Pairs .... 5·50
First Day Cover .... 2·25
Presentation Pack .... 2·50
P.H.Q. Card (No. 972) .... 40·00 25·00

Special First Day of Issue Postmarks

Philatelic Bureau, Edinburgh .... 5·00
London WC .... 7·00

457 Charlotte Square, Edinburgh   **458** The Rows, Chester

T **457/8** were printed horizontally *se-tenant* within the sheet.

459 Royal Observatory,   **460** St. George's Chapel,
Greenwich   Windsor

461 National Theatre, London

(Des P. Gauld)

1975 (23 Apr). **European Architectural Heritage Year.** *"All-over"*
phosphor. P 15 × 14.
975 **457** 7p. greenish yellow, brt orange, grey-black,
red-brown, new blue, lavender & gold .. 25 25
a. Pair. Nos. 975/6 .... 80 1·00
976 **458** 7p. grey-black, greenish yellow, new blue,
brt orange, red-brown & gold 25 25

977 **459** 8p. magenta, dp slate, pale magenta, lt
yellow-olive, grey-black & gold 25 30
978 **460** 10p. bistre-brown, greenish yellow, dp slate,
emerald-green, grey-black & gold 25 30
979 **461** 12p. grey-black, new blue, pale magenta &
gold 30 35
Set of 5 .... 1·40 1·25
Set of 5 Gutter Pairs .... 5·50
Set of 5 Traffic Light Gutter Pairs .... 22·00
First Day Cover .... 3·75
Presentation Pack .... 3·00
P.H.Q. Cards (Nos. 975/7) .... 10·00 27·00

Special First Day of Issue Postmark

Philatelic Bureau, Edinburgh .... 7·00

462 Sailing Dinghies   **463** Racing Keel Yachts

464 Cruising Yachts   **465** Multihulls

(Des A. Restall. Recess and photo)

1975 (11 June). **Sailing.** *"All-over"* phosphor. P 15 × 14.
980 **462** 7p. black, bluish violet, scarlet, orange-vermilion, orange & gold 15 10
981 **463** 8p. black, orange-vermilion, orange, lavender, brt mauve, brt blue, dp ultramarine
& gold 30 30
a. Black omitted .... 60·00
982 **464** 10p. black, orange, bluish emerald, lt olive-
drab, chocolate & gold 30 35
983 **465** 12p. black, ultramarine, turquoise-blue, rose,
grey, steel-blue & gold 50 50
Set of 4 .... 1·10 1·10
Set of 4 Gutter Pairs .... 2·50
Set of 4 Traffic Light Gutter Pairs .... 15·00
First Day Cover .... 2·50
Presentation Pack .... 2·50
P.H.Q. Card (No. 981) .... 5·00 25·00
On No. 981a the recess-printed black colour is completely omitted.

Special First Day of Issue Postmark

Special First Day of Issue Postmarks

Philatelic Bureau, Edinburgh .... 4·50
A First Day of Issue handstamp was provided at Weymouth for this issue.

Stephenson's Locomotion **7**p

1825 Stockton and Darlington Railway

466 Stephenson's *Locomotion*, 1825

Waverley Class **8**p

1876 North British Railway Drummond

467 *Abbotsford*, 1876

Caerphilly Castle **10**p

1923 Great Western Railway Castle Class

468 *Caerphilly Castle*, 1923

High-Speed Train **12**p

1975 British Rail Inter-City Service HST

469 High Speed Train, 1975

(Des B. Craker)

1975 (13 Aug). **150th Anniv of Public Railways.** *"All-over"* phosphor. P 15 × 14.

984	**466**	7p. red-brown, grey-black, greenish yellow, grey & silver	25	20
985	**467**	8p. brown, orange-yellow, vermilion, grey-black, grey & silver	35	40
986	**468**	10p. emerald-green, grey-black, yellow-orange, vermilion, grey & silver	45	45
987	**469**	12p. grey-black, pale lemon, vermilion, blue, grey & silver	50	50
		Set of 4	1·40	1·40
		Set of 4 Gutter Pairs	3·00	
		Set of 4 Traffic Light Gutter Pairs	8·50	
		First Day Cover		3·50
		Presentation Pack	3·50	
		Souvenir Book	6·00	
		P.H.Q. Cards (set of 4)	60·00	55·00

The souvenir book is an eight-page booklet containing a history of the railways.

GIBBONS STAMP MONTHLY
– finest and most informative magazine for all collectors. Obtainable from your newsagent or by postal subscription – details on request.

SHILDON CO DURHAM FIRST DAY OF ISSUE

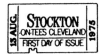

STOCKTON-ON-TEES CLEVELAND FIRST DAY OF ISSUE

Philatelic Bureau, Edinburgh .... 6·50
Darlington, Co. Durham .... 13·00
Shildon, Co. Durham .... 15·00
Stockton-on-Tees, Cleveland .... 13·00

470 Palace of Westminster

(Des R. Downer)

1975 (3 Sept). **62nd Inter-Parliamentary Union Conference.** *"All-over"* phosphor. P 15 × 14.

988	**470**	12p. lt new blue, black, brownish grey & gold	35	40
		Gutter Pair	70	
		Traffic Light Gutter Pair	2·00	
		First Day Cover		1·50
		Presentation Pack	1·60	

Special First Day of Issue Postmark

Philatelic Bureau, Edinburgh .... 3·00

471 Emma and Mr. Woodhouse (*Emma*)

472 Catherine Morland (*Northanger Abbey*)

473 Mr. Darcy (*Pride and Prejudice*)

474 Mary and Henry Crawford (*Mansfield Park*)

(Des Barbara Brown)

1975 (22 Oct). **Birth Bicentenary of Jane Austen (novelist).** *"All-over" phosphor.* P 14 × 15.

989	**471**	8½p. blue, slate, rose-red, lt yellow, dull green, grey-black & gold	15	10
990	**472**	10p. slate, brt magenta, grey, lt yellow, grey-black & gold	40	35
991	**473**	11p. dull blue, pink, olive-sepia, slate, pale greenish yellow, grey-black & gold	40	35
992	**474**	13p. brt magenta, lt new blue, slate, buff, dull blue-green, grey-black & gold	45	50
		Set of 4	1·25	1·10
		Set of 4 Gutter Pairs	2·50	
		Set of 4 Traffic Light Gutter Pairs	7·00	
		First Day Cover		3·50
		Presentation Pack	2·25	
		P.H.Q. Cards (set of 4)	22·00	32·00

Special First Day of Issue Postmark

Philatelic Bureau, Edinburgh .... 4·50
Steventon, Basingstoke, Hants .... 6·00

475 Angels with Harp and Lute

476 Angel with Mandolin

477 Angel with Horn

478 Angel with Trumpet

(Des R. Downer)

1975 (26 Nov). **Christmas.** *One phosphor band (6½p.), phosphor-inked background (8½p.), "all-over" phosphor (others).* P 15 × 14.

993	**475**	6½p. bluish violet, brt reddish violet, light lavender & gold	15	15
994	**476**	8½p. turquoise-green, brt emerald-green, slate, lt turquoise-green & gold	25	30
995	**477**	11p. vermilion, cerise, pink & gold	40	40
996	**478**	13p. drab, brown, brt orange, buff & gold	40	40
		Set of 4	1·10	1·10
		Set of 4 Gutter Pairs	2·50	
		Set of 4 Traffic Light Gutter Pairs	7·00	
		First Day Cover		2·00
		Presentation Pack	2·25	

The 6½p. exists with both ordinary PVA gum and PVA containing added dextrin.

Special First Day of Issue Postmarks

Philatelic Bureau, Edinburgh .... 3·00
Bethlehem, Llandeilo, Dyfed .... 4·00

Collectors Pack 1975

1975 (26 Nov). *Comprises Nos. 970/96.*
CP996a Collectors Pack .... 8·00

479 Housewife

480 Policeman

481 District Nurse   **482** Industrialist

(Des P. Sharland)

1976 (10 Mar). **Telephone Centenary.** *"All-over"* phosphor. *P* 15 × 14.

997	**479**	8½p.	greenish blue, dp rose, black & blue ...	15	10
		a.	Dp rose (vase and picture frame) omitted	£2250	
998	**480**	10p.	greenish blue, black & yellow-olive	30	30
999	**481**	11p.	greenish blue, dp rose, black & brt mauve	40	40
1000	**482**	13p.	olive-brown, dp rose, black & orange-red	45	45
			Set of 4	1·20	1·20
			Set of 4 Gutter Pairs	2·75	
			Set of 4 Traffic Light Gutter Pairs	6·50	
			First Day Cover		2·00
			Presentation Pack	2·50	

Special First Day of Issue Postmark

Philatelic Bureau, Edinburgh .... 3·00

483 Hewing Coal   **484** Machinery (Robert Owen)
(Thomas Hepburn)

 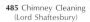

485 Chimney Cleaning   **486** Hands clutching Prison Bars
(Lord Shaftesbury)   (Elizabeth Fry)

(Des D. Gentleman)

1976 (28 Apr). **Social Reformers.** *"All-over"* phosphor. *P* 15 × 14.

1001	**483**	8½p.	lavender-grey, grey-black, black & slate-grey	20	10
1002	**484**	10p.	lavender-grey, grey-black, grey & slate-violet	35	30
1003	**485**	11p.	black, slate-grey & drab	40	35
1004	**486**	13p.	slate-grey, black & dp dull green	40	35
			Set of 4	1·25	1·00
			Set of 4 Gutter Pairs	2·50	
			Set of 4 Traffic Light Gutter Pairs	6·50	
			First Day Cover		2·00
			Presentation Pack	2·50	
			P.H.Q. Card (No. 1001)	5·50	18·00

Special First Day of Issue Postmark

Philatelic Bureau, Edinburgh .... 3·50

487 Benjamin Franklin
(bust by Jean-Jacques Caffieri)

(Des P. Sharland)

1976 (2 June). **Bicentenary of American Revolution.** *"All-over"* phosphor. *P* 14 × 15.

1005	**487**	11p.	pale bistre, slate-violet, pale blue-green, black & gold	35	35
			Gutter Pair	75	
			Traffic Light Gutter Pair	1·75	
			First Day Cover		1·40
			Presentation Pack	1·25	
			P.H.Q. Card	4·00	17·00

Special First Day of Issue Postmark

Philatelic Bureau, Edinburgh .... 2·50

488 "Elizabeth of Glamis"

489 "Grandpa Dickson"

492 Archdruid

493 Morris Dancing

490 "Rosa Mundi"

491 "Sweet Briar"

494 Scots Piper

495 Welsh Harpist

(Des Kristin Rosenberg)

1976 (30 June). **Centenary of Royal National Rose Society.** *"All-over"*
phosphor. P 14 × 15.

1006	**488**	8½p. brt rose-red, greenish yellow, emerald, grey-black & gold	15	10
1007	**489**	10p. greenish yellow, brt green, reddish brown, grey-black & gold	25	30
1008	**490**	11p. brt magenta, greenish yellow, emerald, grey-blue, grey-black & gold	40	40
1009	**491**	13p. rose-pink, lake-brown, yellow-green, pale greenish yellow, grey-black & gold	50	50
		a. Value omitted*	£22000	
		Set of 4	1·25	1·25
		Set of 4 Gutter Pairs	3·00	
		Set of 4 Traffic Light Gutter Pairs	7·00	
		First Day Cover		2·50
		Presentation Pack	2·50	
		P.H.Q. Cards (set of 4)	25·00	30·00

*During repairs to the cylinder the face value on R.1/9 was
temporarily covered with copper. This covering was inadvertently left
in place during printing, but the error was discovered before issue and
most examples were removed from the sheets. Two mint and one used
examples have so far been reported, but only one of the mint remains
in private hands.

(Des Marjorie Saynor)

1976 (4 Aug). **British Cultural Traditions.** *"All-over" phosphor. P* 14 × 15.

1010	**492**	8½p. yellow, sepia, brt rose, dull ultramarine, black & gold	15	10
1011	**493**	10p. dull ultramarine, brt rose-red, sepia, greenish yellow, black & gold	30	30
1012	**494**	11p. bluish green, yellow-brown, yellow-orange, black, brt rose-red & gold	40	40
1013	**495**	13p. dull violet-blue, yellow-orange, yellow, black, bluish green & gold	45	45
		Set of 4	1·20	1·20
		Set of 4 Gutter Pairs	2·75	
		Set of 4 Traffic Light Gutter Pairs	6·50	
		First Day Cover		3·00
		Presentation Pack	2·50	
		P.H.Q. Cards (set of 4)	15·00	20·00

The 8½p. and 13p. commemorate the 800th anniversary of the Royal
National Eisteddfod.

Special First Day of Issue Postmark

Philatelic Bureau, Edinburgh .... 5·00

Special First Day of Issue Postmarks

Philatelic Bureau, Edinburgh .... 4·00
Cardigan, Dyfed .... 5·00

496 Woodcut from
The Canterbury Tales

497 Extract from
The Tretyse of Love

498 Woodcut from
The Game and Playe of Chesse

499 Early Printing Press

(Des R. Gay. Queen's head printed in gold and then embossed)

1976 (29 Sept). **500th Anniv of British Printing.** *"All-over" phosphor.*
P 14 × 15.

1014	496	8½p. black, lt new blue & gold	20	10
1015	497	10p. black, olive-green & gold	35	30
1016	498	11p. black, brownish grey & gold	40	40
1017	499	13p. chocolate, pale ochre & gold	40	45
		Set of 4	1·20	1·10
		Set of 4 Gutter Pairs	2·75	
		Set of 4 Traffic Light Gutter Pairs	6·50	
		First Day Cover		2·75
		Presentation Pack	2·50	
		P.H.Q. Cards (set of 4)	12·00	25·00

Special First Day of Issue Postmarks

Philatelic Bureau, Edinburgh .... 4·00
London SW1 .... 5·00

500 Virgin and Child

501 Angel with Crown

502 Angel appearing to
Shepherds

503 The Three Kings

(Des Enid Marx)

1976 (24 Nov). **Christmas. English Medieval Embroidery.** *One
phosphor band (6½p.) or "all-over" phosphor (others).* P 15 × 14.

1018	500	6½p. blue, bistre-yellow, brown & orange ...	15	15
		a. Imperf (pair)	£425	
1019	501	8½p. sage-green, yellow, brown-ochre, chest-		
		nut & olive-black	30	20
1020	502	11p. dp magenta, brown-orange, new blue,		
		black & cinnamon	35	40
		a. Uncoated paper*	75·00	30·00
1021	503	13p. bright purple, new blue, cinnamon,		
		bronze-green & olive-grey	40	45
		Set of 4	1·10	1·10
		Set of 4 Gutter Pairs	2·25	
		Set of 4 Traffic Light Gutter Pairs	6·00	
		First Day Cover		3·25
		Presentation Pack	2·50	
		P.H.Q. Cards (set of 4)	4·50	20·00

*See footnote after No. 744.

Special First Day of Issue Postmarks

Philatelic Bureau, Edinburgh .... 4·50
Bethlehem, Llandeilo, Dyfed .... 5·50

Collectors Pack 1976

1976 (24 Nov). *Comprises Nos. 997/1021.*
CP1021a Collectors Pack .... 13·00

504 Lawn Tennis

505 Table Tennis

506 Squash   **507** Badminton

(Des A. Restall)

1977 (12 Jan). **Racket Sports.** *Phosphorised paper. P* 15 × 14.

1022	**504**	8$\frac{1}{2}$p. emerald-green, black, grey & bluish green		15	10
		a. Imperf (horiz pair)		£900	
1023	**505**	10p. myrtle-green, black, grey-black & blue-green		30	30
1024	**506**	11p. orange, pale yellow, black, slate-black & grey		40	40
		a. Imperf (horiz pair)		£2000	
1025	**507**	13p. brown, grey-black, grey & brt reddish violet		40	45
		Set of 4		1·10	1·10
		Set of 4 Gutter Pairs		2·50	
		Set of 4 Traffic Light Gutter Pairs		6·00	
		First Day Cover			3·25
		Presentation Pack		2·25	
		P.H.Q. Cards (set of 4)		7·00	20·00

The only known example of No. 1024a is cut close at left.

Special First Day of Issue Postmark

Philatelic Bureau, Edinburgh .... 5·00

508

1977 (2 Feb)–**87**. *P* 14 × 15.

1026	**508**	£1 brt yellow-green & blackish olive	3·00	25
		a. Imperf (pair)	£750	
1026*b*		£1.30 pale drab & dp greenish blue (3.8.83)	5·50	6·00
1026*c*		£1.33 pale mauve & grey-black (28.8.84) ..	7·50	7·00
1026*d*		£1.41 pale drab & dp greenish blue (17.9.85)	8·00	8·50
1026*e*		£1.50 pale mauve & grey-black (2.9.86) ...	6·00	5·00

1026*f*	**508**	£1.60 pale drab & dp greenish blue (15.9.87)	6·50	7·00
1027		£2 light emerald & purple-brown	12·00	50
1028		£5 salmon & chalky blue	29·00	3·00
		a. Imperf (vert pair)	£2750	
		Set of 8	70·00	32·00
		Set of 8 Gutter Pairs	£110	
		Set of 8 Traffic Light Gutter Pairs	£160	
		First Day Cover (1026, 1027/8)		8·00
		First Day Cover (1026b)		6·50
		First Day Cover (1026c)		8·00
		First Day Cover (1026d)		8·50
		First Day Cover (1026e)		5·50
		First Day Cover (1026f)		8·00
		Presentation Pack (P.O. Pack No. 91 (small size)) (1026, 1027/8)	24·00	
		Presentation Pack (P.O. Pack No. 13 (large size)) (1026, 1027/8)	90·00	
		Presentation Pack (P.O. Pack No. 14) (large size) (1026f)	12·00	

Special First Day of Issue Postmarks
(for illustrations see Introduction)

Philatelic Bureau, Edinburgh (Type F) (£1, £2, £5) ..	14·00
Windsor, Berks (Type F) (£1, £2, £5)	20·00
Philatelic Bureau, Edinburgh (Type F) (£1.30)	6·50
Windsor, Berks (Type F) (£1.30)	10·00
British Philatelic Bureau, Edinburgh (Type F) (£1.33)	8·00
Windsor, Berks (Type F) (£1.33)	10·00
British Philatelic Bureau, Edinburgh (Type G) (£1.41)	9·00
Windsor, Berks (Type G) (£1.41)	9·00
British Philatelic Bureau, Edinburgh (Type G) (£1.50)	6·50
Windsor, Berks (Type G) (£1.50)	6·50
British Philatelic Bureau, Edinburgh (Type G) (£1.60)	8·50
Windsor, Berks (Type G) (£1.60)	8·50

509 Steroids—Conformational   **510** Vitamin C—Synthesis
Analysis

511 Starch—Chromatography   **512** Salt—Crystallography

(Des J. Karo)

1977 (2 Mar). **Royal Institute of Chemistry Centenary.** *"All-over" phosphor. P* 15 × 14.

1029	**509**	8$\frac{1}{2}$p. rosine, new blue, olive-yellow, brt mauve, yellow-brown, black & gold ...	15	10
		a. Imperf (horiz pair)	£1250	
1030	**510**	10p. brt orange, rosine, new blue, brt blue, black & gold	35	35

1031	**511**	11p. rosine, greenish yellow, new blue, dp violet, black & gold	35	40
1032	**512**	13p. new blue, brt green, black & gold	35	40
		Set of 4	1·10	1·10
		Set of 4 Gutter Pairs	2·50	
		Set of 4 Traffic Light Gutter Pairs	6·00	
		First Day Cover		2·50
		Presentation Pack	2·25	
		P.H.Q. Cards (set of 4)	7·00	15·00

Special First Day of Issue Postmark

Philatelic Bureau, Edinburgh .... 3·50

513

514

515   516

T **513**/**16** differ in the decorations of "ER".

(Des R. Guyatt)

1977 (11 May–15 June). **Silver Jubilee.** "All-over" phosphor. P 15 × 14.
1033	**513**	8½p. blackish green, black, silver, olive-grey & pale turquoise-green	15	15
		a. Imperf (pair)	£750	
1034		9p. maroon, black, silver, olive-grey & lavender (15 June)	25	15
1035	**514**	10p. blackish blue, black, silver, olive-grey & ochre	25	30
		a. Imperf (horiz pair)	£1500	

1036	**515**	11p. brown-purple, black, silver, olive-grey & rose-pink	35	40
		a. Imperf (horiz pair)	£1500	
1037	**516**	13p. sepia, black, silver, olive-grey & bistre-yellow	40	45
		a. Imperf (pair)	£1100	
		Set of 5	1·40	1·10
		Set of 5 Gutter Pairs	3·00	
		Set of 5 Traffic Light Gutter Pairs	4·00	
		First Day Covers (2)		3·75
		Presentation Pack (Nos. 1033, 1035/7)	2·00	
		Souvenir Book	4·50	
		P.H.Q. Cards (set of 5)	12·00	16·00

The souvenir book is a 16-page booklet containing a history of the Queen's reign.

Special First Day of Issue Postmarks

Philatelic Bureau, Edinburgh (1033, 1035/7) (11 May)	3·00
Philatelic Bureau, Edinburgh (1034) (15 June)	2·00
Windsor, Berks (1033, 1035/7) (11 May)	3·00
Windosr, Berks (1034) (15 June)	2·00

517 "Gathering of Nations"

(Des P. Murdoch. Recess and photo)

1977 (8 June). **Commonwealth Heads of Government Meeting, London.** "All-over" phosphor. P 14 × 15.
1038	**517**	13p. black, blackish green, rose-carmine & silver	35	35
		Gutter Pair	80	
		Traffic Light Gutter Pair	1·25	
		First Day Cover		1·00
		Presentation Pack	1·00	
		P.H.Q. Card	4·00	5·00

111

Special First Day of Issue Postmarks

Philatelic Bureau, Edinburgh .... 2·00
London SW .... 2·00

518 Hedgehog

519 Brown Hare

520 Red Squirrel

521 Otter

522 Badger

T **518/22** were printed horizontally *se-tenant* within the sheet.

(Des P. Oxenham)

1977 (5 Oct). **British Wildlife.** *"All-over"* phosphor. P 14 × 15.

1039	**518**	9p. reddish brown, grey-black, pale lemon, brt turquoise-blue, brt magenta & gold	25	25
		a. Horiz strip of 5. Nos. 1039/43	1·40	2·00
		b. Imperf (vert pair)	£650	
		c. Imperf (horiz pair. Nos. 1039/40)	£1600	
1040	**519**	9p. reddish brown, grey-black, pale lemon, brt turquoise-blue, brt magenta & gold	25	25
1041	**520**	9p. reddish brown, grey-black, pale lemon, brt turquoise-blue, brt magenta & gold	25	25
1042	**521**	9p. reddish brown, grey-black, pale lemon, brt turquoise-blue, brt magenta & gold	25	25
1043	**522**	9p. grey-black, reddish brown, pale lemon, brt turquoise-blue, brt magenta & gold	25	25
		Set of 5	1·60	1·10
		Gutter Strip of 10	3·50	
		Traffic Light Gutter Strip of 10	4·00	
		First Day Cover		3·50
		Presentation Pack	2·50	
		P.H.Q. Cards (set of 5)	4·00	6·00

Special First Day of Issue Postmark

Philatelic Bureau, Edinburgh .... 5·00

523 "Three French Hens, Two Turtle Doves and a Partridge in a Pear Tree"

524 "Six Geese-a-laying, Five Gold Rings, Four Colly Birds"

525 "Eight Maids-a-milking, Seven Swans a-swimming"

526 "Ten Pipers piping, Nine Drummers drumming"

527 "Twelve Lords a-leaping, Eleven Ladies dancing"

T **523/7** depict the card "The Twelve Days of Christmas" and were printed horizontally *se-tenant* within the sheet.

528 "A Partridge in a Pear Tree"

(Des D. Gentleman)

1977 (23 Nov). **Christmas.** *One centre phosphor band (7p.) or "all-over" phosphor (9p.). P* 15 × 14.

1044	**523**	7p. slate, grey, brt yellow-green, new blue, rose-red & gold	20	15
		a. Horiz strip of 5. Nos. 1044/8	1·40	2·00
		ab. Imperf (strip of 5. Nos. 1044/8)	£1750	
1045	**524**	7p. slate, brt yellow-green, new blue & gold	20	15
1046	**525**	7p. slate, grey, brt yellow-green, new blue, rose-red & gold	20	15
1047	**526**	7p. slate, grey, brt yellow-green, new blue, rose-red & gold	20	15
1048	**527**	7p. slate, grey, brt yellow-green, new blue, rose-red & gold	20	15
1049	**528**	9p. pale brown, pale orange, brt emerald, pale greenish yellow, slate-black & gold	25	20
		a. Imperf (pair)	£1100	
		Set of 6	1·10	85
		Set of 6 Gutter Pairs	3·50	
		Traffic Light Gutter Pairs	5·00	
		First Day Cover		3·50
		Presentation Pack	2·25	
		P.H.Q. Cards (set of 6)	3·00	5·00

Special First Day of Issue Postmarks

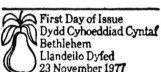

First Day of Issue
Dydd Cyhoeddiad Cyntaf
Bethlehem
Llandeilo Dyfed
23 November 1977

Philatelic Bureau, Edinburgh	5·00	
Bethlehem, Llandeilo, Dyfed	6·00	

Collectors Pack 1977

1977 (23 Nov). *Comprises Nos. 1022/5 and 1029/49.*
CP1049*b* Collectors Pack .... 9·00

529 Oil—North Sea
Production Platform

530 Coal—Modern Pithead

531 Natural Gas—Flame
Rising from Sea

532 Electricity—Nuclear
Power Station and
Uranium Atom

(Des P. Murdoch)

1978 (25 Jan). **Energy Resources.** *"All-over" phosphor. P* 14 × 15.

1050	**529**	9p. dp brown, orange-vermilion, grey-black, greenish yellow, rose-pink, new blue & silver	20	10
1051	**530**	10½p. lt emerald-green, grey-black, red-brown, slate-grey, pale apple-green & silver	25	25
1052	**531**	11p. greenish blue, brt violet, violet-blue, blackish brown, grey-black & silver	35	35
1053	**532**	13p. orange-vermilion, grey-black, dp brown, greenish yellow, lt brown, lt blue & silver	40	40
		Set of 4	1·10	1·00
		Set of 4 Gutter Pairs	2·25	
		Set of 4 Traffic Light Gutter Pairs	3·75	
		First Day Cover		1·50
		Presentation Pack	2·00	
		P.H.Q. Cards (set of 4)	2·00	4·00

Special First Day of Issue Postmark

Philatelic Bureau, Edinburgh .... 5·50

533 The Tower of London

534 Holyroodhouse

535 Caernarvon Castle

536 Hampton Court Palace

(Des R. Maddox (stamps), J. Matthews (miniature sheet))

1978 (1 Mar). **British Architecture. Historic Buildings.** *"All-over"* *phosphor.* P 15 × 14.

1054 **533**	9p. black, olive-brown, new blue, brt green, lt yellow-olive & rose-red	25	10
1055 **534** 10½p.	black, brown-olive, orange-yellow, brt green, lt yellow-olive & violet-blue	25	30
1056 **535**	11p. black, brown-olive, violet-blue, brt green, lt yellow-olive & dull blue	35	35
1057 **536**	13p. black, orange-yellow, lake-brown, brt green & lt yellow-olive	35	35
	Set of 4	1·10	1·00
	Set of 4 Gutter Pairs	2·25	
	Set of 4 Traffic Light Gutter Pairs	4·00	
	First Day Cover		1·50
	Presentation Pack	2·00	
	P.H.Q. Cards (set of 4)	2·00	4·00
MS1058	121 × 89 mm. Nos. 1054/7 *(sold at* 53½p.*)*.......	1·40	1·40
	a. Imperforate	£4250	
	b. Lt yellow-olive (Queen's head) omitted	£4750	
	c. Rose-red (Union Jack on 9p.) omitted ..	£3750	
	d. Orange-yellow omitted	£3750	
	e. New blue (Union Jack on 9p.) omitted .£12000		
	First Day Cover		1·90

The premium on No. **MS**1058 was used to support the London 1980 International Stamp Exhibition.

No. **MS**1058d is most noticeable on the 10½p. (spheres absent on towers) and around the roadway and arch on the 13p.

539 The Sovereign's Orb   **540** Imperial State Crown

(Des J. Matthews)

1978 (31 May). **25th Anniv of Coronation.** *"All-over"* phosphor. P 14 × 15.

1059 **537**	9p. gold & royal blue	25	15
1060 **538** 10½p.	gold & brown-lake	30	35
1061 **539**	11p. gold & dp dull green	30	35
1062 **540**	13p. gold & reddish violet	40	45
	Set of 4	1·10	1·10
	Set of 4 Gutter Pairs	2·25	
	Set of 4 Traffic Light Gutter Pairs	3·75	
	First Day Cover		1·50
	Presentation Pack	2·00	
	Souvenir Book	5·00	
	P.H.Q. Cards (set of 4)	3·00	4·00

The souvenir book is a 16-page booklet illustrated with scenes from the Coronation.

Special First Day of Issue Postmarks

Philatelic Bureau, Edinburgh (stamps)	3·50
Philatelic Bureau, Edinburgh (miniature sheet)	4·50
London EC (stamps)	3·50
London EC (miniature sheet)	4·50

Special First Day of Issue Postmarks

Philatelic Bureau, Edinburgh	3·00
London SW1	4·00

537 State Coach   **538** St. Edward's Crown

HAVE YOU READ THE NOTES AT THE BEGINNING OF THIS CATALOGUE?

These often provide answers to the enquiries we receive.

541 Shire Horse   **542** Shetland Pony

543 Welsh Pony   **544** Thoroughbred

(Des P. Oxenham)

1978 (5 July). **Horses.** *"All-over" phosphor.* P 15 × 14.

1063 **541** 9p. black, pale reddish brown, grey-black, greenish yellow, lt blue, vermilion & gold 20 10
1064 **542** 10½p. pale chestnut, magenta, brownish grey, greenish yellow, greenish blue, grey-black & gold 35 40
1065 **543** 11p. reddish brown, black, lt green, greenish yellow, bistre, grey-black & gold 35 45
1066 **544** 13p. reddish brown, pale reddish brown, emerald, greenish yellow, grey-black & gold 45 50
Set of 4 .... 1·25 1·25
Set of 4 Gutter Pairs .... 2·75
Set of 4 Traffic Light Gutter Pairs .... 4·00
First Day Cover .... 1·60
Presentation Pack .... 1·75
P.H.Q. Cards (set of 4) .... 2·00 5·00

Special First Day of Issue Postmarks

Philatelic Bureau, Edinburgh .... 3·00
Peterborough .... 4·00

545 "Penny-farthing" and 1884 Safety Bicycle

546 1920 Touring Bicycles

547 Modern Small-wheel Bicycles

548 1978 Road-racers

(Des F. Wegner)

1978 (2 Aug). **Centenaries of Cyclists Touring Club and British Cycling Federation.** *"All-over" phosphor.* P 15 × 14.

1067 **545** 9p. brown, dp dull blue, rose-pink, pale olive, grey-black & gold 20 10
  a. Imperf (pair) £375
1068 **546** 10½p. olive, pale yellow-orange, orange-vermilion, rose-red, lt brown, grey-black & gold 30 35

1069 **547** 11p. orange-vermilion, greenish blue, lt brown, pale greenish yellow, dp grey, grey-black & gold 35 35
1070 **548** 13p. new blue, orange-vermilion, lt brown, olive-grey, grey-black & gold 40 40
  a. Imperf (pair) £1100
Set of 4 .... 1·10 1·10
Set of 4 Gutter Pairs .... 2·50
Set of 4 Traffic Light Gutter Pairs .... 4·00
First Day Cover .... 1·75
Presentation Pack .... 1·75
P.H.Q. Cards (set of 4) .... 2·00 4·50

Special First Day of Issue Postmarks

Philatelic Bureau, Edinburgh .... 3·00
Harrogate, North Yorkshire .... 3·00

549 Singing Carols round the Christmas Tree

550 The Waits

551 18th-century Carol Singers

552 "The Boar's Head Carol"

(Des Faith Jaques)

1978 (22 Nov). **Christmas.** *One centre phosphor band (7p.) or "all-over" phosphor (others).* P 15 × 14.

1071 **549** 7p. brt green, greenish yellow, magenta, new blue, black & gold 15 10
  a. Imperf (vert pair) £500
1072 **550** 9p. magenta, greenish yellow, new blue, sage-green, black & gold 30 15
  a. Imperf (pair) £875
1073 **551** 11p. magenta, new blue, greenish yellow, yellow-brown, black & gold 35 40
  a. Imperf (horiz pair) £875

1074 552	13p. salmon-pink, new blue, greenish yellow, magenta, black & gold	40	45
	Set of 4	1·10	1·00
	Set of 4 Gutter Pairs	2·25	
	Set of 4 Traffic Light Gutter Pairs	3·50	
	First Day Cover		1·50
	Presentation Pack	1·75	
	P.H.Q. Cards (set of 4)	2·75	4·50

Special First Day of Issue Postmarks

Philatelic Bureau, Edinburgh	2·00
Bethlehem, Llandeilo, Dyfed	3·00

Collectors Pack 1978

1978 (22 Nov). *Comprises Nos. 1050/7 and 1059/74.*
CP1074a   Collectors Pack .... 9·00

553 Old English Sheepdog

554 Welsh Springer Spaniel

555 West Highland Terrier

556 Irish Setter

(Des P. Barrett)

1979 (7 Feb).   **Dogs.** *"All-over" phosphor. P 15 × 14.*

1075 553	9p. grey-black, sepia, turquoise-green, pale greenish yellow, pale greenish blue & grey	15	10
1076 554	10½p. grey-black, lake-brown, apple-green, pale greenish yellow, pale greenish blue & grey	35	30
1077 555	11p. grey-black, claret, yellowish green, pale greenish yellow, cobalt & grey	35	40
	a. Imperf (horiz pair)	£1500	
1078 556	13p. grey-black, lake-brown, green, pale greenish yellow & dp turquoise-blue	35	40
	Set of 4	1·10	1·00
	Set of 4 Gutter Pairs	2·25	
	Set of 4 Traffic Light Gutter Pairs	3·50	
	First Day Cover		1·60
	Presentation Pack	1·60	
	P.H.Q. Cards (set of 4)	3·00	5·50

Special First Day of Issue Postmarks

Philatelic Bureau, Edinburgh	2·50
London SW	3·50

557 Primrose

558 Daffodil

559 Bluebell

560 Snowdrop

(Des P. Newcombe)

1979 (21 Mar).   **Spring Wild Flowers.** *"All-over" phosphor. P 14 × 15.*

1079 557	9p. slate-black, dp brown, pale greenish yellow, dp olive, pale new blue & silver	15	10
	a. Imperf (pair)	£425	
1080 558	10½p. greenish yellow, grey-green, steel-blue, slate-black, new blue & silver	30	35
	a. Imperf (vert pair)	£1600	
1081 559	11p. slate-black, dp brown, ultramarine, lt greenish blue, pale greenish yellow & silver	40	35
	a. Imperf (horiz pair)	£1400	
1082 560	13p. slate-black, indigo, grey-green, sepia, ochre & silver	40	30
	a. Imperf (horiz pair)	£875	
	Set of 4	1·10	1·00
	Set of 4 Gutter Pairs	2·25	
	Set of 4 Traffic Light Gutter Pairs	3·50	
	First Day Cover		1·75
	Presentation Pack	1·90	
	P.H.Q. Cards (set of 4)	3·00	4·50

Special First Day of Issue Postmark

Philatelic Bureau, Edinburgh .... 2·75

Special First Day of Issue Postmarks

Philatelic Bureau, Edinburgh .... 3·50
London SW .... 3·50

561   562

563   564

T **561/4** show Hands placing National Flags in Ballot Boxes.

(Des S. Cliff)

1979 (9 May). **First Direct Elections to European Assembly.** *Phosphorised paper.* P 15 × 14.

1083	561	9p. grey-black, vermilion, cinnamon, pale greenish yellow, pale turquoise-green & dull ultramarine	15	10
1084	562	10½p. grey-black, vermilion, cinnamon, pale greenish yellow, dull ultramarine, pale turquoise-green & chestnut	30	30
1085	563	11p. grey-black, vermilion, cinnamon, pale greenish yellow, dull ultramarine, pale turquoise-green & grey-green	35	35
1086	564	13p. grey-black, vermilion, cinnamon, pale greenish yellow, dull ultramarine, pale turquoise-green & brown	40	35
		Set of 4	1·10	1·00
		Set of 4 Gutter Pairs	2·25	
		Set of 4 Traffic Light Gutter Pairs	3·50	
		First Day Cover		1·75
		Presentation Pack	1·90	
		P.H.Q. Cards (set of 4)	1·75	4·50

565 "Saddling 'Mahmoud' for the Derby, 1936" (Sir Alfred Munnings)

566 "The Liverpool Great National Steeple Chase, 1839" (aquatint by F. C. Turner)

567 "The First Spring Meeting, Newmarket, 1793" (J. N. Sartorius)

568 "Racing at Dorsett Ferry, Windsor, 1684" (Francis Barlow)

(Des S. Rose)

1979 (6 June). **Horseracing Paintings. Bicentenary of the Derby (9p.).** *"All-over" phosphor.* P 15 × 14.

1087	565	9p. lt blue, red-brown, rose-pink, pale greenish yellow, grey-black & gold	20	10
1088	566	10½p. bistre-yellow, slate-blue, salmon-pink, lt blue, grey-black & gold	30	30
1089	567	11p. rose, vermilion, pale greenish yellow, new blue, grey-black & gold	35	35
1090	568	13p. bistre-yellow, rose, turquoise, grey-black & gold	35	35
		Set of 4	1·10	1·00
		Set of 4 Gutter Pairs	2·25	
		Set of 4 Traffic Light Gutter Pairs	3·50	
		First Day Cover		1·75
		Presentation Pack	1·90	
		P.H.Q. Cards (set of 4)	1·90	4·00

Philatelic Bureau, Edinburgh .... 3·50
Epsom, Surrey .... 3·50

Philatelic Bureau, Edinburgh .... 3·00
First Day of Issue handstamps were provided at Hartfield, East Sussex and Stourbridge, West Midlands for this issue.

569 *The Tale of Peter Rabbit* (Beatrix Potter)

570 *The Wind in the Willows* (Kenneth Grahame)

573 Sir Rowland Hill

574 Postman, *circa* 1839

571 *Winnie-the-Pooh* (A. A. Milne)

572 *Alice's Adventures in Wonderland* (Lewis Carroll)

575 London Postman, *circa* 1839

576 Woman and Young Girl with Letters, 1840

(Des E. Stemp)

(Des E. Hughes)

1979 (11 July). **International Year of the Child. Children's Book Illustrations.** *"All-over" phosphor.* P 14 × 15.

1091	**569**	9p. dp bluish green, grey-black, bistre-brown, brt rose, greenish yellow & silver	30	25
1092	**570**	10½p. dull ultramarine, grey-black, olive-brown, brt rose, yellow-orange, pale greenish yellow & silver	35	35
1093	**571**	11p. drab, grey-black, greenish yellow, new blue, yellow-orange, agate & silver	40	40
1094	**572**	13p. pale greenish yellow, grey-black, brt rose, dp bluish green, olive-brown, new blue & silver	60	60
		Set of 4	1·50	1·50
		Set of 4 Gutter Pairs	3·00	
		Set of 4 Traffic Light Gutter Pairs	4·00	
		First Day Cover		2·00
		Presentation Pack	2·25	
		P.H.Q. Cards (set of 4)	2·50	4·50

1979 (22 Aug–24 Oct). **Death Centenary of Sir Rowland Hill.** *"All-over" phosphor.* P 14 × 15.

1095	**573**	10p. grey-black, brown-ochre, myrtle-green, pale greenish yellow, rosine, brt blue & gold	25	15
		a. Imperf (horiz pair)	£2400	
1096	**574**	11½p. grey-black, brown-ochre, brt blue, rosine, bistre-brown, pale greenish yellow & gold	30	30
1097	**575**	13p. grey-black, brown-ochre, brt blue, rosine, bistre-brown, pale greenish yellow & gold	35	40
1098	**576**	15p. grey-black, brown-ochre, myrtle-green, bistre-brown, rosine, pale greenish yellow & gold	60	45
		Set of 4	1·40	1·20
		Set of 4 Gutter Pairs	2·40	
		Set of 4 Traffic Light Gutter Pairs	3·75	
		First Day Cover		1·75
		Presentation Pack	1·90	
		P.H.Q. Cards (set of 4)	2·00	3·50

MS1099 89 × 121 mm. Nos. 1095/8 (*sold at* 59½p.) (24 Oct)   1·40   1·25

   a. Imperforate £1600
   b. Brown-ochre (15p. background, etc.)
      omitted £1800
   c. Gold (Queen's head) omitted £260
   d. Brown-ochre, myrtle-green & gold
      omitted £5500
   e. Brt blue (13p. background, etc.) omitted £3500
   f. Myrtle-green (10p. (background), 15p.)
      omitted £1800
   g. Pale greenish yellow omitted £275
   h. Rosine omitted £800
   i. Bistre-brown omitted £800
   j. Grey-black and pale greenish yellow
      omitted £14000
     First Day Cover .... 2·00

The premium on No. **MS**1099 was used to support the London 1980 International Stamp Exhibition.

Examples of No. **MS**1099 showing face values on the stamps of 9p., 10½p., 11p. and 13p., with a sheet price of 53½p., were prepared, but not issued.

Special First Day of Issue Postmarks

Philatelic Bureau, Edinburgh (stamps) (22 Aug) ..... 2·25
Philatelic Bureau, Edinburgh (miniature sheet) (24 Oct) 2·25
London EC (stamps) (22 Aug) .... 2·25
London EC (miniature sheet) (24 Oct) .... 2·25

First Day of Issue handstamps were provided at Kidderminster, Worcs on 22 August (pictorial) and 24 October (Type C) and at Sanquhar, Dumfriesshire on 22 August and 24 October (both Type C).

577 Policeman on the Beat   578 Policeman directing Traffic

579 Mounted Policewoman   580 River Patrol Boat

(Des B. Sanders)

1979 (26 Sept). **150th Anniv of Metropolitan Police.** *Phosphorised paper. P* 15 × 14.

1100 **577** 10p. grey-black, red-brown, emerald, green-
     ish yellow, brt blue & magenta   25   10
1101 **578** 11½p. grey-black, brt orange, purple-brown,
     ultramarine, greenish yellow & dp bluish
     green   30   35
1102 **579** 13p. grey-black, red-brown, magenta, olive-
     green, greenish yellow & dp dull blue .   40   45
1103 **580** 15p. grey-black, magenta, brown, slate-blue,
     dp brown & greenish black   60   45
     Set of 4 ....   1·40   1·20
     Set of 4 Gutter Pairs ....   2·50
     Set of 4 Traffic Light Gutter Pairs ....   3·75
     First Day Cover ....   1·75
     Presentation Pack ....   1·90
     PHQ Cards (set of 4) ....   1·75   3·50

Special First Day of Issue Postmarks

Philatelic Bureau, Edinburgh .... 2·00
London SW .... 2·00

581 The Three Kings   582 Angel appearing to the Shepherds

583 The Nativity   584 Mary and Joseph travelling to Bethlehem

585 The Annunciation

(Des F. Wegner)

1979 (21 Nov). **Christmas.** *One centre phosphor band* (8p.) *or phosphorised paper* (others). *P* 15 × 14.

1104	**581**	8p. blue, grey-black, ochre, slate-violet & gold	15	15
		a. Imperf (pair)	£500	
1105	**582**	10p. brt rose-red, grey-black, chestnut, chrome-yellow, dp violet & gold	20	25
		a. Imperf between (vert pair)	£450	
		b. Imperf (pair)	£850	
1106	**583**	11½p. orange-vermilion, steel-blue, drab, grey-black, dp blue-green & gold	30	35
1107	**584**	13p. brt blue, orange-vermilion, bistre, grey-black & gold	50	40
1108	**585**	15p. orange-vermilion, blue, bistre, grey-black, green & gold	55	45
		Set of 5	1·50	1·50
		Set of 5 Gutter Pairs	3·00	
		Set of 5 Traffic Light Gutter Pairs	4·00	
		First Day Cover		1·75
		Presentation Pack	2·00	
		P.H.Q. Cards (set of 5)	1·50	3·50

Special First Day of Issue Postmarks

Philatelic Bureau, Edinburgh .... 2·00
Bethlehem, Llandeilo, Dyfed .... 2·00

Collectors Pack 1979

1979 (21 Nov). *Comprises Nos. 1075/98 and 1100/8.*
CP1108a Collectors Pack .... 12·00

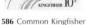

586 Common Kingfisher   **587** Dipper

588 Moorhen   **589** Yellow Wagtails

(Des M. Warren)

1980 (16 Jan). **Centenary of Wild Bird Protection Act.** *Phosphorised paper. P* 14 × 15.

1109	**586**	10p. brt blue, brt yellow-green, vermilion, pale greenish yellow, grey-black & gold	20	10
1110	**587**	11½p. sepia, grey-black, dull ultramarine, vermilion, grey-green, pale greenish yellow & gold	40	35
1111	**588**	13p. emerald-green, grey-black, brt blue, vermilion, pale greenish yellow & gold	50	45
1112	**589**	15p. greenish yellow, brown, lt green, slate-blue, grey-black & gold	50	45
		Set of 4	1·50	1·25
		Set of 4 Gutter Pairs	3·75	
		First Day Cover		1·75
		Presentation Pack	2·00	
		P.H.Q. Cards (set of 4)	1·60	4·00

Special First Day of Issue Postmarks

Philatelic Bureau, Edinburgh .... 2·50
Sandy, Beds .... 2·50

590 *Rocket* approaching Moorish Arch, Liverpool   **591** First and Second Class Carriages passing through Olive Mount Cutting

592 Third Class Carriage and Sheep Truck crossing Chat Moss   **593** Horsebox and Carriage Truck near Bridgewater Canal

594 Goods Truck and Mail-Coach at Manchester

T **590/4** were printed together, *se-tenant*, in horizontal strips of 5 throughout the sheet.

(Des D. Gentleman)

1980 (12 Mar). **150th Anniv of Liverpool and Manchester Railway.** *Phosphorised paper. P 15 x 14.*

1113	**590**	12p. lemon, lt brown, rose-red, pale blue & grey-black	20	20
	a.	Strip of 5. Nos. 1113/17	1·50	1·75
	ab.	Imperf (horiz strip of 5. Nos. 1113/17)	£1750	
	ac.	Lemon omitted (horiz strip of 5. Nos. 1113/17)	£15000	
1114	**591**	12p. rose-red, lt brown, lemon, pale blue & grey-black	20	20
1115	**592**	12p. pale blue, rose-red, lemon, lt brown & grey-black	20	20
1116	**593**	12p. lt brown, lemon, rose-red, pale blue & grey-black	20	20
1117	**594**	12p. lt brown, rose-red, pale blue, lemon & grey-black	20	20
		Set of 5	1·50	90
		Gutter Block of 10	3·50	
		First Day Cover		1·75
		Presentation Pack	2·40	
		P.H.Q. Cards (set of 5)	1·60	4·00

Special First Day of Issue Postmarks

Philatelic Bureau, Edinburgh	2·25
Liverpool	2·25
Manchester	2·25

595 Montage of London Buildings

During the printing of No. 1118 the die was re-cut resulting in the following two types:

Type I (original). Top and bottom lines of shading in portrait oval broken. Hatched shading below left arm of Tower Bridge and hull of ship below right arm. Other points: Hatched shading on flag on Westminster Abbey, bottom right of Post Office Tower and archway of entrance to Westminster Abbey.

Type II (re-engraved). Lines in oval unbroken. Solid shading on bridge and ship. Also solid shading on flag, Post Office Tower and archway.

(Des J. Matthews. Eng G. Holt. Recess)

1980 (9 Apr–7 May). **"London 1980" International Stamp Exhibition.** *Phosphorised paper. P* 14½ × 14.

1118	595	50p. agate (I)	1·25	1·10
		Ea. Type II	1·25	1·25
		Gutter Pair	3·25	
		First Day Cover		2·00
		Presentation Pack	2·25	
		P.H.Q. Card	80	2·25
MS1119		90 × 123 mm. No. 1118 Ea (*sold at 75p.*) (7 May)	1·40	1·50
		a. Error. Imperf	£1000	
		First Day Cover		2·25

Examples of No 1118 are known in various shades of green. Such shades result from problems with the drying of the printed sheets on the press, but are not listed as similar colours can be easily faked.

Special First Day of Issue Postmarks

Philatelic Bureau, Edinburgh (stamp) (9 Apr.) .... 2·50
Philatelic Bureau, Edinburgh (miniature sheet) (7 May) 2·50
London SW (stamp) (9 Apr.) .... 2·50
London SW (miniature sheet) (7 May) .... 2·50

596 Buckingham Palace

597 The Albert Memorial

598 Royal Opera House

599 Hampton Court

600 Kensington Palace

(Des Sir Hugh Casson)

1980 (7 May). **London Landmarks.** *Phosphorised paper. P* 14 × 15.

1120	596	10½p. grey, pale blue, rosine, pale greenish yellow, yellowish green & silver	25	10
1121	597	12p. grey-black, bistre, rosine, yellowish green, pale greenish yellow & silver ...	25	15
		a. Imperf (vert pair)	£1000	
1122	598	13½p. grey-black, pale salmon, pale olive-green, slate-blue & silver	35	40
		a. Imperf (pair)	£1000	
1123	599	15p. grey-black, pale salmon, slate-blue, dull yellowish green, olive-yellow & silver ..	45	50
1124	600	17½p. grey, slate-blue, red-brown, sepia, yellowish green, pale greenish yellow & silver .	60	50
		a. Silver (Queen's head) omitted	£275	
		Set of 5	1·70	1·50
		Set of 5 Gutter Pairs	3·50	
		First Day Cover		1·75
		Presentation Pack	2·00	
		P.H.Q. Cards (set of 5)	1·60	2·75

No. 1124a shows the Queen's head in pale greenish yellow, this colour being printed beneath the silver for technical reasons.

Special First Day of Issue Postmarks

Philatelic Bureau, Edinburgh .... 2·00
Kingston-upon-Thames .... 2·00

601 Charlotte Brontë
(*Jane Eyre*)

602 George Eliot
(*The Mill on the Floss*)

603 Emily Brontë
(*Wuthering Heights*)

604 Mrs. Gaskell
(*North and South*)

T **601/4** show authoresses and scenes from their novels. T **601/2** also include the "Europa" C.E.P.T. emblem.

(Des Barbara Brown)

1980 (9 July). **Famous Authoresses.** *Phosphorised paper. P* 15 × 14.

1125 **601**	12p.	red-brown, brt rose, brt blue, greenish yellow, grey & gold	25	10
	Ea.	Missing "p" in value (R.4/6)	25·00	
1126 **602**	13½p.	red-brown, dull vermilion, pale blue, pale greenish yellow, grey & gold	30	35
	a.	Pale blue omitted	£3200	
1127 **603**	15p.	red-brown, vermilion, blue, lemon, grey & gold	40	35
1128 **604**	17½p.	dull vermilion, slate-blue, ultramarine, pale greenish yellow, grey & gold	50	40
	a.	Imperf and slate-blue omitted (pair) ...	£800	
		Set of 4	1·25	1·10
		Set of 4 Gutter Pairs	3·25	
		First Day Cover		1·75
		Presentation Pack	2·00	
		P.H.Q. Cards (set of 4)	2·50	2·75

Special First Day of Issue Postmarks

Philatelic Bureau, Edinburgh .... 2·50
Haworth, Keighley, W. Yorks .... 2·50

605 Queen Elizabeth the Queen Mother

(Des J. Matthews from photograph by N. Parkinson)

1980 (4 Aug). **80th Birthday of Queen Elizabeth the Queen Mother.** *Phosphorised paper. P* 14 × 15.

1129 **605**	12p.	brt rose, greenish yellow, new blue, grey & silver	75	75
	a.	Imperf (horiz pair)	£1600	
		Gutter Pair	1·90	
		First Day Cover		1·50
		P.H.Q. Card	1·00	1·75

Special First Day of Issue Postmarks

Philatelic Bureau, Edinburgh .... 2·50
Glamis Castle, Forfar .... 4·00

606 Sir Henry Wood

607 Sir Thomas Beecham

608 Sir Malcolm Sargent

609 Sir John Barbirolli

(Des P. Gauld)

1980 (10 Sept). **British Conductors.** *Phosphorised paper. P* 14 × 15.

1130 **606**	12p.	slate, rose-red, greenish yellow, bistre & gold	20	10
1131 **607**	13½p.	grey-black, vermilion, greenish yellow, pale carmine-rose & gold	35	35
1132 **608**	15p.	grey-black, brt rose-red, greenish yellow, turquoise-green & gold	40	40
1133 **609**	17½p.	black, brt rose-red, greenish yellow, dull violet-blue & gold	45	40
		Set of 4	1·25	1·10
		Set of 4 Gutter Pairs	3·50	
		First Day Cover		1·90
		Presentation Pack	2·00	
		P.H.Q. cards (set of 4)	1·60	3·25

Special First Day of Issue Postmarks

Philatelic Bureau, Edinburgh .... 2·25
London SW .... 2·25

Special First Day of Issue Postmarks

Philatelic Bureau, Edinburgh .... 2·25
Cardiff .... 2·25

610 Running   **611** Rugby

614 Christmas Tree

615 Candles

612 Boxing   **613** Cricket

616 Apples and Mistletoe

617 Crown, Chains and Bell

(Des R. Goldsmith. Litho Questa)

1980 (10 Oct). **Sport Centenaries.** *Phosphorised paper.* P 14 × 14½.
1134 **610** 12p. pale new blue, greenish yellow, magen-
ta, lt brown, reddish purple & gold   20   10
a. Gold (Queen's head) omitted £12000
1135 **611** 13½p. pale new blue, olive-yellow, brt purple,
orange-vermilion, blackish lilac & gold .   40   40
1136 **612** 15p. pale new blue, greenish yellow, brt
purple, chalky blue & gold   35   35
a. Gold (Queen's head) omitted £12000
1137 **613** 17½p. pale new blue, greenish yellow, magenta, dp olive, grey-brown & gold   45   40
Set of 4 ....   1·25   1·10
Set of 4 Gutter Pairs ....   3·50
First Day Cover ....   1·90
Presentation Pack ....   2·00
P.H.Q. Cards (set of 4) ....   1·60   3·25
Centenaries:—12p. Amateur Athletics Association; 13½p. Welsh
Rugby Union; 15p. Amateur Boxing Association; 17½p. First England–
Australia Test Match.
Nos. 1134a and 1136a were caused by paper folds.

618 Holly

(Des J. Matthews)

1980 (19 Nov). **Christmas.** *One centre phosphor band* (10p.) *or
phosphorised paper* (others). P 15 × 14.
1138 **614** 10p. black, turquoise-green, greenish yellow,
vermilion & blue   20   10
a. Imperf (horiz pair) £1100
1139 **615** 12p. grey, magenta, rose-red, greenish grey
& pale orange   20   20
1140 **616** 13½p. grey-black, dull yellow-green, brown,
greenish yellow & pale olive-bistre   40   40
1141 **617** 15p. grey-black, bistre-yellow, brt orange,
magenta & new blue   55   55

1142 **618** 17½p.	black, vermilion, dull yellowish green & greenish yellow	55	55
	Set of 5	1·75	1·60
	Set of 5 Gutter Pairs	4·25	
	First Day Cover		1·90
	Presentation Pack	2·00	
	P.H.Q. Cards (set of 5)	1·60	4·50

Special First Day of Issue Postmarks

Philatelic Bureau, Edinburgh	2·25
Bethlehem, Llandeilo, Dyfed	3·00

Collectors Pack 1980

1980 (19 Nov). *Comprises Nos. 1109/18 and 1120/42.*
CP1142a   Collectors Pack .... 15·00

619 St. Valentine's Day   **620** Morris Dancers

621 Lammastide   **622** Medieval Mummers

T **619/20** also include the "Europa" C.E.P.T. emblem.

(Des F. Wegner)

1981 (6 Feb). **Folklore.** *Phosphorised paper.* P 15 × 14.

1143 **619** 14p.	cerise, green, yellow-orange, salmon-pink, black & gold	25	10
1144 **620** 18p.	dull ultramarine, lemon, lake-brown, brt green, black & gold	35	50
1145 **621** 22p.	chrome-yellow, rosine, brown, new blue, black & gold	60	55
1146 **622** 25p.	brt blue, red-brown, brt rose-red, greenish yellow, black & gold	70	65
	Set of 4	1·75	1·60
	Set of 4 Gutter Pairs	4·25	
	First Day Cover		2·00
	Presentation Pack	2·25	
	P.H.Q. Cards (set of 4)	1·60	3·00

Special First Day of Issue Postmarks

Philatelic Bureau, Edinburgh	2·50
London WC	2·50

623 Blind Man with Guide Dog   **624** Hands spelling "Deaf" in Sign Language

625 Disabled Man in Wheelchair   **626** Disabled Artist painting with Foot

(Des J. Gibbs)

1981 (25 Mar). **International Year of the Disabled.** *Phosphorised paper.* P 15 × 14.

1147 **623** 14p.	drab, greenish yellow, brt rose-red, dull purple & silver	35	20
	a. Imperf (pair)	£600	
1148 **624** 18p.	dp blue-green, brt orange, dull vermilion, grey-black & silver	45	60
1149 **625** 22p.	brown-ochre, rosine, purple-brown, greenish blue, black & silver	60	75
1150 **626** 25p.	vermilion, lemon, pale salmon, olive-brown, new blue, black & silver	70	85
	Set of 4	2·00	2·20
	Set of 4 Gutter Pairs	3·75	
	First Day Cover		2·25
	Presentation Pack	2·25	
	P.H.Q. Cards (set of 4)	1·60	3·00

All known examples of No. 1147a are creased.

GIBBONS STAMP MONTHLY
– finest and most informative magazine for all collectors. Obtainable from your newsagent or by postal subscription – details on request.

Special First Day of Issue Postmarks

Philatelic Bureau, Edinburgh .... 2·50
Windsor .... 2·50

Special First Day of Issue Postmarks

Philatelic Bureau, Edinburgh .... 3·00
London SW .... 3·00

631 Glenfinnan, Scotland

632 Derwentwater, England

627 *Aglais urticae*

628 *Maculinea arion*

633 Stackpole Head, Wales

634 Giant's Causeway, Northern Ireland

629 *Inachis io*

630 *Carterocephalus palaemon*

635 St. Kilda, Scotland

(Des G. Beningfield)

1981 (13 May). **Butterflies.** *Phosphorised paper. P* 14 × 15.
1151 **627** 14p. greenish yellow, yellow-green, brt rose,
   brt blue, emerald & gold 25   20
   a. Imperf (pair) £2100
1152 **628** 18p. black, greenish yellow, dull yellowish
   green, brt mauve, brt blue, brt green &
   gold 55   60
1153 **629** 22p. black, greenish yellow, bronze-green,
   rosine, ultramarine, lt green & gold 65   70
1154 **630** 25p. black, greenish yellow, bronze-green,
   brt rose-red, ultramarine, brt emerald
   & gold 70   75
   Set of 4 .... 1·90 2·10
   Set of 4 Gutter Pairs .... 4·75
   First Day Cover .... 2·75
   Presentation Pack .... 2·25
   P.H.Q. Cards (set of 4) .... 1·75 5·00

(Des M. Fairclough)

1981 (24 June). **50th Anniv of National Trust for Scotland. British Landscapes.** *Phosphorised paper. P* 15 × 14.
1155 **631** 14p. lilac, dull blue, reddish brown, bistre-
   yellow, black & gold 25   15
1156 **632** 18p. bottle green, brt blue, brown, bistre-
   yellow, black & gold 45   45
1157 **633** 20p. dp turquoise-blue, dull blue, greenish
   yellow, reddish brown, black & gold ... 65   70
1158 **634** 22p. chrome-yellow, reddish brown, new
   blue, yellow-brown, black & gold 70   75
1159 **635** 25p. ultramarine, new blue, olive-green,
   olive-grey & gold 80   90
   Set of 5 .... 2·50 2·70
   Set of 5 Gutter Pairs .... 6·00
   First Day Cover .... 2·75
   Presentation Pack .... 3·00
   P.H.Q. Cards (set of 5) .... 2·50 5·00

Special First Day of Issue Postmarks

Special First Day of Issue Postmarks

Philatelic Bureau, Edinburgh	3·50
Glenfinnan	3·50
Keswick	3·50

Philatelic Bureau, Edinburgh	5·00
Caernarfon, Gwynedd	5·00
London EC	5·00

637 "Expeditions"   **638** "Skills"

636 Prince Charles and Lady Diana Spencer

639 "Service"   **640** "Recreation"

(Des P. Sharland. Litho J.W.)

(Des J. Matthews from photograph by Lord Snowdon)

1981 (22 July).   **Royal Wedding.** *Phosphorised paper.* P 14 × 15.

1160 **636**	14p. grey-black, greenish yellow, brt rose-red, ultramarine, pale blue, blue & silver	65	40
1161	25p. drab, greenish yellow, brt rose-red, ultramarine, grey-brown, grey-black & silver	1·25	1·60
	Set of 2	1·90	2·00
	Set of 2 Gutter Pairs	4·75	
	First Day Cover		3·50
	Presentation Pack	3·50	
	Souvenir Book	5·00	
	P.H.Q. Cards (set of 2)	3·00	5·00

The souvenir book is a 12-page illustrated booklet with a set of mint stamps in a sachet attached to the front cover.

HAVE YOU READ THE NOTES AT THE BEGINNING OF THIS CATALOGUE?
These often provide answers to the enquiries we receive.

1981 (12 Aug).   **25th Anniv of Duke of Edinburgh Award Scheme.** *Phosphorised paper.* P 14.

1162 **637**	14p. greenish yellow, magenta, pale new blue, black, emerald & silver	25	10
1163 **638**	18p. greenish yellow, magenta, pale new blue, black, cobalt & gold	45	50
1164 **639**	22p. greenish yellow, magenta, pale new blue, black, red-orange & gold	70	70
1165 **640**	25p. brt orange, mauve, pale new blue, black, flesh & bronze	80	80
	Set of 4	2·00	1·90
	Set of 4 Gutter Pairs	5·00	
	First Day Cover		2·40
	Presentation Pack	2·75	
	P.H.Q. Cards (set of 4)	1·75	4·00

Special First Day of Issue Postmarks

Special First Day of Issue Postmarks

Philatelic Bureau, Edinburgh .... 2·75
London W2 .... 2·75

Philatelic Bureau, Edinburgh .... 2·75
Hull .... 2·75

641 Cockle-dredging from *Linsey II*   **642** Hauling in Trawl Net

645 Father Christmas   **646** Jesus Christ

643 Lobster Potting   **644** Hoisting Seine Net

647 Flying Angel   **648** Joseph and Mary arriving
at Bethlehem

(Des B. Sanders)

1981 (23 Sept). **Fishing Industry.** *Phosphorised paper. P* 15 × 14.

1166	**641**	14p. slate, greenish yellow, magenta, new blue, orange-brown, olive-grey & bronze-green	25	10
1167	**642**	18p. slate, greenish yellow, brt crimson, ultramarine, black & greenish slate	45	50
1168	**643**	22p. grey, greenish yellow, brt rose, dull ultramarine, reddish lilac & black	65	50
1169	**644**	25p. grey, greenish yellow, brt rose, cobalt & black	75	60
		Set of 4	1·90	1·50
		Set of 4 Gutter Pairs	4·75	
		First Day Cover		2·40
		Presentation Pack	2·75	
		P.H.Q. Cards (set of 4)	1·75	4·00

Nos. 1166/9 were issued on the occasion of the centenary of the Royal National Mission to Deep Sea Fishermen.

649 Three Kings approaching Bethlehem

(Des Samantha Brown (11½p.), Tracy Jenkins (14p.), Lucinda Blackmore (18p.), Stephen Moore (22p.), Sophie Sharp (25p.))

1981 (18 Nov). **Christmas. Children's Pictures.** *One phosphor band* (11½p.) *or phosphorised paper* (*others*). P 15 × 14.

1170	**645**	11½p. ultramarine, black, red, olive-bistre, brt green & gold	25	20
1171	**646**	14p. bistre-yellow, brt magenta, blue, greenish blue, brt green, black & gold	35	20
1172	**647**	18p. pale blue-green, bistre-yellow, brt magenta, ultramarine, black & gold	50	60
1173	**648**	22p. dp turquoise-blue, lemon, magenta, black & gold	75	70

1174 **649** 25p. royal blue, lemon, brt magenta, black &
gold 85 75
Set of 5 .... 2·40 2·40
Set of 5 Gutter Pairs .... 5·25
First Day Cover .... 2·25
Presentation Pack .... 3·00
P.H.Q. Cards (set of 5) .... 2·00 5·00

Special First Day of Issue Postmarks

Philatelic Bureau, Edinburgh .... 2·50
Bethlehem, Llandeilo, Dyfed .... 2·50

Collectors Pack 1981

1981 (18 Nov). *Comprises Nos. 1143/74.*
CP1174a Collectors Pack .... 17·00

650 Charles Darwin and   **651** Darwin and Marine Iguanas
Giant Tortoises

652 Darwin, Cactus Ground   **653** Darwin and Prehistoric Skulls
Finch and Large Ground Finch

(Des D. Gentleman)

1982 (10 Feb). **Death Centenary of Charles Darwin.** *Phosphorised paper.* P 15 × 14.
1175 **650** 15½p. dull purple, drab, bistre, black & grey-
black 40 20
1176 **651** 19½p. violet-grey, bistre-yellow, slate-black,
red-brown, grey-black & black 50 60
1177 **652** 26p. sage green, bistre-yellow, orange,
chalky blue, grey-black, red-brown &
black 65 85
1178 **653** 29p. grey-brown, yellow-brown, brown-
ochre, black & grey-black 70 90
Set of 4 .... 2·10 2·40
Set of 4 Gutter Pairs .... 4·75
First Day Cover .... 2·50
Presentation Pack .... 3·00
P.H.Q. Cards (set of 4) .... 2·50 6·50

Special First Day of Issue Postmarks

Philatelic Bureau, Edinburgh .... 3·00
Shrewsbury .... 3·00

654 Boys' Brigade   **655** Girls' Brigade

656 Boy Scout Movement   **657** Girl Guide Movement

(Des B. Sanders)

1982 (24 Mar). **Youth Organizations.** *Phosphorised paper.* P 15 × 14.
1179 **654** 15½p. gold, greenish yellow, pale orange,
mauve, dull blue & grey-black 25 15
1180 **655** 19½p. gold, greenish yellow, pale orange, brt
rose, dp ultramarine, olive-bistre &
grey-black 45 55
1181 **656** 26p. gold, greenish yellow, olive-sepia, rosine, dp blue, dp dull green & grey-black 60 75
1182 **657** 29p. gold, yellow, dull orange, cerise, dull
ultramarine, chestnut & grey-black 75 80
Set of 4 .... 1·90 2·00
Set of 4 Gutter Pairs .... 5·00
First Day Cover .... 2·75
Presentation Pack .... 3·00
P.H.Q. Cards (set of 4) .... 2·50 6·50
Nos. 1179/82 were issued on the occasion of the 75th anniversary of
the Boy Scout Movement; the 125th birth anniversary of Lord Baden-
Powell and the centenary of the Boys' Brigade (1983).

Special First Day of Issue Postmarks

Edinburgh Philatelic Bureau	3·00
Glasgow	3·00
London SW	3·00

658 Ballerina

659 Harlequin

660 Hamlet

661 Opera Singer

(Des A. George)

1982 (28 Apr). **Europa. British Theatre.** *Phosphorised paper.* P 15 × 14.
1183 **658** 15½p. carmine-lake, greenish blue, greenish yellow, grey-black, bottle green & silver ... 25 15
1184 **659** 19½p. rosine, new blue, greenish yellow, black, ultramarine & silver ... 40 50
1185 **660** 26p. carmine-red, brt rose-red, greenish yellow, black, dull ultramarine, lake-brown & silver ... 70 70

1186 **661** 29p. rose-red, greenish yellow, brt blue, grey-black & silver ... 75 90
Set of 4 ... 1·90 2·00
Set of 4 Gutter Pairs ... 5·00
First Day Cover ... 2·75
Presentation Pack ... 3·00
P.H.Q. Cards (set of 4) ... 2·50 6·50

Special First Day of Issue Postmarks

Philatelic Bureau, Edinburgh	3·00
Stratford-upon-Avon	3·00

662 Henry VIII and *Mary Rose*

663 Admiral Blake and *Triumph*

664 Lord Nelson and H.M.S. *Victory*

665 Lord Fisher and H.M.S. *Dreadnought*

666 Viscount Cunningham and H.M.S. *Warspite*

(Des Marjorie Saynor. Eng C. Slania. Recess and photo)

1982 (16 June). **Maritime Heritage.** *Phosphorised paper.* P 15 × 14.
1187 **662** 15½p. black, lemon, brt rose, pale orange, ultramarine & grey ... 35 20
a. Imperf (pair) ... £1100
1188 **663** 19½p. black, greenish yellow, brt rose-red, pale orange, ultramarine & grey ... 50 50
1189 **664** 24p. black, orange-yellow, brt rose-red, lake-brown, dp ultramarine & grey ... 65 75

1190 **665** 26p. black, orange-yellow, brt rose, lemon,
ultramarine & grey 80 85
   a. Imperf (pair) £2000
1191 **666** 29p. black, olive-yellow, brt rose, orange-
yellow, ultramarine & grey 85 90
   Set of 5 . . . . 2·90 3·00
   Set of 5 Gutter Pairs . . . . 7·00
   First Day Cover . . . . 3·00
   Presentation Pack . . . . 3·50
   P.H.Q. Cards (set of 5) . . . . 3·00 7·00

Nos. 1187/91 were issued on the occasion of Maritime England Year, the Bicentenary of the Livery Grant by the City of London to the Worshipful Company of Shipwrights and the raising of the *Mary Rose* from Portsmouth Harbour.

Several used examples of the 15½p. have been seen with the black recess (ship and waves) omitted.

Special First Day of Issue Postmarks

Philatelic Bureau, Edinburgh . . . . 3·50
Portsmouth . . . . 3·50

667 "Strawberry Thief"
(William Morris)

668 Untitled (Steiner and Co)

669 "Cherry Orchard"
(Paul Nash)

670 "Chevron"
(Andrew Foster)

(Des Peter Hatch Partnership)

1982 (23 July). **British Textiles.** *Phosphorised paper. P* 14 × 15.
1192 **667** 15½p. blue, olive-yellow, rosine, dp blue-
green, bistre & Prussian blue 25 10
   a. Imperf (horiz pair) £1000
1193 **668** 19½p. olive-grey, greenish yellow, brt magenta, dull green, yellow-brown & black . . 50 55
   a. Imperf (vert pair) £1500
1194 **669** 26p. brt scarlet, dull mauve, dull ultramarine
& brt carmine 65 75
1195 **670** 29p. bronze-green, orange-yellow, turquoise-
green, stone, chestnut & sage-green . . . 75 90
   Set of 4 . . . . 1·90 2·00
   Set of 4 Gutter Pairs . . . . 5·00
   First Day Cover . . . . 2·50
   Presentation Pack . . . . 2·75
   P.H.Q. Cards (set of 4) . . . . 3·00 6·50

Nos. 1192/5 were issued on the occasion of the 250th birth anniversary of Sir Richard Arkwright (inventor of spinning machine).

Special First Day of Issue Postmarks

Philatelic Bureau, Edinburgh . . . . 3·00
Rochdale . . . . 3·00

671 Development of Communications

672 Modern Technological Aids

(Des Delaney and Ireland)

1982 (8 Sept). **Information Technology.** *Phosphorised paper. P* 14 × 15.
1196 **671** 15½p. black, greenish yellow, brt rose-red,
bistre-brown, new blue & lt ochre 40 10
   a. Imperf (pair) £250
1197 **672** 26p. black, greenish yellow, brt rose-red,
olive-bistre, new blue & lt olive-grey . . . 60 90
   a. Imperf (pair) £1300
   Set of 2 . . . . 1·00 1·00
   Set of 2 Gutter Pairs . . . . 2·50
   First Day Cover . . . . 1·75
   Presentation Pack . . . . 1·60
   P.H.Q. cards (set of 2) . . . . 1·50 4·50

Philatelic Bureau, Edinburgh .... 2·50
London WC .... 2·50

673 Austin "Seven" and "Metro"   **674** Ford "Model T" and "Escort"

675 Jaguar "SS 1" and "XJ6"   **676** Rolls-Royce "Silver Ghost" and
"Silver Spirit"

(Des S. Paine. Litho Questa)

1982 (13 Oct).   **British Motor Cars.** *Phosphorised paper. P* 14½ × 14.
1198 **673** 15½p. slate, orange-vermilion, brt orange,
drab, yellow-green, olive-yellow, bluish
grey & black 30 10
1199 **674** 19½p. slate, brt orange, olive-grey, rose-red,
dull vermilion, grey & black 55 55
Ea. Rose-red, grey and black ptgs double .. £650
1200 **675** 26p. slate, red-brown, brt orange, turquoise-
green, myrtle-green, dull blue-green,
grey & olive 65 70
1201 **676** 29p. slate, brt orange, carmine-red, reddish
purple, grey & black .... 1·00 90
Ea. Black ptg quadruple £450
Eb. Brt orange, carmine-red, grey and black
ptgs double £800
Set of 4 .... 2·25 2·00
Set of 4 Gutter Pairs .... 5·75
First Day Cover .... 2·50
Presentation Pack .... 3·00
P.H.Q. cards (set of 4) .... 3·00 6·75

Philatelic Bureau, Edinburgh .... 3·75
Birmingham .... 3·75
Crewe .... 3·75

677 "While Shepherds Watched"   **678** "The Holly and the Ivy"

679 "I Saw Three Ships"   **680** "We Three Kings"

681 "Good King Wenceslas"

(Des Barbara Brown)

1982 (17 Nov).   **Christmas. Carols.** *One phosphor band* (12½p.) *or
phosphorised paper* (others). *P* 15 × 14.
1202 **677** 12½p. black, greenish yellow, brt scarlet, steel
blue, red-brown & gold 25 20
1203 **678** 15½p. black, bistre-yellow, brt rose-red, brt
blue, brt green & gold 35 20
a. Imperf (pair) £1250

1204	**679** 19½p.	black, bistre-yellow, brt rose-red, dull blue, dp brown & gold	65	70
	a.	Imperf (pair)		£1600
1205	**680** 26p.	black, bistre-yellow, brt magenta, brt blue, chocolate, gold & orange-red	75	80
1206	**681** 29p.	black, bistre-yellow, magenta, brt blue, chestnut, gold & brt magenta	80	90
		Set of 5	2·50	2·50
		Set of 5 Gutter Pairs	5·75	
		First Day Cover		2·75
		Presentation Pack	3·00	
		P.H.Q. cards (set of 5)	3·00	7·00

Special Day of Issue Postmarks

Philatelic Bureau, Edinburgh .... 3·25
Bethlehem, Llandeilo, Dyfed .... 3·25

Collectors Pack 1982

1982 (17 Nov). Comprises Nos. 1175/1206.
CP1206a   Collectors Pack .... 22·00

682 Atlantic Salmon   683 Northern Pike

684 Brown Trout   685 Eurasian Perch

(Des A. Jardine)

1983 (26 Jan). **British River Fishes.** Phosphorised paper. P 15 × 14.

1207	**682** 15½p.	grey-black, bistre-yellow, brt purple, new blue & silver	30	10
	a.	Imperf (pair)		£1300
1208	**683** 19½p.	black, bistre-yellow, olive-bistre, dp claret, silver & dp bluish green	60	60
1209	**684** 26p.	grey-black, bistre-yellow, chrome-yellow, magenta, silver & pale blue	75	75
	a.	Imperf (pair)		£950

1210	**685** 29p.	black, greenish yellow, brt carmine, new blue & silver	90	90
		Set of 4	2·25	2·10
		Set of 4 Gutter Pairs	5·75	
		First Day Cover		2·75
		Presentation Pack	3·00	
		P.H.Q. Cards (set of 4)	3·00	7·00

All known examples of No. 1209a are creased.

Special First Day of Issue Postmarks

Philatelic Bureau, Edinburgh .... 3·00
Peterborough .... 3·00

686 Tropical Island   687 Desert

688 Temperate Farmland   689 Mountain Range

(Des D. Fraser)

1983 (9 Mar). **Commonwealth Day. Geographical Regions.** Phosphorised paper. P 14 × 15.

1211	**686** 15½p.	greenish blue, greenish yellow, brt rose, lt brown, grey-black, dp claret & silver	30	10
1212	**687** 19½p.	brt lilac, greenish yellow, magenta, dull blue, grey-black, dp dull blue & silver .	55	60
1213	**688** 26p.	lt blue, greenish yellow, brt magenta, new blue, grey-black, violet & silver ...	75	80
1214	**689** 29p.	dull violet-blue, reddish violet, slate-lilac, new blue, myrtle-green, black & silver	85	85
		Set of 4	2·25	2·25
		Set of 4 Gutter Pairs	5·25	
		First Day Cover		2·50
		Presentation Pack	3·00	
		P.H.Q. Cards (set of 4)	3·00	6·50

Special First Day of Issue Postmarks

Philatelic Bureau, Edinburgh .... 3·00
London SW .... 3·00

690 Humber Bridge   **691** Thames Flood Barrier

692 *Iolair* (oilfield emergency support vessel)

(Des M. Taylor)

1983 (25 May). **Europa. Engineering Achievements.** *Phosphorised paper.* P 15 × 14.
1215 **690** 16p. silver, orange-yellow, ultramarine, black
    & grey 30   10
1216 **691** 20½p. silver, greenish yellow, brt purple, blue,
    grey-black & grey 80   1·00
1217 **692** 28p. silver, lemon, brt rose-red, chestnut,
    dull ultramarine, black & grey 90   1·00
    Set of 3 .... 1·75   1·90
    Set of 3 Gutter Pairs .... 4·50
    First Day Cover ....   2·40
    Presentation Pack .... 3·00
    P.H.Q. Cards (set of 3) .... 2·50   5·00

Special First Day of Issue Postmarks

Philatelic Bureau, Edinburgh .... 2·75
Hull .... 2·75

693 Musketeer and Pikeman,   **694** Fusilier and Ensign,
The Royal Scots (1633)   The Royal Welch Fusiliers
                                   (mid-18th century)

695 Riflemen, 95th Rifles (The   **696** Sergeant (khaki service)
Royal Green Jackets) (1805)   and Guardsman (full dress),
                              The Irish Guards (1900)

697 Paratroopers, The Parachute Regiment (1983)

(Des E. Stemp)

1983 (6 July). **British Army Uniforms.** *Phosphorised paper.* P 14 × 15.
1218 **693** 16p. black, buff, dp brown, slate-black, rose-
    red, gold & new blue 30   10
1219 **694** 20½p. black, buff, greenish yellow, slate-black,
    brown-rose, gold & brt blue 45   60
1220 **695** 26p. black, buff, slate-purple, green, bistre &
    gold 70   90
    a. Imperf (pair) £1600
1221 **696** 28p. black, buff, lt brown, grey, dull rose,
    gold & new blue 75   90
1222 **697** 31p. black, buff, olive-yellow, grey, dp ma-
    genta, gold & new blue 75   80
    Set of 5 .... 2·75   3·00
    Set of 5 Gutter Pairs .... 7·00
    First Day Cover ....   3·00
    Presentation Pack .... 4·00
    P.H.Q. Cards (set of 5) .... 3·00   7·50
Nos. 1218/22 were issued on the occasion of the 350th anniversary
of the Royal Scots, the senior line regiment of the British Army.

Special First Day of Issue Postmarks

6 JULY 1983

6 JULY 1983

Philatelic Bureau, Edinburgh .... 3·75
Aldershot .... 3·75

Special First Day of Issue Postmarks

24 AUGUST 1983

24 AUGUST 1983

Philatelic Bureau, Edinburgh .... 3·50
Oxford .... 3·50

20TH CENTURY GARDEN
SISSINGHURST

698 20th-century Garden, Sissinghurst

19TH CENTURY GARDEN
BIDDULPH GRANGE

699 19th-century Garden, Biddulph Grange

702 Merry-go-round   **703** Big Wheel, Helter-skelter and Performing Animals

18TH CENTURY GARDEN
BLENHEIM

700 18th-century Garden, Blenheim

17TH CENTURY GARDEN
PITMEDDEN

701 17th-century Garden, Pitmedden

704 Side Shows   **705** Early Produce Fair

(Des A. Restall)

1983 (5 Oct). **British Fairs.** *Phosphorised paper.* P 15 × 14.

1227	**702**	16p. grey-black, greenish yellow, orange-red, ochre & turquoise-blue	35	15
1228	**703**	20½p. grey-black, yellow-ochre, yellow-orange, brt magenta, violet & black	60	70
1229	**704**	28p. grey-black, bistre-yellow, orange-red, violet & yellow-brown	75	80
1230	**705**	31p. grey-black, greenish yellow, red, dp turquoise-green, slate-violet & brown ..	85	85
		Set of 4	2·40	2·40
		Set of 4 Gutter Pairs	5·00	
		First Day Cover		2·50
		Presentation Pack	3·25	
		P.H.Q. Cards (set of 4)	3·00	6·00

(Des Liz Butler. Litho J.W.)

1983 (24 Aug). **British Gardens.** *Phosphorised paper.* P 14.

1223	**698**	16p. greenish yellow, brt purple, new blue, black, brt green & silver	30	10
1224	**699**	20½p. greenish yellow, brt purple, new blue, black, brt green & silver	40	55
1225	**700**	28p. greenish yellow, brt purple, new blue, black, brt green & silver	75	90
1226	**701**	31p. greenish yellow, brt purple, new blue, black, brt green & silver	80	90
		Set of 4	2·00	2·25
		Set of 4 Gutter Pairs	5·00	
		First Day Cover		2·75
		Presentation Pack	3·25	
		P.H.Q. Cards (set of 4)	3·00	6·00

Nos. 1223/6 were issued on the occasion of the death bicentenary of "Capability" Brown (landscape gardener).

Special First Day of Issue Postmarks

5 OCT 1983

5 OCT 1983

Philatelic Bureau, Edinburgh .... 3·00
Nottingham .... 3·00

For full information on all future British issues, collectors should write to the British Post Office Philatelic Bureau, 21 South Gyle Crescent, Edinburgh EH12 9PB

706 "Christmas Post" (pillar-box)

707 "The Three Kings" (chimney-pots)

708 "World at Peace" (Dove and Blackbird)

709 "Light of Christmas" (street lamp)

710 "Christmas Dove" (hedge sculpture)

(Des T. Meeuwissen)

1983 (16 Nov). **Christmas.** *One phosphor band (12½p.) or phosphorised paper (others). P 15 × 14.*

1231 **706** 12½p. black, greenish yellow, brt rose-red, brt blue, gold & grey-black 25 10
   a. Imperf (horiz pair) £1000
1232 **707** 16p. black, greenish yellow, rose, pale new blue, gold & brown-purple 30 10
   a. Imperf (pair) £850
1233 **708** 20½p. black, greenish yellow, brt rose, new blue, gold & blue 55 75
1234 **709** 28p. black, lemon, brt carmine, bluish violet, gold, dp turquoise-green & purple 75 80
1235 **710** 31p. black, greenish yellow, brt rose, new blue, gold, green & brown-olive .... 90 1·00
   Set of 5 .... 2·50 2·50
   Set of 5 Gutter Pairs .... 6·25
   First Day Cover .... 3·00
   Presentation Pack .... 3·50
   P.H.Q. Cards (set of 5) .... 3·00 6·00

Special First Day of Issue Postmarks

Philatelic Bureau, Edinburgh .... 3·25
Bethlehem, Llandeilo, Dyfed .... 3·25

Collectors Pack 1983

1983 (16 Nov). *Comprises Nos. 1207/35.*
CP1235a Collectors Pack .... 28·00

711 Arms of the College of Arms

712 Arms of King Richard III (founder)

713 Arms of the Earl Marshal 714 Arms of the City of London of England

(Des J. Matthews)

1984 (17 Jan). **500th Anniv of College of Arms.** *Phosphorised paper. P 14½.*

1236 **711** 16p. black, chrome-yellow, reddish brown, scarlet-vermilion, brt blue & grey-black 35 15
1237 **712** 20½p. black, chrome-yellow, rosine, brt blue & grey-black 45 65
1238 **713** 28p. black, chrome-yellow, rosine, brt blue, dull green & grey-black 90 90
1239 **714** 31p. black, chrome-yellow, rosine, brt blue & grey-black .... 1·00 1·00
   a. Imperf (horiz pair) £2000
   Set of 4 .... 2·50 2·50
   Set of 4 Gutter Pairs .... 5·75
   First Day Cover .... 3·25
   Presentation Pack .... 3·25
   P.H.Q. Cards .... 3·00 7·50

Special First Day of Issue Postmarks

Philatelic Bureau, Edinburgh .... 3·75
London EC .... 4·00

715 Highland Cow

716 Chillingham Wild Bull

717 Hereford Bull

718 Welsh Black Bull

719 Irish Moiled Cow

(Des B. Driscoll)

1984 (6 Mar). **British Cattle.** *Phosphorised paper. P* 15 × 14.
1240 **715** 16p. grey-black, bistre-yellow, rosine, yellow-
    orange, new blue & pale drab 35 15
    a. Imperf (vert pair) £3500
1241 **716** 20½p. grey-black, greenish yellow, magenta,
    bistre, dull blue-green, pale drab & lt
    green 55 60
1242 **717** 26p. black, chrome-yellow, rosine, reddish
    brown, new blue & pale drab 75 75
1243 **718** 28p. black, greenish yellow, brt carmine,
    orange-brown, dp dull blue & pale drab 75 85
1244 **719** 31p. grey-black, bistre-yellow, rosine, red-
    brown, lt blue & pale drab .... 1·00 90
    Set of 5 .... 3·00 3·00
    Set of 5 Gutter Pairs .... 7·50
    First Day Cover .... 3·75
    Presentation Pack .... 4·00
    P.H.Q. Cards (set of 5) .... 3·00 7·00
    Nos. 1240/4 were issued on the occasion of the centenary of the
Highland Cattle Society and the bicentenary of the Royal Highland and
Agricultural Society of Scotland.

Special First Day of Issue Postmarks

Philatelic Bureau, Edinburgh .... 4·50
Oban, Argyll .... 4·50

720 Garden Festival Hall,
    Liverpool

721 Milburngate Centre, Durham

722 Bush House, Bristol

723 Commercial Street
    Development, Perth

(Des R. Maddox and Trickett and Webb Ltd)

1984 (10 Apr). **Urban Renewal.** *Phosphorised paper. P* 15 × 14.
1245 **720** 16p. brt emerald, greenish yellow, cerise,
    steel-blue, black, silver & flesh 30 10
1246 **721** 20½p. brt orange, greenish yellow, dp dull
    blue, yellowish green, azure, black &
    silver 50 60
    a. Imperf (horiz pair) £2000
1247 **722** 28p. rosine, greenish yellow, Prussian blue,
    pale blue-green, black & silver .... 90 1·00
1248 **723** 31p. blue, greenish yellow, cerise, grey-blue,
    brt green, black & silver .... 1·00 1·00
    a. Imperf (pair) £1000
    Set of 4 .... 2·40 2·40
    Set of 4 Gutter Pairs .... 6·00
    First Day Cover .... 3·00
    Presentation Pack .... 3·00
    P.H.Q. Cards (set of 4) .... 3·00 6·00
    Nos. 1245/8 were issued on the occasion of 150th anniversaries of
the Royal Institute of British Architects and the Chartered Institute of
Building, and to commemorate the first International Gardens Festival,
Liverpool.

Special First Day of Issue Postmarks

Philatelic Bureau, Edinburgh .... 3·50
Liverpool .... 3·50

724 C.E.P.T. 25th Anniversary Logo

725 Abduction of Europa

(Des J. Larrivière (T **724**), F. Wegner (T **725**))

1984 (15 May). **25th Anniv of C.E.P.T. ("Europa")** (T **724**) **and Second Elections to European Parliament** (T **725**). *Phosphorised paper.* P 15 × 14.

1249	**724**	16p. greenish slate, dp blue & gold	30	15
		a. Horiz pair. Nos. 1249/50	1·00	1·25
		ab. Imperf (horiz pair)	£2000	
1250	**725**	16p. greenish slate, dp blue, black & gold ..	30	15
1251	**724**	20½p. Venetian red, dp magenta & gold	70	75
		a. Horiz pair. Nos. 1251/2	2·00	2·50
		ab. Imperf (horiz pair)	£2000	
1252	**725**	20½p. Venetian red, dp magenta, black & gold	70	75
		Set of 4	2·75	1·60
		Set of 2 Gutter Blocks of 4	6·75	
		First Day Cover		4·00
		Presentation Pack	4·50	
		P.H.Q. Cards (set of 4)	3·00	6·00

Nos. 1249/50 and 1251/2 were each printed together, *se-tenant*, in horizontal pairs throughout the sheets.

Special First Day of Issue Postmarks

Philatelic Bureau, Edinburgh	4·50
London SW	4·50

726 Lancaster House

(Des P. Hogarth)

1984 (5 June). **London Economic Summit Conference.** *Phosphorised paper.* P 14 × 15.

1253	**726**	31p. silver, bistre-yellow, brown-ochre, black, rosine, brt blue & reddish lilac ..	85	85
		Gutter Pair	2·00	
		First Day Cover		2·00
		P.H.Q. Card	1·00	3·25

Special First Day of Issue Postmarks

Philatelic Bureau, Edinburgh	2·50
London SW	2·50

727 View of Earth from "Apollo 11"

728 Navigational Chart of English Channel

729 Greenwich Observatory

730 Sir George Airy's Transit Telescope

GIBBONS STAMP MONTHLY

– finest and most informative magazine for all collectors. Obtainable from your newsagent or by postal subscription – details on request.

(Des H. Waller. Litho Questa)

1984 (26 June). **Centenary of the Greenwich Meridian.** *Phosphorised paper.* P 14 × 14½.

1254	727	16p. new blue, greenish yellow, magenta, black, scarlet & blue-black	40	10
	Ea.	Black ptg double	†	
1255	728	20½p. olive-sepia, lt brown, pale buff, black & scarlet	75	55
1256	729	28p. new blue, greenish yellow, scarlet, black & brt purple	85	75
1257	730	31p. dp blue, cobalt, scarlet & black	1·10	90
		Set of 4	2·75	2·10
		Set of 4 Gutter Pairs	6·00	
		First Day Cover		2·50
		Presentation Pack	3·25	
		P.H.Q. Cards (set of 4)	3·00	6·00

On Nos. 1254/7 the Meridian is represented by a scarlet line.

Special First Day of Issue Postmarks

Philatelic Bureau, Edinburgh .... 3·25
London SE10 .... 3·25

(Des K. Bassford and S. Paine. Eng C. Slania. Recess and photo)

1984 (31 July). **Bicentenary of First Mail Coach Run, Bath and Bristol to London.** *Phosphorised paper.* P 15 × 14.

1258	731	16p. pale stone, black, grey-black & brt scarlet	40	35
	a.	Horiz strip of 5. Nos. 1258/62	2·50	2·75
1259	732	16p. pale stone, black, grey-black & brt scarlet	40	35
1260	733	16p. pale stone, black, grey-black & brt scarlet	40	35
1261	734	16p. pale stone, black, grey-black & brt scarlet	40	35
1262	735	16p. pale stone, black, grey-black & brt scarlet	40	35
		Set of 5	2·50	1·60
		Gutter Block of 10	6·00	
		First Day Cover		3·50
		Presentation Pack	3·50	
		Souvenir Book	7·00	
		P.H.Q. Cards (set of 5)	3·00	7·50

Nos. 1258/62 were printed together, *se-tenant*, in horizontal strips of 5 throughout the sheet.

The souvenir book is a 24-page illustrated booklet with a set of mint stamps in a sachet attached to the front cover.

Special First Day of Issue Postmarks

Philatelic Bureau, Edinburgh .... 4·00
Bristol .... 4·00

731 Bath Mail Coach, 1784   **732** Attack on Exeter Mail, 1816

733 Norwich Mail in Thunderstorm, 1827   **734** Holyhead and Liverpool Mails leaving London, 1828

736 Nigerian Clinic   **737** Violinist and Acropolis, Athens

735 Edinburgh Mail Snowbound, 1831

738 Building Project, Sri Lanka   **739** British Council Library, Middle East

(Des F. Newell and J. Sorrell)

1984 (25 Sept).   **50th Anniv of the British Council.** *Phosphorised paper.*
  P 15 × 14.

1263 **736** 17p. grey-green, greenish yellow, brt purple,
dull blue, black, pale green & yellow-
green 35   10

1264 **737** 22p. crimson, greenish yellow, brt rose-red,
dull green, black, pale drab & slate-
purple 55   75

1265 **738** 31p. sepia, olive-bistre, red, black, pale stone
& olive-brown 70   1·00

1266 **739** 34p. steel blue, yellow, rose-red, new blue,
black, azure & pale blue 75   90
  Set of 4 .... 2·10   2·50
  Set of 4 Gutter Pairs .... 5·25
  First Day Cover .... 3·00
  Presentation Pack .... 3·25
  P.H.Q. Cards (set of 4) .... 3·00   6·00

Special First Day of Issue Postmarks

Philatelic Bureau, Edinburgh .... 3·50
London SW .... 3·50

740 The Holy Family

741 Arrival in Bethlehem

742 Shepherd and Lamb

743 Virgin and Child

744 Offering of Frankincense

(Des Yvonne Gilbert)

1984 (20 Nov).   **Christmas.** *One phosphor band (13p.) or phosphorised
paper (others). P* 15 × 14.

1267 **740** 13p. pale cream, grey-black, bistre-yellow,
magenta, red-brown & lake-brown 25   20
  Eu. Underprint Type 4 50

1268 **741** 17p. pale cream, grey-black, yellow, magenta, dull blue & dp dull blue 45   25
  a. Imperf (pair) £2000

1269 **742** 22p. pale cream, grey-black, olive-yellow, brt
magenta, brt blue & brownish grey 55   80

1270 **743** 31p. pale cream, grey-black, bistre-yellow,
magenta, dull blue & lt brown 75   1·00

1271 **744** 34p. pale cream, olive-grey, bistre-yellow,
magenta, turquoise-green & brown-ol-
ive .... 1·00   1·10
  Set of 5 .... 2·75   3·00
  Set of 5 Gutter Pairs .... 6·00
  First Day Cover .... 3·25
  Presentation Pack .... 3·50
  P.H.Q. Cards (set of 5) .... 3·00   6·00

Examples of No. 1267Eu from the 1984 Christmas booklet (No. FX7)
show a random pattern of blue double-lined stars printed on the
reverse over the gum.

Special First Day of Issue Postmarks

Philatelic Bureau, Edinburgh .... 3·50
Bethlehem, Llandeilo, Dyfed .... 3·50

Collectors Pack 1984

1984 (20 Nov).   *Comprises Nos. 1236/71.*
CP1271a Collectors Pack .... 35·00

Post Office Yearbook

1984.   *Comprises Nos. 1236/71 in 24-page hardbound book with slip
case, illustrated in colour* .... 90·00

745 "Flying Scotsman"

746 "Golden Arrow"

747 "Cheltenham Flyer"

748 "Royal Scot"

749 "Cornish Riviera"

(Des T. Cuneo)

1985 (22 Jan). **Famous Trains.** *Phosphorised paper. P* 15 × 14.

1272 **745** 17p. black, lemon, magenta, dull blue, grey-
black & gold 50 20
a. Imperf (pair) £1900
1273 **746** 22p. black, greenish yellow, brt rose, dp dull
blue, grey-black & gold 80 80
1274 **747** 29p. black, greenish yellow, magenta, blue,
grey-black & gold .... 90 1·00
1275 **748** 31p. black, bistre-yellow, brt magenta, new
blue, slate-black & gold .... 1·10 1·20
1276 **749** 34p. black, greenish yellow, brt rose, blue,
slate-black & gold .... 1·35 1·20
Set of 5 .... 4·25 4·25
Set of 5 Gutter Pairs .... 9·25
First Day Cover .... 6·00
Presentation Pack .... 6·00
P.H.Q. Cards (set of 5) .... 5·50 16·00

Nos. 1272/6 were issued on the occasion of the 150th anniversary of the Great Western Railway Company.

Special First Day of Issue Postmarks

Philatelic Bureau, Edinburgh .... 6·50
Bristol .... 6·50

750 *Bombus terrestris*
(bee)

751 *Coccinella septempunctata*
(ladybird)

752 *Decticus verrucivorus*
(bush-cricket)

753 *Lucanus cervus*
(stag beetle)

754 *Anax imperator* (dragonfly)

(Des G. Beningfield)

1985 (12 Mar). **Insects.** *Phosphorised paper. P* 14 × 15.

1277 **750** 17p. black, greenish yellow, magenta, blue,
azure, gold & slate-black 40 10
1278 **751** 22p. black, greenish yellow, brt rose-red, dull
blue-green, slate-black & gold 60 55
1279 **752** 29p. black, greenish yellow, brt rose, greenish blue, grey-black, gold & bistre-
yellow 85 90
1280 **753** 31p. black, greenish yellow, rose, pale new
blue & gold .... 1·10 1·00
1281 **754** 34p. black, greenish yellow, magenta, greenish blue, grey-black & gold .... 1·10 90
Set of 5 .... 3·75 3·25
Set of 5 Gutter Pairs .... 8·75
First Day Cover .... 4·00
Presentation Pack .... 4·50
P.H.Q. Cards (set of 5) .... 3·00 8·00

Nos. 1277/81 were issued on the occasion of the centenaries of the Royal Entomological Society of London's Royal Charter, and of the Selborne Society.

Special First Day of Issue Postmarks

Philatelic Bureau, Edinburgh .... 4·50
London SW .... 4·50

755 "Water Music"
(George Frederick Handel)

756 "The Planets Suite"
(Gustav Holst)

759 R.N.L.I. Lifeboat and
Signal Flags

760 Beachy Head Lighthouse
and Chart

761 "Marecs A"
Communications Satellite and
Dish Aerials

762 Buoys

757 "The First Cuckoo"
(Frederick Delius)

758 "Sea Pictures" (Edward
Elgar)

(Des F. Newell and J. Sorrell. Litho J.W.)

1985 (18 June).   **Safety at Sea.** *Phosphorised paper.* P 14.

1286 **759**	17p. black, azure, emerald, ultramarine, orange-yellow, vermilion, brt blue & chrome-yellow	40	15
1287 **760**	22p. black, azure, emerald, ultramarine, orange-yellow, vermilion, brt blue & chrome-yellow	60	70
1288 **761**	31p. black, azure, emerald, ultramarine, orange-yellow, vermilion & brt blue	90	1·00
1289 **762**	34p. black, azure, emerald, ultramarine, orange-yellow, vermilion, brt blue & chrome-yellow	1·00	1·20
	Set of 4	2·75	2·75
	Set of 4 Gutter Pairs	6·00	
	First Day Cover		3·25
	Presentation Pack	4·00	
	P.H.Q. Cards (set of 4)	3·00	6·00

Nos. 1286/9 were issued on the occasion of the bicentenary of the unimmersible lifeboat and the 50th anniversary of radar.

(Des W. McLean)

1985 (14 May).   **Europa. European Music Year. British Composers.**
Phosphorised paper. P 14 × 14½.

1282 **755**	17p. black, brt yellow-green, dp magenta, new blue, grey & gold	55	10
	a. Imperf (vert pair)	£1500	
1283 **756**	22p. black, greenish yellow, brt magenta, new blue, grey-black & gold	75	90
	a. Imperf (pair)	£1600	
1284 **757**	31p. black, greenish yellow, magenta, greenish blue, grey-black & gold	1·40	1·25
1285 **758**	34p. black, olive-yellow, bistre, turquoise-blue, slate & gold	1·40	1·25
	Set of 4	3·75	3·25
	Set of 4 Gutter Pairs	8·75	
	First Day Cover		4·50
	Presentation Pack	4·75	
	P.H.Q. Cards (set of 4)	3·00	6·00

Nos. 1282/5 were issued on the occasion of the 300th birth anniversary of Handel.

Special First Day of Issue Postmarks

Philatelic Bureau, Edinburgh .... 3·50
Eastbourne .... 3·50

HAVE YOU READ THE NOTES AT THE BEGINNING OF THIS CATALOGUE?
These often provide answers to the enquiries we receive.

Special First Day of Issue Postmarks

Philatelic Bureau, Edinburgh .... 4·75
Worcester .... 4·75

763 Datapost Motorcyclist, City of London   **764** Rural Postbus

765 Parcel Delivery in Winter   **766** Town Letter Delivery

(Des P. Hogarth)

1985 (30 July). **350 Years of Royal Mail Public Postal Service.** *Phosphorised paper.* P 14 × 15.

1290	763	17p. black, greenish yellow, brt carmine, greenish blue, yellow-brown, grey-black & silver	35	10
		a. Imperf on 3 sides (vert pair)	£1700	
		Eu. Underprint Type 5	1·00	
1291	764	22p. black, greenish yellow, cerise, steel-blue, lt green, grey-black & silver	55	70
1292	765	31p. black, greenish yellow, brt carmine, dull blue, drab, grey-black & silver	80	1·00
		a. Imperf (vert pair)	£1700	
1293	766	34p. black, greenish yellow, cerise, ultramarine, lt brown, grey-black & silver	1·00	1·00
		a. Imperf between (vert pair)	£800	
		Set of 4	2·40	2·50
		Set of 4 Gutter Pairs	6·00	
		First Day Cover		3·25
		Presentation Pack	3·75	
		P.H.Q. Cards (set of 4)	3·00	6·00

No. 1290a shows perforation indentations at right, but is imperforate at top, bottom and on the left-hand side.

Examples of No. 1290Eu from the 1985 £1.70 booklet (sold at £1.53) (No. FT4) show a blue double-lined D in a random pattern, on the reverse over the gum.

Special First Day of Issue Postmarks

Philatelic Bureau, Edinburgh	3·75
Bagshot, Surrey	3·75

767 King Arthur and Merlin   **768** Lady of the Lake

769 Queen Guinevere and Sir Lancelot   **770** Sir Galahad

(Des Yvonne Gilbert)

1985 (3 Sept). **Arthurian Legends.** *Phosphorised paper.* P 15 × 14.

1294	767	17p. grey-black, lemon, brown-lilac, ultramarine, grey-black & silver	35	10
		a. Imperf (pair)	£2500	
1295	768	22p. black, lemon, brown-lilac, pale blue, grey-black, silver & grey-black	55	70
1296	769	31p. black, lemon, magenta, turquoise-blue, grey-black, silver & grey-black	90	1·10
1297	770	34p. grey, lemon, magenta, new blue, grey-black, silver & grey-black	1·00	1·10
		Set of 4	2·50	2·75
		Set of 4 Gutter Pairs	6·25	
		First Day Cover		3·50
		Presentation Pack	4·50	
		P.H.Q. Cards (set of 4)	3·00	7·00

Nos. 1294/7 were issued on the occasion of the 500th anniversary of the printing of Sir Thomas Malory's *Morte d'Arthur*.

Special First Day of Issue Postmarks

Philatelic Bureau, Edinburgh	4·00
Tintagel, Cornwall	4·00

GIBBONS STAMP MONTHLY

– finest and most informative magazine for all collectors. Obtainable from your newsagent or by postal subscription – details on request.

771 Peter Sellers (from photo by Bill Brandt) **772** David Niven (from photo by Cornell Lucas)

773 Charlie Chaplin (from photo by Lord Snowdon) **774** Vivien Leigh (from photo by Angus McBean)

775 Alfred Hitchcock (from photo by Howard Coster)

(Des K. Bassford)

1985 (8 Oct). **British Film Year.** *Phosphorised paper. P* 14½.

1298	771	17p. grey-black, olive-grey, gold & silver	45	10
1299	772	22p. black, brown, gold & silver	60	70
1300	773	29p. black, lavender, gold & silver	1·00	1·10
1301	774	31p. black, pink, gold & silver	1·10	1·25
1302	775	34p. black, greenish blue, gold & silver	1·40	1·40
		Set of 5	4·00	4·00
		Set of 5 Gutter Pairs	9·25	
		First Day Cover		5·00
		Presentation Pack	6·00	
		Souvenir Book	10·00	
		P.H.Q. Cards (set of 5)	3·00	9·50

The souvenir book is a 24-page illustrated booklet with a set of mint stamps in a sachet attached to the front cover.

Special First Day of Issue Postmarks

Philatelic Bureau, Edinburgh .... 5·50
London WC .... 5·50

776 Principal Boy **777** Genie

778 Dame **779** Good Fairy

780 Pantomime Cat

(Des A. George)

1985 (19 Nov). **Christmas. Pantomine Characters.** *One phosphor band* (12p.) *or phosphorised paper* (others). *P* 15 × 14.

1303	776	12p. new blue, greenish yellow, brt rose, gold, grey-black & silver	35	15
		a. Imperf (pair)	£1300	
		Eu. Underprint Type 4	1·00	
1304	777	17p. emerald, greenish yellow, brt rose, new blue, black, gold & silver	40	25
		a. Imperf (pair)	£2000	
1305	778	22p. brt carmine, greenish yellow, pale new blue, grey, gold & silver	65	90
1306	779	31p. brt orange, lemon, rose, slate-purple, silver & gold	1·00	1·10
1307	780	34p. brt reddish violet, brt blue, brt rose, black, grey-brown, gold & silver	1·10	1·25
		Set of 5	3·00	3·25
		Set of 5 Gutter Pairs	7·00	
		First Day Cover		3·75
		Presentation Pack	4·25	
		P.H.Q. Cards (set of 5)	3·00	8·00
		Christmas Folder (contains No. 1303 × 50)	20·00	

Examples of No. 1303Eu from the 1985 Christmas booklet (No. FX8) show a random pattern of blue double-lined stars printed on the reverse over the gum.

Special First Day of Issue Postmarks

Philatelic Bureau, Edinburgh .... 4·00
Bethlehem, Llandeilo, Dyfed .... 4·00

Collectors Pack 1985

1985 (19 Nov). *Comprises Nos.* 1272/1307.
CP1307a   Collectors Pack .... 35·00

Post Office Yearbook

1985. *Comprises Nos.* 1272/1307 *in 32-page hardbound book with slip case, illustrated in colour* .... 80·00

781 Light Bulb and North Sea Oil Drilling Rig (Energy)

782 Thermometer and Pharmaceutical Laboratory (Health)

783 Garden Hoe and Steelworks (Steel)

784 Loaf of Bread and Cornfield (Agriculture)

(Des K. Bassford. Litho Questa)

1986 (14 Jan).   **Industry Year.** *Phosphorised paper. P* 14½ × 14.
1308 **781** 17p. gold, black, magenta, greenish yellow & new blue   40   10
1309 **782** 22p. gold, pale turquoise-green, magenta, greenish yellow & blue   60   70
1310 **783** 31p. gold, black, magenta, greenish yellow & new blue .... 1·05   1·10
1311 **784** 34p. gold, black, magenta, greenish yellow & new blue .... 1·30   1·25
             Set of 4 ....   3·00   3·00
             Set of 4 *Gutter Pairs* ....   6·75
             First Day Cover ....   3·75
             Presentation Pack .... 3·75
             P.H.Q. Cards (set of 4) .... 3·00   6·00

Special First Day of Issue Postmarks

Philatelic Bureau, Edinburgh .... 4·00
Birmingham .... 4·00

785 Dr. Edmond Halley as Comet

786 *Giotto* Spacecraft approaching Comet

787 "Maybe Twice in a Lifetime"

788 Comet orbiting Sun and Planets

(Des R. Steadman)

1986 (18 Feb).   **Appearance of Halley's Comet.** *Phosphorised paper. P* 15 × 14.
1312 **785** 17p. black, bistre, rosine, blue, grey-black, gold & dp brown 35   10
1313 **786** 22p. orange-vermilion, greenish yellow, brt purple, new blue, black & gold   60   75
1314 **787** 31p. black, greenish yellow, brt purple, dp turquoise-blue, grey-black & gold   90   1·00
1315 **788** 34p. blue, greenish yellow, magenta, dp turquoise-blue, black & gold .... 1·10   1·10
             Set of 4 .... 2·75   2·75
             Set of 4 *Gutter Pairs* .... 6·75
             First Day Cover ....   4·00
             Presentation Pack .... 3·75
             P.H.Q. Cards (set of 4) .... 4·00   6·00

ALBUM LISTS

Write for our latest list of albums and accessories.
These will be sent on request.

Special First Day of Issue Postmarks

Philaelic Bureau, Edinburgh .... 4·50
London SE10 .... 4·50

789 Queen Elizabeth in 1928, 1942 and 1952

790 Queen Elizabeth in 1958, 1973 and 1982

T **789/90** were printed horizontally se-tenant within the sheet

791 Barn Owl

792 Pine Marten

793 Wild Cat

794 Natterjack Toad

(Des J. Matthews)

1986 (21 Apr). **60th Birthday of Queen Elizabeth II.** *Phosphorised paper. P* 15 × 14.

1316	**789**	17p. grey-black, turquoise-green, brt green, green & dull blue	60	50
		a. Pair. Nos. 1316/17	1·50	1·50
1317	**790**	17p. grey-black, dull blue, greenish blue & indigo	60	50
1318	**789**	34p. grey-black, dp dull purple, yellow-orange & red	1·40	1·75
		a. Pair. Nos. 1318/19	3·00	3·75
1319	**790**	34p. grey-black, olive-brown, yellow-brown, olive-grey & red	1·40	1·75
		Set of 4	4·50	4·00
		Set of 2 Gutter Blocks of 4	11·00	
		First Day Cover		4·50
		Presentation Pack	6·50	
		Souvenir Book	9·00	
		P.H.Q. Cards (set of 4)	3·00	7·00

The souvenir book is a special booklet, fully illustrated and containing a mint set of stamps.

(Des K. Lilly)

1986 (20 May). **Europa. Nature Conservation – Endangered Species.** *Phosphorised paper. P* $14\frac{1}{2}$ × 14.

1320	**791**	17p. gold, greenish yellow, rose, yellow-brown, olive-grey, new blue & black ...	40	10
1321	**792**	22p. gold, greenish yellow, reddish brown, olive-yellow, turquoise-blue, grey-black & black	80	1·00
1322	**793**	31p. gold, brt yellow-green, magenta, lt brown, ultramarine, olive-brown & black	1·25	1·25
1323	**794**	34p. gold, greenish yellow, brt rose-red, brt green, grey-black & black	1·40	1·40
		Set of 4	3·50	3·50
		Set of 4 Gutter Pairs	8·75	
		First Day Cover		4·25
		Presentation Pack	4·25	
		P.H.Q. Cards (set of 4)	3·00	7·00

Special First Day of Issue Postmarks

Philatelic Bureau, Edinburgh .... 5·00
Windsor .... 5·00

Special First Day of Issue Postmarks

Philatelic Bureau, Edinburgh .... 4·75
Lincoln .... 4·75

795 Peasants working in Fields

796 Freemen working
at Town Trades

797 Knight and Retainers

798 Lord at Banquet

(Des Tayburn Design Consultancy)

1986 (17 Jun). **900th Anniv of Domesday Book.** *Phosphorised paper.*
P 15 × 14.

1324	**795**	17p.	yellow-brown, vermilion, lemon, brt emerald, orange-brown, grey & brownish grey	40	10
1325	**796**	22p.	yellow-ochre, red, greenish blue, chestnut, grey-black & brownish grey	70	85
1326	**797**	31p.	yellow-brown, vermilion, green, Indian red, grey-black & brownish grey	1·10	1·40
1327	**798**	34p.	yellow-ochre, bright scarlet, greybrown, new blue, lake-brown, greyblack & grey	1·25	1·40
			Set of 4	3·00	3·50
			Set of 4 Gutter Pairs	7·00	
			First Day Cover		4·25
			Presentation Pack	4·00	
			P.H.Q. Cards (set of 4)	3·00	6·00

Special First Day of Issue Postmarks

Philatelic Bureau, Edinburgh .... 4·50
Gloucester .... 4·50

799 Athletics

800 Rowing

801 Weightlifting

802 Rifle Shooting

803 Hockey

(Des N. Cudworth)

1986 (15 July). **Thirteenth Commonwealth Games, Edinburgh and World
Hockey Cup for Men, London** (34p.). *Phosphorised paper.* P 15 × 14.

1328	**799**	17p.	black, greenish yellow, orange-vermilion, ultramarine, chestnut & emerald .	40	10
1329	**800**	22p.	black, lemon, scarlet, new blue, royal blue, chestnut & dp ultramarine	55	70
1330	**801**	29p.	grey-black, greenish yellow, scarlet, new blue, brown-ochre, brown-rose & pale chestnut	75	80
1331	**802**	31p.	black, greenish yellow, rose, blue, dull yellow-green, chestnut & yellow-green .	1·00	1·10
1332	**803**	34p.	black, lemon, scarlet, brt blue, brt emerald, red-brown & vermilion	1·25	1·25
		a.	Imperf (pair)	£2000	
			Set of 5	3·50	3·50
			Set of 5 Gutter Pairs	8·75	
			First Day Cover		4·75
			Presentation Pack	4·50	
			P.H.Q. Cards (set of 5)	4·00	8·00

No. 1332 also commemorates the centenary of the Hockey
Association.

Special First Day of Issue Postmarks

Philatelic Bureau, Edinburgh .... 5·00
Head Post Office, Edinburgh .... 5·00

For full information on all future British issues, collectors
should write to the British Post Office Philatelic Bureau,
21 South Gyle Crescent, Edinburgh EH12 9PB

804   805

Prince Andrew and Miss Sarah Ferguson (from photo by Gene Nocon)

(Des J. Matthews)

1986 (22 July). **Royal Wedding.** *One phosphor band* (12p.) *or phosphorised paper* (17p.). *P* 14 × 15.

1333	**804** 12p. lake, greenish yellow, cerise, ultramarine, black & silver	50	30
1334	**805** 17p. steel blue, greenish yellow, cerise, ultramarine, black & gold	1·00	95
	a. Imperf (pair)	£950	
	Set of 2	1·50	1·25
	Set of 2 Gutter Pairs	3·50	
	First Day Cover		2·25
	Presentation Pack	2·00	
	P.H.Q. Cards (set of 2)	1·75	5·00

Special First Day of Issue Postmarks

Philatelic Bureau, Edinburgh .... 2·75
London, SW1 .... 2·75

806 Stylised Cross on Ballot Paper

(Des J. Gibbs. Litho Questa)

1986 (19 Aug). **32nd Commonwealth Parliamentary Association Conference.** *Phosphorised paper. P* 14 × 14½.

1335	**806** 34p. pale grey-lilac, black, vermilion, yellow & ultramarine	1·00	1·00
	Gutter Pair	2·50	
	First Day Cover		1·60
	P.H.Q. Card	1·00	2·50

Special First Day of Issue Postmarks

Philatelic Bureau, Edinburgh .... 2·00
London, SW1 .... 2·00

807 Lord Dowding and   808 Lord Tedder and Hawker
Hawker Hurricane Mk I   Typhoon IB

809 Lord Trenchard and   810 Sir Arthur Harris and
De Havilland D.H.9A   Avro Type 683 Lancaster

811 Lord Portal and De Havilland
D.H.98 Mosquito

(Des B. Sanders)

1986 (16 Sept). **History of the Royal Air Force.** *Phosphorised paper. P* 14½.

1336	**807** 17p. pale blue, greenish yellow, brt rose, blue, black & grey-black	70	10
	a. Imperf (pair)	£1100	
1337	**808** 22p. pale turquoise-green, greenish yellow, magenta, new blue, black & grey-black	90	95
	a. Face value omitted*	£450	
	b. Queen's head omitted*	£450	

1338	**809**	29p.	pale drab, olive-yellow, magenta, blue, grey-black & black	1·25	1·10
1339	**810**	31p.	pale flesh, greenish yellow, magenta, ultramarine, black & grey-black	1·50	1·40
1340	**811**	34p.	buff, greenish yellow, magenta, blue, grey-black & black	1·75	1·50
			Set of 5	5·50	4·50
			Set of 5 Gutter Pairs	13·00	
			First Day Cover		5·25
			Presentation Pack	6·00	
			P.H.Q. Cards (set of 5)	4·00	10·00

Nos. 1336/40 were issued to celebrate the 50th anniversary of the first R.A.F. Commands.

*Nos. 1337a/b come from three consecutive sheets on which the stamps in the first vertical row are without the face value and those in the second vertical row the Queen's head.

Special First Day of Issue Postmarks

Philatelic Bureau, Edinburgh	6·00
Farnborough	6·00

812 The Glastonbury Thorn   **813** The Tanad Valley Plygain

814 The Hebrides Tribute   **815** The Dewsbury Church Knell

816 The Hereford Boy Bishop

(Des Lynda Gray)

1986 (18 Nov–2 Dec). **Christmas. Folk Customs.** *One phosphor band (12p., 13p.) or phosphorised paper (others). P* 15 × 14.

1341	**812**	12p.	gold, greenish yellow, vermilion, dp brown, emerald & dp blue (2.12)	50	30
		a.	Imperf (pair)	£1500	
1342		13p.	dp blue, greenish yellow, vermilion, dp brown, emerald & gold	25	10
		Eu.	Underprint Type 4 (2.12)	1·00	
1343	**813**	18p.	myrtle-green, yellow, vermilion, dp blue, black, reddish brown & gold	45	10
1344	**814**	22p.	vermilion, olive-bistre, dull blue, dp brown, dp green & gold	80	95
1345	**815**	31p.	dp brown, yellow, vermilion, violet, dp dull green, black & gold	95	1·00
1346	**816**	34p.	violet, lemon, vermilion, dp dull blue, reddish brown & gold	1·25	1·10
			Set of 6	3·75	3·25
			Set of 6 Gutter Pairs	8·50	
			First Day Covers (2)		5·75
			Presentation Pack (Nos. 1342/6)	5·00	
			P.H.Q. Cards (Nos. 1342/6) (Set of 5)	3·00	7·00
			Christmas Folder (contains No. 1342Eu × 36)	17·00	

No. 1341 represented a discount of 1p., available between 2 and 24 December 1986, on the current second class postage rate.

Special First Day of Issue Postmarks

Philatelic Bureau, Edinburgh (Nos. 1342/6) (18 Nov)	4·00
Bethlehem, Llandeilo, Dyfed (Nos. 1342/6) (18 Nov)	4·00
Philatelic Bureau, Edinburgh (No. 1341) (2 Dec)	2·00

Collectors Pack 1986

1986 (18 Nov). *Comprises Nos. 1308/40 and 1342/6.*
CP1346a Collectors Pack .... 35·00

Post Office Yearbook

1986 (18 Nov). *Comprises Nos. 1308/46 in 32-page hardbound book with slip case, illustrated in colour* .... 75·00

817 North American
Blanket Flower

818 Globe Thistle

821 The Principia
Mathematica

822 Motion of Bodies
in Ellipses

819 Echeveria

820 Autumn Crocus

823 Optick Treatise

824 The System of the World

(Adapted J. Matthews)

1987 (20 Jan).   **Flower Photographs by Alfred Lammer.** *Phosphorised paper.* P 14½ × 14.

1347	**817**	18p. silver, greenish yellow, rosine, dp green & black	40	10
1348	**818**	22p. silver, greenish yellow, new blue, greenish blue & black	70	85
1349	**819**	31p. silver, greenish yellow, scarlet, blue-green, dp green & black	1·00	1·25
		a. Imperf (pair)	£2000	
1350	**820**	34p. silver, greenish yellow, magenta, dull blue, dp green & black	1·10	1·25
		Set of 4	3·00	3·25
		Set of 4 Gutter Pairs	7·50	
		First Day Cover		3·75
		Presentation Pack	4·50	
		P.H.Q. Cards (set of 4)	3·00	7·00

(Des Sarah Godwin)

1987 (24 Mar).   **300th Anniv of "The Principia Mathematica" by Sir Isaac Newton.** *Phosphorised paper.* P 14 × 15.

1351	**821**	18p. black, greenish yellow, cerise, blue-green, grey-black & silver	60	15
1352	**822**	22p. black, greenish yellow, brt orange, blue, brt emerald, silver & bluish violet	85	90
1353	**823**	31p. black, greenish yellow, scarlet, new blue, bronze-green, silver & slate-green	1·40	1·60
1354	**824**	34p. black, greenish yellow, red, brt blue, grey-black & silver	1·50	1·50
		Set of 4	4·00	3·75
		Set of 4 Gutter Pairs	9·00	
		First Day Cover		4·25
		Presentation Pack	4·50	
		P.H.Q. Cards (set of 4)	3·00	6·25

Special First Day of Issue Postmarks

Philatelic Bureau, Edinburgh	4·50
Richmond, Surrey	4·50

Special First Day of Issue Postmarks

Philatelic Bureau, Edinburgh	4·25
Woolsthorpe, Lincs	4·25

825 Willis Faber and Dumas
Building, Ipswich

826 Pompidou Centre, Paris

827 Staatsgalerie, Stuttgart

828 European Investment Bank,
Luxembourg

829 Brigade Members with
Ashford Litter, 1887

830 Bandaging Blitz
Victim, 1940

831 Volunteer with
fainting Girl, 1965

832 Transport of Transplant
Organ by Air Wing, 1987

(Des B. Tattersfield)

1987 (12 May). **Europa. British Architects in Europe.** *Phosphorised paper.* P 15 × 14.

1355	**825**	18p. black, bistre-yellow, cerise, brt blue, dp grey & grey-black	55	15
1356	**826**	22p. black, greenish yellow, carmine, brt blue, dp grey & grey-black	80	90
1357	**827**	31p. grey-black, bistre-yellow, cerise, brt blue, brt green, black & dull violet	1·40	1·50
		a. Imperf (horiz pair)	£1300	
1358	**828**	34p. black, greenish yellow, cerise, brt blue, grey-black & dp grey	1·50	1·50
		Set of 4	3·75	3·75
		Set of 4 Gutter Pairs	8·50	
		First Day Cover		4·25
		Presentation Pack	4·50	
		P.H.Q. Cards (set of 4)	3·00	6·25

Special First Day of Issue Postmarks

Philatelic Bureau, Edinburgh . . . . 4·00
Ipswich . . . . 4·00

HAVE YOU READ THE NOTES AT THE BEGINNING OF THIS CATALOGUE?
These often provide answers to the enquiries we receive.

(Des Debbie Cook. Litho Questa)

1987 (16 June). **Centenary of St. John Ambulance Brigade.** *Phosphorised paper.* P 14 × 14½.

1359	**829**	18p. new blue, greenish yellow, magenta, black, silver & pink	40	10
		Ea. Black ptg double	†	£850
		Eb. Black ptg triple	†	£1500
1360	**830**	22p. new blue, greenish yellow, magenta, black, silver & cobalt	60	70
1361	**831**	31p. new blue, greenish yellow, magenta, black, silver & bistre-brown	1·00	1·10
1362	**832**	34p. new blue, greenish yellow, magenta, black, silver & greenish grey	1·25	1·25
		Set of 4	3·00	3·00
		Set of 4 Gutter Pairs	7·50	
		First Day Cover		3·75
		Presentation Pack	4·50	
		P.H.Q. Cards (set of 4)	3·00	6·25

Special First Day of Issue Postmarks

Philatelic Bureau, Edinburgh . . . . 4·00
London, EC1 . . . . 4·00

833 Arms of the Lord Lyon King of Arms

834 Scottish Heraldic Banner of Prince Charles

837 Crystal Palace, "Monarch of the Glen" (Landseer) and Grace Darling

838 *Great Eastern, Beeton's Book of Household Management* and Prince Albert

835 Arms of Royal Scottish Academy of Painting, Sculpture and Architecture

836 Arms of Royal Society of Edinburgh

839 Albert Memorial, Ballot Box and Disraeli

840 Diamond Jubilee Emblem, Newspaper Placard for Relief of Mafeking and Morse Key

(Des J. Matthews)

1987 (21 July). **300th Anniv of Revival of Order of the Thistle.** *Phosphorised paper. P* 14½.

1363	833	18p. black, lemon, scarlet, blue, dp green, slate & brown	50	10
1364	834	22p. black, greenish yellow, carmine, new blue, dp green, grey & lake-brown	75	90
1365	835	31p. black, greenish yellow, scarlet, new blue, dull green, grey & grey-black	1·40	1·40
1366	836	34p. black, greenish yellow, scarlet, dp ultramarine, dull green, grey & yellow-brown	1·50	1·40
		Set of 4	3·75	3·50
		Set of 4 Gutter Pairs	9·00	
		First Day Cover		4·00
		Presentation Pack	4·50	
		P.H.Q. Cards (set of 4)	3·00	7·50

(Des M. Dempsey. Eng C. Slania. Recess and photo)

1987 (8 Sept). **150th Anniv of Queen Victoria's Accession.** *Phosphorised paper. P* 15 × 14.

1367	837	18p. pale stone, dp blue, lemon, rose, greenish blue, brown-ochre & grey-black	50	10
1368	838	22p. pale stone, dp brown, lemon, rose, grey-black & brown-ochre	80	90
1369	839	31p. pale stone, dp lilac, lemon, cerise, brown-ochre, greenish blue & grey-black	1·50	1·50
1370	840	34p. pale stone, myrtle-green, yellow-ochre, reddish brown & brown-ochre	1·60	1·60
		Set of 4	4·00	3·75
		Set of 4 Gutter Pairs	10·00	
		First Day Cover		4·00
		Presentation Pack	4·50	
		P.H.Q. Cards (set of 4)	3·00	7·00

Special First Day of Issue Postmarks

Special First Day of Issue Postmarks

Philatelic Bureau, Edinburgh .... 4·50
Rothesay, Isle of Bute .... 4·50

Philatelic Bureau, Edinburgh .... 4·50
Newport, Isle of Wight .... 4·50

841 Pot by Bernard Leach   **842** Pot by Elizabeth Fritsch

843 Pot by Lucie Rie   **844** Pot by Hans Coper

(Des T. Evans)

1987 (13 Oct).   **Studio Pottery.** *Phosphorised paper. P* 14½ × 14.

1371	**841**	18p.	gold, lemon, lt red-brown, chestnut, lt grey & black	50	10
1372	**842**	26p.	blue over silver, yellow-orange, brt purple, lavender, bluish violet, grey-brown & black	70	70
1373	**843**	31p.	rose-lilac over silver, greenish yellow, cerise, new blue, grey-lilac & black	1·25	1·10
1374	**844**	34p.	copper, yellow-brown, reddish brown, grey-lilac & black	1·40	1·40
			Set of 4	3·50	3·00
			Set of 4 Gutter Pairs	8·50	
			First Day Cover		3·50
			Presentation Pack	4·50	
			P.H.Q. Cards (set of 4)	3·00	6·00

Special First Day of Issue Postmarks

Philatelic Bureau, Edinburgh .... 4·00
St. Ives, Cornwall .... 4·00

845 Decorating the   **846** Waiting for Father
Christmas Tree   Christmas

847 Sleeping Child and   **848** Child reading
Father Christmas in Sleigh

849 Child playing Recorder
and Snowman

(Des M. Foreman)

1987 (17 Nov).   **Christmas.** *One phosphor band* (13p.) *or phosphorised paper* (others). P 15 × 14.

1375	**845**	13p.	gold, greenish yellow, rose, greenish blue & black	30	10
			Eu. Underprint Type 4	95	
1376	**846**	18p.	gold, greenish yellow, brt purple, greenish blue, brt blue & black	40	20
1377	**847**	26p.	gold, greenish yellow, brt purple, new blue, brt blue & black	80	1·00
1378	**848**	31p.	gold, greenish yellow, scarlet, brt magenta, dull rose, greenish blue & black	1·10	1·50
1379	**849**	34p.	gold, greenish yellow, dull rose, greenish blue, brt blue & black	1·25	1·50
			Set of 5	3·50	4·00
			Set of 5 Gutter Pairs	8·50	
			First Day Cover		4·50
			Presentation Pack	4·50	
			P.H.Q. Cards (set of 5)	3·00	6·00
			Christmas Folder (contains No. 1375Eu × 36)	17·00	

Examples of the 13p. value from special folders, containing 36 stamps and sold for £4.60, show a blue underprint of double-lined stars printed on the reverse over the gum.

Special First Day of Issue Postmarks

Philatelic Bureau, Edinburgh .... 5·00
Bethlehem, Llandeilo, Dyfed .... 5·00

Collectors Pack 1987

1987 (17 Nov). *Comprises Nos. 1347/79.*
CP1379a Collectors Pack .... 40·00

Post Office Yearbook

1987 (17 Nov). *Comprises Nos. 1347/79 in 32-page hardbound book with slip case, illustrated in colour* . . . . 40·00

850 Short-spined Seascorpion ("Bull-rout") (Jonathan Couch)

851 Yellow Waterlily (Major Joshua Swatkin)

852 Whistling ("Bewick's") Swan (Edward Lear)

853 *Morchella esculenta* (James Sowerby)

854 Revd William Morgan (Bible translator, 1588)

855 William Salesbury (New Testament translator, 1567)

856 Bishop Richard Davies (New Testament translator, 1567)

857 Bishop Richard Parry (editor of Revised Welsh Bible, 1620)

(Des. E. Hughes)

1988 (19 Jan). **Bicentenary of Linnean Society. Archive Illustrations.** *Phosphorised paper. P 15 × 14.*

1380	**850**	18p. grey-black, stone, orange-yellow, brt purple, olive-bistre & gold	55	10
1381	**851**	26p. black, stone, bistre-yellow, dull orange, greenish blue, gold & pale bistre	85	1·00
1382	**852**	31p. black, stone, greenish yellow, rose-red, dp blue, gold & olive-bistre	1·10	1·25
		a. Imperf (horiz pair)	£1500	
1383	**853**	34p. black, stone, yellow, pale bistre, olive-grey, gold & olive-bistre	1·25	1·40
		Set of 4	3·25	3·25
		Set of 4 Gutter Pairs	8·00	
		First Day Cover		3·75
		Presentation Pack	4·50	
		P.H.Q. Cards (set of 4)	3·00	6·00

(Des K. Bowen)

1988 (1 Mar). **400th Anniv of Welsh Bible.** *Phosphorised paper. P 14½ × 14.*

1384	**854**	18p. grey-black, greenish yellow, cerise, blue, black & emerald	40	10
		a. Imperf (pair)	£1500	
1385	**855**	26p. grey-black, yellow, brt rose-red, turquoise-blue, black & orange	70	95
1386	**856**	31p. black, chrome-yellow, carmine, new blue, grey-black & blue	1·25	1·25
1387	**857**	34p. grey-black, greenish yellow, cerise, turquoise-green, black & brt violet	1·40	1·25
		Set of 4	3·25	3·25
		Set of 4 Gutter Pairs	8·00	
		First Day Cover		3·75
		Presentation Pack	4·50	
		P.H.Q. Cards (set of 4)	3·00	6·00

Special First Day of Issue Postmarks

Special First Day of Issue Postmarks

Philatelic Bureau, Edinburgh . . . . 4·50
London, W1 . . . . 4·50

Philatelic Bureau, Edinburgh . . . . 4·50
Ty Mawr, Wybrnant, Gwynedd . . . . 4·50

858 Gymnastics (Centenary of British Amateur Gymnastics Association)

859 Downhill Skiing (Ski Club of Great Britain)

860 Tennis (Centenary of Lawn Tennis Association)

861 Football (Centenary of Football League)

(Des. J. Sutton)

1988 (22 Mar). **Sports Organizations.** *Phosphorised paper. P* 14½.

1388	858	18p. violet-blue, greenish yellow, rosine, brt rose, new blue & silver	40	15
1389	859	26p. violet-blue, greenish yellow, vermilion, carmine, yellow-orange & silver	70	80
1390	860	31p. violet-blue, greenish yellow, rose, blue, pale greenish blue, silver & brt orange .	1·10	1·25
1391	861	34p. violet-blue, greenish yellow, vermilion, blue, brt emerald, silver & pink	1·25	1·25
		Set of 4	3·25	3·25
		Set of 4 Gutter Pairs	8·00	
		First Day Cover		3·50
		Presentation Pack	4·25	
		P.H.Q. Cards (set of 2)	2·50	6·00

Special First Day of Issue Postmarks

Philatelic Bureau, Edinburgh .... 4·50
Wembley .... 5·00

GIBBONS STAMP MONTHLY
– finest and most informative magazine for all collectors. Obtainable from your newsagent or by postal subscription – details on request.

862 *Mallard* and Mailbags on Pick-up Arms

863 Loading Transatlantic Mail on Liner *Queen Elizabeth*

864 Glasgow Tram No. 1173 and Pillar Box

865 Imperial Airways Handley Page H.P.45 *Horatius* and Airmail Van

(Des M. Dempsey)

1988 (10 May). **Europa. Transport and Mail Services in 1930s.** *Phosphorised paper. P* 15 × 14.

1392	862	18p. brown, yellow, rose-red, dull blue, dp brown, reddish violet & black	50	15
1393	863	26p. brown, yellow, orange-vermilion, dull blue, violet-blue, brt emerald & black .	1·00	1·00
1394	864	31p. brown, yellow-orange, carmine, dull purple, violet-blue, brt green & black .	1·25	1·60
1395	865	34p. brown, orange-yellow, carmine-rose, bluish violet, brt blue, sepia & black ...	1·60	1·75
		Set of 4	4·00	4·00
		Set of 4 Gutter Pairs	9·00	
		First Day Cover		4·50
		Presentation Pack	5·00	
		P.H.Q. Cards (set of 4)	2·00	5·00

Special First Day of Issue Postmarks

Philatelic Bureau, Edinburgh .... 4·50
Glasgow .... 4·50

866 Early Settler and Sailing Clipper

867 Queen Elizabeth II with British and Australian Parliament Buildings

868 W.G. Grace (cricketer) and Tennis Racquet

868 Shakespeare, John Lennon (entertainer) and Sydney Opera House

(Des G. Emery. Litho Questa)

1988 (21 June). **Bicentenary of Australian Settlement.** *Phosphorised paper.* P 14½.

1396	**866**	18p. dp ultramarine, orange-yellow, scarlet, black, bluish grey & emerald	50	25
		a. Horiz pair. Nos. 1396/7	1·25	1·50
1397	**867**	18p. dp ultramarine, orange-yellow, black, bluish grey & emerald	50	25
1398	**868**	34p. dp ultramarine, orange-yellow, scarlet, black, bluish grey & emerald	1·00	80
		a. Horiz pair. Nos. 1398/9	2·25	2·75
1399	**869**	34p. dp ultramarine, orange-yellow, black, bluish grey & emerald	1·00	80
		Set of 4	3·50	1·90
		Set of 2 Gutter Blocks of 4	8·75	
		First Day Cover		3·50
		Presentation Pack	4·25	
		Souvenir Book	10·00	
		P.H.Q. Cards (set of 4)	2·00	6·50

Nos. 1396/7 and 1398/9 were each printed together, *se-tenant,* in horizontal pairs throughout the sheets, each pair showing a background design of the Australian flag.

The 40 page souvenir book contains the British and Australian sets which were issued on the same day in similar designs.

Special First Day of Issue Postmarks

Philatelic Bureau, Edinburgh	4·00
Portsmouth	4·00

870 Spanish Galeasse off The Lizard

871 English Fleet leaving Plymouth

872 Engagement off Isle of Wight

873 Attack of English Fire-ships, Calais

874 Armada in Storm, North Sea

(Des G. Evernden)

1988 (19 July). **400th Anniv of Spanish Armada.** *Phosphorised paper.* P 15 × 14.

1400	**870**	18p. slate-black, yellow-orange, brt carmine, brt blue, turquoise-blue, yellow-green & gold	70	40
		a. Horiz strip of 5. Nos. 1400/4	3·50	3·75
1401	**871**	18p. slate-black, yellow-orange, brt carmine, brt blue, turquoise-blue, yellow-green & gold	70	40
1402	**872**	18p. slate-black, yellow-orange, brt carmine, brt blue, turquoise-blue, yellow-green & gold	70	40
1403	**873**	18p. slate-black, yellow-orange, brt carmine, brt blue, turquoise-blue, yellow-green & gold	70	40
1404	**874**	18p. slate-black, yellow-orange, brt carmine, brt blue, turquoise-blue, yellow-green & gold	70	40
		Set of 5	3·50	1·75
		Gutter block of 10	8·75	
		First Day Cover		3·75
		Presentation Pack	3·75	
		P.H.Q. Cards (set of 5)	2·75	8·00

Nos. 1400/4 were printed together, *se-tenant,* in horizontal strips of 5 throughout the sheet, forming a composite design.

Special First Day of Issue Postmarks

Philatelic Bureau, Edinburgh	5·00
Plymouth	5·00

875 "The Owl and the Pussy-cat"

876 "Edward Lear as a Bird" (self-portrait)

879 Carrickfergus Castle

880 Caernarfon Castle

877 "Cat" (from alphabet book)

878 "There was a Young Lady whose Bonnet . . ." (limerick)

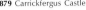

881 Edinburgh Castle

882 Windsor Castle

(Des M. Swatridge and S. Dew)

1988 (6–27 Sept). **Death Centenary of Edward Lear (artist and author).** *Phosphorised paper.* P 15 × 14.

1405	**875**	19p. black, pale cream & carmine	65	20
1406	**876**	27p. black, pale cream & yellow	1·00	1·00
1407	**877**	32p. black, pale cream & emerald	1·25	1·40
1408	**878**	35p. black, pale cream & blue	1·40	1·40
		Set of 4	4·00	3·50
		Set of 4 Gutter Pairs	10·00	
		First Day Cover		4·00
		Presentation Pack	4·50	
		P.H.Q. Cards (set of 4)	2·00	7·00
MS1409	22 × 90 mm. Nos. 1405/8 (*sold at £1.35*) (27 Sept)		7·00	7·50
		First Day Cover		7·50

The premium on No. **MS**1409 was used to support the "Stamp World London 90" International Stamp Exhibition.

(Des from photos by Prince Andrew, Duke of York. Eng C. Matthews. Recess Harrison)

1988 (18 Oct). *Ordinary paper.* P 15 × 14.

1410	**879**	£1 dp green	3·25	60
1411	**880**	£1.50 maroon	4·50	1·25
1412	**881**	£2 indigo	8·00	1·50
1413	**882**	£5 dp brown	25·00	5·50
		Set of 4	37·00	8·00
		Set of 4 Gutter Pairs	65·00	
		First Day Cover		35·00
		Presentation Pack	35·00	

For similar designs, but with silhouette of Queen's head see Nos. 1611/14 and 1993/6.

Special First Day of Issue Postmarks
(For illustrations see Introduction)

Philatelic Bureau, Edinburgh (Type H)	40·00
Windsor, Berkshire (Type I)	45·00

Special First Day of Issue Postmarks

Philatelic Bureau, Edinburgh (stamps) (6 Sept)	5·00
Philatelic Bureau, Edinburgh (miniature sheet) (27 Sept)	8·00
London N7 (stamps) (6 Sept)	5·00
London N22 (miniature sheet) (27 Sept)	8·00

883 Journey to Bethlehem

884 Shepherds and Star

885 Three Wise Men

886 Nativity

887 The Annunciation

888 Atlantic Puffin

889 Avocet

(Des L. Trickett)

1988 (15 Nov). **Christmas. Christmas Cards.** *One phosphor band
(14p.) or phosphorised paper (others). P* 15 × 14.

1414	**883**	14p.	gold, orange-yellow, brt mauve, bluish violet, brt blue & grey-black	45	20
		a.	Error. "13p" instead of "14p"	£6500	
		b.	Imperf (pair)	£1000	
1415	**884**	19p.	gold, yellow-orange, brt violet, ultramarine, rose-red, grey-black & brt blue	50	20
		a.	Imperf (pair)	£800	
1416	**885**	27p.	gold, red, dp lavender, dp lilac, emerald, grey-black & brt blue	90	1·00
1417	**886**	32p.	gold, orange-yellow, brt rose, dp mauve, violet, grey-black & brt blue	1·10	1·10
1418	**887**	35p.	gold, green, reddish violet, brt blue, brt purple & grey-black	1·40	1·10
			Set of 5	4·00	3·25
			Set of 5 Gutter Pairs	10·00	
			First Day Cover		4·25
			Presentation Pack	4·50	
			P.H.Q. Cards (set of 5)	2·50	7·00

Examples of No. 1414a were found in some 1988 Post Office
Yearbooks.

890 Oystercatcher

891 Northern Gannet

Special First Day of Issue Postmarks

Philatelic Bureau, Edinburgh .... 5·00
Bethlehem, Llandeilo, Dyfed .... 5·00

(Des D. Cordery)

1989 (17 Jan). **Centenary of Royal Society for the Protection of Birds.**
Phosphorised paper. P 14 × 15.

1419	**888**	19p.	grey, orange-yellow, orange-red, dull ultramarine, grey-black & silver	45	20
1420	**889**	27p.	grey, bistre, rose, steel-blue, lavender, silver & grey-black	1·25	1·25
1421	**890**	32p.	grey, bistre, scarlet, orange-red, lavender, silver & black	1·25	1·25
1422	**891**	35p.	grey, lemon, rose-carmine, green, new blue, silver & black	1·40	1·40
			Set of 4	4·00	3·75
			Set of 4 Gutter Pairs	10·00	
			First Day Cover		4·25
			Presentation Pack	4·50	
			P.H.Q. Cards (set of 4)	2·50	8·00

Collectors Pack 1988

1988 (15 Nov). *Comprises Nos.* 1380/1408, 1414/18.
CP1418a Collectors Pack .... 40·00

Post Office Yearbook

1988 (15 Nov). *Comprises Nos.* 1380/1404, **MS**1409, 1414/18 *in 32-page
hardbound book with slip case, illustrated in colour* . 40·00

Special First Day of Issue Postmarks

Philatelic Bureau, Edinburgh .... 5·25
Sandy, Bedfordshire .... 5·25

892 Rose

893 Cupid

897 Fruit and Vegetables

898 Meat Products

894 Yachts

895 Fruit

899 Dairy Products

900 Cereal Products

896 Teddy Bear

(Des Sedley Place Ltd)

1989 (7 Mar). **Food and Farming Year.** *Phosphorised paper. P* 14 × 14½.

1428	**897**	19p. brownish grey, greenish yellow, rose, new blue, black, pale grey & emerald .	45	15
1429	**898**	27p. brownish grey, greenish yellow, brt carmine, new blue, black, pale grey & brt orange	90	85
1430	**899**	32p. brownish grey, greenish yellow, rose-red, new blue, black, pale grey & bistre-yellow	1·25	1·40
1431	**900**	35p. brownish grey, greenish yellow, brt carmine, new blue, black, pale grey & brown-red	1·40	1·50
		Set of 4	3·50	3·50
		Set of 4 Gutter Pairs	8·50	
		First Day Cover		4·00
		Presentation Pack	4·50	
		P.H.Q. Cards (set of 4)	2·00	7·50

(Des P. Sutton)

1989 (31 Jan). **Greetings Stamps.** *Phosphorised paper. P* 15 × 14.

1423	**892**	19p. black, greenish yellow, brt rose, red, new blue, lt green & gold	5·50	5·50
		a. Booklet pane. Nos. 1423/7 × 2 plus 12 half stamp-size labels	50·00	
1424	**893**	19p. black, greenish yellow, brt rose, red, new blue, lt green & gold	5·50	5·50
1425	**894**	19p. black, greenish yellow, brt rose, red, new blue, lt green & gold	5·50	5·50
1426	**895**	19p. black, greenish yellow, brt rose, red, new blue, lt green & gold	5·50	5·50
1427	**896**	19p. black, greenish yellow, brt rose, red, new blue, lt green & gold	5·50	3·75
		Set of 5	25·00	25·00
		First Day Cover		25·00

Nos. 1423/7 were only issued in £1.90 booklets.

Special First Day of Issue Postmarks

Philatelic Bureau, Edinburgh	5·00
Stoneleigh, Kenilworth, Warwicks	5·00

Special First Day of Issue Postmarks

Philatelic Bureau, Edinburgh	25·00
Lover, Salisbury, Wilts	25·00

For full information on all future British issues, collectors should write to the British Post Office Philatelic Bureau, 21 South Gyle Crescent, Edinburgh EH12 9PB

901 Mortar Board (150th Anniv of Public Education in England)

902 Cross on Ballot Paper (3rd Direct Elections to European Parliament)

905 Toy Train and Airplane

906 Building Bricks

903 Posthorn (26th Postal, Telegraph and Telephone International Congress, Brighton)

904 Globe (Inter-Parliamentary Union Centenary Conference, London)

907 Dice and Board Games

908 Toy Robot, Boat and Doll's House

(Des Lewis Moberly from firework set-pieces. Litho Questa)

1989 (11 Apr).   **Anniversaries.** *Phosphorised paper.* P $14 \times 14\frac{1}{2}$.

1432	**901**	19p. new blue, greenish yellow, magenta & black	1·00	50
		a. Horiz pair. Nos. 1432/3	2·00	2·00
1433	**902**	19p. new blue, greenish yellow, magenta & black	1·00	50
1434	**903**	35p. new blue, greenish yellow, magenta & black	1·50	1·75
		a. Horiz pair. Nos. 1434/5	3·00	4·00
1435	**904**	35p. new blue, greenish yellow, magenta & black	1·50	1·75
		Set of 4	4·50	4·00
		Set of 2 Gutter Strips of 4	11·00	
		First Day Cover		4·50
		Presentation Pack	6·00	
		P.H.Q. Cards (set of 4)	2·00	6·50

Nos. 1432/3 and 1434/5 were each printed together, *se-tenant*, in horizontal pairs throughout the sheets.

Stamps as No. 1435, but inscribed "ONE HUNDREDTH CONFERENCE" were prepared, but not issued.

(Des D. Fern)

1989 (16 May).   **Europa. Games and Toys.** *Phosphorised paper.* P 14×15.

1436	**905**	19p. black, greenish yellow, vermilion, blue-green, blue, gold & pale ochre	65	20
1437	**906**	27p. black, greenish yellow, reddish orange, blue-green, blue & gold	95	1·00
1438	**907**	32p. black, greenish yellow, orange-red, blue-green, blue, gold & pale ochre	1·40	1·40
1439	**908**	35p. black, greenish yellow, reddish orange, blue-green, blue, gold & stone	1·50	1·50
		Set of 4	4·00	3·75
		Set of 4 Gutter Pairs	10·00	
		First Day Cover		4·25
		Presentation Pack	4·50	
		P.H.Q. Cards (set of 4)	2·00	7·00

Special First Day of Issue Postmarks

Philatelic Bureau, Edinburgh	6·00
London SW	6·00

Special First Day of Issue Postmarks

Philatelic Bureau, Edinburgh	5·25
Leeds	5·25

909 Ironbridge, Shropshire

910 Tin Mine, St. Agnes Head, Cornwall

911 Cotton Mills, New Lanark, Strathclyde

912 Pontcysyllte Aqueduct, Clwyd

912a Horizontal versions of T **909/12**

1442	**911**	32p.	black, yellow-orange, apple-green, dull blue, grey-black & dp reddish violet .	1·10	1·25
1443	**912**	35p.	black, yellow, brt rose, apple-green, dull blue, grey-black & vermilion	1·25	1·50

Set of 4	3·50	3·50
Set of 4 Gutter Pairs	8·50	
First Day Cover		4·00
Presentation Pack	4·50	
P.H.Q. Cards (set of 4)	2·25	6·50

MS1444 **912a** 122 × 90 mm. As Nos. **1440/3**, but horizontal. Each black, olive-yellow, brt rose-red, dull blue, apple-green, grey-black & vermilion (sold at £1.40) (25 July) ... 5·50 5·50
First Day Cover .... 6·00

The premium on No. **MS**1444 was used to support the "Stamp World London 90" International Stamp Exhibition.

Special First Day of Issue Postmarks

Philatelic Bureau, Edinburgh (stamps) (4 July) ...... 5·00
Philatelic Bureau, Edinburgh (miniature sheet) (25 July) 5·50
Telford (stamps) (4 July) .... 5·00
New Lanark (miniature sheet) (25 July) .... 5·50

913

914

1989 (22 Aug)–93. Booklet Stamps.

(a) Photo Harrison. P 15 x 14.

1445	**913**	(2nd)	brt blue (1 centre band)	1·00	1·00

a. Booklet pane. No. 1445 × 10 with horizontal edges of pane imperf .... 8·00
b. Booklet pane. No. 1445 × 4 with three edges of pane imperf (28.11.89) .... 22·00

| 1446 | | (2nd) | brt blue (1 band at right) (20.3.90) ..... | 3·00 | 3·25 |

(Des R. Maddox)

1989 (4–25 July). **Industrial Archaeology.** Phosphorised paper. P 14 × 15.

1440	**909**	19p.	black, bistre-yellow, rose-red, apple-green, lt blue, grey-black & emerald ...	60	15
1441	**910**	27p.	black, bistre-yellow, rose-red, apple-green, lt blue, grey-black & dull blue ..	1·00	1·10

1447	**914**	(1st) brownish black (phosphorised paper) ..	1·75	1·75
		a. Booklet pane. No. 1447 × 10 with horizontal edges of pane imperf	15·00	
		b. Booklet pane. No. 1447 × 4 with three edges of pane imperf (5.12.89)	35·00	
1448		(1st) brownish black (2 phosphor bands) (20.3.90)	3·25	3·25
		First Day Cover (Nos. 1445, 1447)		5·00

(b) Litho Walsall. P 14

1449	**913**	(2nd) brt blue (1 centre band)	90	90
		a. Imperf between (vert pair)		
		b. Booklet pane. No. 1449 × 4 with three edges of pane imperf	7·00	
		c. Booklet pane. No. 1449 × 4 with horiz edges of pane imperf (6.8.91)	3·50	
		d. Booklet pane. No. 1449 × 10 with horiz edges of pane imperf (6.8.91)	6·00	
1450	**914**	(1st) blackish brown (2 phosphor bands) ...	2·50	2·40
		a. Booklet pane. No. 1450 × 4 with three edges of pane imperf	8·50	
		Ey. Phosphor omitted	£600	

(c) Litho Questa. P 15 × 14.

1451	**913**	(2nd) brt blue (1 centre band) (19.9.89)	1·00	1·00
		Ey. Phosphor omitted	£150	
1451a		(2nd) brt blue (1 band at right) (25.2.92)	3·00	3·00
		aEb. Band at left (10.8.93)	2·00	2·00
		al. Booklet pane. Nos. 1451aEb and 1514a, each × 3, with margins all round (10.8.93)	10·00	
1452	**914**	(1st) brownish black (phosphorised paper) (19.9.89)	2·50	2·50

Nos. 1445, 1447 and 1449/52 were initially sold at 14p. (2nd) and 19p. (1st), but these prices were later increased to reflect new postage rates.

Nos. 1446 and 1448 come from the *se-tenant* pane in the London Life £5 Booklet. This pane is listed under No. X906m in the Decimal Machin section.

No. 1451a comes from the *se-tenant* panes in the Wales and Tolkien £6 booklet. These panes are listed under Nos. X1012l and W49a (Wales Regionals). No. 1451aEb comes from the £6 (£5.64) Beatrix Potter booklet.

Nos. 1445, 1447 and 1449/50 do not exist perforated on all four sides, but come with either one or two adjacent sides imperforate.

No. 1450Ey comes from a pane in which one stamp was without phosphor bands due to a dry print.

For illustrations showing the differences between photogravure and lithography see above Type **367**.

For similar designs, but in changed colours, see Nos. 1511/16, for those with elliptical perforations, Nos. 1663a/6, and for self-adhesive versions Nos. 2039/40 and 2295.

Special First Day of Issue Postmarks
(for illustrations see Introduction)

Philatelic Bureau, Edinburgh (Type G) (in red) ...... 6·00
Windsor, Berks (Type G) (in red) .... 6·00

915 Snowflake (× 10)

916 *Calliphora erythrocephala* (× 5) (fly)

917 Blood Cells (× 500)

918 Microchip (× 600)

(Des K. Bassford. Litho Questa)

1989 (5 Sept). **150th Anniv of Royal Microscopical Society** *Phosphorised paper. P 14½ × 14.*

1453	**915**	19p. gold, lemon, pale blue, grey, black & grey-black	45	15
1454	**916**	27p. gold, lemon, drab, black & grey-black .	95	1·10
1455	**917**	32p. gold, lemon, orange-vermilion, flesh, black & grey-black	1·10	1·40
1456	**918**	35p. gold, lemon, black, brt green & grey-black	1·25	1·40
		Set of 4	3·50	3·75
		Set of 4 Gutter Pairs	8·50	
		First Day Cover		4·00
		Presentation Pack	4·50	
		P.H.Q. Cards (set of 4)	2·00	6·00

Special First Day of Issue Postmarks

Philatelic Bureau, Edinburgh .... 4·50
Oxford .... 4·50

919 Royal Mail Coach

920 Escort of Blues and Royals

HAVE YOU READ THE NOTES AT THE BEGINNING OF THIS CATALOGUE?
These often provide answers to the enquiries we receive.

921 Lord Mayor's Coach   922 Passing St. Paul's

923 Blues and Royals Drum Horse

(Des P. Cox)

924 14th-century Peasants from   925 Arches and Roundels,
Stained-glass Window   West Front

926 Octagon Tower   927 Arcade from West
                             Transept

928 Triple Arch from West Front

(Des D. Gentleman)

1989 (17 Oct). **Lord Mayor's Show, London.** *Phosphorised paper. P* 14 × 15.

1457 919	20p. gold, lemon, rose, orange, pale blue & black	70	40
	a. Horiz strip of 5. Nos. 1457/61	3·25	3·50
	ab. Imperf (horiz strip of 5. Nos. 1457/61) ..	£6000	
	ac. Imperf (horiz strip of 4. Nos. 1457/60) ..	£3750	
	ad. Imperf (horiz strip of 3. Nos. 1457/9) ...	£2000	
1458 920	20p. gold, lemon, rose, orange, pale blue & black	70	40
1459 921	20p. gold, lemon, rose, orange, pale blue & black	70	40
1460 922	20p. gold, lemon, rose, orange, pale blue & black	70	40
1461 923	20p. gold, lemon, rose, orange, pale blue & black	70	40
	Set of 5	3·25	1·75
	Gutter Strip of 10	8·00	
	First Day Cover		4·00
	Presentation Pack	3·75	
	P.H.Q. Cards (set of 5)	2·50	7·00

Nos. 1457/61 were printed together, *se-tenant*, in horizontal strips of 5 throughout the sheet. This issue commemorates the 800th anniversary of the installation of the first Lord Mayor of London.

Nos. 1457ab/ad come from a sheet partly imperf at left.

Stamps of Types **919/23**, but each with face value of 19p., were prepared but not issued. One mint *se-tenant* strip has been recorded.

Special First Day of Issue Postmarks

Philatelic Bureau, Edinburgh	4·50
London, EC4	4·50

1989 (14 Nov). **Christmas. 800th Anniv of Ely Cathedral.** *One phosphor band* (15p., 15p. + 1p.) *or phosphorised paper* (others). *P* 15 × 14.

1462 924	15p. gold, silver & blue	40	15
1463 925	15p. +1p. gold, silver & blue	50	40
	a. Imperf (pair)	£1300	
1464 926	20p. +1p. gold, silver & rosine	65	80
	a. Imperf (pair)	£1300	
1465 927	34p. +1p. gold, silver & emerald	1·25	1·75
1466 928	37p. +1p. gold, silver & yellow-olive	1·40	1·90
	Set of 5	3·75	4·50
	Set of 5 Gutter Pairs	8·50	
	First Day Cover		4·50
	Presentation Pack	5·00	
	P.H.Q. Cards (set of 5)	2·50	7·00

Special First Day of Issue Postmarks

Philatelic Bureau, Edinburgh	5·00
Bethlehem, Llandeilo, Dyfed	5·00
Ely	5·00

Collectors Pack 1989

1989 (14 Nov). *Comprises Nos. 1419/22, 1428/43 and 1453/66.*

CP1466a Collectors Pack .... 42·00

Post Office Yearbook

1989 (14 Nov). *Comprises Nos. 1419/22, 1428/44 and 1453/66 in hardbound book with slip case, illustrated in colour* . 42·00

929 Queen Victoria and Queen Elizabeth II

(Des J. Matthews (after Wyon and Machin))

1990 (10 Jan–12 June). **150th Anniv of the Penny Black.**

(a) *Photo Harrison. P 15 × 14.*

1467	**929**	15p. brt blue (1 centre band)	80	80
		a. Imperf (pair)	£1500	
		l. Booklet pane. No. 1467 × 10 with horizontal edges of pane imperf (30.1.90)	10·00	
1468		15p. brt blue (1 side band at left) (30.1.90)	3·75	3·50
		Ea. Band at right (20.3.90)	3·25	3·25
		l. Booklet pane. No. 1468 × 2 and 1470 plus label	9·50	
1469		20p. brownish black & cream (phosphorised paper)	80	80
		a. Imperf (pair)	£1250	
		l. Booklet pane. No. 1469 × 5 plus label with vertical edges of pane imperf (30.1.90)	8·00	
		m. Booklet pane. No. 1469 × 10 with horizontal edges of pane imperf (30.1.90)	11·00	
		n. Booklet pane. No. 1469 × 6 with margins all round (20.3.90)	5·00	
		r. Booklet pane. No. 1469 × 4 with three edges of pane imperf (17.4.90)	8·00	
1470		20p. brownish black & cream (2 bands) (30.1.90)	2·75	2·75
1471		29p. dp mauve (phosphorised paper)	1·75	1·75
1472		29p. dp mauve (2 bands) (20.3.90)	9·00	9·00
1473		34p. dp bluish grey (phosphorised paper)	2·00	2·00
1474		37p. rosine (phosphorised paper)	2·25	2·25

(b) *Litho Walsall. P 14 (from booklets)*

1475	**929**	15p. brt blue (1 centre band) (30.1.90)	1·50	1·75
		l. Booklet pane. No. 1475 × 4 with three edges of pane imperf	7·00	
		m. Booklet pane. No. 1475 × 10 with three edges of pane imperf (12.6.90)	12·00	
1476		20p. brownish black & cream (phosphorised paper) (30.1.90)	1·60	1·60
		l. Booklet pane. No. 1476 × 5 plus label with vertical edges of pane imperf	10·00	
		m. Booklet pane. No. 1476 × 4 with three edges of pane imperf	10·00	
		n. Booklet pane. No. 1476 × 10 with three edges of pane imperf (12.6.90)	15·00	

(c) *Litho Questa. P 15 × 14*

1477	**929**	15p. brt blue (1 centre band) (17.4.90)	2·25	2·25
1478		20p. brownish black (phosphorised paper) (17.4.90)	1·75	2·00
		Set of 5 (Nos. 1467, 1469, 1471, 1473/4)	7·00	7·00
		First Day Cover (Nos. 1467, 1469, 1471, 1473/4)		7·00
		Presentation Pack (Nos. 1467, 1469, 1471, 1473/4)	9·00	

Nos. 1475/6 do not exist perforated on all four sides, but come with either one or two adjacent sides imperforate.

Nos. 1468, 1468Ea, 1470, 1472 and 1475/8 were only issued in stamp booklets. Nos. 1468Ea, 1470 and 1472 occur in the *se-tenant* pane from the 1990 London Life £5 booklet. This pane is listed as No. X906m.

For illustrations showing the difference between photogravure and lithography see beneath Type **367**.

For No. 1469 in miniature sheet see No. **MS**1501.

For Type **929** redrawn with "1st" face value see No. 2133.

Special First Day of Issue Postmark

Philatelic Bureau, Edinburgh (in red)		8·00
Windsor, Berks (Type G, see Introduction) (in red)	.	8·00

930 Kitten   **931** Rabbit

932 Duckling   **933** Puppy

(Des T. Evans. Litho Questa)

1990 (23 Jan). **150th Anniv of Royal Society for Prevention of Cruelty to Animals.** *Phosphorised paper. P 14 × 14½.*

1479	**930**	20p. new blue, greenish yellow, brt magenta, black & silver	60	15
		a. Silver (Queen's head and face value) omitted	£250	
1480	**931**	29p. new blue, greenish yellow, brt magenta, black & silver	1·10	1·10
		a. Imperf (horiz pair)	£2500	
1481	**932**	34p. new blue, greenish yellow, brt magenta, black & silver	1·25	1·25
		a. Silver (Queen's head and face value) omitted	£500	
1482	**933**	37p. new blue, greenish yellow, brt magenta, black & silver	1·40	1·40
		Set of 4	4·00	3·75
		Set of 4 Gutter Pairs	8·00	
		First Day Cover		4·00
		Presentation Pack	5·00	
		P.H.Q. Cards (set of 4)	3·00	8·00

Philatelic Bureau, Edinburgh .... 5·00
Horsham .... 5·00

934 Teddy Bear

935 Dennis the Menace

936 Punch

937 Cheshire Cat

938 The Man in the Moon

939 The Laughing Policeman

940 Clown

941 Mona Lisa

942 Queen of Hearts

943 Stan Laurel (comedian)

(Des Michael Peters and Partners Ltd)

1990 (6 Feb). **Greetings Stamps. "Smiles".** *Two phosphor bands. P* 15 × 14.
1483 **934** 20p. gold, greenish yellow, brt rose-red, new
blue & grey-black .... 3·50 2·50
   a. Booklet pane. Nos. 1483/92 with margins all round .... 30·00
1484 **935** 20p. gold, greenish yellow, brt rose-red, new
blue, dp blue & grey-black .... 3·50 2·50
1485 **936** 20p. gold, greenish yellow, brt rose-red, new
blue, dp blue & grey-black .... 3·50 2·50
1486 **937** 20p. gold, greenish yellow, brt rose-red, new
blue & grey-black .... 3·50 2·50
1487 **938** 20p. gold, greenish yellow, brt rose-red, new
blue & grey-black .... 3·50 2·50
1488 **939** 20p. gold, greenish yellow, brt rose-red, new
blue & grey-black .... 3·50 2·50
1489 **940** 20p. gold, greenish yellow, brt rose-red, new
blue & grey-black .... 3·50 2·50
1490 **941** 20p. gold, greenish yellow, brt rose-red, new
blue & grey-black .... 3·50 2·50
1491 **942** 20p. gold, greenish yellow, brt rose-red, new
blue & grey-black .... 3·50 2·50
1492 **943** 20p. gold & grey-black .... 3·50 2·50
   Set of 10 .... 30·00 24·00
   First Day Cover .... 25·00
Nos. 1483/92 were only issued in £2 booklets. The design of Nos.
1483, 1485/7, 1489 and 1492 extend onto the pane margin.
For Types **934/43** inscribed (1st), see Nos. 1550/59.

Philatelic Bureau, Edinburgh .... 26·00
Giggleswick, North Yorkshire .... 26·00

944 Alexandra Palace
("Stamp World London 90"
Exhibition)

945 Glasgow School of
Art

165

946 British Philatelic
Bureau, Edinburgh

947 Templeton Carpet
Factory, Glasgow

(Des P. Hogarth)

1990 (6–20 Mar). **Europa** (*Nos. 1493 and 1495*) **and "Glasgow 1990 European City of Culture"** (*Nos. 1494 and 1496*). *Phosphorised paper.* P 14 × 15.

1493	**944**	20p. silver, lemon, flesh, grey-brown, blue, grey-black & black	60	20
		a. Booklet pane. No. 1493 × 4 with margins all round (20 Mar)	3·50	
1494	**945**	20p. silver, greenish yellow, dull orange, blue, grey-black & black	60	20
1495	**946**	29p. silver, stone, orange, olive-sepia, grey-blue, grey-black & black	1·40	1·60
1496	**947**	37p. silver, greenish-yellow, brt emerald, salmon, olive-sepia, brt blue & black	1·50	1·60
		Set of 4	3·75	3·25
		Set of 4 Gutter Pairs	9·50	
		First Day Cover		3·50
		Presentation Pack	4·00	
		P.H.Q. Cards (set of 4)	2·50	6·50

Special First Day of Issue Postmarks

Philatelic Bureau, Edinburgh .... 5·00
Glasgow .... 5·00

948 Export Achievement
Award

949 Technological Achievement
Award

(Des S. Broom. Litho Questa)

1990 (10 Apr). **25th Anniv of Queen's Awards for Export and Technology.** P 14 × 14½.

1497	**948**	20p. new blue, greenish yellow, magenta, black & silver	70	45
		a. Horiz pair. Nos. 1497/8	1·40	1·60
1498	**949**	20p. new blue, greenish yellow, magenta, black & silver	70	45
1499	**948**	37p. new blue, greenish yellow, magenta, black & silver	1·25	1·25
		a. Horiz pair. Nos. 1499/500	2·50	3·25
1500	**949**	37p. new blue, greenish yellow, magenta, black & silver	1·25	1·25
		Set of 4	3·50	3·00
		Set of 2 Gutter Strips of 4	8·50	
		First Day Cover		4·25
		Presentation Pack	4·50	
		P.H.Q. Cards (set of 4)	2·50	6·50

Nos. 1497/8 and 1499/1500 were each printed together, *se-tenant,* in horizontal pairs throughout the sheets.

Special First Day of Issue Postmarks

Philatelic Bureau, Edinburgh .... 5·00
London, SW .... 5·00

949a

(Des Sedley Place Design Ltd. Eng C. Matthews. Recess and photo Harrison)

1990 (3 May). **"Stamp World 90" International Stamp Exhibition.** *Sheet* 122 × 89 *mm containing No. 1469. Phosphorised paper.* P 15 × 14.

MS1501	**949a**	20p. brownish black & cream (*sold at* £1)	4·50	4·50
		a. Error. Imperf	£6500	
		b. Black (recess-printing) omitted	£12000	
		c. Black (recess-printing) inverted	£8000	
		First Day Cover		5·50
		Souvenir Book (*Nos.* 1467, 1469, 1471, 1473/4 *and* **MS**1501)		22·00

The premium on No. **MS**1501 was used to support the "Stamp World London '90" International Stamp Exhibition. In No. **MS**1501 only the example of the 20p. is perforated.

No. **MS**1501b shows an albino impression on the reverse. The 1d. black and Seahorse background were omitted due to one sheet becoming attached to the underside of another prior to recess-printing.

No. **MS**1501c shows the recess part of the design inverted in relation to the photogravure of Type **929**.

Special First Day of Issue Postmarks

Philatelic Bureau, Edinburgh (in red) .... 6·00
City of London (in red) .... 6·00
A First Day of Issue handstamp as Type B was provided at Alexandra Palace; London N22 for this issue.

950 Cycad and Sir Joseph   **951** Stone Pine and Princess of
   Banks Building   Wales Conservatory

952 Willow Tree and Palm   **953** Cedar Tree and Pagoda
   House

(Des P. Leith)

1990 (5 June). **150th Anniv of Kew Gardens.** *Phosphorised paper. P* 14 × 15.

1502 **950** 20p. black, brt emerald, pale turquoise-green, lt brown & lavender	55	15
1503 **951** 29p. black, brt emerald, turquoise-green, reddish orange & grey-black	90	1·00
1504 **952** 34p. Venetian red, brt green, cobalt, dull purple, turquoise-green & yellow-green	1·40	1·60
1505 **953** 37p. pale violet-blue, brt emerald, red-brown, steel-blue & brown-rose	1·60	1·50
Set of 4	4·00	3·75
Set of 4 Gutter Pairs	10·00	
First Day Cover		4·00
Presentation Pack	4·50	
P.H.Q. Cards (set of 4)	2·50	6·50

Special First Day of Issue Postmarks

Philatelic Bureau, Edinburgh .... 5·50
Kew, Richmond .... 5·50

954 Thomas Hardy and Clyffe Clump, Dorset

(Des J. Gibbs)

1990 (10 July). **150th Birth Anniv of Thomas Hardy (author).** *Phosphorised paper. P* 14 × 15.

1506 **954** 20p. vermilion, greenish yellow, pale lake-brown, dp brown, lt red-brown & black	80	70
a. Imperf (pair)	£1400	
Gutter Pair	2·00	
First Day Cover		1·50
Presentation Pack	1·50	
P.H.Q. Card	1·00	2·00

Special First Day of Issue Postmarks

Philatelic Bureau, Edinburgh .... 2·50
Dorchester .... 2·50

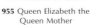

955 Queen Elizabeth the   **956** Queen Elizabeth
   Queen Mother

957 Elizabeth, Duchess of York **958** Lady Elizabeth Bowes-Lyon

(Des J. Gorham from photographs by N. Parkinson (20p.), Dorothy Wilding (29p.), B. Park (34p.), Rita Martin (37p.))

1990 (2 Aug). **90th Birthday of Queen Elizabeth the Queen Mother.** *Phosphorised paper. P 14 × 15.*

1507	**955**	20p. silver, greenish yellow, magenta, turquoise-blue & grey-black	95	20
1508	**956**	29p. silver, indigo & grey-blue	1·40	1·50
1509	**957**	34p. silver, lemon, red, new blue & grey-black	2·00	2·10
1510	**958**	37p. silver, sepia & stone	2·25	2·20
		Set of 4	6·00	5·50
		Set of 4 Gutter Pairs	14·00	
		First Day Cover		6·50
		Presentation Pack	7·00	
		P.H.Q. Cards (set of 4)	5·00	8·00

For these designs with Queen's head and frame in black see Nos. 2280/3.

Special First Day of Issue Postmarks

Philatelic Bureau, Edinburgh	7·00
Westminster, SW1	7·00

1990 (7 Aug)–**92**. *Booklet stamps. As T* **913/14**, *but colours changed.*

(a) Photo Harrison. P 15 × 14

1511	**913**	(2nd) dp blue (1 centre band)	1·25	1·25
		a. Booklet pane. No. 1511 × 10 with horiz edges of pane imperf	12·00	
1512	**914**	(1st) brt orange-red (phosphorised paper) ..	1·10	1·10
		a. Booklet pane. No. 1512 × 10 with horiz edges of pane imperf	10·00	

(b) Litho Questa. P 15 × 14

1513	**913**	(2nd) dp blue (1 centre band)	2·50	2·50
1514	**914**	(1st) brt orange-red (phosphorised paper) ..	90	1·00
1514a		(1st) brt orange-red (2 bands) (25.2.92)	2·25	2·25

(c) Litho Walsall. P 14

1515	**913**	(2nd) dp blue (1 centre band)	80	80
		a. Booklet pane. No. 1515 × 4 with horiz edges of pane imperf	3·75	
		b. Booklet pane. No. 1515 × 10 with horiz edges of pane imperf	8·50	

1516	**914**	(1st) brt orange-red (phosphorised paper)	90	90
		a. Booklet pane. No. 1516 × 4 with horiz edges of pane imperf	4·00	
		b. Booklet pane. No. 1516 × 10 with horiz edges of pane imperf	8·00	
		c. Perf 13	2·75	3·00
		ca. Booklet pane. No. 1516c × 4 with horiz edges of pane imperf	11·00	
		First Day Cover (Nos. 1515/16)		5·00

Nos. 1511/14 and 1515/16 were initially sold at 15p. (2nd) and 20p. (1st), but these prices were later increased to reflect new postage rates.

No. 1514a comes from the *se-tenant* panes in the £6 Wales, £6 Tolkien and £5.64 Beatrix Potter booklets. These panes are listed under Nos. X1012l, 1451al and W49a (Wales Regionals). No. 1514a exists with phosphor omitted (*Price £700 unused*).

No. 1516c was caused by the use of an incorrect perforation comb. Nos. 1511/12 and 1515/16 do not exist with perforations on all four sides, but come with either the top or the bottom edge imperforate.

For similar stamps with elliptical perforations see Nos. 1663a/6.

Special First Day of Issue Postmarks
(For illustration see Introduction)

Philatelic Bureau, Edinburgh (Type G)	5·50
Windsor, Berks (Type G)	7·00

959 Victoria Cross   **960** George Cross

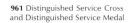

961 Distinguished Service Cross and Distinguished Service Medal   **962** Military Cross and Military Medal

963 Distinguished Flying Cross and Distinguished Flying Medal

(Des J. Gibbs and J. Harwood)

1990 (11 Sept). **Gallantry Awards.** *Phosphorised paper. P* 14 × 15 *(vert) or* 15 × 14 *(horiz).*

1517	**959**	20p. grey-black, pale stone, stone, bistre-brown & brt carmine	80	65
1518	**960**	20p. grey-black, pale stone, flesh, grey & ultramarine	80	65
1519	**961**	20p. grey-black, pale stone, flesh, pale blue & ultramarine	80	65
		a. Imperf (pair)	£1400	
1520	**962**	20p. grey-black, pale stone, ochre, pale blue, ultramarine, scarlet & violet	80	65
1521	**963**	20p. grey-black, pale stone, yellow-brown, bluish grey & purple	80	65
		Set of 5	3·75	3·00
		Set of 5 Gutter Pairs	8·50	
		First Day Cover		3·75
		Presentation Pack	4·00	
		P.H.Q. Cards (set of 5)	3·00	8·00

Special First Day of Issue Postmarks

Philatelic Bureau, Edinburgh .... 4·75
Westminster, SW1 .... 4·75

964 Armagh Observatory, Jodrell Bank Radio Telescope and La Palma Telescope

965 Newton's Moon and Tides Diagram and Early Telescopes

966 Greenwich Old Observatory and Early Astronomical Equipment

967 Stonehenge, Gyroscope and Navigation by Stars

(Des J. Fisher. Litho Questa)

1990 (16 Oct). **Astronomy.** *Phosphorised paper. P* 14 × 14½.

1522	**964**	22p. cream, grey, dull blue-green, slate-blue, blue-green, orange-red, gold & black ..	65	15
		a. Gold (Queen's head) omitted	£375	

1523	**965**	26p. black, yellow, dull purple, pale cream, brown-rose, new blue, greenish yellow, vermilion & gold	1·00	1·10
1524	**966**	31p. black, cream, pale cream, yellow-orange, salmon, lemon, vermilion & gold	1·25	1·40
1525	**967**	37p. black, pale buff, olive-bistre, pale cream, pale flesh, flesh, grey, rose-red & gold	1·50	1·40
		Set of 4	4·00	3·75
		Set of 4 Gutter Pairs	9·00	
		First Day Cover		4·25
		Presentation Pack	4·50	
		P.H.Q. Cards (set of 4)	2·50	7·00

Special First Day of Issue Postmarks

Philatelic Bureau, Edinburgh .... 5·25
Armagh .... 5·25

968 Building a Snowman **969** Fetching the Christmas Tree

970 Carol Singing **971** Tobogganing

972 Ice-skating

(Des J. Gorham and A. Davidson)

1990 (13 Nov). **Christmas.** *One phosphor band* (17p.) *or phosphorised paper (others). P* 15 × 14.

1526	**968**	17p. gold, greenish yellow, rose, new blue & grey-black	50	15
		a. Booklet pane of 20	10·00	

1527 **969** 22p. gold, greenish yellow, magenta, new
blue & black 70 20
    a. Imperf (horiz pair) £450
1528 **970** 26p. gold, olive-yellow, pale magenta, agate,
new blue, dull violet-blue & black ..... 95 1·10
1529 **971** 31p. gold, greenish yellow, brt rose-red, dull
mauve, new blue, turquoise-blue &
grey-black .... 1·25 1·50
1530 **972** 37p. gold, greenish yellow, rose, new blue &
slate-green .... 1·40 1·50
    Set of 5 .... 4·50 4·00
    Set of 5 Gutter Pairs .... 10·00
    First Day Cover .... 4·25
    Presentation Pack .... 4·75
    P.H.Q. Cards (set of 5) .... 3·25 7·00

Booklet pane No. 1526a has the horizontal edges of the pane imperforate.

Special First Day of Issue Postmarks

Philatelic Bureau, Edinburgh .... 5·25
Bethlehem, Llandeilo, Dyfed .... 5·25

Collectors Pack 1990

1990 (13 Nov). *Comprises Nos. 1479/82, 1493/1510 and 1517/30.*
CP1530a Collectors Pack .... 55·00

Post Office Yearbook

1990 (13 Nov). *Comprises Nos. 1479/82, 1493/1500, 1502/10, 1517/30 in
hardbound book with slip case, illustrated in colour* . 55·00

KING CHARLES SPANIEL
GEORGE STUBBS

973 "King Charles Spaniel"

A POINTER
GEORGE STUBBS

974 "A Pointer"

TWO HOUNDS IN A LANDSCAPE
GEORGE STUBBS

975 "Two Hounds in a
Landscape"

A ROUGH DOG
GEORGE STUBBS

976 "A Rough Dog"

FINO AND TINY
GEORGE STUBBS

977 "Fino and Tiny"

(Des Carroll, Dempsey and Thirkell Ltd)

1991 (8 Jan). **Dogs. Paintings by George Stubbs.** *Phosphorised paper.*
P 14 × 14½.
1531 **973** 22p. gold, greenish yellow, magenta, new
blue, black & drab 85 15
    a. Imperf (pair) £950
1532 **974** 26p. gold, greenish yellow, magenta, new
blue, black & drab .... 1·10 1·25
1533 **975** 31p. gold, greenish yellow, magenta, new
blue, black & drab .... 1·25 1·25
    a. Imperf (pair) £950
1534 **976** 33p. gold, greenish yellow, magenta, new
blue, black & drab .... 1·40 1·40
1535 **977** 37p. gold, greenish yellow, magenta, new
blue, black & drab .... 1·50 1·40
    Set of 5 .... 5·50 5·00
    Set of 5 Gutter Pairs .... 12·00
    First Day Cover .... 5·25
    Presentation Pack .... 6·00
    P.H.Q. Cards (set of 5) .... 3·50 7·00

Special First Day of Issue Postmarks

Philatelic Bureau, Edinburgh .... 5·50
Birmingham .... 5·50

978 Thrush's Nest

979 Shooting Star
and Rainbow

980 Magpies and
Charm Bracelet

981 Black Cat

982 Common Kingfisher
with Key

983 Mallard and Frog

984 Four-leaf Clover
in Boot and Match Box

985 Pot of Gold at
End of Rainbow

986 Heart-shaped Butterflies

987 Wishing Well and Sixpence

(Des T. Meeuwissen)

1991 (5 Feb). **Greetings Stamps. "Good Luck".** *Two phosphor bands.*
P 15 × 14.

1536	978	(1st) silver, greenish yellow, magenta, new blue, olive-brown & black	1·90	1·90
		a. Booklet pane. Nos. 1536/45 plus 12 half stamp-size labels with margins on 3 sides	17·00	
1537	979	(1st) silver, greenish yellow, magenta, new blue, olive-brown & black	1·90	1·90
1538	980	(1st) silver, greenish yellow, magenta, new blue, olive-brown & black	1·90	1·90
1539	981	(1st) silver, greenish yellow, magenta, new blue, olive-brown & black	1·90	1·90
1540	982	(1st) silver, greenish yellow, magenta, new blue, olive-brown & black	1·90	1·90
1541	983	(1st) silver, greenish yellow, magenta, new blue, olive-brown & black	1·90	1·90
1542	984	(1st) silver, greenish yellow, magenta, new blue, olive-brown & black	1·90	1·90
1543	985	(1st) silver, greenish yellow, magenta, new blue, olive-brown & black	1·90	1·90
1544	986	(1st) silver, greenish yellow, magenta, new blue, olive-brown & black	1·90	1·90
1545	987	(1st) silver, greenish yellow, magenta, new blue, olive-brown & black	1·90	1·90
		Set of 10	17·00	17·00
		First Day Cover		19·00

Nos. 1536/45 were only issued in £2.20 booklets (sold at £2.40 from
16 September 1991). The backgrounds of the stamps form a composite
design.

Special First Day of Issue Postmarks

Philatelic Bureau, Edinburgh	19·00
Greetwell, Lincs	19·00

988 Michael Faraday
(inventor of electric motor)
(Birth Bicentenary)

989 Charles Babbage
(computer science pioneer)
(Birth Bicentenary)

990 Radar Sweep of East
Anglia (50th Anniv of
Operational Radar Network)

991 Gloster Whittle E28/39
Airplane over East Anglia (50th
Anniv of First Flight of Sir
Frank Whittle's Jet Engine)

(Des P. Till (Nos. 1546/7), J. Harwood (Nos. 1548/9))

1991 (5 Mar). **Scientific Achievements.** *Phosphorised paper.* P 14 × 15.

1546	988	22p. silver, olive-brown, greenish yellow, magenta, slate-blue, grey & black	60	30
		a. Imperf (pair)	£400	
1547	989	22p. silver, chrome-yellow, red, grey-black, brownish grey & sepia	60	30

1548 **990** 31p. silver, dp turquoise-green, violet-blue,
steel-blue & dp dull blue ..... 1·20   1·35
1549 **991** 37p. silver, olive-bistre, rose-red, turquoise-
blue, new blue & grey-black .... 1·35   1·75
        Set of 4 ..... 3·50   3·50
        Set of 4 Gutter Pairs ..... 7·50
        First Day Cover ..... 3·75
        Presentation Pack ..... 4·00
        P.H.Q. Cards (set of 4) ..... 3·00   6·50

Special First Day of Issue Postmarks

Philatelic Bureau, Edinburgh ..... 4·75
South Kensington, London, SW7 ..... 4·75

992 Teddy Bear

1991 (26 Mar).   **Greeting Stamps.** *As Nos. 1483/92, but inscribed "1st"
as T* **992**. *Two phosphor bands. P* 15 × 14.
1550 **992** (1st) gold, greenish yellow, brt rose-red, new
blue & grey-black ..... 1·25   1·50
      a. Booklet pane. Nos. 1550/9 plus 12 half
stamp-size labels with margins on 3
sides ..... 11·00
1551 **935** (1st) gold, greenish yellow, brt rose-red, new
blue, dp blue & grey-black ..... 1·25   1·50
1552 **936** (1st) gold, greenish yellow, brt rose-red, new
blue, dp blue & grey-black ..... 1·25   1·50
1553 **937** (1st) gold, greenish yellow, bright rose-red,
new blue & grey-black ..... 1·25   1·50
1554 **938** (1st) gold, greenish yellow, brt rose-red, new
blue & grey-black ..... 1·25   1·50
1555 **939** (1st) gold, greenish yellow, brt rose-red, new
blue & grey-black ..... 1·25   1·50
1556 **940** (1st) gold, greenish yellow, brt rose-red, new
blue & grey-black ..... 1·25   1·50
1557 **941** (1st) gold, greenish yellow, brt rose-red, new
blue & grey-black ..... 1·25   1·50
1558 **942** (1st) gold, greenish yellow, brt rose-red, new
blue & grey-black ..... 1·25   1·50
1559 **943** (1st) gold & grey-black ..... 1·25   1·50
        Set of 10 ..... 11·00   13·50
        First Day Cover ..... 14·00
     Nos. 1550/9 were originally issued in £2.20 booklets (sold at £2.40
from 16 September 1991 and at £2.50 from 1 November 1993). The
designs of Nos. 1550, 1552/4, 1556 and 1559 extend onto the pane
margin.
     The stamps were re-issued in sheets of 10, printed in photogravure
by Questa, each with *se-tenant* label on 22 May 2000 in connection
with "customised" stamps available at "Stamp Show 2000". The labels
show either a pattern of ribbons at £2.95, or a personal photograph for
£5.95.

A similar sheet, but printed in lithography by Questa instead of in
photogravure, appeared on 3 July 2001. Stamps from this sheet were
perforated 14½ × 14 instead of the previous 15 × 14. Sheets showing
greetings on the labels were available from the Bureau or Postshops at
£2.95 each or with personal photographs at £12.95 for two. Similar
sheets each containing ten examples of Nos. 1550/1 and 1555/7 were
only available with personal photograph. From 29 October 2001 sheets
with personal photographs could also be purchased, on an experimental basis, from photo-booths situated at six post offices.
     On 1 October 2002 three further sheets appeared printed in
lithography by Questa. One contained Nos. 1550/1 each × 10 with
greetings labels and cost £5.95. Both designs were also available in
sheets of 20 with personal photographs at £14.95 a sheet.

Special First Day of Issue Postmarks

Philatelic Bureau, Edinburgh ..... 14·00
Laugherton, Lincs ..... 14·00

993   **994**
Man Looking at Space

995   **996**
Space Looking at Man

(Des J.-M. Folon)

1991 (23 Apr).   **Europa. Europe in Space.** *Phosphorised paper. P* 14 × 15.
1560 **993** 22p. silver-mauve, greenish yellow, scarlet,
violet-blue, brt blue & brt green & black 75   50
      a. Horiz pair. Nos. 1560/1 ..... 1·50   1·50
1561 **994** 22p. silver-mauve, greenish yellow, scarlet,
violet-blue, brt blue & black 75   50
1562 **995** 37p. silver-mauve, bistre-yellow, dull vermilion, blue & black ..... 2·00   1·40
      a. Horiz pair. Nos. 1562/3 ..... 4·00   2·75

1563 **996** 37p. silver-mauve, bistre-yellow, dull vermilion, blue & black .... 2·00 1·40
Set of 4 .... 5·00 3·25
Set of 2 Gutter Strips of 4 .... 12·00
First Day Cover .... 4·00
Presentation Pack .... 5·50
P.H.Q. Cards (set of 4) .... 3·00 6·50

Nos. 1560/1 and 1562/3 were each printed together, *se-tenant*, in horizontal pairs throughout the sheets, each pair forming a composite design.

Special First Day of Issue Postmarks

Philatelic Bureau, Edinburgh .... 5·50
Cambridge .... 5·50

997 Fencing   **998** Hurdling

999 Diving   **1000** Rugby

(Des Huntley Muir Partners)

1991 (11 June). **World Student Games, Sheffield** (*Nos.* 1564/6) **and World Cup Rugby Championship, London** (*No.* 1567). *Phosphorised paper.* P 14½ × 14.

1564 **997** 22p. black, greenish yellow, vermilion, brt orange, ultramarine & grey 60 20
1565 **998** 26p. pale blue, greenish yellow, red, brt blue & black .... 1·00 1·00
1566 **999** 31p. brt blue, bistre-yellow, rose, vermilion, new blue & black .... 1·25 1·25
1567 **1000** 37p. yellow-orange, greenish yellow, rose, brt blue, emerald & black .... 1·50 1·50
Set of 4 .... 4·00 3·50
Set of 4 Gutter Pairs .... 10·00
First Day Cover .... 4·00
Presentation Pack .... 4·50
P.H.Q. Cards (set of 4) .... 2·50 6·50

Special First Day of Issue Postmarks

Philatelic Bureau, Edinburgh .... 4·75
Sheffield .... 4·75

1001 "Silver Jubilee"   **1002** "Mme Alfred Carrière"

1003 Rosa moyesii   **1004** "Harvest Fayre"

1005 "Mutabilis"

(Des Yvonne Skargon. Litho Questa)

1991 (16 July). **9th World Congress of Roses, Belfast.** *Phosphorised paper.* P 14½ × 14.

1568 **1001** 22p. new blue, greenish yellow, magenta, black & silver 95 20
a. Silver (Queen's head) omitted £1100
Eb. Black printing double .... — £2800
1569 **1002** 26p. new blue, greenish yellow, magenta, black & silver .... 1·10 1·25
1570 **1003** 31p. new blue, greenish yellow, magenta, black & silver .... 1·25 1·25
1571 **1004** 33p. new blue, greenish yellow, magenta, black & silver .... 1·50 1·50

1572	**1005**	37p. new blue, greenish yellow, magenta, black & silver	1·60	1·50
		Set of 5	5·75	5·00
		Set of 5 Gutter Pairs	12·00	
		First Day Cover		6·00
		Presentation Pack	6·25	
		P.H.Q. Cards (set of 5)	3·00	8·50

Special First Day of Issue Postmarks

| Philatelic Bureau, Edinburgh | 7·00 |
| Belfast | 7·00 |

1006 Iguanodon

1007 Stegosaurus

1008 Tyrannosaurus

1009 Protoceratops

1010 Triceratops

(Des B. Kneale)

1991 (20 Aug). **150th Anniversary of Dinosaurs' Identification by Owen.** *Phosphorised paper.* P 14½ × 14

| 1573 | **1006** | 22p. grey, pale blue, magenta, brt blue, dull violet & grey-black | 90 | 20 |
| | | a. Imperf (pair) | £1500 | |

1574	**1007**	26p. grey, greenish yellow, pale emerald, brt blue-green, pale brt blue, grey-black & black	1·10	1·25
1575	**1008**	31p. grey, lt blue, magenta, brt blue, pale blue, brown & grey-black	1·25	1·25
1576	**1009**	33p. grey, dull rose, pale brt blue, brt rose-red, yellow-orange, grey-black & black	1·50	1·50
1577	**1010**	37p. grey, greenish yellow, turquoise-blue, dull violet, yellow-brown & black	1·60	1·50
		Set of 5	5·75	5·00
		Set of 5 Gutter Pairs	12·00	
		First Day Cover		6·00
		Presentation Pack	6·50	
		P.H.Q. Cards (set of 5)	3·25	8·50

Special First Day of Issue Postmarks

| Philatelic Bureau, Edinburgh | 7·00 |
| Plymouth | 7·00 |

1011 Map of 1816

1012 Map of 1906

1013 Map of 1959

1014 Map of 1991

(Des H. Brown. Recess and litho Harrison (24p.), litho Harrison (28p.), Questa (33p., 39p.))

1991 (17 Sept). **Bicentenary of Ordnance Survey. Maps of Hamstreet, Kent.** *Phosphorised paper.* P 14½ × 14.

1578	**1011**	24p. black, magenta & cream	60	20
		Ea. Black (litho) printing treble & magenta printing double	£1000	
		Eb. Black (litho) & magenta printing double	£1500	
1579	**1012**	28p. black, brt yellow-green, new blue, reddish orange, magenta, olive-sepia & cream	1·00	95
1580	**1013**	33p. dull blue-green, orange-brown, magenta, olive-grey, greenish yellow, vermilion, greenish grey, pale blue, blue, dull orange, apple green & black	1·25	1·40

1581 **1014** 39p. black, magenta, greenish yellow & new
blue .... 1·50 1·40
Set of 4 .... 4·00 3·50
Set of 4 Gutter Pairs .... 10·00
First Day Cover .... 4·25
Presentation Pack .... 4·50
P.H.Q. Cards (set of 4) .... 3·00 6·00
Mint examples of Type **1012** exist with a face value of 26p.

Special First Day of Issue Postmarks

Philatelic Bureau, Edinburgh .... 5·50
Southampton .... 5·50

1015 Adoration of the Magi   **1016** Mary and Jesus in Stable

1017 Holy Family and Angel   **1018** The Annunciation

1019 The Flight into Egypt

(Des D. Driver)

1991 (12 Nov). **Christmas. Illuminated Letters from "Acts of Mary and Jesus" Manuscript in Bodleian Library, Oxford.** *One phosphor band* (18p.) *or phosphorised paper* (others). P 15 × 14.
1582 **1015** 18p. steel-blue, greenish yellow, rose-red,
orange-red, black & gold 75 10
a. Imperf (pair) £2000
b. Booklet pane of 20 .... 8·25
1583 **1016** 24p. brt rose-red, greenish yellow, vermilion, slate-blue, yellow-green, grey-
black & gold 90 10
1584 **1017** 28p. reddish brown, bistre-yellow, orange-
vermilion, orange-red, dp dull blue,
grey-black & gold .... 95 1·25

1585 **1018** 33p. green, greenish yellow, red, orange-
red, blue, grey & gold .... 1·10 1·40
1586 **1019** 39p. orange-red, greenish yellow, orange-
vermilion, dp dull blue, olive-sepia,
black & gold .... 1·25 1·60
Set of 5 .... 4·50 4·00
Set of 5 Gutter Pairs .... 11·00
First Day Cover .... 5·00
Presentation Pack .... 5·00
P.H.Q. Cards (set of 5) .... 3·00 7·50
Booklet pane No. 1582b has margins at left, top and bottom.

Special First Day of Issue Postmarks

Philatelic Bureau, Edinburgh .... 5·50
Bethlehem, Landeilo, Dyfed .... 5·50

Collectors Pack 1991

1991 (12 Nov). *Comprises Nos. 1531/5, 1546/9 and 1560/86.*
CP1586a Collectors Pack .... 55·00

Post Office Yearbook

1991 (13 Nov). *Comprises Nos. 1531/5, 1546/9 and 1560/86 in hardbound book with slip case, illustrated in colour* . 60·00

1020 Fallow Deer in Scottish   **1021** Hare on North Yorkshire
Forest   Moors

1022 Fox in the Fens   **1023** Redwing and Home Counties
Village

1024 Welsh Mountain Sheep in Snowdonia

(Des J. Gorham and K. Bowen)

1992 (14 Jan-25 Feb). **The Four Seasons. Wintertime.** *One phosphor band* (18p.) *or phosphorised paper* (*others*). *P* 15 × 14.

1587	**1020**	18p. silver, greenish yellow, grey, dull rose, new blue & black	55	15
1588	**1021**	24p. silver, lemon, rose, blue & grey-black .	75	20
		a. Imperf (pair)	£400	
1589	**1022**	28p. silver, greenish yellow, bright rose, steel-blue & grey-black	1·00	1·10
1590	**1023**	33p. silver, greenish yellow, brt orange, brt purple, greenish blue & grey	1·25	1·40
1591	**1024**	39p. silver, yellow, yellow-orange, grey, vermilion, new blue & black	1·40	1·60
		a. Booklet pane. No. 1591 × 4 with margins all round (25 Feb)	4·75	
		Set of 5	4·50	4·00
		Set of 5 Gutter Pairs	11·00	
		First Day Cover		4·75
		Presentation Pack	4·75	
		P.H.Q. Cards (*set of 5*)	3·50	8·00

Booklet pane No. 1591a comes from the £6 "Cymru–Wales" booklet.

Philatelic Bureau, Edinburgh .... 5·50
Brecon .... 5·50

1025 Flower Spray   **1026** Double Locket

1027 Key   **1028** Model Car and Cigarette Cards

1029 Compass and Map   **1030** Pocket Watch

1031 1854 1d. Red Stamp and Pen   **1032** Pearl Necklace

1033 Marbles   **1034** Bucket, Spade and Starfish

(Des Trickett and Webb Ltd)

1992 (28 Jan). **Greetings Stamps. "Memories".** *Two phosphor bands. P* 15 × 14.

1592	**1025**	(1st) gold, greenish yellow, magenta, ochre, lt blue & grey-black	1·40	1·40
		a. Booklet pane. Nos. 1592/1601 plus 12 half stamp-size labels with margins on 3 sides	12·00	
1593	**1026**	(1st) gold, greenish yellow, magenta, ochre, lt blue & grey-black	1·40	1·40
1594	**1027**	(1st) gold, greenish yellow, magenta, ochre, lt blue & grey-black	1·40	1·40
1595	**1028**	(1st) gold, greenish yellow, magenta, ochre, lt blue & grey-black	1·40	1·40
1596	**1029**	(1st) gold, greenish yellow, magenta, ochre, lt blue & grey-black	1·40	1·40
1597	**1030**	(1st) gold, greenish yellow, magenta, ochre, lt blue & grey-black	1·40	1·40
1598	**1031**	(1st) gold, greenish yellow, magenta, ochre, lt blue & grey-black	1·40	1·40
1599	**1032**	(1st) gold, greenish yellow, magenta, ochre, lt blue & grey-black	1·40	1·40
1600	**1033**	(1st) gold, greenish yellow, magenta, ochre, lt blue & grey-black	1·40	1·40
1601	**1034**	(1st) gold, greenish yellow, magenta, ochre, lt blue & grey-black	1·40	1·40
		Set of 10	12·00	12·00
		First Day Cover		14·00
		Presentation Pack	15·00	

Nos. 1592/1601 were only issued in £2.40 booklets (sold at £2.50 from 1 November 1993 and at £2.60 from 8 July 1996). The backgrounds of the stamps form a composite design.

Philatelic Bureau, Edinburgh .... 12·00
Whimsey, Gloucestershire .... 12·00

1035 Queen Elizabeth in Coronation Robes and Parliamentary Emblem

1036 Queen Elizabeth in Garter Robes and Archiepiscopal Arms

1040 Tennyson in 1888 and "The Beguiling of Merlin" (Sir Edward Burne-Jones)

1041 Tennyson in 1856 and "April Love" (Arthur Hughes)

1037 Queen Elizabeth with Baby Prince Andrew and Royal Arms **1038** Queen Elizabeth at Trooping the Colour and Service Emblems

1042 Tennyson in 1864 and "I am Sick of the Shadows" (John Waterhouse)

1043 Tennyson as a Young Man and "Mariana" (Dante Gabriel Rossetti)

(Des Irene von Treskow)

1039 Queen Elizabeth and Commonwealth Emblem

(Des Why Not Associates. Litho Questa)

1992 (6 Feb). **40th Anniv of Accession.** *Two phosphor bands.* P 14½ × 14.
1602 **1035** 24p. new blue, greenish yellow, magenta, black, silver & gold .... 1·10 1·10
    a. Horiz strip of 5. Nos. 1602/6 .... 6·00 7·00
1603 **1036** 24p. new blue, greenish yellow, magenta, black, silver & gold .... 1·10 1·10
1604 **1037** 24p. new blue, greenish yellow, magenta, black & silver .... 1·10 1·10
1605 **1038** 24p. new blue, greenish yellow, magenta, black, silver & gold .... 1·10 1·10
1606 **1039** 24p. new blue, greenish yellow, magenta, black, silver & gold .... 1·10 1·10
    Set of 5 .... 6·00 5·00
    Gutter Block of 10 .... 13·00
    First Day Cover .... 7·00
    Presentation Pack .... 7·00
    P.H.Q. Cards (set of 5) .... 3·50 7·50
Nos. 1602/6 were printed together, *se-tenant*, in horizontal strips of five throughout the sheet.

Special First Day of Issue Postmarks

Philatelic Bureau, Edinburgh .... 7·50
Buckingham Palace, London SW1 .... 7·50

1992 (10 Mar). **Death Centenary of Alfred, Lord Tennyson (poet).** *Phosphorised paper.* P 14½ × 14.
1607 **1040** 24p. gold, greenish yellow, magenta, new blue & black 60 20
1608 **1041** 28p. gold, greenish yellow, magenta, new blue & black 85 85
1609 **1042** 33p. gold, greenish yellow, magenta, new blue & black .... 1·40 1·60
1610 **1043** 39p. gold, greenish yellow, magenta, new blue, bistre & black .... 1·50 1·60
    Set of 4 .... 4·00 3·75
    Set of 4 Gutter Pairs .... 10·00
    First Day Cover .... 4·25
    Presentation Pack .... 4·50
    P.H.Q. Cards (set of 4) .... 3·00 6·50

Special First Day of Issue Postmarks

Philatelic Bureau, Edinburgh .... 4·50
Isle of Wight .... 4·50

For full information on all future British issues, collectors should write to the British Post Office Philatelic Bureau, 21 South Gyle Crescent, Edinburgh EH12 9PB

1044 Carrickfergus Castle

Elliptical hole in vertical perforations

CASTLE

Harrison Plates (Nos. 1611/14)

CASTLE

Enschedé Plates (Nos. 1993/6)

(Des from photos by Prince Andrew, Duke of York. Eng C. Matthews. Recess Harrison)

1992 (24 Mar)–**95**. *Designs as Nos. 1410/13, but showing Queen's head in silhouette as T* **1044**. *P* 15 × 14 *(with one elliptical hole on each vertical side).*

1611	**1044**	£1 bottle green & gold†	5·50	1·00
1612	**880**	£1.50 maroon & gold†	5·00	1·00
1613	**881**	£2 indigo & gold†	6·75	1·00
1613a	**1044**	£3 reddish violet & gold† (22.8.95)	20·00	3·00
1614	**882**	£5 dp brown & gold†	17·00	3·00
		a. Gold† (Queen's head) omitted	£350	
		Set of 5	48·00	8·00
		Set of 5 Gutter Pairs	95·00	
		First Day Cover (Nos. 1611/13, 1614) ..		35·00
		First Day Cover (No. 1613a)		10·00
		Presentation Pack (P.O. Pack No. 27)		
		(Nos. 1611/13, 1614)	38·00	
		Presentation Pack (P.O. Pack No. 33) (No.		
		1613a)	20·00	
		P.H.Q. Cards†† *(Nos. 1611/13, 1614)* ...	12·00	
		P.H.Q. Cards (No. 1613a)	6·00	22·00

†The Queen's head on these stamps is printed in optically variable ink which changes colour from gold to green when viewed from different angles.

††The P.H.Q. cards for this issue did not appear until 16 February 1993. They do not exist used on the first day of issue of Nos. 1611/13 and 1614.

The £1.50 (5 March 1996), £2 (2 May 1996), £3 (February 1997) and £5 (17 September 1996) subsequently appeared on PVA (white gum) instead of the tinted PVAD previously used.

See also Nos. 1993/6.

Special First Day of Issue Postmarks
(for illustrations see Introduction)

Philatelic Bureau, Edinburgh (Type H) (£1, £1.50, £2, £5)	35·00
Windsor, Berkshire (Type I) (£1, £1.50, £2, £5)	35·00
Philatelic Bureau, Edinburgh (Type H) (£3)	12·00
Carrickfergus, Antrim (as Type I) (£3)	15·00

1045 British Olympic Association Logo (Olympic Games, Barcelona)

1046 British Paralympic Association Symbol (Paralympics '92, Barcelona)

1047 *Santa Maria* (500th Anniv of Discovery of America by Columbus)

1048 *Kaisei* (Japanese cadet brigantine) (Grand Regatta Columbus, 1992)

1049 British Pavilion, "EXPO '92", Seville

(Des K. Bassford (Nos. 1615/16, 1619), K. Bassford and S. Paine. Eng C. Matthews (Nos. 1617/18). Litho Questa (Nos. 1615/16, 1619) or recess and litho Harrison (Nos. 1617/18))

1992 (7 Apr). **Europa. International Events.** *Phosphorised paper. P* 14 × 14½.

1615	**1045**	24p. new blue, lemon, magenta & black ...	1·00	65
		a. Horiz pair. Nos. 1615/16	2·25	1·75
1616	**1046**	24p. new blue, lemon, magenta & black ...	1·00	65
1617	**1047**	24p. black, grey, carmine, cream & black ...	1·00	55
1618	**1048**	39p. black, grey, carmine, cream & gold ...	1·40	1·30
1619	**1049**	39p. new blue, lemon, magenta & black ...	1·40	1·30
		Set of 5	5·50	4·00
		Set of 3 Gutter Pairs and a Gutter Strip of 4	11·50	
		First Day Cover		5·00
		Presentation Pack	5·75	
		PHQ Cards (set of 5)	3·50	6·50

Nos. 1615/16 were printed together, *se-tenant*, throughout the sheet.

No. 1617 is known with the cream omitted used from Cornwall in September 1992.

Philatelic Bureau, Edinburgh .... 4·50
Banbury, Oxfordshire .... 4·50

Special First Day of Issue Postmarks

Philatelic Bureau, Edinburgh .... 5·50
Liverpool .... 5·50

1054 *The Yeomen of the Guard*

1055 *The Gondoliers*

1050 Pikeman

1051 Drummer

1056 *The Mikado*

1057 *The Pirates of Penzance*

1052 Musketeer

1053 Standard Bearer

1058 *Iolanthe*

(Des J. Sancha)

1992 (16 June). **350th Anniv of the Civil War.** *Phosphorised paper.*
P $14\frac{1}{2} \times 14$.

1620	**1050**	24p.	black, stone, bistre, scarlet, indigo, grey-green & yellow-ochre	60	20
		a.	Imperf (pair)	£250	
1621	**1051**	28p.	black, yellow-ochre, ochre, rose-pink, blue, dull yellow-green & slate-lilac ...	85	85
1622	**1052**	33p.	black, ochre, pale orange, lemon, reddish orange, new blue & olive-green	1·40	1·40
1623	**1053**	39p.	black, yellow-ochre, yellow, greenish yellow, vermilion, indigo & orange-brown	1·50	1·50
			Set of 4	4·00	3·50
			Set of 4 Gutter Pairs	10·00	
			First Day Cover		4·00
			Presentation Pack	4·50	
			P.H.Q. Cards (set of 4)	3·50	6·00

(Des Lynda Gray)

1992 (21 July). **150th Birth Anniv of Sir Arthur Sullivan (composer). Gilbert and Sullivan Operas.** *One phosphor band* (18p.) *or phosphorised paper* (others). P $14\frac{1}{2} \times 14$.

1624	**1054**	18p.	bluish violet, bistre-yellow, scarlet, stone, blue & grey-black	50	20
1625	**1055**	24p.	purple-brown, lemon, scarlet, stone, blue, olive-bistre & black	80	20
		a.	Imperf (pair)	£250	
1626	**1056**	28p.	rose-red, lemon, stone, new blue, bluish violet, brt emerald & black	95	1·00

1627 **1057** 33p. blue-green, orange-yellow, scarlet, olive-bistre, blue, brown-purple & black 1·50 1·60
1628 **1058** 39p. dp blue, lemon, scarlet, stone, lavender, olive-bistre & lake-brown .... 1·60 1·60
Set of 5 .... 4·75 4·25
Set of 5 Gutter Pairs .... 10·50
First Day Cover .... 4·75
Presentation Pack .... 5·00
P.H.Q. Cards (set of 5) .... 3·50 6·00

Special First Day of Issue Postmarks

Philatelic Bureau, Edinburgh .... 5·25
Birmingham .... 5·25

1059 "Acid Rain Kills"

1060 "Ozone Layer"

1061 "Greenhouse Effect"

1062 "Bird of Hope"

(Des Christopher Hall (24p.), Lewis Fowler (28p.), Sarah Warren (33p.), Alice Newton-Mold (39p.). Adapted Trickett and Webb Ltd)

1992 (15 Sept). **Protection of the Environment. Children's Paintings.** *Phosphorised paper. P 14 × 14½.*
1629 **1059** 24p. emerald, greenish yellow, pale olive-yellow, brt carmine & black 70 20
1630 **1060** 28p. vermilion, lemon, brt blue, new blue, brt green, ultramarine & black .... 1·10 1·10
1631 **1061** 33p. greenish blue, greenish yellow, brt rose-red, brt green, emerald, blue & black .... 1·25 1·25
1632 **1062** 39p. emerald, greenish yellow, brt magenta, brt orange, brt blue & black .... 1·40 1·25
Set of 4 .... 4·00 3·50
Set of 4 Gutter Pairs .... 10·00
First Day Cover .... 4·50
Presentation Pack .... 4·75
P.H.Q. Cards (set of 4) .... 3·50 5·50

Special First Day of Issue Postmarks

Philatelic Bureau, Edinburgh (in green) .... 5·00
Torridon (in green) .... 5·00

1063 European Star

(Des D. Hockney)

1992 (13 Oct). **Single European Market.** *Phosphorised paper. P 15 × 14.*
1633 **1063** 24p. gold, greenish yellow, brt magenta, dull ultramarine & black 90 80
Gutter Pair .... 2·00
First Day Cover .... 1·90
Presentation Pack .... 1·90
P.H.Q. Card .... 90 3·50

Special First Day of Issue Postmarks

Philatelic Bureau, Edinburgh .... 2·50
Westminster .... 2·50

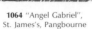

1064 "Angel Gabriel", St. James's, Pangbourne

1065 "Madonna and Child", St. Mary's, Bibury

1066 "King with Gold", Our Lady and St. Peter, Leatherhead

1067 "Shepherds", All Saints, Porthcawl

1068 "Kings with Frankincense and Myrrh", Our Lady and St. Peter, Leatherhead

(Des Carroll, Dempsey and Thirkell Ltd from windows by Karl Parsons (18, 24, 33p.) and Paul Woodroffe (28p. 39p.))

1992 (10 Nov). **Christmas. Stained Glass Windows.** *One centre band* (18p.) *or phosphorised paper* (others). P 15 × 14.

1634	**1064**	18p. black, greenish yellow, mauve, ultra-marine, brt emerald & gold	45	15
		a. Booklet pane of 20	7·50	
1635	**1065**	24p. black, greenish yellow, brt purple, ultramarine, new blue, brt greenish yellow & gold	75	15
1636	**1066**	28p. black, lemon, rosine, ultramarine, red-dish lilac, red-orange & gold	90	1·10
1637	**1067**	33p. brt ultramarine, greenish yellow, ro-sine, brown, yellow-orange, black & gold	1·10	1·50
1638	**1068**	39p. black, lemon, rosine, brt blue, dp violet, yellow-orange & gold	1·25	1·40
		Set of 5	4·25	4·00
		Set of 5 Gutter Pairs	10·00	
		First Day Cover		4·75
		Presentation Pack	4·75	
		P.H.Q. Cards (set of 5)	3·50	7·50

Booklet pane No. 1634a comes from a special £3.60 Christmas booklet and has margins at left, top and bottom.

Special First Day of Issue Postmarks

Philatelic Bureau, Edinburgh	5·00
Bethlehem, Llandeilo, Dyfed	5·00
Pangbourne	5·00

Collectors Pack 1992

1992 (10 Nov). *Comprises Nos. 1587/91, 1602/10 and 1615/38.*
CP1638a Collectors Pack .... 55·00

Post Office Yearbook

1992 (11 Nov). *Comprises Nos. 1587/91, 1602/10 and 1615/38 in hardbound book with slip case, illustrated in colour* . 60·00

1069 Mute Swan Cob and St. Catherine's Chapel, Abbotsbury

1070 Cygnet and Decoy

1071 Swans and Cygnet

1072 Eggs in Nest and Tithe Barn, Abbotsbury

1073 Young Swan and the Fleet

(Des D. Gentleman)

1993 (19 Jan). **600th Anniv of Abbotsbury Swannery.** *One phosphor band* (18p.) *or phosphorised paper* (others). P 14 × 15.

1639	**1069**	18p. gold, greenish yellow, bistre, green, vermilion & black	1·25	30
1640	**1070**	24p. gold, cream, brt green, grey-brown, dull blue & grey-black	1·10	30
1641	**1071**	28p. gold, greenish grey, yellow-brown, myrtle-green, brown, vermilion & black	1·40	1·80

1642 **1072** 33p. gold, ochre, apple-green, olive-brown,
brt orange & grey-black .... 1·75 2·45
1643 **1073** 39p. gold, cream, brt green, cobalt, lt brown
& black .... 1·90 2·45
Set of 5 .... 6·50 6·75
Set of 5 Gutter Pairs .... 16·00
First Day Cover .... 7·00
Presentation Pack .... 8·00
P.H.Q. Cards (set of 5) .... 4·00 9·00

Special First Day of Issue Postmarks

Philatelic Bureau, Edinburgh .... 7·50
Abbotsbury, Dorset .... 7·50

1074 Long John Silver and
Parrot (*Treasure Island*)

1075 Tweedledum and
Tweedledee (*Alice Through
the Looking-Glass*)

1076 William (*William* books)

1077 Mole and Toad (*The
Wind in the Willows*)

1078 Teacher and Wilfrid
("The Bash Street Kids")

1079 Peter Rabbit and Mrs.
Rabbit (*The Tale of Peter
Rabbit*)

1080 Snowman (*The Snowman*)
and Father Christmas
(*Father Christmas*)

1081 The Big Friendly Giant
and Sophie (*The BFG*)

1082 Bill Badger and Rupert
Bear

1083 Aladdin and the Genie

(Des Newell and Sorell)

1993 (2 Feb–10 Aug). **Greetings Stamps. "Gift Giving".** *Two phosphor
bands.* P 15 × 14 *(with one elliptical hole in each horizontal side).*
1644 **1074** (1st) gold, greenish yellow, magenta, pale
brown, lt blue & black .... 1·25 1·25
a. Booklet pane. Nos. 1644/53 .... 11·00
1645 **1075** (1st) gold, cream & black .... 1·25 1·25
1646 **1076** (1st) gold, greenish yellow, magenta, cream,
new blue & black .... 1·25 1·25
1647 **1077** (1st) gold, greenish yellow, magenta, cream,
new blue & black .... 1·25 1·25
1648 **1078** (1st) gold, greenish yellow, magenta, cream,
new blue & black .... 1·25 1·25
1649 **1079** (1st) gold, greenish yellow, magenta, cream,
new blue & black .... 1·25 1·25
a. Booklet pane. No. 1649 × 4 with margins all round (10 Aug) .... 4·75
1650 **1080** (1st) gold, greenish yellow, magenta, cream,
new blue & black .... 1·25 1·25
1651 **1081** (1st) gold, greenish yellow, magenta, cream,
new blue & black .... 1·25 1·25
1652 **1082** (1st) gold, greenish yellow, magenta, cream,
new blue & black .... 1·25 1·25
1653 **1083** (1st) gold, greenish yellow, magenta, cream,
new blue & black .... 1·25 1·25
Set of 10 .... 11·00 11·00
First Day Cover .... 12·00
Presentation Pack .... 15·00
P.H.Q. Cards (set of 10) .... 7·00 20·00
Nos. 1644/53 were issued in £2.40 booklets (sold at £2.50 from 1
November 1993), together with a pane of 20 half stamp-sized labels.
The stamps and labels were affixed to the booklet cover by a common
gutter margin.
Booklet pane No. 1649a comes from the £6 (£5.64) Beatrix Potter
booklet.

Special First Day of Issue Postmarks

Philatelic Bureau, Edinburgh (No. 1644a) (2 Feb) ... 12·00
Greetland (No. 1644a) (2 Feb) .... 12·00
Philatelic Bureau, Edinburgh (No. 1649a) (10 Aug) .. 6·00
Keswick (No. 1649a) (10 Aug) .... 6·00

Philatelic Bureau, Edinburgh .... 4·75
Greenwich .... 4·75

1084 Decorated Enamel
Dial

1085 Escapement,
Remontoire and Fusée

1088 Britannia

(Des B. Craddock, adapted Roundel Design Group. Litho (silver die-stamped, Braille symbol for "10" embossed) Questa)

1993 (2 Mar). *Granite paper. P* $14 \times 14\frac{1}{2}$ *(with two elliptical holes on each horizontal side).*

1658 **1088** £10 greenish grey, rosine, yellow, new blue,
reddish violet, vermilion, violet, brt
green & silver .... 28·00 12·00
a. Silver omitted £1200
b. Braille symbol for "10" omitted ....
First Day Cover .... 25·00
Presentation Pack .... 28·00
P.H.Q. Card .... 5·00 35·00

The paper used for No. 1658 contains fluorescent coloured fibres which, together with the ink used on the shield, react under U.V. light.

1086 Balance, Spring and
Temperature
Compensator

1087 Back of Movement

Philatelic Bureau, Edinburgh .... 28·00
Windsor .... 28·00

(Des H. Brown and D. Penny. Litho Questa)

1993 (16 Feb). **300th Birth Anniv of John Harrison (inventor of the marine chronometer). Details of "H4" Clock.** *Phosphorised paper. P* $14\frac{1}{2} \times 14$.

1654 **1084** 24p. new blue, greenish yellow, magenta,
black, grey-black & pale cream 60 20
1655 **1085** 28p. new blue, greenish yellow, magenta,
black, grey-black & pale cream .... 1·00 1·10
1656 **1086** 33p. new blue, greenish yellow, magenta,
black, grey-black & pale cream .... 1·40 1·25
1657 **1087** 39p. new blue, greenish yellow, magenta,
black, grey-black & pale cream .... 1·50 1·40
Set of 4 .... 4·00 3·50
Set of 4 Gutter Pairs .... 10·00
First Day Cover .... 4·25
Presentation Pack .... 4·25
P.H.Q. Cards (set of 4) .... 3·50 8·00

1089 *Dendrobium
hellwigianum*

1090 *Paphiopedilum Maudiae
"Magnificum"*

1091 *Cymbidium lowianum*   1092 *Vanda* Rothschildiana

1093 *Dendrobium vexillarius*
var *albiviride*

(Des Pandora Sellars)

1993 (16 Mar). **14th World Orchid Conference, Glasgow.** *One phosphor band (18p.) or phosphorised paper (others). P 15 × 14.*

1659	**1089**	18p. green, greenish yellow, magenta, pale blue, apple-green & slate	45	20
		a. Imperf (pair)	£1250	
1660	**1090**	24p. green, greenish yellow, brt green & grey-black	75	20
1661	**1091**	28p. green, greenish yellow, red, brt turquoise-blue & drab	1·00	1·10
1662	**1092**	33p. green, greenish yellow, pale magenta, brt violet, brt green & grey	1·25	1·50
1663	**1093**	39p. green, greenish yellow, red, pale olive-yellow, brt green, violet & grey-black .	1·60	1·40
		Set of 5	4·50	4·00
		Set of 5 Gutter Pairs	10·00	
		First Day Cover		5·00
		Presentation Pack	5·50	
		P.H.Q. Cards (set of 5)	5·00	8·00

Special First Day of Issue Postmarks

Philatelic Bureau, Edinburgh	5·50
Glasgow	5·50

GIBBONS STAMP MONTHLY
– finest and most informative magazine for all
collectors. Obtainable from your newsagent or by
postal subscription – details on request.

FLUORESCENT PHOSPHOR BANDS. Following the introduction of new automatic sorting machinery in 1991 it was found necessary to substantially increase the signal emitted by the phosphor bands. This was achieved by adding a fluorescent element to the phosphor which appears yellow under U.V. light. This combination was first used on an experimental sheet printing of the 18p., No. X913, produced by Enschedé in 1991. All values with phosphor bands from the elliptical perforations issue, including the No Value Indicated design, originally showed this yellow fluor.

From mid-1995 printings of current sheet and booklet stamps began to appear with the colour of the fluorescent element changed to blue. As such differences in fluor colour can only be identified by use of a U.V. lamp they are outside the scope of this catalogue, but full details will be found in the *Great Britain Specialised Catalogue Volume 4.*

The first commemorative/special stamp issue to show the change to blue fluor was the Centenary of Rugby League set, Nos. 1891/5.

COMPUTER-ENGRAVED CYLINDERS. In 1991 Enschedé introduced a new method of preparing photogravure cylinders for Great Britain stamps. This new method utilised computer-engraving instead of the traditional acid-etching and produced cylinders without the minor flaws which had long been a feature of the photogravure process. Such cylinders were first used on Great Britain stamps for the printing of the 18p. released on 19 November 1991 (see No. X913).

Harrison and Sons continued to use the acid-etching method until mid-1996 after which most Machin values, including N.V.I.'s, were produced from computer-engraved cylinders using a very similar process to that of Enschedé. Some values exist in versions from both cylinder production methods and can often be identified by minor differences. Such stamps are, however, outside the scope of this listing, but full details can be found in the current edition of the *Great Britain Specialised Catalogue Volume 4.*

For commemorative stamps the first Harrison issue to use computer-engraved cylinders was the Centenary of Cinema set (Nos. 1920/4).

When Walsall introduced photogravure printing in 1997 their cylinders were produced using a similar computer-engraved process.

1093*a*

1993 (6 Apr)–**2003**. *Booklet Stamps. As T **913/14**, and **1093**a. P 14 (No. 1663c) or 15 × 14 (others) (both with one elliptical hole on each vertical side).*

(a) *Photo*
  Harrison – No. 1664
  Questa – Nos. 1663ab, 1664ab
  Walsall – No. 1663b
  Harrison/De La Rue, Questa or Walsall – No. 1664a
  Harrison/De La Rue, Enschedé, Questa or Walsall – Nos. 1663a, 1664b, 1664c

1663a	**913**	(2nd) brt blue (1 centre band) (7.9.93)	90	90
		ab. Perf 14 (1.12.98)	1·00	1·00
		al. Booklet pane. Nos. 1663a and 1664a × 3 plus 4 labels ("postcode" on top right label) (27.4.00)	4·50	
		ala. As No. 1663al, but inscr "postcodes" on top right label (17.4.01)	4·50	
		am. Booklet pane. Nos. 1663a × 2 and 1664a × 6 (27.4.00)	6·50	
		an. Booklet pane. Nos. 1663a and 1664c, each × 4, with central label and margins all round (6.2.02)	6·00	
		ao. Booklet pane. Nos. 1663a and 1664b, each × 4, with central label and margins all round (2.6.03)	3·50	

1663*b*	**913**	(2nd) bright blue (1 band at right) (13.10.98)	1·10	1·10
	b*E*c.	Band at left	1·00	1·00
	bl.	Booklet pane. Nos. 1663*b* × 3 and Nl81*b*, S91*a* and W80*a* with margins all round	7·50	
1664	**914**	(1st) brt orange-red (phosphorised paper) ..	1·50	1·25
1664*a*		(1st) brt orange-red (2 phosphor bands) (4.4.95)	90	90
	ab.	Perf 14 (1.12.98)	1·50	1·50
	al.	Booklet pane. No. 1664*a* × 8 with centre label and margins all round (16.2.99)	6·50	
	am.	Booklet pane. No. 1664*a* × 4 plus commemorative label at right (12.5.99)	4·50	
1664*b*		(1st) gold (2 phosphor bands) (21.4.97) ...	45	50
	bl.	Booklet pane. Nos. 1664*b* and Y1683*b*, each × 4, and centre label with margins all round (23.9.97)	7·00	
	bm.	Booklet pane. Nos. 1664*b/c, each* × 4, with centre label and margins all round (24.9.02)	6·00	
	bn.	Booklet pane. Nos. 1664*b/c, each* × 4, with centre label and margins all round (25.2.03)	6·00	
	bo.	Booklet pane. Nos. 1664*b* and Y1691*a* each × 4, with centre label and margins all round (16.3.04)	4·00	
1664*c*	**1093***a*	(E) deep blue (2 phosphor bands) (19.1.99)	60	65

(b) Litho Questa or Walsall (2nd), Enschedé, Questa or Walsall (1st)

1665	**913**	(2nd) brt blue (1 centre band)	80	80
	E*y*.	Phosphor omitted		
1666	**914**	(1st) brt orange-red (2 phosphor bands) ...	90	90
	E*y*.	Phosphor omitted	£190	
	l.	Booklet pane. No. 1666 × 4 plus commemorative label at left (27.7.94)	8·50	
	l*a*.	Ditto, but with commemorative label at right (16.5.95)	6·00	
	l*E*y.	Phosphor omitted		
	m.	Pane. No. 1666 with margins all round (roul 8 across top corners of pane) (Boots logo on margin) (17.8.94)	2·50	
	m*E*y.	Phosphor omitted		
	m*a*.	Without Boots logo above stamp (11.9.95)	1·25	
	mb.	Ditto, but roul 10 across top corners of pane (20.2.97)	1·40	
	n.	Booklet pane. No. 1666 × 9 with margins all round (16.2.99)	6·00	

For details of sheets, booklets, etc containing these stamps see Decimal Machin Index following the "Y" numbers.

Nos. 1663*a*/6 were issued in booklet panes showing perforations on all four edges.

On 6 September 1993 Nos. 1665/6 printed in lithography by Questa were made available in sheets from post offices in Birmingham, Coventry, Falkirk and Milton Keynes. These sheet stamps became available nationally on 5 October 1993. On 29 April 1997 No. 1663*a* printed in photogravure by Walsall became available in sheets. On the same date Nos. 1663*a* and 1664*a* were issued in coils printed by Harrison. Sheets of No. 1664*a* were printed by Walsall from 18 November 1997.

No. 1663*b* exists with the phosphor band at the left or right of the stamp from separate panes of the £6.16 Speed stamp booklet No. DX21. For pane containing No. 1663*b*E*c see No. Y1674*a*l.

No. 1664*b* was originally printed by Harrisons in booklets and Walsall in sheets and booklets for The Queen's Golden Wedding and issued on 21 April 1997.

No. 1664*c* was intended for the basic European air mail rate, initially 30p., and was at first only available from Barcode booklet No. HF1, printed by Walsall. It appeared in sheets printed by De La Rue on 5 October 1999.

No. 1666m, printed by Questa, was provided by the Royal Mail for inclusion in single pre-packed greetings cards. The pane shows large

margins at top and sides with lines of roulette gauging 8 stretching from the bottom corners to the mid point of the top edge. Examples included with greetings cards show the top two corners of the pane folded over. Unfolded examples were available from the British Philatelic Bureau and from other Post Office philatelic outlets. The scheme was originally limited to Boots and their logo appeared on the pane margin. Other card retailers subsequently participated and later supplies omitted the logo.

A further printing by Enschedé in 1997 showed the roulettes gauging 10 (No. 1666mb). Blank pieces of gummed paper have been found showing the perforation and rouletting of No. 1666mb, but no printing.

In mid-1994 a number of postal forgeries of the 2nd bright blue printed in lithography were detected after having been rejected by the sorting equipment. These show the Queen's head in bright greenish blue, have a fluorescent, rather than a phosphor, band and show matt, colourless gum on the reverse. These forgeries come from booklets of ten which also have forged covers.

For self-adhesive versions in these colours see Nos. 2039/40 and 2295/6.

COMMEMORATIVE BOOKLET PANES. Booklets of four 1st Class stamps with *se-tenant* commemorative label were issued for the following anniversaries or events:

300th Anniversary of the Bank of England (No. 1666*l*)
Birth Centenary of R. J. Mitchell (No. 1666*l*a)
70th Birthday of Queen Elizabeth II (No. 1666*l*a)
"Hong Kong '97" International Stamp Exhibition (No. 1666*l*a)
Commonwealth Heads of Government Meeting, Edinburgh (No. 1666*l*a)
50th Birthday of Prince of Wales (No. 1666*l*a)
50th Anniversary of Berlin Airlift (No. 1664*a*m)
Rugby World Cup (No. 1664*a*m)

First Day Covers

21.4.97	1st (No. 1664*b*), 26p. (Y1683*b*) (Type G) (Philatelic Bureau or Windsor)	3·50
23.9.97	B.B.C. label pane 1st × 4, 26p × 4 (No. 1664*b*l), (Philatelic Bureau or London W1)	15·00
19.1.99	E (No. 1664*c*) (Type G) (Philatelic Bureau or Windsor)	3·50
16.2.99	"Profile on Print" label pane 1st × 8 (No. 1666*n*) (see Nos. 2077/9) (Philatelic Bureau or London SW1)	5·50
6.2.02	"A Gracious Accession" label pane 2nd × 4 and E × 4 (No. 1663*a*n) (see Nos. 2253/7) (Tallents House or Windsor)	5·00
24.9.02	"Across the Universe" label pane 1st × 4, E × 4 (No. 1664*b*m) (Tallents House or Star, Glenrothes)	5·00
25.2.03	"Microcosmos" label pane 1st × 4, E × 4 (No. 1664*b*n) (Tallents House or Cambridge)	5·00
2.6.03	"A Perfect Coronation" label pane 2nd × 4, 1st × 4 (No. 1663*a*o) (Tallents House or London SW1)	4·00
16.3.04	"Letters by Night A Tribute to the Travelling Post Office" label pane 1st × 4, 37p × 4 (No. 1664*b*o) (Tallents House or London NW10)	5·25

Special First Day of Issue Postmarks

1993 (27 Apr)–**2003**. *As Nos. X841, etc, but P 15 × 14 (with one elliptical hole on each vertical side).*

(a) Photo

Enschedé: – 20p. (Y1677), 29p., 35p. (Y1688), 36p., 38p. (Y1692), 41p. (Y1696), 43p. (Y1699)

Harrison/De La Rue: – 7p., 8p., 20p. (Y1679/80), 25p. (Y1681), 33p., 35p. (Y1689), 37p. (Y1691a), 41p. (Y1697/8), 42p., 43p. (Y1700), 44p., 45p., 47p., 68p.

Walsall: – 10p. (Y1674a), 19p. (Y1676), 38p. (Y1693a), 43p. (Y1700a)

Enschedé or Harrison/De La Rue or Questa: – 4p., 5p., 6p., 10p. (Y1674), 25p. (Y1682), 31p., 39p., 50p., £1

Enschedé, Harrison/De La Rue or Questa: – 1p., 2p.

Enschedé, Harrison/De La Rue or Walsall: – 30p., 37p. (Y1691), 63p.

Harrison/De La Rue or Questa: – 19p. (Y1675), 20p. (Y1678), 26p. (Y1683/b)

De La Rue or Walsall: – 38p. (Y1693), 40p., 64p., 65p.

De La Rue: – 34p. (Y1687a), £1.50, £2, £3, £5

Y1667	**367**	1p. crimson (2 bands) (8.6.93)	15	15
		l. Booklet pane. Nos. Y1667 × 2, Y1678 and Y1683 × 3 plus 2 labels (1.12.98) ..	8·50	
		m. Booklet pane. Nos. Y1667/8, Y1675, Y1683 × 3 plus 2 labels (26.4.99)	6·00	
		n. Booklet pane. Nos. Y1667 × 4, Y1675 × 3 and Y1683 with central label and margins all round (21.9.99)	3·25	
Y1668		2p. dp green (2 bands) (11.4.95)	15	15
Y1669		4p. new blue (2 bands) (14.12.93)	15	15
Y1670		5p. dull red-brown (2 bands) (8.6.93)	20	20
Y1671		6p. yellow-olive (2 bands)	25	30
Y1672		Ey. Phosphor omitted		
		7p. grey (2 bands) (20.4.99)	35	35
Y1673		8p. yellow (2 bands) (25.4.00)	35	35
Y1674		10p. dull orange (2 bands) (8.6.93)	30	30
		a. Perf 14 (13.10.98)	2·00	2·00
		al. Booklet pane. Nos. Y1674a × 2, 1663bEc and Y1700a, each × 3, with centre label and margins all round	12·00	
Y1675		19p. bistre (1 centre band) (26.10.93)	60	60
		a. Imperf (pair)	£400	
		l. Booklet pane. Nos. Y1675 and Y1683 × 7 (26.4.99)	6·50	
		Ey. Phosphor omitted	75·00	
Y1676		19p. bistre (1 band at right) (p 14) (15.2.00)	2·00	2·00
		l. Booklet pane. Nos. Y1676 × 4 and Y1693a × 2 with margins all round ...	14·00	
Y1677		20p. turquoise-green (2 bands) (14.12.93) ..	90	90
Y1678		20p. brt green (1 centre band) (25.6.96)	70	70
		a. Imperf (horiz pair)	£250	
		l. Booklet pane. Nos. Y1678 and Y1683 × 7 (1.12.98)	14·00	
Y1679		20p. brt green (1 band at right) (23.9.97) ...	1·40	1·40
		l. Booklet pane. Nos. Y1679 and Y1683, each × 3 with margins all round	6·50	
Y1680		20p. brt green (2 bands) (20.4.99)	30	35
Y1681		25p. rose-red (phosphorised paper) (26.10.93)	1·10	1·10
		a. Imperf (pair)	£450	
		l. Booklet pane. No. Y1681 × 2 plus 2 labels (1.11.93)	2·25	
Y1682		25p. rose-red (2 bands) (20.12.94)	1·10	1·10
		l. Booklet pane. No. Y1682 × 2 plus 2 labels (6.6.95)	3·50	
Y1683		26p. red-brown (2 bands) (25.6.96)	1·10	1·10
		a. Imperf (pair)		
Y1683b		26p. gold (2 bands) (21.4.97)	1·00	1·00
		ba. Imperf (horiz pair)	£2000	
Y1684		29p. grey (2 bands) (26.10.93)	1·25	1·25
Y1685		30p. dp olive-grey (2 bands) (27.7.93)	1·10	1·10
Y1686		31p. dp mauve (2 bands) (25.6.96)	1·10	1·10
Y1687		33p. grey-green (2 bands) (25.4.00)	1·20	1·20
Y1687a		34p. yellow-olive (2 bands) (6.5.03)	55	60

Y1688	**367**	35p. yellow (2 bands) (17.8.93)	1·40	1·50
Y1689		35p. yellow (phosphorised paper) (1.11.93) .	6·75	6·75
Y1690		36p. brt ultramarine (2 bands) (26.10.93) ...	1·50	1·50
Y1691		37p. brt mauve (2 bands) (25.6.96)	1·40	1·40
Y1691a		37p. grey-black (2 bands) (4.7.02)	1·10	1·10
Y1692		38p. rosine (2 bands) (26.10.93)	1·50	1·50
		a. Imperf (pair)	£250	
Y1693		38p. ultramarine (2 bands) (20.4.99)	1·50	1·50
		a. Perf 14 (15.2.00)	6·00	6·00
Y1694		39p. brt magenta (2 bands) (25.6.96)	1·25	1·40
		a. Imperf (pair)		
Y1695		40p. dp azure (2 bands) (25.4.00)	1·20	1·20
Y1696		41p. grey-brown (2 bands) (26.10.93)	1·40	1·40
Y1697		41p. drab (phosphorised paper) (1.11.93) ...	6·75	6·75
Y1698		41p. rosine (2 bands) (25.4.00)	1·20	1·20
Y1698a		42p. dp olive-grey (2 bands) (4.7.02)	1·20	1·20
Y1699		43p. dp olive-brown (2 bands) (25.6.96)	1·75	1·75
Y1700		43p. sepia (2 bands) (8.7.96)	2·00	2·00
		a. Perf 14 (13.10.98)	2·00	2·00
Y1701		44p. grey-brown (2 bands) (20.4.99)	1·90	1·90
Y1702		45p. brt mauve (2 bands) (25.4.00)	1·20	1·20
Y1702a		47p. turquoise-green (2 bands) (4.7.02)	1·40	1·40
Y1703		50p. ochre (2 bands) (14.12.93)	1·40	1·00
		a. Imperf (pair)		
Y1704		63p. lt emerald (2 bands) (25.6.96)	2·00	2·00
Y1705		64p. turquoise-green (2 bands) (20.4.99)	2·10	2·10
Y1706		65p. greenish blue (2 bands) (25.4.00)	1·80	1·80
Y1706a		68p. grey-brown (2 bands) (4.7.02)	1·80	1·80
Y1707		£1 bluish violet (2 bands) (22.8.95)	3·00	2·70
		a. Imperf (horiz pair)	£1100	
Y1708		£1.50 brown-red (2 bands) (1.7.03)	2·25	2·40
Y1709		£2 deep blue-green (2 bands) (1.7.03)	3·00	3·25
		a. Missing "£" in value (R. 18/19), Cyl D1 no dot)		
Y1710		£3 deep mauve (2 bands) (1.7.03)	4·50	4·75
Y1711		£5 azure (2 bands) (1.7.03)	7·50	7·75

(b) Litho Walsall (37p., 60p., 63p.), Questa or Walsall (25p., 35p., 41p.), Questa (others)

Y1743	**367**	1p. lake (2 bands) (8.7.96)	40	40
		Ey. Phosphor omitted	£350	
		l. Booklet pane. Nos. Y1743 × 2, Y1751 and Y1753 × 3 plus 2 labels	5·00	
		lEy. Booklet pane. Phosphor omitted		
Y1748		6p. yellow-olive (2 bands) (26.7.94)	12·00	13·00
		l. Booklet pane. Nos. Y1748, Y1750 and Y1752 × 4 with margins all round	15·00	
		la. 6p. value misplaced		
Y1749		10p. dull orange (2 bands) (25.4.95)	4·75	4·75
		l. Booklet pane. Nos. Y1749, Y1750/Ea, Y1752 × 2, Y1754/5, Y1757Ea and centre label with margins all round	18·00	
		lEy. Booklet pane. Phosphor omitted		
Y1750		19p. bistre (1 band at left) (26.7.94)	1·90	1·75
		Ea. Band at right (25.4.95)	2·50	2·50
		l. Booklet pane. Nos. Y1750/Ea, each × 3 with margins all round (25.4.95)	14·00	
Y1751		20p. brt yellow-green (1 centre band) (8.7.96)	1·90	1·90
		Ey. Phosphor omitted	£200	
		l. Booklet pane. Nos. Y1751 and Y1753 × 7	8·00	
		lEy. Booklet pane. Phosphor omitted		
Y1752		25p. red (2 bands) (1.11.93)	1·00	1·00
		l. Booklet pane. Nos. Y1752, NI72, S84 and W73, each × 2, with centre label and margins all round (14.5.96)	7·50	
Y1753		26p. chestnut (2 bands) (8.7.96)	1·00	1·00
		Ey. Phosphor omitted	50·00	

Y1754	30p. olive-grey (2 bands) (25.4.95)	4·00	4·00
Y1755	35p. yellow (2 bands) (1.11.93)	1·60	1·60
Y1756	37p. brt mauve (2 bands) (8.7.96)	2·40	2·40
Y1757	41p. drab (2 bands) (1.11.93)	1·75	1·75
	Ea. Grey-brown (25.4.95)	3·50	3·50
	Ey. Phosphor omitted		
Y1758	60p. dull blue-grey (2 bands) (9.8.94)	2·50	2·50
Y1759	63p. lt emerald (2 bands) (8.7.96)	3·00	3·00
	Ey. Phosphor omitted		

(c) Eng C. Slania. Recess Enschedé (until Mar 2000) *or De La Rue (from* 11 Apr 2000)

Y1800	**367**	£1.50, red (9.3.99)	4·80	2·00
Y1801		£2 dull blue (9.3.99)	6·00	2·25
Y1802		£3 dull violet (9.3.99)	9·00	3·00
Y1803		£5 brown (9.3.99)	15·00	5·00
		P.H.Q. Card (No. Y1707)	40	3·00

No. Y1682 exists with the phosphor bands omitted, but can only be identified by the use of a u.v. lamp (*Price £24 unused*).

Nos. Y1707/11 are printed in Iriodin ink which gives a shiny effect to the solid part of the background behind the Queen's head.

No. Y1748la shows the 6p. value printed 22 mm to the left so that its position on the booklet pane is completely blank except for the phosphor bands. Other more minor misplacements exist.

The De La Rue printings of the high values, Nos. Y1800/3, cannot easily be identified from the original Enschedé issue as single stamps. For self-adhesive versions of the 42p. and 68p. see Nos. 2297/8.

First Day Covers

26.10.93	19p., 25p., 29p., 36p., 38p., 41p. (Y1675, Y1681, Y1684, Y1690, Y1692, Y1696) ...	6·00
9.8.94	60p. (Y1758)	4·00
25.4.95	National Trust *se-tenant* pane 10p., 19p., 25p., 30p., 35p., 41p. (Y1749l)	5·00
22.8.95	£1 (Y1707)	3·50
14.5.96	European Football Championship *se-tenant* pane 25p. × 8 (Y1752l)	7·50
25.6.96	20p., 26p., 31p., 37p., 39p., 43p., 63p. (Y1678, Y1683, Y1686, Y1691, Y1694, Y1699, Y1704)	8·00
13.10.98	Speed *se-tenant* pane 10p., 2nd, 43p. (Y1674al)	6·50
9.3.99	£1·50, £2, £3, £5 (Y1800/3) (Type G) (Philatelic Bureau or Windsor)	27·00
20.4.99	7p., 38p., 44p., 64p. (Y1672, Y1693, Y1701, Y1705) (Type G) (Philatelic Bureau or Windsor)	5·00
21.9.99	World Changers *se-tenant* pane 1p., 19p., 26p. (Y1667n) (Philatelic Bureau or Downe, Orpington)	4·00
25.4.00	8p., 33p., 40p., 41p., 45p., 65p. (Y1673, Y1687, Y1695, Y1698, Y1702, Y1706) (Type G) (Philatelic Bureau or Windsor) .	5·00
4.7.02	37p., 42p., 47p., 68p. (Y1691a, Y1698a, Y1702a, Y1706a) (Type K) (Tallents House or Windsor)	4·00
6.5.03	34p., (Y1687a) (Type K) (Tallents House or Windsor)	1·25
1.7.03	£1·50, £2, £3, £5 (Nos. Y1708/11) (Type K) (Tallents House or Windsor)	21·00

Post Office Presentation Packs

26.10.93	P.O. Pack No. 30. 19p. (1 centre band), 25p. (phos paper), 29p., 36p., 38p. rosine, 41p. grey-brown (Nos. Y1675, Y1681, Y1684, Y1690, Y1692, Y1696)	8·00

21.11.95	P.O. Pack No. 34. 1p. (photo), 2p., 4p., 5p., 6p. (photo), 10p. (photo), 19p. (1 centre band), 20p. turquoise-green, 25p. (photo) (2 bands), 29p., 30p. (photo), 35p. (photo) (2 bands), 36p., 38p. rosine, 41p. grey-brown, 50p., 60p., £1 (Nos. Y1667/71, Y1674/5, Y1677, Y1682, Y1684/5, Y1688, Y1690, Y1692, Y1696, Y1703, Y1758, Y1707)	17·00
25.6.96	P.O. Pack No. 35. 20p. brt green (1 centre band), 26p. (photo), 31p., 37p. (photo), 39p., 43p. deep olive-brown, 63p. (photo) (Nos. Y1678, Y1683, Y1686, Y1691, Y1694, Y1699, Y1704)	8·00
21.4.97	P.O. Pack No. 38. 1st, 26p. gold (Nos. 1664b, Y1683b)	3·50
20.10.98	P.O. Pack No. 41. 2nd brt blue (1 centre band), 1st brt orange-red (2 phosphor bands), 1p., 2p., 4p., 5p., 6p., 10p., 20p. brt green (1 centre band), 26p., 30p., 31p., 37p., 39p., 43p. sepia, 50p., 63p., £1, (Nos. 1663a, 1664a, Y1667/71, Y1674, Y1678, Y1683, Y1685/6, Y1691, Y1694, Y1700, Y1703/4, Y1707)	12·00
9.3.99	P.O. Pack No. 43 or 43a. £1·50, £2, £3, £5 (Nos. Y1800/3)	35·00
20.4.99	P.O. Pack No. 44. 7p., 19p., 38p. ultramarine, 44p., 64p. (Nos. Y1672, Y1675, Y1693, Y1701, Y1705)	5·50
25.4.00	P.O. Pack No. 49. 8p., 33p., 40p., 41p. rosine, 45p., 65p. (Nos. Y1673, Y1687, Y1695, Y1698, Y1702, Y1706)	7·50
12.3.02	P.O. Pack No. 57. 2nd, 1st, E, 1p., 2p., 4p., 5p., 8p., 10p., 20p., 33p., 40p., 41p., 45p., 50p., 65p., £1. (Nos. 1663a, 1664a/b., Y1667/70, Y1673/4, Y1680, Y1687, Y1695, Y1698, Y1702/3, Y1706/7)	12·00
4.7.02	P.O. Pack No. 58. 37p., 42p., 47p., 68p. (Nos. Y1691a, Y1698a, Y1702a, Y1706a) .	5·00
1.7.03	P.O. Pack No. 62. £1·50, £2, £3, £5 (Nos. Y1708/11)	18·00

187

Advert on this page 188
—SG London Stamps (Full Page)
—GBC 12

DECIMAL MACHIN, INCLUDING N.V.Is., WITH ELLIPTICAL PERFORATIONS INDEX

Val.	Process and Printer	Colour	Phosphor	Cat No.	Source
2nd	litho Questa or Walsall	brt blue	1 centre band	1665	sheets (Questa), booklets of 4 (Walsall–HA6, Walsall HA9/11), booklets of 10 (Questa–HC11, HC13, HC16, HC18, HC20, Walsall–HC12)
2nd	photo Harrison/De La Rue), Enschedé, Questa or Walsall	brt blue	1 centre band	1663a	sheets (Walsall), horizontal coil (Harrison/De La Rue), vertical coils (Harrison/De La Rue or Enschedé) booklets of 4 (Harrison–HA7/8, Walsall–HA12), booklets of 10 (Harrison/ De La Rue–HC14/15, HC17, HC19, HC21), £1 booklet (Questa–FH44/a), £2 booklet (Questa–FW12), £7.29 "A Gracious Accession" booklet (Enschedé–DX28), £7.46 "A Perfect Coronation" booklet (Walsall–DX31)
2nd	photo Walsall (p 14)	brt blue	1 band at right	1663b	£6.16 British Land Speed Record Holders booklet (DX21)
2nd	photo Walsall (p 14)	brt blue	1 band at left	1663bEc	£6.16 British Land Speed Record Holders booklet (DX21)
2nd	photo Questa (p 14)	brt blue	1 centre band	1663ab	booklets of 10 (HC22)
1st	litho Enschedè, Questa or Walsall	brt orange-red	2 bands	1666	sheets (Questa), greetings card panes (Questa–Y1666m/ma, Enschedé–Y1666mb), booklets of 4 (Walsall–HB6, HB8/13, HB15/16, Questa–HB7), booklets of 10 (Walsall–HD10, HD12/19, HD22/3, HD25, HD28, HD34, HD36/8, HD40, Questa–HD11, HD21, HD26, HD50), £7.54 "Profile on Print" booklet (Questa–DX22)
1st	photo Harrison	brt orange-red	phos paper	1664	booklets of 4 (HB5), booklets of 10 (HD9, HD20)
1st	photo Harrison/De La Rue, Questa or Walsall	brt orange-red	2 bands	1664a	sheets (Walsall), horizontal and vertical coils (Harrison, De La Rue), booklets of 4 (Walsall–HB14, HB17/18), booklets of 8 with 2 Millennium commems (Walsall–HBA1/2), booklets of 10 (Harrison/De La Rue–HD24, HD27, HD29/33, HD35, HD39, HD45/9, Walsall–HD44), £1 booklet (Questa–FH44/a), £2 booklet (Questa–FW12), £7.54 "Profile on Print" booklet (De La Rue - DX22)
1st	photo Questa (p 14)	brt orange-red	2 bands	1664ab	booklets of 10 (HD51)
1st	photo De La Rue, Enschedé, Harrison, Questa or Walsall	gold	2 bands	1664b	sheets (Walsall, De La Rue), vertical coils (Enschedé, De La Rue), booklets of 10 (Harrison–HD41, HD43, Walsall–HD42), £6.15 B.B.C. booklet (Harrison–DX19), £6.83 "Across the Universe" booklet (Questa–DX29), £6.99 "Microcosmos" booklet (Enschedé–DX30), £7.46 "A Perfect Coronation" booklet (Walsall–DX31), £7.44 "Letters by Night" booklet (De La Rue–DX32)
E	photo De La Rue, Enschedé, Questa or Walsall	deep blue	2 bands	1664c	sheets (De La Rue), booklets of 4 (Walsall–HF1), £7.29 "A Gracious Accession" booklet (Enschedé–DX28), £6.83 "Across the Universe" booklet (Questa–DX29), £6.99 "Microcosmos" booklet (Enschedé–DX30
1p.	photo De La Rue Enschedé, Harrison or Questa	crimson	2 bands	Y1667	sheets, £1 booklets (Questa–FH42/3), £6.91 World Changers booklet (Questa–DX23)
1p.	litho Questa	lake	2 bands	Y1743	£1 booklet (FH41)
2p.	photo De La Rue, Enschedé, Harrison or Questa	dp green	2 bands	Y1668	sheets, £1 booklet (Questa–FH43)
4p.	photo De La Rue, Enschedé or Harrison	new blue	2 bands	Y1669	sheets
4p.	photo De La Rue	new blue	phos paper	MS2146	Jeffrey Matthews Colour Palette miniature sheet
5p.	photo De La Rue, Enschedé or Harrison	dull red-brown	2 bands	Y1670	sheets
5p.	photo De La Rue	dull red-brown	phos paper	MS2146	Jeffrey Matthews Colour Palette miniature sheet
6p.	photo Enschedé or Harrison	yellow-olive	2 bands	Y1671	sheets
6p.	litho Questa	yellow-olive	2 bands	Y1748	£6.04 Northern Ireland booklet (DX16)
6p.	photo De La Rue	yellow-olive	phos paper	MS2146	Jeffrey Matthews Colour Palette miniature sheet
7p.	photo De La Rue	grey	2 bands	Y1672	sheets
8p.	photo De La Rue	yellow	2 bands	Y1673	sheets
10p.	photo De La Rue, Enschedé or Harrison	dull orange	2 bands	Y1674	sheets

Val.	Process and Printer	Colour	Phosphor	Cat No.	Source
10p.	litho Questa	dull orange	2 bands	Y1749	£6 National Trust booklet (DX17)
10p.	photo Walsall (p 14)	dull orange	2 bands	Y1674a	£6.16 British Land Speed Record Holders booklet (DX21)
10p.	photo De La Rue	dull orange	phos paper	**MS**2146	Jeffrey Matthews Colour Palette miniature sheet
19p.	photo Harrison or Questa	bistre	1 centre band	Y1675	sheets, vertical coils, £1 booklet (Questa–FH43), £2 booklet (Questa–FW11), £6.99 World Changers booklet (Questa–DX23)
19p.	litho Questa	bistre	1 band at left	Y1750	£6.04 Northern Ireland booklet (DX16), £6 National Trust booklet (DX17)
19p.	litho Questa	bistre	1 band at right	Y1750Ea	£6 National Trust booklet (DX17)
19p.	photo Walsall (p 14)	bistre	1 band at right	Y1676	£7.50 "Special by Design" booklet (DX24)
20p.	photo Enschedé	turquoise-green	2 bands	Y1677	sheets
20p.	photo Harrison or Questa	brt green	1 centre band	Y1678	sheets, £1 booklet (Questa–FH42), £2 booklet (Questa–FW10)
20p.	litho Questa	brt yellow-green	1 centre band	Y1751	£1 booklet (FH41), £2 booklet (FW9)
20p.	photo Harrison	brt green	1 band at right	Y1679	£6.15 B.B.C. booklet (DX19)
20p.	photo De La Rue	brt green	2 bands	Y1680	sheets
25p.	photo Harrison	rose-red	phos paper	Y1681	sheets, vertical coils, 50p booklets (FB67/73), £1 booklets (FH33/7), £2 booklets (FW1/5)
25p	litho Walsall or Questa	red	2 bands	Y1752	£1 booklets (Walsall–FH31/2), (Questa–FH40), £2 booklet (Questa–FW8), £6.04 Northern Ireland booklet (Questa–DX16), £6 National Trust booklet (Questa–DX17), £6.84 European Football Championship (Questa–DX18)
25p.	photo Harrison or Enschedé	rose-red	2 bands	Y1682	sheets (Harrison or Enschedé), vertical coils (Harrison), 50p booklets (Harrison–FB74/5), £1 booklets (Harrison–H38/9)), £2 booklets (Harrison–FW6/7)
26p.	photo Harrison or Questa	red-brown	2 bands	Y1683	sheets, £1 booklets (Questa–FH42/3), £2 booklets (Questa–FW10/11), £6.15 B.B.C. booklet (Harrison–DX19), £6.99 World Changers booklet (Questa–DX23)
26p.	litho Questa	chestnut	2 bands	Y1753	£1 booklet (FH41), £2 booklet (FW9)
26p.	photo Harrison	gold	2 bands	Y1683b	sheets, £6.15 B.B.C. booklet (Harrison–DX19)
29p.	photo Enschedé	grey	2 bands	Y1684	sheets
30p.	photo Enschedé, Harrison or Walsall	dp olive-grey	2 bands	Y1685	sheets, £1.20 booklets (Walsall–GGA1/2)
30p.	litho Questa	olive-grey	2 bands	Y1754	£6 National Trust booklet (DX17)
31p.	photo Enschedé or Harrison	dp mauve	2 bands	Y1686	sheets
31p.	photo De La Rue	dp mauve	phos paper	**MS**2146	Jeffrey Matthews Colour Palette miniature sheet
33p.	photo De La Rue	grey-green	2 bands	Y1687	sheets
34p.	photo De La Rue	yellow-olive	2 bands	Y1687a	sheets
35p.	photo Enschedé	yellow	2 bands	Y1688	sheets
35p.	photo Harrison	yellow	phos paper	Y1689	vertical coils
35p.	litho Walsall or Questa	yellow	2 bands	Y1755	£1.40 booklets (Walsall–GK5/7), £6 National Trust booklet (Questa–DX17)
36p.	photo Enschedé	brt ultramarine	2 bands	Y1690	sheets
37p.	photo Enschedé, Harrison or Walsall	brt mauve	2 bands	Y1691	sheets (Enschedé or Harrison), vertical coils (Harrison), £1.48 booklets (Walsall–GL3/4)
37p.	litho Walsall	brt mauve	2 bands	Y1756	£1.48 booklets (GL1/2)
37p.	photo De La Rue	grey-black	2 bands	Y1691a	sheets, £7.44 "Letters by Night" booklet (De La Rue–DX32)
38p.	photo Enschedé	rosine	2 bands	Y1692	sheets
38p.	photo De La Rue or Walsall	ultramarine	2 bands	Y1693	sheets (D.L.R.), £1.52 booklet (Walsall–GLA1)
38p.	photo Walsall (p 14)	ultramarine	2 bands	Y1693a	£7.50 "Special by Design" booklet (DX24)
39p.	photo Enschedé or Harrison	brt magenta	2 bands	Y1694	sheets
39p.	photo De La Rue	brt magenta	phos paper	**MS**2146	Jeffrey Matthews Colour Palette miniature sheet
40p.	photo De La Rue or Walsall	deep azure	2 bands	Y1695	sheets (D.L.R.), £1.60 booklet (Walsall–GMA1)
41p.	photo Enschedé	grey-brown	2 bands	Y1696	sheets
41p.	photo Harrison	drab	phos paper	Y1697	vertical coils
41p.	photo De La Rue	rosine	2 bands	Y1698	sheets
41p.	litho Walsall	drab	2 bands	Y1757	£1.64 booklets (GN1/3)
41p.	litho Questa	grey-brown	2 bands	Y1757Ea	£6 National Trust booklet (DX17)
42p.	photo De La Rue	dp olive-grey	2 bands	Y1698a	sheets

Val.	Process and Printer	Colour	Phosphor	Cat No.	Source
43p.	photo Enschedé	dp olive-brown	2 bands	Y1699	sheets
43p.	photo Harrison	sepia	2 bands	Y1700	sheets, vertical coils
43p.	photo Walsall (p 14)	sepia	2 bands	Y1700a	£6.16 British Land Speed Record Holders booklet (DX21)
44p.	photo De La Rue	grey-brown	2 bands	Y1701	sheets
45p.	photo De La Rue	brt mauve	2 bands	Y1702	sheets
47p.	photo De La Rue	turquoise-green	2 bands	Y1702a	sheets
50p.	photo Enschedé or Harrison	ochre	2 bands	Y1703	sheets
60p.	litho Walsall	dull blue-grey	2 bands	Y1758	£2.40 booklets (GQ1/4)
63p.	photo Enschedé, Harrison or Walsall	lt emerald	2 bands	Y1704	sheets (Enschedé or Harrison), vertical coils (Harrison), £2.52 booklets (Walsall–GR3/4)
63p.	litho Walsall	lt emerald	2 bands	Y1759	£2.52 booklets (GR1/2)
64p.	photo De La Rue or Walsall	turquoise-green	2 bands	Y1705	sheets (D.L.R.), £2.56 booklet (Walsall–GS1)
64p.	photo De La Rue	turquoise-green	phos paper	**MS**2146	Jeffrey Matthews Colour Palette miniature sheet
65p.	photo De La Rue or Walsall	greenish blue	2 bands	Y1706	sheets (D.L.R.), £2.60 booklet (Walsall–GT1)
68p.	photo De La Rue	grey-brown	2 bands	Y1706a	sheets
£1	photo Enschedé or Harrison	bluish violet	2 bands	Y1707	sheets
£1	photo De La Rue	bluish violet	phos paper	**MS**2146	Jeffrey Matthews Colour Palette miniature sheet
£1.50	recess	red	—	Y1800	sheets (Enschedé then D.L.R.)
£1.50	photo De La Rue	brown-red	2 bands	Y1708	sheets
£2	recess	dull blue	—	Y1801	sheets (Enschedé then D.L.R.)
£2	photo De La Rue	deep blue-green	2 bands	Y1709	sheets
£3	recess	dull violet	—	Y1802	sheets (Enschedé then D.L.R.)
£3	photo De La Rue	deep mauve	2 bands	Y1710	sheets
£5	recess	brown	—	Y1803	sheets (Enschedé then D.L.R.)
£5	photo De La Rue	azure	2 bands	Y1711	sheets

Note. Harrison and Sons became De La Rue Security Print on 8 September 1997.

1094 "Family Group"
(bronze sculpture)
(Henry Moore)

1095 "Kew Gardens"
(lithograph)
(Edward Bawden)

1098 Emperor Claudius
(from gold coin)

1099 Emperor Hadrian
(bronze head)

1100 Goddess Roma
(from gemstone)

1101 Christ
(Hinton St. Mary mosaic)

(Des J. Gibbs)

1096 "St. Francis and the Birds"
(Stanley Spencer)

1097 "Still Life: Odyssey I"
(Ben Nicholson)

1993 (15 June). **Roman Britain.** *Phosphorised paper with two phosphor bands.* P 14 × 14½.

1771	**1098**	24p. black, pale orange, lt brown & silver ..	60	20
1772	**1099**	28p. black, greenish yellow, brt rose-red, silver, brt blue & grey-black	90	1·00
1773	**1100**	33p. black, greenish yellow, brt rose-red, silver & grey	1·25	1·40
1774	**1101**	39p. black, greenish yellow, rosine, silver, pale violet & grey	1·40	1·40
		Set of 4	3·75	3·50
		Set of 4 Gutter Pairs	8·00	
		First Day Cover		4·00
		Presentation Pack	4·50	
		PHQ Cards (set of 4)	4·00	6·50

(Des. A. Dastor)

1993 (11 May). **Europa. Contemporary Art.** *Phosphorised paper.* P 14 × 14½.

1767	**1094**	24p. brownish grey, lemon, magenta, turquoise-blue & grey-black	60	20
1768	**1095**	28p. brownish grey, buff, lt green, yellow-brown, brt orange, new blue & grey-black	90	1·00
1769	**1096**	33p. brownish grey, cream, greenish yellow, magenta, new blue & grey-black	1·25	1·40
1770	**1097**	39p. brownish grey, cream, yellow-ochre, rose-lilac, red, lt blue & grey-black ...	1·40	1·40
		Set of 4	3·75	3·50
		Set of 4 Gutter Pairs	8·00	
		First Day Cover		4·00
		Presentation Pack	4·50	
		PHQ Cards (set of 4)	4·00	6·50

Special First Day of Issue Postmarks

British Philatelic Bureau, Edinburgh .... 4·50
Caerllion .... 4·50

Special First Day of Issue Postmarks

British Philatelic Bureau, Edinburgh .... 4·50
London SW .... 4·50

1102 *Midland Maid* and
other Narrow Boats,
Grand Junction Canal

1103 *Yorkshire Lass* and
other Humber Keels,
Stainforth and Keadby Canal

1104 *Valley Princess* and other Horse-drawn Barges, Brecknock and Abergavenny Canal

1105 Steam Barges, including *Pride of Scotland,* and Fishing Boats, Crinan Canal

(Des T. Lewery. Litho Questa)

1993 (20 July). **Inland Waterways.** *Two phosphor bands.* P 14½ × 14.

1775	**1102**	24p.	new blue, greenish yellow, brt magenta, black, blue, vermilion, brownish grey & sage-green	60	20
1776	**1103**	28p.	new blue, greenish yellow, brt magenta, black, blue, bluish grey, vermilion & sage-green	95	1·00
1777	**1104**	33p.	new blue, greenish yellow, brt magenta, black, blue, vermilion, greenish grey & sage-green	1·25	1·25
1778	**1105**	39p.	new blue, greenish yellow, brt magenta, black, blue, vermilion, sage-green & dull mauve	1·50	1·40
			Set of 4	4·00	3·50
			Set of 4 Gutter Pairs	9·00	
			First Day Cover		4·25
			Presentation Pack	4·50	
			PHQ Cards (set of 4)	4·00	8·00

Nos. 1775/8 commemorate the bicentenary of the Acts of Parliament authorising the canals depicted.

Special First Day of Issue Postmarks

British Philatelic Bureau, Edinburgh	4·50
Gloucester	4·50

1106 Horse Chestnut

1107 Blackberry

1108 Hazel

1109 Rowan

1110 Pear

(Des Charlotte Knox)

1993 (14 Sept). **The Four Seasons. Autumn. Fruits and Leaves.** *One phosphor band* (18p.) *or phosphorised paper* (others). P 15 × 14.

1779	**1106**	18p.	black, greenish yellow, cerise, brt green, gold & chestnut	50	20
1780	**1107**	24p.	black, lemon, cerise, myrtle-green, gold, brt green & brown	75	20
1781	**1108**	28p.	grey, lemon, emerald, lake-brown & gold	1·10	1·25
1782	**1109**	33p.	grey-black, greenish yellow, rosine, lt green, gold & brown	1·40	1·50
1783	**1110**	39p.	myrtle-green, greenish yellow, rosine, olive-sepia, gold, apple-green & dp myrtle-green	1·50	1·50
			Set of 5	4·75	4·25
			Set of 5 Gutter Pairs	10·50	
			First Day Cover		5·00
			Presentation Pack	5·25	
			PHQ Cards (set of 5)	5·00	8·00

Special First Day of Issue Postmarks

British Philatelic Bureau, Edinburgh	5·25
Taunton	5·25

1111 *The Reigate Squire*

1112 *The Hound of the Baskervilles*

SHERLOCK HOLMES & LESTRADE
"THE SIX NAPOLEONS"

SHERLOCK HOLMES & MYCROFT
"THE GREEK INTERPRETER"

1113 *The Six Napoleons*   **1114** *The Greek Interpreter*

SHERLOCK HOLMES & MORIARTY
"THE FINAL PROBLEM"

1115 *The Final Problem*

(Des A. Davidson. Litho Questa)

1993 (12 Oct).   **Sherlock Holmes. Centenary of the Publication of
"The Final Problem".** *Phosphorised paper. P* 14 × 14½.

1784	**1111**	24p. new blue, greenish yellow, magenta, black & gold	1·10	1·10
		a. Horiz strip of 5. Nos. 1784/8	5·00	5·00
1785	**1112**	24p. new blue, greenish yellow, magenta, black & gold	1·10	1·10
1786	**1113**	24p. new blue, greenish yellow, magenta, black & gold	1·10	1·10
1787	**1114**	24p. new blue, greenish yellow, magenta, black & gold	1·10	1·10
1788	**1115**	24p. new blue, greenish yellow, magenta, black & gold	1·10	1·10
		Set of 5	5·00	5·00
		Gutter strip of 10	11·00	
		First Day Cover		6·50
		Presentation Pack	6·00	
		PHQ Cards (set of 5)	5·00	10·00

Nos. 1784/8 were printed together, *se-tenant*, in horizontal strips of 5
throughout the sheet.

Special First Day of Issue Postmarks

British Philatelic Bureau, Edinburgh .... 6·50
London NW1 .... 6·50
A First Day of Issue handstamp was provided at Autumn Stampex,
London SW1, for this issue.

1116

(Des J. Matthews. Litho Walsall)

1993 (19 Oct)   *Self-adhesive. Two phosphor bands. Die-cut P* 14 × 15
(with one elliptical hole on each vertical side).

1789	**1116**	(1st) orange-red	1·25	1·40
		Ey. Phosphor omitted		
		a. Booklet pane. No. 1789 × 20	18·00	
		aEy. Booklet pane. Phosphor omitted		
		First Day Cover (No. 1789)		4·50
		Presentation Pack (No. 1789a)	20·00	
		PHQ Card	4·00	8·00

No. 1789 was initially sold at 24p. which was increased to 25p. from
November 1993. It was only issued in booklets containing 20 stamps,
each surrounded by die-cut perforations.

For similar 2nd and 1st designs printed in photogravure by Enschedé
see Nos. 1976/7.

Special First Day of Issue Postmarks

British Philatelic Bureau, Edinburgh .... 5·00
Newcastle upon Tyne .... 5·00

1117 Bob Cratchit and Tiny Tim   **1118** Mr. and Mrs. Fezziwig

1119 Scrooge   **1120** The Prize Turkey

1121 Mr. Scrooge's Nephew

(Des Q. Blake)

1993 (9 Nov). **Christmas. 150th Anniv of Publication of "A Christmas Carol" by Charles Dickens.** *One phosphor band* (19p.) *or phosphorised paper* (others). *P* 15 × 14.

1790	**1117**	19p. new blue, yellow, magenta, salmon, brt emerald & grey-black	60	15
		a. Imperf (pair)	£1700	
1791	**1118**	25p. yellow-orange, brown-lilac, steel-blue, lake-brown, lt green, grey-black & black	90	15
1792	**1119**	30p. cerise, bistre-yellow, dull blue, brown-rose, pale green, grey-black & black ..	1·25	1·50
1793	**1120**	35p. dp turquoise-green, lemon, vermilion, dull ultramarine, Indian red, bluish grey & black	1·40	1·60
1794	**1121**	41p. reddish purple, lemon, purple, lt blue, salmon, brt green & black	1·50	1·60
		Set of 5	5·00	4·50
		Set of 5 Gutter Pairs	11·00	
		First Day Cover		5·50
		Presentation Pack	5·75	
		PHQ Cards (set of 5)	5·00	9·00

Special First Day of Issue Postmarks

British Philatelic Bureau, Edinburgh .... 5·75
Bethlehem, Llandeilo .... 5·75
A First Day of Issue handstamp (pictorial) was provided at the City of London for this issue.

Collectors Pack 1993

1993 (9 Nov). *Comprises Nos.* 1639/43, 1654/7, 1659/63, 1767/88 *and* 1790/4.
CP1794a Collectors Pack .... 60·00

Post Office Yearbook

1993 (9 Nov). *Comprises Nos.* 1639/43, 1654/7, 1659/63, 1767/88 *and* 1790/4 *in hardbound book with slip case, illustrated in colour* .... 65·00

GIBBONS STAMP MONTHLY
– finest and most informative magazine for all collectors. Obtainable from your newsagent or by postal subscription – details on request.

1122 Class 5 No. 44957
and Class B1 No. 61342
on West Highland Line

1123 Class A1 No.
60149 *Amadis* at
Kings Cross

1124 Class 4 No. 43000 on
Turntable at Blyth North

1125 Class 4 No. 42455
near Wigan Central

1126 Class "Castle"
No. 7002 *Devizes Castle* on Bridge
crossing Worcester and Birmingham Canal

(Des B. Delaney)

1994 (18 Jan). **The Age of Steam. Railway Photographs by Colin Gifford.** *One phosphor band* (19p.) *or phosphorised paper with two bands* (others). *P* 14½.

1795	**1122**	19p. dp blue-green, grey-black & black	55	25
1796	**1123**	25p. slate-lilac, grey-black & black	90	95
1797	**1124**	30p. lake-brown, grey-black & black	1·40	1·40
1798	**1125**	35p. dp claret, grey-black & black	1·50	1·60
1799	**1126**	41p. indigo, grey-black & black	1·60	1·50
		Set of 5	5·50	5·00
		Set of 5 Gutter Pairs	12·00	
		First Day Cover		5·50
		Presentation Pack	6·25	
		PHQ Cards (set of 5)	5·00	9·00

Nos. 1796/9 are on phosphorised paper and also show two phosphor bands.

Special First Day of Issue Postmarks

Philatelic Bureau, Edinburgh .... 5·75
York .... 5·75
A First Day of Issue handstamp (pictorial) was provided at Bridge of Orchy for this issue.

1127 Dan Dare and the Mekon

1128 The Three Bears

1129 Rupert Bear

1130 Alice (Alice in Wonderland)

1131 Noggin and the Ice Dragon

1132 Peter Rabbit posting Letter

1133 Red Riding Hood and Wolf

1134 Orlando the Marmalade Cat

1135 Biggles

1136 Paddington Bear on Station

(Des Newell and Sorrell)

1994 (1 Feb). **Greetings Stamps. "Messages".** *Two phosphor bands.*
P 15 × 14 (*with one elliptical hole on each vertical side*).

1800	**1127**	(1st) gold, greenish yellow, brt purple, bistre-yellow, new blue & black	1·00	90
		a. Booklet pane. Nos. 1800/9	11·00	
1801	**1128**	(1st) gold, greenish yellow, brt purple, bistre-yellow, new blue & black	1·00	90
1802	**1129**	(1st) gold, greenish yellow, brt purple, bistre-yellow, new blue & black	1·00	90
1803	**1130**	(1st) gold, bistre-yellow & black	1·00	90
1804	**1131**	(1st) gold, greenish yellow, brt purple, bistre-yellow, new blue & black	1·00	90
1805	**1132**	(1st) gold, greenish yellow, brt purple, bistre-yellow, new blue & black	1·00	90
1806	**1133**	(1st) gold, greenish yellow, brt purple, bistre-yellow, new blue & black	1·00	90
1807	**1134**	(1st) gold, greenish yellow, brt purple, bistre-yellow, new blue & black	1·00	90
1808	**1135**	(1st) gold, greenish yellow, brt purple, bistre-yellow, new blue & black	1·00	90
1809	**1136**	(1st) gold, greenish yellow, brt purple, bistre-yellow, new blue & black	1·00	90
		Set of 10	11·00	8·00
		First Day Cover		12·00
		Presentation Pack	20·00	
		PHQ Cards (set of 10)	10·00	22·00

Nos. 1800/9 were issued in £2.50 stamp booklets (sold at £2.60 from 8 July 1996), together with a pane of 20 half stamp-sized labels. The stamps and labels were attached to the booklet cover by a common gutter margin.

Special First Day of Issue Postmarks

British Philatelic Bureau, Edinburgh .... 15·00
Penn, Wolverhampton .... 15·00

1137 Castell Y Waun (Chirk Castle), Clwyd, Wales

1138 Ben Arkle, Sutherland, Scotland

1139 Mourne Mountains, County Down, Northern Ireland

1140 Dersingham, Norfolk, England

1141 Dolwyddelan, Gwynedd, Wales

1994 (1 Mar–26 July). **25th Anniv of Investiture of the Prince of Wales. Paintings by Prince Charles.** *One phosphor band (19p.) or phosphorised paper (others).* P 15 × 14.

1810	**1137**	19p.	grey-black, greenish yellow, magenta, new blue, black & silver	55	20
1811	**1138**	25p.	grey-black, orange-yellow, brt magenta, new blue, silver & black	1·00	20
1812	**1139**	30p.	grey-black, greenish yellow, magenta, new blue, silver & black	1·10	1·40
		a.	Booklet pane. No. 1812 × 4 with margins all round (26 July)	5·00	
1813	**1140**	35p.	grey-black, greenish yellow, magenta, new blue, silver & black	1·40	1·50
1814	**1141**	41p.	grey-black, lemon, magenta, new blue, silver & black	1·50	1·50
			Set of 5	5·00	4·50
			Set of 5 Gutter Pairs	11·00	
			First Day Cover		5·00
			Presentation Pack	5·25	
			PHQ Cards (set of 5)	5·00	9·00

Booklet pane No. 1812a comes from the £6.04 "Northern Ireland" booklet.

Special First Day of Issue Postmarks

British Philatelic Bureau, Edinburgh .... 5·50
Caernarfon .... 5·50

1142 Bather at Blackpool   **1143** "Where's my Little Lad?"

1144 "Wish You were Here!"   **1145** Punch and Judy Show

1146 "The Tower Crane" Machine

(Des M. Dempsey and B. Dare. Litho Questa)

1994 (12 Apr). **Centenary of Picture Postcards.** *One side band (19p.) or two phosphor bands (others).* P 14 × 14½.

1815	**1142**	19p.	new blue, greenish yellow, magenta & black	60	20
1816	**1143**	25p.	new blue, greenish yellow, magenta & black	90	20
1817	**1144**	30p.	new blue, greenish yellow, magenta & black	1·10	1·25
1818	**1145**	35p.	new blue, greenish yellow, magenta & black	1·40	1·50
1819	**1146**	41p.	new blue, greenish yellow, magenta & black	1·50	1·50
			Set of 5	5·00	4·25
			Set of 5 Gutter Pairs	11·00	
			First Day Cover		4·75
			Presentation Pack	5·50	
			PHQ Cards (set of 5)	5·00	9·00

Special First Day of Issue Postmarks

British Philatelic Bureau, Edinburgh .... 5·00
Blackpool .... 5·00

1147 British Lion and French Cockerel
over Tunnel

1149 Groundcrew replacing
Smoke Canisters on
Douglas Boston of 88 Sqn

1150 H.M.S. *Warspite*
(battleship) shelling
Enemy Positions

1148 Symbolic Hands over Train

(Des G. Hardie (T **1147**), J.-P. Cousin (T **1148**))

1151 Commandos landing
on Gold Beach

1152 Infantry regrouping
on Sword Beach

1994 (3 May)   **Opening of Channel Tunnel.** *Phosphorised paper.* P 14 × 14$\frac{1}{2}$.
1820	**1147**	25p. ultramarine, brt orange, scarlet, new		
		blue, emerald, turquoise-blue & silver	80	70
		a. Horiz pair. Nos. 1820/1	1·75	1·60
1821	**1148**	25p. ultramarine, scarlet, new blue, emerald		
		& silver	80	70
1822	**1147**	41p. new blue, brt orange, scarlet, turquoise-		
		blue, emerald, ultramarine & silver	1·50	1·50
		a. Horiz pair. Nos. 1822/3	3·25	3·25
		ab. Imperf (horiz pair)	£1400	
1823	**1148**	41p. ultramarine, scarlet, new blue, emerald		
		& silver	1·50	1·50
		Set of 4	4·50	4·00
		First Day Cover		5·50
		Presentation Pack	5·50	
		Souvenir Book	27·00	
		PHQ Cards (set of 4)	4·00	8·00

Nos. 1820/1 and 1822/3 were printed together, *se-tenant*, in
horizontal pairs throughout the sheets.

Stamps in similar designs were also issued by France. These are
included in the souvenir book.

1153 Tank and Infantry
advancing, Ouistreham

(Des K. Bassford from contemporary photographs. Litho Questa)

1994 (6 June).   **50th Anniv of D-Day.** *Two phosphor bands.* P 14$\frac{1}{2}$ × 14.
1824	**1149**	25p. pink, greenish yellow, blackish lilac,		
		slate-black, brt scarlet & silver-grey	1·10	1·10
		a. Horiz strip of 5. Nos. 1824/8	5·00	5·50
1825	**1150**	25p. pink. greenish yellow, blackish lilac,		
		slate-black, brt scarlet & silver-grey	1·10	1·10
1826	**1151**	25p. pink, greenish yellow, blackish lilac,		
		slate-black, brt scarlet & silver-grey	1·10	1·10
1827	**1152**	25p. pink, greenish yellow, blackish lilac,		
		slate-black, brt scarlet & silver-grey	1·10	1·10
1828	**1153**	25p. pink, greenish yellow, blackish lilac,		
		slate-black, brt scarlet & silver-grey	1·10	1·10
		Set of 5	5·00	5·00
		Gutter block of 10	11·00	
		First Day Cover		5·25
		Presentation Pack	5·50	
		PHQ Cards (set of 5)	5·00	9·00

Nos. 1824/8 were printed together, *se-tenant*, in horizontal strips of 5
throughout the sheet.

Special First Day of Issue Postmarks

British Philatelic Bureau, Edinburgh .... 6·00
Folkestone .... 6·00

Special First Day of Issue Postmarks

British Philatelic Bureau, Edinburgh .... 5·50
Portsmouth .... 5·50

1154 The Old Course,
St. Andrews

1155 The 18th Hole, Muirfield

1156 The 15th Hole
("Luckyslap"),
Carnoustie

1157 The 8th Hole
("The Postage Stamp"),
Royal Troon

1158 The 9th Hole,
Turnberry

(Des P. Hogarth)

1994 (5 July).   **Scottish Golf Courses.** *One phosphor band* (19p.) or
phosphorised paper (others). *P* 14½ × 14.

1829	**1154**	19p. yellow-green, olive-grey, orange-vermilion, apple-green, blue & grey-black	50	20
1830	**1155**	25p. yellow-green, lemon, brt orange, apple-green, blue, magenta & grey-black	75	20
1831	**1156**	30p. yellow-green, yellow, rosine, emerald, blue-green, new blue & grey-black	1·10	1·40

1832	**1157**	35p. yellow-green, yellow, rosine, apple-green, new blue, dull blue & grey-black	1·25	1·40
1833	**1158**	41p. yellow-green, lemon, magenta, apple-green, dull blue, new blue & grey-black	1·40	1·40
		Set of 5	4·50	4·25
		Set of 5 Gutter Pairs	10·00	
		First Day Cover		5·00
		Presentation Pack	5·25	
		PHQ Cards (set of 5)	5·00	10·00

Nos. 1829/33 commemorate the 250th anniversary of golf's first set
of rules produced by the Honourable Company of Edinburgh Golfers.

Special First Day of Issue Postmarks

British Philatelic Bureau, Edinburgh .... 5·50
Turnberry .... 5·50

1159 Royal Welsh Show,
Llanelwedd

1160 All England Tennis
Championships, Wimbledon

1161 Cowes Week

1162 Test Match, Lord's

1163 Braemar Gathering

(Des M. Cook)

1994 (2 Aug).   **The Four Seasons. Summertime.** *One phosphor band*
(19p.) or *phosphorised paper* (others). *P* 15 × 14.

1834	**1159**	19p. black, greenish yellow, magenta, brown, yellow-brown & new blue ...	50	20
1835	**1160**	25p. black, greenish yellow, magenta, reddish violet, yellow-green, myrtle-green & new blue	75	20
1836	**1161**	30p. black, greenish yellow, brt magenta, yellow-ochre, dp slate-blue, blue-green & blue	1·10	1·25

1837	**1162**	35p. black, greenish yellow, magenta, slate-lilac, yellow-green, dp bluish green & brt blue	1·25	1·60
1838	**1163**	41p. black, greenish yellow, brt magenta, dp claret, lt brown, myrtle-green & brt blue	1·40	1·60
		Set of 5	4·50	4·25
		Set of 5 Gutter Pairs	10·00	
		First Day Cover		4·75
		Presentation Pack	5·00	
		PHQ Cards (set of 5)	5·00	9·00

Special First Day of Issue Postmarks

British Philatelic Bureau, Edinburgh		5·00
Wimbledon		5·00

1164 Ultrasonic Imaging   **1165** Scanning Electron Microscopy

1166 Magnetic Resonance Imaging   **1167** Computed Tomography

(Des P. Vermier and J.-P. Tibbles. Photo Enschedé)

1994 (27 Sept). **Europa. Medical Discoveries.** *Phosphorised paper.* P 14 × 14½.

1839	**1164**	25p. greenish yellow, brt magenta, new blue, black & silver	80	20
		a. Imperf (vert pair)	£1800	
1840	**1165**	30p. greenish yellow, brt magenta, new blue, black & silver	1·25	1·10
1841	**1166**	35p. greenish yellow, brt magenta, new blue, black & silver	1·25	1·40
1842	**1167**	41p. greenish yellow, brt magenta, new blue, black & silver	1·50	1·40
		Set of 4	4·25	3·75
		Set of 4 Gutter Pairs	8·50	
		First Day Cover		4·50
		Presentation Pack	4·75	
		PHQ Cards (set of 4)	4·50	8·00

Special First Day of Issue Postmarks

British Philatelic Bureau, Edinburgh		5·00
Cambridge		5·00

1168 Mary and Joseph   **1169** Three Wise Men

1170 Mary with Doll   **1171** Shepherds

1172 Angels

(Des Yvonne Gilbert)

1994 (1 Nov). **Christmas. Children's Nativity Plays.** *One phosphor band* (19p.) *or phosphorised paper* (others). P 15 × 14.

1843	**1168**	19p. turquoise-green, greenish yellow, brt magenta, new blue, dull blue & grey-black	65	15
		a. Imperf (pair)	£160	
1844	**1169**	25p. orange-brown, greenish yellow, brt magenta, new blue, lt blue, bistre & grey-black	90	15
1845	**1170**	30p. lt brown, greenish yellow, brt magenta, blue, turquoise-blue, new blue & brownish grey	1·10	1·40
1846	**1171**	35p. dp grey-brown, greenish yellow, brt magenta, turquoise-blue, dull violet-blue, ochre & brown	1·25	1·40
1847	**1172**	41p. blue, greenish yellow, brt magenta, turquoise-blue, lt blue & dp grey	1·50	1·40
		Set of 5	4·75	4·00
		Set of 5 Gutter Pairs	10·50	
		First Day Cover		4·50
		Presentation Pack	5·25	
		PHQ Cards (set of 5)	5·00	9·00

Special First Day of Issue Postmarks

British Philatelic Bureau, Edinburgh .... 5·00
Bethlehem, Llandeilo .... 5·00

Collectors Pack 1994

1994 (14 Nov). *Comprises Nos. 1795/1847*
CP1847a Collectors Pack .... 55·00

Post Office Yearbook

1994 (14 Nov). *Comprises Nos. 1795/9 and 1810/47 in hardbound book with slip case, illustrated in colour* .... 60·00

1173 Sophie (black cat)

1174 Puskas (Siamese) and Tigger (tabby)

1175 Chloe (ginger cat)

1176 Kikko (tortoiseshell) and Rosie (Abyssinian)

1177 Fred (black and white cat)

(Des Elizabeth Blackadder. Litho Questa)

1995 (17 Jan). **Cats.** *One phosphor band (19p.) or two phosphor bands (others). P 14½ × 14.*

1848	**1173**	19p. new blue, greenish yellow, magenta, black & brown-red	80	20
1849	**1174**	25p. new blue, greenish yellow, magenta, black & dull yellow-green	95	25
1850	**1175**	30p. new blue, greenish yellow, magenta, black & yellow-brown	1·10	1·40

1851	**1176**	35p. new blue, greenish yellow, magenta, black & yellow	1·25	1·50
1852	**1177**	41p. new blue, greenish yellow, magenta, black & reddish orange	1·60	1·60
		Set of 5	5·00	4·50
		Set of 5 Gutter Pairs	11·00	
		First Day Cover		5·00
		Presentation Pack	5·50	
		PHQ Cards (set of 5)	6·00	10·00

Special First Day of Issue Postmarks

British Philatelic Bureau, Edinburgh .... 5·50
Kitts Green .... 5·50

1178 Dandelions

1179 Chestnut Leaves

1180 Garlic Leaves

1181 Hazel Leaves

1182 Spring Grass

1995 (14 Mar). **The Four Seasons. Springtime. Plant Sculptures by Andy Goldsworthy.** *One phosphor band (19p.) or two phosphor bands (others). P 15 × 14.*

1853	**1178**	19p. silver, greenish yellow, magenta, green & grey-black	80	15
1854	**1179**	25p. silver, greenish yellow, magenta, new blue & black	95	15
1855	**1180**	30p. silver, greenish yellow, magenta, new blue & black	1·25	1·40

1856	**1181**	35p. silver, greenish yellow, magenta, new blue & black	1·25	1·40
1857	**1182**	41p. silver, greenish yellow, magenta, new blue, blue-green & black	1·60	1·60
		Set of 5	5·25	4·25
		Set of 5 Gutter Pairs	11·50	
		First Day Cover		5·00
		Presentation Pack	5·50	
		PHQ Cards (set of 5)	6·00	8·00

Special First Day of Issue Postmarks

British Philatelic Bureau, Edinburgh .... 5·50
Springfield .... 5·50

1183 "La Danse a la Campagne" (Renoir)

1184 "Troilus and Criseyde" (Peter Brookes)

1185 "The Kiss" (Rodin)

1186 "Girls on the Town" (Beryl Cook)

1187 "Jazz" (Andrew Mockett)

1188 "Girls performing a Kathak Dance" (Aurangzeb period)

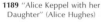

1189 "Alice Keppel with her Daughter" (Alice Hughes)

1190 "Children Playing" (L. S. Lowry)

1191 "Circus Clowns" (Emily Firmin and Justin Mitchell)

1192 Decoration from "All the Love Poems of Shakespeare" (Eric Gill)

(Des Newell and Sorrell. Litho Walsall)

1995 (21 Mar). **Greetings Stamps. "Greetings in Art".** *Two phosphor bands.* P $14\frac{1}{2} \times 14$ *(with one elliptical hole on each vertical side).*

1858	**1183**	(1st) greenish yellow, new blue, magenta, black & silver	1·00	80
		a. Booklet pane. Nos. 1858/67	11·00	
		ab. Silver (Queen's head and "1ST") and phosphor omitted	£9000	
1859	**1184**	(1st) greenish yellow, new blue, magenta, black & silver	1·00	80
1860	**1185**	(1st) greenish yellow, new blue, magenta, black & silver	1·00	80
1861z	**1186**	(1st) greenish yellow, new blue, magenta, black & silver	1·00	80
1862	**1187**	(1st) greenish yellow, new blue, magenta, black & silver	1·00	80
1863	**1188**	(1st) greenish yellow, new blue, magenta, black & silver	1·00	80
1864	**1189**	(1st) purple-brown & silver	1·00	80
1865	**1190**	(1st) greenish yellow, new blue, magenta, black & silver	1·00	80
1866	**1191**	(1st) greenish yellow, new blue, magenta. black & silver	1·00	80
1867	**1192**	(1st) black, greenish yellow & silver	1·00	80
		Set of 10	11·00	7·25
		First Day Cover		9·00
		Presentation Pack	12·00	
		PHQ Cards (set of 10)	9·00	22·00

Nos. 1858/67 were issued in £2.50 stamp booklets (sold at £2.60 from 8 July 1996), together with a pane of 20 half stamp-sized labels. The stamps and labels were attached to the booklet cover by a common gutter margin.

Special First Day of Issue Postmarks

British Philatelic Bureau, Edinburgh .... 10·00
Lover .... 10·00

The National Trust
Celebrating 100 Years 19

1193 Fireplace Decoration,
Attingham Park, Shropshire

The National Trust
Protecting Land 25

1194 Oak Seedling

The National Trust
Conserving Art 30

1195 Carved Table Leg,
Attingham Park

The National Trust
Saving Coast 35

1196 St. David's Head,
Dyfed, Wales

The National Trust
Repairing Buildings 41

1197 Elizabethan Window, Little
Moreton Hall, Cheshire

(Des T. Evans)

1995 (11–25 Apr). **Centenary of The National Trust.** *One phosphor band (19p.), two phosphor bands (25p, 35p) or phosphorised paper (30p, 41p). P 14 × 15.*

1868	**1193**	19p. grey-green, stone, grey-brown, grey-black & gold	60	20
1869	**1194**	25p. grey-green, greenish yellow, magenta, new blue, gold & black	80	20
		a. Booklet pane. No. 1869×6 with margins all round (25 Apr)	4·50	
1870	**1195**	30p. grey-green, greenish yellow, magenta, new blue, gold, black & slate-black	1·00	1·25
1871	**1196**	35p. grey-green, greenish yellow, magenta, blue, gold & black	1·25	1·50
1872	**1197**	41p. grey-green, greenish yellow, brt green, slate-green, gold, blackish brown & black	1·40	1·50
		Set of 5	4·50	4·25
		Set of 5 Gutter Pairs	10·00	
		First Day Cover		4·75
		Presentation Pack	5·25	
		PHQ Cards (set of 5)	6·00	8·00

Booklet pane No. 1869a comes from the £6 "National Trust" booklet.

Special First Day of Issue Postmarks

British Philatelic Bureau, Edinburgh .... 5·25
Alfriston .... 5·25

1198 British Troops and
French Civilians
celebrating

1199 Symbolic Hands and
Red Cross

1200 St. Paul's Cathedral
and Searchlights

1201 Symbolic Hand releasing
Peace Dove

1202 Symbolic Hands

(Des J. Gorham (Nos. 1873, 1875), J-M. Folon (others))

1995 (2 May). **Europa. Peace and Freedom.** *One phosphor band (Nos. 1873/4) or two phosphor bands (others). P 14½ × 14.*

1873	**1198**	19p. silver, bistre-brown & grey-black	70	40
1874	**1199**	19p. silver, bistre-yellow, brt rose-red, vermilion, brt blue & slate-blue	70	40
1875	**1200**	25p. silver, blue & grey-black	1·00	60

1876	**1201**	25p. silver, vermilion, brt blue & grey-black	1·00	60
		a. Imperf (vert pair)	£3500	
1877	**1202**	30p. silver, bistre-yellow, brt magenta, pale		
		greenish blue, grey-black & flesh	1·25	1·75
		Set of 5	4·25	3·50
		Set of 5 Gutter Pairs	9·00	
		First Day Cover		4·00
		Presentation Pack	5·00	
		PHQ Cards (set of 5)	6·00	9·00

Nos. 1873 and 1875 commemorate the 50th anniversary of the end of the Second World War, No. 1874 the 125th anniversary of the British Red Cross Society and Nos. 1876/7 the 50th anniversary of the United Nations.

Nos. 1876/7 include the "EUROPA" emblem.

Special First Day of Issue Postmarks

British Philatelic Bureau, Edinburgh .... 4·75
London SW .... 4·75

A First Day of Issue handstamp (pictorial) was provided at London EC4 for this issue.

1203 *The Time Machine*

1204 *The First Men in the Moon*

1205 *The War of the Worlds*

1206 *The Shape of Things to Come*

(Des Siobhan Keaney. Litho Questa)

1995 (6 June). **Science Fiction. Novels by H. G. Wells.** *Two phosphor bands.* P 14½ × 14.

1878	**1203**	25p. new blue, greenish yellow, magenta,		
		black & rosine	95	25
1879	**1204**	30p. new blue, greenish yellow, black,		
		rosine & violet	1·40	1·50

1880	**1205**	35p. rosine, greenish yellow, violet, black &		
		lt blue-green	1·50	1·60
1881	**1206**	41p. new blue, greenish yellow, magenta,		
		black & rosine	1·60	1·60
		Set of 4	5·00	4·50
		Set of 4 Gutter Pairs	11·00	
		First Day Cover		5·25
		Presentation Pack	5·50	
		PHQ Cards (set of 4)	5·00	10·00

Nos. 1878/81 commemorate the centenary of publication of Wells's *The Time Machine.*

Special First Day of Issue Postmarks

British Philatelic Bureau, Edinburgh .... 5·50
Wells .... 5·50

1207 The Swan, 1595

1208 The Rose, 1592

1209 The Globe, 1599

1210 The Hope, 1613

1211 The Globe, 1614

(Des C. Hodges. Litho Walsall)

1995 (8 Aug). **Reconstruction of Shakespeare's Globe Theatre.** *Two phosphor bands.* P 14½.

1882	**1207**	25p. brownish grey, black, magenta, new blue & greenish yellow	90	90
		a. Horiz strip of 5. Nos. 1882/6	4·25	4·25
1883	**1208**	25p. brownish grey, black, magenta, new blue & greenish yellow	90	90
1884	**1209**	25p. brownish grey, black, magenta, new blue & greenish yellow	90	90
1885	**1210**	25p. brownish grey, black, magenta, new blue & greenish yellow	90	90
1886	**1211**	25p. brownish grey, black, magenta, new blue & greenish yellow	90	90
		Set of 5	4·25	4·00
		Gutter Strip of 10	10·50	
		First Day Cover		5·50
		Presentation Pack	5·25	
		PHQ Cards (set of 5)	6·00	9·00

Nos. 1882/6 were issued together, *se-tenant*, in horizontal strips of 5 throughout the sheet with the backgrounds forming a composite design.

Special First Day of Issue Postmarks

British Philatelic Bureau, Edinburgh	5·75
Stratford-upon-Avon	5·75

1212 Sir Rowland Hill and Uniform Penny Postage Petition

1213 Hill and Penny Black

1214 Guglielmo Marconi and Early Wireless

1215 Marconi and Sinking of *Titanic* (liner)

(Des The Four Hundred, Eng C. Slania. Recess and litho Harrison)

1995 (5 Sept). **Pioneers of Communications.** *One phosphor band* (19p.) *or phosphorised paper (others).* P 14½ × 14.

1887	**1212**	19p. silver, red & black	65	30
1888	**1213**	25p. silver, brown & black	90	35
		a. Silver (Queen's head and face value) omitted	£300	
1889	**1214**	41p. silver, grey-green & black	1·50	1·60
1890	**1215**	60p. silver, dp ultramarine & black	1·75	1·90
		Set of 4	4·25	3·75
		Set of 4 Gutter Pairs	9·50	
		First Day Cover		4·50
		Presentation Pack	5·00	
		PHQ Cards (set of 4)	5·00	9·00

Nos. 1887/8 mark the birth bicentenary of Sir Rowland Hill and Nos. 1889/90 the centenary of the first radio transmissions.

Special First Day of Issue Postmarks

British Philatelic Bureau, Edinburgh	5·00
London EC	5·00

1216 Harold Wagstaff

1217 Gus Risman

1218 Jim Sullivan

1219 Billy Batten

1220 Brian Bevan

(Des C. Birmingham)

1995 (3 Oct). **Centenary of Rugby League**. *One phosphor band (19p.) or two phosphor bands (others).* P $14\frac{1}{2}$ × 14.

1891	**1216**	19p.	blue, greenish yellow, magenta, new blue, grey-black & black	85	25
1892	**1217**	25p.	slate-purple, greenish yellow, magenta, new blue, grey-black & black	1·00	30
1893	**1218**	30p.	slate-green, greenish yellow, brt purple, new blue, grey-black & black .	1·25	1·50
1894	**1219**	35p.	slate-black, greenish yellow, magenta, new blue & black	1·25	1·60
1895	**1220**	41p.	bluish grey, orange-yellow, magenta, new blue, grey-black & black	1·60	1·75
			Set of 5	5·25	5·00
			Set of 5 Gutter Pairs	11·00	
			First Day Cover		5·50
			Presentation Pack	6·00	
			PHQ Cards (set of 5)	6·00	9·00

Special First Day of Issue Postmarks

British Philatelic Bureau, Edinburgh	. . . .	5·75
Huddersfield	. . . .	5·75

A First Day of Issue handstamp (pictorial) was provided at Headingly, Leeds for this issue.

1221 European Robin in Mouth of Pillar Box

1222 European Robin on Railings and Holly

1223 European Robin on Snow-covered Milk Bottles

1224 European Robin on Road Sign

1225 European Robin on Door Knob and Christmas Wreath

(Des K. Lilly)

1995 (30 Oct). **Christmas. Christmas Robins**. *One phosphor band (19p.) or two phosphor bands (others).* P 15 × 14.

1896	**1221**	19p.	silver, greenish yellow, vermilion, orange-vermilion, bistre & black	60	20
1897	**1222**	25p.	silver, greenish yellow, scarlet, pale blue, ochre & black	85	30
1898	**1223**	30p.	silver, greenish yellow, rose-carmine, lt green, olive-brown & grey	1·25	1·40
1899	**1224**	41p.	silver, greenish yellow, rose-red, dull blue, bistre & black	1·60	1·60
1900	**1225**	60p.	silver, orange-yellow, red-orange, bistre & black	1·75	1·90
			Set of 5	5·50	4·75
			Set of 5 Gutter Pairs	12·00	
			First Day Cover		5·25
			Presentation Pack	6·00	
			PHQ Cards (set of 5)	6·00	9·00

The 19p. value was re-issued on 3 October 2000 in sheets of 20, each with a *se-tenant* label showing Christmas greetings (sold for £3.99) or a personal photograph (sold for £7.99). These sheets were printed in photogravure by Questa and were sold by the Philatelic Bureau and selected philatelic outlets. Similar sheets were available from 9 October 2001 when the price for a personalised version was increased to £8.75. These could also be purchased, on an experimental basis, from photo-booths at six post offices.

Special First Day of Issue Postmarks

British Philatelic Bureau, Edinburgh	. . . .	5·50
Bethlehem, Llandeilo	. . . .	5·50

Collectors Pack 1995

1995 (30 Oct). *Comprises Nos. 1848/1900*
CP1900a Collectors Pack . . . . 55·00

Post Office Yearbook

1995 (30 Oct). *Comprises Nos. 1848/57 and 1868/1900 in hardback book with slip case, illustrated in colour* . . . . 60·00

1226 Opening Lines of "To a Mouse" and Fieldmouse

1227 "O my Luve's like a red, red rose" and Wild Rose

1228 "Scots, wha hae wi Wallace bled" and Sir William Wallace

1229 "Auld Lang Syne" and Highland Dancers

(Des Tayburn Design Consultancy. Litho Questa)

1996 (25 Jan). **Death Bicentenary of Robert Burns (Scottish poet).** *One phosphor band (19p.) or two phosphor bands (others).* P 14½.

1901	**1226**	19p. cream, bistre-brown & black	60	25
1902	**1227**	25p. cream, bistre-brown, black, magenta, bistre-yellow & new blue	90	30
1903	**1228**	41p. cream, bistre-brown, black, magenta, bistre-yellow & new blue	1·40	1·50
1904	**1229**	60p. cream, bistre-brown, black, magenta, bistre-yellow & new blue	1·75	1·90
		Set of 4	4·25	3·50
		Set of 4 Gutter Pairs	9·50	
		First Day Cover		5·00
		Presentation Pack	5·00	
		PHQ Cards (set of 4)	6·00	7·00

Special First Day of Issue Postmarks

British Philatelic Bureau, Edinburgh	5·25
Dumfries	5·25

1230 "MORE! LOVE" (Mel Calman)

1231 "Sincerely" (Charles Barsotti)

1232 "Do you have something for the HUMAN CONDITION?" (Mel Calman)

1233 "MENTAL FLOSS" (Leo Cullum)

1234 "4.55 P.M." (Charles Barsotti)

1235 "Dear lottery prize winner" (Larry)

1236 "I'm writing to you because...." (Mel Calman)

1237 "FETCH THIS, FETCH THAT" (Charles Barsotti)

1238 "My day starts before I'm ready for it" (Mel Calman)

1239 "THE CHEQUE IN THE POST" (Jack Ziegler)

(Des M. Wolff. Litho Walsall)

1996 (26 Feb–11 Nov). **Greetings Stamps. Cartoons.** *"All-over" phosphor.* P 14½ × 14 (with one elliptical hole on each vertical side).

1905	**1230**	(1st) black & bright mauve	80	75
		a. Booklet pane. Nos. 1905/14	9·00	
		p. Two phosphor bands (11 Nov)	1·25	1·25
		pa. Booklet pane. Nos. 1905p/14p	15·00	
1906	**1231**	(1st) black & blue-green	80	75
		p. Two phosphor bands (11 Nov)	1·25	1·25
1907	**1232**	(1st) black & new blue	80	75
		p. Two phosphor bands (11 Nov)	1·25	1·25
1908	**1233**	(1st) black & brt violet	80	75
		p. Two phosphor bands (11 Nov)	1·25	1·25
1909	**1234**	(1st) black & vermilion	80	75
		p. Two phosphor bands (11 Nov)	1·25	1·25
1910	**1235**	(1st) black & new blue	80	75
		p. Two phosphor bands (11 Nov)	1·25	1·25
1911	**1236**	(1st) black & vermilion	80	75
		p. Two phosphor bands (11 Nov)	1·25	1·25
1912	**1237**	(1st) black & brt violet	80	75
		p. Two phosphor bands (11 Nov)	1·25	1·25
1913	**1238**	(1st) black & blue-green	80	75
		p. Two phosphor bands (11 Nov)	1·25	1·25
1914	**1239**	(1st) black & brt mauve	80	75
		p. Two phosphor bands (11 Nov)	1·25	1·25
		Set of 10 (Nos. 1905/14)	9·00	6·75
		Set of 10 (Nos. 1905p/14p)	15·00	11·00
		First Day Cover (1905/14)		8·00
		Presentation Pack (1905/14)	10·00	
		PHQ Cards (set of 10)	10·00	20·00

Nos. 1905/14 were issued in £2.50 stamp booklets (sold at £2.60 from 8 July 1996), together with a pane of twenty half stamp-sized labels. The stamps and labels were attached to the booklet cover by a common gutter margin.

These designs were re-issued on 18 December 2001 in sheets of 10, each with a *se-tenant* label showing cartoon comments (sold for £2.95).

They were re-issued again on 29 July 2003 in sheets of 20 sold for £6.15 containing two of each design, each stamp accompanied by a half stamp-size label showing a crossword grid (clues printed on the bottom sheet margin). Sheets of 20 with personal photographs on the labels and a crossword puzzle in the bottom sheet margin were also available, at £14.95 a sheet from Royal Mail, Edinburgh and Post Office philatelic outlets, or £15 a sheet from photo booths.

All these sheets were printed in lithography by Questa with two phosphor bands and perforated 14½ × 14 (without elliptical holes), and were available from the bureau and other selected philatelic outlets.

Special First Day of Issue Postmarks

British Philatelic Bureau, Edinburgh .... 9·00
Titterhill, Haytons Bent, Ludlow .... 9·00

1240 "Muscovy Duck"

1241 "Lapwing"

1242 "White-fronted Goose"

1243 "Bittern"

1244 "Whooper Swan"

(Des Moseley Webb)

1996 (12 Mar). **50th Anniv of the Wildfowl and Wetlands Trust. Bird Paintings by C. F. Tunnicliffe.** *One phosphor band* (19p.) *or phosphorised paper* (others). P 14 × 14½.

1915	**1240**	19p. sepia, orange-yellow, brown, pale buff, grey & gold	70	25
1916	**1241**	25p. bistre-brown, greenish yellow, magenta, new blue, pale buff, gold & black	90	30
1917	**1242**	30p. bistre-brown, greenish yellow, magenta, new blue, pale buff, gold & grey-black	1·00	1·25
1918	**1243**	35p. sepia, pale orange, lake-brown, brown-olive, pale buff, gold & grey-black	1·10	1·50
1919	**1244**	41p. sepia, greenish yellow, magenta, new blue, pale buff, gold & grey-black	1·50	1·60
		Set of 5	4·75	4·50
		Set of 5 Gutter Pairs	10·50	
		First Day Cover		5·25
		Presentation Pack	5·25	
		PHQ Cards (set of 5)	6·00	9·00

Special First Day of Issue Postmarks

British Philatelic Bureau, Edinburgh .... 5·50
Slimbridge, Gloucester .... 5·50

1245 The Odeon, Harrogate

1246 Laurence Olivier and Vivien Leigh in *Lady Hamilton* (film)

1247 Old Cinema Ticket

1248 Pathé News Still

208

1249 Cinema Sign, The Odeon, Manchester

(Des The Chase)

1996 (16 Apr). **Centenary of Cinema.** One phosphor band (19p.) or two phosphor bands (others). P 14 × 14½.

1920	**1245**	19p. black, greenish yellow, silver, brt magenta & new blue	50	25
1921	**1246**	25p. black, greenish yellow, silver, brt magenta & new blue	70	30
1922	**1247**	30p. black, greenish yellow, silver, brt magenta & new blue	90	1·10
1923	**1248**	35p. black, red & silver	1·25	1·25
1924	**1249**	41p. black, greenish yellow, silver, brt magenta & new blue	1·60	1·60
		Set of 5	4·50	4·00
		Set of 5 Gutter Pairs	10·00	
		First Day Cover		5·00
		Presentation Pack	5·00	
		PHQ Cards (set of 5)	6·00	9·00

Special First Day of Issue Postmarks

British Philatelic Bureau, Edinburgh .... 5·50
London, WC2 .... 5·50

1250 Dixie Dean

1252 Duncan Edwards

1251 Bobby Moore

1253 Billy Wright

1254 Danny Blanchflower

(Des H. Brown. Litho Questa)

1996 (14 May). **European Football Championship.** One phosphor band (19p.) or two phosphor bands (others). P 14½ × 14.

1925	**1250**	19p. vermilion, black, pale grey & grey	40	20
		a. Booklet pane. No. 1925 × 4 with margins all round	3·25	
1926	**1251**	25p. brt emerald, black, pale grey & grey	70	20
		a. Booklet pane. No. 1926 × 4 with margins all round	3·25	
1927	**1252**	35p. orange-yellow, black, pale grey & grey	1·25	1·60
		a. Booklet pane. Nos. 1927/9, each × 2, with margins all round	8·00	
1928	**1253**	41p. new blue, black, pale grey & grey	1·40	1·60
1929	**1254**	60p. brt orange, black, pale grey & grey	1·75	1·90
		Set of 5	5·00	5·00
		Set of 5 Gutter Pairs	11·00	
		First Day Cover		5·50
		Presentation Pack	5·50	
		PHQ Cards (set of 5)	6·00	9·00

Special First Day of Issue Postmarks

British Philatelic Bureau, Edinburgh .... 6·00
Wembley .... 6·00

1255 Athlete on Starting Blocks

1256 Throwing the Javelin

1257 Basketball

1258 Swimming

209

1259 Athlete celebrating and Olympic Rings

(Des N. Knight. Litho Questa)

1996 (9 July). **Olympic and Paralympic Games, Atlanta.** *Two phosphor bands.* P 14½ × 14.

1930	**1255**	26p. greenish grey, silver, rosine, black, magenta, bistre-yellow & new blue ...	1·10	1·00
		a. Horiz strip of 5. Nos. 1930/4	5·00	5·50
1931	**1256**	26p. greenish grey, silver, rosine, black, magenta, bistre-yellow & new blue ...	1·10	1·00
1932	**1257**	26p. greenish grey, silver, rosine, black, magenta, bistre-yellow & new blue ...	1·10	1·00
1933	**1258**	26p. greenish grey, silver, rosine, black, magenta, bistre-yellow & new blue ...	1·10	1·00
1934	**1259**	26p. greenish grey, silver, rosine, black, magenta, bistre-yellow & new blue ...	1·10	1·00
		Set of 5	5·00	4·50
		Gutter Strip of 10	11·00	
		First Day Cover		5·75
		Presentation Pack	5·50	
		PHQ Cards (set of 5)	6·00	9·00

Nos. 1930/4 were printed together, *se-tenant*, in horizontal strips of 5 throughout the sheet.

Special First Day of Issue Postmarks

British Philatelic Bureau, Edinburgh	....	6·00
Much Wenlock	....	6·00

1260 Prof. Dorothy Hodgkin (scientist)

1261 Dame Margot Fonteyn (ballerina)

1262 Dame Elisabeth Frink (sculptress)

1263 Dame Daphne du Maurier (novelist)

1264 Dame Marea Hartman (sports administrator)

(Des Stephanie Nash)

1996 (6 Aug). **Europa. Famous Women.** *One phosphor band (20p.) or two phosphor bands (others).* P 14½.

1935	**1260**	20p. dull blue-green, brownish grey & black	60	25
1936	**1261**	26p. dull mauve, brownish grey & black ...	75	25
		a. Imperf (horiz pair)	£300	
1937	**1262**	31p. bronze, brownish grey & black	95	1·10
1938	**1263**	37p. silver, brownish grey & black	1·25	1·40
1939	**1264**	43p. gold, brownish grey & black	1·40	1·50
		Set of 5	4·50	4·50
		Set of 5 Gutter Pairs	9·00	
		First Day Cover		5·75
		Presentation Pack	5·25	
		PHQ Cards (set of 5)	6·00	9·00

Nos. 1936/7 include the "EUROPA" emblem.

Special First Day of Issue Postmarks

British Philatelic Bureau, Edinburgh	....	6·00
Fowey	....	6·00

1265 *Muffin the Mule*

1266 *Sooty*

1267 *Stingray*

1268 *The Clangers*

1272 Austin-Healey 100

1273 Jaguar XK120

1269 *Dangermouse*

(Des Tutssels. Photo Harrison (No. 1940a) or Enschedé (others))

1996 (3 Sept)–**97. 50th Anniv of Children's Television.** *One phosphor band* (20p.) *or two phosphor bands* (others). *P* 14½ × 14.

1940	**1265**	20p. dp claret, black, magenta, rosine & greenish yellow	55	20
		a. Perf 15 × 14 (23.9.97)	2·00	2·00
		ab. Booklet pane. No. 1940a × 4 with margins all round	8·00	
1941	**1266**	26p. brt blue, black, dp grey-blue, magenta & greenish yellow	80	20
1942	**1267**	31p. greenish blue, black, new blue, magenta & greenish yellow	1·00	1·50
1943	**1268**	37p. dull violet-blue, black, new blue, magenta & greenish yellow	1·40	1·60
1944	**1269**	43p. brt purple, black, new blue, magenta & greenish yellow	1·60	1·75
		Set of 5	4·75	4·75
		Set of 5 Gutter Pairs	10·50	
		First Day Cover		5·50
		Presentation Pack	5·25	
		PHQ Cards (set of 5)	6·00	9·00

No. 1940a comes from the 1997 £6.15 B.B.C. stamp booklet.

Special First Day of Issue Postmarks

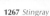

British Philatelic Bureau, Edinburgh .... 6·00
Alexandra Palace, London .... 6·00

1270 Triumph TR3   **1271** MG TD

1274 Morgan Plus 4

(Des S. Clay)

1996 (1 Oct). **Classic Sports Cars.** *One phosphor band* (20p.) *or two phosphor bands* (others). *P* 14½.

1945	**1270**	20p. silver, greenish yellow, brt scarlet, vermilion, new blue & black	55	20
1946	**1271**	26p. silver, greenish yellow, magenta, greenish blue & black	80	20
		a. Imperf (pair)		
1947	**1272**	37p. silver, greenish yellow, brt magenta, dp turquoise-blue, new blue & black	1·40	1·50
		a. Imperf (pair)	£650	
1948	**1273**	43p. silver, greenish yellow, magenta, greenish blue & black	1·40	1·50
		a. Imperf (horiz pair)		
1949	**1274**	63p. silver, greenish yellow, magenta, greenish blue, stone & black	1·75	1·50
		Set of 5	5·25	4·50
		Set of 5 Gutter Pairs	11·00	
		First Day Cover		6·00
		Presentation Pack	5·50	
		PHQ Cards (set of 5)	6·00	9·00

On Nos. 1946/9 the right-hand phosphor band on each stamp is three times the width of that on the left.

Special First Day of Issue Postmarks

British Philatelic Bureau, Edinburgh .... 6·25
Beaulieu, Brockenhurst .... 6·25

A pictorial First Day of Issue handstamp was provided at London E1 for this issue.

1275 The Three Kings

1276 The Annunciation

1277 The Journey to Bethlehem

1278 The Nativity

1279 The Shepherds

(Des Laura Stoddart)

1996 (28 Oct). **Christmas.** *One phosphor band (2nd) or two phosphor bands (others).* P 15 × 14.

1950	**1275**	(2nd)	gold, greenish yellow, magenta, blue, black & lt brown	75	20
1951	**1276**	(1st)	gold, yellow, cerise, new blue, black & lt brown	1·00	35
1952	**1277**	31p.	gold, orange-yellow, cerise, blue, black & lt brown	1·10	1·50
1953	**1278**	43p.	gold, greenish yellow, magenta, new blue, grey-black & lt brown	1·25	1·50
1954	**1279**	63p.	gold, greenish yellow, magenta, new blue, black & lt brown	1·60	1·75
			Set of 5	5·25	4·75
			Set of 5 Gutter Pairs	11·00	
			First Day Cover		5·75
			Presentation Pack	5·75	
			PHQ Cards (set of 5)	6·00	9·00

Special First Day of Issue Postmarks

British Philatelic Bureau, Edinburgh .... 6·25
Bethlehem, Llandeilo .... 6·25

Collectors Pack 1996

1996 (28 Oct). *Comprises Nos. 1901/4 and 1915/54*
CP1954a Collectors Pack............................ 55·00

Post Office Yearbook

1996 (28 Oct). *Comprises Nos. 1901/4 and 1915/54 in hardback book with slip case, illustrated in colour*............... 65·00

1280 *Gentiana acaulis* (Georg Ehret)

1281 *Magnolia grandiflora* (Ehret)

1282 *Camellia japonica* (Alfred Chandler)

1283 *Tulipa* (Ehret)

1284 *Fuchsia "Princess of Wales"* (Augusta Withers)

1285 *Tulipa gesneriana* (Ehret)

1286 *Guzmania splendens* (Charlotte Sowerby)

1287 *Iris latifolia* (Ehret)

1288 *Hippeastrum rutilum* (Pierre-Joseph Redoute)

1289 *Passiflora coerulea* (Ehret)

(Des Tutssels. Litho Walsall)

1997 (6 Jan). **Greeting Stamps. 19th-century Flower Paintings.** *Two phosphor bands. P 14½ × 14 (with one elliptical hole on each vertical side).*

1955	**1280**	(1st) greenish yellow, new blue, magenta, black, blue-green & gold	85	90
		a. Booklet pane. Nos. 1955/64	9·00	
		ab. Gold, blue-green and phosphor omitted £17000		
1956	**1281**	(1st) greenish yellow, new blue, magenta, black, blue-green & gold	85	90
1957	**1282**	(1st) greenish yellow, new blue, magenta, black, blue-green & gold	85	90
1958	**1283**	(1st) greenish yellow, new blue, magenta, black, blue-green & gold	85	90
1959	**1284**	(1st) greenish yellow, new blue, magenta, black, blue-green & gold	85	90
1960	**1285**	(1st) greenish yellow, new blue, magenta, black, blue-green & gold	85	90
1961	**1286**	(1st) greenish yellow, new blue, magenta, black, blue-green & gold	85	90
1962	**1287**	(1st) greenish yellow, new blue, magenta, black, blue-green & gold	85	90
1963	**1288**	(1st) greenish yellow, new blue, magenta, black, blue-green & gold	85	90
1964	**1289**	(1st) greenish yellow, new blue, magenta, black, blue-green & gold	85	90
		Set of 10	9·00	8·00
		First Day Cover		10·00
		Presentation Pack	10·00	
		PHQ Cards (set of 10)	10·00	18·00

Nos. 1955/64 were issued in £2.60 stamp booklets together with a pane of twenty half-sized labels. The stamps and labels were attached to the booklet cover by a common gutter margin.

Nos. 1955/64 were re-issued on 21 January 2003 in *se-tenant* sheets of 20, each accompanied by a label showing further flowers (sold at £5.95) or personal photographs (sold at £14.95). These stamps were printed in lithography by Questa and are without elliptical holes in the perforations.

Special First Day of Issue Postmarks

British Philatelic Bureau, Edinburgh .... 11·00
Kew, Richmond, Surrey .... 11·00

1290 "King Henry VIII"

1291 "Catherine of Aragon"

1292 "Anne Boleyn"

1293 "Jane Seymour"

1294 "Anne of Cleves"

1295 "Catherine Howard"

1296 "Catherine Parr"

(Des Kate Stephens from contemporary paintings)

1997 (21 Jan). **450th Death Anniv of King Henry VIII.** *Two phosphor bands. P 15 (No. 1965) or 14 × 15 (others).*

1965	**1290**	26p. gold, greenish yellow, brt purple, new blue and black	1·00	90
		a. Imperf (pair)	£800	
1966	**1291**	26p. gold, greenish yellow, brt carmine, new blue and black	1·25	1·00
		a. Horiz strip of 6. Nos. 1966/71	7·50	8·50
1967	**1292**	26p. gold, greenish yellow, brt carmine, new blue and black	1·25	1·00
1968	**1293**	26p. gold, greenish yellow, brt carmine, new blue and black	1·25	1·00
1969	**1294**	26p. gold, greenish yellow, brt carmine, new blue and black	1·25	1·00
1970	**1295**	26p. gold, greenish yellow, brt carmine, new blue and black	1·25	1·00
1971	**1296**	26p. gold, greenish yellow, brt carmine, new blue and black	1·25	1·00
		Set of 7	7·75	6·25
		Set of 1 Gutter Pair and a Gutter Strip of 12	17·00	
		First Day Cover		9·00
		Presentation Pack	10·00	
		PHQ Cards (set of 7)	10·00	14·00

Nos. 1966/71 were printed together, *se-tenant*, in horizontal strips of six throughout the sheet.

Special First Day of Issue Postmarks

British Philatelic Bureau, Edinburgh .... 9·00
Hampton Court, East Molesey .... 9·00

1297 St. Columba in Boat   **1298** St. Columba on Iona

1299 St. Augustine with   **1300** St. Augustine with
King Ethelbert   Model of Cathedral

(Des Claire Melinsky. Photo Enschedé)

1997 (11 Mar). **Religious Anniversaries**. *Two phosphor bands*. P 14½.
1972 **1297** 26p. greenish yellow, magenta, new blue,
grey-black and gold 75   35
   a. Imperf (pair) £250
1973 **1298** 37p. greenish yellow, magenta, new blue,
grey-black and gold .... 1·10   1·50
1974 **1299** 43p. greenish yellow, magenta, new blue,
grey-black and gold .... 1·50   1·50
1975 **1300** 63p. greenish yellow, magenta, new blue,
grey-black and gold .... 2·00   2·10
   Set of 4 .... 4·75   5·00
   Set of 4 Gutter Pairs .... 10·50
   First Day Cover .... 6·00
   Presentation Pack .... 5·25
   PHQ Cards (set of 4) .... 5·00   8·00
Nos. 1972/3 commemorate the 1400th death anniversary of St.
Columba and Nos. 1974/5 the 1400th anniversary of the arrival of St.
Augustine of Canterbury in Kent.

Special First Day of Issue Postmarks

British Philatelic Bureau, Edinburgh .... 6·00
Isle of Iona .... 6·00

1301   **1302**

(Des J. Matthews. Photo Enschedé)

1997 (18 Mar). **Self-adhesive**. *One centre phosphor band (2nd) or two
phosphor bands (1st). P 14 × 15 die-cut (with one elliptical hole on
each vertical side).*
1976 **1301** (2nd) bright blue .... 2·00   2·50
1977 **1302** (1st) bright orange-red .... 2·00   2·75
   Set of 2 .... 4·00   5·25
   First Day Cover .... 5·50
   Presentation Pack (P.O. Pack No. 37) .. 4·00
Nos. 1976/7, which were sold at 20p. and 26p., were in rolls of 100
with the stamps separate on the backing paper.

Special First Day of Issue Postmarks

British Philatelic Bureau, Edinburgh .... 5·50
Glasgow .... 5·50

1303 *Dracula*   **1304** *Frankenstein*

1305 *Dr. Jekyll and Mr. Hyde*

1306 *The Hound of the Baskervilles*

(Des I. Pollock. Photo Walsall)

1997 (13 May). **Europa. Tales and Legends. Horror Stories.** *Two phosphor bands. P 14 × 15.*

1980	**1303**	26p. grey-black, black, new blue, magenta and greenish yellow	1·00	40
1981	**1304**	31p. grey-black, black, new blue, magenta and greenish yellow	1·10	1·40
1982	**1305**	37p. grey-black, black, new blue, magenta and greenish yellow	1·35	1·50
1983	**1306**	43p. grey-black, black, new blue, magenta and greenish yellow	1·75	1·60
		Set of 4	4·75	4·50
		Set of 4 Gutter Pairs	9·50	
		First Day Cover		6·00
		Presentation Pack	5·50	
		PHQ Cards (set of 4)	5·00	8·00

Nos. 1980/3 commemorate the birth bicentenary of Mary Shelley (creator of Frankenstein) with the 26p. and 31p. values incorporating the "EUROPA" emblem.

Each value has features printed in fluorescent ink which are visible under ultra-violet light.

Special First Day of Issue Postmarks

British Philatelic Bureau, Edinburgh .... 6·00
Whitby .... 6·00

1307 Reginald Mitchell and Supermarine Spitfire MkIIA

1308 Roy Chadwick and Avro Lancaster MkI

1309 Ronald Bishop and De Havilland Mosquito B MkXVI

1310 George Carter and Gloster Meteor T Mk7

1311 Sir Sidney Camm and Hawker Hunter FGA Mk9

(Des Turner Duckworth)

1997 (10 June). **British Aircraft Designers.** *One phosphor band (20p.) or two phosphor bands (others). P 15 × 14.*

1984	**1307**	20p. silver, greenish yellow, magenta, new blue, black and grey	75	40
1985	**1308**	26p. silver, greenish yellow, magenta, new blue, black and grey	1·10	1·10
1986	**1309**	37p. silver, greenish yellow, magenta, new blue, black and grey	1·35	1·10
1987	**1310**	43p. silver, greenish yellow, magenta, new blue, black and grey	1·50	1·40
1988	**1311**	63p. silver, greenish yellow, magenta, new blue, black and grey	2·00	1·90
		Set of 5	6·00	5·25
		Set of 5 Gutter Pairs	12·00	
		First Day Cover		6·50
		Presentation Pack	6·25	
		PHQ Cards (set of 5)	6·00	10·00

Special First Day of Issue Postmarks

British Philatelic Bureau, Edinburgh .... 6·50
Duxford, Cambridge .... 6·50

GIBBONS STAMP MONTHLY
– finest and most informative magazine for all collectors. Obtainable from your newsagent or by postal subscription – details on request.

1312 Carriage Horse and Coachman

1313 Lifeguards Horse and Trooper

1314 Blues and Royals Drum Horse and Drummer

1315 Duke of Edinburgh's Horse and Groom

(Des J.-L. Benard. Litho Walsall)

1997 (8 July). **"All the Queen's Horses". 50th Anniv of the British Horse Society.** *One phosphor band* (20p.) *or two phosphor bands* (others). P 14½.

1989	**1312**	20p. scarlet-vermilion, black, magenta, new blue and greenish yellow	80	45
1990	**1313**	26p. scarlet-vermilion, black, magenta, new blue and greenish yellow	1·10	1·40
1991	**1314**	43p. scarlet-vermilion, black, magenta, new blue and greenish yellow	1·50	1·50
1992	**1315**	63p. scarlet-vermilion, black, magenta, new blue and greenish yellow	2·00	2·00
		Set of 4	5·00	4·75
		Set of 4 Gutter Pairs	10·50	
		First Day Cover		5·75
		Presentation Pack	5·50	
		PHQ Cards (set of 4)	5·00	8·00

Special First Day of Issue Postmarks

British Philatelic Bureau, Edinburgh .... 6·00
Windsor, Berks .... 6·00

CASTLE   CASTLE

Harrison plates (Nos. 1611/14)   Enschedé plates (Nos. 1993/6)

216

Differences between Harrison and Enschedé:

Harrison - "C" has top serif and tail of letter points to right. "A" has flat top. "S" has top and bottom serifs.

Enschedé - "C" has no top serif and tail of letter points upwards. "A" has pointed top. "S" has no serifs.

(Des from photos by Prince Andrew, Duke of York. Eng Inge Madle Recess (Queen's head by silk screen process) Enschedé)

1997 (29 July). *Designs as Nos.* 1612/14 *with Queen's head in silhouette as T* **1044**, *but re-engraved with differences in inscription as shown above.* P 15 × 14 (*with one elliptical hole on each vertical side*).

1993	**880**	£1.50, deep claret and gold†	7·50	4·00
1994	**881**	£2 indigo and gold†	8·50	2·25
		a. Gold (Queen's head) omitted	£600	
1995	**1044**	£3 violet and gold†	25·00	3·50
		a. Gold (Queen's head) omitted	£2800	
1996	**882**	£5 deep brown and gold†	25·00	10·00
		a. Gold (Queen's head) omitted	£2800	
		Set of 4	60·00	18·00
		Set of 4 Gutter Pairs	£100	
		Presentation Pack (P.O. Pack No. 40)	60·00	

† The Queen's head on these stamps is printed in optically variable ink which changes colour from gold to green when viewed from different angles.

A used example of the £1.50 value is known showing the gold Queen's head omitted.

No. 1996a occurs on R. 5/8 and 6/8 from some sheets.

1316 Haroldswick, Shetland   **1317** Painswick, Gloucestershire

1318 Beddgelert, Gwynedd   **1319** Ballyroney, County Down

(Des T. Millington. Photo Enschedé)

1997 (12 Aug). **Sub-Post Offices.** *One phosphor band* (20p.) *or two phosphor bands* (others). P 14½.

1997	**1316**	20p. greenish yellow, bright magenta, new blue, grey-black, rosine and blue-green	75	50
1998	**1317**	26p. greenish yellow, bright magenta, new blue, grey-black, rosine and blue-green	1·00	60
1999	**1318**	43p. greenish yellow, bright magenta, new blue, grey-black, rosine and blue-green	1·50	1·50
2000	**1319**	63p. greenish yellow, bright magenta, new blue, grey-black, rosine and blue-green	2·25	2·10
		Set of 4	5·50	4·25
		Set of 4 Gutter Pairs	9·50	
		First Day Cover		5·75
		Presentation Pack	5·00	
		PHQ Cards (set of 4)	5·00	8·00

Nos. 1997/2000 were issued on the occasion of the Centenary of the National Federation of Sub-Postmasters.

Special First Day of Issue Postmarks

British Philatelic Bureau, Edinburgh .... 6·00
Wakefield .... 6·00

PRINTERS. Harrison and Sons Ltd became De La Rue Security Print on 8 September 1997. This was not reflected in the sheet imprints until mid-1998.

Enid Blyton's *Noddy*

1320 Noddy

Enid Blyton's *Famous Five*

1321 Famous Five

Enid Blyton's *Secret Seven*

1322 Secret Seven

Enid Blyton's *Faraway Tree*

1323 Faraway Tree

Enid Blyton's *Malory Towers*

1324 Malory Towers

(Des C. Birmingham. Photo Enschedé)

1997 (9 Sept). **Birth Centenary of Enid Blyton (children's author).** *One phosphor band (20p.) or two phosphor bands (others).* P 14 × 14½.

2001	**1320**	20p. greenish yellow, magenta, new blue, grey-black and deep grey-blue	60	45
2002	**1321**	26p. greenish yellow, magenta, new blue, grey-black and deep grey-blue	1·00	1·25
2003	**1322**	37p. greenish yellow, magenta, new blue, grey-black and deep grey-blue	1·25	1·25
2004	**1323**	43p. greenish yellow, magenta, new blue, grey-black and deep grey-blue	1·50	1·50
2005	**1324**	63p. greenish yellow, magenta, new blue, grey-black and deep grey-blue	2·00	2·00
		Set of 5	5·75	5·75
		Set of 5 Gutter Pairs	12·00	
		First Day Cover		6·50
		Presentation Pack	6·00	
		PHQ Cards (set of 5)	6·00	10·00

Special First Day of Issue Postmarks

British Philatelic Bureau, Edinburgh .... 6·50
Beaconsfield .... 6·50

1325 Children and Father Christmas pulling Cracker

1326 Father Christmas with Traditional Cracker

1327 Father Christmas riding Cracker

1328 Father Christmas on Snowball

1329 Father Christmas and Chimney

217

(Des J. Gorham and M. Thomas (1st), J. Gorham (others))

1997 (27 Oct). **Christmas. 150th Anniv of the Christmas Cracker.** *One phosphor band (2nd) or two phosphor bands (others).* P 15 × 14.

2006	**1325**	(2nd) gold, greenish yellow, bright magenta, new blue and grey-black	75	20
		a. Imperf (pair)	£1400	
2007	**1326**	(1st) gold, greenish yellow, bright magenta, new blue and grey-black	90	30
2008	**1327**	31p. gold, greenish yellow, bright magenta, new blue, bright blue and grey-black .	1·00	1·60
		a. Imperf (pair)	£1250	
2009	**1328**	43p. gold, greenish yellow, bright magenta, pale new blue and grey-black	1·25	1·75
2010	**1329**	63p. gold, greenish yellow, bright magenta, new blue and grey-black	1·60	1·90
		Set of 5	5·00	5·00
		Set of 5 Gutter Pairs	11·00	
		First Day Cover		6·00
		Presentation Pack	5·75	
		PHQ Cards (set of 5)	6·00	9·00

The 1st value was re-issued on 3 October 2000 in sheets of 10, each with a *se-tenant* label showing Christmas greetings (sold for £2.95) or a personal photograph (sold for £5.95). These sheets were printed in photogravure by Questa and were sold by the Philatelic Bureau and selected philatelic outlets. Similar sheets were available from 9 October 2001 when the price for the personalised version was increased to £12.95 for two sheets. These could also be purchased, on an experimental basis, from photo-booths situated at six post offices.

From 1 October 2002 the size of the sheet was increased to 20 either with greetings labels (sold at £5.95) or personal photographs (sold at £14.95). These stamps were printed by Questa in lithography and perforated 14½ × 14.

Special First Day of Issue Postmarks

British Philatelic Bureau, Edinburgh .... 6·25
Bethlehem, Llandeilo .... 6·25

(Des D. Driver (20p., 43p.), Lord Snowdon (26p., 63p.))

1997 (13 Nov). **Royal Golden Wedding.** *One phosphor band (20p.) or two phosphor bands (others).* P 15.

2011	**1330**	20p. gold, yellow-brown and grey-black ...	85	45
		a. Imperf (pair)	£2750	
2012	**1331**	26p. gold, bistre-yellow, magenta, new blue, grey-black and greenish grey	1·10	70
2013	**1330**	43p. gold, bluish green and grey-black	1·90	2·25
2014	**1331**	63p. gold, bistre-yellow, magenta, new blue, grey-black and lavender-grey	2·50	3·00
		Set of 4	5·75	5·75
		Set of 4 Gutter Pairs	12·00	
		First Day Cover		6·50
		Presentation Pack	6·25	
		Souvenir Book (contains Nos. 1979, 1989/92 and 2011/14)	18·00	
		PHQ Cards (set of 4)	5·00	8·00

For 26p. and (1st) Machin printed in gold, see Nos. 1664b and Y1683b.

Special First Day of Issue Postmarks

British Philatelic Bureau, Edinburgh .... 6·50
London, SW1 .... 6·50

Collectors Pack 1997

1997 (13 Nov). *Comprises Nos. 1965/75, 1980/92 and 1997/2014*
CP2014a Collectors Pack .... 60·00

Post Office Yearbook

1997 (13 Nov). *Comprises Nos. 1965/75, 1980/92 and 1997/2014 in hardback book with slip case* .... 60·00

1330 Wedding Photograph, 1947

1331 Queen Elizabeth II and Prince Philip, 1997

1332 Common Dormouse

1333 Lady's Slipper Orchid

31 ENDANGERED SPECIES
Song thrush
Turdus philomelos

37 ENDANGERED SPECIES
Shining ram's-horn snail
Segmentina nitida

1334 Song Thrush

1335 Shining Ram's-horn Snail

43 ENDANGERED SPECIES
Mole cricket
Gryllotalpa gryllotalpa

63 ENDANGERED SPECIES
Devil's bolete
Boletus satanas

1336 Mole Cricket

1337 Devil's Bolete

(Des R. Maude. Litho Questa)

1998 (20 Jan). **Endangered Species**. *One side phosphor band (20p.) or two phosphor bands (others).* P 14 × 14½.

2015	**1332**	20p. black, new blue, magenta, greenish yellow, deep blue and pale lavender-grey	60	40
2016	**1333**	26p. black, new blue, magenta, greenish yellow, deep blue and pale yellow-olive	75	40
2017	**1334**	31p. black, new blue, magenta, greenish yellow, deep blue and pale bluish grey	1·00	1·00
2018	**1335**	37p. black, new blue, magenta, greenish yellow, deep blue and pale greenish grey	1·25	1·10
2019	**1336**	43p. black, new blue, magenta, greenish yellow, deep blue and pale dull mauve	1·40	1·25
2020	**1337**	63p. black, new blue, magenta, greenish yellow, deep blue and pale grey-brown	1·90	1·75

Set of 6 .... 6·25 5·25
Set of 6 *Gutter Pairs* ...... 13·50
First Day Cover .... 5·75
Presentation Pack ...... 6·75
PHQ Cards (set of 6) ..... 8·00 10·00

Special First Day of Issue Postmarks

British Philatelic Bureau, Edinburgh ...... 5·75
Selborne, Alton .... 5·75

1338 Diana, Princess of Wales (photo by Lord Snowdon)

1339 At British Lung Foundation Function, April 1997 (photo by John Stillwell)

1340 Wearing Tiara, 1991 (photo by Lord Snowdon)

1341 On Visit to Birmingham, October 1995 (photo by Tim Graham)

1342 In Evening Dress, 1987 (photo by Terence Donavan)

(Des B. Robinson)

1998 (3 Feb). **Diana, Princess of Wales Commemoration**. *Two phosphor bands.* P 14 × 15.

2021	**1338**	26p. purple, greenish yellow, magenta, new blue and black	90	90
		a. Horiz strip of 5. Nos. 2021/5	4·00	4·50
		ab. Imperf (horiz strip of 5. Nos. 2021/5)		
		ac. Imperf (horiz strip of 4. Nos. 2021/4)		
		ad. Imperf (horiz strip of 3. Nos. 2021/3)		
2022	**1339**	26p. purple, greenish yellow, magenta, new blue and black	90	90
2023	**1340**	26p. purple, greenish yellow, magenta, new blue and black	90	90
2024	**1341**	26p. purple, greenish yellow, magenta, new blue and black	90	90
2025	**1342**	26p. purple, greenish yellow, magenta, new blue and black	90	90

Set of 5 .... 4·00 4·00
Gutter Strip of 10 ...... 9·00
First Day Cover .... 6·00
Presentation Pack ...... 15·00
Presentation Pack (Welsh) £150

219

Nos. 2021/5 were printed together, *se-tenant*, in horizontal strips of five throughout the sheet.

No. 2021ac shows No. 2025 perforated at right only.

In addition to the generally issued Presentation Pack a further pack with all text printed in English and Welsh was available.

Special First Day of Issue Postmarks

British Philatelic Bureau, Edinburgh	6·00
Kensington, London	6·00

1343 Lion of England and Griffin of Edward III

1344 Falcon of Plantagenet and Bull of Clarence

1345 Lion of Mortimer and Yale of Beaufort

1346 Greyhound of Richmond and Dragon of Wales

1347 Unicorn of Scotland and Horse of Hanover

(Des J. Matthews. Recess and litho Harrison)

1998 (24 Feb). **650th Anniv of the Order of the Garter. The Queen's Beasts.** *Two phosphor bands. P 15 × 14.*

2026	**1343**	26p. silver, green, bright blue, carmine-red, vermilion, lemon, grey-black and black	90	90
		a. Horiz strip of 5. Nos. 2026/30	4·00	4·50
		ab. Missing green (on Nos. 2026, 2028/9) (horiz strip of 5)	£7500	
		Eay. Horiz strip of 5. Phosphor omitted	25·00	
2027	**1344**	26p. silver, bright blue, carmine-red, vermilion, lemon, grey, grey-black and black	90	90

2028	**1345**	26p. silver, green, bright blue, carmine-red, vermilion, lemon, grey, grey-black and black	90	90
2029	**1346**	26p. silver, green, bright blue, carmine-red, vermilion, lemon, grey, grey-black and black	90	90
2030	**1347**	26p. silver, green, bright blue, vermilion, lemon, grey, grey-black and black	90	90
		Set of 5	4·00	4·00
		Gutter Block of 10	9·00	
		First Day Cover		5·25
		Presentation Pack	5·00	
		PHQ Cards (set of 5)	6·00	9·00

Nos. 2026/30 were printed together, *se-tenant*, in horizontal strips of five throughout the sheet.

The phosphor bands on Nos 2026/30 are only half the height of the stamps and do not cover the silver parts of the designs.

Special First Day of Issue Postmarks

British Philatelic Bureau, Edinburgh	5·50
London SW1	5·50

1348

(Des G. Knipe, adapted Dew Gibbons Design Group. Photo Walsall)

1998 (10 Mar). *As T* **157** *(Wilding Definitive of 1952-54) but with face values in decimal currency as T* **1348**. *One side phosphor band (20p.) or two phosphor bands (others). P 14 (with one elliptical hole on each vertical side).*

2031	**1348**	20p. light green (1 band at right)	70	75
		Ea. Band at left	70	75
		b. Booklet pane. Nos. 2031/Ea each × 3 with margins all round	4·75	
		c. Booklet pane. Nos. 2031/Ea and 2032/3, all × 2, and central label with margins all round	9·50	
2032		26p. red-brown	90	95
		a. Booklet pane. No. 2032 × 9 with margins all round	9·50	
		b. Booklet pane. Nos. 2032/3, each × 3 with margins all round	9·50	
2033		37p. light purple	2·75	2·75
		Set of 3 (cheapest)	4·00	4·00
		First Day Cover (No. 2031c)		7·00

Nos. 2031/3 were only issued in the 1998 £7·49 Wilding Definitives stamp booklet No. DX20.

For further Wilding designs with decimal face values and on paper watermarked W**1565** see Nos. 2258/9 and **MS**2326.

Special First Day of Issue Postmarks

British Philatelic Bureau, Edinburgh .... 7·00
London SW1 .... 7·00

1349 St. John's Point Lighthouse, County Down

1350 Smalls Lighthouse, Pembrokeshire

1351 Needles Rock Lighthouse, Isle of Wight, c 1900

1352 Bell Rock Lighthouse, Arbroath, mid-19th-century

1353 Original Eddystone Lighthouse, Plymouth, 1698

(Des D. Davis and J. Boon. Litho Questa)

1998 (24 Mar). **Lighthouses**. *One side phosphor band* (20p.) *or two phosphor bands* (others). P 14½ × 14.

2034	**1349**	20p. gold, greenish yellow, magenta, new blue and black	50	40
2035	**1350**	26p. gold, greenish yellow, magenta, new blue and black	75	50
2036	**1351**	37p. gold, greenish yellow, magenta, new blue and black	1·10	1·25

2037	**1352**	43p. gold, greenish yellow, magenta, new blue and black	1·50	1·50
2038	**1353**	63p. gold, greenish yellow, magenta, new blue and black	2·10	2·10
		Set of 5	5·50	5·25
		Set of 5 Gutter Pairs	12·00	
		First Day Cover		5·75
		Presentation Pack	6·00	
		PHQ Cards (set of 5)	7·00	10·00

Nos. 2034/8 commemorate the 300th anniversary of the first Eddystone Lighthouse and the final year of manned lighthouses.

Special First Day of Issue Postmarks

British Philatelic Bureau, Edinburgh .... 6·00
Plymouth .... 6·00

(Photo Enschedé, Questa or Walsall)

1998 (6 Apr)–**2001**. **Self-adhesive**. *Designs as T* **913/14**. *One centre phosphor band* (2nd), *or two phosphor bands* (1st). *P* 15 × 14 *die-cut (with one elliptical hole on each vertical side).*

2039	(2nd)	bright blue	30	35
		a. Imperf (pair)	75·00	
		b. Perf 14½ × 14 die-cut (22.6.98)	£150	
2040	(1st)	bright orange-red	40	45
		a. Imperf (pair)	75·00	
		b. Perf 14½ × 14 die-cut (22.6.98)	£150	
		Ey. Phosphor omitted		
		l. Booklet pane. No. 2040 × 6 plus commemorative label at left (29.1.01) .	7·00	

Nos. 2039/40, initially sold for 20p. and 26p., were in rolls of 200 printed by Enschedé with the surplus self-adhesive paper removed.

2nd and 1st self-adhesive stamps as Nos. 2039/40 were issued in sheets, printed in photogravure by Walsall Security Printers, on 22 June 1998. These are similar to the previous coil printings, but the sheets retain the surplus self-adhesive paper around each stamp. Stamps from these sheets have square perforation tips instead of the rounded versions to be found on the coils.

Nos. 2039b and 2040b come from initial stocks of these Walsall sheet printings sent to the Philatelic Bureau and supplied to collectors requiring single stamps.

A further printing in sheets appeared on 4 September 2000 printed by Walsall (2nd) or Questa (1st). These sheets were slightly re-designed to provide a block of 4, rather than a strip, in the top panel. Individual stamps cannot be identified as coming from these new sheets as they have rounded perforation tips similar to those on the original coil printings.

The sheets of 100 were re-issued on 9 May 2002 printed by Enschedé in the same format as used in September 2000. The individual stamps are similar to the Enschedé coil printings of April 1998. A further printing of No. 2039 in sheets of 100 appeared on 4 July 2002 printed by Enschedé. On this printing the top panel reverted to a strip of 4 with the typography on the label matching that of contemporary stamp booklets.

No. 2039 was issued on 18 March 2003 in stripped matrix sheets of 100, printed by Walsall.

Both values appeared in stamp booklets from 29 January 2001. No. 2040l comes from self-adhesive booklet No. MB2. The label commemorates the death centenary of Queen Victoria.

See also Nos. 2295/8.

1354 Tommy Cooper

1355 Eric Morecambe

1356 Joyce Grenfell

1357 Les Dawson

1358 Peter Cook

Special First Day of Issue Postmarks

British Philatelic Bureau, Edinburgh .... 6·50
Morecambe .... 6·50

1359 Hands forming Heart

1360 Adult and Child holding Hands

1361 Hands forming Cradle

1362 Hand taking Pulse

(Des G. Scarfe. Litho Walsall)

1998 (23 Apr). **Comedians.** *One side phosphor band* (20p.) *or two phosphor bands* (*others*). P 14½ × 14.

2041	**1354**	20p. vermilion, black, rose-pink, new blue and greenish yellow	50	50
		Ea. Vermilion printed double		£1500
		Eb. Vermilion and black both printed quadruple with rose-pink and new blue both printed double	†	£2500
		Ec. Vermilion and black both printed double	†	£2000
2042	**1355**	26p. vermilion, black, rose-pink and new blue	90	85
		Ea. Vermilion printed double	£250	
		Eb. Vermilion printed triple	£550	
		Ec. Black and vermilion printed double ...	£2000	
2043	**1356**	37p. vermilion, black, rose-pink, new blue and greenish yellow	1·25	1·25
2044	**1357**	43p. vermilion, black, rose-pink, new blue and pale orange	1·50	1·50
2045	**1358**	63p. vermilion, black, deep rose-pink, new blue and greenish yellow	2·10	2·10
		Set of 5	5·75	5·50
		Set of 5 Gutter Pairs	12·50	
		First Day Cover		6·50
		Presentation Pack	6·00	
		PHQ Cards (set of 5)	6·50	10·00

Stamps as Type **1356**, but with a face value of 30p., were prepared but not issued. Mint examples and a first day cover have been reported.

1998 (23 June). **50th Anniv of the National Health Service.** *One side phosphor band* (20p.) *or two phosphor bands* (*others*). P 14 × 14½.

2046	**1359**	20p. deep claret, black, grey-brown, pale cream and cream	50	50
2047	**1360**	26p. deep grey-green, black, grey-brown, pale cream and cream	90	90
2048	**1361**	43p. deep lilac, black, grey-brown, pale cream and cream	1·50	1·50
2049	**1362**	63p. deep dull blue, black, grey-brown, pale cream and cream	2·10	2·10
		Set of 4	4·50	4·50
		Set of 4 Gutter Pairs	10·00	
		First Day Cover		5·00
		Presentation Pack	4·75	
		PHQ Cards (set of 4)	5·00	8·00

British Philatelic Bureau, Edinburgh .... 5·50
Tredegar, Wales .... 5·50

1363 *The Hobbit* (J. R. R. Tolkien)

1364 *The Lion, The Witch and the Wardrobe* (C. S. Lewis)

1365 *The Phoenix and the Carpet* (E. Nesbit)

1366 *The Borrowers* (Mary Norton)

1367 *Through the Looking Glass* (Lewis Carroll)

(Des P. Malone. Photo D.L.R.)

1998 (21 July). **Famous Children's Fantasy Novels**. *One centre phosphor band* (20p.) *or two phosphor bands* (others). P 15 × 14.
2050 **1363** 20p. silver, greenish yellow, bright magenta, new blue, black and gold 50 45
2051 **1364** 26p. silver, greenish yellow, bright magenta, new blue, black and gold 85 55
 a. Imperf (pair) £800
2052 **1365** 37p. silver, greenish yellow, bright magenta, new blue, black and gold .... 1·25 1·50
2053 **1366** 43p. silver, greenish yellow, bright magenta, new blue, black and gold .... 1·40 1·50
2054 **1367** 63p. silver, greenish yellow, bright magenta, new blue, black and gold .... 2·10 2·00
 Set of 5 .... 5·50 5·50
 Set of 5 Gutter Pairs .... 12·00
 First Day Cover .... 6·25
 Presentation Pack .... 6·00
 PHQ Cards (set of 5) .... 6·00 10·00
Nos. 2050/4 commemorate the birth centenary of C. S. Lewis and the death centenary of Lewis Carroll.

British Philatelic Bureau, Edinburgh .... 6·50
Oxford .... 6·50

1368 Woman in Yellow Feathered Costume

1369 Woman in Blue Costume and Headdress

1370 Group of Children in White and Gold Robes

1371 Child in "Tree" Costume

(Des T. Hazael. Photo Walsall)

1998 (25 Aug). **Europa. Festivals. Notting Hill Carnival.** *One centre phosphor band* (20p.) *or two phosphor bands* (others). P 14 × 14½.
2055 **1368** 20p. gold, black, new blue, bright magenta and greenish yellow 75 45
2056 **1369** 26p. gold, grey-black, new blue, bright magenta and greenish yellow 95 55
2057 **1370** 43p. gold, grey-black, new blue, bright magenta and bistre-yellow .... 1·50 1·60

2058 **1371**	63p. gold, grey-black, new blue, bright magenta and greenish yellow	2·00	2·10
	Set of 4	4·75	4·25
	Set of 4 Gutter Pairs	10·50	
	First Day Cover		5·00
	Presentation Pack	5·25	
	PHQ Cards (set of 4)	5·00	9·00

The 20p. and 26p. incorporate the "EUROPA" emblem.

Special First Day of Issue Postmarks

British Philatelic Bureau, Edinburgh	5·50
London W11	5·50

1372 Sir Malcolm Campbell's
Bluebird, 1925

1373 Sir Henry Segrave's
Sunbeam, 1926

1374 John G. Parry Thomas's
Babs, 1926

1375 John R. Cobb's *Railton
Mobil Special*, 1947

1376 Donald Campbell's
Bluebird CN7, 1964

(Des Roundel Design Group. Photo De La Rue)

1998 (29 Sept–13 Oct). **British Land Speed Record Holders.** One phosphor band (20p.) or two phosphor bands (others). P 15 × 14.

2059 **1372**	20p. rosine, greenish yellow, magenta, new blue, black and silver (1 centre band) .	70	25
	a. Perf $14\frac{1}{2} \times 13\frac{1}{2}$ (1 side band at right) (13.10.98)	1·00	1·00
	aEb. Band at left	1·00	1·00
	ac. Booklet pane. Nos. 2059a and 2059aEb, each × 2, with margins all round	5·00	
2060 **1373**	26p. rosine, greenish yellow, magenta, new blue, black and silver	85	30
	a. Rosine (face value) omitted	£2500	
	Eb. "2" from face value omitted	£2000	
	Ec. "6" from face value omited	£2000	
2061 **1374**	30p. rosine, greenish yellow, magenta, new blue, black and silver	1·25	1·50
2062 **1375**	43p. rosine, greenish yellow, magenta, new blue, black and silver	1·50	1·60
2063 **1376**	63p. rosine, greenish yellow, magenta, new blue, black and silver	2·25	2·40
	Set of 5	6·00	5·50
	Set of 5 Gutter Pairs	13·00	
	First Day Cover		6·50
	Presentation Pack	6·50	
	PHQ Cards (set of 5)	7·00	9·00

Nos. 2059/63 commemorate the 50th death anniversary of Sir Malcolm Campbell.

Nos. 2060a/Ec occur on the fourth vertical row of several sheets. Other examples show one or other of the figures partially omitted.

Nos. 2059a/aEb come from the £6.16 British Land Speed Record Holders stamp booklet, No. DX21, and were printed by Walsall. There are minor differences of design between No. 2059 (sheet stamp printed by De La Rue) and Nos. 2059a/aEb (booklet stamps printed by Walsall), which omit the date and copyright symbol.

Special First Day of Issue Postmarks

British Philatelic Bureau, Edinburgh	6·50
Pendine	6·50

1377 Angel with Hands raised
in Blessing

1378 Angel praying

1379 Angel playing Flute

1380 Angel playing Lute

1381 Angel praying

(Des Irene von Treskow. Photo De La Rue)

1998 (2 Nov). **Christmas. Angels.** *One centre phosphor band (20p.) or two phosphor bands (others).* P 15 × 14.

2064	**1377**	20p. gold, greenish yellow, magenta, new blue and grey-black	70	50
		a. Imperf (pair)	£425	
2065	**1378**	26p. gold, greenish yellow, magenta, new blue and grey-black	85	60
		a. Imperf (pair)	£800	
2066	**1379**	30p. gold, greenish yellow, magenta, new blue and grey-black	1·25	1·50
2067	**1380**	43p. gold, greenish yellow, magenta, new blue and grey-black	1·40	1·60
		a. Imperf (pair)	£1400	
2068	**1381**	63p. gold, greenish yellow, magenta, new blue and grey-black	2·00	2·25
		Set of 5	5·50	5·75
		Set of 5 Gutter Pairs	12·00	
		First Day Cover		6·00
		Presentation Pack	6·00	
		PHQ Cards (set of 5)	6·00	9·00

Special First Day of Issue Postmarks

British Philatelic Bureau, Edinburgh	6·25
Bethlehem	6·25

Collectors Pack 1998

1998 (2 Nov). *Comprises Nos. 2015/30, 2034/8 and 2041/68*
CP2068a Collectors Pack .... 55·00

Post Office Yearbook

1998 (2 Nov). *Comprises Nos. 2015/30, 2034/8 and 2041/68 in hardback book with slip case* .... 60·00

1382 Greenwich Meridian and Clock (John Harrison's chronometer)

1383 Industrial Worker and Blast Furnace (James Watt's discovery of steam power)

1384 Early Photos of Leaves (Henry Fox-Talbot's photographic experiments)

1385 Computer inside Human Head (Alan Turing's work on computers)

(Des D. Gentleman (20p.), P. Howson (26p.), Z. and Barbara Baran (43p.), E. Paolozzi (63p.). Photo Enschedé (26p.), Questa (63p. No. 2072a) or De La Rue (others))

1999 (12 Jan–21 Sept). **Millennium Series. The Inventors' Tale.** *One centre phosphor band (20p.) or two phosphor bands (others).* P 14 × 14½.

2069	**1382**	20p. silver, deep grey, pale olive-grey, greenish grey, grey-black and bright rose-red	75	70
		a. Imperf (horiz pair)	£1500	
2070	**1383**	26p. silver, black, new blue, bright magenta and greenish yellow	95	1·00
2071	**1384**	43p. silver, greenish yellow, bright crimson, new blue, black and bright magenta	1·50	1·60
2072	**1385**	63p. greenish blue, greenish yellow, cerise, new blue, black and pale lemon	2·25	2·40
		a. Perf 13½ × 14 (21 Sept)	3·00	3·00
		ab. Booklet pane. No. 2072a × 4 with margins all round	10·00	
		Set of 4	5·00	5·25
		Set of 4 Gutter Pairs	10·00	
		First Day Cover (Philatelic Bureau) (Type J, see Introduction)		6·50
		First Day Cover (Greenwich, London SE)		6·50
		Presentation Pack	5·50	
		PHQ Cards (set of 4)	5·00	10·00

No. 2072a comes from the £6.99 World Changers booklet, No. DX23.

Special First Day of Issue Postmark

1386 Airliner hugging Globe
(International air travel)

1387 Woman on Bicycle
(Development of the bicycle)

1390

1388 Victorian Railway Station
(Growth of public transport)

1389 Captain Cook and Maori
(Captain James Cook's voyages)

(Des G. Hardie (20p.), Sara Fanelli (26p.), J. Lawrence (43p.), A. Klimowski (63p.). Photo Enschedé (20p., 63p.) or De La Rue (26p.). Litho Enschedé (43p.))

1999 (2 Feb). **Millennium Series. The Travellers' Tale.** *One centre phosphor band* (20p.) *or two phosphor bands* (others). P 14 × 14½.

2073	**1386**	20p. silver, vermilion, grey-black, bluish violet, greenish blue and pale grey ...	75	70
2074	**1387**	26p. silver, greenish yellow, cerise, new blue, black and vermilion	95	1·00
2075	**1388**	43p. grey-black, stone and bronze	1·50	1·60
2076	**1389**	63p. silver, grey-black, new blue, bright magenta and greenish yellow	2·25	2·40
		Set of 4	5·00	5·25
		Set of 4 Gutter Pairs	10·00	
		First Day Cover (Philatelic Bureau) (Type J, see Introduction)		6·00
		First Day Cover (Coventry)		6·00
		Presentation Pack	5·50	
		PHQ Cards (set of 4)	5·00	10·00

Special First Day of Issue Postmark

1999 (16 Feb). (a) *Embossed and litho Walsall. Self-adhesive. Die-cut perf* 14 × 15.

2077	**1390**	(1st) grey (face value) (Queen's head in colourless relief) (phosphor background around head)	2·25	2·25
		l. Booklet pane. No. 2077 × 4 with margins all round	8·00	
		(b) *Eng C. Slania. Recess Enschedé. P* 14 × 14½.		
2078	**1390**	(1st) grey-black (2 phosphor bands)	2·25	2·25
		l. Booklet pane. No. 2078 × 4 with margins all round	8·00	
		(c) *Typo Harrison. P* 14 × 15		
2079	**1390**	(1st) black (2 phosphor bands)	2·25	2·25
		Ey. Phosphor omitted		
		l. Booklet pane. No. 2079 × 4 with margins all round	8·00	
		Ely. Booklet pane. Phosphor omitted		
		First Day Covers (3 covers with Nos. 2077l, 2078l, 2079l) (Philatelic Bureau)		12·00
		First Day Covers (3 covers with Nos. 2077l, 2078l, 2079l) (London SW1) ...		12·00

Nos. 2077/9 were only issued in the £7·54 "Profile on Print" booklet, No. DX22.

Special First Day of Issue Postmarks

1391 Vaccinating Child (pattern in cow markings) (Jenner's development of smallpox vaccine)

1392 Patient on Trolley (nursing care)

1393 Penicillin Mould (Fleming's discovery of penicillin)

1394 Sculpture of Test-tube Baby (development of in-vitro fertilization)

1397 Sailing Ship and Aspects of Settlement (19th-century migration to Australia)

1398 Hummingbird and Superimposed Stylised Face (20th-century migration to Great Britain)

(Des P. Brookes (20p.), Susan Macfarlane (26p.), M. Dempsey (43p.), A. Gormley (63p.). Photo Questa)

1999 (2 Mar–21 Sept). **Millennium Series. The Patients' Tale.** *One centre phosphor band (20p.) or two phosphor bands (others).* P 13½ × 14.

2080	**1391**	20p.	greenish yellow, bright magenta, new blue, black and silver	75	70
		a.	Booklet pane. No. 2080 × 4 with margins all round (21 Sept)	2·50	
2081	**1392**	26p.	greenish yellow, bright magenta, new blue, black, silver and deep turquoise-blue	95	1·00
		a.	Imperf (pair)	£1500	
2082	**1393**	43p.	greenish yellow, bright magenta, new blue, black, deep bluish green and silver	1·50	1·60
2083	**1394**	63p.	greenish yellow, bright magenta, new blue, black, silver and blue-black	2·25	2·40
			Set of 4	5·00	5·25
			Set of 4 Gutter Pairs	10·00	
			First Day Cover (Philatelic Bureau) (Type J, see Introduction)	6·00	
			First Day Cover (Oldham)	6·00	
			Presentation Pack	5·50	
			PHQ Cards (set of 4)	5·00	10·00

No. 2080a comes from the £6.99 World Changers booklet, No. DX23.

(Des J. Byrne (20p.), W. McLean (26p.), J. Fisher (43p.), G. Powell (63p.). Litho (20p.) or photo (others) Walsall)

1999 (6 Apr–12 May). **Millennium Series. The Settlers' Tale.** *One centre phosphor band (20p.) or two phosphor bands (others).* P 14 × 14½.

2084	**1395**	20p.	gold, silver, black, magenta, blue and greenish yellow	75	70
2085	**1396**	26p.	greenish yellow, magenta, new blue, grey-black and silver	95	1·00
		a.	Booklet pane. Nos. 2085 and 2089 with margins all round (12 May)	6·00	
2086	**1397**	43p.	greenish yellow, magenta, new blue, grey-black, gold and chocolate	1·50	1·60
2087	**1398**	63p.	greenish yellow, magenta, new blue, reddish violet, deep reddish violet and gold	2·25	2·40
			Set of 4	5·00	5·25
			Set of 4 Gutter Pairs	10·00	
			First Day Cover (Philatelic Bureau) (Type J, see Introduction)	6·00	
			First Day Cover (Plymouth)	6·00	
			Presentation Pack	5·50	
			PHQ Cards (set of 4)	5·00	10·00

No. 2085a comes from the £2.60 booklet, No. HBA1.

Special First Day of Issue Postmark

Special First Day of Issue Postmark

1395 Dove and Norman Settler (medieval migration to Scotland)

1396 Pilgrim Fathers and Red Indian (17th-century migration to America)

1399 Woven Threads (woollen industry)

1400 Salts Mill, Saltaire (worsted cloth industry)

1401 Hull on Slipway
(shipbuilding)

1402 Lloyd's Building (City
of London finance centre)

1405 Dalek from *Dr. Who*
(science-fiction series)
("Television")

1406 Charlie Chaplin (film star)
("Cinema")

(Des P. Collingwood (19p.), D. Hockney (26p.), B. Sanderson (44p.), B.
Neiland (64p.). Litho (19p.) or photo (others) De La Rue)

1999 (4 May). **Millennium Series. The Workers' Tale**. *One centre
phosphor band* (19p.) *or two phosphor bands* (others). *P* 14 × 14½.

2088	**1399**	19p. drab, greenish yellow, cerise, new blue, grey-black and bronze	75	70
		a. Bronze (Queen's head) omitted	£350	
		a£y. Bronze and phosphor omitted	£500	
2089	**1400**	26p. silver, greenish yellow, rosine, new blue and grey-black	95	1·00
2090	**1401**	44p. silver, greenish yellow, orange-red, bright blue, yellow-brown and grey-black	1·50	1·60
2091	**1402**	64p. silver, greenish yellow, rosine, new blue and grey-black	2·25	2·40
		Set of 4	5·00	5·25
		Set of 4 Gutter Pairs	10·00	
		First Day Cover (Philatelic Bureau) (Type J, see Introduction)		6·00
		First Day Cover (Belfast)		6·00
		Presentation Pack	5·50	
		PHQ Cards (set of 4)	5·00	10·00

For No. 2089, printed by Walsall in photogravure, see booklet pane
No. 2085a.

(Des P. Blake (19p.), M. White (26p.), Lord Snowdon (44p.), R. Steadman
(64p.). Photo Enschedé)

1999 (1 June). **Millennium Series. The Entertainers' Tale**. *One centre
phosphor band* (19p.) *or two phosphor bands* (others). *P* 14 × 14½.

2092	**1403**	19p. greenish yellow, bright magenta, new blue, grey-black and gold	75	70
2093	**1404**	26p. greenish yellow, bright magenta, new blue, grey-black, gold and stone	95	1·00
2094	**1405**	44p. greenish yellow, bright magenta, new blue, grey-black and silver	1·50	1·60
2095	**1406**	64p. greenish yellow, bright magenta, new blue, grey-black and silver	2·25	2·40
		Set of 4	5·00	5·25
		Set of 4 Gutter Pairs	10·00	
		First Day Cover (Philatelic Bureau) (Type J, see Introduction)		6·00
		First Day Cover (Wembley)		6·00
		Presentation Pack	5·50	
		PHQ Cards (set of 4)	5·00	10·00

Special First Day of Issue Postmark

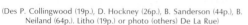

Special First Day of Issue Postmark

1407 Prince Edward and Miss Sophie Rhys-Jones **1408**
(from photos by John Swannell)

(Adapted J. Gibbs. Photo De La Rue)

1999 (15 June). **Royal Wedding**. *Two phosphor bands*. *P* 15 × 14.

2096	**1407**	26p. vermilion, black, grey-black and silver	85	85
		a. Imperf (pair)	£850	
2097	**1408**	64p. new blue, black, grey-black and silver	1·90	1·90
		Set of 2	2·75	2·75
		Set of 2 Gutter Pairs	6·75	
		First Day Cover (Philatelic Bureau)		4·25
		First Day Cover (Windsor)		4·25
		Presentation Pack	3·25	
		PHQ Cards (set of 2)	4·00	6·00

1403 Freddie Mercury
(lead singer of Queen)
("Popular Music")

1404 Bobby Moore with
World Cup, 1966 ("Sport")

Special First Day of Issue Postmarks

Special First Day of Issue Postmark

1409 Suffragette behind Prison Window (Equal Rights for Women)

1410 Water Tap (Right to Health)

1413 Molecular Structures (DNA Decoding)

1414 Galapagos Finch and Fossilized Skeleton (Darwin's Theory of Evolution)

1415 Rotation of Polarized Light by Magnetism (Faraday's work on Electricity)

1416 Saturn (development of astronomical telescopes)

1411 Generations of School Children (Right to Education)

1412 "MAGNA CARTA" (Human Rights)

(Des Natasha Kerr (19p.), M. Craig-Martin (26p.), A. Drummond (44p.), A. Kitching (64p.). Photo De La Rue)

1999 (6 July). **Millennium Series**. *The Citizens' Tale*. *One centre phosphor band* (19p.) *or two phosphor bands* (others). P 14 × 14½.

2098	**1409**	19p. silver, greenish yellow, cerise, new blue and grey-black	75	70
2099	**1410**	26p. grey-black, new blue, bright mauve, rosine, turquoise-green and apple-green	95	1·00
2100	**1411**	44p. bright blue, greenish yellow, cerise, new blue and grey-black	1·50	1·60
2101	**1412**	64p. gold, greenish yellow, cerise, new blue and grey-black	2·25	2·40
		Set of 4	5·00	5·25
		Set of 4 Gutter Pairs	10·00	
		First Day Cover (Philatelic Bureau) (Type J, see Introduction)		6·00
		First Day Cover (Newtown, Powis)		6·00
		Presentation Pack	5·50	
		PHQ Cards (set of 4)	5·00	10·00

(Des M. Curtis (19p.), R. Harris Ching (26p.), C. Gray (44p.), from Hubble Space Telescope photograph (64p.). Photo (19p., 64p.) or litho (26p., 44p.) Questa)

1999 (3 Aug–21 Sept). **Millennium Series**. *The Scientists' Tale*. *One centre phosphor band* (19p.) *or two phosphor bands* (others). P 13½ × 14 (19p., 64p.) or 14 × 14½ (26p., 44p.).

2102	**1413**	19p. bright magenta, greenish yellow, new blue, black, black and silver	75	70
2103	**1414**	26p. greenish yellow, bright magenta, new blue, black, bronze and reddish violet	95	1·00
		a. Imperf (pair)	£750	
		b. Perf 14½ × 14 (21 Sept)	3·00	3·00
		ba. Booklet pane. No. 2103b × 4 with margins all round	8·00	
2104	**1415**	44p. greenish yellow, bright magenta, new blue, black and gold	1·50	1·60
		a. Perf 14½ × 14 (21 Sept)	3·00	3·00
		ab. Booklet pane. No. 2104a × 4 with margins all round	9·00	
2105	**1416**	64p. bright magenta, greenish yellow, new blue, black and silver	2·25	2·40
		Set of 4	5·00	5·25
		Set of 4 Gutter Pairs	10·00	
		First Day Cover (Philatelic Bureau) (Type J, see Introduction)		6·00
		First Day Cover (Cambridge)		6·00
		Presentation Pack	5·50	
		PHQ Cards (set of 4)	5·00	10·00

Nos. 2103b and 2104a come from the £6.99 World Changers booklet, No. DX23.

Special First Day of Issue Postmark

(Photo De La Rue)

1999 (11 Aug). **Solar Eclipse**. *Sheet* 89 × 121 *mm. Two phosphor bands.* P 14 × 14½.

MS2106	No. 2105 × 4 (*sold at* £2.56)	18·00	18·00
	a. Imperf	£3250	
	First Day Cover (Philatelic Bureau)	62·00	
	First Day Cover (Falmouth)	62·00	

(Des D. Tress (19p.), C. Wormell (26p.), Tessa Traeger (44p.), R. Cooke (64p.). Photo Walsall (No. 2108a) or De La Rue (others))

1999 (7–21 Sept). **Millennium Series. The Farmers' Tale**. *One centre phosphor band* (19p.) *or two phosphor bands* (others). P 14 × 14½.

2107	**1417**	19p. grey-black, greenish yellow, cerise, new blue and silver	75	70
2108	**1418**	26p. chestnut, orange-brown, violet-blue, grey-black, pale turquoise-green and silver	95	1·00
		a. Booklet pane. No. 2108 × 2 with margins all round (21 Sept)	6·00	
2109	**1419**	44p. silver, yellow-brown, brown and grey-black	1·50	1·60
2110	**1420**	64p. deep brown, greenish yellow, magenta, new blue and silver	2·25	2·40
		Set of 4	5·00	5·25
		Set of 4 Gutter Pairs	10·00	
		First Day Cover (Philatelic Bureau) (Type J, see Introduction)		6·00
		First Day Cover (Laxton, Newark)		6·00
		Presentation Pack	5·50	
		PHQ Cards (set of 4)	5·00	10·00

The 19p. includes the "EUROPA" emblem.
No. 2108a comes from the £2.60 booklet, No. HBA2.

Special First Day of Issue Postmarks

Special First Day of Issue Postmark

1417 Upland Landscape (Strip Farming)

1418 Horse-drawn Rotary Seed Drill (Mechanical Farming)

1421 Robert the Bruce (Battle of Bannockburn, 1314)

1422 Cavalier and Horse (English Civil War)

1419 Man peeling Potato (Food Imports)

1420 Aerial View of Combine Harvester (Satellite Agriculture)

1423 War Graves Cemetery, The Somme (World Wars)

1424 Soldiers with Boy (Peace-keeping)

(Des A. Davidson (19p.), R. Kelly (26p.), D. McCullin (44p.), C. Corr (64p.). Litho (19p.) or photo (others) Walsall)

1999 (5 Oct). **Millennium Series. The Soldiers' Tale.** *One centre phosphor band (19p.) or two phosphor bands (others). P 14 × 14½.*

2111	**1421**	19p. black, stone and silver	75	70
2112	**1422**	26p. lemon, black, grey, silver, black and gold	95	1·00
2113	**1423**	44p. grey-black, black and silver	1·50	1·60
2114	**1424**	64p. greenish yellow, red-orange, bright magenta, pale new blue, black and bright blue	2·25	2·40
		Set of 4	5·00	5·25
		Set of 4 Gutter Pairs	10·00	
		First Day Cover (Philatelic Bureau) (Type J, see Introduction)		6·00
		First Day Cover (London SW)		6·00
		Presentation Pack	5·50	
		PHQ Cards (set of 4)	5·00	10·00

Special First Day of Issue Postmark

5-10-1999

2116	**1426**	26p. gold, greenish yellow, bright scarlet, emerald, dull violet and black	95	1·00
2117	**1427**	44p. gold, greenish yellow, bright magenta, new blue, black and ultramarine	1·50	1·60
2118	**1428**	64p. gold, bistre-yellow, cerise, bright emerald, bistre, slate-blue, pale new blue and black	2·25	2·40
		Set of 4	5·00	5·25
		Set of 4 Gutter Pairs	10·00	
		First Day Cover (Philatelic Bureau) (Type J, see Introduction)		6·00
		First Day Cover (St. Andrews, Fife)		6·00
		Presentation Pack	5·50	
		PHQ Cards (set of 4)	5·00	10·00

Special First Day of Issue Postmark

2-11-1999

1425 "Hark the herald angels sing" and Hymnbook (John Wesley)

1426 King James I and Bible (Authorised Version of Bible)

1429 "World of the Stage" (Allen Jones)

1430 "World of Music" (Bridget Riley)

1427 St. Andrews Cathedral, Fife ("Pilgrimage")

1428 Nativity ("First Christmas")

1431 "World of Literature" (Lisa Milroy)

1432 "New Worlds" (Sir Howard Hodgkin)

(Des B. Neuenschwander (19p.), Clare Melinsky (26p.), Catherine Yass (44p.), C. Aitchison (64p.). Photo De La Rue)

1999 (2 Nov). **Millennium Series. The Christians' Tale.** *One centre phosphor band (19p.) or two phosphor bands (others). P 14 × 14½.*

2115	**1425**	19p. gold, stone, greenish yellow, bright crimson, deep dull blue, black and yellow-ochre	75	70

(Photo Walsall)

1999 (7 Dec). **Millennium Series. The Artists' Tale.** *One centre phosphor band (19p.) or two phosphor bands (others). P 14 × 14½.*

2119	**1429**	19p. greenish yellow, bright magenta, new blue, black and silver	75	70
2120	**1430**	26p. lemon, orange, pale new blue, violet-blue and black	95	1·00
2121	**1431**	44p. greenish yellow, bright magenta, new blue, black and gold	1·50	1·60

2122 **1432** 64p. greenish yellow, yellow, bright turquoise-green, bright magenta, new blue, black, gold and silver .... 2·25 2·40
    Set of 4 .... 5·00 5·25
    Set of 4 Gutter Pairs .... 10·00
    First Day Cover (Philatelic Bureau) (Type J, see Introduction) .... 6·00
    First Day Cover (Stratford-upon-Avon) 6·00
    Presentation Pack .... 5·50
    PHQ Cards (set of 4) .... 5·00 10·00

Special First Day of Issue Postmark

Collectors Pack 1999

1999 (7 Dec). *Comprises Nos. 2069/76, 2080/105 and 2107/22*
CP2122a Collectors Pack .... 55·00

Post Office Yearbook

1999 (7 Dec). *Comprises Nos. 2069/76, 2080/105 and 2107/22 in hardback book with slip case* .... 60·00

1433a

(Des D. Gentleman. Photo De La Rue)

1999 (14 Dec). **Millennium Series. "Millennium Timekeeper"**. *Sheet 120 × 89 mm. Each design silver, deep grey, pale olive-grey, greenish grey, grey-black and bright rose-red. Two phosphor bands. P 14 × 14½.*
MS2123 **1433a** 64p. Clock face and map of North America; 64p. Clock face and map of Asia; 64p. Clock face and map of Middle East; 64p. Clock face and map of Europe .... 17·00 17·00
    First Day Cover (Philatelic Bureau) .... 18·00
    First Day Cover (Greenwich SE) .... 18·00
    Presentation Pack .... 24·00
    PHQ Cards (set of 5) .... 8·00 22·00

No. **MS**2123 also exists overprinted "EARLS COURT, LONDON 22–28 MAY 2000 THE STAMP SHOW 2000" from Exhibition Premium Passes, costing £10, available from 1 March 2000.

Special First Day of Issue Postmarks

1437 Queen Elizabeth II

(Des A. Machin, adapted R. Scholey. Photo De La Rue, Questa or Walsall (No. 2124), Walsall (Nos. 2124bl, 2124dl), Questa or Walsall (No. 2124d))

2000 (6 Jan-4 Aug). **New Millennium**. *Two phosphor bands. P 15 × 14 (with one elliptical hole on each vertical side).*
2124 **1437** (1st) olive-brown 80 90
    a. Imperf (pair) £700
    bl. Booklet pane. No. 2124 × 4 plus commemorative label at right (21.3.00) .... 4·50
    bm. Booklet pane. No. 2124 × 9 with margins all round (4 Aug) .... 7·00
    cEy. Phosphor omitted ....
    d. Perf 14 .... 80 90
    dEa. Phosphor omitted ....
    dl. Booklet pane. No. 2124d × 8 with central label and margins all round (15.2.00) .... 6·50
    First Day Cover (No. 2124) (Philatelic Bureau) (Type G, see Introduction) .. 3·00
    First Day Cover (No. 2124) (Windsor) (Type G) .... 3·00
    First Day Cover (No. 2124bm) (Philatelic Bureau) .... 6·00
    First Day Cover (No. 2124bm) (London SW1) .... 6·00
    First Day Cover (No. 2124dl) (Philatelic Bureau) .... 6·00
    First Day Cover (No. 2124dl) (London SW5) .... 6·00
    Presentation Pack .... 3·25
    PHQ Card (23 May) .... 5·00 16·00

No. 2124d comes from stamp booklets printed by Questa. Similar booklets produced by Walsall have the same perforation as the sheet stamps.

The labels on booklet pane No. 2124bl show either Postman Pat, publicising "The Stamp Show 2000", or the National Botanic Garden of Wales.

For special first day of issue postmarks used on No. 2124bm see below No. **MS**2161.

2127	**1440**	44p.	black, bistre-brown, buff and silver ...	1·50	1·60
2128	**1441**	64p.	greenish yellow, magenta, blue, black, silver and orange	2·25	2·40

Set of 4 (ex No. 2126a) .... 5·00 5·25
Set of 4 Gutter Pairs .... 10·00
First Day Cover (Nos. 2125/8) (Philatelic Bureau) (Type J, see Introduction) ... 6·00
First Day Cover (Nos. 2125/8) (Muncaster, Ravenglass) .... 6·00
First Day Cover (No. 2126ab) (Philatelic Bureau) .... 6·00
First Day Cover (No. 2126ab) (Leicester) 6·00
Presentation Pack .... 5·50
PHQ Cards (set of 4) .... 5·00 10·00

No. 2126a comes from the £2.70 Millennium booklet, No. HBA3, and the "Across the Universe" sponsored booklet, No. DX29.

1438 Barn Owl (World Owl Trust, Muncaster)

1439 Night Sky (National Space Science Centre, Leicester)

1440 River Goyt and Textile Mills (Torrs Walkway, New Mills)

1441 Cape Gannets (Seabird Centre, North Berwick)

1442 Millennium Beacon (Beacons across The Land)

1443 Garratt Steam Locomotive No. 143 pulling Train (Rheilffordd Eryri, Welsh Highland Railway)

(Litho (44p.), photo (others) Walsall (No. 2126a/ab) or Questa (others))

2000 (18 Jan)–**02. Millennium Projects (1st series)**. **"Above and Beyond"**. *One centre phosphor band* (19p.) *or two phosphor bands* (others). P 14 × 14½ (1st, 44p.) *or* 13½ × 14 (others).

2125	**1438**	19p.	greenish yellow, magenta, pale new blue, black and silver	75	70
2126	**1439**	26p.	greenish yellow, magenta, pale new blue, black and silver	95	1·00
2126a		(1st)	greenish yellow, magenta, pale new blue, black and silver (26.5.00)	3·50	3·50
		ab.	Booklet pane. Nos. 2126a and 2139 with margins all round	6·00	
		ac.	Booklet pane. No. 2126a × 4 with margins all round (24.9.02)	4·00	

1444 Lightning (Dynamic Earth Centre, Edinburgh)

1445 Multicoloured Lights (Lighting Croydon's Skyline)

(Photo De La Rue)

2000 (1 Feb). **Millennium Projects (2nd series)**. **"Fire and Light"**. *One centre phosphor band (19p.) or two phosphor bands (others). P 14 × 14½.*

2129	**1442**	19p. silver, greenish yellow, bright magenta, new blue and black	75	70
2130	**1443**	26p. silver, greenish yellow, bright magenta, new blue and black	95	1·00
2131	**1444**	44p. silver, greenish yellow, bright magenta, new blue and black	1·50	1·60
2132	**1445**	64p. silver, greenish yellow, bright magenta, pale greenish blue and black	2·25	2·40
		Set of 4	5·00	5·25
		Set of 4 Gutter Pairs	10·00	
		First Day Cover (Philatelic Bureau) (Type J, see Introduction)		6·00
		First Day Cover (Edinburgh 3°10'W) ...		6·00
		Presentation Pack	5·50	
		PHQ Cards (set of 4)	5·00	10·00

Special First Day of Issue Postmark

1-2-2000

1446 Queen Victoria and Queen Elizabeth II

(Des J. Matthews. Photo Walsall)

2000 (15 Feb). *T* **929** *redrawn with "1st" face value as T* **1446**. *Two phosphor bands. P 14 (with one elliptical hole on each vertical side).*

2133	**1446**	(1st) brownish black and cream	1·10	1·25
		l. Booklet pane. No. 2133 × 6 with margins all round	6·00	
		First Day Cover (No. 2133l) (Philatelic Bureau)		4·00
		First Day Cover (No. 2133l) (London SW5)		4·00

No. 2133 was only issued in £7.50 stamp booklets.
For illustrations of first day cover cancellations see below No. 2124.

1449 Cliff Boardwalk (Parc Arfordirol, Llanelli Coast)

1450 Reflections in Water (Portsmouth Harbour Development)

(Litho (44p.), photo (others) Walsall)

2000 (7 Mar). **Millennium Projects (3rd series)**. **"Water and Coast"**. *One centre phosphor band (19p.) or two phosphor bands (others). P 14 × 14½.*

2134	**1447**	19p. silver, black, dull blue, sage-green, olive-grey, orange-yellow and pale grey	75	70
2135	**1448**	26p. new blue, silver, black, greenish yellow and magenta	95	1·00
2136	**1449**	44p. black, grey and silver	1·50	1·60
2137	**1450**	64p. black, grey, deep bluish green, greenish blue, cobalt, grey-green and brownish grey	2·25	2·40
		Set of 4	5·00	5·25
		Set of 4 Gutter Pairs	10·00	
		First Day Cover (Philatelic Bureau) (Type J, see Introduction)		6·00
		First Day Cover (Llanelli)		6·00
		Presentation Pack	5·50	
		PHQ Cards (set of 4)	5·00	10·00

Special First Day of Issue Postmark

7-3-2000

1447 Beach Pebbles (Turning the Tide, Durham Coast)

1448 Frog's Legs and Water Lilies (National Pondlife Centre, Merseyside)

1451 Reed Beds, River Braid (ECOS, Ballymena)

1452 South American Leaf-cutter Ants ("Web of Life" Exhibition, London Zoo)

1453 Solar Sensors (Earth Centre, Doncaster)

1454 Hydroponic Leaves (Project SUZY, Teesside)

1457 Road Marking (Cycle Network Artworks)

1458 People of Salford (Lowry Centre, Salford)

(Photo De La Rue)

2000 (4 Apr). **Millennium Projects (4th series)**. **"Life and Earth"**. *One centre phosphor band* (2nd) *or two phosphor bands* (others). P 14 × 14½.

2138	**1451**	(2nd) silver, greenish yellow, magenta, new blue, black and grey	75	70
2139	**1452**	(1st) silver, greenish yellow, magenta, new blue and black	95	1·00
2140	**1453**	44p. silver, greenish yellow, magenta, new blue and black	1·50	1·60
2141	**1454**	64p. silver, greenish yellow, magenta, new blue and grey-black	2·25	2·40
		Set of 4	5·00	5·25
		Set of 4 Gutter Pairs	10·00	
		First Day Cover (Philatelic Bureau) (Type J, see Introduction)		6·00
		First Day Cover (Doncaster)		6·00
		Presentation Pack	5·50	
		PHQ Cards (set of 4)	5·00	10·00

For No. 2139 printed by Walsall in photogravure, see booklet pane No. 2126ab.

Types **1453/4** with face values of 45p. and 65p. were prepared, but not issued.

2000 (2 May). **Millennium Projects (5th series)**. **"Art and Craft"**. *One centre phosphor band* (2nd) *or two phosphor bands* (others). P 14 × 14½.

2142	**1455**	(2nd) greenish yellow, magenta, new blue, black, silver and grey-brown	75	70
2143	**1456**	(1st) greenish yellow, magenta, new blue, black and silver	95	1·00
2144	**1457**	45p. greenish yellow, magenta, new blue, black and silver	1·50	1·60
2145	**1458**	65p. greenish yellow, magenta, new blue, black, dull silver and silver	2·25	2·40
		Set of 4	5·00	5·25
		Set of 4 Gutter Pairs	10·00	
		First Day Cover (Philatelic Bureau) (Type J, see Introduction)		6·00
		First Day Cover (Salford)		6·00
		Presentation Pack	5·50	
		PHQ Cards (set of 4)	5·00	10·00

Special First Day of Issue Postmark

Special First Day of Issue Postmark

1455 Pottery Glaze (Ceramica Museum, Stoke-on-Trent)

1456 Bankside Galleries (Tate Modern, London)

(Des J. Matthews. Photo De La Rue)

2000 (22 May). **"Stamp Show 2000" International Stamp Exhibition, London. Jeffrey Matthews Colour Palette**. *Sheet, 124 × 70 mm, containing stamps as* T **367** *with two labels. Phosphorised paper.* P 15 × 14 (*with one elliptical hole on each vertical side*).

MS2146	4p. new blue; 5p. dull red-brown; 6p. yellow-olive; 10p. dull orange; 31p. deep mauve; 39p. bright magenta; 64p. turquoise-green; £1 bluish violet	13·00	12·00
	First Day Cover (Philatelic Bureau)		12·00
	First Day Cover (Earls Court, London SW5)		12·00
	Exhibition Card (wallet, sold at £4·99, containing one mint sheet and one cancelled on postcard)		20·00

The £1 value is printed in Iriodin ink which gives a shiny effect to the solid part of the background behind the Queen's head.

Special First Day of Issue Postmarks

1460 Children playing
(Millennium Greens Project)

1461 Millennium Bridge,
Gateshead

1459a

(Des Delaney Design Consultants. Photo De La Rue)

1462 Daisies (Mile End Park,
London)

1463 African Hut and Thatched
Cottage ("On the Meridian Line"
Project)

(Photo (2nd, 45p.) or litho (1st, 65p.) Walsall)

2000 (23 May). **"Stamp Show 2000" International Stamp Exhibition, London. "Her Majesty's Stamps".** *Sheet 121 × 89 mm. Phosphorised paper. P 15 × 14 (with one elliptical hole on each vertical side of stamps as T* **1437**).

MS2147 **1459**a (1st) olive-brown (Type **1437**) × 4; £1
slate-green (as Type **163**) .... 18·00   12·00
   First Day Cover (Philatelic Bureau) .....   14·00
   First Day Cover (City of Westminster,
   London SW1) ....   14·00
   Presentation Pack .... 70·00
   PHQ Cards (set of 2) .... 12·00   25·00

The £1 value is an adaptation of the 1953 Coronation 1s. 3d. stamp originally designed by Edmund Dulac. It is shown on one of the PHQ cards with the other depicting the complete miniature sheet.

2000 (6 June). **Millennium Projects (6th series). "People and Places".** *One centre phosphor band (2nd) or two phosphor bands (others). P 14 × 14½.*

2148 **1460** (2nd) bistre-yellow, bright magenta, new
   blue, grey-black and silver   75   70
2149 **1461** (1st) deep ultramarine, silver, black, new
   blue, bright magenta and greenish
   yellow   95   1·00
2150 **1462** 45p. greenish yellow, magenta, pale new
   blue, grey-black, silver and deep
   turquoise-green ....   1·50   1·60
2151 **1463** 65p. silver, black, new blue, bright magenta
   and greenish yellow ....   2·25   2·40
   Set of 4 ....   5·00   5·25
   Set of 4 Gutter Pairs .... 10·00
   First Day Cover (Philatelic Bureau)
   (Type J, see Introduction) ....   6·00
   First Day Cover (Gateshead) ....   6·00
   Presentation Pack .... 5·50
   PHQ Cards (set of 4) .... 5·00   10·00

Special First Day of Issue Postmarks

Special First Day of Issue Postmark

1464 Raising the Stone
(Strangford Stone, Killyleagh)

1465 Horse's Hooves (Trans
Pennine Trail, Derbyshire)

1468 Tree Roots ("Yews for
the Millennium" Project)

1469 Sunflower ("Eden"
Project, St. Austell)

1466 Cyclist (Kingdom of Fife
Cycle Ways, Scotland)

1467 Bluebell Wood
(Groundwork's "Changing
Places" Project)

1470 Sycamore Seeds
(Millennium Seed Bank,
Wakehurst Place, Surrey)

1471 Forest, Doire Dach
("Forest for Scotland")

(Photo Walsall (Nos. 2156a, 2158a, 2159a) or De La Rue (others))

(Photo Walsall (Nos. 2153a, 2155a) or Enschedé (others))

2000 (4 July–18 Sept). **Millennium Projects (7th series). "Stone and
Soil".** *One centre phosphor band* (2nd) *or two phosphor bands*
(others). P $14 \times 14\frac{1}{2}$.

2152	**1464**	(2nd) brownish black, grey-black and silver .	75	70
2153	**1465**	(1st) greenish yellow, bright magenta, new blue, grey-black, silver and grey	95	1·00
		a. Booklet pane. Nos. 2153 and 2157 with margins all round (5 Sept)	7·00	
2154	**1466**	45p. brownish black, grey-black, black and silver	1·50	1·60
2155	**1467**	65p. greenish yellow, bright magenta, new blue, black and silver	2·25	2·40
		a. Booklet pane. No. 2155 × 2 with margins all round (18 Sept)	3·75	
		Set of 4	5·00	5·25
		Set of 4 Gutter Pairs	10·00	
		First Day Cover (Philatelic Bureau) (Type J, see Introduction)		6·00
		First Day Cover (Killyleagh)		6·00
		Presentation Pack	5·50	
		PHQ Cards (set of 4)	5·00	10·00

No. 2155a comes from the £7 Treasury of Trees booklet, No. DX26.

Special First Day of Issue Postmark

2000 (1 Aug–18 Sept). **Millennium Projects (8th series). "Tree and
Leaf".** *One centre phosphor band* (2nd) *or two phosphor bands*
(others). P $14 \times 14\frac{1}{2}$.

2156	**1468**	(2nd) silver, greenish yellow, magenta, new blue and black	75	70
		a. Booklet pane. No. 2156 × 4 with margins all round (18 Sept)	3·50	
2157	**1469**	(1st) greenish yellow, magenta, new blue, black and silver	95	1·00
2158	**1470**	45p. black, greenish yellow, magenta, new blue, grey-black and silver	1·50	1·60
		a. Booklet pane. No. 2158 × 4 with margins all round (18 Sept)	5·50	
2159	**1471**	65p. greenish yellow, magenta, new blue, black and black	2·25	2·40
		a. Booklet pane. No. 2159 × 2 with margins all round (18 Sept)	4·00	
		Set of 4	5·00	5·25
		Set of 4 Gutter Pairs	10·00	
		First Day Cover (Philatelic Bureau) (Type J, see Introduction)		6·00
		First Day Cover (St Austell)		6·00
		Presentation Pack	5·50	
		PHQ Cards (set of 4)	5·00	10·00

Nos. 2156a, 2158a and 2159a come from the £7 Treasury of Trees
booklet, No. DX26.

For No. 2157 printed by Walsall in photogravure, see booklet pane
No. 2153a.

Special First Day of Issue Postmark

1472 Queen Elizabeth
the Queen Mother

1473 Head of *Gigantiops
destructor* (Ant) (Wildscreen at
Bristol)

1474 Gathering Water Lilies on
Broads (Norfolk and Norwich
Project)

1472a Royal Family on Queen Mother's 99th Birthday

(Des J. Gibbs from photo by J. Swannell. Photo Questa (Nos. 2160, MS2161a) or De La Rue (No. MS2161))

2000 (4 Aug). **Queen Elizabeth the Queen Mother's 100th Birthday.**
Phosphorised paper plus two phosphor bands. P 14½.
2160 **1472** 27p. silver, greenish yellow, magenta, new
  blue and black .... 2·50   2·50
  a. Booklet pane. No. 2160×4 with mar-
    gins all round .... 7·50
MS2161 121×89 mm. **1472a** 27p.×4, silver, greenish
  yellow, magenta, new blue and black .... 10·00 10·00
  a. Booklet pane. As No. **MS**2161, but
    larger, 150×95 mm, and with addi-
    tional silver frame .... 8·00   8·00
  First Day Cover (No. 2160a) (Philatelic
    Bureau) .... 8·00
  First Day Cover (No. 2160a) (London
    SW1) .... 8·00
  First Day Cover (**MS**2161) (Philatelic
    Bureau) .... 12·00
  First Day Cover (**MS**2161) (London SW1) 12·00
  Presentation Pack (**MS**2161) .... 15·00
  PHQ Cards (*set of 5*) .... 6·00 18·00
  No. 2160 was only issued in £7.03 stamp booklets and as part of
Nos. **MS**2161/a.
  The complete miniature sheet is shown on one of the PHQ cards
with the others depicting individual stamps.

Special First Day of Issue Postmarks

1475 X-ray of Hand holding
Computer Mouse (Millennium
Point, Birmingham)

1476 Tartan Wool Holder
(Scottish Cultural Resources
Access Network)

(Litho Walsall)

2000 (5 Sept). **Millennium Projects (9th series). "Mind and Matter"**. *One
centre phosphor band* (2nd) *or two phosphor bands* (others).
P 14×14½.
2162 **1473** (2nd) black, orange-yellow, slate-green and
  silver 75   70
2163 **1474** (1st) black, sage-green, ochre and gold .... 95 1·00
2164 **1475** 45p. silver, black, new blue, magenta and
  greenish yellow .... 1·50 1·60
2165 **1476** 65p. silver, black, new blue, magenta and
  greenish yellow .... 2·25 2·40
  Set of 4 .... 5·00 5·25
  Set of 4 Gutter Pairs .... 10·00
  First Day Cover (Philatelic Bureau)
    (Type J, see Introduction) ....   6·00
  First Day Cover (Norwich) ....   6·00
  Presentation Pack .... 5·50
  PHQ Cards (set of 4) .... 5·00 10·00

Special First Day of Issue Postmark

5-9-2000

1477 Acrobatic Performers (Millennium Dome)

1478 Football Players (Hampden Park, Glasgow)

1481 Virgin and Child Stained Glass Window, St. Edmundsbury Cathedral (Suffolk Cathedral Millennium Project)

1482 Floodlit Church of St. Peter and St. Paul, Overstowey (Church Floodlighting Trust)

1479 Bather (Bath Spa Project)

1480 Hen's Egg under Magnification (Centre for Life, Newcastle)

1483 12th-cent Latin Gradual (St. Patrick Centre, Downpatrick)

1484 Chapter House Ceiling, York Minster (York Millennium Mystery Plays)

(Photo De La Rue)

(Litho (2nd) or photo (others) Questa)

2000 (3 Oct). **Millennium Projects (10th series). "Body and Bone"**. One centre phosphor band (2nd) or two phosphor bands (others). P 14 × 14½ (2nd) or 13½ × 14 (others).

2166	**1477**	(2nd) black, slate-blue and silver	75	70
2167	**1478**	(1st) magenta, new blue, greenish yellow, black and silver	95	1·00
2168	**1479**	45p. mauve, olive-grey, greenish yellow, grey-black and silver	1·50	1·60
2169	**1480**	65p. magenta, pale new blue, greenish yellow, grey-black and silver	2·25	2·40
		Set of 4	5·00	5·25
		Set of 4 Gutter Pairs	10·00	
		First Day Cover (Philatelic Bureau) (Type J, see Introduction)		6·00
		First Day Cover (Glasgow)		6·00
		Presentation Pack	5·50	
		PHQ Cards (set of 4)	5·00	10·00

Special First Day of Issue Postmark

2000 (7 Nov). **Millennium Projects (11th series). "Spirit and Faith"**. One centre phosphor band (2nd) or two phosphor bands (others). P 14 × 14½.

2170	**1481**	(2nd) gold, greenish yellow, cerise, new blue and grey-black	75	70
2171	**1482**	(1st) gold, greenish yellow, cerise, new blue, bright blue, black and grey-black	95	1·00
		a. Imperf (pair)	£550	
2172	**1483**	45p. deep reddish purple, olive-sepia, red, black and gold	1·50	1·60
2173	**1484**	65p. gold, greenish yellow, cerise, new blue, grey-black and black	2·25	2·40
		Set of 4	5·00	5·25
		Set of 4 Gutter Pairs	10·00	
		First Day Cover (Philatelic Bureau) (Type J, see Introduction)		6·00
		First Day Cover (Downpatrick)		6·00
		Presentation Pack	5·50	
		PHQ Cards (set of 4)	5·00	10·00

Special First Day of Issue Postmark

Post Office Yearbook

2000 (7 Nov). Comprises Nos. 2125/6, 2127/32, 2134/45, 2148/59 and **MS**2161/81 in hardback book with slip case .... 75·00

The last two issues in the Millennium Projects Series were supplied for insertion into the above at a later date.

1485 Church Bells (Ringing in the Millennium)

1486 Eye (Year of the Artist)

1489 "Flower" ("Nurture Children")

1490 "Tiger" ("Listen to Children")

1487 Top of Harp (Canolfan Mileniwm, Cardiff)

1488 Silhouetted Figure within Latticework (TS2K Creative Enterprise Centres, London)

1491 "Owl" ("Teach Children")

1492 "Butterfly" ("Ensure Children's Freedom")

(Photo De La Rue)

2000 (5 Dec). **Millennium Projects (12th series). "Sound and Vision".** One centre phosphor band (2nd) or two phosphor bands (others). P 14 × 14½.

2174 **1485** (2nd) silver, greenish yellow, magenta, new blue and black	75	70
2175 **1486** (1st) silver, magenta, blue, black and brownish grey	95	1·00
2176 **1487** 45p. silver, greenish yellow, magenta, new blue and black	1·50	1·60
2177 **1488** 65p. black, greenish yellow, magenta, new blue, grey-black and silver	2·25	2·40
Set of 4	5·00	5·25
Set of 4 Gutter Pairs	10·00	
First Day Cover (Philatelic Bureau) (Type J, see Introduction)		6·00
First Day Cover (Cardiff)		6·00
Presentation Pack	5·50	
PHQ Cards (set of 4)	5·00	10·00

Special First Day of Issue Postmark

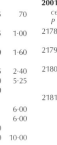

Collectors Pack 2000

2000 (5 Dec). Comprises Nos. 2125/6, 2127/32, 2134/45, 2148/59 and **MS**2161/81.
CP2181a Collectors Pack .... 65·00

(Des Why Not Associates. Photo De La Rue)

2001 (16 Jan). **New Millennium. Rights of the Child. Face Paintings.** One centre phosphor band (2nd) or two phosphor bands (others). P 14 × 14½.

2178 **1489** (2nd) bright violet, greenish yellow, cerise, new blue, rosine, grey-black and silver	75	75
2179 **1490** (1st) lemon, greenish yellow, cerise, new blue, emerald, grey-black and silver	1·00	1·10
2180 **1491** 45p. orange-yellow, greenish yellow, cerise, new blue, pale violet-blue, grey-black and silver	1·60	1·75
2181 **1492** 65p. bright violet, greenish yellow, cerise, new blue, lemon, grey-black and silver	2·40	2·50
Set of 4	5·25	5·50
Set of 4 Gutter Pairs	11·00	
First Day Cover (Philatelic Bureau)		6·25
First Day Cover (Hope, Hope Valley)		6·25
Presentation Pack	6·25	
PHQ Cards (set of 4)	5·00	10·00

Special First Day of Issue Postmarks

1493 "Love"

1494 "THANKS"

1495 "abc" (New Baby)

1496 "WELCOME"

1498 Dog and Owner on
Bench

1499 Dog in Bath

1497 "Cheers"

1500 Boxer at Dog Show

1501 Cat in Handbag

(Des Springpoint Design. Photo Enschedé)

2001 (6 Feb). **"Occasions" Greetings Stamps.** *Two phosphor bands.*
P 14 × 14½.

2182	**1493**	(1st)	silver, greenish yellow, magenta, pale greenish blue, black and silver-grey ..	90	90
2183	**1494**	(1st)	silver, greenish yellow, magenta, pale greenish blue, black and silver-grey ..	90	90
2184	**1495**	(1st)	silver, greenish yellow, magenta, pale greenish blue, black and silver-grey ..	90	90
2185	**1496**	(1st)	silver, greenish yellow, magenta, pale greenish blue, black and silver-grey ..	90	90
2186	**1497**	(1st)	silver, greenish yellow, magenta, pale greenish blue, black and silver-grey ..	90	90

Set of 5	4·00	4·00
Set of 5 Gutter Pairs	8·00	
First Day Cover (Philatelic Bureau)		4·75
First Day Cover (Merry Hill, Wolverhampton)		4·75
Presentation Pack (13 Feb)	4·50	
PHQ Cards (set of 5)	6·00	10·00

The silver-grey backgrounds are printed in Iriodin ink which gives a
shiny effect.

Nos. 2182/6 were re-issued on 1 May 2001 in sheets of 20 with
se-tenant half stamp-size labels, printed by Questa in lithography, in
connection with the "customised" stamps scheme. Such sheets
contained twenty examples of either Nos. 2182, 2184 or 2185, or ten
each of Nos. 2183 and 2186. Sheets with personal photographs printed
on the labels were available from Royal Mail in Edinburgh at £12.95
each. From 5 June 2001 a similar sheet containing four of each design
in horizontal strips, with postal symbols on the labels, was sold at
£5.95.

1502 Cat on Gate

1503 Dog in Car

1504 Cat at Window

1505 Dog Behind Fence

1506 Cat watching Bird

1507 Cat in Washbasin

(Des johnson banks. Photo Walsall)

2001 (13 Feb). **Cats and Dogs**. *Self-adhesive. Two phosphor bands.*
P 15 × 14 *die-cut.*

2187	**1498**	(1st) black, grey and silver	1·50	1·00
		a. Sheetlet. Nos. 2187/96	15·00	
		aa. Imperf (sheetlet)		
		b. Booklet pane. Nos. 2187/96 plus No.		
		2040 × 2	15·00	
		ba. Imperf (pane)		
2188	**1499**	(1st) black, grey and silver	1·50	1·00
2189	**1500**	(1st) black, grey and silver	1·50	1·00
2190	**1501**	(1st) black, grey and silver	1·50	1·00
2191	**1502**	(1st) black, grey and silver	1·50	1·00
2192	**1503**	(1st) black, grey and silver	1·50	1·00
2193	**1504**	(1st) black, grey and silver	1·50	1·00
2194	**1505**	(1st) black, grey and silver	1·50	1·00
2195	**1506**	(1st) black, grey and silver	1·50	1·00
2196	**1507**	(1st) black, grey and silver	1·50	1·00
2187/96		*Set of 10*	15·00	9·00
		First Day Cover (Philatelic Bureau)		12·00
		First Day Cover (Petts Wood, Orping-		
		ton)		12·00
		Presentation Pack	12·00	
		PHQ Cards (set of 10)	8·00	20·00

Nos. 2187/96 were printed together in sheetlets of 10 (5 × 2), with
the surplus self-adhesive paper around each stamp retained. The pane
has vertical roulettes between rows 2/3 and 4/5 with the design on the
reverse of the backing paper similar to Booklet No. PM1.

(Des H. Brown and T. Meeuwissen. Photo De La Rue)

2001 (13 Mar). **The Weather**. *One side phosphor band (19p.) or two
phosphor bands (others).* P 14½.

2197	**1508**	19p. black, greenish yellow, bright magenta,		
		new blue and gold	70	75
2198	**1509**	27p. black, greenish yellow, bright magenta,		
		new blue and gold	85	90
2199	**1510**	45p. black, greenish yellow, bright magenta,		
		new blue and gold	1·50	1·60
2200	**1511**	65p. black, greenish yellow, bright magenta,		
		new blue and gold	2·40	2·50
		Set of 4	5·00	5·25
		Set of 4 Gutter Pairs	11·00	
		First Day Cover (Philatelic Bureau)		6·25
		First Day Cover (Fraserburgh)		6·25
		Presentation Pack	6·25	
MS2201		105 × 105 mm. Nos. 2197/200	11·50	9·00
		First Day Cover (Philatelic Bureau)		10·00
		First Day Cover (Fraserburgh)		10·00
		PHQ Cards (set of 5)	7·00	12·00

Nos. 2197/200 show the four quadrants of a barometer dial which
are combined on the miniature sheet. The reddish violet on both the
27p. and the miniature sheet is printed in thermochromic ink which
changes from reddish violet to light blue when exposed to heat.

The PHQ cards depict the four values and the miniature sheet.

Special First Day of Issue Postmarks

Special First Day of Issue Postmarks

1508 "RAIN"   1509 "FAIR"

1512 *Vanguard* Class Submarine, 1992   1513 *Swiftsure* Class Submarine, 1973

1510 "STORMY"   1511 "VERY DRY"

1514 *Unity* Class Submarine, 1939   1515 "Holland" Type Submarine, 1901

1516 White Ensign

1517 Union Jack

1518 Jolly Roger flown by H.M.S. *Proteus* (submarine)

1519 Flag of Chief of Defence Staff

(Des D. Davis. Photo Questa)

2001 (10 Apr–22 Oct). **Centenary of Royal Navy Submarine Service.**
One centre phosphor band (2nd) or two phosphor bands (others).

(a) *Submarines. PVA gum. P* 15 × 14

2202	**1512**	(2nd) black, brownish black, dull purple and gold		70	75
		a. Perf 15½ × 15 (22 Oct)		3·75	3·00
		ab. Booklet pane. Nos. 2202a and 2204a, each × 2, with margins all round		12·00	
2203	**1513**	(1st) black, azure, slate-blue and gold		85	90
		a. Perf 15½ × 15 (22 Oct)		3·75	3·00
		ab. Booklet pane. Nos. 2203a and 2205a, each × 2, with margins all round		12·00	
2204	**1514**	45p. magenta, chrome yellow, new blue, black and gold		1·50	1·60
		a. Perf 15½ × 15 (22 Oct)		3·75	3·00
2205	**1515**	65p. magenta, chrome yellow, new blue, black and gold		2·40	2·50
		a. Perf 15½ × 15 (22 Oct)		3·75	3·00
		Set of 4		5·00	5·25
		Set of 4 Gutter Pairs		11·00	
		First Day Cover (Philatelic Bureau)			6·00
		First Day Cover (Portsmouth)			6·00
		Presentation Pack		5·00	
		PHQ Cards (set of 4)		6·00	10·00

(b) *Flags. PVA gum. P* 14½

MS2206	92 × 97 mm. **1516** (1st) bright scarlet, blue and silver; **1517** (1st) bright scarlet, blue and silver; **1518** (1st) black, blue and silver; **1519** (1st) bright scarlet, blue, greenish yellow, black and silver (22 Oct)		7·50	6·00
	First Day Cover (Tallents House)			9·00
	First Day Cover (Rosyth, Dunfermline)			9·00
	Presentation Pack		9·00	
	PHQ Cards (set of 5)		5·00	12·00

(c) *Self-adhesive. Die-cut p* 15½ × 14 (No. 2207) *or* 14½ (*others*)

2207	**1513**	(1st) black, azure, slate-blue and gold (17 Apr)		35·00	20·00
		a. Booklet pane. No. 2207 × 2 plus No. 2040 × 4		75·00	
		ab. Booklet pane. Imperf		£1500	
2208	**1516**	(1st) bright scarlet, blue and silver (22 Oct)		8·50	7·50
		a. Booklet pane. Nos. 2208/9 plus No. 2040 × 4		17·00	
2209	**1518**	(1st) black, blue and silver (22 Oct)		8·50	7·50

The five PHQ cards depict the four designs and the complete
miniature sheet.

Nos. 2202a/5a were only issued in the £6.76 "Unseen and Unheard"
booklet, No. DX27, and Nos. 2207/9 only come from two different
£1.62 self-adhesive booklets.

Special First Day of Issue Postmarks

1520 Leyland X2 Open-top,
London General B Type,
Leyland Titan TD1 and AEC
Regent 1

1521 AEC Regent 1, Daimler
COG5, Utility Guy Arab Mk II
and AEC Regent III RT Type

1522 AEC Regent III RT Type,
Bristol KSW5G Open-top, AEC
Routemaster and Bristol
Lodekka FSF6G

1523 Bristol Lodekka FSF6G,
Leyland Titan PD3/4, Leyland
Atlantean PDR1/1 and Daimler
Fleetline CRG6LX-33

1524 Daimler Fleetline CRG6LX-33,
MCW Metrobus DR102/43,
Leyland Olympian ONLXB/1R
and Dennis Trident

(Des M. English. Litho Questa)

2001 (15 May). **150th Anniv of First Double-decker Bus.** *"All-over"* phosphor. P 14½ × 14.

2210	**1520**	(1st) new blue, greenish yellow, magenta, black and grey	1·10	1·10
		a. Horiz strip of 5. Nos. 2210/14	5·00	5·75
		ab. Imperf (horiz strip of 5)	£2000	
2211	**1521**	(1st) new blue, greenish yellow, magenta, black and grey	1·10	1·10
2212	**1522**	(1st) new blue, greenish yellow, magenta, black and grey	1·10	1·10
2213	**1523**	(1st) new blue, greenish yellow, magenta, black and grey	1·10	1·10
2214	**1524**	(1st) new blue, greenish yellow, magenta, black and grey	1·10	1·10
		Set of 5	5·00	5·00
		Gutter Strip of 10	11·00	
		First Day Cover (Philatelic Bureau)		6·00
		First Day Cover (Covent Garden, London WC2)		6·00
		Presentation Pack	6·00	
		PHQ Cards (set of 5)	7·00	14·00
MS2215	120 × 105 mm. Nos. 2210/14		8·25	8·25
	First Day Cover (Philatelic Bureau)			8·50
	First Day Cover (Covent Garden, London WC2)			8·50

Nos. 2210/14 were printed together, *se-tenant*, in horizontal strips of 5 throughout the sheet. The illustrations of the first bus on No. 2210 and the last bus on No. 2214 continue onto the sheet margins.

In No. **MS**2215 the illustrations of the AEC Regent III RT Type and the Daimler Fleetline CRG6LX-33 appear twice.

1527 Top Hat by Stephen Jones

1528 Spiral Hat by Philip Treacy

(Des Rose Design from photos by N. Knight. Litho Enschedé)

2001 (19 June). **Fashion Hats.** *"All-over"* phosphor. P 14½.

2216	**1525**	(1st) greenish yellow, bright magenta, new blue, grey-black and silver	85	90
2217	**1526**	(E) greenish yellow, bright magenta, new blue, grey-black and silver	1·10	1·25
2218	**1527**	45p. greenish yellow, bright magenta, new blue, grey-black and silver	1·50	1·60
2219	**1528**	65p. greenish yellow, bright magenta, new blue, grey-black and silver	2·40	2·50
		Set of 4	5·25	5·50
		Set of 4 Gutter Pairs	11·00	
		First Day Cover (Tallents House)		5·75
		First Day Cover (Ascot)		5·75
		Presentation Pack	5·50	
		PHQ Cards (set of 4)	5·00	10·00

Special First Day of Issue Postmarks

Special First Day of Issue Postmarks

1529 Common Frog

1530 Great Diving Beetle

1525 Toque Hat by Pip Hackett

1526 Butterfly Hat by Dai Rees

1531 Three-Spined Stickleback

1532 Southern Hawker Dragonfly

(Des J. Gibbs. Photo De La Rue)

2001 (10 July). **Europa. Pond Life.** *Two phosphor bands.* P 15 × 14.

2220	**1529**	(1st)	black, greenish yellow, bright magenta, new blue, bluish silver and silver	75	85
2221	**1530**	(E)	black, greenish yellow, bright magenta, new blue, bluish silver and silver	95	1·00
2222	**1531**	45p.	black, greenish yellow, bright magenta, new blue, bluish silver, dull silver and silver	1·25	1·40
2223	**1532**	65p.	black, greenish yellow, bright magenta, new blue, bluish silver and silver	2·00	2·10
			Set of 4	4·50	4·75
			Set of 4 Gutter Pairs	10·00	
			First Day Cover (Tallents House)		6·00
			First Day Cover (Oundle, Peterborough)		6·00
			Presentation Pack	5·00	
			PHQ Cards (set of 4)	5·00	10·00

The 1st and E values incorporate the "EUROPA" emblem.

The bluish silver on all four values is in Iriodin ink and was used as a background for those parts of the design below the water line.

Special First Day of Issue Postmarks

1533 Policeman

1534 Clown

1535 Mr. Punch

1536 Judy

1537 Beadle

1538 Crocodile

(Des K. Bernstein from puppets by Bryan Clarkez)

2001 (4 Sept). **Punch and Judy Show Puppets.** *Two phosphor bands.*

(a) Photo Walsall. PVA gum. P 14 × 15.

2224	**1533**	(1st)	greenish yellow, bright magenta, new blue, grey-black, violet, deep magenta, ultramarine and silver	80	75
		a.	Horiz strip of 6. Nos. 2224/9	4·50	4·75
2225	**1534**	(1st)	greenish yellow, bright magenta, new blue, grey-black, violet, deep magenta, ultramarine and silver	80	75
2226	**1535**	(1st)	greenish yellow, bright magenta, new blue, grey-black, violet, deep magenta, ultramarine and silver	80	75
2227	**1536**	(1st)	greenish yellow, bright magenta, new blue, grey-black, violet, deep magenta, ultramarine and silver	80	75
2228	**1537**	(1st)	greenish yellow, bright magenta, new blue, grey-black, violet, deep magenta, ultramarine and silver	80	75
2229	**1538**	(1st)	greenish yellow, bright magenta, new blue, grey-black, violet, deep magenta, ultramarine and silver	80	75
			Set of 6	4·50	4·00
			Gutter Block of 12	10·00	
			First Day Cover (Tallents House)		5·00
			First Day Cover (Blackpool)		5·00
			Presentation Pack	5·00	
			PHQ Cards (set of 6)	8·00	12·00

(b) Photo Questa. Self-adhesive. Die-cut p 14 × 15½.

2230	**1535**	(1st)	greenish yellow, bright magenta, new blue, grey-black, violet, deep magenta, ultramarine and silver (4 Sept)	7·50	7·50
		a.	Booklet pane. Nos. 2230/1 plus No. 2040 × 4	16·00	
2231	**1536**	(1st)	greenish yellow, bright magenta, new blue, grey-black, violet, deep magenta, ultramarine and silver (4 Sept)	7·50	7·50

Nos. 2224/9 were printed together, *se-tenant,* as horizontal strips of 6 in sheets of 60 (6 × 10).

Nos. 2230/1 were only issued in £1.62 stamp booklets.

Special First Day of Issue Postmarks

1539 Carbon 60 Molecule (Chemistry)

1540 Globe (Economic Sciences)

Special First Day of Issue Postmarks

1541 Embossed Dove (Peace)

1542 Crosses (Physiology or Medicine)

1545 Robins with Snowman

1546 Robins on Bird Table

1547 Robins skating on Bird Bath

1548 Robins with Christmas Pudding

1543 Poem "The Ad-dressing of Cats" by T. S. Eliot in Open Book (Literature)

1544 Hologram of Boron Molecule (Physics)

1549 Robins in Paper Chain Nest

(Des A. Robins and H. Brown. Photo De La Rue)

(Des P. Vermier. Eng Ing Madle (1st). Litho and silk-screen ptg (2nd), litho and recess (1st), litho and embossed (E), litho (45p.), litho and hologram (65p.) Enschedé)

2001 (2 Oct). **Centenary of Nobel Prizes.** *One side phosphor band (2nd) or phosphor frame (others).* P 14½.

2232	**1539**	(2nd) black, silver and grey-black	60	55
2233	**1540**	(1st) black, silver, dull mauve, blue and rosine	80	90
2234	**1541**	(E) black, silver and bright green	1·00	1·10
2235	**1542**	40p. black, silver, new blue and greenish yellow	1·00	1·10
2236	**1543**	45p. black, silver, yellow-ochre and pale grey	1·40	1·50
2237	**1544**	65p. black and silver	2·10	2·25
		Set of 6	6·25	6·75
		Set of 6 Gutter Pairs	12·50	
		First Day Cover (Tallents House)		7·50
		First Day Cover (Cambridge)		7·50
		Presentation Pack	6·75	
		PHQ Cards (set of 6)	8·00	12·00

The grey-black on No. 2232 is printed in thermochromic ink which temporarily changes to pale grey when exposed to heat.

The centre of No. 2235 is coated with a eucalyptus scent.

2001 (6 Nov). **Christmas. Robins.** *Self-adhesive. One centre phosphor band (2nd) or two phosphor bands (others). Die-cut p 14½.*

2238	**1545**	(2nd) new blue, blue, greenish yellow, bright magenta, vermilion and black	75	70
		a. Booklet pane. No. 2238 × 24	12·00	
		b. Imperf (pair)	£950	
2239	**1546**	(1st) red-orange, blue, greenish yellow, bright magenta, new blue and black ..	95	1·00
		a. Booklet pane. No. 2239 × 12	8·00	
2240	**1547**	(E) indigo, azure, greenish yellow, bright magenta, new blue, vermilion and black	1·00	1·10
2241	**1548**	45p. bright purple, blue, greenish yellow, bright magenta, new blue, vermilion and black	1·40	1·50

2242 **1549** 65p. greenish blue, blue, greenish yellow,
bright magenta, new blue, vermilion
and black .... 2·10 2·25
   a. Imperf (pair) (die-cut perforations and
     roulettes omitted) £900
   b. Imperf backing paper (pair) (roulettes
     omitted) £275
     Set of 5 .... 5·50 6·00
     First Day Cover (Tallents House) ...... 7·00
     First Day Cover (Bethlehem, Llandeilo) 7·00
     Presentation Pack .... 6·00
     PHQ Cards (set of 5) .... 6·00 10·00

Nos. 2238/40 were printed in sheets of 50 with the surplus backing
paper around each stamp retained and separated by gauge 9 roulettes.

The 1st value was re-issued on 30 September 2003 in sheets of 20
(sold at £6.15) printed in lithography instead of photogravure, each
stamp accompanied by a stamp-size label showing a snowman. Sheets
with personal photographs printed on the labels were available from
Royal Mail, Edinburgh for £14.95 or photo-booths at selected post
offices and Safeway stores for £15.

No. 2238b shows both the die-cut perforations and the roulettes
omitted.

Stamps from booklet panes Nos. 2238a and 2239a differ from those
in sheets by omitting the roulettes in the backing paper between each
stamp. Instead there are roulettes after the first and then every
alternate horizontal row to assist with the folding of the booklets.

Special First Day of Issue Postmarks

Collectors Pack 2001

2001 (6 Nov). *Comprises Nos. 2178/2200, 2202/6, 2210/14, 2216/29 and
2232/42.*
CP242a Collectors Pack .... 57·00

Post Office Yearbook

2001 (6 Nov). *Comprises Nos. 2178/96, **MS**2201/6, 2210/14, 2216/29 and
2232/42 in hardback book with slip case* .... 65·00

1550 "How the Whale got his
Throat"

1551 "How the Camel got his
Hump"

1552 "How the Rhinoceros
got his Skin"

1553 "How the Leopard got
his Spots"

1554 "The Elephant's Child"

1555 "The Sing-Song of Old
Man Kangaroo"

1556 "The Beginning of the
Armadillos"

1557 "The Crab that played
with the Sea"

1558 "The Cat that walked by
Himself"

1559 "The Butterfly that
stamped"

(Des I. Cohen. Photo Walsall)

2002 (15 Jan). **Centenary of Publication of Rudyard Kipling's *Just So
Stories**. *Self-adhesive. Two phosphor bands. Die-cut p* 15 × 14.
2243 **1550** (1st) new blue, magenta, greenish yellow
and black 95 85
   a. Sheetlet. Nos. 2243/52 .... 9·00
2244 **1551** (1st) new blue, magenta, greenish yellow
and black 95 85
2245 **1552** (1st) new blue, magenta, greenish yellow
and black 95 85
2246 **1553** (1st) new blue, magenta, greenish yellow
and black 95 85
2247 **1554** (1st) new blue, magenta, greenish yellow
and black 95 85
2248 **1555** (1st) new blue, magenta, greenish yellow
and black 95 85
2249 **1556** (1st) new blue, magenta, greenish yellow
and black 95 85
2250 **1557** (1st) new blue, magenta, greenish yellow
and black 95 85

2251 **1558** (1st) new blue, magenta, greenish yellow
and black 95 85
2252 **1559** (1st) new blue, magenta, greenish yellow
and black 95 85
Set of 10 .... 9·00 7·75
First Day Cover (Tallents House) ...... 8·00
First Day Cover (Burwash, Etchingham) 8·00
Presentation Pack .... 10·00
PHQ Cards (set of 10) .... 7·00 15·00

Nos. 2243/52 were printed together in sheetlets of 10 (5 × 2), with
the surplus self-adhesive paper around each stamp retained. The pane
shows vertical roulettes between rows 2/3 and 4/5 and has illustrations
on the reverse of the backing paper.

Special First Day of Issue Postmarks

1560 Queen Elizabeth II,
1952 (Dorothy Wilding)

1561 Queen Elizabeth II,
1968 (Cecil Beaton)

1562 Queen Elizabeth II,
1978 (Lord Snowdon)

1563 Queen Elizabeth II,
1984 (Yousef Karsh)

1564 Queen Elizabeth II,
1996 (Tim Graham)

1565

(Des Kate Stephens. Photo De La Rue)

2002 (6 Feb). **Golden Jubilee. Studio portraits of Queen Elizabeth II by
photographers named.** *One centre phosphor band* (2nd) *or two
phosphor bands* (others). W **1565** (sideways). P $14\frac{1}{2}$ × 14.
2253 **1560** (2nd) silver, pale turquoise-green, black and
deep grey 55 55
a. Watermark upright .... 2·50 70
b. Booklet pane. Nos. 2253a/6a with
margins all round .... 8·00
2254 **1561** (1st) silver, pale turquoise-green, black and
grey-black 80 80
a. Watermark upright .... 1·25 1·00
b. Booklet pane. Nos. 2254a/7a with
margins all round .... 9·50
2255 **1562** (E) silver, pale turquoise-green, black and
grey-black .... 1·00 1·00
a. Watermark upright .... 1·75 1·40
2256 **1563** 45p. silver, pale turquoise-green, black and
grey-black .... 1·40 1·40
a. Watermark upright .... 2·50 1·50
2257 **1564** 65p. silver, pale turquoise-green, black and
grey-black .... 2·10 2·00
a. Watermark upright .... 4·00 2·25
Set of 5 .... 5·25 5·25
Set of 5 Gutter Pairs .... 10·50
First Day Cover (Tallents House) ...... 6·00
First Day Cover (Windsor) .... 6·00
Presentation Pack .... 5·75
PHQ Cards (set of 5) .... 4·00 9·00

The turquoise-green is used as an underlay for the black colour on
all five values.
Nos. 2253a/7a were only available in £7.29 stamp booklets.

Special First Day of Issue Postmarks

1566

(Des M. Farrar-Bell (2nd), Enid Marx (1st). Photo Enschedé)

2002 (6 Feb). As *T* **154/5** (*Wilding definitive of 1952–54*), *but with service
indicator as* T **1566**. *One centre phosphor band* (2nd) *or two
phosphor bands* (1st). W **1565**. *Uncoated paper.* P 15 × 14 (*with one
elliptical hole on each vertical side*).
2258 **1566** (2nd) carmine-red .... 1·00 1·00
Ea. Watermark diagonal .... 4·50 3·25
b. Booklet pane. Nos. 2258 × 4, 2258Ea
and 2259 × 4 with centre blank label
and margins all round .... 12·00

2259 — (1st) green .... 1·25   1·25
      First Day Cover (No. 2258b) (Tallents
          House) ....   10·00
      First Day Cover (No. 2258b) (Windsor) .   10·00
    Nos. 2258/9 were only issued in the £7.29 "A Gracious Accession"
booklet, No. DX28.
    No. 2258b contains a block of 8, four of each value, with a blank
central label, plus an additional 2nd value shown to the left at such an
angle so as to produce a diagonal watermark.
    First day cover postmarks were as Nos. 2253/7.

1567 Rabbits ("a new baby")

1568 "LOVE"

1569 Aircraft Sky-writing "hello"

1570 Bear pulling Potted
Topiary Tree (Moving Home)

1571 Flowers ("best wishes")

(Des I. Bilbey (Nos. 2260, 2264), A. Kitching (No. 2261), Hoop Associates
(No. 2262) and G. Percy (No. 2263)

2002 (5 Mar)–**03**. **"Occasions". Greetings Stamps.** *Two phosphor bands.*

(a) *Litho Questa.* P 15 × 14.

2260	**1567**	(1st) greenish yellow, magenta, new blue, black and lilac	80	90
2261	**1568**	(1st) greenish yellow, magenta, new blue, black and silver	80	90
2262	**1569**	(1st) greenish yellow, magenta, new blue and black	80	90
2263	**1570**	(1st) greenish yellow, magenta, new blue and black	80	90
2264	**1571**	(1st) greenish yellow, magenta, new blue, black and cobalt	80	90
		Set of 5	3·50	4·00
		Set of 5 Gutter Pairs	8·00	
		First Day Cover (Tallents House)		5·00
		First Day Cover (Merry Hill, Wolver- hampton)		5·00
		Presentation Pack	4·50	
		PHQ Cards (set of 5)	3·25	9·00

(b) *Photo Questa. Self-adhesive. Die-cut* p 15 × 14
2264a **1569** (1st) greenish yellow, magenta, new blue
          and black (4.3.03) .... 1·00   1·00
      ab. Booklet pane. No. 2264a × 2 plus No.
          2295 × 4 .... 2·50
    Nos. 2260/4 were re-issued on 23 April in sheets of 20 with half
stamp-size labels, with either the five designs *se-tenant* with greetings
on the labels (sold at £5.95) or in sheets of one design with personal
photographs on the labels (sold at £12.95). These stamps, printed by
Questa in lithography, were perforated 14½ × 14 instead of 15 × 14.
    No. 2264a was only issued in £1.62 stamp booklets, No. PM8, in
which the surplus self-adhesive paper around each stamp was
removed.

Special First Day of Issue Postmarks

1572 Studland Bay, Dorset

1573 Luskentyre, South Harris

1574 Cliffs, Dover, Kent

1575 Padstow Harbour,
Cornwall

1576 Broadstairs, Kent

1577 St. Abb's Head, Scottish
Borders

1578 Dunster Beach, Somerset

1579 Newquay Beach, Cornwall

1582 Slack Wire Act

1583 Lion Tamer

1580 Portrush, County Antrim

1581 Sand-spit, Conwy

1584 Trick Tri-cyclists

1585 Krazy Kar

(Des R. Cooke. Litho Walsall)

2002 (19 Mar). **British Coastlines.** *Two phosphor bands.* P $14\frac{1}{2}$.

2265	1572	27p. silver, black, greenish yellow, bright magenta and new blue	75	80
		a. Block of 10. Nos. 2265/74	7·00	
2266	1573	27p. silver, black, greenish yellow, bright magenta and new blue	75	80
2267	1574	27p. silver, black, greenish yellow, bright magenta and new blue	75	80
2268	1575	27p. silver, black, greenish yellow, bright magenta and new blue	75	80
2269	1576	27p. silver, black, greenish yellow, bright magenta and new blue	75	80
2270	1577	27p. silver, black, greenish yellow, bright magenta and new blue	75	80
2271	1578	27p. silver, black, greenish yellow, bright magenta and new blue	75	80
2272	1579	27p. silver, black, greenish yellow, bright magenta and new blue	75	80
2273	1580	27p. silver, black, greenish yellow, bright magenta and new blue	75	80
2274	1581	27p. silver, black, greenish yellow, bright magenta and new blue	75	80
		Set of 10	7·00	7·25
		Gutter Block of 20	15·00	
		First Day Cover (Tallents House)		8·50
		First Day Cover (Poolewe, Achnasheen)		8·50
		Presentation Pack	7·50	
		PHQ Cards (set of 10)	7·00	15·00

Nos. 2265/74 were printed together, *se-tenant*, in blocks of 10 (5 × 2) throughout the sheet.

Special First Day of Issue Postmarks

1586 Equestrienne

(Des R. Fuller. Photo Questa)

2002 (10 Apr*). **Europa. Circus.** *One centre phosphor band* (2nd) *or two phosphor bands* (others). P $14\frac{1}{2}$.

2275	1582	(2nd)	greenish yellow, magenta, new blue, black, bright orange, emerald and silver	55	60
2276	1583	(1st)	greenish yellow, magenta, new blue, black, bright orange, emerald and silver	75	85
2277	1584	(E)	greenish yellow, magenta, new blue, black, bright orange, emerald and silver	1·00	1·10
2278	1585	45p.	greenish yellow, magenta, new blue, black, bright orange, emerald and silver	1·25	1·40
2279	1586	65p.	greenish yellow, magenta, new blue, black, bright orange, emerald and silver	1·90	2·00
			Set of 5	4·90	5·25
			Set of 5 Gutter Pairs	10·50	
			First Day Cover (Tallents House)		6·00
			First Day Cover (Clowne, Chesterfield)		6·00
			Presentation Pack	5·75	
			PHQ Cards (set of 5)	4·00	9·00

The 1st and E values incorporate the "EUROPA" emblem.

*Due to the funeral of the Queen Mother, the issue of Nos. 2275/9 was delayed from 9 April, the date which appears on first day covers.

Special First Day of Issue Postmarks

1590 Trident (1964) **1591** VC 10 (1964)

1587 Queen Elizabeth
the Queen Mother

1592 Comet (1952)

(Des J. Gorham from photographs by N. Parkinson (1st), Dorothy Wilding (E), B. Park (45p.), Rita Martin (65p.). Photo De La Rue)

2002 (25 Apr). **Queen Elizabeth the Queen Mother Commemoration.** *Vert designs as T* **955/8** *with changed face values and showing both the Queen's head and frame in black as in T* **1587**. *Two phosphor bands.* P 14 × 15.

2280	**1587**	(1st)	black, greenish yellow, magenta, new blue and grey-black	75	85
2281	**956**	(E)	black and indigo	1·00	1·10
2282	**957**	45p.	black, greenish yellow, magenta, new blue and grey-black	1·25	1·40
2283	**958**	65p.	black, stone and sepia	1·90	2·00
			Set of 4	4·25	4·75
			Set of 4 Gutter Pairs	9·50	
			First Day Cover (Tallents House)		6·00
			First Day Cover (London SW1)		6·00
			Presentation Pack		4·75

Special First Day of Issue Postmarks

1588 Airbus A340-600 (2002)

1589 Concorde (1976)

(Des Roundel)

2002 (2 May). **50th Anniv of Passenger Jet Aviation. Airliners.** One centre phosphor band (2nd) or two phosphor bands (others).

(a) *Photo De La Rue. PVA gum.* P 14½.

2284	**1588**	(2nd)	greenish yellow, bright magenta, new blue, black and silver	50	55
2285	**1589**	(1st)	greenish yellow, bright magenta, new blue, black and silver	70	80
2286	**1590**	(E)	greenish yellow, bright magenta, new blue, black and silver	90	1·00
2287	**1591**	45p.	greenish yellow, bright magenta, new blue, black and silver	1·25	1·40
2288	**1592**	65p.	greenish yellow, bright magenta, new blue, black and silver	1·90	2·00
			Set of 5	4·75	5·25
			Set of 5 Gutter Pairs	9·50	
			First Day Cover (Tallents House)		6·00
			First Day Cover (Heathrow Airport, London)		6·00
			Presentation Pack		5·25
MS2289	120 × 105 mm. Nos. 2284/8			5·00	5·25
			First Day Cover (Tallents House)		6·00
			First Day Cover (Heathrow Airport, London)		6·00
			PHQ Cards (set of 6)	5·00	7·00

(b) *Photo Questa. Self-adhesive. Die-cut p* 14½.

2290	**1589**	(1st)	greenish yellow, bright magenta, new blue, black and silver	1·60	1·60
			a. Booklet pane. No. 2040 × 4 and No. 2290 × 2	3·50	

No. 2290 was only issued in £1.62 stamp booklets.

Special First Day of Issue Postmarks

1593 Crowned Lion with Shield of St. George

1594 Top Left Quarter of English Flag, and Football

1595 Top Right Quarter of English Flag, and Football

1596 Bottom Left Quarter of English Flag, and Football

1597 Bottom Right Quarter of English Flag, and Football

(Des Sedley Place (No. 2291), H. Brown (No. **MS**2292). Photo Walsall)

2002 (21 May). **World Cup Football Championship, Japan and Korea.** *Two phosphor bands.* P 14½ × 14. (a) *PVA gum.*

2291 **1593** (1st) deep turquoise-blue, scarlet-vermilion and silver .... 1·50 1·25
    Gutter Pair .... 1·50
MS2292 145 × 74 mm. No. 2291; **1594** (1st) deep turquoise-blue, indigo, deep blue, black, silver, scarlet-vermilion and pale bluish grey; **1595** (1st) deep turquoise-blue, indigo, deep blue, black, silver, scarlet-vermilion and pale bluish grey; **1596** (1st) deep turquoise-blue, indigo, deep blue, black, silver, scarlet-vermilion and pale bluish grey; **1597** (1st) deep turquoise-blue, indigo, deep blue, black, silver, scarlet-vermilion and pale bluish grey. P 14½ (square) or 15 × 14 (horiz) .... 3·50 4·00
    First Day Cover (**MS**2292) (Tallents House) .... 4·50
    First Day Cover (**MS**2292) (Wembley) .. 4·50
    Presentation Pack (**MS**2292) .... 4·50
    PHQ Cards (set of 6) .... 5·00 9·00

    (b) *Self-adhesive. Die-cut p* 15 × 14.
2293 **1594** (1st) deep turquoise-blue, indigo, deep blue, black, silver, scarlet-vermilion and pale bluish grey .... 1·50 1·50
    a. Booklet pane. Nos. 2293/4 plus No. 2040 × 4 .... 3·50
2294 **1595** (1st) deep turquoise-blue, indigo, deep blue, black, silver, scarlet-vermilion and pale bluish grey .... 1·50 1·50
The complete miniature sheet is shown on one of the PHQ cards with the others depicting individual stamps from No. **MS**2292 and No. 2291.

Nos. 2293/4 were only issued in £1.62 stamp booklets.

Stamps as Type **1597** also exist in sheets of 20 with *se-tenant* labels, printed by lithography. Such sheets, with the labels showing match scenes or supporters, were available at £5.95 from philatelic outlets, or with personal photographs at £12.95 from Royal Mail in Edinburgh.

Special First Day of Issue Postmarks

(Photo Questa, Walsall, Enschedé or De La Rue (1st), Walsall (others))

2002 (5 June–4 July). **Self-adhesive.** *Two phosphor bands.* P 15 × 14 *die-cut* (*with one elliptical hole on each vertical side*).

2295 **914** (1st) gold 45 50
2296 **1093**a (E) deep blue (4 July) 60 65
2297 **367**a 42p. deep olive-grey (4 July) 65 70
2298 68p. grey-brown (4 July) .... 1·10 1·25
    Set of 4 .... 2·75 3·00
No. 2295, sold for 27p., was initially only available in booklets of 6 or 12, printed by Questa or Walsall, with the surplus self-adhesive paper around each stamp removed. Later booklets were also printed by De La Rue. Nos. 2296/8 were only issued in separate booklets, each containing six stamps with the surplus self-adhesive paper around each stamp removed.

A further printing of No. 2295 in sheets of 100 appeared on 4 July 2002 produced by Enschedé and on 18 March 2003 in stripped matrix sheets of 100 printed by Walsall. The top panel shows a strip of four with the typography of the label matching that of booklet Type ME 2.

1598 Swimming

1599 Running

1600 Cycling

1601 Long Jumping

1602 Wheelchair Racing

(Des Madeleine Bennett. Photo Enschedé)

2002 (16 July). **17th Commonwealth Games, Manchester**. *One side phosphor band* (2nd) *or two phosphor bands* (others). P 14½.

2299 **1598** (2nd) greenish yellow, magenta, greenish blue, black, silver and new blue 50 55
2300 **1599** (1st) greenish yellow, magenta, new blue, black and silver 70 80
2301 **1600** (E) greenish yellow, magenta, new blue, black and silver .... 90 1·00
2302 **1601** 47p. greenish yellow, magenta, new blue, black and silver .... 1·25 1·40
2303 **1602** 68p. greenish yellow, magenta, new blue, black and silver .... 1·90 2·00
Set of 5 .... 4·75 5·25
Set of 5 Gutter Pairs .... 9·50
First Day Cover (Tallents House) ...... 6·00
First Day Cover (Manchester) .... 6·00
Presentation Pack .... 5·25
PHQ Cards (set of 5) .... 4·00 8·00

On Nos. 2300/3 the phosphor bands appear at the right and the centre of each stamp.

Special First Day of Issue Postmarks

1603 Tinkerbell

1604 Wendy, John and Michael Darling in front of Big Ben

1605 Crocodile and Alarm Clock

1606 Captain Hook

1607 Peter Pan

(Des Tutssels. Photo De La Rue.)

2002 (20 Aug). **150th Anniv of Great Ormond Street Children's Hospital. "Peter Pan" by Sir James Barrie**. *One centre phosphor band* (2nd) *or two phosphor bands* (others). P 15 × 14.

2304 **1603** (2nd) gold, deep ultramarine, greenish yellow and grey-black 50 55
2305 **1604** (1st) gold, purple, greenish yellow, deep violet and grey-black 70 80
2306 **1605** (E) gold, blue-green, greenish yellow, bright carmine, new blue grey-black and orange-brown .... 90 1·00
2307 **1606** 47p. gold, pale new blue, greenish yellow, bright carmine and grey-black .... 1·25 1·40
2308 **1607** 68p. gold, bright rose-red, orange-brown, emerald and grey-black .... 1·90 2·00
Set of 5 .... 4·75 5·25
Set of 5 Gutter Pairs .... 9·50
First Day Cover (Tallents House) ...... 6·00
First Day Cover (Hook) .... 6·00
Presentation Pack .... 5·25
PHQ Cards (set of 5) .... 4·00 8·00

Special First Day of Issue Postmarks

1608 Millennium Bridge, 2001

1609 Tower Bridge, 1894

1610 Westminster Bridge, 1864

1611 "Blackfriars Bridge, c1800" (William Marlow)

1612 "London Bridge, c1670"
(Wenceslaus Hollar)

(Des Sarah Davies and R. Maude)

2002 (10 Sept). **Bridges of London**. *One centre phosphor band* (2nd) *or two phosphor bands* (others). (a) *Litho Questa. PVA gum.* P 15 × 14.

2309	**1608**	(2nd) greenish yellow, magenta, new blue and black	50	55
2310	**1609**	(1st) grey-brown, black, brown-purple and pale grey-brown	70	80
2311	**1610**	(E) greenish yellow, magenta, new blue, black and reddish brown	90	1·00
2312	**1611**	47p. greenish yellow, magenta, new blue and black	1·25	1·40
2313	**1612**	68p. greenish yellow, magenta, new blue, black and reddish brown	1·90	2·00
		Set of 5	4·75	5·25
		Set of 5 Gutter Pairs	9·50	
		First Day Cover (Tallents House)		6·00
		First Day Cover (London SE1)		6·00
		Presentation Pack	5·25	
		PHQ Cards (set of 5)	4·00	7·00

(b) *Photo Questa. Self-adhesive. Die-cut p* 15 × 14.

2314	**1609**	(1st) grey-brown, black, brown-purple and pale grey-brown	1·50	1·50
		a. Booklet pane. No. 2314 × 2, and No. 2295 × 4	4·00	

No. 2314 was only issued in £1.62 stamp booklets in which the surplus self-adhesive paper around each stamp was removed.

Special First Day of Issue Postmarks

1613*a* Galaxies and Nebula
(*Illustration reduced. Actual size* 120 × 89 *mm*)

(Des Rose Design. Photo Questa)

2002 (24 Sept). **Astronomy**. *Sheet* 120 × 89 *mm. Multicoloured. Two phosphor bands.* P 14½ × 14.

MS2315	**1613***a* (1st) Planetary nebula in Aquila; (1st) Seyfert 2 galaxy in Pegasus; (1st) Planetary nebula in Norma; (1st) Seyfert 2 galaxy in Circinus	2·75	3·00
	a. Booklet pane. As No. **MS**2315, but larger, 150 × 95 mm	1·60	
	First Day Cover (Tallents House)		3·50
	First Day Cover (Star, Glenrothes)		3·50
	Presentation Pack	3·25	
	PHQ Cards (set of 5)	4·00	6·00

The five PHQ cards depict the four designs and the complete miniature sheet.

Special First Day of Issue Postmarks

1614 Green Pillar Box, 1857

1615 Horizontal Aperture Box, 1874

1616 Air Mail Box, 1934

1617 Double Aperture Box, 1939

1618 Modern Style Box, 1980

(Des Silk Pearce. Eng C. Slania. Recess and litho Enschedé)

2002 (8 Oct). **150th Anniv of the First Pillar Box**. *One centre phosphor band (2nd) or two phosphor bands (others)*. P 14 × 14½.

2316	**1614**	(2nd)	greenish black, new blue, bright magenta, greenish yellow, grey and silver	50	55
2317	**1615**	(1st)	deep blue, new blue, bright magenta, greenish yellow, grey and silver	70	80
2318	**1616**	(E)	deep blue, new blue, bright magenta, greenish yellow, grey and silver	90	1·00
2319	**1617**	47p.	brown-purple, new blue, bright magenta, greenish yellow, grey and silver	1·25	1·40
2320	**1618**	68p.	deep brown-red, new blue, bright magenta, greenish yellow, grey and silver	1·90	2·00
			Set of 5	4·75	5·25
			Set of 5 Gutter Pairs	9·50	
			First Day Cover (Tallents House)		6·00
			First Day Cover (Bishops Caundle, Sherborne)		6·00
			Presentation Pack	5·25	
			PHQ Cards (set of 5)	4·00	7·00

Special First Day of Issue Postmarks

1619 Blue Spruce Star

1620 Holly

1621 Ivy

1622 Mistletoe

1623 Pine Cone

(Des Rose Design. Photo De La Rue)

2002 (5 Nov). **Christmas**. *Self-adhesive. One centre phosphor band (2nd) or two phosphor bands (others). Die-cut p 14½ × 14.*

2321	**1619**	(2nd)	lilac, greenish yellow, bright carmine, new blue and black	50	55
			a. Booklet pane. No. 2321 × 24	6·75	
			b. Imperf (pair)	80·00	
2322	**1620**	(1st)	greenish grey, greenish yellow, bright carmine, new blue and black	70	80
			a. Booklet pane. No. 2322 × 12	4·75	
			b. Imperf (pair)	£325	
2323	**1621**	(E)	dull mauve, greenish yellow, bright carmine, new blue and black	90	1·00
2324	**1622**	47p.	silver, greenish yellow, bright carmine, new blue and black	1·25	1·40
2325	**1623**	68p.	light blue, greenish yellow, bright carmine, new blue and black	1·90	2·00
			Set of 5	4·75	5·25
			First Day Cover (Tallents House)		6·00
			First Day Cover (Bethlehem, Llandeilo)		6·00
			Presentation Pack	5·25	
			PHQ Cards (set of 5)	4·00	7·00

Nos. 2321/5 were printed in sheets of 50, with the surplus backing paper around each stamp retained, separated by gauge 9 roulettes.

Nos. 2321b and 2322b show both the die-cut perforations and the roulettes omitted.

Special First Day of Issue Postmarks

Collectors Pack 2002

2002 (5 Nov). *Comprises Nos. 2243/57, 2260/88, 2291/2, 2299/313 and* **MS**2315/25

CP2325a Collectors Pack .... 42·00

Post Office Yearbook

2002 (5 Nov). *Comprises Nos. 2243/57, 2260/88, 2291/2, 2299/313 and* **MS**2315/25 *in hardback book with slip case* .... 50·00

(Des Rose Design. Photo De La Rue)

2002 (5 Dec). **50th Anniv of Wilding Definitives (1st issue)**. *Sheet, 124 × 70 mm containing designs as T* **154/5** *and* **157/60** *(1952-54 issue), but with values in decimal currency as T* **1348** *or with service indicator as T* **1566**, *printed on pale cream. One centre phosphor band (2nd) or two phosphor bands (others). W* **1565**. *P 15 × 14 (with one elliptical hole on each vertical side).*

MS2326	1p. orange-red; 2p. ultramarine; 5p. red-brown; (2nd) carmine-red; (1st) green; 33p. brown; 37p. magenta; 47p. bistre-brown; 50p. green and label showing national emblems	6·25	6·50
	First Day Cover (Tallents House)		7·00
	First Day Cover (Windsor)		7·00
	Presentation Pack	£100	
	PHQ Cards (set of 5)	3·00	12·00

The five PHQ cards depict the 1st, 2nd, 33p., 37p. and 47p. stamps.

Special First Day of Issue Postmarks

1632 Kestrel with Wings partly extended downwards

1633 Kestrel with Wings fully extended downwards

(Des J. Gibbs from photographs by S. Dalton. Litho Walsall)

1624 Barn Owl landing

1625 Barn Owl with folded Wings and Legs down

2003 (14 Jan). **Birds of Prey**. *Phosphor background.* P $14\frac{1}{2}$.

2327	**1624**	(1st) brownish grey, black, greenish yellow, magenta and new blue	70	80
		a. Block of 10. Nos. 2327/36	6·25	
		ab. Brownish grey and phosphor omitted .	£2000	
2328	**1625**	(1st) brownish grey, black, greenish yellow, magenta and new blue	70	80
2329	**1626**	(1st) brownish grey, black, greenish yellow, magenta and new blue	70	80
2330	**1627**	(1st) brownish grey, black, greenish yellow, magenta and new blue	70	80
2331	**1628**	(1st) brownish grey, black, greenish yellow, magenta and new blue	70	80
2332	**1629**	(1st) brownish grey, black, greenish yellow, magenta and new blue	70	80
2333	**1630**	(1st) brownish grey, black, greenish yellow, magenta and new blue	70	80
2334	**1631**	(1st) brownish grey, black, greenish yellow, magenta and new blue	70	80
2335	**1632**	(1st) brownish grey, black, greenish yellow, magenta and new blue	70	80
2336	**1633**	(1st) brownish grey, black, greenish yellow, magenta and new blue	70	80
		Set of 10	6·25	7·25
		Gutter Block of 20	13·00	
		First Day Cover (Tallents House)		8·00
		First Day Cover (Hawkshead, Ambleside)		8·00
		Presentation Pack	6·50	
		PHQ Cards (set of 10)	5·75	12·00

1626 Barn Owl with extended Wings and Legs down

1627 Barn Owl in Flight with Wings lowered

Nos. 2327/36 were printed together, *se-tenant*, in blocks of 10 (5 × 2) throughout the sheet.

No. 2327ab shows the owl white on Nos. 2327/31 and the face value with Queen's head omitted on Nos. 2332/6.

1628 Barn Owl in Flight with Wings raised

1629 Kestrel with Wings folded

Special First Day of Issue Postmarks (applied in silver)

1630 Kestrel with Wings fully extended upwards

1631 Kestrel with Wings horizontal

For full information on all future British issues, collectors should write to the British Post Office Philatelic Bureau, 21 South Gyle Crescent, Edinburgh EH12 9PB

1634 "Gold star, See me, Playtime"

1635 "I♥U, XXXX, S.W.A.L.K."

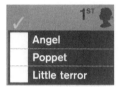

1636 "Angel, Poppet, Little terror"

1637 "Yes, No, Maybe"

Genome **The End of the Beginning**

1640 Completing the Genome Jigsaw

Genome **Comparative Genetics**

1641 Ape with Moustache and Scientist

1638 "Oops!, Sorry, Will try harder"

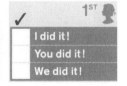

1639 "I did it!, You did it!, We did it!"

(Des UNA, Sara Wiegand and M. Exon. Litho Questa)

Genome **Cracking the Code**

1642 DNA Snakes and Ladders

Genome **Genetic Engineering**

1643 "Animal Scientists"

2003 (4 Feb). **"Occasions" Greetings Stamps.** *Two phosphor bands.* P 14½ × 14.

2337	**1634**	(1st) lemon and new blue	70	80
		a. Block of 6. Nos. 2337/42	3·75	
		b. Imperf block of 6		
2338	**1635**	(1st) red and deep ultramarine	70	80
2339	**1636**	(1st) purple and bright yellow-green	70	80
2340	**1637**	(1st) bright yellow-green and red	70	80
2341	**1638**	(1st) deep ultramarine and lemon	70	80
2342	**1639**	(1st) new blue and purple	70	80
		Set of 6	3·75	4·25
		Gutter Block of 12	7·00	
		First Day Cover (Tallents House)		4·50
		First Day Cover (Merry Hill, Wolverhampton)		4·50
		Presentation Pack	4·00	
		PHQ Cards (set of 6)	3·50	7·00

Nos. 2337/42 were printed together, *se-tenant* in blocks of 6 (3 × 2) throughout the sheet.

Nos. 2337/42 were also issued in sheets of 20 (containing four of Nos. 2338 and 2340 and three each of the others) with *se-tenant* labels. Such sheets with the labels showing printed faces were available at £5.95 from philatelic outlets, or with personalised photographs at £14.95 from Royal Mail in Edinburgh.

Genome **Medical Futures**

1644 Genome Crystal Ball

(Des Williams Murray Hamm and P. Brookes. Litho Enschedé)

2003 (25 Feb). **50th Anniv of Discovery of DNA.** *One centre phosphor band (2nd) or two phosphor bands (others).* P 14½.

2343	**1640**	(2nd) azure, black, new blue, magenta and greenish yellow	50	55
		a. Booklet pane. Nos. 2343/4, each × 2, with margins all round	2·00	
2344	**1641**	(1st) bright apple-green, black, new blue, magenta and greenish yellow	70	80
2345	**1642**	(E) yellow-orange, black, new blue, magenta and greenish yellow	90	1·00
		a. Booklet pane. No. 2345 × 4 with margins all round	3·00	

2346	**1643**	47p. bistre-yellow, black, new blue, magenta and greenish yellow	1·25	1·40
2347	**1644**	68p. lavender, black, new blue, magenta and greenish yellow	1·90	2·00
		Set of 5	4·75	5·25
		Set of 5 Gutter Pairs	9·50	
		First Day Cover (Tallents House)		6·00
		First Day Cover (Cambridge)		6·00
		Presentation Pack	5·25	
		PHQ Cards (set of 5)	4·00	7·00

Special First Day of Issue Postmarks

'Our fate
is in our
genes'
JAMES WATSON
25·2·2003

'We have
discovered
the secret
of life'
FRANCIS CRICK
25·2·2003

1651 Tomato

1652 Lemon

1645 Strawberry   **1646** Potato

1653 Brussels Sprout

1654 Aubergine

(Des Johnson Banks. Photo Walsall)

2003 (25 Mar). **Fruit and Vegetables**. *Self-adhesive. Two phosphor bands. P* $14\frac{1}{2} \times 14$ *die-cut (without teeth around protruding tops or bottoms of the designs).*

1647 Apple   **1648** Red Pepper

2348	**1645**	(1st) greenish yellow, magenta, new blue, black and silver	70	80
		a. Sheetlet. Nos. 2348/57 and pane of decorative labels	6·25	
		ab. Imperf block of 10		
2349	**1646**	(1st) greenish yellow, magenta, new blue, black and silver	70	80
2350	**1647**	(1st) greenish yellow, magenta, new blue, black and silver	70	80
2351	**1648**	(1st) greenish yellow, magenta, new blue, black and silver	70	80
2352	**1649**	(1st) greenish yellow, magenta, new blue, black and silver	70	80
2353	**1650**	(1st) greenish yellow, magenta, new blue, black and silver	70	80
2354	**1651**	(1st) greenish yellow, magenta, new blue, black and silver	70	80
2355	**1652**	(1st) greenish yellow, magenta, new blue, black and silver	70	80
2356	**1653**	(1st) greenish yellow, magenta, new blue, black and silver	70	80
2357	**1654**	(1st) greenish yellow, magenta, new blue, black and silver	70	80
		Set of 10	6·25	7·25
		First Day Cover (Tallents House)		8·00
		First Day Cover (Pear Tree, Derby)		8·00
		Presentation Pack	6·50	
		PHQ Cards (set of 10)	5·75	12·00

1649 Pear   **1650** Orange

Nos. 2348/57 were printed together in sheets of 10 with the surplus self-adhesive paper around each stamp retained. The stamp pane is accompanied by a similar-sized pane of self-adhesive labels showing ears, eyes, mouths, hats etc which are intended for the adornment of fruit and vegetables depicted. This pane is separated from the stamps by a line of roulettes.

Special First Day of Issue Postmarks

1655

(Des Sedley Place. Photo Walsall)

2003 (27 Mar). **Overseas Booklet Stamps**. *Self-adhesive. Two phosphor bands. P 15 × 14 die-cut with one elliptical hole on each vertical side.*

2358	**1655**	(Europe) new blue and rosine	80	85
2359		(Worldwide) rosine and new blue	1·60	1·70
		First Day Cover (Tallents House) (Type K, see Introduction)		5·25
		First Day Cover (Windsor) (Type K)		5·25
		Presentation Pack (P.O. Pack No. 60)		3·00
		PHQ Cards (set of 2)	1·00	6·00

Nos. 2358/9 were intended to pay postage on mail up to 40 grams to either Europe (52p.) or to foreign destinations outside Europe (£1.12). Operationally they were only available in separate booklets of 4, initially sold at £2.08 and £4.48, with the surplus self-adhesive paper around each stamp removed. Single examples of the stamps were available from philatelic outlets as sets of two or in presentation packs.

1656 Amy Johnson (pilot) and Bi-plane

1657 Members of 1953 British Team on Everest

1658 Freya Stark (traveller and writer) and Desert

1659 Ernest Shackleton (Antarctic explorer) and Wreck of Endurance

1660 Francis Chichester (yachtsman) and Gipsy Moth IV

1661 Robert Falcon Scott (Antarctic explorer) and Norwegian Expedition at the Pole

(Des H. Brown)

2003 (29 Apr). **Extreme Endeavours (British Explorers)**. *One centre phosphor band* (2nd) *or two phosphor bands* (others). *(a) Photo Questa. PVA gum. P 15 × 14½.*

2360	**1656**	(2nd) gold, black, magenta, greenish yellow, and new blue	45	50
2361	**1657**	(1st) gold, black, magenta, greenish yellow, and new blue	70	75
2362	**1658**	(E) gold, black, magenta, greenish yellow, and new blue	90	95
2363	**1659**	42p. gold, black, magenta, greenish yellow, and new blue	1·00	1·10
2364	**1660**	47p. gold, black, magenta, greenish yellow, and new blue	1·10	1·20
2365	**1661**	68p. gold, black, magenta, greenish yellow, and new blue	1·60	1·80
		Set of 6	5·50	5·75
		Set of 6 Gutter Pairs	11·50	
		First Day Cover (Tallents House)		6·75
		First Day Cover (Plymouth)		6·75
		Presentation Pack	6·00	
		PHQ Cards (set of 6)	3·25	9·50

(b) Photo De La Rue. Self-adhesive. Die-cut P 14½

2366	**1657**	(1st) gold, black, magenta, greenish yellow and new blue	1·00	1·00
		a. Booklet pane. No. 2366 × 2 plus No. 2295 × 4	3·00	

The phosphor bands on Nos. 2361/5 are at the centre and right of each stamp.

No. 2366 was only issued in £1.62 stamp booklets, No. PM9, in which the surplus self-adhesive paper around each stamp was removed.

Special First Day of Issue Postmarks

(Des Rose Design. Photo De La Rue)

2003 (20 May). **50th Anniv of Wilding Definitives** (2nd issue). *Sheet 124 × 70 mm, containing designs as T **155/8** and **160** (1952-54 issue), but with values in decimal currency as T **1348** or with service indicator as T **1566**, printed on pale cream. One centre phosphor band (20p.) or two phosphor bands (others). W **1565**. P 15 × 14 (with one elliptical hole on each vertical side).*

MS2367 4p. deep lilac; 8p. ultramarine; 10p. reddish
    purple; 20p. bright green; 28p. bronze-
    green; 34p. brown-purple; (E) chestnut;
    42p. Prussian blue; 68p. grey-blue and
    label showing national emblems .... 9·50   9·75
    First Day Cover (Tallents House) ......   10·00
    First Day Cover (Windsor) ....   10·00
    Presentation Pack ....   10·00

Special First Day of Issue Postmarks

1662 Guardsmen in
Coronation Procession

1663 East End Children reading
Coronation Party Poster

1664 Queen Elizabeth II in
Coronation Chair with Bishops
of Durham and Bath and Wells

1665 Children in Plymouth
working on Royal Montage

1666 Queen Elizabeth II in
Coronation Robes (photograph
by Cecil Beaton)

1667 Children's Race at East
End Street Party

1668 Coronation Coach passing
through Marble Arch

1669 Children in Fancy Dress

1670 Coronation Coach
outside Buckingham Palace

1671 Children eating at
London Street Party

(Des Kate Stephens. Photo De La Rue (sheets) or Walsall (booklets))

2003 (2 June). **50th Anniv of Coronation**. W **1565**. *Two phosphor bands. P 14½ × 14.*

2368 **1662** (1st) greenish yellow, bright magenta, new
             blue, grey-black, deep turquoise-blue
             and gold   45   50
     a. Block of 10. Nos. 2368/77 .... 4·50
     b. Booklet pane. Nos. 2368, 2370, 2373
        and 2375 with margins all round ..... 1·70

2369	**1663**	(1st) black and gold	45	50
		b. Booklet pane. Nos. 2369, 2372, 2374 and 2377 with margins all round	1·70	
2370	**1664**	(1st) greenish yellow, bright magenta, new blue, grey-black, deep turquoise-blue and gold	45	50
2371	**1665**	(1st) black and gold	45	50
2372	**1666**	(1st) greenish yellow, bright magenta, new blue, grey-black and deep turquoise-blue	45	50
2373	**1667**	(1st) black and gold	45	50
2374	**1668**	(1st) greenish yellow, bright magenta, new blue, grey-black, deep turquoise-blue and gold	45	50
2375	**1669**	(1st) black and gold	45	50
2376	**1670**	(1st) greenish yellow, bright magenta, new blue, grey-black, deep turquoise-blue and gold	45	50
2377	**1671**	(1st) black and gold	45	50
		Set of 10	4·50	5·00
		Gutter Block of 20	9·25	
		First Day Cover (Tallents House)		5·50
		First Day Cover (London SW1)		5·50
		Presentation Pack	4·75	
		PHQ Cards (set of 10)	3·75	8·00

Nos. 2368/77 were printed together, se-tenant, in blocks of 10 (5 × 2) throughout sheets of 60.

No. 2372 does not show a silhouette of the Queen's head in gold as do the other nine designs.

1672 Prince William in September 2001 (Brendan Beirne)

1673 Prince William in September 2000 (Tim Graham)

1674 Prince William in September 2001 (Camera Press)

1675 Prince William in September 2001 (Tim Graham)

(Des Madeleine Bennett. Litho Walsall)

2003 (17 June). **21st Birthday of Prince William of Wales**. *Phosphor backgrounds*. P $14\frac{1}{2}$.

2381	**1672**	28p. silver, black, grey-black, and light green	45	50
2382	**1673**	(E) dull mauve, grey-black and light green	60	65
2383	**1674**	47p. greenish grey, grey-black, black and light green	75	80
2384	**1675**	68p. sage-green, black and bright green ...	1·10	1·20
		Set of 4	2·75	3·00
		Set of 4 Gutter Pairs	5·75	
		First Day Cover (Tallents House)		3·75
		First Day Cover (Cardiff)		3·75
		Presentation Pack	3·25	
		PHQ Cards (set of 4)	1·50	4·25

Special First Day of Issue Postmarks

(Photo Walsall)

2003 (2 June). **50th Anniv of Coronation**. *Booklet stamps. Designs as* T **160** *(Wilding definitive of 1952) and* **163** *(Coronation commemorative of 1953), but with values in decimal currency as* T **1348**. W **1565**. *Two phosphor bands*. P 15 × 14 *(with one elliptical hole on each vertical side for Nos. 2378/9)*.

2378	**160**	47p. bistre-brown	2·50	2·50
		a. Booklet pane. Nos. 2378/9, each × 2, and 2380 with margins all round	50·00	
2379		68p. grey-blue	2·50	2·50
2380	**163**	£1 deep yellow-green	45·00	45·00
		Set of 3	45·00	45·00

Nos. 2378/80 were only available in £7.46 stamp booklets, No. DX31. Stamps as Nos. 2378/9, but on pale cream, were also included in the Wilding miniature sheets, Nos. **MS**2326 or **MS**2367. A £1 design as No. 2380, but on phosphorised paper, was previously included in the "Stamp Show 2000" miniature sheet, No. **MS**2147.

Special First Day of Issue Postmarks

GIBBONS STAMP MONTHLY
– finest and most informative magazine for all collectors. Obtainable from your newsagent or by postal subscription – details on request.

1676 Loch Assynt, Sutherland

1677 Ben More, Isle of Mull

1678 Rothiemurchus,
Cairngorms

1679 Dalveen Pass, Lowther
Hills

1680 Glenfinnan Viaduct,
Lochaber

1681 Papa Little, Shetland
Islands

(Des Phelan Barker. Photo De La Rue)

2003 (15 July). **A British Journey: Scotland**. *One centre phosphor band (2nd) or two phosphor bands (others).* P 14½. (a) *PVA gum*

2385	**1676**	(2nd) silver, black, bright magenta, greenish yellow and new blue		30	35
2386	**1677**	(1st) silver, black, bright magenta, greenish yellow and new blue		45	50
2387	**1678**	(E) silver, black, bright magenta, greenish yellow and new blue		60	65
2388	**1679**	42p. silver, black, bright magenta, greenish yellow and new blue		65	70
2389	**1680**	47p. silver, black, bright magenta, greenish yellow and new blue		75	80
2390	**1681**	68p. silver, black, bright magenta, greenish yellow and new blue		1·10	1·20
		Set of 6		3·75	4·00
		Set of 6 Gutter Pairs		7·75	
		First Day Cover (Tallents House)			5·00
		First Day Cover (Baltasound, Unst, Shetland)			5·00
		Presentation Pack		4·25	
		PHQ Cards (set of 6)		2·20	6·25

(b) *Self-adhesive. Die-cut perf* 14½

2391	**1677**	(1st) silver, black, bright magenta, greenish yellow and new blue		1·00	1·00
		a. Booklet pane. No. 2391 × 2, and No. 2295 × 4		2·50	

No. 2391 was only issued in £1.68 stamp booklets, No. **PM**10, in which the surplus self-adhesive paper around each stamp was removed.

Special First Day of Issue Postmarks

1682 "The Station"
(Andrew Davidson)   **1683** "Black Swan"
(Stanley Chew)

1684 "The Cross Keys"
(George Mackenney)

1685 "The Mayflower"
(Ralph Ellis)

1687 Meccano Constructor
Biplane, c. 1931

1688 Wells-Brimtoy Clockwork
Double-decker Omnibus,
c. 1938

1686 "The Barley Sheaf"
(Joy Cooper)

1689 Hornby M1 Clockwork
Locomotive and Tender,
c. 1948

1690 Dinky Toys Ford Zephyr,
c. 1956

(Des Elmwood. Photo De La Rue)

2003 (12 Aug)–**04. British Pub Signs.** *Two phosphor bands.* P $14 \times 14z\frac{1}{2}$.

2392	**1682**	(1st)	silver, black, magenta, greenish yellow and new blue	45	50
		a.	Booklet pane. No. 2392 × 4 with margins all round (16.3.04)	1·60	
2393	**1683**	(E)	silver, black, magenta, greenish yellow and new blue	60	65
2394	**1684**	42p.	silver, black, magenta, greenish yellow and new blue	65	70
2395	**1685**	47p.	silver, black, magenta, greenish yellow and new blue	75	80
2396	**1686**	68p.	silver, black, magenta, greenish yellow and new blue	1·10	1·20
			Set of 5	3·50	3·75
			Set of 5 Gutter Pairs	7·25	
			First Day Cover (Tallents House)		4·50
			First Day Cover (Cross Keys, Hereford)		4·50
			Presentation Pack	4·00	
			PHQ Cards (set of 5)	1·90	5·50

No. 2392a comes from the £7.44 "Letters by Night" booklet, No. **DX**32.

Special First Day of Issue Postmarks

1691 Mettoy Friction Drive
Space Ship Eagle, c. 1960

(Des Trickett and Webb)

2003 (18 Sept). **Classic Transport Toys.** *Two phosphor bands.* (a) *Photo Enschedé. PVA gum.* P $14\frac{1}{2} \times 14$

2397	**1687**	(1st)	silver, blue-black, black, new blue, magenta and greenish yellow	45	50
2398	**1688**	(E)	silver, blue-black, black, new blue, magenta and greenish yellow	60	65
2399	**1689**	42p.	silver, blue-black, black, new blue, magenta and greenish yellow	65	70
2400	**1690**	47p.	silver, blue-black, black, new blue, magenta and greenish yellow	75	80
2401	**1691**	68p.	silver, blue-black, black, new blue, magenta and greenish yellow	1·10	1·20
			Set of 5	3·50	3·75
			Set of 5 Gutter Pairs	7·25	
			First Day Cover (Tallents House)		4·50
			First Day Cover (Toye, Downpatrick)		4·50
			Presentation Pack	4·00	
			PHQ Cards (set of 6)	2·75	6·25
MS2402			115 × 105 mm. Nos. 2397/401	3·50	3·75
			First Day Cover		4·50

(b) *Photo De La Rue. Self-adhesive. Die-cut* P $14\frac{1}{2} \times 14$

2403	**1687**	(1st)	silver, blue-black, black, new blue, magenta and greenish yellow	45	50
		a.	Booklet pane. No. 2403 × 2 and No. 2295 × 4	2·50	

The complete miniature sheet is shown on one of the PHQ cards with the others depicting individual stamps.

No. 2403 was only issued in £1.68 stamp booklets, No. **PM**11, in which the surplus self-adhesive paper around each stamp was removed.

Special First Day of Issue Postmarks

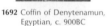

1692 Coffin of Denytenamun, Egyptian, c. 900BC

1693 Alexander the Great, Greek, c. 200BC

1694 Sutton Hoo Helmet, Anglo-Saxon, c. AD600

1695 Sculpture of Parvati, South Indian, c. AD1550

1696 Mask of Xiuhtecuhtli, Mixtec-Aztec, c. AD1500

1697 Hoa Hakananai'a, Easter Island, c. AD1000

(Des Rose Design. Photo Walsall)

2003 (7 Oct). **250th Anniv of the British Museum**. *One side phosphor band (2nd), two phosphor bands ((1st), (E), 47p.) or phosphor background at left and band at right (42p., 68p.). P 14 × 14½.*

2404	**1692**	(2nd) brownish grey, black, greenish yellow, magenta and pale new blue	30	35
2405	**1693**	(1st) brownish grey, black, greenish yellow, magenta and pale new blue	45	50
2406	**1694**	(E) brownish grey, black, greenish yellow, magenta and pale new blue	60	65
2407	**1695**	42p. brownish grey, black, greenish yellow, magenta and pale new blue	65	70
2408	**1696**	47p. brownish grey, black, greenish yellow, magenta and pale new blue	75	80
2409	**1697**	68p. brownish grey, black, greenish yellow, magenta and pale new blue	1·10	1·20
		Set of 6	3·75	4·00
		Set of 6 Gutter Pairs	7·75	
		First Day Cover (Tallents House)		4·75
		First Day Cover (London WC1)		4·75
		Presentation Pack	4·25	
		PHQ Cards (set of 6)	2·75	6·50

Special First Day of Issue Postmarks

1698 Ice Spiral

1699 Icicle Star

1700 Wall of Ice Blocks

1701 Ice Ball

1702 Ice Hole

1703 Snow Pyramids

(Des D. Davis. Photo De La Rue)

2003 (4 Nov). **Christmas. Ice Sculptures by Andy Goldsworthy.** *Self-adhesive. One side phosphor band (2nd), "all-over" phosphor (1st) or two bands (others). Die-cut perf 14½ × 14.*

2410	**1698**	(2nd) magenta, greenish yellow, new blue and black	30	35
		a. Booklet pane. No. 2410 × 24	7·25	
2411	**1699**	(1st) magenta, greenish yellow, new blue and black	45	50
		a. Booklet pane. No. 2411 × 12	5·00	
2412	**1700**	(E) magenta, greenish yellow, new blue and black	60	65
2413	**1701**	53p. magenta, greenish yellow, new blue and black	80	85
2414	**1702**	68p. magenta, greenish yellow, new blue and black	1·10	1·20
2415	**1703**	£1.12 magenta, greenish yellow, new blue and black	1·60	1·70
		Set of 6	4·75	5·25
		First Day Cover (Tallents House)		6·25
		First Day Cover (Bethlehem, Llandeilo)		6·25
		Presentation Pack	5·25	
		PHQ Cards (set of 6)	2·75	

Nos. 2410/15 were each printed in sheets of 50 with the surplus backing paper around each stamp removed.

The 2nd and 1st class were also issued in separate sheets of 20 printed in lithography instead of photogravure, each stamp accompanied by a half stamp-size *se-tenant* label showing either ice sculptures (2nd) or animals (1st). The 2nd class sheet was sold for £4.20 and the 1st class for £6.15. These sheets were also available with personal photographs instead of labels at £14.95 from Royal Mail, Edinburgh or £15 from photo-booths at selected post offices and Safeway stores.

1704 (*Illustration reduced. Actual size 115 × 88 mm*)

(Des Why Not Associates. Litho Walsall)

2003 (19 Dec). **England's Victory in Rugby World Cup Championship, Australia.** *Sheet 115 × 85 mm. Multicoloured. Two phosphor bands. P 14.*

MS2416	**1704**	(1st) England flags and fans; (1st) England team standing in circle before match; 68p. World Cup trophy; 68p. Victorious England players after match	4·50	4·50
		First Day Cover (Tallents House)		4·50
		First Day Cover (Twickenham)		4·50
		Presentation Pack	4·75	

Special First Day of Issue Postmarks

Special First Day of Issue Postmarks

Collectors Pack 2003

2003 (4 Nov). Comprises Nos. 2327/57, 2360/5, 2368/77, 2381/90, 2392/401 and 2404/15
Collectors Pack .... 45·00

Post Office Yearbook

2003 (4 Nov). Comprises Nos. 2327/57, 2360/5, 2368/77, 2381/90, 2392/401 and 2404/15
Yearbook .... 50·00

GIBBONS STAMP MONTHLY
– finest and most informative magazine for all collectors. Obtainable from your newsagent or by postal subscription – details on request.

1705 Dolgoch, Rheilffordd Talyllyn Railway, Gwynedd

1706 CR Class 439, Bo'ness and Kinneil Railway, West Lothian

1707 GCR Class 8K, Leicestershire

1708 GWR Manor Class Bradley Manor, Severn Valley Railway, Worcestershire

1709 SR West Country class Blackmoor Vale, Bluebell Railway, East Sussex

1710 BR Standard class, Keighley and Worth Valley Railway, Yorkshire

(Des Roundel. Litho De La Rue)

2004 (13 Jan–16 Mar). **Classic Locomotives**. *One side phosphor band (20p) or two phosphor bands (others). P* 14½.

2417	**1705**	20p. greenish yellow, magenta, new blue, silver and black	30	35
2418	**1706**	28p. greenish yellow, magenta, new blue, silver and black	45	50
		a. Booklet pane. Nos. 2418/20 with margins all round (16 Mar)	1·60	
2419	**1707**	(E) greenish yellow, magenta, new blue, silver and black	60	65
2420	**1708**	42p. greenish yellow, magenta, new blue, silver and black	65	70
2421	**1709**	47p. greenish yellow, magenta, new blue, silver and black	75	80
2422	**1710**	68p. greenish yellow, magenta, new blue, silver and black	1·10	1·20
		Set of 6	3·75	4·00
		Set of 6 Gutter Pairs	7·75	
		First Day Cover (Tallents House)		4·75
		First Day Cover (York)		4·75
		Presentation Pack	4·50	
		PHQ Cards (set of 6)	2·50	6·25
MS2423		190 × 67 mm. Nos. 2417/22	3·75	4·25
		First Day Cover (Tallents House)		4·75
		First Day Cover (York)		4·75

No. 2418a comes from the £7.44 "Letters by Night" booklet, No. DX32.

Special First Day of Issue Postmarks

1711 Postman   **1712** Face

1713 Duck   **1714** Baby

1715 Aircraft

(Des S. Kambayashi. Litho De La Rue)

2004 (3 Feb). **Occasions**. *Two phosphor bands. P* 14½ × 14.

2424	**1711**	(1st) bright mauve and black	45	50
		a. Horiz strip of 5. Nos. 2424/8	2·20	
		ab. Imperf strip of 5		
2425	**1712**	(1st) magenta and black	45	50
2426	**1713**	(1st) lemon and black	45	50
2427	**1714**	(1st) pale turquoise-green and black	45	50
2428	**1715**	(1st) bright new blue and black	45	50
		Set of 5	2·20	2·50
		Gutter Block of 10	4·75	
		First Day Cover (Tallents House)		3·00
		First Day Cover (Merry Hill, Wolverhampton)		3·00
		Presentation Pack	2·75	
		PHQ Cards (set of 5)	2·20	4·25

Nos. 2424/8 were printed together, *se-tenant*, as horizontal strips of 5 in sheets of 25 (5 × 5).

Nos. 2424/8 were also issued in sheets of 20 containing vertical strips of the five designs alternated with half stamp-size labels. These sheets with printed labels were available at £6.15 from philatelic outlets, or with personalised photographs at £14.95 from Royal Mail in Edinburgh.

Special First Day of Issue Postmarks

1722 Doors of Durin

1723 Barad-dûr

1716 Map showing Middle Earth

1717 Forest of Lothlórien in Spring

1724 Minas Tirth

1725 Fangorn Forest

(Des HGV Design. Litho Walsall)

1718 Dust-jacket for The Fellowship of the Ring

1719 Rivendell

2004 (26 Feb). **50th Anniv of Publication of The Fellowship of the Ring and The Two Towers by J. R. R. Tolkien.** *Two phosphor bands.* P 14½.

2429	**1716**	(1st) pale stone, sepia, black, greenish yellow, magenta and new blue	45	50
		a. Block of 10. Nos. 2429/38	4·50	
2430	**1717**	(1st) pale stone, sepia, black, greenish yellow, magenta and new blue	45	50
2431	**1718**	(1st) pale stone, sepia, black, greenish yellow, magenta and new blue	45	50
2432	**1719**	(1st) pale stone, sepia, black, greenish yellow, magenta and new blue	45	50
2433	**1720**	(1st) pale stone, sepia, black, greenish yellow, magenta and new blue	45	50
2434	**1721**	(1st) pale stone, sepia, black, greenish yellow, magenta and new blue	45	50
2435	**1722**	(1st) pale stone, sepia, black, greenish yellow, magenta and new blue	45	50
2436	**1723**	(1st) pale stone, sepia, black, greenish yellow, magenta and new blue	45	50
2437	**1724**	(1st) pale stone, sepia, black, greenish yellow, magenta and new blue	45	50
2438	**1725**	(1st) pale stone, sepia, black, greenish yellow, magenta and new blue	45	50
		Set of 10	4·50	5·00
		Gutter Block of 20	9·25	
		First Day Cover (Tallents House)		5·50
		First Day Cover (Oxford)		5·50
		Presentation Pack	5·00	
		PHQ Cards (set of 10)	4·50	9·00

1720 The Hall at Bag End

1721 Orthanc

Nos. 2429/38 were printed together, *se-tenant*, in blocks of 10 (5 × 2) throughout the sheet.

Special First Day of Issue Postmarks

1726 Ely Island, Lower Lough Erne

1727 Giant's Causeway, Antrim Coast

1728 Slemish, Antrim Mountains

1729 Banns Road, Mourne Mountains

1730 Glenelly Valley, Sperrins

1731 Islandmore, Strangford Lough

(Des Phelan Barker. Photo Enschedé)

2004 (16 Mar). **A British Journey: Northern Ireland**. *One phosphor band* (2nd) *or two phosphor bands* (others). P 14½. (a) *PVA gum.*

2439	**1726**	(2nd) silver, black, new blue, magenta and greenish yellow	30	35
2440	**1727**	(1st) silver, black, new blue, magenta and greenish yellow	45	50
2441	**1728**	(E) silver, black, new blue, magenta and greenish yellow	60	65
2442	**1729**	42p. silver, black, new blue, magenta and greenish yellow	65	70

2443	**1730**	47p. silver, black, new blue, magenta and greenish yellow	75	80
2444	**1731**	68p. silver, black, new blue, magenta and greenish yellow	1·10	1·20
		Set of 6	3·75	4·00
		Set of 6 Gutter Pairs	7·75	
		First Day Cover (Tallents House)		5·00
		First Day Cover (Garrison, Enniskillen)		5·00
		Presentation Pack	4·50	
		PHQ Cards (set of 6)	2·75	6·75

(b) *Self-adhesive. Die-cut perf* 14½

2445	**1727**	(1st) silver, black, new blue, magenta and greenish yellow	45	50
		a. Booklet pane. No. 2445 × 2 and No. 2295 × 4	2·50	

No. 2445 was only issued in £1.68 stamp booklets No. PM12 in which the surplus self-adhesive paper around each stamp was removed.

Special First Day of Issue Postmarks

ROYAL MAIL POSTAGE LABELS

These imperforate labels were issued as an experiment by the Post Office. Special microprocessor controlled machines were installed at post offices in Cambridge, London, Shirley (Southampton) and Windsor to provide an after-hours sales service to the public. The machines printed and dispensed the labels according to the coins inserted and the buttons operated by the customer. Values were initially available in $\frac{1}{2}$p. steps to 16p. and in addition, the labels were sold at philatelic counters in two packs containing either 3 values ($3\frac{1}{2}$, $12\frac{1}{2}$, 16p.) or 32 values ($\frac{1}{2}$p. to 16p.).

From 28 August 1984 the machines were adjusted to provide values up to 17p. After 31 December 1984 labels including $\frac{1}{2}$p. values were withdrawn. The machines were taken out of service on 30 April 1985.

Machine postage-paid impression in red on phosphorised paper with grey-green background design. No watermark. Imperforate.

1984 (1 May–28 Aug).
Set of 32 ($\frac{1}{2}$p. to 16p.)	12·00	15·00
Set of 3 ($3\frac{1}{2}$p., $12\frac{1}{2}$p., 16p.)	2·00	2·25
Set of 3 on First Day Cover (1.5.84)	4·00	
Set of 2 ($16\frac{1}{2}$p., 17p.) (28.8.84)	2·50	2·50

REGIONAL ISSUES

CHANNEL ISLANDS

GENERAL ISSUE

C **1** Gathering Vraic   C **2** Islanders gathering Vraic

(Des J. R. R. Stobie (1d.) or from drawing by E. Blampied ($2\frac{1}{2}$d.). Photo Harrison)

1948 (10 May).   *Third Anniv of Liberation. W* **127** *of Great Britain. P* 15 × 14.
C1	C **1**	1d. scarlet	25	30
C2	C **2**	$2\frac{1}{2}$d. ultramarine	25	30
		First Day Cover	35·00	

PRINTERS (£.s.d. stamps of all regions):—Photo Harrison & Sons. Portrait by Dorothy Wilding Ltd.

DATES OF ISSUE. Conflicting dates of issue have been announced for some of the regional issues, partly explained by the stamps being released on different dates by the Philatelic Bureau in Edinburgh or the Philatelic Counter in London and in the regions. We have adopted the practice of giving the earliest known dates, since once released the stamps could have been used anywhere in the U.K.

I. ENGLAND

EN **1** Three Lions   EN **2** Crowned Lion with Shield of St. George

EN **3** Oak Tree   EN **4** Tudor Rose

(Des Sedley Place, from sculptures by D. Dathan. Photo Questa (No. EN1b) or De La Rue (others))

2001 (23 Apr)–**02**. *One centre phosphor band (2nd) or two phosphor bands (others). P* 15 × 14 *(with one elliptical hole on each vertical side).*
EN1	EN **1**	(2nd) slate-green and silver	30	35
		a. Imperf (pair)		
		b. Booklet pane. Nos. EN1/2, each × 4, and No. S95, with margins all round (24.9.02)	4·75	
EN2	EN **2**	(1st) lake-brown and silver	45	50
EN3	EN **3**	(E) olive-green and silver	60	65
EN4	EN **4**	65p. deep reddish lilac and silver	1·60	1·75
EN5		68p. deep reddish lilac and silver (4.7.02)	1·10	1·25
		Presentation Pack (Nos. EN1/4) (P.O. Pack No. 54)	2·75	
		PHQ Cards (Nos. EN1/4) (set of 4)	1·50	10·00

Nos. EN1/3 were initially sold at 19p., 27p. and 36p., the latter representing the basic European airmail rate.

First Day Covers
23.4.01	2nd, 1st, E, 65p. (EN1/4)		
	Philatelic Bureau (Type G, see Introduction)	3·25	
	Windsor	3·25	
4.7.02	68p. (EN5)		
	Tallents House (Type K, see Introduction)	1·75	
	London (as Windsor)	1·75	

Special First Day of Issue Postmark

Combined Presentation Packs for England, Northern Ireland, Scotland and Wales
4.7.02	P.O. Pack No. 59. 68p. from England, Northern Ireland, Scotland and Wales (Nos. EN5, NI93, S99, W88)	4·50

(Photo De La Rue)

2003 (14 Oct). **As Nos. EN1/3 and EN5 but with white borders.** *One centre phosphor band (2nd) or two phosphor bands (others). P 15 × 14 (with one elliptical hole on each vertical side).*

EN6	EN1	(2nd) slate-green and silver	30	35
EN7	EN2	(1st) lake-brown and silver	45	50
EN8	EN3	(E) olive-green and silver	60	65
EN9	EN4	68p. deep reddish lilac and silver	1·10	1·20
		Presentation Pack (P.O. Pack No. 63)	2·75	
		PHQ Cards (set of 4)	1·70	4·00

First Day Covers
14.10.03   2nd, 1st, E, 68p. (EN6/9)
Tallents House (Type K, see Introduction) .... 3·25
London (as Windsor) .... 3·25

II. NORTHERN IRELAND

N 1

N 2

N 3

(Des W. Hollywood (3d., 4d., 5d.), L. Pilton (6d., 9d.), T. Collins (1s. 3d., 1s. 6d.))

1958–67. W 179. P 15 × 14.

NI1	N 1	3d. deep lilac (18.8.58)	15	10
		p. One centre phosphor band (9.6.67)	15	15
NI2		4d. ultramarine (7.2.66)	15	15
		p. Two phosphor bands (10.67)	15	15
NI3	N 2	6d. deep claret (29.9.58)	20	25
NI4		9d. bronze-green (2 phosphor bands) (1.3.67)	30	70
NI5	N 3	1s. 3d. green (29.9.58)	30	70
NI6		1s. 6d. grey-blue (2 phosphor bands) (1.3.67)	30	70
		Ey. Phosphor omitted	£200	

First Day Covers

18.8.58	3d. (NI1)	30·00
29.9.58	6d., 1s. 3d. (NI3, NI5)	35·00
7.2.66	4d. (NI2)	7·00
1.3.67	9d., 1s. 6d. (NI4, NI6)	4·00

For Nos. NI1, NI3 and NI5 in Presentation Pack, see below Wales No. W6.

1968–69. *No watermark. Chalk-surfaced paper. One centre phosphor band (Nos. NI8/9) or two phosphor bands (others). Gum arabic (No. NI7) or PVA gum (others). P 15 × 14.*

NI 7	N 1	4d. dp brt blue (27.6.68)	15	15
		Ev. PVA gum* (23.10.68)	12·00	
NI 8		4d. olive-sepia (4.9.68)	15	15
		Ey. Phosphor omitted		
NI 9		4d. brt vermilion (26.2.69)	20	20
		Ey. Phosphor omitted	4·50	
NI10		5d. royal blue (4.9.68)	20	20
		Ey. Phosphor omitted	25·00	
NI11	N 3	1s. 6d. grey-blue (20.5.69)	2·25	2·50
		Ey. Phosphor omitted	£500	

4.9.68   *First Day Cover (NI8, NI10)* .... 3·00
Presentation Pack (containing Nos. NI1p, NI4/6, NI8/10) (9.12.70) .... 3·25

*No. NI7Ev was never issued in Northern Ireland. After No. NI7 (gum arabic) had been withdrawn from Northern Ireland but whilst still on sale at the philatelic counters elsewhere, about fifty sheets with PVA gum were sold over the London Philatelic counter on 23 October, 1968, and some were also on sale at the British Philatelic Exhibition Post Office.

N 4

I   II

Redrawn design of Type N 4 (litho ptgs.)

Two Types of Crown

Type I:–Crown with all pearls individually drawn.

Type II:–Crown with clear outlines, large pearls and strong white line below them. First 3 pearls at left are joined, except on Nos. NI39 and NI49.

The following stamps printed in lithography show a screened background behind and to the left of the emblem: 11½p., 12½p., 14p. (No. NI38), 15½p., 16p., 18p. (No. NI45), 19½p., 22p. (No. NI53) and 28p. (No. NI62). The 13p. and 17p. (No. NI43) also showed screened backgrounds in Type I, but changed to solid backgrounds for Type II. The 31p. had a solid background in Type I, but changed to a screened background for Type II. All other values printed in lithography have solid backgrounds.

(Des J. Matthews after plaster cast by Arnold Machin)

1971 (7 July)–**93.** *Decimal Currency. Chalk-surfaced paper. Type N* **4.**

(a) Photo Harrison. With phosphor bands. P 15 × 14.

NI12	2½p. brt magenta (1 centre band)	70	45
NI13	3p. ultramarine (2 bands)	25	25
	Ey. Phosphor omitted	50·00	
NI14	3p. ultramarine (1 centre band) (23.1.74)	20	15
NI15	3½p. olive-grey (2 bands) (23.1.74)	20	25
NI16	3½p. olive-grey (1 centre band) (6.11.74)	20	25
NI17	4½p. grey-blue (2 bands) (6.11.74)	30	25
NI18	5p. reddish violet (2 bands)	1·25	1·25
NI19	5½p. violet (2 bands) (23.1.74)	20	20
	Ey. Phosphor omitted	£225	
NI20	5½p. violet (1 centre band) (21.5.75)	20	25
NI21	6½p. greenish blue (1 centre band) (14.1.76).	20	20
NI22	7p. purple-brown (1 centre band) (18.1.78)	35	25
NI23	7½p. chestnut (2 bands)	1·75	1·75
	Ey. Phosphor omitted	55·00	
NI24	8p. rosine (2 bands) (23.1.74)	35	35
	Ey. Phosphor omitted	75·00	
NI25	8½p. yellow-green (2 bands) (14.1.76)	35	40
NI26	9p. dp violet (2 bands) (18.1.78)	40	40
	Ey. Phosphor omitted	25·00	
NI27	10p. orange-brown (2 bands) (20.10.76)	40	50
NI28	10p. orange-brown (1 centre band) (23.7.80)	50	50
NI29	10½p. steel-blue (2 bands) (18.1.78)	40	50
NI30	11p. scarlet (2 bands) (20.10.76)	50	50
	Ey. Phosphor omitted	4·50	

(b) Photo Harrison. On phosphorised paper. P 15 × 14.

NI31	12p. yellowish green (23.7.80)	50	50
NI32	13½p. purple-brown (23.7.80)	60	70
NI33	15p. ultramarine (23.7.80)	60	70

(c) Litho Questa (Type II, unless otherwise stated). P 14 (11½p., 12½p., 14p.
(No. NI38), 15½p., 16p., 18p. (No. NI45), 19½p., 20½p., 22p. (No. NI53),
26p. (No. NI60), 28p. (No. NI62)) *or* 15 × 14 *(others)*

NI34	11½p.	drab (Type I) (1 side band) (8.4.81)	85	85
NI35	12p.	brt emerald (1 side band) (7.1.86)	70	80
NI36	12½p.	lt emerald (Type I) (1 side band) (24.2.82)	60	60
		a. Perf 15 × 14 (28.2.84)	4·25	4·00
NI37	13p.	pale chestnut (Type I) (1 side band) (23.10.84)	80	50
		Ea. Type II (28.11.86)	1·00	30
		Ey. Phosphor omitted (Type I)		
NI38	14p.	grey-blue (Type I) (phosphorised paper) (8.4.81)	75	75
NI39	14p.	dp blue (1 centre band) (8.11.88)	75	60
NI40	15p.	brt blue (1 centre band) (28.11.89)	90	60
NI41	15½p.	pale violet (Type I) (phosphorised paper) (24.2.82)	80	80
NI42	16p.	drab (Type I) (phosphorised paper) (27.4.83)	1·00	1·00
		a. Perf 15 × 14 (28.2.84)	7·50	7·50
NI43	17p.	grey-blue (Type I) (phosphorised paper) (23.10.84)	90	95
		Ea. Type II (9.9.86)	£140	90·00
NI44	17p.	dp blue (1 centre band) (4.12.90)	1·00	80
NI45	18p.	dp violet (Type I) (phosphorised paper) (8.4.81)	1·00	1·00
NI46	18p.	dp olive-grey (phosphorised paper) (6.1.87)	1·00	90
NI47	18p.	brt green (1 centre band) (3.12.91)	1·00	95
		a. Perf 14 (31.12.92*)	1·90	1·60
NI48	18p.	brt green (1 side band) (10.8.93)	2·25	2·25
		l. Booklet pane. Nos. NI48, NI59, S61, S71, W49Eb and W60 with margins all round	14·00	
NI49	19p.	brt orange-red (phosphorised paper) (8.11.88)	1·00	1·00
NI50	19½p.	olive-grey (Type I) (phosphorised paper) (24.2.82)	1·90	1·90
NI51	20p.	brownish black (phosphorised paper) (28.11.89)	1·00	80
NI52	20½p.	ultramarine (Type I) (phosphorised paper) (27.4.83)	3·00	3·50
NI53	22p.	blue (Type I) (phosphorised paper) (8.4.81)	1·10	1·10
NI54	22p.	yellow-green (Type I) (phosphorised paper) (23.10.84)	1·10	1·10
NI55	22p.	brt orange-red (phosphorised paper) (4.12.90)	1·25	90
NI56	23p.	brt green (phosphorised paper) (8.11.88)	1·25	1·10
NI57	24p.	Indian red (phosphorised paper) (28.11.89)	1·50	1·00
NI58	24p.	chestnut (phosphorised paper) (3.12.91)	1·10	90
NI59	24p.	chestnut (2 bands) (10.8.93)	2·50	2·25
NI60	26p.	rosine (Type I) (phosphorised paper) (24.2.82)	1·25	1·25
		a. Perf 15 × 14 (Type II) (27.1.87)	4·00	3·50
NI61	26p.	drab (phosphorised paper) (4.12.90)	1·50	1·25
NI62	28p.	dp violet-blue (Type I) (phosphorised paper) (27.4.83)	1·40	1·25
		a. Perf 15 × 14 (Type II) (27.1.87)	1·50	1·25
NI63	28p.	dp bluish grey (phosphorised paper) (3.12.91)	1·60	1·40
NI64	31p.	brt purple (Type I) (phosphorised paper) (23.10.84)	1·60	1·60
		Ea. Type II (14.4.87)	1·90	1·75
NI65	32p.	greenish blue (phosphorised paper) (8.11.88)	1·75	1·75
NI66	34p.	dp bluish grey (phosphorised paper) (28.11.89)	1·90	1·90
NI67	37p.	rosine (phosphorised paper) (4.12.90)	1·90	1·90
NI68	39p.	brt mauve (phosphorised paper) (3.12.91)	1·90	1·90

*Earliest known date of use.

No. NI47a was caused by the use of a reserve perforating machine
for some printings in the second half of 1992.

Nos. NI48 and NI59 only come from booklets.

From 1972 printing were made on fluorescent white paper and from
1973 most printings had dextrin added to the PVA gum (see notes after
1971 Decimal Machin issue).

First Day Covers

7.7.71	2½p., 3p., 5p., 7½p. (NI12/13, NI18, NI23)	3·75
23.1.74	3p., 3½p., 5½p., 8p. (NI14/15, NI19, NI24)	2·00
6.11.74	4½p. (NI17)	1·50
14.1.76	6½p., 8½p. (NI21, NI25)	1·50
20.10.76	10p., 11p. (NI27, NI30)	1·50
18.1.78	7p., 9p., 10½p. (NI22, NI26, NI29)	1·75
23.7.80	12p., 13½p., 15p. (NI31/3)	2·25
8.4.81	11½p., 14p., 18p., 22p. (NI34, NI38, NI45, NI53)	3·50
24.2.82	12½p., 15½p., 19½p., 26p. (NI36, NI41, NI50, NI60)	5·00
27.4.83	16p., 20½p., 28p. (NI42, NI52, NI62)	6·00
23.10.84	13p., 17p., 22p., 31p. (NI37, NI43, NI54, NI64)	4·75
7.1.86	12p. (NI35)	1·50
6.1.87	18p. (NI46)	1·50
8.11.88	14p., 19p., 23p., 32p. (NI39, NI49, NI56, NI65)	4·00
28.11.89	15p., 20p., 24p., 34p. (NI40, NI51, NI57, NI66)	4·50
4.12.90	17p., 22p., 26p., 37p. (NI44, NI55, NI61, NI67)	4·75
3.12.91	18p., 24p., 28p., 39p. (NI47, NI58, NI63, NI68)	5·50

Presentation Packs

7.7.71	P.O. Pack No. 29. 2½p., 3p. (2 bands), 5p., 7½p. (Nos. NI12/13, NI18, NI23)	4·25
29.5.74	P.O. Pack No. 61. 3p. (1 centre band), 3½p. (2 bands) or (1 centre band), 5½p. (2 bands) or (1 centre band), 8p. (Nos. NI14, NI15 or NI16, NI19 or NI20, NI24). The 4½p. (No. NI17) was added later	2·75
20.10.76	P.O. Pack No. 84. 6½p., 8½p., 10p. (2 bands), 11p. (Nos. NI21, NI25, NI27, NI30)	2·00
28.10.81	P.O. Pack No. 129d. 7p., 9p., 10½p., 12p. (photo), 13½p., 15p. (photo), 11½p., 14p. grey-blue, 18p. dp violet, 22p. blue (Nos. NI22, NI26, NI29, NI31/4, NI38, NI45, NI53)	9·00
3.8.83	P.O. Pack No. 4. 10p. (1 centre band), 12½p., 16p., 20½p., 26p. rosine, 28p. dp violet-blue (Nos. NI28, NI36, NI42, NI52, NI60, NI62)	12·00
23.10.84	P.O. Pack No. 8. 10p. (1 centre band), 13p., 16p., 17p. grey-blue, 22p. yellow-green, 26p. rosine, 28p. dp violet-blue, 31p. (Nos. NI28, NI37, NI42a, NI43, NI54, NI60, NI62, NI64)	17·00
3.3.87	P.O. Pack No. 12. 12p. (litho), 13p., 17p. grey-blue, 18p. dp olive-grey, 22p. yellow-green, 26p. rosine, 28p. dp violet-blue, 31p. (Nos. NI35, NI37, NI43, NI46, NI54, NI60a, NI62a, NI64)	15·00

Presentation Packs for Northern Ireland, Scotland and Wales

8.11.88	P.O. Pack No. 17. 14p. dp blue, 19p., 23p., 32p. (Nos. NI39, NI49, NI56, NI65), 14p. (1 centre band), 19p. (phosphorised paper), 23p. (phosphorised paper), 32p. (Nos. S54, S62, S67, S77), 14p. dp blue, 19p., 23p., 32p. (Nos. W40, W50, W57, W66)	16·00

28.11.89 P.O. Pack No. 20. 15p. (litho) 20p., 24p.
Indian red, 34p. (Nos. NI40, NI51, NI57,
NI66), 15p. (litho), 20p., 24p. Indian red,
34p. (Nos. S56, S64, S69, S78), 15p. (litho),
20p., 24p. Indian red, 34p. (Nos. W41,
W52, W58, W67) .... 18·00

4.12.90 P.O. Pack No. 23. 17p. dp blue, 22p. brt
orange-red, 26p. drab, 37p., (Nos. NI44,
NI55, NI61, NI67), 17p. dp blue, 22p. brt
orange-red, 26p. drab, 37p. (Nos. S58,
S66, S73, S79), 17p. dp blue, 22p. brt
orange-red, 26p. drab, 37p. (Nos. W45,
W56, W62, W68) .... 18·00

3.12.91 P.O. Pack No. 26. 18p. brt green, 24p.
chestnut, 28p. dp bluish grey, 39p. (Nos.
NI47, NI58, NI63, NI68), 18p. brt green,
24p. chestnut, 28p. dp bluish grey, 39p.
(Nos. S60, S70, S75, S80), 18p. brt green,
24p. chestnut, 28p. dp bluish grey, 39p.
(Nos. W48, W59, W64, W69) .... 18·00

(Des J. Matthews after plaster cast by Arnold Machin)

1993 (7 Dec)–**2000**. *Chalk-surfaced paper. (a) Litho Questa. P* 15 × 14
(with one elliptical hole on each vertical side).

NI69	N **4**	19p. bistre (1 centre band)	90	80
NI70		19p. bistre (1 band at left) (26.7.94)	1·50	1·75
		a. Booklet pane. Nos. NI70 × 2, NI72 × 4, NI74, NI76 and centre label with margins all round	8·00	
		b. Booklet pane. Nos. NI70, NI72, NI74 and NI76 with margins all round	6·00	
		bEy. Booklet pane. Phosphor omitted		
		Ec. Band at right (25.4.95)	2·50	2·50
		d. Booklet pane. Nos. NI70Ec, NI72, S82, S84, W71 and W73 with margins all round (25.4.95)	10·00	
		da. Part perf pane*		
NI71		20p. brt green (1 centre band) (23.7.96)	1·50	1·25
NI72		25p. red (2 bands)	75	75
		Ey. Phosphor omitted		
NI73		26p. red-brown (2 bands) (23.7.96)	1·40	1·40
NI74		30p. dp olive-grey (2 bands)	1·50	1·40
NI75		37p. brt mauve (2 bands) (23.7.96)	2·25	2·25
NI76		41p. grey-brown (2 bands)	1·50	1·50
		Ey. Phosphor omitted		
NI77		63p. lt emerald (2 bands) (23.7.96)	3·50	3·50

*(b) Photo Walsall (*19p., 20p., 26p. *(No. NI81b), 38p., 40p., 63p., 64p.,
65p.), Harrison or Walsall (*26p. *(No. NI81), 37p.). P* 14 *(No. NI80) or*
15 × 14 *(others) (both with one elliptical hole on each vertical side)*

NI78	N **4**	19p. bistre (1 centre band) (8.6.99)	1·25	70
NI79		20p. brt green (1 centre band) (1.7.97)	75	70
NI80		20p. brt green (1 side band at right) (13.10.98)	1·75	1·90
		al. Booklet pane. Nos. NI80, S90a, W79a and Y1700a × 3 with margins all round	10·00	
NI81		26p. chestnut (2 bands) (1.7.97)	1·25	1·00
		al. Booklet pane. Nos. NI81/2, S91/2 and W80/1 with margins all round (23.9.97) .	6·00	
		b. Perf 14 (13.10.98)	2·25	1·75
NI82		37p. brt mauve (2 bands) (1.7.97)	1·50	1·25
NI83		38p. ultramarine (2 bands) (8.6.99)	2·10	2·10
NI84		40p. dp azure (2 bands) (25.4.00)	1·10	1·10
NI85		63p. lt emerald (2 bands) (1.7.97)	2·40	2·25
NI86		64p. turquoise-green (2 bands) (8.6.99)	2·25	2·00
NI87		65p. greenish blue (2 bands) (25.4.00)	2·00	2·00

* No. NI70da, which comes from the 1995 National Trust £6 booklet,
shows the top two values in the pane of 6 (Nos. S82, S84) completely
imperforate and the two Wales values below partly imperforate.
Nos. NI70, NI80 and NI81b only come from booklets.

The listed booklet panes come from the following Sponsored
Booklets:

NI70a/b – Booklet DX16
NI70d – Booklet DX17
NI80al – Booklet DX21
NI81al – Booklet DX19

First Day Covers

7.12.93	19p., 25p., 30p., 41p. (NI69, NI72, NI74, NI76)	5·50
26.7.94	Northern Ireland *se-tenant* pane 19p., 25p., 30p., 41p. (NI70a)	6·00
23.7.96	20p., 26p., 37p., 63p. (NI71, NI73, NI75, NI77)	8·75
8.6.99	38p., 64p. (NI83, NI86)	4·00
25.4.00	1st, 40p., 65p. (NI84, NI87, NI88b)	4·25

Presentation Packs

8.6.99	P.O. Pack No. 47. 19p., 26p., 38p., 64p. (Nos. NI78, NI81, NI83, NI86)	4·50
25.4.00	P.O. Pack No. 52. 1st, 40p., 65p. (Nos. NI88b, NI84, NI87)	4·00

Presentation Packs for Northern Ireland, Scotland and Wales

7.12.93	P.O. Pack No. 31. 19p., 25p., 30p., 41p., each × 3 (Nos. NI69, NI72, NI74, NI76, S81, S84, S86, S88, W70, W73, W75, W77)	18·00
23.7.96	P.O. Pack No. 36. 20p., 26p., 37p., 63p., each × 3 (Nos. NI71, NI73, NI75, NI77, S83, S85, S87, S89, W72, W74, W76, W78)	22·00
20.10.98	P.O. Pack No. 42. 20p. (1 centre band), 26p., 37p., 63p., each × 3 (Nos. NI79/82, NI85, S90/3, W79/82)	12·00

N **5**

(Des J. Matthews. Photo Walsall)

2000 (15 Feb–25 Apr). *Type* N **4** *redrawn with "1st" face value as Type*
N **5**. *Two phosphor bands. P* 14 *(with one elliptical hole on each
vertical side).*

NI88	N **5**	(1st) bright orange-red	1·90	1·90
		al. Booklet pane. Nos. NI88, S108 and W97, each × 3 with margins all round	13·00	
		b. Perf 15 × 14 (25 Apr)	2·00	2·00
		First Day Cover (se-tenant pane No. NI88al) (Philatelic Bureau)		13·00
		First Day Cover (se-tenant pane No. NI88al) (London SW5)		13·00

No. NI88 was issued in £7.50 stamp booklets (No. DX24) and No.
NI88b in sheets.

N **6** Basalt Columns, Giant's Causeway

N **7** Aerial View of Patchwork Fields

N 8 Linen Pattern   **N 9** Vase Pattern
from Belleck

(Des Rodney Miller Associates. Litho De La Rue or Enschedé (1st, 2nd), De La Rue or Walsall (E), Walsall (65p.), De La Rue (68p.)).

2001 (6 Mar)–**03**. *One centre phosphor band (2nd) or two phosphor bands (others). P 15 × 14 (with one elliptical hole on each vertical side).*

NI89	N 6	(2nd) black, new blue, bright magenta and greenish yellow	30	35
		a. Booklet pane No. NI89 × 5 and No. NI90 × 4 with margins all round (25.2.03)	4·50	
NI90	N 7	(1st) black, new blue and greenish yellow .	45	50
NI91	N 8	(E) black, new blue and pale orange	60	70
NI92	N 9	65p. black, bright magenta and greenish yellow	1·60	1·75
NI93		68p. black, bright magenta and greenish yellow (4.7.02)	1·10	1·25
		Presentation Pack (Nos. NI89/92) (P.O. Pack No. 53)	2·75	
		PHQ Cards (Nos. NI89/92) (set of 4) ...	1·50	10·00

Nos. NI89, NI90 and NI91 were initially sold at 19p., 27p. and 36p., the latter representing the basic European airmail rate.

A new printing of No. NI91, produced by De La Rue instead of Walsall, was issued on 15 October 2002. Stamps from this printing do not differ from those produced by Walsall. Booklet pane No. NI89a was printed by Enschedé.

For combined presentation pack for all four Regions, see under England.

First Day Covers

6.3.01	2nd, 1st, E, 65p. (*NI89/92*)		
	Philatelic Bureau	3·25	
	Belfast	3·25	
4.7.02	68p. (*NI93*)		
	Tallents House (Type K, see Introduction)	1·75	
	Belfast	1·75	

Special First Day of Issue Postmarks

(Litho De La Rue)

2003 (14 Oct). **As Nos. NI89/91 and NI93 but with white borders.** *One centre phosphor band (2nd) or two phosphor bands (others). P 15 × 14 (with one elliptical hole on each vertical side).*

NI94	N 6	(2nd) black, new blue, bright magenta and greenish yellow	30	35
NI95	N 7	(1st) black, new blue and greenish yellow .	45	50
NI96	N 8	(E) black and new blue	60	65

NI97	N 9	68p. black, bright magenta* and greenish yellow	1·10	1·20
		Presentation Pack (P.O. Pack No. 66) ...	2·75	
		PHQ Cards (set of 4)	1·70	4·00

*The bright magenta used on the 68p. is fluorescent.

First Day Cover

14.10.03	2nd, 1st, E, 68p. (NI94/7)		
	Tallents House (Type K, see Introduction)		3·25
	Belfast		3·25

III. SCOTLAND

S **1**   S **2**   S **3**

(Des. G. Huntly (3d., 4d., 5d.), J. Fleming (6d., 9d.), A. Imrie (1s., 3d., 1s. 6d.))

1958–67. *W* 179. *P* 15 × 14.

S1	S **1**	3d. dp lilac (18.8.58)	15	15
		p. Two phosphor bands (29.1.63)	16·00	2·00
		pa. One side phosphor band (30.4.65)	20	25
		pb. One centre phosphor band (9.11.67)	15	15
S2		4d. ultramarine (7.2.66)	15	15
		p. Two phosphor bands	15	15
S3	S **2**	6d. dp claret (29.9.58)	20	15
		p. Two phosphor bands (29.1.63)	20	20
S4		9d. bronze-green (2 phosphor bands) (1.3.67)	35	40
S5	S **3**	1s. 3d. green (29.9.58)	40	40
		p. Two phosphor bands (29.1.63)	40	40
S6		1s. 6d. grey-blue (2 phosphor bands) (1.3.67) .	45	50

First Day Covers

18.8.58	3d. (*S1*)	12·00
29.9.58	6d., 1s. 3d. (*S3, S5*)	25·00
7.2.66	4d. (*S2*)	7·00
1.3.67	9d., 1s. 6d. (*S4, S6*)	4·00

The one phosphor band on No. S1pa was produced by printing broad phosphor bands across alternate vertical perforations. Individual stamps show the band at right or left (same prices either way).

For Nos. S1, S3 and S5 in Presentation Pack, see below Wales No. W6.

1967–70. *No watermark. Chalk-surfaced paper. One centre phosphor band (S7, S9/10) or two phosphor bands (others). Gum arabic (Nos. S7, S8) or PVA gum (others). P* 15 × 14.

S 7	S **1**	3d. dp lilac (16.5.68)	10	15
		Ey. Phosphor omitted	6·00	
		Ev. PVA gum	10	
		Eya. Phosphor omitted (No. S7Ev)	3·00	
S 8		4d. dp brt blue (28.11.67)	10	15
		Ey. Phosphor omitted	8·00	
		Ev. PVA gum (25.7.68)	10	
S 9		4d. olive-sepia (4.9.68)	10	10
		Ey. Phosphor omitted	2·50	
S10		4d. brt vermilion (26.2.69)	10	10
		Ey. Phosphor omitted	2·50	
S11		5d. royal blue (4.9.68)	20	10
		Ey. Phosphor omitted	50·00	
S12	S **2**	9d. bronze-green (28.9.70)	4·00	4·50
		Ey. Phosphor omitted	£200	
S13	S **3**	1s. 6d. grey-blue (12.12.68)	1·40	1·40
		Ey. Phosphor omitted	£120	

4.9.68	*First Day Cover* (*S9, S11*)	3·00
	Presentation Pack (*containing Nos. S3, S5p., S7, S9/13*) (9.12.70)	10·00

S **4**

I   II

Redrawn design of Type S 4 (litho ptgs.)

The introduction of the redrawn lion took place in 1983 when Waddington's had the contract and therefore the 13, 17, 22 and 31p. exist in both types and perforated 14. The Questa printings, perforated 15 × 14, are all Type II.

The Types of Lion.

Type I:–The eye and jaw appear larger and there is no line across the bridge of the nose.

Type II:–The tongue is thick at the point of entry to the mouth and the eye is linked to the background by a solid line.

The following stamps printed in lithography show a screened background behind and to the left of the emblem: $12\frac{1}{2}$p., $15\frac{1}{2}$p., 16p., $19\frac{1}{2}$p., 28p. (Nos. S50 and S74) and 31p. (Nos. S51 and S76). The 13p. and 17p. (No. S43) also showed screened backgrounds for both Type I and II of the John Waddington printings, but changed to solid backgrounds for the Questa Type II. All other values printed in lithography have solid backgrounds.

(Des J. Matthews after plaster cast by Arnold Machin)

1971 (7 July)–**93**. *Decimal Currency. Chalk-surfaced paper. Type S* **4**.

(a) Photo Harrison. With phosphor bands. P 15 × 14.

S14	$2\frac{1}{2}$p. brt magenta (1 centre band)	25	20
	Ey. Phosphor omitted	20·00	
	Eg. Gum arabic (22.9.72)	30	
S15	3p. ultramarine (2 bands)	35	15
	Ey. Phosphor omitted	10·00	
	Eg. Gum arabic (14.12.72)	10	
	Ega. Imperf (pair)	£425	
S16	3p. ultramarine (1 centre band) (23.1.74)	15	15
S17	$3\frac{1}{2}$p. olive-grey (2 bands) (23.1.74)	20	25
	Ey. Phosphor omitted	50·00	
S18	$3\frac{1}{2}$p. olive-grey (1 centre band) (6.11.74)	20	25
S19	$4\frac{1}{2}$p. grey-blue (2 bands) (6.11.74)	30	25
S20	5p. reddish violet (2 bands)	85	1·00
S21	$5\frac{1}{2}$p. violet (2 bands) (23.1.74)	20	20
S22	$5\frac{1}{2}$p. violet (1 centre band) (21.5.75)	20	25
	a. Imperf (pair)	£375	
S23	$6\frac{1}{2}$p. greenish blue (1 centre band) (14.1.76).	20	20
S24	7p. purple-brown (1 centre band) (18.1.78) ..	30	30
S25	$7\frac{1}{2}$p. chestnut (2 bands)	95	1·25
	Ey. Phosphor omitted	5·00	
S26	8p. rosine (2 bands) (23.1.74)	45	40
S27	$8\frac{1}{2}$p. yellow-green (2 bands) (14.1.76)	40	40
S28	9p. dp violet (2 bands) (18.1.78)	40	40
S29	10p. orange-brown (2 bands) (20.10.76)	45	50
S30	10p. orange-brown (1 centre band) (23.7.80)	40	50
S31	$10\frac{1}{2}$p. steel-blue (2 bands) (18.1.78)	45	50
S32	11p. scarlet (2 bands) (20.10.76)	50	50
	Ey. Phosphor omitted	2·00	

(b) Photo Harrison. On phosphorised paper. P 15 × 14

S33	12p. yellowish green (23.7.80)	50	50
S34	$13\frac{1}{2}$p. purple-brown (23.7.80)	70	80
S35	15p. ultramarine (23.7.80)	60	70

(c) *Litho J.W. (Type I unless otherwise stated). One side phosphor band*
(11½p., 12p., 12½p., 13p.) or phosphorised paper (others). P 14

S36	11½p. drab (8.4.81)	80	80
	Ey. Phosphor omitted	£700	
S37	12p. brt emerald (Type II) (7.1.86)	2·00	1·60
S38	12½p. lt emerald (24.2.82)	60	70
S39	13p. pale chestnut (Type I) (23.10.84)	75	75
	Ea. Type II (1.85)	8·00	4·25
S40	14p. grey-blue (8.4.81)	75	75
S41	15½p. pale violet (24.2.82)	80	80
S42	16p. drab (Type II) (27.4.83)	80	85
S43	17p. grey-blue (Type I) (23.10.84)	3·00	2·25
	Ea. Type II (1.85)	1·25	1·00
S44	18p. dp violet (8.4.81)	80	80
S45	19½p. olive-grey (24.2.82)	1·50	1·50
S46	20½p. ultramarine (Type II) (27.4.83)	3·75	3·75
S47	22p. blue (8.4.81)	1·10	1·10
S48	22p. yellow-green (Type I) (23.10.84)	3·00	3·25
	Ea. Type II (1.86)	50·00	30·00
S49	26p. rosine (24.2.82)	1·25	1·25
S50	28p. dp violet-blue (Type II) (27.4.83)	1·25	1·25
S51	31p. brt purple (Type I) (23.10.84)	2·25	2·25
	Ea. Type II (11.85*)	£100	70·00

(d) *Litho Questa (Type II). P 15 × 14*

S52	12p. brt emerald (1 side band) (29.4.86)	2·00	2·00
S53	13p. pale chestnut (1 side band) (4.11.86)	70	75
S54	14p. dp blue (1 centre band) (8.11.88)	60	70
	l. Booklet pane. No. S54 × 6 with margins all round (21.3.89)	3·50	
S55	14p. dp blue (1 side band) (21.3.89)	80	90
	l. Booklet pane. No. S55 × 5, S63 × 2, S68 and centre label with margins all round	18·00	
	la. Error. Booklet pane imperf		
S56	15p. brt blue (1 centre band) (28.11.89)	70	70
	a. Imperf (three sides) (block of four)	£275	
S57	17p. grey-blue (phosphorised paper) (29.4.86)	4·00	4·00
S58	17p. dp blue (1 centre band) (4.12.90)	1·00	1·10
S59	18p. dp olive-grey (phosphorised paper) (6.1.87)	1·10	85
S60	18p. brt green (1 centre band) (3.12.91)	1·25	90
	a. Perf 14 (26.9.92*)	1·40	1·50
	aEy. Phosphor omitted		
S61	18p. brt green (1 side band) (10.8.93)	2·25	2·25
S62	19p. brt orange-red (phosphorised paper) (8.11.88)	70	70
	l. Booklet pane. No. S62 × 9 with margins all round (21.3.89)	5·50	
	m. Booklet pane. No. S62 × 6 with margins all round (21.3.89)	4·50	
S63	19p. brt orange-red (2 bands) (21.3.89)	1·75	1·75
S64	20p. brownish black (phosphorised paper) (28.11.89)	95	95
S65	22p. yellow-green (phosphorised paper) (27.1.87)	1·40	1·50
S66	22p. brt orange-red (phosphorised paper) (4.12.90)	1·25	90
S67	23p. brt green (phosphorised paper) (8.11.88)	1·25	1·10
S68	23p. brt green (2 bands) (21.3.89)	12·00	12·00
S69	24p. Indian red (phosphorised paper) (28.11.89)	1·50	1·00
S70	24p. chestnut (phosphorised paper) (3.12.91)	1·40	1·25
	a. Perf 14 (10.92*)	2·75	2·75
S71	24p. chestnut (2 bands) (10.8.93)	3·00	2·75
S72	26p. rosine (phosphorised paper) (27.1.87)	3·25	3·00
S73	26p. drab (phosphorised paper) (4.12.90)	1·25	1·25
S74	28p. dp violet-blue (phosphorised paper) (27.1.87)	1·25	1·25
S75	28p. dp bluish grey (phosphorised paper) (3.12.91)	1·50	1·40
	a. Perf 14 (18.2.93*)	5·50	4·50
S76	31p. brt purple (phosphorised paper) (29.4.86)	2·00	1·90
S77	32p. greenish blue (phosphorised paper) (8.11.88)	1·75	1·60
S78	34p. dp bluish grey (phosphorised paper) (28.11.89)	1·90	1·90
S79	37p. rosine (phosphorised paper) (4.12.90)	1·90	1·90
S80	39p. brt mauve (phosphorised paper) (3.12.91)	2·00	1·90
	a. Perf 14 (11.92)	3·50	3·50

*Earliest known date of use.

Nos. S55, S61, S63, S68 and S71 only come from booklets.
The listed booklet panes come from the following Sponsored Booklets:

S54l	– Booklet DX10
S55l	– Booklet DX10
S62l/m	– Booklet DX10

No. S56a occured in the second vertical row of two sheets. It is best collected as a block of four including the left-hand vertical pair imperforate on three sides.

Nos. S60a, S70a, S75a and S80a were caused by the use of a reserve perforating machine for some printings in the second half of 1992.

From 1972 printings were on fluorescent white paper. From 1973 most printings had dextrin added to the PVA gum (see notes after the 1971 Decimal Machin issue).

First Day Covers

7.7.71	2½p., 3p., 5p., 7½p. (*S14/15, S20, S25*)	3·00
23.1.74	3p., 3½p., 5½p., 8p. (*S16/17, S21, S26*)	2·00
6.11.74	4½p. (*S19*)	1·50
14.1.76	6½p., 8½p. (*S23, S27*)	1·50
20.10.76	10p., 11p. (*S29, S32*)	1·50
18.1.78	7p., 9p., 10½p. (*S24, S28, S31*)	1·75
23.7.80	12p., 13½p., 15p. (*S33/5*)	2·25
8.4.81	11½p., 14p., 18p., 22p. (*S36, S40, S44, S47*)	3·50
24.2.82	12½p., 15½p., 19½p., 26p. (*S38, S41, S45, S49*)	4·50
27.4.83	16p., 20½p., 28p. (*S42, S46, S50*)	6·00
23.10.84	13p., 17p., 22p., 31p. (*S39, S43, S48, S51*)	7·50
7.1.86	12p. (*S37*)	1·50
6.1.87	18p. (*S59*)	1·50
8.11.88	14p., 19p., 23p., 32p. (*S54, S62, S67, S77*)	4·25
21.3.89	Scots Connection *se-tenant* pane 14p., 19p., 23p. (*S55l*)	14·00
28.11.89	15p., 20p., 24p., 34p. (*S56, S64, S69, S78*)	4·75
4.12.90	17p., 22p., 26p., 37p. (*S58, S66, S73, S79*)	4·75
3.12.91	18p., 24p., 28p., 39p. (*S60, S70, S75, S80*)	5·50

Presentation Packs

7.7.71	P.O. Pack No. 27. 2½p., 3p. (2 bands) 5p., 7½p. (*Nos. S14/15, S20, S25*)	4·25
29.5.74	P.O. Pack No. 62. 3p. (1 centre band), 3½p. (2 bands) *or* (1 centre band), 5½p. (2 bands) *or* (1 centre band), 8p. (*Nos. S16, S17 or S18, S21 or S22, S26*). The 4½p. (No. S19) was added later	2·75
20.10.76	P.O. Pack No. 85. 6½p., 8½p., 10p. (2 bands), 11p. (*Nos. S23, S27, S29, S32*)	2·00
28.10.81	P.O. Pack No. 129b. 7p., 9p., 10½p., 12p. (photo), 13½p., 15p. (photo), 11½p., 14p. grey-blue, 18p. dp violet, 22p. blue (*Nos. S24, S28, S31, S33/6, S40, S44, S47*)	9·00
3.8.83	P.O. Pack No. 2. 10p. (1 centre band), 12½p., 16p., 20½p., 26p. (J.W.), 28p. (J.W.), (*Nos. S30, S38, S42, S46, S49/50*)	12·00
23.10.84	P.O. Pack No. 6. 10p. (1 centre band), 13p. (J.W.), 16p., 17p. (J.W.), 22p. yellow-green, 26p. (J.W.), 28p. (J.W.), 31p. (J.W.), (*Nos. S30, S39, S42/3, S48/51*)	13·00
3.3.87	P.O. Pack No. 12. (litho), 13p. (Questa), 17p. grey-blue (Questa), 18p. dp olive-grey, 22p. yellow-green, 26p. rosine (Questa), 28p. dp violet-blue (Questa), 31p. (Questa) (*Nos. S52/3, S57, S59, S65, S72, S74, S76*)	15·00

Presentation Packs containing stamps of Northern Ireland, Scotland and Wales are listed after those for Northern Ireland.

1977–78 EXPERIMENTAL MACHINE PACKETS. These are small cartons containing loose stamps for sale in vending machines. The experiment was confined to the Scottish Postal Board area, where six vending machines were installed, the first becoming operational in Dundee about February 1977.

The cartons carry labels inscribed "ROYAL MAIL STAMPS", their total face value (30p. or 60p.) and their contents.

At first the 30p. packet contained two 6½p. and two 8½p. Scottish Regional stamps and the 60p. packet had four of each. The stamps could be in pairs or blocks, but also in strips or singles.

With the change in postal rates on 13 June 1977 these packets were withdrawn on 11 June and on 13 June the contents were changed, giving three 7p. and one 9p. for the 30p. packet and double this for the 60p. packet. However, this time ordinary British Machin stamps were used. Moreover the Edinburgh machine, situated in an automatic sorting area, was supplied with 7p. stamps with two phosphor bands instead of the new centre band 7p. stamps, despite instructions having been given to withdraw the two band stamps. However, the demand for these packets was too great to be filled and by 27 June the machine was closed down. It was brought back into use on 16 August 1977, supplying 7p. stamps with the centre band.

The 6½p. and 8½p. Scottish Regional packets were put on sale at the Edinburgh Philatelic Bureau in June 1977 and withdrawn in April 1978. The packets with the 7p. and 9p. Machin stamps were put on sale at the Bureau in June 1977 and withdrawn in December 1978.

Such machine packets are outside the scope of this catalogue.

(Des J. Matthews after plaster cast by Arnold Machin)

1993 (7 Dec)–**98**. *Chalk-surfaced paper. (a) Litho Questa. P 15 × 14 (with one elliptical hole on each vertical side).*

S81	S **4**	19p. bistre (1 centre band)	80	70
S82		19p. bistre (1 band at right) (25.4.95)	2·40	2·40
S83		20p. brt green (1 centre band) (23.7.96)	1·25	1·00
S84		25p. red (2 bands)	1·10	1·00
S85		26p. red-brown (2 bands) (23.7.96)	1·50	1·50
S86		30p. dp olive-grey (2 bands)	1·50	1·25
S87		37p. brt mauve (2 bands) (23.7.96)	2·50	2·25
S88		41p. grey-brown (2 bands)	1·90	1·90
		Ey. Phosphor omitted		
S89		63p. lt emerald (2 bands) (23.7.96)	3·50	3·25

(b) *Photo Walsall (20p., 26p. (No. S91a), 63p.), Harrison or Walsall (26p. (No. S91), 37p.). P 14 (No. S90a) or 15 × 14 (others) (both with one elliptical hole on each vertical side).*

S90	S **4**	20p. brt green (1 centre band) (1.7.97)	60	60
S90a		20p. brt green (1 side band at right) (13.10.98)	2·00	1·75
S91		26p. chestnut (2 bands) (1.7.97)	1·00	1·00
		a. Perf 14 (13.10.98)	2·25	2·00
S92		37p. brt mauve (2 bands) (1.7.97)	1·25	90
S93		63p. lt emerald (2 bands) (1.7.97)	2·25	2·00

Nos. S82, S90a and S91a only come from booklets.
The Harrison printings of Nos. S91/2 come from booklet pane No. NI81al.

First Day Covers

7.12.93	19p., 25p., 30p., 41p. (S81, S84, S86, S88) .	5·50	
23.7.96	20p. 26p., 37p., 63p. (S83, S85, S87, S89) .	8·75	

For Presentation Pack containing stamps of Northern Ireland, Scotland and Wales see after No. NI85 of Northern Ireland.

S **5** Scottish Flag

S **6** Scottish Lion

S **7** Thistle

S **8** Tartan

(Des A. Morris (2nd), F. Pottinger and T. Chalk (1st, E). Adapted Tayburn. Photo Questa (Nos. S94a, S95a), De La Rue (No. S99), De La Rue or Walsall (Nos. S94/5), Walsall (others))

1999 (8 June)–**2004**. *One centre phosphor band (2nd) or two phosphor bands (others). P 15 × 14 (with one elliptical hole on each vertical side).*

S94	S **5**	(2nd) new blue, blue and silver	30	35
		a. Booklet pane. Nos. S94 × 6 and S98 × 2 with centre label and margins all round (4.8.00)	7·00	
		b. Booklet pane. No. S94 and EN5, each × 3, with margins all round (16.3.04)	4·00	
S95	S **6**	(1st) greenish yellow, dp rose-red, rose-red and silver	40	45
		a. Booklet pane. Nos. S95/6, each × 4, with centre label and margins all round (22.10.01)	7·75	
S96	S **7**	(E) brt lilac, dp lilac and silver	60	70
S97	S **8**	64p. greenish yellow, brt magenta, new blue, grey-black and silver	3·00	2·25
S98		65p. greenish yellow, brt magenta, new blue, grey-black and silver (25.4.00) . . .	1·60	1·75
S99		68p. greenish yellow, bright magenta, new blue, grey-black and silver (4.7.02) . . .	1·10	1·25
		Presentation Pack (P.O. Pack No. 45) (2nd, 1st, E, 64p.) (Nos. S94/7)	4·00	
		Presentation Pack (P.O. Pack No. 50) (65p.) (No. S98)	3·00	
		Presentation Pack (P.O. Pack No. 55) (2nd, 1st, E, 65p.) (Nos. S94/6, S98) . .	2·75	
		PHQ Cards (set of 4) (Nos. S94/7)	1·50	10·00

Nos. S94, S95 and S96 were initially sold at 19p., 26p. and 30p., the latter representing the basic European airmail rate.

New printings of Nos. S94/5, produced by De La Rue instead of Walsall were issued on 5 June 2002. Stamps from this printing do not differ from those produced by Walsall.

No. S94a comes from booklet No. DX25.

No. S94b comes from booklet No. DX32.

No. S95a comes from booklet No. DX27.

For combined presentation pack for all four Regions, see under England.

First Day Covers

8.6.99	2nd, 1st, E, 64p. (S94/7)	
	Philatelic Bureau	4·00
	Edinburgh	4·00
25.4.00	65p. (S98)	
	Philatelic Bureau	1·90
	Edinburgh	1·90
4.8.00	Queen Elizabeth the Queen Mother *se-tenant* pane 2nd, 65p. (S94a)	
	Philatelic Bureau (as for Nos. 2160/1) . . .	4·75
	London SW1 (as for Nos. 2160/1)	4·75
22.10.01	Unseen and Unheard *se-tenant* pane (1st), E, (S95a) Philatelic Bureau (as for **MS**2206)	7·00
	Rosyth, Dunfermline (as for **MS**2206) . . .	7·00

4.7.02   68p. (S99)
         Tallents House (Type K) (see Introduction) .... 1·75
         Edinburgh .... 1·75

Special First Day of Issue Postmarks
(for use on Nos. S94, S95/8)

S 9

(Des J. Matthews. Photo Walsall)

2000 (15 Feb). Type S **4** redrawn with "1st" face value as Type S **9**. Two phosphor bands. P 14 (with one elliptical hole on each vertical side).
S108 S **9** (1st) bright orange-red .... 2·00 2·00
No. S108 was only issued in £7.50 stamp booklets (No. DX24).

(Photo De La Rue)

2003 (14 Oct). **As Nos. S94/6 and S99 but with white borders.** One centre phosphor band (2nd) or two phosphor bands (others). P 15 × 14 (with one elliptical hole on each vertical side).
S109 S **5** (2nd) new blue, blue and silver 30 35
S110 S **6** (1st) rose-red, greenish yellow, deep rose-red and silver 45 50
S111 S **7** (E) bright lilac, deep lilac and silver 60 65
S112 S **8** 68p. bright magenta, greenish yellow, new blue, grey-black and silver .... 1·10 1·20
         Presentation Pack (P.O. Pack No. 64) ... 2·75
         PHQ Cards (set of 4) .... 1·70 4·00

First Day Covers
14.10.03 2nd, 1st, E, 68p. (S109/12)
         Tallents House (Type K, see Introduction) 3·25
         Edinburgh .... 3·25

IV. WALES

From the inception of the Regional stamps, the Welsh versions were tendered to members of the public at all Post Offices within the former County of Monmouthshire but the national alternatives were available on request. By August 1961 the policy of "dual stocking" of definitive stamps was only maintained at Abergavenny, Chepstow, Newport and Pontypool. Offices with a Monmouthshire postal address but situated outside the County, namely Beachley, Brockweir, Redbrook, Sedbury, Tutshill, Welsh Newton and Woodcroft, were not supplied with the Welsh Regional stamps.

With the re-formation of Counties, Monmouthshire became known as Gwent and was also declared to be part of Wales. From 1 July 1974, therefore, except for the offices mentioned above, only Welsh Regional stamps were available at the offices under the jurisdiction of Newport, Gwent.

W **4** With "p"

| | |
| I | II |

Redrawn design of Type W 4 (litho ptgs.)

W **1**

W **2**

W **3**

(Des R. Stone)

1958–67. *W 179. P* 15 × 14.

W1	W **1**	3d. dp lilac (18.8.58)	15	15
		p. One centre phosphor band (16.5.67) ...	20	15
W2		4d. ultramarine (7.2.66)	20	15
		p. Two phosphor bands (10.67)	20	15
W3	W **2**	6d. dp claret (29.9.58)	35	30
W4		9d. bronze-green (2 phosphor bands) (1.3.67)		
			40	35
		Ey. Phosphor omitted	£325	
W5	W **3**	1s. 3d. green (29.9.58)	40	40
W6		1s. 6d. grey-blue (2 phosphor bands) (1.3.67)	40	40
		Ey. Phosphor omitted	45·00	

First Day Covers

18.8.58	3d. (*W1*)	12·00
29.9.58	6d., 1s. 3d. (*W3*, *W5*)	25·00
7.2.66	4d. (*W2*)	7·00
1.3.67	9d., 1s. 6d. (*W4*, *W6*)	4·00
	*Presentation Pack**	£100

*This was issued in 1960 and comprises Guernsey No. 7, Jersey No. 10, Isle of Man No. 2, Northern Ireland Nos. NI1, NI3 and NI5, Scotland Nos. S1, S3 and S5 and Wales Nos. W1, W3 and W5 together with a 6-page printed leaflet describing the stamps. There exist two forms: (*a*) inscribed "7s.3d." for sale in the U.K.; and (*b*) inscribed "$1.20" for sale in the U.S.A.

1967–69. *No wmk. Chalk-surfaced paper. One centre phosphor band (W7, W9/10) or two phosphor bands (others). Gum arabic (3d.) or PVA gum (others). P* 15 × 14.

W 7	W **1**	3d. dp lilac (6.12.67)	10	15
		Ey. Phosphor omitted	50·00	
W 8		4d. ultramarine (21.6.68)	10	15
W 9		4d. olive-sepia (4.9.68)	15	15
W10		4d. brt vermilion (26.2.69)	15	15
		Ey. Phosphor omitted	2·00	
W11		5d. royal blue (4.9.68)	15	15
		Ey. Phosphor omitted	2·50	
W12	W **3**	1s. 6d. grey-blue (1.8.69)	3·50	3·50

4.9.68	*First Day Cover (W9, W11)*	3·00
	Presentation Pack (containing Nos. W4, W6/7, W9/11) (9.12.70)	3·75

Two Types of Dragon

Type I:–The eye is complete with white dot in the centre. Wing-tips, tail and tongue are thin.

Type II:–The eye is joined to the nose by a solid line. Tail, wing-tips, claws and tongue are wider than in Type I.

The following stamps printed in lithography show a screened background behind and to the left of the emblem: 11½p., 12½p., 14p. (No. W39), 15½p., 16p., 18p. (No. W46), 19½p., 22p. (No. W54) and 28p. (No. W63). The 13p. and 17p. (No. W44) also show screened backgrounds in Type I, but changed to solid backgrounds for Type II. All other values printed in lithography have solid backgrounds.

(Des J. Matthews after plaster cast by Arnold Machin)

1971 (7 July)–**93.** *Decimal Currency. Chalk-surfaced paper. Type W* **4**.

(a) Photo Harrison. With phosphor bands. P 15 × 14.

W13	2½p. brt magenta (1 centre band)	20	20
	Ey. Phosphor omitted	7·50	
	Eg. Gum arabic (22.9.72)	20	
	Ega. Imperf (pair)	£375	
W14	3p. ultramarine (2 bands)	25	20
	Ey. Phosphor omitted	20·00	
	Eg. Gum arabic (6.6.73)	25	
	Eya. Phosphor omitted (No. W14Eg)	12·00	
W15	3p. ultramarine (1 centre band) (23.1.74)	25	25
W16	3½p. olive-grey (2 bands) (23.1.74)	20	30
W17	3½p. olive-grey (1 centre band) (6.11.74)	20	30
W18	4½p. grey-blue (2 bands) (6.11.74)	30	30
W19	5p. reddish violet (2 bands)	1·00	1·10
	Ey. Phosphor omitted	15·00	
W20	5½p. violet (2 bands) (23.1.74)	25	30
	Ey. Phosphor omitted	£160	
W21	5½p. violet (1 centre band) (21.5.75)	25	30
	a. Imperf (pair)	£425	
W22	6½p. greenish blue (1 centre band) (14.1.76)	20	20
W23	7p. purple-brown (1 centre band) (18.1.78)	25	25
W24	7½p. chestnut (2 bands)	90	1·25
	Ey. Phosphor omitted	95·00	
W25	8p. rosine (2 bands) (23.1.74)	30	35
	Ey. Phosphor omitted	£650	
W26	8½p. yellow-green (2 bands) (14.1.76)	30	35
W27	9p. dp violet (2 bands) (18.1.78)	40	40
W28	10p. orange-brown (2 bands) (20.10.76)	40	40
W29	10p. orange-brown (1 centre band) (23.7.80)	40	40
W30	10½p. steel-blue (2 bands) (18.1.78)	40	45
W31	11p. scarlet (2 bands) (20.10.76)	40	45

(b) Photo Harrison. On phosphorised paper. P 15 × 14

W32	12p. yellowish green (23.7.80)	40	50
W33	13½p. purple-brown (23.7.80)	60	70
W34	15p. ultramarine (23.7.80)	60	70

(c) Litho Questa (Type II unless otherwise stated). P 14 (11½p., 12½p., 14p. (No. W39), 15½p., 16p., 18p. (No. W46), 19½p., 20½p., 22p. (No. W54), 26p. (No. W61), 28p. (No. W63) *or* 15 × 14 *(others)*

W35	11½p. drab (Type I) (1 side band) (8.4.81)	90	80
W36	12p. brt emerald (1 side band) (7.1.86)	1.50	1.25
W37	12½p. lt emerald (Type I) (1 side band) (24.2.82) ...	70	70
	a. Perf 15 × 14 (10.1.84)	4.50	5.00
W38	13p. drab (Type I) (1 side band) (23.10.84)	60	60
	Ea. Type II (1.87)	1.90	1.75
W39	14p. grey-blue (Type I) (phosphorised paper) (8.4.81)	70	70
W40	14p. dp blue (1 centre band) (8.11.88)	75	75
W41	15p. brt blue (1 centre band) (28.11.89)	80	75
	Ey. Phosphor omitted		
W42	15½p. pale violet (Type I) (phosphorised paper) (24.2.82)	75	75
W43	16p. drab (Type I) (phosphorised paper) (27.4.83) .	1.50	1.60
	a. Perf 15 × 14 (10.1.84)	1.75	1.90
W44	17p. grey-blue (Type I) (phosphorised paper) (23.10.84)	70	80
	Ea. Type II (18.8.86)	35.00	20.00
W45	17p. dp blue (1 centre band) (4.12.90)	90	80
	Ey. Phosphor omitted	18.00	
W46	18p. dp violet (Type I) (8.4.81)	1.00	95
W47	18p. dp olive-grey (phosphorised paper) (6.1.87) .	95	90
W48	18p. brt green (1 centre band) (3.12.91)	75	75
	Ey. Phosphor omitted	£180	
	a. Booklet pane. No. W48 × 6 with margins all round (25.2.92)	3.25	
	aEy. Phosphor omitted		
	b. Perf 14 (12.1.93*)	4.50	4.50
W49	18p. brt green (1 side band at right) (25.2.92)	2.25	2.25
	a. Booklet pane. No. X1020 × 2, 1451a, 1514a, W49 × 2, W60 × 2 and centre label with margins all round	11.00	
	aEy. Phosphor omitted		
	Eb. Band at left (10.8.93)	2.00	2.00
W50	19p. brt orange-red (phosphorised paper) (8.11.88)	1.00	80
W51	19½p. olive-grey (Type I) (phosphorised paper) (24.2.82)	1.50	1.50
W52	20p. brownish black (phosphorised paper) (28.11.89)	90	90
W53	20½p. ultramarine (Type I) (phosphorised paper) (27.4.83)	3.25	3.25
W54	22p. blue (Type I) (phosphorised paper) (8.4.81) ..	1.10	1.10
W55	22p. yellow-green (Type I) (phosphorised paper) (23.10.84)	95	1.10
W56	22p. brt orange-red (phosphorised paper) (4.12.90)	1.00	1.10
W57	22p. brt green (phosphorised paper) (8.11.88)	1.00	1.10
W58	24p. Indian red (phosphorised paper) (28.11.89) ..	95	1.10
W59	24p. chestnut (phosphorised paper) (3.12.91)	75	75
	a. Booklet pane. No. W59 × 6 with margins all round (25.2.92)	5.00	
	b. Perf 14 (14.9.92*)	3.50	3.75
W60	24p. chestnut (2 bands) (25.2.92)	1.40	1.40
W61	26p. rosine (Type I) (phosphorised paper) (24.2.82)	1.10	1.10
	a. Perf 15 × 14 (27.1.87)	5.50	5.00
W62	26p. drab (phosphorised paper) (4.12.90)	1.40	1.40
W63	28p. dp violet-blue (Type I) (phosphorised paper) (27.4.83)	1.25	1.25
	a. Perf 15 × 14 (Type II) (27.1.87)	1.40	1.40
W64	28p. dp bluish grey (phosphorised paper) (3.12.91)	1.50	1.40
W65	31p. brt purple (Type I) (phosphorised paper) (23.10.84)	1.40	1.40
W66	32p. greenish blue (phosphorised paper) (8.11.88)	1.60	1.40

W67	34p. dp bluish grey (phosphorised paper) (28.11.89)	1.60	1.60
W68	37p. rosine (phosphorised paper) (4.12.90)	1.90	1.90
W69	39p. brt mauve (phosphorised paper) (3.12.91) ...	2.00	2.00

*Earliest known date of use.

Nos. W48b and W59b were caused by the use of a reserve perforating machine for some printings in the second half of 1992.

Nos. W49, W49Eb and W60 only come from booklets.

The listed booklet panes come from the following Sponsored Booklets:

W48a – Booklet DX13
W49a – Booklet DX13
W59a – Booklet DX13

No. W60 exists with the phosphor omitted, but cannot be identified without the use of u.v. light (*Price £375 unused*).

From 1972 printings were on fluorescent white paper. From 1973 most printings had dextrin added to the PVA gum (see notes after 1971 Decimal Machin issue).

First Day Covers

7.7.71	2½p., 3p., 5p., 7½p., (W13/14, W19, W24)	3.00
23.1.74	3p., 3½p., 5½p., 8p. (W15/16, W20, W25)	2.00
6.11.74	4½p. (W18)	1.50
14.1.76	6½p., 8½p. (W22, W26)	1.50
20.10.76	10p., 11p. (W28, W31)	1.50
18.1.78	7p., 9p., 10½p (W23, W27, W30)	1.75
23.7.80	12p., 13½p., 15p. (W32/4)	2.25
8.4.81	11½p., 14p., 18p., 22p. (W35, W39, W46, W54)	3.75
24.2.82	12½p., 15½p., 19½p., 26p. (W37, W42, W51, W61)	4.50
27.4.83	16p., 20½p., 28p. (W43, W53, W63)	6.50
23.10.84	13p., 17p., 22p., 31p. (W38, W44, W55, W65)	4.25
7.1.86	12p. (W36)	1.50
6.1.87	18p. (W47)	1.50
8.11.88	14p., 19p., 23p., 32p. (W40, W50, W57, W66)	4.50
28.11.89	15p., 20p., 24p., 34p. (W41, W52, W58, W67)	4.75
4.12.90	17p., 22p., 26p., 37p (W45, W56, W62, W68)	4.75
3.12.91	18p., 24p., 28p., 39p. (W48, W59, W64, W69)	5.50
25.2.92	Cymru–Wales *se-tenant* pane 18p., (2nd), 24p., (1st), 33p. (W49a)	12.00

Presentation Packs

7.7.71	P.O. Pack No. 28. 2½p., 3p. (2 bands), 5p., 7½p. (*Nos.* W13/14, W19, W24)	4.25
29.5.74	P.O. Pack No. 63. 3p. (1 centre band), 3½p. (2 bands) *or* (1 centre band), 5½p. (2 bands) *or* (1 centre band), 8p. (*Nos.* W15, W16 or W17, W20 *or* W21, W25). The 4½p. (No. W18) was added later	2.75
20.10.76	P.O. Pack No. 86. 6½p., 8½p., 10p. (2 bands), 11p. (*Nos.* W22, W26, W28, W31)	2.00
28.10.81	P.O. Pack No. 129c. 7p., 10½p., 12p. (photo), 13½p., 15p. (photo), 11½p., 14p. grey-blue, 18p. dp violet, 22p. blue (*Nos.* W23, W27, W30, W32/5, W39, W46, W54)	9.00
3.8.83	P.O. Pack No. 3. 10p. (1 centre band), 12½p., 16p., 20½p., 26p. rosine, 28p. dp violet-blue (*Nos.* W29, W37, W43, W53, W61, W63)	10.00

23.10.84 P.O. Pack No. 7. 10p. (1 centre band),
13p., 16p., 17p. grey-blue, 22p. yellow-
green, 26p. rosine, 28p. dp violet-blue,
31p. (Nos. W29, W38, W43a, W44, W55,
W61, W63, W65) .... 13·00

3.3.87 P.O. Pack No. 11. 12p. (litho), 13p., 17p.
grey-blue, 18p. dp olive-grey, 22p. yellow-green, 26p. rosine, 28p. dp violet-
blue, 31p. (Nos. W36, W38, W44, W47,
W55, W61a, W63a, W65) .... 15·00

Presentation Packs containing stamps of Northern Ireland, Scotland
and Wales are listed after those for Northern Ireland.

(Des J. Matthews after plaster cast by Arnold Machin. Litho Questa)

1993 (7 Dec)–**96**. *Chalk-surfaced paper. P 15 × 14 (with one elliptical
hole on each vertical side).*
W70 W **4** 19p. bistre (1 centre band) 80 70
W71   19p. bistre (1 band at right) (25.4.95) .... 3·25 3·00
W72   20p. brt green (1 centre band) (23.7.96) ..... 1·25 1·40
W73   25p. red (2 bands) .... 1·25 1·00
W74   26p. red-brown (2 bands) (23.7.96) .... 1·60 1·50
W75   30p. dp olive-grey (2 bands) .... 1·10 1·25
W76   37p. brt mauve (2 bands) (23.7.96) .... 2·40 2·40
W77   41p. grey-brown (2 bands) .... 1·75 1·90
W78   63p. lt emerald (2 bands) (23.7.96) .... 3·75 3·75
No. W71 only comes from booklets.

First Day Covers

7.12.93 19p., 25p., 30p., 41p. (W70, W73, W75,
W77) .... 5·75
23.7.96 20p., 26p., 37p., 63p., (W72, W74, W76,
W78) .... 9·50

For Presentation Packs containing stamps of Northern Ireland,
Scotland and Wales see after No. NI85 of Northern Ireland.

W **5** Without "p"

(Photo Walsall (20p., 26p. (No. W80a), 63p.), Harrison or Walsall (26p.
(No. W80), 37p.))

1997 (1 July)–**98**. *Chalk-surfaced paper. P 14 (No. W79a) or 15 × 14
(others) (both with one elliptical hole on each vertical side).*
W79 W **5** 20p. brt green (1 centre band) 80 80
W79a   20p. brt green (1 side band at right) (13.10.98) 2·25 2·00
W80   26p. chestnut (2 bands) .... 1·00 1·00
          a. Perf 14 (13.10.98) .... 2·00 2·00
W81   37p. brt mauve (2 bands) .... 1·75 1·75
W82   63p. lt emerald (2 bands) .... 2·50 2·50
No. W79a and W80a were only issued in booklets.
The Harrison printings of Nos. W80/1 come from booklet pane No.
NI81al.

First Day Cover

1.7.97 20p., 26p., 37p., 63p. (W79/82) .... 5·50

Presentation Pack

1.7.97 P.O. Pack No. 39. 20p., 26p., 37p., 63p.
(Nos. W79/82) .... 6·50

W **6** Leek   W **7** Welsh Dragon

W **8** Daffodil   W **9** Prince of Wales
Feathers

(Des D. Petersen (2nd), T. & G. Petersen (1st), I. Rees (E), R. Evans (64p.,
65p.). Adapted Tutssels. Photo De La Rue or Walsall (2nd, 1st), De La
Rue (68p.), Walsall (others))

1999 (8 June)–**2002**. *One phosphor band (2nd) or two phosphor bands
(others). P 14 (No. W83a) or 15 × 14 (others) (both with one elliptical
hole on each vertical side).*
W83 W **6** (2nd) orange-brown, yellow-orange and
          black (1 centre band) 30 35
W83a   (2nd) orange-brown, yellow-orange and
          black (1 band at right) (p 14) (18.9.00) 2·50 2·50
          al. Booklet pane. No. 2124d and W83a,
          each × 4, with centre label and
          margins all round .... 12·00
W84 W **7** (1st) blue-green, greenish yellow, silver and
          black 40 45
W85 W **8** (E) greenish blue, dp greenish blue and
          grey-black 60 70
W86 W **9** 64p. violet, gold, silver and black .... 2·75 2·40
W87   65p. violet, gold, silver and black (25.4.00) 1·60 1·75
W88   68p. violet, gold, silver and black (4.7.02) . 1·10 1·25
          Presentation Pack (P.O. Pack No. 46)
          (2nd, 1st, E, 64p.) (Nos. W83, W84/6)) 4·50
          Presentation Pack (P.O. Pack No. 51)
          (65p.) (No. W87)) .... 3·00
          Presentation Pack (P.O. Pack No. 56)
          (2nd, 1st, E, 65p.) (Nos. W83, W84/5,
          W87)) .... 2·75
          PHQ Cards (set of 4) (Nos. W83,
          W84/6) .... 1·50 10·00
Nos. W83, W84 and W85 were initially sold at 19p., 26p. and 30p.,
the latter representing the basic European airmail rate.
New printings of Nos. W83 and W84, produced by De La Rue
instead of Walsall, were issued on 28 May 2003 and 4 March 2003.
Stamps from these printings do not differ from those produced by
Walsall.
No. W83a comes from the £7 Treasury of Trees booklet (No. DX26).
For combined presentation pack for all four Regions, see under
England.

First Day Covers

8.6.99 2nd (centre band), 1st, E, 64p. (W83,
W84/6)
          Philatelic Bureau .... 4·00
          Cardiff .... 4·00
25.4.00 65p. (W87)
          Philatelic Bureau .... 1·90
          Cardiff .... 1·90
18.9.00 Treasury of Trees *se-tenant* pane 1st
          (Millennium), 2nd (2124d, W83a)
          Philatelic Bureau .... 5·00
          Llangernyw, Abergele .... 5·00

4.7.02   68p. (*W88*)
          Tallents House (Type K) (see Introduc-
          tion) ....   1·75
          Cardiff ....   1·75

Special First Day of Issue Postmarks

W **10**

(Des J. Matthews. Photo Walsall)

2000 (15 Feb). *Type W* **4** *redrawn with "1af/st" face value as Type W* **10**.
Two phosphor bands. P 14 *(with one elliptical hole on each vertical
side)*
W97 W **10** (1st) bright orange-red ....   1·75   1·75
          No. W97 was only issued in £7.50 stamp booklets (No. DX24).

(Photo De La Rue)

2003 (14 Oct). **As Nos. W83, W84/5 and W88, but with white borders.**
One centre phosphor band (2nd) *or two phosphor bands* (others).
P 15 × 14 *(with one elliptical hole on each vertical side)*.
W 98 W **6** (2nd) yellow-orange, orange-brown and
                    black   30   35
W 99 W **7** (1st) blue-green, greenish yellow, silver and
                    black   45   50
W100 W **8** (E) greenish blue, deep greenish blue and
                    grey-black   60   65
W101 W **9** 68p. violet, gold, silver and black ....   1·10   1·20
                    Presentation Pack (P.O. Pack No. 65) ..   2·75
                    PHQ Cards (set of 4) ....   1·70   4·00

First Day Cover

14.10.03   2nd, 1st, E, 68p. (*W98/101*)
          Tallents House (Type K, see Introduc-
          tion) ....   3·25
          Cardiff ....   3·25

Regional Issues (Guernsey)

V. GUERNSEY

War Occupation Issues

BISECTS. On 24 December 1940 authority was given, by Post Office notice, that prepayment of penny postage could be effected by using half a British 2d. stamp, diagonally bisected. Such stamps were first used on 27 December 1940.

The 2d. stamps generally available were those of the Postal Centenary issue, 1940 (S.G. 482) and the first colour of the King George VI issue (S.G. 465). These are listed under Nos. 482a and 465b. A number of the 2d. King George V, 1912–22, and of the King George V photogravure stamp (S.G. 442) which were in the hands of philatelists, were also bisected and used.

1

1a Loops (half actual size)

(Des E. W. Vaudin. Typo Guernsey Press Co Ltd)

1941–44. Rouletted. (a) White paper. No wmk.
1	1	½d. light green (7.4.41)	3·00	1·75
		a. Emerald-green (6.41)	3·50	1·50
		b. Bluish green (11.41)	30·00	13·00
		c. Brt green (2.42)	18·00	9·00
		d. Dull green (9.42)	3·00	1·75
		e. Olive-green (2.43)	25·00	10·00
		f. Pale yellowish green (7.43 and later) (shades)	3·00	1·50
		g. Imperf (pair)	£200	
		h. Imperf between (horiz pair)	£700	
		i. Imperf between (vert pair)	£800	
2		1d. scarlet (18.2.41)	2·00	90
		a. Pale vermilion (7.43)	2·50	75
		b. Carmine (1943)	2·00	75
		c. Imperf (pair)	£150	75·00
		d. Imperf between (horiz pair)	£700	
		da. Imperf vert (centre stamp of horiz strip of 3)		
		e. Imperf between (vert pair)	£800	
		f. Printed double (scarlet shade)	£100	
3		2½d. ultramarine (12.4.44)	3·25	4·00
		a. Pale ultramarine (7.44)	3·25	5·00
		b. Imperf (pair)	£500	
		c. Imperf between (horiz pair)	£1000	
		Set of 3	7·00	6·50

First Day Covers
18.2.41	1d.	12·00	
7.4.41	½d.	6·00	
12.4.44	2½d.	8·00	

(b) Bluish French bank-note paper. W **1**a (sideways)
4	1	½d. bright green (11.3.42)	20·00	18·00
5		1d. scarlet (9.4.42)	10·00	16·00

First Day Covers
11.3.42	½d.	80·00
9.4.42	1d.	45·00

The dates given for the shades of Nos. 1/3 are the months in which they were printed as indicated on the printer's imprints. Others are issue dates.

Regional Issues

2 **3**

(Des E. A. Piprell. Portrait by Dorothy Wilding Ltd. Photo Harrison & Sons)

1958 (18 Aug)–**67**. W **179** of Great Britain. P 15 × 14.
6	2	2½d. rose-red (8.6.64)	35	40
7	3	3d. dp lilac	30	30
		p. One centre phosphor band (24.5.67)	15	20
8		4d. ultramarine (7.2.66)	25	30
		p. Two phosphor bands (24.10.67)	15	20
		Set of 3 (cheapest)	70	80

First Day Covers
18.8.58	3d.	17·00
8.6.64	2½d.	30·00
7.2.66	4d.	8·00

For No. 7 in Presentation Pack, see Regional Issues below Wales No. W6.

1968–69. No wmk. Chalk-surfaced paper. PVA gum*. One centre phosphor band (Nos. 10/11) or two phosphor bands (others). P 15 × 14.
9	3	4d. pale ultramarine (16.4.68)	10	20
		Ey. Phosphor omitted	45·00	
10		4d. olive-sepia (4.9.68)	10	15
		Ey. Phosphor omitted	45·00	
11		4d. brt vermilion (26.2.69)	20	25
12		5d. royal blue (4.9.68)	20	30
		Set of 4	50	1·00

First Day Cover
4.9.68	4d., 5d.	3·00

No. 9 was not issued in Guernsey until 22 April.
*PVA Gum. See note after No. 722 of Great Britain.

282

VI. ISLE OF MAN

Although specifically issued for use in the Isle of Man, these issues were also valid for use throughout Great Britain.

DATES OF ISSUE. The note at the beginning of Northern Ireland also applies here.

Nos. 8/11 and current stamps of Great Britain were withdrawn from sale on the island from 5 July 1973 when the independent postal administration was established but remained valid for use there for a time. They also remained on sale at the Philatelic Sales counters in the United Kingdom until 4 July 1974.

1   **2**

(Des J. Nicholson. Portrait by Dorothy Wilding Ltd. Photo Harrison)

1958 (18 Aug)–**68.** W **179.** P 15 × 14.
1	1	2½d. carmine-red (8.6.64)	40	1·25
2	2	3d. dp lilac	20	20
		a. Chalk-surfaced paper (17.5.63)	10·00	10·00
		p. One centre phosphor band (27.6.68)	20	50
3		4d. ultramarine (7.2.66)	1·40	1·40
		p. Two phosphor bands (5.7.67)	20	30
		Set of 3 (cheapest)	80	1·60

First Day Covers
18.8.58	3d.	32·00	
8.6.64	2½d.	45·00	
7.2.66	4d.	10·00	

No. 2a was released in London sometime after 17 May 1963, this being the date of issue in Douglas.

For No. 2 in Presentation Pack, see Regional Issues below Wales No. W6.

1968–69. *No wmk. Chalk-surfaced paper. PVA gum. One centre phosphor band* (Nos. 5/6) *or two phosphor bands* (others). P 15 × 14.
4	2	4d. blue (24.6.68)	25	30
5		4d. olive-sepia (4.9.68)	25	40
		Ey. Phosphor omitted	22·00	
6		4d. brt vermilion (26.2.69)	45	75
7		5d. royal blue (4.9.68)	45	75
		Ey. Phosphor omitted	£150	
		Set of 4	1·25	2·00

First Day Cover
4.9.68	4d., 5d.	4·00	

3

(Des J. Matthews. Portrait after plaster cast by Arnold Machin. Photo Harrison)

1971 (7 July). *Decimal Currency. Chalk-surfaced paper. One centre phosphor band* (2½p.) *or two phosphor bands* (others). P 15 × 14.
8	3	2½p. brt magenta	20	15
		Ey. Phosphor omitted	£1500	

9	3	3p. ultramarine	20	15
10		5p. reddish violet	40	60
		Ey. Phosphor omitted	£250	
11		7½p. chestnut	40	75
		Set of 4	1·10	1·50
		Presentation Pack	2·75	

First Day Cover
7.7.71	2½p., 3p., 5p., 7½p.	3·00	

All values exist with PVA gum on ordinary cream paper and the 2½p. and 3p. also on fluorescent white paper.

VII. JERSEY

War Occupation Issues

(Des Major N. V. L. Rybot. Typo *Evening Post,* Jersey)

1941–43. *White paper* (thin to thick). *No wmk.* P 11.
1	1	½d. brt green (29.1.42)	4·00	3·25
		a. Imperf between (vert pair)	£800	
		b. Imperf between (horiz pair)	£700	
		c. Imperf (pair)	£250	
		d. On greyish paper (1.43)	5·50	5·50
2		1d. scarlet (1.4.41)	4·50	2·50
		a. Imperf between (vert pair)	£800	
		b. Imperf between (horiz pair)	£700	
		c. Imperf (pair)	£275	
		d. On chalk-surfaced paper	42·00	38·00
		e. On greyish paper (1.43)	5·50	5·75

First Day Covers
1.4.41	1d.	7·00	
29.1.42	½d.	7·00	

2 Old Jersey Farm   **3** Portelet Bay

4 Corbière Lighthouse   **5** Elizabeth Castle

6 Mont Orgueil Castle   **7** Gathering Vraic (seaweed)

(Des E. Blampied. Eng H. Cortot. Typo French Govt Ptg Works, Paris)

1943–44. *No wmk. P 13½.*

3	**2**	½d. green (1 June)		7·50	5·50
		a. Rough, grey paper (6.10.43)		7·50	5·50
4	**3**	1d. scarlet (1 June)		2·00	75
		a. On newsprint (28.2.44)		2·50	75
5	**4**	1½d. brown (8 June)		3·50	3·25
6	**5**	2d. orange-yellow (8 June)		4·75	3·25
7	**6**	2½d. blue (29 June)		2·00	1·00
		a. On newsprint (25.2.44)		1·00	1·10
		ba. Thin paper*		£225	
8	**7**	3d. violet (29 June)		1·25	3·00
		Set of 6		18·00	15·00
		First Day Covers (3)			30·00
		Set of 6 Gutter Pairs		40·00	

*On No. 7ba the design shows clearly through the back of the stamp.

Regional Issues

8   9

(Des. E. Blampied (T **8**), W. Gardner (T **9**). Portrait by Dorothy Wilding Ltd. Photo Harrison & Sons).

1958 (18 Aug)–**67.** *W* **179** *of Great Britain. P 15 × 14.*

9	**8**	2½d. carmine-red (8.6.64)		20	45
		a. Imperf three sides (pair)		£2000	
10	**9**	3d. dp lilac		20	25
		p. One centre phosphor band (9.6.67)		15	15
11		4d. ultramarine (7.2.66)		25	30
		p. Two phosphor bands (5.9.67)		15	25
		Set of 3 (cheapest)		45	75

First Day Covers

18.8.58	3d.		17·00
8.6.64	2½d.		30·00
7.2.66	4d.		8·00

For No.10 in Presentation Pack, see Regional Issues below Wales No. W6.

1968–69. *No wmk. Chalk-surfaced paper. PVA gum*. One centre phosphor band (4d. values) or two phosphor bands (5d.). P 15 × 14.*

12	**9**	4d. olive-sepia (4.9.68)		15	25
		Ey. Phosphor omitted		£750	
13		4d. brt vermilion (26.2.69)		15	25
14		5d. royal blue (4.9.68)		15	50
		Set of 3		40	1·10

First Day Cover

4.9.68	4d., 5d.		3·00

*PVA Gum. See note after No. 722 of Great Britain.

POSTAGE DUE STAMPS

PERFORATIONS. All postage due stamps to No. D101 are perf 14 × 15.

WATERMARK. The watermark always appears sideways and this is the "normal" listed in this Catalogue for Nos. D1/D68. Varieties occur as follows. The point of identification is which way the top of the crown points, but (where they occur) the disposition of the letters needs to be noted also.

The meaning of the terms is given below: (1) as described and illustrated in the Catalogue, i.e. as read through the front of the stamp, and (2) what is seen during watermark detection when the stamp is face down and the back is under examination.

Watermark	Crown pointing	Letters reading
(1) As described		
Sideways	left	upwards
Sideways-inverted	right	downwards
Sideways and reversed	left	downwards, back to front
Sideways-inverted and reversed	right	upwards, back to front
(2) As detected (stamp face down)		
Sideways	right	upwards, back to front
Sideways-inverted	left	downwards, back to front
Sideways and reversed	right	downwards
Sideways-inverted and reversed	left	upwards

D 1   D 2

(Des G. Eve. Typo Somerset House (early trial printings of ½d., 1d., 2d. and 5d.; all printings of 1s.) or Harrison (later printings of all values except 1s.))

1914 (20 Apr)–**22.** *W* **100** *(Simple Cypher) (sideways).*

			Unmtd mint	Mtd mint	Used
D1	D 1	½d. emerald	1·00	50	25
		Wi. Watermark sideways-inverted	2·00	1·00	1·00
		Wj. Watermark sideways and reversed	18·00	12·00	15·00
		Wk. Watermark sideways-inverted and reversed			
D2		1d. carmine	1·50	50	25
		a. *Pale carmine*	1·50	75	50
		Wi. Watermark sideways-inverted	2·00	1·00	1·00
		Wj. Watermark sideways and reversed			
		Wk. Watermark sideways-inverted and reversed	15·00	12·00	12·00
D3		1½d. chestnut (1922)	£140	48·00	20·00
		Wi. Watermark sideways-inverted	£175	70·00	20·00
D4		2d. agate	1·50	50	25
		Wi. Watermark sideways-inverted	3·00	2·00	2·00
		Wj. Watermark sideways-inverted and reversed	9·00	6·00	6·00
D5		3d. violet (1918)	24·00	5·00	75
		a. *Bluish violet*	24·00	6·00	2·75
		Wi. Watermark sideways-inverted	24·00	7·50	2·00
		Wj. Watermark sideways-inverted and reversed			
D6		4d. dull grey-green (12.20)	£120	18·00	5·00
		Wi. Watermark sideways-inverted	£140	40·00	5·00
D7		5d. brownish cinnamon	14·00	6·00	3·50
		Wi. Watermark sideways-inverted	40·00	16·00	16·00
D8		1s. brt blue (1915)	£130	40·00	4·75
		a. *Dp brt blue*	£130	40·00	5·00
		Wi. Watermark sideways-inverted	70·00	20·00	20·00
		Wj. Watermark sideways-inverted and reversed			
		Set of 8	£365	£110	32·00

Stamps from the above issue are known bisected and used for half their face value at the following sorting offices:

1d. Barrhead (1922), Bristol (1918), Cowes (1923), Elgin (1921), Kidlington (1922, 1923), Kilburn, London NW (1923), Malvern (1915), Palmers Green, London N (1922), Plaistow, London E (1916), River, Dover (1922), Rock Ferry, Birkenhead (1915, 1918), St. Owens, Jersey (1924), Salford, Manchester (1914), South Tottenham, London N (1921), Warminster (1922), Wavertree, Liverpool (1921), Whitchurch (1922), Winton, Bournemouth (1921), Wood Green, London N (1921)

2d. Anerley, London SE (1921), Bethnal Green, London E (1918), Christchurch (1921), Didcot (1919), Ealing, London W (1921), Hythe, Southampton (1923), Kirkwall (1922), Ledbury (1922), Malvern (1921, 1923), Sheffield (1921), Shipley (1922), Streatham, London SW (1921), Victoria Docks & North Woolwich (1921), West Kensington, London W (1921, 1922)

3d. Malvern (trisected and used for 1d.) (1921), Warminster (1922)

(Typo Waterlow)

1924. *As 1914–22, but on thick chalk-surfaced paper.*

D9	D **1**	1d. carmine	7·50	2·25	3·50

(Typo Waterlow and (from 1934) Harrison)

1924–31. W **111** (*Block Cypher*) *sideways.*

			Unmtd mint	Used	
D10	D **1**	½d. emerald (6.25)	2·50	1·25	75
		Wi. Watermark sideways-inverted	6·00	3·00	1·50
D11		1d. carmine (4.25)	2·50	60	25
		Wi. Watermark sideways-inverted	—	—	10·00
D12		1½d. chestnut (10.24)	£130	45·00	18·00
		Wi. Watermark sideways-inverted	—	—	30·00
D13		2d. agate (7.24)	9·00	1·00	25
		Wi. Watermark sideways-inverted	—	—	10·00
D14		3d. dull violet (10.24)	10·00	1·50	25
		a. Printed on gummed side	£125	75·00	†
		b. Experimental paper W **111**a	80·00	38·00	35·00
		Wi. Watermark sideways-inverted	10·00	5·00	2·00
D15		4d. dull grey-green (10.24)	50·00	15·00	3·00
		Wi. Watermark sideways-inverted	55·00	16·00	25·00
D16		5d. brownish cinnamon (1.31)	90·00	32·00	28·00
D17		1s. dp blue (9.24)	30·00	10·00	1·00
		Wi. Watermark sideways-inverted			
D18	D **2**	2s. 6d. purple/*yellow* (5.24)	£200	45·00	2·00
		Wi. Watermark sideways-inverted			
		Set of 9	£475	£140	48·00

Stamps from the above issue are known bisected and used for half their face value at the following sorting offices:

1d. Ashton under Lyne (1932), Hastings (1930), Penryn, Cornwall (1928), Shenfield (1926), Wimbledon, London SW (1925)

2d. Perranwell Station (1932)

1936–37. W **125** (E 8 R) *sideways.*

			Unmtd mint	Used
D19	D **1**	½d. emerald (6.37)	7·50	8·00
D20		1d. carmine (5.37)	1·50	2·00
D21		2d. agate (5.37)	8·00	11·00
D22		3d. dull violet (3.37)	1·50	2·25
D23		4d. dull grey-green (12.36)	35·00	35·00
D24		5d. brownish cinnamon (11.36)	55·00	25·00
		a. Yellow-brown (1937)	16·00	23·00
D25		1s. dp blue (12.36)	11·00	9·00
D26	D **2**	2s. 6d. purple/*yellow* (5.37)	£300	9·00
		Set of 8	£350	90·00

The 1d. of the above issue is known bisected and used for half its face value at the following sorting office:

1d. Solihull (1937)

1937–38. W **127** (G VI R) *sideways.*

D27	D **1**	½d. emerald (5.38)	9·00	5·00
D28		1d. carmine (5.38)	3·00	75
		Wi. Watermark sideways-inverted	£130	
D29		2d. agate (5.38)	2·50	75
		Wi. Watermark sideways-inverted	12·00	
D30		3d. violet (12.37)	12·00	1·00
		Wi. Watermark sideways-inverted	30·00	
D31		4d. dull grey-green (9.37)	75·00	13·00
		Wi. Watermark sideways-inverted	£130	
D32		5d. yellow-brown (11.38)	14·00	75
		Wi. Watermark sideways-inverted	35·00	
D33		1s. dp blue (10.37)	75·00	2·00
		Wi. Watermark sideways-inverted	65·00	
D34	D **2**	2s. 6d. purple/*yellow* (9.38)	75·00	2·50
		Set of 8	£250	23·00

The 2d. from the above issue is known bisected and used for half its face value at the following sorting offices:

2d. Boreham Wood (1951), Camberley (1951), Harpenden (1951, 1954), St. Albans (1951)

DATES OF ISSUE. The dates for Nos. D35/68 are those on which stamps were first issued by the Supplies Department to postmasters.

1951–52. *Colours changed and new value (1½d.).* W **127** (G VI R) *sideways.*

D35	D **1**	½d. orange (18.9.51)	1·00	3·00
D36		1d. violet-blue (6.6.51)	1·50	1·50
		Wi. Watermark sideways-inverted		
D37		1½d. green (11.2.52)	1·75	3·00
		Wi. Watermark sideways-inverted	10·00	
D38		4d. blue (14.8.51)	32·00	12·00
D39		1s. ochre (6.12.51)	38·00	14·00
		Wi. Watermark sideways-inverted		
		Set of 5	70·00	30·00

The 1d. of the above issue is known bisected and used for half its face value at the following sorting offices:

1d. Camberley (1954), Capel, Dorking (1952)

1954–55. W **153** (*Mult Tudor Crown and* E 2 R) *sideways.*

D40	D **1**	½d. orange (8.6.55)	4·50	8·00
		Wi. Watermark sideways-inverted	12·00	
D41		2d. agate (28.7.55)	10·00	12·00
		Wi. Watermark sideways-inverted		
D42		3d. violet (4.5.55)	55·00	38·00
D43		4d. blue (14.7.55)	20·00	23·00
		a. Imperf (pair)	£250	
D44		5d. yellow-brown (19.5.55)	25·00	12·00
D45	D **2**	2s. 6d. purple/*yellow* (11.54)	£110	7·00
		Wi. Watermark sideways-inverted		
		Set of 6	£200	90·00

1955–57. W **165** (*Mult St. Edward's Crown and* E 2 R) *sideways.*

D46	D **1**	½d. orange (16.7.56)	2·00	4·00
		Wi. Watermark sideways-inverted	12·00	
D47		1d. violet-blue (7.6.56)	5·50	1·75
D48		1½d. green (13.2.56)	6·00	5·00
		Wi. Watermark sideways-inverted	15·00	
D49		2d. agate (22.5.56)	45·00	3·75
D50		3d. violet (5.3.56)	7·00	2·00
		Wi. Watermark sideways-inverted	30·00	
D51		4d. blue (24.4.56)	20·00	4·00
		Wi. Watermark sideways-inverted	35·00	
D52		5d. brown-ochre (23.3.56)	32·00	2·25
D53		1s. ochre (22.11.55)	70·00	2·00
		Wi. Watermark sideways-inverted		
D54	D **2**	2s. 6d. purple/*yellow* (28.6.57)	£150	10·00
		Wi. Watermark sideways-inverted		
D55		5s. scarlet/*yellow* (25.11.55)	80·00	26·00
		Wi. Watermark sideways-inverted		
		Set of 10	£375	55·00

Postage Due

Stamps from the above issue are known bisected and used for half their face value at the following sorting offices:
   1d. Beswick, Manchester (1958), Huddersfield (1956), London SE (1957)
   2d. Eynsham, Oxford (1956), Garelochhead, Helensburgh (1956), Harpenden (1956), Hull (1956), Kingston on Thames (1956), Leicester Square, London WC (1956), London WC (1956)
   3d. London SE (1957)
   4d. Poplar, London E (1958)

1959–63. *W* **179** *(Mult St. Edward's Crown) sideways.*

D56	D **1**	½d. orange (18.10.61)	15	1·25
		Wi. Watermark sideways-inverted	2·00	
D57		1d. violet-blue (9.5.60)	15	50
		Wi. Watermark sideways-inverted	16·00	
D58		1½d. green (5.10.60)	90	3·50
D59		2d. agate (14.9.59)	1·10	50
		Wi. Watermark sideways-inverted	50·00	
D60		3d. violet (24.3.59)	30	30
		Wi. Watermark sideways-inverted	12·00	
D61		4d. blue (17.12.59)	30	30
		Wi. Watermark sideways-inverted	35·00	
D62		5d. yellow-brown (6.11.61)	45	60
		Wi. Watermark sideways-inverted	5·00	
D63		6d. purple (29.3.62)	50	30
		Wi. Watermark sideways-inverted	45·00	
D64		1s. ochre (11.4.60)	90	30
		Wi. Watermark sideways-inverted	10·00	
D65	D **2**	2s. 6d. purple/*yellow* (11.5.61)	4·75	75
		Wi. Watermark sideways-inverted	9·00	
D66		5s. scarlet/*yellow* (8.5.61)	6·50	1·00
		Wi. Watermark sideways-inverted	15·00	
D67		10s. blue/*yellow* (2.9.63)	10·00	5·50
		Wi. Watermark sideways-inverted	35·00	
D68		£1 black/*yellow* (2.9.63)	40·00	7·50
		Set of 13	60·00	20·00

Whiter paper. The note after No. 586 also applies to Postage Due stamps.

Stamps from the above issue are known bisected and used for half their face value at the following sorting offices:
   1d. Chieveley, Newbury (1962, 1963), Henlan, Llandyssil (1961), Mayfield (1962), St. Albans (1964)
   2d. Doncaster (?)

1968–69. *Typo. No wmk. Chalk-surfaced paper.*

D69	D **1**	2d. agate (11.4.68)	25	75
		Ev. PVA gum (26.11.68)	75	
D70		3d. violet (9.9.68)	30	75
D71		4d. blue (6.5.68)	40	75
		Ev. PVA gum	£1500	
D72		5d. orange-brown (3.1.69)	5·00	10·00
D73		6d. purple (9.9.68)	60	1·00
D74		1s. ochre (19.11.68)	2·00	1·00
		Set of 6	7·50	13·00

The 2d. and 4d. exist with gum arabic and PVA gum; the remainder with PVA gum only.

Stamps from the above issue are known bisected and used for half their face value at the following sorting offices:
   4d. Northampton (1970)
   6d. Kilburn, London NW (1968)

1968–69. *Photo. No wmk. Chalk-surfaced paper. PVA gum.*

D75	D **1**	4d. blue (12.6.69)	6·00	6·00
D76		8d. red (3.10.68)	1·25	1·00

Nos. D75/6 are smaller, 21½ × 17½mm.

       D **3**   D **4**

(Des J. Matthews. Photo Harrison)

1970 (17 June)–**75.** *Decimal Currency. Chalk-surfaced paper.*

D77	D **3**	½p. turquoise-blue (15.2.71)	15	50
D78		1p. dp reddish purple (15.2.71)	15	15
D79		2p. myrtle-green (15.2.71)	20	15
D80		3p. ultramarine (15.2.71)	20	15
D81		4p. yellow-brown (15.2.71)	25	15
D82		5p. violet (15.2.71)	25	15
D83		7p. red-brown (21.8.74)	35	80
D84	D **4**	10p. carmine	30	30
D85		11p. slate-green (18.6.75)	50	1·00
D86		20p. olive-brown	60	25
D87		50p. ultramarine	1·75	25
D88		£1 black	3·25	25
D89		£5 orange-yellow and black (2.4.73)	35·00	1·50
		Set of 13	38·00	5·25
		Presentation Pack (P.O. Pack No. 36) (Nos. D77/82, D84, D86/8 (3.11.71)	9·00	
		Presentation Pack (P.O. Pack No. 93) (Nos. D77/88) (30.3.77)	9·00	

Later printings were on fluorescent white paper, some with dextrin added to the PVA gum (see notes after X1058).

The 2p. from the above issue is known bisected and used for half its face value at the following sorting office:
   2p. Exeter (1977)

       D **5**   D **6**

(Des Sedley Place Design Ltd. Photo Harrison)

1982 (9 June). *Chalk-surfaced paper.*

D 90	D **5**	1p. lake	10	30
D 91		2p. brt blue	30	30
D 92		3p. dp mauve	15	30
D 93		4p. dp blue	15	25
D 94		5p. sepia	20	25
D 95	D **6**	10p. lt brown	30	40
D 96		20p. olive-green	50	60
D 97		25p. dp greenish blue	80	90
D 98		50p. grey-black	1·50	1·10
D 99		£1 red	3·00	1·25
D100		£2 turquoise-blue	6·00	2·40
D101		£5 dull orange	14·00	8·00
		Set of 12	24·00	8·50
		Set of 12 *Gutter Pairs*	48·00	
		Presentation Pack	26·00	

        D **7**

(Des Sedley Place Design Ltd. Litho Questa)

1994 (15 Feb). *P* 15 × 14 (*with one elliptical hole on each vertical side*).

D102	D **7**	1p. red, yellow & black	10	50
D103		2p. magenta, purple & black	10	50
D104		5p. yellow, red-brown & black	15	35
D105		10p. yellow, emerald & black	30	45
D106		20p. blue-green, violet & black	50	70
D107		25p. cerise, rosine & black	70	75
D108		£1 violet, magenta & black	3·00	2·50
D109		£1.20, greenish blue, blue-green & black .	3·75	3·50
D110		£5 greenish black, blue-green & black	14·00	12·00
		Set of 9	20·00	19·00
		First Day Cover		22·00
		Presentation Pack	28·00	

Special First Day of Issue Postmark

London EC3 .... 22·00

Following changes in the method of collecting money due on unpaid or underpaid mail the use of postage due stamps was restricted from April 1995 to mail addressed to business customers and to Customs/V.A.T. charges levied by the Royal Mail on behalf of the Customs and Excise. The use of postage due stamps ceased on 28 January 2000.

OFFICIAL STAMPS

In 1840 the 1d. black (Type **1**), with "V R" in the upper corners, was prepared for official use, but was never issued for postal purposes. Obliterated specimens are those which were used for experimental trials of obliterating inks, or those that passed through the post by oversight.

V **1**

1840. *Prepared for use but not issued; "V" "R" in upper corners. Imperf.*

			Used on
		Un	*Used cover*
V1	V **1** 1d. black	£10000	£16000

The following Official stamps would be more correctly termed Departmental stamps as they were exclusively for the use of certain government departments. Until 1882 official mail used ordinary postage stamps purchased at post offices, the cash being refunded once a quarter. Later the government departments obtained Official stamps by requisition.

Official stamps were on sale to the public for a short time at Somerset House but they were not sold from post offices. The system of only supplying the Government departments with stamps was open to abuse so that all official stamps were withdrawn on 13 May 1904.

OVERPRINTS, PERFORATIONS, WATERMARKS. All official stamps were overprinted by Thomas De La Rue & Co. and are perf 14. Except for the 5s., and 10s. on Anchor, they are on Crown watermarked paper unless otherwise stated.

INLAND REVENUE

These stamps were used by revenue officials in the provinces, mail to and from Head Office passing without a stamp. The London Office used these stamps only for foreign mail.

I.R.   **I. R.**

OFFICIAL   **OFFICIAL**

(O **1**)   (O **2**)

Optd with Types O **1** (½d. to 1s.) *or* O **2** (*others*)

1882–1901. *Stamps of Queen Victoria.* (a) *Issues of 1880–81.*

				★ *Used on*
		Un	*Used*	*cover*
O1	½d. dp green (1.11.82)	60·00	20·00	60·00
O2	½d. pale green	60·00	20·00	
O3	1d. lilac (Die II) (1.10.82)	4·00	2·00	20·00
	a. Optd in blue-black	£150	50·00	
	b. "OFFICIAL" omitted	—	£5000	
	Wi. Watermark inverted	—	£800	
O4	6d. grey (Plate 18) (3.11.82)	£250	65·00	

No. O3 with the lines of the overprint transposed is an essay.

(b) *Issues of 1884–88.*

O 5	½d. slate-blue (8.5.85)	60·00	22·00	90·00
O 6	2½d. lilac (12.3.85)	£250	80·00	£850
O 7	1s. dull green (12.3.85)	£3500	£850	
O 8	5s. rose (*blued paper*) (wmk Anchor) (12.3.85)	£3750	£1500	
O 9	5s. rose (wmk Anchor) (3.90)	£2500	£750	
	a. Raised stop after "R"	£3000	£850	
	b. Optd in blue-black	£3500	£850	
O 9c	10s. cobalt (*blued paper*) (wmk Anchor) (12.3.85)	£8000	£2000	
O 9d	10s. ultramarine (*blued paper*) (wmk Anchor) (12.3.85)	£7500	£2500	
O10	10s. ultramarine (wmk Anchor) (3.90) ...	£3750	£1000	
	a. Raised stop after "R"	£4250	£1500	
	b. Optd in blue-black	£4500	£1500	
O11	£1 brown-lilac (wmk Crowns) (12.3.85) .£27000	£14000	
	a. Frame broken £32000	
	b. Optd in blue-black	
O12	£1 brown-lilac (wmk Orbs) (3.90) £40000	£20000	
	a. Frame broken £45000	

(c) *Issues of 1887–92.*

O13	½d. vermilion (15.5.88)	5·00	2·00	60·00
	a. Without "I.R."	£2500	
	b. Imperf	£1700	
	c. Opt double (imperf)	£2000	
O14	2½d. purple/*blue* (2.92)	£100	10·00	£300
O15	1s. dull green (9.89)	£350	£125	£2000
O16	£1 green (6.92)	£5500	£950	
	a. No stop after "R"	—	£1500	
	b. Frame broken	£8000	£2000	

Nos. O3, O13, O15 and O16 may be found showing worn impressions of the overprints with thicker letters.

(d) Issues of 1887 and 1900

O17	½d. blue-green (4.01)	10·00	6·00	£200
O18	6d. purple/rose-red (1.7.01)	£250	60·00	
O19	1s. green and carmine (12.01)	£1400	£450	
★O1/19	**For well-centred, lightly used**	+35%		

1902–04. *Stamps of King Edward VII. Ordinary paper.*

O20	½d. blue-green (4.2.02)	22·00	3·00	£110
O21	1d. scarlet (4.2.02)	15·00	2·00	75·00
O22	2½d. ultramarine (19.2.02)	£500	£125	
O23	6d. pale dull purple (14.3.04)	£120000		
O24	1s. dull green & carmine (29.4.02)	£1250	£250	
O25	5s. brt carmine (29.4.02)	£7500	£4500	
	a. Raised stop after "R"	£8000	£5000	
O26	10s. ultramarine (29.4.02) £35000 £18000			
	a. Raised stop after "R" £40000 £20000			
O27	£1 blue-green (29.4.02) £25000 £12000			

OFFICE OF WORKS

These were issued to Head and Branch (local) offices in London and to Branch (local) offices at Birmingham, Bristol, Edinburgh, Glasgow, Leeds, Liverpool, Manchester and Southampton. The overprints on stamps of value 2d. and upwards were created later in 1902, the 2d. for registration fees and the rest for overseas mail.

O. W.

OFFICIAL

(O 3)

Optd with Type O **3**

1896 (24 Mar)–**02.** *Stamps of Queen Victoria.*

				★ *Used on*
		Un	*Used*	*cover*
O31	½d. vermilion	£150	75·00	£400
O32	½d. blue-green (2.02)	£200	£100	
O33	1d. lilac (Die II)	£250	75·00	£500
O34	5d. dull purple & blue (II) (29.4.02)	£1250	£400	
O35	10d. dull purple & carmine (28.5.02) ...	£2000	£600	

1902 (11 Feb)–**03.** *Stamps of King Edward VII. Ordinary paper.*

O36	½d. blue-green (2.02)	£500	£150	£1500
O37	1d. scarlet	£500	£150	£350
O38	2d. yellowish green & carmine-red (27.4.02)	£1000	£300	£2000
O39	2½d. ultramarine (29.4.02)	£1250	£500	
O40	10d. dull purple & carmine (28.5.03) £12000 £4250			
★O31/40	**For well-centred, lightly used**	+25%		

ARMY

Letters to and from the War Office in London passed without postage. The overprinted stamps were distributed to District and Station Paymasters nationwide, including Cox and Co., the Army Agents, who were paymasters to the Household Division.

ARMY ARMY ARMY

OFFICIAL OFFICIAL OFFICIAL

(O **4**)   (O **5**)   (O **6**)

1896 (1 Sept)–**01.** *Stamps of Queen Victoria optd with Type* O **4** (½d., 1d.) *or* O **5** (2½d., 6d.).

O41	½d. vermilion	3·50	1·50	40·00
	a. "OFFICIAI" (R.13/7)	£100	50·00	
	b. Lines of opt transposed	£1750		
	Wi. Watermark inverted	£280	£140	
O42	½d. blue-green (6.00)	3·50	6·00	
	Wi. Watermark inverted	£220	£110	
O43	1d. lilac (Die II)	3·50	2·50	65·00
	a. "OFFICAI" (R.13/7)	£100	50·00	
O44	2½d. purple/blue	15·00	8·00	£450
O45	6d. purple/rose-red (20.9.01)	50·00	30·00	£975

Nos. O41a and O43a occur in sheets overprinted by Forme 1.

1902-03. *Stamps of King Edward VII optd with Type* O **4** (*Nos.* O48/50) *or Type* O **6** (O52). *Ordinary paper.*

O48	½d. blue-green (11.2.02)	5·00	2·00	90·00
O49	1d. scarlet (11.2.02)	5·00	2·00	90·00
	a. "ARMY" omitted	†		
O50	6d. pale dull purple (23.8.02)	£120	50·00	
O52	6d. pale dull purple (12.03)	£1250	£450	

GOVERNMENT PARCELS

These stamps were issued to all departments, including Head Office, for use on parcels weighing over 3 lb. Below this weight government parcels were sent by letter post to avoid the 55% of the postage paid from accruing to the railway companies, as laid down by parcel-post regulations. Most government parcels stamps suffered heavy postmarks in use.

GOVT
PARCELS

(O **7**)

Optd as Type O **7**

1883 (1 Aug)–**86.** *Stamps of Queen Victoria.*

		★	
		Un	*Used*
O61	1½d. lilac (1.5.86)	£200	45·00
	a. No dot under "T"	£275	55·00
	b. Dot to left of "T"	£250	55·00
O62	6d. dull green (1.5.86)	£1200	£400
O63	9d. dull green	£1000	£400
O64	1s. orange-brown (watermark Crown, Pl 13) ...	£600	£100
	a. No dot under "T"	£850	£125
	b. Dot to left of "T"	£850	£125
O64c	1s. orange-brown (Pl 14)	£1000	£200
	ca. No dot under "T"	£1100	£225
	cb. Dot to left of "T"		

1887–90. *Stamps of Queen Victoria.*

O65	1½d. dull purple & pale green (29.10.87)	50·00	5·00	
	a. No dot under "T"	70·00	10·00	
	b. Dot to right of "T"	70·00	10·00	
	c. Dot to left of "T"	70·00	10·00	
O66	6d. purple/*rose-red* (19.12.87)	£100	18·00	
	a. No dot under "T"	£140	22·00	
	b. Dot to right of "T"	£140	22·00	
	c. Dot to left of "T"	£140	22·00	
O67	9d. dull purple & blue (21.8.88)	£150	25·00	
O68	1s. dull green (25.3.90)	£250	£100	
	a. No dot under "T"	£300	£120	
	b. Dot to right of "T"	£300	£120	
	c. Dot to left of "T"	£325	£120	
	d. Optd in blue-black			

1891–1900 *Stamps of Queen Victoria.*

O69	1d. lilac (Die II) (18.6.97)	50·00	10·00	
	a. No dot under "T"	65·00	25·00	
	b. Dot to left of "T"	65·00	25·00	
	c. Opt inverted	£2500	£1200	
	d. Ditto. Dot to left of "T"	£2750	£1400	
	Wi. Watermark inverted	—	£150	
O70	2d. grey-green & carmine (24.10.91)	£100	15·00	
	a. No dot under "T"	£140	25·00	
	b. Dot to left of "T"	£140	25·00	
O71	4½d. green & carmine (29.9.92)	£160	£125	
	b. Dot to right of "T"			
	Wi. Watermark inverted			
O72	1s. green & carmine (11.00)	£250	90·00	
	a. Opt inverted	†	£5000	
★O61/72	**For well-centred lightly used**		+ **100%**	

1902. *Stamps of King Edward VII. Ordinary paper.*

O74	1d. scarlet (30.10.02)	30·00	12·00	
O75	2d. yellowish green & carmine-red (29.4.02)	90·00	22·00	
O76	6d. pale dull purple (19.2.02)	£160	25·00	
	a. Opt double, one albino	£9000		
O77	9d. dull purple & ultramarine (28.8.02)	£350	75·00	
O78	1s. dull green & carmine (17.12.02)	£550	£125	

The "no dot under T" variety occured on R.12/3 and 20/2. The "dot to left of T" comes four times in the sheet on R.2/7, 6/7, 7/9 and 12/9. The best example of the "dot to right of T" is on R.20/1. All three varieties were corrected around 1897.

BOARD OF EDUCATION

BOARD

OF

EDUCATION

(O **8**)

Optd with Type O **8**

1902 (19 Feb). *Stamps of Queen Victoria.*

			Used on
		Un	Used cover
O81	5d. dull purple & blue (II) £1000	£225	
O82	1s. green & carmine £3000	£1800	

1902 (19 Feb)–**04** *Stamps of King Edward VII. Ordinary paper.*

O83	½d. blue-green	£100	35·00	£350
O84	1d. scarlet	£100	35·00	£375
O85	2½d. ultramarine	£1500	£110	
O86	5d. dull purple & ultramarine (6.2.04)	£6000	£2000	
O87	1s. dull green & carmine (23.12.02) £60000			

ROYAL HOUSEHOLD

R.H.

OFFICIAL

(O **9**)

1902. *Stamps of King Edward VII optd with Type O **9**. Ordinary paper.*

O91	½d. blue-green (29.4.02)	£200	£140	£750
O92	1d. scarlet (19.2.02)	£175	£120	£600

ADMIRALTY

ADMIRALTY ADMIRALTY

OFFICIAL OFFICIAL

(O **10**)   (O **11**)
(with different "M")

1903 (1 Apr). *Stamps of King Edward VII optd with Type O **10**. Ordinary paper.*

O101	½d. blue-green	15·00	12·00	
O102	1d. scarlet	10·00	6·00	£275
O103	1½d. dull purple & green	£110	70·00	
O104	2d. yellowish green & carmine-red	£185	85·00	
O105	2½d. ultramarine	£200	70·00	
O106	3d. purple/*yellow*	£185	70·00	

1903–04. *Stamps of King Edward VII optd with Type O **11**. Ordinary paper.*

O107	½d. blue-green (9.03)	30·00	15·00	£450
O108	1d. scarlet (12.03)	30·00	15·00	£100
O109	1½d. dull purple & green (2.04)	£500	£300	
O110	2d. yellowish green & carmine-red (3.04)	£750	£325	
O111	2½d. ultramarine (3.04)	£850	£500	
O112	3d. dull purple/*orange-yellow* (12.03) ...	£600	£160	

Stamps of various issues perforated with a Crown and initials ("H.M.O.W.", "O.W.", "B.T." or "S.O.") or with initials only ("H.M.S.O." or "D.S.I.R.") have also been used for official purposes, but these are outside the scope of this catalogue.

POSTAL FISCAL STAMPS

PRICES. Prices in the used column are for stamps with genuine postal cancellations dated from the time when they were authorised for use as postage stamps. Beware of stamps with fiscal cancellations removed and fraudulent postmarks applied.

VALIDITY. The 1d. surface-printed stamps were authorised for postal use from 1 June 1881 and at the same time the 1d. postage issue, No. 166, was declared valid for fiscal purposes. The 3d. and 6d. values together with the embossed issues were declared valid for postal purposes by another Act effective from 1 January 1883.

SURFACE-PRINTED ISSUES

(Typo Thomas De La Rue & Co.)

F **1** Rectangular Buckle

F **2**

F **3** Octagonal Buckle

F **4**

F **5** Double-lined Anchor

F **6** Single-lined Anchor

1853–57. P 15½ × 15.   (a) Wmk F **5** (inverted) (1853–55).

			Un	Used	Used on cover
F1	F **1**	1d. lt blue (10.10.53)	32·00	40·00	£160
		Wi. Watermark upright	£100		
		Wj. Watermark reversed (large loop to right)	£100		
F2	F **2**	1d. ochre (10.53)	95·00	£110	£425
		a. Tête-bêche (in block of four)	£15000		
F3	F **3**	1d. pale turquoise-blue (12.53)	25·00	38·00	£225
		Wi. Watermark upright	70·00		
F4		1d. lt blue/blue (12.53)	65·00	65·00	£375
		Wi. Watermark upright	£110	£175	
F5	F **4**	1d. reddish lilac/blue glazed paper (25.3.55)	95·00	£100	£325
		Wi. Watermark upright	£140	£190	

Only one example is known of No. F2a outside the National Postal Museum and the Royal Collection.

(b) Wmk F **6** (1856–57)

F6	F **4**	1d. reddish lilac (shades)	8·50	7·00	£125
		Wi. Watermark inverted	£110		
		Wj. Watermark reversed	£125		
F7		1d. reddish lilac/bluish (shades) (1857)	8·50	7·00	£125
		Wj. Watermark reversed	£125		

(text in top right: INLAND REVENUE)

(F **7**)

1860 (3 Apr).   No. F7 optd with Type F **7**, in red.

F8	F **4**	1d. dull reddish lilac/blue	£625	£525	£1000
		Wj. Wmk reversed			

BLUE PAPER. In the following issues we no longer distinguish between bluish and white paper. There is a range of papers from white or greyish to bluish.

F **8**

F **9**

F **10**

1860–67.   Bluish to white paper. P 15½ × 15.   (a) Wmk F **6** (1860).

F9	F **8**	1d. reddish lilac (May)	10·00	10·00	£125
		Wi. Watermark inverted	90·00		
F10	F **9**	3d. reddish lilac (June)	£325	£200	£375
F11	F **10**	6d. reddish lilac (Oct)	£150	£125	£325
		Wi. Watermark inverted	£190	£150	
		Wj. Watermark reversed	£180	£150	

(b) W **40**. (Anchor 16mm high) (1864)

F12	F **8**	1d. pale reddish lilac (Nov)	8·50	8·50	£125
		Wi. Watermark inverted			
F13	F **9**	3d. pale reddish lilac	£185	£125	£375
F14	F **10**	6d. pale reddish lilac	£150	£125	£325
		Wi. Watermark inverted	£220		

(c) W **40** (Anchor 18mm high) (1867)

F15	F **8**	1d. reddish lilac	16·00	16·00	£185
F16	F **9**	3d. reddish lilac	85·00	80·00	£325
F17	F **10**	6d. reddish lilac	75·00	60·00	£210

For stamps perf 14, see Nos. F24/7.

F **11**

F **12**

Four Dies of Type F 12

Nos. F19/21 show "O" of "ONE" circular. No. F22 (Die 4) shows a horizontal oval and is the only Die to have this plus heavy shading on hair ribbons.

Die 1. Four lines of shading in left band of ribbon opposite "Y" of "PENNY". Small ornaments and heavy shading under chin

Die 2. Two lines of shading in left band of ribbon. Clear lines of shading under chin. Small ornaments

Die 3. Mid-size ornaments: line shading under chin extended halfway down neck

Die 4. Large size ornaments: straight line of shading continued to bottom of neck

1867–81. *White to bluish paper.* P 14. *(a)* W **47** *(Small Anchor).*

F18	F **11**	1d. purple (1.9.67)	15·00	15·00	£100	
		Wi. Watermark inverted	95·00	£100		
F19	F **12**	1d. purple (Die I) (6.68)	4·50	5·00	£100	
		Wi. Watermark inverted	65·00			
F20		1d. purple (Die 2) (6.76)	18·00	13·00	£225	
F21		1d. purple (Die 3) (3.77)	9·00	9·00	£150	
F22		1d. purple (Die 4) (7.78)	6·00	6·00	95·00	

(b) W **48** *(Orb)*

F23	F **12**	1d. purple (Die 4) (1.81)	6·00	3·00	80·00	
		Wi. Watermark inverted	90·00			

1881. *White to bluish paper.* P 14.

(a) W **40** *(Anchor 18mm high)* (Jan)

F24	F **9**	3d. reddish lilac	£600	£325	£675
F25	F **10**	6d. reddish lilac	£275	£130	£325

(b) W **40** *(Anchor 20mm high)* (May)

F26	F **9**	3d. reddish lilac	£450	£250	£500
F27	F **10**	6d. reddish lilac	£250	£130	£325

ISSUES EMBOSSED IN COLOUR

(Made at Somerset House)

The embossed stamps were struck from dies not appropriated to any special purpose on paper which had the words "INLAND REVENUE" previously printed, and thus became available for payment of any duties for which no special stamps had been provided.

The die letters are included in the embossed designs and holes were drilled for the insertion of plugs showing figures indicating dates of striking.

F **13**   F **14**

INLAND
REVENUE
(F **15**)

INLAND
REVENUE
(F **16**)

1860 (3 Apr)–**71.** *Types F **13/14** and similar types embossed on bluish paper. Underprint Type F **15**. No wmk. Imperf.*

			Un	Used
F28	2d. pink (Die A) (1.1.71)		£500	
F29	3d. pink (Die C)		£125	
	a. *Tête-bêche* (vert pair)		£1000	
F30	3d. pink (Die D)		£500	
F31	6d. pink (Die T)			

F32	6d. pink (Die U)	£250
	a. Tête-bêche (vert pair)	
F33	9d. pink (Die C) (1.1.71)	£625
F34	1s. pink (Die E) (28.6.61)	£500
	a. Tête-bêche (vert pair)	
F35	1s. pink (Die F) (28.6.61)	£180
	a. Tête-bêche (vert pair)	£750
F36	2s. pink (6.8.61)	£500
F37	2s. 6d. pink (Die N) (28.6.61)	
F38	2s. 6d. pink (Die O) (28.6.61)	£250

1871 (Aug).   *As last but perf 12½.*

F39	2d. pink (Die A)	£325
F42	9d. pink (Die C)	£750
F43	1s. pink (Die E)	£500
F44	1s. pink (Die F)	£425
F45	2s. 6d. pink (Die O)	£250

1874 (Nov).   *Types as before embossed on white paper. Underprint Type F* **16**, *in green. W* **47** *(Small Anchor). P 12½.*

F46	2d. pink (Die A)	
F47	9d. pink (Die C)	
F48	1s. pink (Die F)	£500
F49	2s. 6d. pink (Die O)	

It is possible that the 2d., 9d. and 2s. 6d. may not exist with the thin underprint, Type F **16**, in this shade.

1875 (Nov)–**80**.   *As last but colour changed and on white or bluish paper.*

F50	2d. vermilion (Die A) (1880)	£375
F51	9d. vermilion (Die C) (1876)	£500
F52	1s. vermilion (Die E)	£325
F53	1s. vermilion (Die F)	£750
F54	2s. 6d. vermilion (Die O) (1878)	£325

1882 (Oct).   *As last but W* **48** *(Orbs).*

F55	2d. vermilion (Die A)		
F56	9d. vermilion (Die C)		
F57	1s. vermilion (Die E)		
F58	2s. 6d. vermilion (Die O)	£650	£500

Although specimen overprints of Nos. F55/7 are known there is some doubt if these values were issued.

The sale of Inland Revenue stamps up to the 2s. value ceased from 30 December 1882 and stocks were called in and destroyed. The 2s. 6d. value remained on sale until 2 July 1883 when it was replaced by the 2s. 6d. "Postage & Revenue" stamps. Inland Revenue stamps still in the hands of the public continued to be accepted for revenue and postal purposes.

POSTMASTER AND U.P.U. SPECIMEN OVERPRINTS

At various times since 1847 the British Post Office, or its printers, has applied "SPECIMEN" or "CANCELLED" overprints to certain stamp issues.

Many of these overprints were purely intended for internal record purposes, but some had a wider use connected to the postal service. Between 1847 and 1873 the G.P.O. circulated examples of new stamps

overprinted "SPECIMEN" to its postmasters and from 1879 similar overprints were applied to samples forwarded to the Universal Postal Union for distribution to member administrations. After 1892 such U.P.U. overprints were restricted to stamps with a face value of 1 shilling or above and they were discontinued altogether after March 1948.

In the listings below Types P **1** to P **6** are postmaster specimens and the remainder for the U.P.U.

For a complete listing of all other "SPECIMEN" overprints see the *Great Britain Specialised Catalogue.*

SPECIMEN	SPECIMEN (vertical)	SPECIMEN
P **1**	P **3**	P **4**

SPECIMEN	SPECIMEN	SPECIMEN
P **5**	P **6**	P **9**

SPECIMEN	*SPECIMEN*	SPECIMEN
P **16**	P **23**	P **26**

SPECIMEN

P **32**

1847–54.   *Embossed issues.*

No.	Type No.	Specimen	Unused Price
SP1	P **1**	1s. pale green (No. 54) (red opt)	£1250
		a. Black opt	£1250
SP2		10d. brown (No. 57)	£1250
SP3		6d. mauve (No. 58)	£1500

1855–57.   *Surface-printed issues. No corner letters.*

SP4	P **3**	4d. carmine/blued (No. 62)	£550
SP5	P **4**	4d. rose/white (No. 65)	
SP6		6d. dp lilac/white (No. 69)	£250
		a. On azure paper	£350
SP7		1s. dp green (No. 71)	£400

No.	Type No.	Specimen	Unused Price
		1858–70. *Line-engraved issues.*	
SP 8	P **9**	½d. rose-red (pl 10) (No. 48)	£150
SP 9		1d. rose-red (pl 146) (No. 43)	£150
SP10		1½d. rose-red (pl 3) (No. 51)	£200
SP11		2d. blue (pl 15) (No. 46)	£200
		1862–64. *Surface-printed issue. Small uncoloured corner letters.*	
SP12	P **5**	3d. dp carmine-rose (No. 75)	£200
SP13		4d. brt red (No. 79)	£200
SP14	P **6**	9d. bistre (No. 86)	£300
		1867–80. *Large uncoloured corner letters. Wmk Spray of Rose.*	
SP15	P **5**	10d. red-brown (No. 112)	£250
SP16		2s. dull blue (pl 1) (No. 118)	£250
SP17	P **9**	2s. dull blue (pl 1) (No. 118)	£250
SP18		2s. brown (No. 121)	£1500
		1867–83. *Wmk Maltese Cross or Anchor* (£5).	
SP19	P **9**	5s. rose (pl 1) (No. 126)	£650
SP20	P **9**	5s. pale rose (pl 2) (No. 127)	£700
SP21		10s. greenish grey (No. 128)	£2000
SP22		£1 brown-lilac (No. 129)	£4000
SP23		£5 orange/blued (No. 133)	£2000
		1872–73. *Uncoloured letters in corner. Wmk Spray of Rose.*	
SP24	P **6**	6d. chestnut (pl 11) (No. 123)	£200
SP25		6d. grey (pl 12) (No. 125)	£200
		1873–80. *Large coloured corner letters.*	
SP26	P **9**	2½d. rosy-mauve (pl 6) (No. 141)	£140
SP27		2½d. blue (pl 17) (No. 142)	£120
SP28		3d. rose (pl 18) (No. 143)	£180
SP29		4d. sage-green (pl 15) (No. 153)	£250
SP30		4d. grey-brown (pl 17) (No. 154)	£250
SP31		6d. grey (pl 16) (No. 147)	£200
SP32		8d. orange (pl 1) (No. 156)	£200
SP33		1s. green (pl 12) (No. 150)	£200
SP34		1s. orange-brown (pl 13) (No. 151)	£300
		1880–83. *Wmk Imperial Crown.*	
SP35	P **9**	3d. on 3d. lilac (No. 159)	£180
SP36		6d. on 6d. lilac (No. 162)	£180
		1880–81. *Wmk Imperial Crown.*	
SP37	P **9**	½d. dp green (No. 164)	50·00
SP38		1d. Venetian red (No. 166)	50·00
SP39		1½d. Venetian red (No. 167)	60·00
SP40		2d. pale rose (No. 168)	85·00
SP41		5d. indigo (No. 169)	£120
		1881. *Wmk Imperial Crown.*	
SP42	P **9**	1d. lilac (14 dots) (No. 170)	50·00
SP43		1d. lilac (16 dots) (No. 172)	50·00
		1883–84. *Wmk Anchor or Three Imperial Crowns* (£1).	
SP44	P **9**	2s. 6d. lilac/blued (No. 175)	£400
SP45		5s. crimson (No. 181)	£350
SP46		10s. ultramarine (No. 183)	£375
SP47		£1 brown-lilac (No. 185)	£1100
		1883–84. *Wmk Imperial Crown.*	
SP48	P **9**	½d. slate-blue (No. 187)	40·00
SP49		1½d. lilac (No. 188)	70·00
SP50		2d. lilac (No. 189)	70·00
SP51		2½d. lilac (No. 190)	70·00
SP52		3d. lilac (No. 191)	70·00

No.	Type No.	Specimen	Unused Price
SP53	P **9**	4d. dull green (No. 192)	£150
SP54		5d. dull green (No. 193)	£150
SP55		6d. dull green (No. 194)	£180
SP56		9d. dull green (No. 195)	£200
SP57		1s. dull green (No. 196)	£180
		1887–91. *"Jubilee" issue.*	
SP58	P **9**	½d. vermilion (No. 197)	30·00
SP59		1½d. dull purple & pale green (No. 198)	40·00
SP60		2d. green & scarlet (No. 199)	45·00
SP61		2½d. purple/blue (No. 201)	55·00
SP62		3d. purple/yellow (No. 202)	40·00
SP63		4d. green & purple-brown (No. 205)	40·00
SP64		5d. dull purple & blue (Die I) (No. 207)	80·00
SP65		6d. purple/rose-red (No. 208)	45·00
SP66		9d. dull purple & blue (No. 209)	50·00
SP67		10d. dull purple & carmine (No. 210)	75·00
SP68		1s. dull green (No. 211)	50·00
		1902–10. *King Edward VII. De La Rue printings.*	
SP69	P **16**	2s. 6d. lilac (No. 260)	£200
SP70		5s. brt carmine (No. 263)	£220
SP71		10s. ultramarine (No. 265)	£325
SP72		£1 dull blue-green (No. 266)	£850
		1913. *King George V. Wmk Royal Cypher.*	
SP73	P **26**	1s. bistre-brown (No. 395)	£250
		1913. *"Seahorse" high values. Printed by Waterlow.*	
SP74	P **26**	2s. 6d. dp sepia-brown (No. 399)	£350
SP75		5s. rose-carmine (No. 401)	£350
SP76		10s. indigo-blue (No. 402)	£600
SP77		£1 green (No. 403)	£1800
		1929. *Ninth U. P. U. Congress.*	
SP78	P **32**	£1 black (No. 438) (opt in red)	£1400
		1936. *Photogravure.*	
SP79	P **32**	1s. bistre-brown (No. 449)	90·00
		1939. *King George VI.*	
SP80	P **23**	1s. bistre-brown (No. 475)	£125
SP81		2s. 6d. brown (No. 476)	£300
SP82		2s. 6d. yellow-green (No. 476a)	£300
SP83		5s. red (No. 477)	£300
SP84		10s. dark blue (No. 478)	£500
SP85		10s. ultramarine (No. 478a)	£425

POSTAGE DUE STAMPS

		1915. *Wmk Simple Cypher.*	
SP86	P **23**	1s. brt blue (No. D8)	45·00
		1924. *Wmk Block Cypher.*	
SP87	P **23**	2s. 6d. purple/yellow (No. D18)	60·00

OFFICIAL STAMPS

		1887–91. *Optd "GOVT PARCELS".*	
SP88	P **9**	1½d. dull purple & pale green (No. O65)	£150
SP89		2d. grey-green & carmine (No. O70)	£150
SP90		6d. purple/rose-red (No. O66)	£150
SP91		9d. dull purple & blue (No. O67)	£150
SP92		1s. dull green (No. O68)	£150

POST OFFICE STAMP BOOKLETS

The following listing covers all booklets sold by post offices from 1904.

All major variations of contents and cover are included, but minor changes to the covers and differences on the interleaves have been ignored.

From 1913 each booklet carried an edition number, linked to an internal Post Office system of identification which divided the various booklets into series. In 1943 these edition numbers were replaced by edition dates. No attempt has been made to list separate edition numbers for booklets prior to 1943, although notes giving their extent are provided for each booklet. Edition dates from August 1943 are listed separately and exist for all £.s.d. and most Decimal Stitched booklets (except for the 1s. booklets, the 2s. booklets (N1/3), the 5s. ''Philympia'' booklets (No. HP34), the £1 ''Stamps for Cooks'' booklet (No. ZP1) and the Decimal Sponsored booklets). They are those found printed upon the booklets, either on the outer back cover or on the white leaves.

ERRORS OF MAKE-UP of booklets exist but we do not list them here. More detailed listings can be found in the 2nd, 3rd and 4th volumes of the *Great Britain Specialised Catalogue.*

ILLUSTRATIONS. The illustrations of the covers are $\frac{3}{4}$ size except where otherwise stated. Those in Queen Elizabeth II Decimal Sections C to H are $\frac{2}{3}$ size, except where otherwise stated.

Type BA2

1906 (June). *Red cover printed in black as Type BA2. As before but make-up changed to include 12 × 1d. and 23 × $\frac{1}{2}$d. and label showing one green cross (Nos. 217 and 219).*
BA2 .... £775

1907 (Aug). *Red cover printed in black as Type BA2. Make-up changed to include 18 × 1d. and 11 × $\frac{1}{2}$d. and label showing one green cross (Nos. 217 and 219).*
BA3 .... £950

PRICES quoted are for complete booklets containing stamps with ''average'' perforations (i.e. full perforations on two edges of the pane only). Booklets containing panes with complete perforations are worth more.

KING EDWARD VII

2s. Booklets

Type BA1

1904 (Mar). *Red cover printed in black as Type BA1. Pages of six stamps: 24 × 1d. Wmk Imperial Crown (No. 219).*
BA1 .... £250

Type BA6

1911 (June). *Red cover printed in black as Type BA2 but showing a larger Post Office cypher on cover. As before, but containing stamps by Harrison & Sons (Nos. 267 and 272).*
BA6 .... £925

KING GEORGE V

2s. Booklets

Type BB1

HAVE YOU READ THE NOTES AT THE BEGINNING OF THIS CATALOGUE?
These often provide answers to the enquiries we receive.

1911 (Aug). *Red cover printed in black as Type BA2 showing King George V cypher. Pages of six stamps: 18 × 1d. and 12 × ½d. Wmk Crown (Nos. 325, 329) Die 1B.*
BB1 .... £550

Type BB2

1912 (April). *As before, but red cover printed in black as Type BB2.*
BB2 .... £800

1912 (Sept). *As before, but wmk Simple Cypher (Nos. 334, 336) Die 1B.*
BB3 .... £675

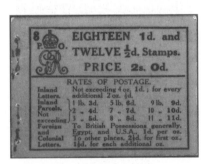

Type BB5

1913 (Jan). *As before, but red cover printed in black as Type BB5.*
BB5   No Edition number or 8 or 9 .... £700

1913 (April). *As before, but 1912–22 Wmk Simple Cypher (Nos. 351, 357).*
BB6   Edition numbers 10 to 45 .... £400

1916 (July). *As before, but orange cover printed in black as Type BB5.*
BB9   Edition numbers 46 to 64 .... £400

Type BB10

1917 (Sept). *As before, but orange cover printed in black as Type BB10.*
BB10   Edition numbers 65 to 81 .... £375

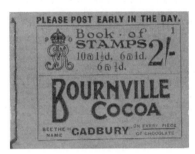

Type BB11

1924 (Feb). *Blue cover printed in black as Type BB11. Pages of six stamps: 10 × 1½d. (first completed by two perforated labels), 6 × 1d. and 6 × ½d. 1912–22 Wmk Simple Cypher (Nos. 351, 357, 362).*
BB11   Edition numbers 1 or 2 .... £1000

1933 (Oct). *As before, but 1924–26 Wmk Block Cypher (Nos. 418/20).*
BB12   Edition numbers 3 to 102 & 108 to 254 .... £375

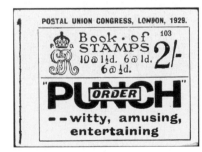

Type BB13

1929 (May). *Postal Union Congress issue. Cover of special design as Type BB13 printed in blue on buff as before but containing stamps of the P.U.C. issue (Nos. 434/6).*
BB13   Edition numbers 103 to 107 .... £475

1934 (Feb). *Blue cover printed in black as Type BB11, but containing stamps with Block Cypher wmk printed by Harrison & Sons (Nos. 418/20).*
BB14   Edition numbers 255 to 287 .... £400

1935 (Jan). *As before, but containing stamps of the photogravure issue with the se-tenant advertisements printed in brown (Nos. 439/41).*
BB15   Edition numbers 288 to 297 .... £900

Type BB16

1935 (May). *Silver Jubilee issue. Larger size cover printed in blue on buff as Type BB16 and containing pages of four stamps with no se-tenant advertisements: $12 \times 1\frac{1}{2}d.$, $4 \times 1d.$ and $4 \times \frac{1}{2}d.$ (Nos. 453/5).*
BB16   Edition numbers 298 to 304 .... 85·00

1935 (July). *As No. BB15, but containing stamps of the photogravure issue with se-tenant advertisements printed in black (Nos. 439/41).*
BB17   Edition numbers 305 to 353 .... £275

3s. Booklets

1918 (Oct). *Orange cover printed in black as Type BB18. Pages of six stamps: $12 \times 1\frac{1}{2}d.$, $12 \times 1d.$ and $12 \times \frac{1}{2}d.$ 1912–22 Wmk Simple Cypher (Nos. 351, 357, 362).*
BB18   Edition numbers 1 to 11 .... £500

Type BB19

1919 (July). *As before, but make-up altered to contain $18 \times 1\frac{1}{2}d.$, $6 \times 1d.$ and $6 \times \frac{1}{2}d.$*
BB19   Edition numbers 12 to 26 .... £500

Type BB20

1921 (April). *Experimental booklet bound in blue covers as Type BB20, containing pages of six stamps: $18 \times 2d.$ (Die I) (No. 368).*
BB20   Edition numbers 35 and part 37 .... £600

1921 (Dec). *As before, but containing 2d. (Die II) (No. 370).*
BB21   Edition numbers 12, 13 and part 37 .... £650

Type BB22

1922 (May). *Scarlet cover printed in black as Type BB22. Pages of six stamps: $18 \times 1\frac{1}{2}d.$, $6 \times 1d.$ and $6 \times \frac{1}{2}d.$ (Nos. 351, 357, 362).*
BB22   Edition numbers 19, 20, 22, 23 and 25 to 54 .... £650

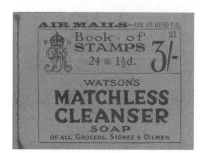

Type BB23

1922 (June). *Experimental booklet as Edition numbers 12 and 13 bound in blue covers as Type BB22, containing pages of six stamps: $24 \times 1\frac{1}{2}d.$ (No. 362).*
BB23   Edition numbers 21 or 24 .... £575

1924 (Feb). *Scarlet cover printed in black as Type BB22, but containing stamps with Block Cypher wmk, printed by Waterlow & Sons (Nos. 418/20).*
BB24   Edition numbers 55 to 167 & 173 to 273 .... £250

1929 (May). *Postal Union Congress issue. Cover of special design as Type BB13 printed in red on buff as before but containing stamps of the P.U.C. issue (Nos. 434/6).*
BB25   Edition numbers 168 to 172 .... £350

1934 (Mar). *Scarlet cover printed in black as Type BB22, but containing stamps with the Block Cypher wmk printed by Harrison & Sons (Nos. 418/20).*
BB26   Edition numbers 274 to 288 .... £300

1935 (May). *Silver Jubilee issue. Larger size cover printed in red on buff as Type BB16 and containing pages of four stamps: 20 × 1½d., 4 × 1d. and 4 × ½d. (Nos. 453/5).*
BB28   Edition numbers 294 to 297 .... 85·00

1935 (July). *As No. BB26, but containing stamps of the photogravure issue (Nos. 439/41).*
BB29   Edition numbers 289 to 293 & 298 to 319 .... £275

3s. 6d. Booklets

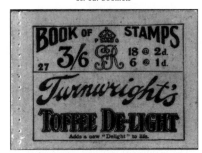

Type BB30

1920 (July). *Orange cover printed in black as Type BB30, containing pages of six stamps: 18 × 2d. and 6 × 1d. (Nos. 357, 368).*
BB30   Edition numbers 27 to 32 .... £625

Type BB31

1921 (Jan). *Orange-red cover printed in black as Type BB31, as before but make-up changed to include stamps of 1912–22 issue with the Simple Cypher wmk: 12 × 2d., 6 × 1½d., 6 × 1d. and 6 × ½d. (Nos. 351, 357, 362, 368 or 370).*
BB31   Edition numbers 1 to 11, 14 to 18, 33, 34, 36 & 38 .... £625

5s. Booklets

Type BB33

1931 (Aug). *Green cover printed in black as Type BB33. Pages of six stamps: 34 × 1½d., 6 × 1d. and 6 × ½d. The first 1½d. pane completed by two se-tenant advertisements. Printed by Waterlow & Sons on paper with Block Cypher wmk (Nos. 418/20).*
BB33   Edition number 1 .... £2500

1932 (June). *As before, but buff cover printed in black.*
BB34   Edition numbers 2 to 6 .... £1250

1934 (July). *As before, but containing stamps with Block Cypher wmk printed by Harrison & Sons (Nos. 418/20).*
BB35   Edition numbers 7 or 8 .... £775

1935 (Feb). *As before, but containing stamps of the photogravure issue with se-tenant advertisements printed in brown (Nos. 439/41).*
BB36   Edition number 9 .... £1700

1935 (July). *As before, but containing stamps of the photogravure issue with se-tenant advertisements printed in black (Nos. 439/41).*
BB37   Edition numbers 10 to 15 .... £300

KING EDWARD VIII

6d. Booklet

1936. *Buff unglazed cover without inscription containing 4 × 1½d. stamps, in panes of two (No. 459).*
BC1 .... 60·00

2s. Booklet

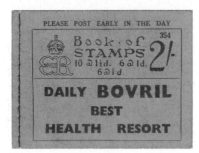

Type BC2

1936 (Oct). *As No. BB17. except for the K.E.VIII cypher on the cover and containing Nos. 457/9.*
BC2   Edition numbers 354 to 385 .... 95·00

3s. Booklet

1936 (Nov). *As No. BB29, except for the K.E.VIII cypher on the cover but without "P" and "O" on either side of the crown, and containing Nos. 457/9.*
BC3   Edition numbers 320 to 332 .... 85·00

5s. Booklet

1937 (Mar). *As No. BB37, but with the K.E.VIII cypher on the cover and containing Nos. 457/9.*
BC4   Edition numbers 16 or 17 .... £190

KING GEORGE VI

6d. Booklets

1938 (Jan). *As No. BC1, but containing stamps in the original dark colours. Buff cover without inscription (No. 464).*
BD1 .... 60·00

1938 (Feb). *As before, but pink unprinted cover and make-up changed to contain 2 × 1½d., 2 × 1d. and 2 × ½d. in the original dark colours (Nos. 462/4).*
BD2 .... £275

1940 (June). *Pale green unprinted cover and make-up changed to include two panes of four stamps with wmk sideways. Stamps in original dark colours with binding margin either at the top or bottom of the pane: 4 × 1d., 4 × ½d. (Nos. 462a/3a).*
BD3 .... £120

1s. Booklets with Panes of 2

1947 (Dec). *Cream cover, unglazed and without inscription containing panes of two stamps in pale shades, all with wmk normal. Panes of two stamps: 4 × ½d., 4 × 1d. and 4 × 1½d. (Nos. 485/7).*
BD4 .... 24·00

1951 (May). *As before, but containing stamps in changed colours (Nos. 503/5).*
BD5 .... 24·00

1s. Booklets with Panes of 4

1948. *Cream cover as before, but make-up changed to contain 4 × 1½d., 4 × 1d. and 4 × ½d. in panes of four of the pale shades with wmk normal (Nos. 485/7).*
BD6 .... £4500

1951 (May). *As before, but stamps in new colours all wmk normal, margins at either top or at the bottom. (Nos. 503/5).*
BD7 .... 28·00

Type BD8

1952 (Dec). *Cream cover printed in black as Type BD8. Make-up as before but with wmk either upright or inverted and margins only at the top (Nos. 503/5).*
BD8 .... 18·00

Type BD10

1954. *As before but cover showing GPO emblem with St. Edward's crown and oval frame as Type BD10 (Nos. 503/5).*
BD10 .... 28·00

2s. Booklets

Type BD11

1937 (Aug). *Blue cover printed in black as Type BB11, but with K.G.VI cypher on the cover and containing stamps in the original dark colours. Panes of six stamps: 10 × 1½d., 6 × 1d. and 6 × ½d. The first 1½d. pane completed by two se-tenant advertisements. (Nos. 462/4).*
BD11   Edition numbers 386 to 412 . . . . £325

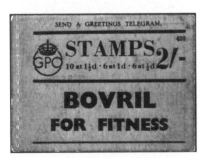

Type BD12

1938 (Mar). *Blue cover printed in black as Type BD12 (Nos. 462/4).*
BD12   Edition numbers 413 to 508 . . . . £325

2s. 6d. Booklets

Type BD13

1940 (June). *Scarlet cover printed in black as Type BD13, containing panes of six stamps in original dark colours: 6 × 2½d., 6 × 2d. and 6 × ½d. (Nos. 462, 465/6).*
BD13   Edition numbers 1 to 7 . . . . £825

1940 (Sept). *As before, but blue cover printed in black as Type BD13.*
BD14   Edition numbers 8 to 13 . . . . £825

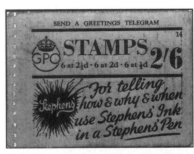

Type BD15

1940 (Oct). *As before, but with green printed in black as Type BD15 (Nos. 462, 465/6).*
BD15   Edition numbers 14 to 94 . . . . £375

1942 (Mar). *As before, but containing stamps in pale shades (Nos. 485, 488/9).*
BD16   Edition numbers 95 to 214 . . . . £400

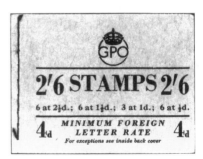

Type A
Circular GPO Cypher

1943 (Aug). *As before, but green cover printed in black as Type A, with different contents details (Nos. 485, 488/9).*

BD18　Edition dates August 1943 to February 1951 .... 45·00

(1) AUG 1943 .... 55·00		(46) MAY 1947 .... 75·00
(2) SEPT 1943 .... 75·00		(47) JUNE 1947 .... 75·00
(3) OCT 1943 .... 75·00		(48) JULY 1947 .... 75·00
(4) NOV 1943 .... 75·00		(49) AUG 1947 .... 75·00
(5) DEC 1943 .... 75·00		(50) SEPT 1947 .... 75·00
(6) JAN 1944 .... 75·00		(51) OCT 1947 .... 75·00
(7) FEB 1944 .... 75·00		(52) NOV 1947 .... 75·00
(8) MAR 1944 .... 75·00		(53) DEC 1947 .... 75·00
(9) APR 1944 .... 75·00		(54) JAN 1948 .... 75·00
(10) MAY 1944 .... 75·00		(55) FEB 1948 .... 75·00
(11) JUNE 1944 .... 75·00		(56) MAR 1948 .... 75·00
(12) JULY 1944 .... 75·00		(57) APR 1948 .... 75·00
(13) AUG 1944 .... 75·00		(58) MAY 1948 .... 75·00
(14) SEPT 1944 .... 75·00		(59) JUNE 1948 .... 75·00
(15) OCT 1944 .... 75·00		(65) JULY 1948 .... 75·00
(16) NOV 1944 .... 75·00		(61) AUG 1948 .... 75·00
(17) DEC 1944 .... 75·00		(62) SEPT 1948 .... 75·00
(18) JAN 1945 .... 75·00		(63) OCT 1948 .... 75·00
(19) FEB 1945 .... 75·00		(64) NOV 1948 .... 75·00
(20) MAR 1945 .... 75·00		(65) DEC 1948 .... 75·00
(21) APR 1945 .... 75·00		(66) JAN 1949 .... 75·00
(22) MAY 1945 .... 75·00		(67) FEB 1949 .... 75·00
(23) JUNE 1945 .... 75·00		(68) MAR 1949 .... 75·00
(24) JULY 1945 .... 75·00		(69) APR 1949 .... 75·00
(25) AUG 1945 .... 75·00		(70) MAY 1949 .... 75·00
(26) SEPT 1945 .... 75·00		(71) JUNE 1949 .... 75·00
(27) OCT 1945 .... 75·00		(72) JULY 1949 .... 75·00
(28) NOV 1945 .... 75·00		(73) AUG 1949 .... 75·00
(29) DEC 1945 .... 75·00		(74) OCT 1949 .... 75·00
(30) JAN 1946 .... 75·00		(75) NOV 1949 .... 75·00
(31) FEB 1946 .... 75·00		(76) DEC 1949 .... 75·00
(32) MAR 1946 .... 75·00		(77) JAN 1950 .... 50·00
(33) APR 1946 .... 75·00		(78) FEB 1950 .... 50·00
(34) MAY 1946 .... 75·00		(79) MAR 1950 .... 50·00
(35) JUNE 1946 .... 75·00		(80) APR 1950 .... 50·00
(36) JULY 1946 .... 75·00		(81) MAY 1950 .... 50·00
(37) AUG 1946 .... 75·00		(82) JUNE 1950 .... 50·00
(38) SEPT 1946 .... 75·00		(83) JULY 1950 .... 50·00
(39) OCT 1946 .... 75·00		(84) AUG 1950 .... 50·00
(40) NOV 1946 .... 75·00		(85) SEPT 1950 .... 50·00
(41) DEC 1946 .... 75·00		(86) OCT 1950 .... 50·00
(42) JAN 1947 .... 75·00		(87) NOV 1950 .... 50·00
(43) FEB 1947 .... 75·00		(88) DEC 1950 .... 45·00
(44) MAR 1947 .... 75·00		(89) JAN 1951 .... 50·00
(45) APR 1947 .... 75·00		(90) FEB 1951 .... 50·00

1951 (May). *As before, but containing stamps in the new colours (Nos. 503, 506/7).*

BD19　Edition dates May 1951 to February 1952 .... 35·00

(1) MAY 1951 .... 35·00	(6) OCT 1951 .... 35·00
(2) JUNE 1951 .... 35·00	(7) NOV 1951 .... 35·00
(3) JULY 1951 .... 35·00	(8) DEC 1951 .... 35·00
(4) AUG 1951 .... 35·00	(9) JAN 1952 .... 35·00
(5) SEPT 1951 .... 45·00	(10) FEB 1952 .... 35·00

1952 (March). *As before, but make-up changed to contain:* $6 \times 2\frac{1}{2}d.$, $6 \times 1\frac{1}{2}d.$, $3 \times 1d.$ *and* $6 \times \frac{1}{2}d.$ *The 1d. pane was completed by three perforated labels in the lower row inscribed "MINIMUM INLAND PRINTED PAPER RATE* $1\frac{1}{2}d$." *(Nos. 503/5, 507).*

BD20　Edition dates March 1952 to May 1953 .... 32·00

(1) MAR 1952 .... 33·00	(9) NOV 1952 .... 33·00
(2) APR 1952 .... 40·00	(10) DEC 1952 .... 33·00
(3) MAY 1952 .... 32·00	(11) JAN 1953 .... 33·00
(4) JUNE 1952 .... 43·00	(12) FEB 1953 .... 33·00
(5) JULY 1952 .... 40·00	(13) MAR 1953 .... 33·00
(6) AUG 1952 .... 33·00	(14) APR 1953 .... 33·00
(7) SEPT 1952 .... 33·00	(15) MAY 1953 .... 40·00
(8) OCT 1952 .... 32·00	

3s. Booklets

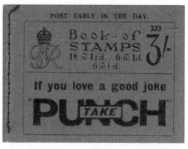

Type BD21

1937 (Aug). *Scarlet cover printed in black as Type BB22 (without "P" and "O") except for K.G.VI cypher on the cover and containing stamps in the original dark colours (Nos. 462/4).*

BD21　Edition numbers 333 to 343 .... £625

Type BD22

1938 (April). *As before, but scarlet cover printed in black as Type BD12 (Nos. 462/4).*

BD22　Edition numbers 344 to 377 .... £625

5s. Booklets

1937 (Aug). *Buff cover printed in black as Type BB33, containing stamps of the new reign in the original dark colours. Pages of six stamps:* $34 \times 1\frac{1}{2}d.$, $6 \times 1\frac{1}{2}d.$ *and* $6 \times \frac{1}{2}d.$ *The first* $1\frac{1}{2}d.$ *pane completed by two se-tenant advertisements. (Nos. 462/4).*

BD23　Edition numbers 18 to 20 .... £750

Type BD24

1938 (May).   *As before, but with redesigned front cover showing GPO emblem as Type BD24 instead of royal cypher.*
BD24   Edition numbers 21 to 29 .... £700

1940 (July).   *As before, but make-up changed to contain: $18 \times 2\frac{1}{2}d.$, $6 \times 2d.$ and $6 \times \frac{1}{2}d.$ in the original dark colours (Nos. 462, 465/6).*
BD25   Edition numbers 1 to 16 (part) £725

1942 (Mar).   *As before, but containing stamps in pale shades (Nos. 485, 488/9).*
BD26   Edition numbers 16 (part) to 36 .... £700

1943 (Sept).   *As before, but buff cover printed in black as Type A (see No. BD18, 2s. 6d.) (Nos. 485, 488/9).*
BD28   Edition dates September 1943 to December 1950 ..... 80·00

(1) SEPT 1943 .... 95·00	(26) JUNE 1947 .... 95·00
(2) OCT 1943 .... 95·00	(27) AUG 1947 .... 95·00
(3) NOV 1943 .... 95·00	(28) OCT 1947 .... 95·00
(4) DEC 1943 .... 95·00	(29) DEC 1947 .... 95·00
(5) FEB 1944 .... £105	(30) FEB 1948 .... 95·00
(6) MAR 1944 .... £105	(31) APR 1948 .... 95·00
(7) AUG 1944 .... £105	(32) JUNE 1948 .... 95·00
(8) OCT 1944 .... £105	(33) JULY 1948 .... 95·00
(9) NOV 1944 .... £105	(34) AUG 1948 .... 95·00
(10) JAN 1945 .... £105	(35) OCT 1948 .... 95·00
(11) FEB 1945 .... £105	(36) DEC 1948 .... 95·00
(12) APR 1945 .... £105	(37) FEB 1949 .... 95·00
(13) JUNE 1945 .... £105	(38) APR 1949 .... 95·00
(14) AUG 1945 .... £105	(39) JUNE 1949 .... 95·00
(15) OCT 1945 .... £105	(40) AUG 1949 .... 95·00
(16) DEC 1945 .... £105	(41) SEPT 1949 .... 95·00
(17) JAN 1946 .... 95·00	(42) OCT 1949 .... 95·00
(18) MAR 1946 .... 95·00	(43) DEC 1949 .... 95·00
(19) MAY 1946 .... 95·00	(44) FEB 1950 .... 80·00
(20) JUNE 1946 .... 95·00	(45) APR 1950 .... 80·00
(21) AUG 1946 .... 95·00	(46) JUNE 1950 .... 80·00
(22) OCT 1946 .... 95·00	(47) AUG 1950 .... 80·00
(23) DEC 1946 .... 95·00	(48) OCT 1950 .... 80·00
(24) FEB 1947 .... 95·00	(49) DEC 1950 .... 80·00
(25) APR 1947 .... 95·00	

Type BD29

1944 (Apr).   *As before, but buff cover printed in black as Type BD29 (Nos. 485, 488/9).*
BD29   Edition dates April or June 1944 .... £875

(1) APR 1944 .... £875   (2) JUNE 1944 .... £875

1951 (May).   *As before, but buff cover changed back to Type A (see No. BD18, 2s. 6d.) and containing stamps in the new colours (Nos. 503, 506/7).*
BD30   Edition dates May 1951 to January 1952 .... 55·00

(1) MAY 1951 .... 55·00	(4) NOV 1951 .... 55·00
(2) JULY 1951 .... 55·00	(5) JAN 1952 .... 55·00
(3) SEPT 1951 .... 55·00	

1952 (Mar).   *As before, make-up changed to contain: $18 \times 2\frac{1}{2}d.$, $6 \times 1\frac{1}{2}d.$, $3 \times 1d.$ and $6 \times \frac{1}{2}d.$ The 1d. pane was completed by three perforated labels in the lower row inscribed "MINIMUM INLAND PRINTED PAPER RATE $1\frac{1}{2}d.$" (Nos. 503/5, 507).*
BD31   Edition dates March to November 1952 .... 40·00

(1) MAR 1952 .... 40·00	(4) SEPT 1952 .... 40·00
(2) MAY 1952 .... 40·00	(5) NOV 1952 .... 40·00
(3) JULY 1952 .... 40·00	

1953 (Jan).   *As before, but make-up changed again to include the 2d. value and containing: $12 \times 2\frac{1}{2}d.$, $6 \times 2d.$, $6 \times 1\frac{1}{2}d.$, $6 \times 1d.$ and $6 \times \frac{1}{2}d.$ (Nos. 503/7).*
BD32   Edition dates January or March 1953 .... 55·00

(1) JAN 1953 .... 55·00   (2) MAR 1953 .... 55·00

QUEEN ELIZABETH II

I. £.s.d. Booklets, 1953–70.

TYPES OF BOOKLET COVER WITH GPO CYPHER

Type A
Circular GPO Cypher
(See illustration above No. BD18)

Type B
Oval Type GPO Cypher

Type C
New GPO Cypher (small)

Type D
New GPO Cypher (large)

1s. Booklets

1953 (2 Sept)–**59.**   *I. White unprinted cover. Pages of two stamps:*
$4 \times 1\frac{1}{2}d.$, $4 \times 1d.$, $4 \times \frac{1}{2}d.$ *For use in experimental "D" machines.*

A. *Wmk Tudor Crown (Nos. 515/17)*
E1   No date ....   7·00

B. *Wmk St. Edward's Crown (Nos. 540/2)*
E2   No date (11.57) ....   18·00

II. White printed cover as Type B. Pages of four stamps: $4 \times 1\frac{1}{2}d.$, $4 \times 1d.$,
$4 \times \frac{1}{2}d.$ *For use in "E" machines.*

A. *Wmk Tudor Crown (Nos. 515/17)*
K1   No date (22.7.54) ....   6·00

B. *Wmk St. Edward's Crown (Nos. 540/2)*
K2   No date (5.7.56) ....   6·00

C. *Wmk Crowns (Nos. 570/2)*
K3   No date (13.8.59) ....   6·00

2s. Booklets

1959 (22 Apr)–**65.**   *Pages of four stamps:* $4 \times 3d.$, $4 \times 1\frac{1}{2}d.$, $4 \times 1d.$,
$4 \times \frac{1}{2}d.$

*I. Salmon cover as Type B. Wmk. St. Edward's Crown (Nos. 540/2 and
545).*
N1   No date ....   5·00

II. Salmon cover as Type C. Wmk Crowns (Nos. 570/2 and 575).
N2   No date (2.11.60) ....   7·00

III. Lemon cover as Type C. Wmk Crowns (Nos. 570/2 and 575).
N3   No date (2.61) ....   7·00

*IV. Lemon cover as Type C. Wmk Crowns (sideways) (Nos. 570a, 571a,
572b, 575a) or phosphor (Nos. 610a, 611a, 612a, 615b).*
N 4   APR 1961 ....   25·00
        p. With phosphor bands ....   60·00
N 5   SEPT 1961 ....   38·00
N 6   JAN 1962 ....   40·00
N 7   APR 1962 ....   42·00
N 8   JULY 1962 ....   40·00
        p. With phosphor bands ....   80·00
N 9   NOV 1962 ....   50·00
        p. With phosphor bands ....   85·00
N10   JAN 1963 ....   40·00
        p. With phosphor bands £120
N11   MAR 1963 ....   40·00
N12   JUNE 1963 ....   40·00
        p. With phosphor bands ....   75·00
N13   AUG 1963 ....   40·00
        p. With phosphor bands ....   75·00
N14   OCT 1963 ....   40·00
        p. With phosphor bands £120
N15   FEB 1964 ....   40·00
        p. With phosphor bands ....   75·00
N16   JUNE 1964 ....   40·00
        p. With phosphor bands £100
N17   AUG 1964 ....   50·00
        p. With phosphor bands £100
N18   OCT 1964 ....   40·00
        p. With phosphor bands ....   65·00
N19   DEC 1964 ....   45·00
        p. With phosphor bands ....   65·00
N20   APR 1965 ....   38·00
        p. With phosphor bands ....   60·00

1965 (16 Aug)–**67.** *New Composition. Pages of four stamps: 4 × 4d. and pane of 2 × 1d. and 2 × 3d. arranged se-tenant horiz.*

Orange-yellow cover as Type C printed in black. Wmk Crowns (sideways) (Nos. 571a, 575a and 576ab) or phosphor (Nos. 611a, 615d or 615dEa (one side phosphor band) and 616ab).

N21	JULY 1965	3·00
	p. With phosphor bands	15·00
N22	OCT 1965	3·50
	p. With phosphor bands	14·00
N23	JAN 1966	5·00
	p. With phosphor bands	20·00
N24	APR 1966	5·00
	p. With phosphor bands	9·00
N25	JULY 1966	4·00
	p. With phosphor bands	55·00
N26	OCT 1966	5·00
	p. With phosphor bands	12·00
N27	JAN 1967	6·00
	p. With phosphor bands	6·50
N28p	APR 1967. With phosphor bands	7·50
N29p	JULY 1967. With phosphor bands	5·00
N30p	OCT 1967. With phosphor bands	5·00

In the *se-tenant* pane the 3d. appears at left or right to facilitate the application of phosphor bands.

The following illustration shows how the *se-tenant* stamps with one phosphor band on 3d. were printed and the arrows indicate where the guillotine fell. The result gives 1d. stamps with two bands and the 3d. stamps with one band either at left or right.

| 3d. | 1d. | 1d. | 3d. | 3d. | 1d. | 1d. | 3d. |

1967 (Nov)–**68.** *Composition and cover as Nos. N21/30. Wmk Crowns (sideways) (Nos. 611a, 615b (two phosphor bands) and 616ab).*

N31p	JAN 1968	3·00
N32p	MAR 1968	3·50

2s. Booklets with Machin type stamps

1968 (6 Apr–Aug). *Orange-yellow cover as Type C. Pages of four stamps: 4 × 4d. and pane of 2 × 1d. and 2 × 3d. arranged se-tenant horiz. PVA gum (Nos. 724, 730, 731Ev).*

NP27	MAY 1968	1·25
NP28	JULY 1968	1·00
NP29	AUG 1968	4·00

1968 (16 Sept)–**70.** *Grey cover as Type C. New Composition. 4d. stamps only comprising page of 4 × 4d. with two phosphor bands (No. 731Ev) and page of 2 × 4d. with one centre phosphor band (No. 732) se-tenant with two printed labels.*

NP30	SEPT 1968	90
NP31	JAN 1969	£200

Same composition but all six 4d. stamps have one centre phosphor band (No. 732).

NP31a	SEPT 1968	£500
NP32	NOV 1968	90
NP33	JAN 1969	90

Same composition but change to 4d. bright vermilion with one centre phosphor band (No. 733).

NP34	MAR 1969	1·25
NP35	MAY 1969	1·50
NP36	JULY 1969	2·00

NP37	SEPT 1969	1·50
NP38	NOV 1969	1·50
NP39	JAN 1970	2·00
NP40	MAR 1970	2·00
NP41	MAY 1970	2·00
NP42	JULY 1970	2·25
NP43	AUG 1970	2·00
NP44	OCT 1970	2·00
NP45	DEC 1970	2·00

2s. Booklets for Holiday Resorts

1963 (15 July)–**64.** *I. Lemon cover as Type C printed in red. New composition. Pages of four stamps: two of 4 × 2½d. and one of 3 × ½d. and 1 × 2½d. arranged se-tenant. Chalky paper. Wmk Crowns (Nos. 570k and 574k).*

NR1	No date, black stitching	3·50
	a. White stitching (3.9.63)	4·00

II. Lemon cover as Type C printed in red. Composition changed again. Pages of four stamps 2 × ½d. and 2 × 2½d. arranged sideways, vertically se-tenant. Wmk Crowns (sideways) (No. 570m × 4).

NR2	1964 (1.7.64)	1·60

2s. Booklet for Christmas Cards

1965 (6 Dec). *Orange-yellow cover as Type C printed in red. Two panes of 4 × 3d. arranged sideways. Wmk Crowns (sideways) (No. 575a).*

NX1	1965	80

2s. 6d. Booklets

Green cover. Pages of six stamps: 6 × 2½d., 6 × 1½d., 3 × 1d. (page completed by three perforated labels), 6 × ½d.

LABELS. The wording printed on the labels differs as follows:

"PPR" = "MINIMUM INLAND PRINTED PAPER RATE 1½d." Two types exist:
A. Printed in photogravure, 17 mm high.
B. Typographed, 15 mm high.
"Shorthand" = "SHORTHAND IN 1 WEEK" (covering all three labels).
"Post Early" = "PLEASE POST EARLY IN THE DAY".
"PAP" = "PACK YOUR PARCELS SECURELY" (1st label) "ADDRESS YOUR LETTERS CORRECTLY" (2nd label), "AND POST EARLY IN THE DAY" (3rd label).

1953–54. *Composite booklets containing stamps of King George VI and Queen Elizabeth II.*

A. K.G.VI ½d. and 1d. (Nos. 503/4) and Q.E.II ½d. and 2½d. (Nos. 517 and 519b). Cover as Type A. No interleaving pages.

F 1	MAY 1953 (PPR 17 mm)	25·00
F 2	JUNE 1953 (PPR 17 mm)	28·00
F 3	JULY 1953 (PPR 17 mm)	32·00
F 4	AUG 1953 (PPR 17 mm)	28·00

B. Same composition but with addition of two interleaving pages, one at each end. Cover as Type A.

F 5	SEPT 1953 (PPR 17 mm)	£160
F 6	SEPT 1953 (PPR 15 mm)	£100

C. Same composition and with interleaving pages but with cover as Type B.

F 7	OCT 1953 (PPR 17 mm)	40·00
F 8	OCT 1953 (PPR 15 mm)	90·00
F 9	NOV 1953 (PPR 17 mm)	40·00
F10	NOV 1953 (PPR 15 mm)	£140
F11	DEC 1953 (PPR 17 mm)	45·00
F12	JAN 1954 (Shorthand)	70·00
F13	FEB 1954 (Shorthand)	70·00

D. *New composition: K.G.VI 1d. (No. 504) and Q.E.II ½d., 1½d. and 2½d. (Nos. 515, 517 and 519b).*

F14	MAR 1954 (PPR 17 mm)	£425
F14a	MAR 1954 (Shorthand)	

1954–57. *Booklets containing only Queen Elizabeth II stamps. All covers as Type B.*

A. *Wmk Tudor Crown (Nos. 515/17 and 519b).*

F15	MAR 1954 (PPR 15 mm)	£250
F16	APR 1954 (Post Early)	40·00
F17	MAY 1954 (Post Early)	40·00
F18	JUNE 1954 (Post Early)	40·00
F19	JULY 1954 (Post Early)	40·00
F22	AUG 1954 (Post Early)	40·00
F21	SEPT 1954 (Post Early)	40·00
F22	OCT 1954 (Post Early)	40·00
F23	NOV 1954 (Post Early)	40·00
F24	DEC 1954 (Post Early)	40·00

B. *Same composition but with interleaving pages between each pane of stamps.*

F25	JAN 1955 (Post Early)	45·00
F26	JAN 1955 (PAP)	£100
F27	FEB 1955 (PAP)	40·00
F28	MAR 1955 (PAP)	40·00
F29	APR 1955 (PAP)	40·00
F30	MAY 1955 (PAP)	40·00
F31	JUNE 1955 (PAP)	40·00
F32	JULY 1955 (PAP)	40·00
F33	AUG 1955 (PAP)	40·00

C. *Mixed watermarks. Wmk Tudor Crown (Nos. 515/17 and 519b) and wmk St. Edward's Crown (Nos. 540/2 and 544b) in various combinations.*

F34	SEPT 1955 (PAP)	*From* 45·00

2s. 6d. booklets dated AUGUST, OCTOBER, NOVEMBER and DECEMBER 1955, JANUARY, MAY and JUNE 1956 exist both as listed and with the two watermarks mixed. There are so many different combinations that we do not list them separately, but when in stock selections can be submitted. The SEPTEMBER 1955 booklet (No. F34) only exists in composite form.

D. *Wmk St. Edward's Crown (Nos. 540/2 and 544b).*

F35	OCT 1955 (PAP)	30·00
F36	NOV 1955 (PAP)	30·00
F37	DEC 1955 (PAP)	30·00
F38	JAN 1956 (PAP)	30·00
F39	FEB 1956 (PAP)	30·00
F40	MAR 1956 (PAP)	30·00
F41	APR 1956 (PAP)	35·00
F42	MAY 1956 (PAP)	30·00
F43	JUNE 1956 (PAP)	30·00
F44	JULY 1956 (PAP)	30·00
F45	AUG 1956 (PAP)	20·00
F46	SEPT 1956 (PAP)	35·00
F47	OCT 1956 (PAP)	30·00
F48	NOV 1956 (PAP)	30·00
F49	DEC 1956 (PAP)	30·00
F50	JAN 1957 (PAP)	30·00
F51	FEB 1957 (PAP)	30·00
F52	MAR 1957 (PAP)	22·00

E. *Same wmk but new composition. Pages of six stamps: 6 × 2½d. (No. 544b), 6 × 2d. (No. 543b) and 6 × ½d. (No. 540).*

F53	APR 1957	30·00
F54	MAY 1957	30·00
F55	JUNE 1957	25·00
F56	JULY 1957	25·00
F57	AUG 1957	25·00
F58	SEPT 1957	25·00

F59	OCT 1957	25·00
F60	NOV 1957	20·00
F61	DEC 1957	35·00

3s. Booklets

1958–65. *Pages of six stamps: 6 × 3d., 6 × 1½d., 6 × 1d., 6 × ½d.*

I. *Red cover as Type B.*
A. *Wmk St. Edward's Crown (Nos. 540/2 and 545).*

M1	JAN 1958	18·00
M2	FEB 1958	18·00
M3	MAR 1958	18·00
M4	APR 1958	18·00
M5	MAY 1958	18·00
M6	JUNE 1958	18·00
M7	JULY 1958	18·00
M8	AUG 1958	20·00
M9	NOV 1958	20·00

The 3s. booklets dated NOVEMBER 1958, DECEMBER 1958 and JANUARY 1959 exist both as listed and with mixed St. Edward's Crown and Crowns wmks.

B. *Wmk Crowns (Nos. 570/2 and 575) or graphite lines (Nos. 587/9 and 592).*

M10	DEC 1958	25·00
M11	JAN 1959	20·00
M12	FEB 1959	22·00
M13	AUG 1959	25·00
	g. With graphite lines	£200
M14	SEPT 1959	25·00
	g. With graphite lines	£260

II. *Brick-red cover as Type C. Wmk Crowns (Nos. 570/2 and 575), graphite lines (Nos. 587/9 and 592) or phosphor (Nos. 610/12 and 615).*

M15	OCT 1959	25·00
	g. With graphite lines	£250
M16	NOV 1959	25·00
M17	DEC 1959	25·00
M18	JAN 1960	25·00
M19	FEB 1960	25·00
	g. With graphite lines	£250
M20	MAR 1960	25·00
	g. With graphite lines	£300
M21	APR 1960	25·00
	g. With graphite lines	£260
M22	MAY 1960	25·00
M23	JUNE 1960	25·00
M24	JULY 1960	25·00
M25	AUG 1960	25·00
	p. With phosphor bands	50·00
M26	SEPT 1960	25·00
M27	OCT 1960	25·00
M28	NOV 1960	25·00
	p. With phosphor bands	55·00

III. *Brick-red cover as Type D. Wmk Crowns (Nos. 570/2 and 575) or phosphor (Nos. 610/12 and 615).*

M29	DEC 1960	25·00
	p. With phosphor bands	60·00
M30	JAN 1961	25·00
M31	FEB 1961	25·00
M32	MAR 1961	22·00
M33	APR 1961	25·00
	p. With phosphor bands	50·00
M34	MAY 1961	25·00
M35	JUNE 1961	25·00
M36	JULY 1961	25·00
	p. With phosphor bands	50·00

M37	AUG 1961	25·00
	p. With phosphor bands	50·00
M38	SEPT 1961	25·00
	p. With phosphor bands	55·00
M39	OCT 1961	25·00
	p. With phosphor bands	50·00
M40	NOV 1961	25·00
M41	DEC 1961	25·00
M42	JAN 1962	25·00
M43	FEB 1962	25·00
	p. With phosphor bands	50·00
M44	MAR 1962	25·00
	p. With phosphor bands	50·00
M45	APR 1962	25·00
	p. With phosphor bands	50·00
M46	MAY 1962	25·00
	p. With phosphor bands	48·00
M47	JUNE 1962	25·00
	p. With phosphor bands	48·00
M48	JULY 1962	22·00
M49	AUG 1962	22·00
	p. With phosphor bands	50·00
M50	SEPT 1962	25·00
	p. With phosphor bands	50·00
M51	OCT 1962	26·00
	p. With phosphor bands	48·00
M52	NOV 1962	25·00
	p. With phosphor bands	50·00
M53	DEC 1962	25·00
	p. With phosphor bands	50·00
M54	JAN 1963	25·00
M55	FEB 1963	22·00
	p. With phosphor bands	48·00
M56	MAR 1963	22·00
	p. With phosphor bands	48·00
M57	APR 1963	22·00
	p. With phosphor bands	48·00
M58	MAY 1963	22·00
	p. With phosphor bands	£200
M59	JUNE 1963	22·00
	p. With phosphor bands	36·00
M60	JULY 1963	22·00
	p. With phosphor bands	50·00
M61	AUG 1963	22·00
	p. With phosphor bands	50·00
M62	SEPT 1963	22·00
M63	OCT 1963	22·00
M64	NOV 1963	22·00
	p. With phosphor bands	48·00
M65	DEC 1963	30·00
	p. With phosphor bands	85·00
M66	JAN 1964	30·00
	p. With phosphor bands	40·00
M67	MAR 1964	25·00
	p. With phosphor bands	50·00
M68	MAY 1964	25·00
	p. With phosphor bands	65·00
M69	JULY 1964	25·00
	p. With phosphor bands	50·00
M70	SEPT 1964	30·00
	p. With phosphor bands	50·00
M71	NOV 1964	30·00
	p. With phosphor bands	40·00
M72	JAN 1965	30·00
	p. With phosphor bands	40·00
M73	MAR 1965	20·00
	p. With phosphor bands	40·00
M74	MAY 1965	20·00
	p. With phosphor bands	40·00

3s. 9d. Booklets

1953–57.   *Red cover as Type B. Pages of six stamps: 18 × 2½d.*
A. Wmk Tudor Crown (No. 519b)

G 1	NOV 1953	28·00
G 2	JAN 1954	30·00
G 3	MAR 1954	30·00
G 4	DEC 1954	30·00
G 5	FEB 1955	30·00
G 6	APR 1955	30·00
G 7	JUNE 1955	30·00
G 8	AUG 1955	30·00
G 9	OCT 1955	28·00
G10	DEC 1955	30·00

3s. 9d. booklets dated OCTOBER and DECEMBER 1955 exist both as listed and with the two wkms mixed.

B. Wmk St. Edward's Crown (No. 544b). Same composition but with interleaving pages between each pane of stamps.

G15	FEB 1956	20·00
G13	APR 1956	20·00
G14	JUNE 1956	20·00
G15	AUG 1956	20·00
G16	OCT 1956	20·00
G17	DEC 1956	20·00
G18	FEB 1957	20·00
G19	APR 1957	20·00
G20	JUNE 1957	12·00
G21	AUG 1957	28·00

4s. 6d. Booklets

1957–65.   *Pages of six stamps: 18 × 3d.*

I. Purple cover as Type B.
A. Wmk St. Edward's Crown (No. 545).

L1	OCT 1957	20·00
L2	DEC 1957	20·00
L3	FEB 1958	24·00
L4	APR 1958	20·00
L5	JUNE 1958	22·00
L6	OCT 1958	22·00
L7	DEC 1958	22·00

B. Wmk Crowns (No. 575).

L8	DEC 1958	70·00

II. Purple cover as Type C. Wmk Crowns (No. 575) or graphite lines (No. 592).

L 9	FEB 1959	22·00
L10	JUNE 1959	22·00
L11	AUG 1959	22·00
	g. With graphite lines	28·00
L12	OCT 1959	30·00
L13	DEC 1959	24·00

III. Violet cover as Type C. Wmk Crowns (No. 575), graphite lines (No. 592) or phosphor (No. 615).

L14	FEB 1959	30·00
L15	APR 1959	24·00
	g. With graphite lines	20·00
L16	JUNE 1959	24·00
	g. With graphite lines	20·00
L17	DEC 1959	24·00
L18	FEB 1960	24·00
	g. With graphite lines	24·00
L19	APR 1960	24·00
	g. With graphite lines	24·00

L20	JUNE 1960	24·00
L21	AUG 1960	24·00
	p. With phosphor bands	40·00
L22	OCT 1960	24·00

IV. Violet cover as Type D. Wmk Crowns (No. 575) or phosphor (No. 615).

L23	DEC 1960	40·00
L24	FEB 1961	40·00
	p. With phosphor bands	30·00
L25	APR 1961	28·00
	p. With phosphor bands	30·00
L26	JUNE 1961	28·00
L27	AUG 1961	28·00
	p. With phosphor bands	36·00
L28	OCT 1961	25·00
	p. With phosphor bands	36·00
L29	DEC 1961	25·00
L30	FEB 1962	36·00
	p. With phosphor bands	26·00
L31	APR 1962	36·00
	p. With phosphor bands	36·00
L32	JUNE 1962	36·00
	p. With phosphor bands	45·00
L33	AUG 1962	25·00
	p. With phosphor bands	50·00
L34	OCT 1962	25·00
	p. With phosphor bands	£140
L35	DEC 1962	25·00
	p. With phosphor bands	36·00
L36	FEB 1963	25·00
	p. With phosphor bands	36·00
L37	APR 1963	25·00
	p. With phosphor bands	36·00
L38	JUNE 1963	25·00
	p. With phosphor bands	36·00
L39	AUG 1963	25·00
	p. With phosphor bands	36·00
L40	OCT 1963	25·00
	p. With phosphor bands	36·00
L41	NOV 1963	25·00
	p. With phosphor bands	36·00
L42	DEC 1963	25·00
	p. With phosphor bands	£130
L43	JAN 1964	55·00
L44	FEB 1964	25·00
	p. With phosphor bands	36·00
L45	MAR 1964	55·00
	p. With phosphor bands	70·00
L46	APR 1964	55·00
	p. With phosphor bands	36·00
L47	MAY 1964	25·00
	p. With phosphor bands	36·00
L48	JUNE 1964	25·00
	p. With phosphor bands	36·00
L49	JULY 1964	25·00
	p. With phosphor bands	36·00
L50	AUG 1964	30·00
	p. With phosphor bands	24·00
L51	SEPT 1964	36·00
	p. With phosphor bands	24·00
L52	OCT 1964	25·00
	p. With phosphor bands	36·00
L53	NOV 1964	25·00
	p. With phosphor bands	36·00
L54	DEC 1964	25·00
	p. With phosphor bands	36·00
L55	JAN 1965	20·00
	p. With phosphor bands	36·00
L56	FEB 1965	20·00
	p. With phosphor bands	35·00

L57	MAR 1965	22·00
	p. With phosphor bands	£275
L58	APR 1965	18·00

1965 (26 July)–**67**. *New composition. Pages of six stamps: 12 × 4d., 6 × 1d. Slate-blue cover as Type D. Wmk Crowns (Nos. 571 and 576a) or phosphor (Nos. 611 and 616a).*

L59	JULY 1965	18·00
	p. With phosphor bands	24·00
L60	SEPT 1965	18·00
	p. With phosphor bands	24·00
L61	NOV 1965	18·00
	p. With phosphor bands	24·00
L62	JAN 1966	18·00
	p. With phosphor bands	24·00
L63	MAR 1966	18·00
	p. With phosphor bands	20·00
L64	JAN 1967	15·00
	p. With phosphor bands	15·00
L65	MAR 1967	24·00
	p. With phosphor bands	15·00
L66p	MAY 1967. With phosphor bands	9·00
L67p	JULY 1967. With phosphor bands	10·00
L68p	SEPT 1967. With phosphor bands	10·00
L69p	NOV 1967. With phosphor bands	9·00
L70p	JAN 1968. With phosphor bands	9·00
L71p	MAR 1968. With phosphor bands	8·00

4s. 6d. Booklets with Machin type stamps

1968–70. *Slate-blue cover as Type D. Pages of six stamps: 12 × 4d., 6 × 1d. PVA gum (Nos 724, 731Ev).*

LP45	MAY 1968	6·00

Type LP46
Ships Series with GPO Cypher

(Des S. Rose)

Blue cover as Type LP46. Ships Series. Composition as last.

LP46	JULY 1968 (*Cutty Sark*)	1·50

Same composition but changed to 4d. with one centre phosphor band (No. 732).

LP47	SEPT 1968 (*Golden Hind*)	2·00
LP48	NOV 1968 (*Discovery*)	2·00

Same composition but changed to 4d. bright vermilion with one centre phosphor band (No. 733).

LP49	JAN 1969 (*Queen Elizabeth 2*)	3·25
LP50	MAR 1969 (*Sirius*)	3·00
LP51	MAY 1969 (*Sirius*)	2·50
LP52	JULY 1969 (*Dreadnought*)	3·00
LP53	SEPT 1969 (*Dreadnought*)	5·00
LP54	NOV 1969 (*Mauretania*)	3·50
LP55	JAN 1970 (*Mauretania*)	5·00
LP56	MAR 1970 (*Victory*)	4·00
LP57	MAY 1970 (*Victory*)	10·00

Type LP58
Ships Series with Post Office
Corporation Crown Symbol

(Des S. Rose)

As last but cover changed to Type LP58.
LP58 AUG 1970 (Sovereign of the Seas) . . . . 3·75
LP59 OCT 1970 (Sovereign of the Seas) . . . . 10·00

5s. Booklets

1953–57. *Buff cover. Pages of six stamps.* $12 \times 2\frac{1}{2}$d., 6×2d., $6 \times 1\frac{1}{2}$d., 6×1d., $6 \times \frac{1}{2}$d.

I. Composite booklets containing stamps of King George VI and Queen Elizabeth II.
A. K.G.VI $\frac{1}{2}$d., 1d. and 2d. (Nos 503/4 and 506) and Q.E.II $1\frac{1}{2}$d. and $2\frac{1}{2}$d. (Nos. 517 and 519b). Cover as Type A. No interleaving pages.
H1   MAY 1953 . . . . 35·00
H2   JULY 1953 . . . . 38·00

B. Same composition but with addition of two interleaving pages, one at each end. Cover as Type A.
H3   SEPT 1953 . . . . 38·00

C. Same composition and with interleaving pages but cover as Type B.
H4   NOV 1953 . . . . 36·00
H5   JAN 1954 . . . . 36·00

D. New composition: K.G.VI 1d. and 2d. (Nos. 504 and 506) and Q.E.II $\frac{1}{2}$d., $1\frac{1}{2}$d. and $2\frac{1}{2}$d. (Nos. 515, 517 and 519b).
H6   MAR 1954 . . . . £250

E. New composition: K.G.VI 2d. (No. 506) and Q.E.II $\frac{1}{2}$d., 1d., $1\frac{1}{2}$d. and $2\frac{1}{2}$d. (Nos. 515/17 and 519b).
H7   MAR 1954 . . . . £140

II. Booklets containing only Queen Elizabeth II stamps. Buff cover as Type B. Two interleaving pages as before.
A. Wmk Tudor Crown (Nos. 515/18 and 519b).
H 8 MAR 1954 . . . . £120
H 9 MAY 1954 . . . . 60·00
H10 JULY 1954 . . . . 70·00
H11 SEPT 1954 . . . . 35·00
H12 NOV 1954 . . . . 60·00

B. Same composition but with interleaving pages between each pane of stamps.
H13 JAN 1955 . . . . 60·00
H14 MAR 1955 . . . . 50·00
H15 MAY 1955 . . . . 50·00
H16 JULY 1955 . . . . 50·00

C. Wmk St. Edward's Crown (Nos. 540/3 and 544b).
H17 SEPT 1955 . . . . 28·00
H18 NOV 1955 . . . . 30·00
H19 JAN 1956 . . . . 35·00
H20 MAR 1956 . . . . 40·00
H21 MAY 1956 . . . . 36·00
H22 JULY 1956 . . . . 36·00
H23 SEPT 1956 . . . . 35·00
H24 NOV 1956 . . . . 36·00
H25 JAN 1957 . . . . 40·00

5s. booklets dated SEPTEMBER and NOVEMBER 1955 and JANUARY 1956 exist both as listed and with the two watermarks mixed. There are so many different combinations that we do not list them separately, but when in stock selections can be submitted.

D. Same watermark. Introduction of 2d. light red-brown (No. 543b) in place of No. 543.
H26 JAN 1957 . . . . 36·00
H27 MAR 1957 . . . . 36·00
H28 MAY 1957 . . . . 35·00
H29 JULY 1957 . . . . 30·00
H30 SEPT 1957 . . . . 30·00
H31 NOV 1957 . . . . 30·00

1958–65. E. *New composition. Pages of six stamps:* 12×3d. (No. 545), $6 \times 2\frac{1}{2}$d. (No. 544b), 6×1d. (No. 541), $6 \times \frac{1}{2}$d. (No. 540). *Wmk St. Edward's Crown.*
H32 JAN 1958 . . . . 30·00
H33 MAR 1958 . . . . 30·00
H34 MAY 1958 . . . . 30·00
H35 JULY 1958 (11.58) . . . . 22·00
H36 NOV 1958 . . . . 22·00

5s. booklets dated JULY 1958, NOVEMBER 1958 AND JANUARY 1959 exist with mixed watermarks.

F. Blue cover as Type C. Wmk Crowns (Nos. 570/1, 574/5), graphite lines (Nos. 587/8 and 591/2) or phosphor (Nos. 610/11, 614 and 615).
H37 JAN 1959 . . . . 25·00
H38 MAR 1959 . . . . 30·00
H39 JULY 1959 . . . . 30·00
     g. With graphite lines £120
H40 SEPT 1959 . . . . 30·00
H41 NOV 1959 . . . . 30·00
H42 JAN 1960 . . . . 30·00
H43 MAR 1960 . . . . 30·00
     g. With graphite lines £130
H44 MAY 1960 . . . . 35·00
H45 JULY 1960 . . . . 35·00
H46 SEPT 1960 . . . . 40·00
     g. With graphite lines £130
     p. With phosphor bands . . . . 95·00
H47 NOV 1960 . . . . 40·00

G. As last but blue cover as Type D. Same composition.
I. Phosphor has two bands on $2\frac{1}{2}$d (No. 614).
H48 JAN 1961 . . . . 40·00
H49 MAR 1961 . . . . 40·00
     p. With phosphor bands £120
H50 MAY 1961 . . . . 42·00
H51 JULY 1961 . . . . 42·00
     p. With phosphor bands £130
H52 SEPT 1961 . . . . 42·00
     p. With phosphor bands £130
H53 NOV 1961 . . . . 42·00
H54 JAN 1962 . . . . 42·00
     p. With phosphor bands £130

II. *As last but phosphor has one band on 2½d (No. 614a).*

H55	MAR 1962	42·00
	p. With phosphor bands	£135
H56	MAY 1962	42·00
	p. With phosphor bands	£120
H57	JULY 1962	42·00
	p. With phosphor bands	£120
H58	SEPT 1962	42·00
	p. With phosphor bands	£130
H59	NOV 1962	42·00
	p. With phosphor bands	£130·00
H60	JAN 1963	42·00
	p. With phosphor bands	£400
H61	MAR 1963	42·00
	p. With phosphor bands	£135
H62	MAY 1963	42·00
	p. With phosphor bands	£130
H63	JULY 1963	42·00
	p. With phosphor bands	£130
H64	SEPT 1963	42·00
	p. With phosphor bands	£150
H65	NOV 1963	42·00
	p. With phosphor bands	£130
H66	JAN 1964	42·00
	p. With phosphor bands	90·00
H67	MAR 1964	42·00
	p. With phosphor bands	90·00
H68	MAY 1964	42·00
	p. With phosphor bands	£130
H69	JULY 1964	42·00
	p. With phosphor bands	£120
H70	SEPT 1964	42·00
	p. With phosphor bands	£120
H71	NOV 1964	42·00
	p. With phosphor bands	90·00
H72	JAN 1965	42·00
	p. With phosphor bands	90·00
H73	MAR 1965	36·00
	p. With phosphor bands	£120
H74	MAY 1965	36·00
	p. With phosphor bands	95·00

5s. Booklets with Machin type stamps

Type HP26
English Homes Series
with GPO Cypher

(Des S. Rose)

1968 (27 Nov)–**70.** *Cinnamon cover as Type* HP26 (*English Homes Series*). *Pages of six stamps: 12 × 5d.* (*No.* 735).

HP26	DEC 1968 (Ightham Mote)	2·40
HP27	FEB 1969 (Little Moreton Hall)	2·40
HP28	APR 1969 (Long Melford Hall)	2·50

HP29	JUNE 1969 (Long Melford Hall)	2·50
HP30	AUG 1969 (Long Melford Hall)	4·00

Type HP31
English Homes Series with Post
Office Corporation Crown Symbol

(Des S. Rose)

As last but cover changed to Type HP31.

HP31	OCT 1969 (Mompesson House)	2·50
HP32	DEC 1969 (Mompesson House)	3·00
HP33	FEB 1970 (Cumberland Terrace)	2·50

Type HP34

(Des P. Gauld)

As last but cover changed to Type HP34 (*special edition to advertise "Philympia" International Philatelic Exhibition, London, September 1970*).

HP34	(no date) (3.3.70)	2·50

As last but cover changed to Type HP31.

HP35	JUNE 1970 (The Vineyard, Saffron Walden)	3·00
HP36	AUG 1970 (The Vineyard, Saffron Walden)	4·00
HP37	OCT 1970 (Mereworth Castle)	3·75
HP38	DEC 1970 (Mereworth Castle)	4·00

6s. Booklets

1965 (21 June)–**67.** *Claret cover as Type* D. *Wmk Crowns (No.* 576a) *or phosphor (No.* 616a). *Pages of six stamps: 18 × 4d.*

Q 1	JUNE 1965	24·00
	p. With phosphor bands	24·00
Q 2	JULY 1965	24·00
	p. With phosphor bands	24·00
Q 3	AUG 1965	28·00
	p. With phosphor bands	32·00
Q 4	SEPT 1965	24·00
	p. With phosphor bands	30·00

Q 5	OCT 1965	24·00
	p. With phosphor bands	30·00
Q 6	NOV 1965	24·00
	p. With phosphor bands	30·00
Q 7	DEC 1965	24·00
	p. With phosphor bands	30·00
Q 8	JAN 1966	24·00
	p. With phosphor bands	30·00
Q 9	FEB 1966	24·00
	p. With phosphor bands	30·00
Q10	MAR 1966	24·00
	p. With phosphor bands	30·00
Q11	APR 1966	24·00
	p. With phosphor bands	50·00
Q12	MAY 1966	24·00
	p. With phosphor bands	34·00
Q13	JUNE 1966	24·00
	p. With phosphor bands	30·00
Q14	JULY 1966	28·00
	p. With phosphor bands	42·00
Q15	AUG 1966	28·00
	p. With phosphor bands	£100
Q16	SEPT 1966	24·00
	p. With phosphor bands	24·00
Q17	OCT 1966	28·00
	p. With phosphor bands	60·00
Q18	NOV 1966	28·00
	p. With phosphor bands	24·00
Q19	DEC 1966	24·00
	p. With phosphor bands	28·00
Q20	JAN 1967	35·00
	p. With phosphor bands	35·00
Q21	FEB 1967	35·00
	p. With phosphor bands	24·00
Q22	MAR 1967	28·00
	p. With phosphor bands	24·00
Q23	APR 1967	24·00
	p. With phosphor bands	25·00
Q24p	MAY 1967. With phosphor bands	24·00
Q25p	JUNE 1967. With phosphor bands	24·00
Q26p	JULY 1967. With phosphor bands	30·00
Q27p	AUG 1967. With phosphor bands	36·00

6s. Booklets with Machin type stamps

1967–70. *Claret cover as Type D. Pages of six stamps: 18 × 4d. Two phosphor bands. Gum arabic (No. 731).*

QP28	SEPT 1967	38·00
QP29	OCT 1967	38·00
QP30	NOV 1967	38·00
QP31	DEC 1967	38·00
QP32	JAN 1968	36·00
QP33	FEB 1968 (No. 731Ea)	34·00
QP34	MAR 1968 (No. 731Ea)	34·00
QP35	APR 1968 (No. 731Ea)	30·00
QP36	MAY 1968 (No. 731Ea)	15·00

Change to PVA gum (No. 731Ev).

QP37	MAY 1968	£400

GIBBONS STAMP MONTHLY
– finest and most informative magazine for all collectors. Obtainable from your newsagent or by postal subscription – details on request.

Type QP38
Birds Series with GPO Cypher

(Des S. Rose)

Orange-red cover as Type QP38 (Birds Series). Same composition. Two phosphor bands. PVA gum (No. 731Ev).

QP38	JUNE 1968 (Kingfisher) (4.6.68)	1·80
QP39	JULY 1968 (Kingfisher)	11·00
QP40	AUG 1968 (Peregrine Falcon)	1·50

Change to one centre phosphor band (No. 732).

QP41	SEPT 1968 (Peregrine Falcon) (16.9.68)	1·80
QP42	OCT 1968 (Pied Woodpecker)	1·80
QP43	NOV 1968 (Pied Woodpecker)	1·90
QP44	DEC 1968 (Great Crested Grebe)	1·90
QP45	JAN 1969 (Barn Owl)	3·00

Change to 4d. bright vermilion with one centre phosphor band (No. 733).

QP46	FEB 1969 (Barn Owl) (20.2.69)	3·50
QP47	MAR 1969 (Jay)	3·00
QP48	MAY 1969 (Jay)	3·50
QP49	JULY 1969 (Puffin)	3·00
QP50	SEPT 1969 (Puffin)	5·00

Type QP51
Birds Series with Post Office
Corporation Crown Symbol

(Des S. Rose)

As last but cover changed to Type QP51.

QP51	NOV 1969 (Cormorant)	3·50
QP52	JAN 1970 (Cormorant)	4·00
QP53	APR 1970 (Wren)	3·50
QP54	AUG 1970 (Golden Eagle)	3·50
QP55	OCT 1970 (Golden Eagle)	3·50

10s. Booklets

1961 (10 Apr–Oct).   *Green cover as Type D. Pages of six stamps:*
30 × 3d., 6 × 2d., 6 × 1½d., 6 × 1d., 6 × ½d. Wmk Crowns (Nos. 570/3
and 575).
X1   No date £110
X2   OCT 1961 .... £125

1962–64.   *New Composition. Pages of six stamps: 30 × 3d., 6 × 2½d.,*
6 × 1½d., 6 × 2d., 6 × 1d. (Nos. 571/2 and 574/5).
X3   APR 1962 .... 90·00
X4   AUG 1962 .... £120
X5   MAR 1963 .... £115
X6   JULY 1963 .... £115
X7   DEC 1963 .... £115
X8   JULY 1964 .... 90·00
X9   DEC 1964 .... £225

1965 (23 Aug)**–66.**   *Ochre cover as Type D. Pages of six stamps:*
24 × 4d., 6 × 3d., 6 × 1d. Wmk Crowns (Nos. 571, 575, 576a).
X10   AUG 1965 .... 24·00
X11   DEC 1965 .... 35·00
X12   FEB 1966 .... 35·00
X13   AUG 1966 .... 24·00
X14   NOV 1966 .... 24·00

1967–68.   *Ochre cover as Type D. Pages of six phosphor stamps:*
24 × 4d., 6 × 3d., 6 × 1d. Wmk Crowns (Nos. 611, 615c (one side
phosphor band), 616a).
X15p   FEB 1967 .... 8·00

Composition as No. X15p. Wmk Crowns (Nos. 611, 615e (one centre
phosphor band), 616a).
X16p   AUG 1967 .... 6·00
X17p   FEB 1968 .... 6·75

10s. Booklets with Machin type stamps

Type XP4
Explorers Series with GPO Cypher

(Des S. Rose)

1968 (25 Mar–Aug).   *Bright purple cover as Type XP4 (Explorers Series).*
Pages of six stamps: 24 × 4d., 6 × 3d., 6 × 1d. PVA gum (Nos. 724,
729Ev, 731Ev).
XP4   MAY 1968 (Livingstone) .... 5·00
XP5   AUG 1968 (Livingstone) .... 5·00

1968 (16 Sept)**–70.**   *Yellow-green covers as Type XP4 (Explorers Series)*
New composition. Pages of six stamps: 12 × 5d. (with two phosphor
bands), 12 × 4d. (with one centre phosphor band) and pane
comprising 4 × 1d. se-tenant with vert pair of 4d. (each with one
centre phosphor band). PVA gum (Nos. 725, 732 and 735).
XP6   SEPT 1968 (Scott) .... 4·00

Change to 4d. bright vermilion (one centre band) but se-tenant pane
comprises 1d. with two phosphor bands and 4d. with one left side
phosphor band (Nos. 724 and 733/4).
XP 7   FEB 1969 (Mary Kingsley) (6.1.69) .... 3·00
XP 8   MAY 1969 (Mary Kingsley) .... 4·00
XP 9   AUG 1969 (Shackleton) .... 4·00
XP10   NOV 1969 (Shackleton) .... 6·00

Type XP11
Explorers Series with Post Office
Corporation Crown Symbol

(Des S. Rose)

As last but cover change to Type XP11.
XP11   FEB 1970 (Frobisher) .... 6·00
XP12   NOV 1970 (Captain Cook) .... 6·50

£1 Booklet with Machin type stamps

Type ZP1

1969 (1 Dec).   *"Stamps for Cooks". Type ZP1 (150 × 72 mm) with full*
colour pictorial cover showing "Baked, Stuffed Haddock". Contains 12
recipes on interleaving pages and on se-tenant labels attached to
booklet panes. PVA gum. Stapled.
ZP1   £1 containing panes of fifteen stamps (5 × 3): 15 × 5d.
    (No. 735), 30 × 4d. (No. 733) and pane comprising
    6 × 4d. (three each of Nos. 734 and 734Eb) se-tenant
    with 6 × 1d. (No. 724) and 3 × 5d. (No. 735) £250
ZP1a   As last but booklet is sewn with thread instead of being
    stapled .... 9·00

II. Decimal Booklets, 1971 onwards.

A. Stitched Booklets.

The 25p., 30p., 35p., 45p. and 50p. booklets have pictorial covers
(except for the 35p. and 45p.) without the design inscription.
    This was no longer necessary as the designs and background
information were given on the inside of the front cover. Each series
was numbered.

10p. Booklets

Type DN46
British Pillar Box Series

(Des R. Maddox)

1971 (15 Feb–1 June). *British Pillar Box Series. Orange-yellow cover as Type DN46. Pages of four stamps: 2 × 2p. se-tenant vertically with 2 × ½p. and 2 × 1p. se-tenant vertically with 2 × 1½p. (Nos. X841l and X844l).*
DN46 FEB 1971 (No. 1 1855 type) .... 2·50
DN47 APR 1971 (No. 1 1855 type) (19.3.71) .... 2·00
DN48 JUNE 1971 (No. 2 1856 type) (1.6.71) .... 2·50
In No. DN47 the pillar box is slightly reduced in size.

1971 (14 July)–**74**. *British Pillar Box Series continued. Orange-yellow cover as Type DN46. Contents unchanged but panes are se-tenant horizontally (Nos. X841l/a and X844m).*
DN49 AUG 1971 (No. 2 1856 type) (14.7.71) .... 3·00
DN50 OCT 1971 (No. 3 1857–9 type) (27/8/71) .... 3·00
DN51 DEC 1971 (No. 3 1857–9 type) (6.10.71) .... 4·00
DN52 FEB 1972 (No. 4 1866–79 type) (8.12.71) .... 4·00
DN53 APR 1972 (No. 4 1866–79 type) (24.2.72) .... 2·75
DN54 JUNE 1972 (No. 5 1899 type) (12.4.72) .... 2·50
DN55 AUG 1972 (No. 5 1899 type) (8.6.72) .... 2·75
DN56 OCT 1972 (No. 6 1968 type) (2.8.72) .... 2·75
DN57 DEC 1972 (No. 6 1968 type) (30.10.72) .... 2·75
DN58 FEB 1973 (No. 7 1936 type) (5.1.73) .... 2·75
DN59 APR 1973 (No. 7 1936 type) (2.4.73) .... 4·00
DN60 JUNE 1973 (No. 8 1952 type) (18.4.73) .... 2·75
DN61 AUG 1973 (No. 8 1952 type) (4.7.73) .... 15·00
DN62 OCT 1973 (No. 9 1973 type) (16.8.73) .... 3·50
DN63 DEC 1973 (No. 9 1973 type) (12.11.73) .... 2·50
DN64 FEB 1974 (No. 9 1973 type) (17.12.73) .... 3·25
DN65 APR 1974 (No. 10 1974 type) (22.2.74) .... 2·50
DN66 JUNE 1974 (No. 10 1974 type) (23.4.74) .... 2·25

Type DN67
Postal Uniforms Series

(Des C. Abbott)

1974 (23 July)–**76**. *Postal Uniforms Series. Orange-yellow cover as Type DN67. Contents unchanged.*
DN67 AUG 1974 (No. 1 1793 type) .... 1·80
DN68 OCT 1974 (No. 1 1793 type) (27.8.74) .... 1·80
DN69 DEC 1974 (No. 2 1837 type) (25.10.74) .... 1·80
DN70 FEB 1975 (No. 2 1837 type) (12.12.74) .... 1·60
DN71 APR 1975 (No. 3 1855 type) (26.3.75) .... 1·60
DN72 JUNE 1975 (No. 3 1855 type) (21.5.75) .... 1·75
DN73 AUG 1975 (No. 3 1855 type) (27.6.75) .... 1·75
DN74 OCT 1975 (No. 3 1855 type) (3.10.75) 90
DN75 JAN 1976 (No. 3 1855 type) (16.3.76) 90

25p. Booklets

Type DH39
Veteran Transport Series

(Des D. Gentleman)

1971 (15 Feb). *Veteran Transport Series. Dull purple cover as Type DH39. Pages of six stamps: 5 × 2½p. with one printed label, 4 × 2½p. with two printed labels, 5 × ½p. with one printed label (Nos. X841m and X851l/m).*
DH39 FEB 1971 (No. 1 Knife-board omnibus) .... 3·50

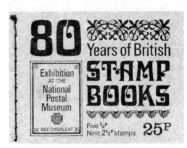

Type DH40

1971 (19 Mar). *Issued to publicise the National Postal Museum Exhibition of 80 Years of British Stamp Booklets. Dull purple cover as Type DH40.*
DH40 APR 1971 .... 4·25

1971 (11 June)–**73**. *Dull purple cover as Type DH39. Veteran Transport Series continued.*
DH41 JUNE 1971 (No. 2 B-type omnibus) .... 4·25
DH42 AUG 1971 (No. 2 B-type omnibus) (17.9.71) .... 11·00
DH43 OCT 1971 (No. 3 Showman's Engine) (22.11.71) .... 11·00
DH44 FEB 1972 (No. 4 Mail Van) (23.12.71) .... 7·25
DH45 APR 1972 (No. 4 Mail Van) (13.3.72) .... 8·75

DH46   JUNE 1972 (No. 5 Motor Wagonette) (24.4.72) ....   6·00
DH47   AUG 1972 (No. 5 Motor Wagonette) (14.6.72) ....   11·00
DH48   OCT 1972 (No. 6 Taxi Cab) (17.7.72) ....   9·00
DH49   DEC 1972 (No. 6 Taxi Cab) (19.10.72) ....   11·00
DH50   DEC 1972 "Issues S" (No. 6 Taxi Cab) (6.11.72) ......   7·25
DH51   FEB 1973 (No. 7 Electric Tramcar) (26.2.73) ....   9·00
    Nos. DH42/51 contain panes showing the perforations omitted
between the label and the binding margin.

Type DH52

1973 (7 June).   *Dull mauve cover as Type DH52.*
DH52   JUNE 1973 ....   9·00
    No. DH52 contains panes showing the perforations omitted
between the label and the binding margin.

30p. Booklets

Type DQ56
British Birds Series

(Des H. Titcombe)

1971 (15 Feb).   *British Birds Series. Bright purple cover as Type DQ56.
Pages of six stamps: 2 panes of 5 × 3p. with one printed label (No.
X855l).*
DQ56   FEB 1971 (No. 1 Curlew) ....   4·50

1971 (19 Mar).   *Bright purple cover as Type DH40.*
DQ57   APR 1971 ....   6·00

1971 (26 May)–**73**.   *Bright purple cover as Type DQ56. British Birds
Series continued.*
DQ58   JUNE 1971 (No. 2 Lapwing) ....   6·00
DQ59   AUG 1971 (No. 2 Lapwing) (23.7.71) ....   6·00
DQ60   OCT 1971 (No. 3 Robin) (1.10.71) ....   6·00
DQ61   DEC 1971 (No. 3 Robin) (10.11.71) ....   7·25
DQ62   FEB 1972 (No. 4 Pied Wagtail) (21.12.71) ....   6·00
DQ63   APR 1972 (No. 4 Pied Wagtail) (9.2.72) ....   6·00
DQ64   JUNE 1972 (No. 5 Kestrel) (12.4.72) ....   6·00
DQ65   AUG 1972 (No. 5 Kestrel) (8.6.72) ....   6·25
DQ66   OCT 1972 (No. 6 Black Grouse) (31.7.72) ....   6·75
DQ67   DEC 1972 (No. 6 Black Grouse) (30.10.72) ....   6·75

DQ68   DEC 1972 "Issue S" (No. 6 Black Grouse) (6.12.72) ....   6·75
DQ69   FEB 1973 (No. 7 Skylark) (29.1.73) ....   6·25
DQ70   APR 1973 (No. 7 Skylark) (2.4.73) ....   5·75
DQ71   JUNE 1973 (No. 8 Oyster-catcher) (8.5.73) ....   6·25
DQ72   AUG 1973 (No. 8 Oyster-catcher) (7.6.73) ....   9·50
DQ72a   As DQ72 but buff cover (10.8.73)* ....   6·75
    Nos. DQ59/72a contain panes showing the perforations omitted
between the label and the binding margin.
    *No. DQ72a was printed with a buff cover because of a shortage of
the original purple-coloured card.

1974 (30 Jan).   *Red cover similar to Type DH52. Make-up as before but
containing panes of 5 × 3p. (1 centre band) (No. X856) with blank
label.*
DQ73   SPRING 1974 ....   5·00

1974 (2 June).   *Red cover similar to Type DT9. Make-up as before.*
DQ74   JUNE 1974 ....   5·00

35p. Booklets

Type DP1
British Coins Series

(Des P Gauld)

1973 (12 Dec)–**74**.   *British Coins Series. Blue cover as Type DP1. Pages
of six stamps: 2 pages of 5 × 3$\frac{1}{2}$p. with one blank label (No. X858Eb).*
DP1   AUTUMN 1973 (No. 1 Cuthred's Penny) ....   3·25
DP2   APR 1974 (No. 1 Cuthred's Penny) (10.4.74) ....   6·50
DP3   JUNE 1974 (No. 2 Silver Groat) (4.7.74) ....   3·75

1974 (23 Oct).   *Blue cover as Type DT9. Make-up as before but with No.
X859.*
DP4   SEPT 1974 ....   3·50

45p. Booklets

1974 (9 Oct–26 Nov).   *British Coins Series continued. Yellow-brown
cover as Type DP1. Pages of six stamps: 2 pages of 5 × 4$\frac{1}{2}$p. (No. X865)
with one blank label.*
DS1   SEPT 1974 (No. 3 Elizabeth Gold Crown) ....   6·00
DS2   DEC 1974 (No. 3 Elizabeth Gold Crown) (1.11.74) ....   6·00
DS2a   As DS2 but orange-brown cover (26.11.74)* ....   14·50
    *No. DS2a was printed with an orange-brown cover because of a
shortage of the original yellow-brown card.

50p. Booklets

Type DT1

(Des Rosalie Southall)

1971 (15 Feb)–72. *British Flowers Series. Turquoise-green cover as Type DT1. Pages of six stamps: 6 × 3p., 4 × 3p. se-tenant horizontally with 2 × 2½p. (side band), 5 × 2½p. (centre band) with one printed label and 5 × ½p. with one printed label (Nos. X841m, X851l, X852l and X855 × 6).*

DT1	FEB 1971 (No. 1 Large Bindweed)	9·00
DT2	MAY 1971 (No. 2 Primrose) (24.3.71)	10·00
DT3	AUG 1971 (No. 3 Honeysuckle) (28.6.71)	10·00
DT4	NOV 1971 (No. 4 Hop) (17.9.71)	11·00
DT5	FEB 1972 (No. 5 Common Violet) (23.12.71)*	11·00
DT6	MAY 1972 (No. 6 Lords-and-Ladies) (13.3.72)	11·00
DT7	AUG 1972 (No. 7 Wood Anemone) (31.5.72)	11·00
DT8	NOV 1972 (No. 8 Deadly Nightshade) (15.9.72)	9·00

Nos. DT4/8 contain panes showing the perforations omitted between the label and the binding margin.

* Although generally released on 24 December, this booklet was put on sale at the London E.C.1 Philatelic Counter and also at one other Philatelic Counter on 23 December.

Type DT9

1973 (19 Jan–June). *Turquoise-green cover as Type DT9.*

DT 9	FEB 1973	9·00
DT10	APR 1973 (26.2.73)	11·00
DT11	MAY 1973 (2.4.73)	11·00
DT12	AUG 1973 (14.6.73)	17·00

1973 (14 Nov)–74. *Moss-green cover similar to Type DT9. Pages of six stamps: 2 pages of 5 × 3½p. with one blank label (No. X858Eb) and 1 page of 5 × 3p. (centre band) and one blank label (No. X856).*

DT13	AUTUMN 1973	8·00
DT14	MAR 1974 (18.2.74)	6·00

85p. Booklet

1974 (13 Nov). *Purple cover similar to Type DT9.*
DW1 Containing 3 pages of 5 × 4½p. (No. X865) with one blank label and 1 page of 5 × 3½p. (No. X859) with one blank label .... 9·00

Sponsored Booklets

Type DX1

(Des J. Wallis)

1972 (24 May). *"The Story of Wedgwood". Full colour pictorial cover, Type DX1 (150 × 72 mm). Containing information and illustrations on interleaving panes and on se-tenant label attached to booklet panes.*
DX1 £1 containing Nos. X841o/p, X851n and X855n booklet panes .... 65·00
Price quoted for No. DX1 is for examples showing the ½p. 1 side band, No. X842, (in pane No. X841p) with full perforations. Examples of the booklet with this ½p. value showing trimmed perforations are priced at £25.

ILLUSTRATIONS. Sponsored booklet covers from No. DX2 are illustrated at one-third linear size *unless otherwise stated.*

Type DX2

(Des J. Wallis)

1980 (16 Apr). *"The Story of Wedgwood". Multicoloured cover, Type DX2 (163 × 97 mm) showing painting "Josiah Wedgwood and his Family" by George Stubbs. Booklet contains text and illustrations on the labels attached to panes and on interleaving pages.*
DX2 £3 containing booklet panes Nos. X849n, X849o, X888l and X895l .... 8·00
No. DX2 is inscribed "January 1980".

Type DX3

(Des B. Dedman)

1982 (19 May). *"Story of Stanley Gibbons". Multicoloured cover, Type DX3 (163 × 97 mm) showing early envelope design on front and stamp album with text on back. Booklet contains text and illustrations on labels attached to panes and on interleaving pages.*

DX3 £4 containing booklet panes Nos. X849p, X899m and X907l/m .... 11·00

No. DX3 is inscribed "February 1982".

Type DX4

(Des B. West)

1983 (14 Sept). *"Story of the Royal Mint". Multicoloured cover, Type DX4 (163 × 97 mm) showing current coins, die and tools. Booklet contains text and illustrations on labels attached to panes and on interleaving pages.*

DX4 £4 containing booklet panes Nos. X899m × 2, X930b and X949l .... 11·00

Type DX5

(Des P. Miles)

1984 (4 Sept). *"The Story of our Christian Heritage". Multicoloured cover, Type DX5 (163 × 97 mm) showing mosaic of Christ from Hinton St. Mary Roman villa. Booklet contains text and illustrations on labels attached to panes and on interleaving pages.*

DX5 £4 containing booklet panes Nos. X886bl, X901m × 2 and X952l .... 32·00

Type DX6

(Des D. Driver)

1985 (8 Jan). *"Story of The Times" (newspaper). Multicoloured cover, Type DX6 (163 × 95 mm) showing "Waiting for The Times" (painting by Haydon). Booklet contains text and illustrations on labels attached to panes and on interleaving pages.*

DX6 £5 containing booklet panes Nos. X864l, X900l, X952l and X952m .... 22·00

Type DX7

(Des Trickett and Webb Ltd)

1986 (18 Mar). *"The Story of British Rail". Multicoloured cover, Type DX7 (162 × 95 mm) showing diesel locomotive. Booklet contains text and illustrations on labels attached to panes and on interleaving pages.*

DX7 £5 containing booklet panes Nos. X896l, X897m, X952l and X952m .... 30·00

Type DX8

(Des Aitken Blakeley Designers)

1987 (3 Mar). *"The Story of P & O". Multicoloured cover, Type DX8 (162 × 95 mm) showing the "William Fawcett". Booklet contains text and illustrations on labels attached to panes and on interleaving pages.*

DX8 £5 containing booklet panes Nos. X847m, X900l, X900m and X955l .... 20·00

Type DX9

(Des The Partners)

1988 (9 Feb). *"The Story of the Financial Times" (newspaper). Multicoloured cover, Type DX9 (162 × 97 mm). Booklet contains text and illustrations on labels attached to the panes and on interleaving pages.*

DX9   £5 containing booklet panes Nos. X1005l, X1006l, X1009l and X1009m .... 30·00

(Des Trickett and Webb Ltd)

1991 (19 Mar). *"Alias Agatha Christie". Multicoloured cover, Type DX12 (162 × 97 mm). Booklet contains text and illustrations on labels attached to the panes and on interleaving pages.*

DX12   £6 containing booklet panes Nos. X1008l × 2, X1016l and X1016m .... 20·00

Type DX10

Type DX13

(Des Tayburn)

1989 (21 Mar). *"The Scots Connection". Multicoloured cover, Type DX10 (162 × 97 mm). Booklet contains text and illustrations on labels attached to the panes and on interleaving pages.*

DX10   £5 containing booklet panes Nos. S54l, S55l, S62l and S62m .... 24·00

(Des G. Evernden and J. Gibbs)

1992 (25 Feb). *"Cymru–Wales". Multicoloured cover, Type DX13 (162 × 97 mm). Booklet contains text and illustrations on labels attached to the panes and on interleaving pages.*

DX13   £6 Containing booklet panes Nos. 1591a, W48a, W49a and W59a. .... 20·00

Type DX11

Type DX14

(Des D. Driver)

1990 (20 Mar). *"London Life". Multicoloured cover, Type DX11 (162 × 97 mm). Booklet contains text and illustrations on labels attached to the panes and on interleaving pages.*

DX11   £5 containing booklet panes Nos. X906m, 1469n × 2 and 1493a .... 30·00

(Des The Partners)

1992 (27 Oct). *Birth Centenary of J. R. R. Tolkien (author). Multicoloured cover, Type DX14 (162 × 97 mm). Booklet contains text and illustrations on labels attached to the panes and on interleaving pages.*

DX14   £6 containing booklet panes Nos. X1011l, X1012l and X1017l × 2 .... 20·00

Type DX12

Type DX15

(Des The Partners)

1993 (10 Aug). *"The Story of Beatrix Potter". Multicoloured cover, Type DX15 (162 × 97 mm). Booklet contains text and illustrations on labels attached to the panes and on interleaving pages.*

DX15   £5.64, containing booklet panes Nos. X1012m, 1451al, 1649a and NI48l .... 24·00

Although inscribed "£6.00" No. DX15 was sold at the face value of its contents, £5.64.

Type DX16

(Des Carroll, Dempsey and Thirkell Ltd)

1994 (26 July). *"Northern Ireland". Multicoloured cover, Type DX16 (162 × 97 mm). Booklet contains text and illustrations on labels attached to the panes and on interleaving pages.*

DX16   £6.04, containing booklet panes Nos. Y1748l, 1812a and NI70a/b, together with a 35p. postal stationery air card   28·00

Type DX17

(Des The Partners)

1995 (25 Apr). *Centenary of the National Trust. Multicoloured cover, Type DX17 (162 × 97 mm). Booklet contains text and illustrations on labels attached to the panes and on interleaving pages.*

DX17   £6 containing booklet panes Nos. Y1749l, Y1750l, 1869a and NI70d .... 28·00

Type DX18

(Des Why Not Associates)

1996 (14 May). *European Football Championship. Multicoloured cover, Type DX18 (162 × 97 mm). Booklet contains text and illustrations on labels attached to the panes and on interleaving pages.*

DX18   £6.48, containing booklet panes Nos. Y1752l, 1925a, 1926a and 1927a .... 18·00

Type DX19

(Des H. Brown)

1997 (23 Sept). *75th Anniv of the B.B.C. Multicoloured cover, Type DX19 (162 × 97 mm). Booklet contains text and illustrations on labels attached to the panes and on interleaving pages.*

DX19   £6.15, containing booklet panes Nos. Y1679l, 1940ab, 1664bl and NI81al .... 20·00

Type DX20

(Des Dew Gibbons Design Group)

1998 (10 Mar). *The Wildings Definitives. Black and gold cover, Type DX20 (162 × 96 mm). Booklet contains text and illustrations on labels attached to the panes and on interleaving pages.*

DX20   £7.49, containing booklet panes Nos. 2031b/c and 2032a/b .... 26·00

Type DX21

(Des Roundel Design Group)

1998 (13 Oct). *"Breaking Barriers". British Speed Record Holders. Multicoloured cover, Type* DX21 *(161 × 96 mm). Booklet contains text and illustrations on labels attached to the panes and on interleaving pages.*
DX21 £6.16, containing booklet panes Nos. 1663bl, Y1674al,
2059ac and Nl80al .... 30·00

(Des Dew Gibbons Design Group)

1999 (16 Feb). *"Profile on Print". Multicoloured cover as Type* DX20 *(162 × 96 mm). Booklet contains text and illustrations on labels attached to the panes and on interleaving pages.*
DX22 £7.54, containing booklet panes Nos. 1664al, 1666n and
2077l/9l .... 32·00

Type DX23

(Des Silk Pearce)

1999 (21 Sept). *"World Changers". Multicoloured cover as Type* DX23 *(163 × 96 mm). Booklet contains text and illustrations on labels attached to the panes and on interleaving pages.*
DX23 £6.99, containing booklet panes Nos. Y1667n, 2072ab,
2080a, 2103ba and 2104ab .... 32·00

(Des Dew Gibbons Design Group)

2000 (15 Feb). *"Special by Design". Multicoloured cover as Type* DX20 *(162 × 96 mm). Booklet contains text and illustrations on labels attached to the panes and on interleaving pages.*
DX24 £7.50, containing booklet panes Nos. Y1676l, 2124dl,
2133l and Nl88al .... 40·00

Type DX25

(Des J. Gibbs)

2000 (4 Aug). *Queen Elizabeth the Queen Mother's 100th Birthday. Brownish grey and grey cover as Type* DX25 *(162 × 96 mm). Booklet contains text and illustrations on labels attached to the panes and on interleaving pages.*
DX25 £7.03, containing booklet panes Nos. 2124bm, 2160a,
MS2161a and S94a .... 26·00

Type DX26

(Des Roundel)

2000 (18 Sept). *A Treasury of Trees. Slate-green and bright green cover as Type* DX26 *(162 × 95 mm). Booklet contains text and illustrations on panes and interleaving pages.*
DX26 £7 containing booklet panes Nos. 2155a, 2156a, 2158a,
2159a and W83al .... 25·00

Type DX27

(Des D. Davis)

2001 (22 Oct). *"Unseen and Unheard". Centenary of Royal Navy Submarine Service. Black, greenish yellow, new blue and red cover as Type* DX27 *(162 × 97 mm). Booklet contains text and illustrations on labels attached to the panes and on interleaving pages.*
DX27 £6.76, containing booklet panes Nos. 2202ab, 2203ab,
MS2206 and S95a .... 32·00

Type DX28

(Des GBH)

2002 (6 Feb). *"A Gracious Accession". Golden Jubilee of Queen Elizabeth II. Multicoloured cover as Type* DX28 *(161 × 96 mm). Booklet contains text and illustrations on labels attached to the panes and interleaving pages.*
DX28 £7.29, containing booklet panes Nos. 1663an, 2253b/4b
and 2258b .... 25·00

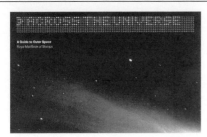

Type DX29

(Des CDT Design)

2002 (24 Sept). *"Across the Universe". Multicoloured cover as Type DX29 (164 × 95 mm). Booklet contains text and illustrations on labels attached to the panes and interleaving pages. Stitched.*
DX29   £6.83, containing booklet panes Nos. 1664bm, 2126ac, **MS**2315a and EN1b .... 20·00

Type DX30

(Des CDT Design)

2003 (25 Feb). *"Microcosmos". 50th Anniv of Discovery of DNA. Multicoloured cover as Type DX30 (164 × 95 mm). Booklet contains text and illustrations on labels attached to the panes and interleaving pages. Stitched.*
DX30   £6.99, containing booklet panes Nos. 1664bn, 2343a, 2345a and NI89a .... 20·00

Type DX31

(Des GBH)

2003 (2 June). *"A Perfect Coronation". 50th Anniv of Coronation. Multicoloured cover as Type DX31 (161 × 96 mm). Booklet contains text and illustrations on labels attached to the panes and on interleaving pages.*
DX31   £7.46, containing booklet panes Nos. 1663ao, 2368b/9b and 2378a .... 45·00

Type DX32

2004 (16 Mar). *"Letters by Night A Tribute to the Travelling Post Office". Multicoloured cover as Type DX32 (164 × 95 mm). Booklet contains text and illustrations on labels attached to the panes and interleaving pages. Stitched.*
DX32   £7.44, containing booklet panes Nos. 1664bo, 2392a, 2418a and S94b .... 11·00

B. Folded Booklets.

NOTE: All panes are attached to the covers by the selvedge. Inscribed dates are those shown with the printer's imprint.
Illustrations for 10p., 50p., £1 and £2 booklets are $\frac{3}{4}$ size; others are $\frac{2}{3}$ size

10p. Booklets

Type FA1

1976 (10 Mar)–**77.**   Cover as Type FA1 printed in dull rose on very pale lavender. Containing booklet pane No. X841r.
FA1	NOV 1975	1·10
FA2	MAR 1976 (9.6.76)	1·20
FA3	JUNE 1977 (13.6.77)	80

Type FA4

(Des N. Battershill)

1978 (8 Feb)–**79.**   Farm Buildings Series. Bistre-brown and turquoise-blue covers as Type FA4, containing booklet pane No. X843m.
FA4	Design No. 1, Oast Houses	70
FA5	Design No. 2, Buildings in Ulster (3.5.78)	80
FA6	Design No. 3, Buildings in Yorkshire (9.8.78)	70
FA7	Design No. 4, Buildings in Wales (25.10.78)	70
FA8	Design No. 5, Buildings in Scotland (10.1.79)	70
FA9	Design No. 6, Buildings in Sussex (4.4.79)	70

Nos. FA4/5 are inscribed "January 1978", FA6 "July 1978", FA7 "October 1978", FA8 "December 1978" and FA9 "March 1979".

Type FA10

(Des Hamper and Purssell)

1979 (17 Oct)–**80.**   "London 1980" International Stamp Exhibition. Red and blue cover as Type FA10 showing Post Office exhibition stand and containing No. X845l.
FA10	Inscr "August 1979"	60
FA11	Inscr "January 1980" (12.1.80)	70

50p. Booklets

All booklets were sold at the cover price of 50p. although some contain stamps to a greater value.

Type FB1

1977 (26 Jan).   Cover as Type FB1 printed in maroon and pale blue.
FB1A	Containing booklet pane X841s	2·40
FB1B	Containing booklet pane X841sa	2·40

1977 (13 June).   Cover as Type FB1. Printed in chestnut and stone.
FB2A	Containing booklet pane X844n	5·00
FB2B	Containing booklet pane X844na	3·00

Type FB3

(Des J. Ireland)

1978 (8 Feb)–**79.**   Commercial Vehicles Series. Olive-yellow and grey covers as Type FB3. A. Containing booklet pane No. X844n. B. Containing booklet pane No. X844na.
		A	B
FB3	Design No. 1, Clement Talbot van	5·00	3·25
FB4	Design No. 2, Austin taxi (3.5.78)	5·00	3·00
FB5	Design No. 3, Morris Royal Mail van (9.8.78)	5·00	3·00
FB6	Design No. 4, Guy Electric dustcart (25.10.78)	6·50	3·25
FB7	Design No. 5, Albion van (10.1.79)	6·50	6·25
FB8	Design No. 6, Leyland fire engine (4.4.79)	5·25	3·50

Nos. FB3/4 are inscribed "January 1978", FB5 "July 1978", FB6 "October 1978", FB7 "December 1978" and FB8 "March 1979".

1979 (28 Aug).   Contents changed. A. Containing booklet pane No. X849l. B. Containing booklet pane No. X849la.
		A	B
FB9	Design No. 6, Leyland fire engine	2·75	2·75

Type FB10

(Des B. Smith)

1979 (3 Oct)–**81**.   *Veteran Cars Series. Orange-red and reddish lilac covers as Type FB10. A. Containing booklet pane No. X849l. B. Containing booklet pane No. X849la.*

		A	B
FB10	Design No. 1, 1907 Rolls-Royce Silver Ghost	2·50	2·50

No. FB10 is inscribed "August 1979".

Contents changed. A. Containing booklet pane No. X849m. B. Containing booklet pane No. X849ma.

		A	B
FB11	Design No. 2, 1908 Grand Prix Austin (4.2.80)	2·75	2·75
FB12	Design No. 3, 1903–5 Vauxhall (25.6.80)	2·75	2·75
FB13	Design No. 4, 1897–1900 Daimler (24.9.80)	2·50	2·50

No. FB11 is inscribed "January 1980", No. FB12 "May 1980" and No. FB13 "July 1980".

Contents changed. A. Containing No. X841t. B. Containing No. X841ta.

		A	B
FB14	Design No. 5, 1896 Lanchester (26.1.81)	2·50	2·50
FB15	Design No. 6, 1913 Bull-nose Morris (18.3.81) ...	3·00	3·00

Nos. FB14/15 are inscribed "January 1981".

Type FB16

(Des R. Downer)

1981 (6 May)–**82**.   *Follies Series. Brown and orange-brown covers as Type FB16. A. Containing No. X841t. B. Containing No. X841ta.*

		A	B
FB16	Design No. 1, Mugdock Castle, Stirlingshire	2·50	2·50

No. FB16 is inscribed "January 1981".

Contents changed. A. Containing No. X854l. B. Containing No. X854la.

		A	B
FB17	Design No. 1, Mugdock Castle, Stirlingshire (26.8.81)	7·25	12·00
FB18	Design No. 2, Mow Cop Castle, Cheshire-Staffs border (30.9.81)	7·00	9·00

Nos. FB17/18 are inscribed "January 1981".

Contents changed. A. Containing No. X841u. B. Containing No. X841ua.

		A	B
FB19	Design No. 3, Paxton's Tower, Llanarthney, Dyfed (1.2.82)	3·00	3·00
FB20	Design No. 4, Temple of the Winds, Mount Stewart, Northern Ireland (6.5.82)	3·00	3·00
FB21	Design No. 5, Temple of the Sun, Stourhead, Wilts (11.8.82)	3·00	3·00
FB22	Design No. 6, Water Garden, Cliveden, Bucks (6.10.82)	3·00	3·00

Nos. FB19/22 are inscribed "February 1982".

Type FB23

(Des H. Titcombe)

1983 (16 Feb–26 Oct).   *Rare Farm Animals Series. Bright green and black covers as Type FB23. A. Containing booklet pane No. X841u. B. Containing booklet pane No. X841ua.*

		A	B
FB23	Design No. 1, Bagot Goat	3·25	3·25

Contents changed. Containing No. X845n.

FB24	Design No. 2, Gloucester Old Spot Pig (5.4.83)	5·25
	b. Corrected rate	15·00
FB25	Design No. 3, Toulouse Goose (27.7.83)	5·00
FB26	Design No. 4, Orkney Sheep (26.10.83)	5·00

No. FB23 is inscribed "February 1982" and Nos. FB24/6 "April 1983". The corrected rate reads, "36p. for 200g" instead of "37p. for 200g".

Type FB27

(Des P. Morter)

1984 (3 Sept)–**85**.   *Orchids Series. Yellow-green and lilac covers as Type FB27. Containing booklet pane No. X845p.*

FB27	Design No. 1, *Dendrobium nobile* and *Miltonia* hybrid .	4·00
FB28	Design No. 2, *Cypripedium calceolus* and *Ophrys apifera* (15.1.85)	4·00
FB29	Design No. 3, *Bifrenaria* and *Vanda tricolor* (23.4.85)	4·00
FB30	Design No. 4, *Cymbidium* and *Arpophyllum* (23.7.85) ..	4·00

Nos. FB27/30 are inscribed "September 1984".

Type FB31

(Des M. Thierens Design)

1985 (4 Nov). *Cover as Type* FB31 *printed in black and bright scarlet. Containing booklet pane No. X909l.*
FB31   Pillar box design .... 4·75
No. FB31 is inscribed "November 1985".

Type FB32

(Des P. Morter)

1986 (20 May–12 Aug). *Pond Life Series. Dull blue and emerald covers as Type* FB32. *Containing booklet pane No. X909l.*
FB32   Design No. 1, Emperor Dragonfly, Four-spotted Libellula
          and Yellow Flag .... 3·00
FB33   Design No. 2. Common Frog, Fennel-leaved Pondweed
          and Long-stalked Pondweed (29.7.86) .... 4·00
          a. Containing booklet pane No. X909Ela (12.8.86) ... 3·75
Nos. FB32/33a are inscribed "November 1985".

Type FB34

(Des N. Battershill)

1986 (29 July). *Roman Britain Series. Brown-ochre and Indian red cover as Type* FB34. *Containing booklet pane No. X845q.*
FB34   Design No. 1, Hadrian's Wall .... 11·00
No. FB34 is inscribed "November 1985".

1986 (20 Oct)–**87**. *Pond Life Series continued. Dull blue and emerald covers as Type* FB32. *Containing booklet pane No. X845s.*
FB35   Design No. 3, Moorhen and Little Grebe .... 4·50
FB36   Design No. 4, Giant Pond and Great Ramshorn Snails
          (27.1.87) .... 4·50
No. FB36 is inscribed "October 1986".

1986 (20 Oct)–**87**. *Roman Britain Series continued. Brown-ochre and Indian red covers as Type* FB34. *Containing booklet pane No. X847l.*
FB37   Design No. 2, Roman Theatre of Verulamium, St. Albans   2·50
FB38   Design No. 3, Portchester Castle, Hampshire (27.1.87) .. 2·50
No. FB38 is inscribed "October 1986".

Type FB39

(Des Patricia Howes)

1987 (14 Apr)–**88**. *Bicentenary of Marylebone Cricket Club Series. Brown and dull ultramarine covers as Type* FB39. *Containing booklet pane No. X847l.*
FB39   Design No. 1, Father Time weather vane .... 3·00
FB40   Design No. 2, Ashes urn and embroidered velvet bag
          (14.7.87) .... 3·00
FB41   Design No. 3, Lord's Pavilion and wrought iron decora-
          tion on roof (29.9.87) .... 3·00
FB42   Design No. 4, England team badge and new stand at
          Lord's (26.1.88) .... 3·00
Nos. FB39/42 are inscribed "October 1986".

Type FB43

(Des G. Evernden)

1987 (14 Apr)–**88**. *Botanical Gardens Series. Covers as Type* FB43. *Containing booklet panes No. X845s (FB43/4) or X845sa (FB45/6).*
FB43   Design No. 1 (cover in ultramarine and rose-red),
          Rhododendron "Elizabeth", Bodnant .... 5·25
FB44   Design No. 2 (cover in deep ultramarine and cobalt),
          Gentiana sino-ornata, Edinburgh (14.7.87) .... 5·00
FB45   Design No. 3 (cover in dull ultramarine and orange-
          yellow), Lilium auratum and "Mount Stuart" (incorrect
          inscr) (29.9.87) .... 3·50
          a. With corrected spelling "Mount Stewart"
          (30.10.87) .... 3·50
FB46   Design No. 4 (cover in dull ultramarine and yellow-
          orange), Strelitzia reginae, Kew (26.1.88) .... 3·50
Nos. FB43/6 are inscribed "October 1986".
The panes from Nos. FB45/6 have imperforate vertical sides.

Type FB47

1988 (12 Apr–5 July). *London Zoo. Children's Drawings Series. Covers as Type FB47.*

FB47 Pigs design (cover in black and rose) containing booklet
       pane No. X847l .... 3·50
FB48 Birds design (cover in black and yellow) containing
       booklet pane No. X845sa .... 3·50
FB49 Elephants design (cover in black and grey) containing
       booklet pane No. X847l (5.7.88) .... 3·50
Nos. FB47/9 are inscribed "October 1986". The pane from No. FB48 has imperforate vertical sides.

Type FB50

(Des P. Morter)

1988 (5 July). *Marine Life Series. Blue and orange-brown cover as Type FB50. Containing booklet pane No. X845sa.*

FB50 Design No. 1, Parasitic Anemone on Common Whelk
       Shell and Umbrella Jellyfish .... 3·50
No. FB50 is inscribed "October 1986" and has the vertical sides of the pane imperforate.

Type FB51

(Des Lynda Gray)

1988 (5 Sept)–**89**. *Gilbert and Sullivan Operas Series. Black and red covers as Type FB51. Containing booklet pane No. X904l.*

FB51 Design No. 1, *The Yeomen of the Guard* .... 7·25
FB52 Design No. 2, *The Pirates of Penzance* (24.1.89) .... 7·25
FB53 Design No. 3, *The Mikado* (25.4.89) .... 7·25

1989 (18 July). *Marine Life Series continued. Blue and orange-brown cover as Type FB50. Containing booklet pane No. X904l.*

FB54 Design No. 2, Common Hermit Crab, Bladder Wrack and
       Laver Spire Shell .... 5·25
For Design No. 3, see £1 Booklet No. FH17.

Type FB55

(Des P. Hutton)

1989 (2 Oct)–**90**. *Aircraft Series. Turquoise-green and light brown covers as Type FB55. Containing booklet pane No. X906l.*

FB55 Design No. 1, HP42, Armstrong Whitworth Atalanta and
       De Havilland Dragon Rapide .... 12·00
No. FB55 was incorrectly inscribed "Atlanta".

As before, but containing Penny Black Anniversary booklet pane No. 1468l.

FB56 Design No. 2, Vickers Viscount 806 and De Havilland
       Comet 4 (30.1.90) .... 9·00

1990 (4 Sept)–**91**. *Aircraft Series continued. Turquoise-green and light brown covers as Type FB55. Containing booklet pane No. X911l.*

FB57 Design No. 3, BAC 1-11 and VC10 .... 5·50
FB58 Design No. 4, BAe ATP, BAe 146 and Aérospatiale–BAC
       Concorde (25.6.91) .... 5·50

Type FB59

(Des A. Drummond)

1991 (10 Sept)–**92**. *Archaeology Series. Covers as Type FB59. Containing booklet pane No. X925m.*

FB59 Design No. 1 (cover in bright blue and lake-brown), Sir
       Arthur Evans at Knossos, Crete .... 3·00
       a. Corrected rate (10.91) .... 3·25
FB60 Design No. 2 (cover in bright blue and yellow), Howard
       Carter in the Tomb of Tutankhamen (21.1.92) .... 3·00
FB61 Design No. 3 (cover in bright blue and yellow), Sir
       Austen Layard at Assyrian site (28.4.92) .... 2·40
FB62 Design No. 4 (cover in new blue and yellow), Sir Flinders
       Petrie surveying the Pyramids and temples of Giza
       (28.7.92) .... 3·00
On the inside front cover of No. FB59 the inland letter rates are shown as 1st class 24, 35, 43, 51p. and 2nd class 18, 28, 33, 39p. These were corrected on No. FB59a to read: 1st class 24, 36, 45, 54p. and 2nd class 18, 28, 34, 41p.

Type FB63

(Des J. Matthews)

1992 (22 Sept). *1000th Anniv of Appointment of Sheriffs. Dull blue and scarlet cover as Type* FB63. *Containing booklet pane No.* X925m.
FB63   Design showing Crest, with Helm and Mantling, and
      Badge of The Shrievalty Association .... 2·00

Type FB64

(Des M. Newton)

1993 (9 Feb–6 July). *Postal History Series. Covers as Type* FB64.
Containing booklet pane No. X925m.
FB64   Design No. 1 (cover in grey-green and grey-black),
      Airmail postmarks .... 2·50
FB65   Design No. 2 (cover in dull orange and black), Ship mail
      postmarks (6.4.93) .... 2·50
FB66   Design No. 3 (cover in blue and grey-black), Registered
      mail postmarks (6.7.93) .... 2·50

1993 (1 Nov). *Postal History Series continued. Rose-red and grey-black cover as Type* FB64 *containing booklet pane No.* Y1681l.
FB67   Design No. 4, "Paid" postmarks .... 2·50

Type FB68

(Des A. Davidson)

1994 (25 Jan–6 Sept). *Coaching Inns Series. Covers as Type* FB68.
Containing booklet pane No. Y1681l.
FB68   Design No. 1 (cover in myrtle-green and pale myrtle-
      green), "Swan with Two Necks" .... 2·50
FB69   Design No. 2 (cover in sepia and buff), "Bull and Mouth"
      (26.4.94) .... 2·50
FB70   Design No. 3 (cover in reddish brown and cinnamon),
      "Golden Cross" (6.6.94) .... 2·50
FB71   Design No. 4 (cover in black and slate-blue), "Pheasant
      Inn", Wiltshire (6.9.94) .... 2·50

Type FB72

(Des D. Davis)

1995 (7 Feb–4 Apr). *Sea Charts Series. Rosine and black covers as Type* FB72, *containing booklet pane No.* Y1681l.
FB72   Design No. 1, John o' Groats, 1800 .... 2·50
FB73   Design No. 2, Land's End, 1808 (4.4.95) .... 2·50

1995 (6 June–4 Sept). *Sea Charts Series continued. Rosine and black covers as Type* FB72, *containing booklet pane No.* Y1682l.
FB74   Design No. 3, St. David's Head, 1812 .... 3·25
FB75   Design No. 4, Giant's Causeway, 1828 (4.9.95) .... 3·25

65p. Booklet

1976 (14 July). *Cover as Type* FB1, *but larger* (90 × 49 mm). *Printed in turquoise-blue and pale buff.* A. *Selvedge at left.* B. *Selvedge at right.*
                                                                A   B
FC1   Containing ten 6½p. (No. X872) .... 16·00   9·00

70p. Booklets

1977 (13 June). *Cover as Type* FB1, *but larger* (90 × 49 mm). *Printed in purple-brown and dull rose.* A. *Selvedge at left.* B. *Selvedge at right.*
                                                                A   B
FD1   Containing ten 7p. (No. X875) .... 6·00   6·00

Type FD2

(Des E. Stemp)

1978 (8 Feb)–**79**.   *Country Crafts Series. Grey-green and red-brown covers as Type FD2 (90 × 49 mm). Containing ten 7p. (No. X875). A. Selvedge at left. B. Selvedge at right.*

		A	B
FD2	Design No. 1, Horse-shoeing	36·00	5·00
FD3	Design No. 2, Thatching (3.5.78)	£200	5·00
FD4	Design No. 3, Dry-stone-walling (9.8.78)	£250	5·00
FD5	Design No. 4, Wheel-making (25.10.78)	9·50	6·75
FD6	Design No. 5, Wattle fence-making (10.1.79)	20·00	7·00

Nos. FD2/3 are inscribed "January 1978", FD4 "July 1978", FD5 "October 1978" and FD6 "December 1978".

Type FD7

(Des F. Wegner)

1979 (5 Feb).   *Official opening of Derby Mechanised Letter Office. Pale yellow-green and lilac cover as Type FD7 (90 × 49 mm). Containing ten 7p. (No. X875). A. Selvedge at left. B. Selvedge at right.*

		A	B
FD7	Kedleston Hall	9·00	9·00

No. FD7 is inscribed "December 1978".
On sale only in the Derby Head Post Office area to promote postcode publicity and also at the Philatelic Bureau and philatelic sales counters.

1979 (4 Apr).   *Country Crafts Series continued. Grey-green and red-brown covers as Type FD2 (90 × 49 mm). A. Selvedge at left. B. Selvedge at right.*

		A	B
FD8	Design No. 6, Basket-making	8·75	5·00

No. FD8 is inscribed "March 1979".

80p. Booklet

Type FE1

(Des P. Hutton)

1979 (3 Oct).   *Military Aircraft Series. Blue and grey cover as Type FE1 (90 × 49 mm). Containing ten 8p. (No. X879) attached by the selvedge. A. Selvedge at left. B. Selvedge at right.*

		A	B
FE1	Design No. 1, BE2B, 1914, & Vickers Gun Bus, 1915	4·00	4·00

No. FE1 is inscribed "August 1979".

85p. Booklet

1976 (14 July).   *Cover as Type FB1 but larger (90 × 49 mm). Printed in light yellow-olive and brownish grey. A. Selvedge at left. B. Selvedge at right.*

		A	B
FF1	Containing ten 8½p. (No. X881)	9·00	10·00

90p. Booklets

1977 (13 June).   *Cover as Type FB1, but larger (90 × 49 mm). Printed in deep grey-blue and cobalt. A. Selvedge at left. B. Selvedge at right.*

		A	B
FG1	Containing ten 9p. (No. X883)	6·00	8·75

Type FG2

(Des R. Maddox)

1978 (8 Feb)–**79**.   *British Canals Series. Yellow-olive and new blue covers as Type FG2 (90 × 49 mm). Containing ten 9p. (No. X883). A. Selvedge at left. B. Selvedge at right.*

		A	B
FG2	Design No. 1, Grand Union	25·00	7·00
FG3	Design No. 2, Llangollen (3.5.78)	5·00	£425
FG4	Design No. 3, Kennet & Avon (9.8.78)	15·00	11·00
FG5	Design No. 4, Caledonian (25.10.78)	7·50	6·00
FG6	Design No. 5, Regents (10.1.79)	17·50	10·00

Nos. FG2/3 are inscribed "January 1978", FG4 "July 1978", FG5 "October 1978" and FG6 "December 1978".

(Des F. Wegner)

1979 (5 Feb).   *Official Opening of Derby Mechanised Letter Office. Violet-blue and rose cover as Type FD7 (90 × 49 mm). Containing ten 9p. (No. X883). A. Selvedge at left. B. Selvedge at right.*

		A	B
FG7	Tramway Museum, Crich	11·00	11·00

No. FG7 is inscribed "December 1978".
On sale only in the Derby Head Post Office area to promote postcode publicity and also at the Philatelic Bureau and philatelic sales counters.

1979 (4 Apr).   *British Canals Series continued. Yellow-olive and new blue cover as Type FG2. A. Selvedge at left. B. Selvedge at right.*

		A	B
FG8	Design No. 6, Leeds & Liverpool	5·00	5·00

No. FG8 is inscribed "March 1979".

For full information on all future British issues, collectors should write to the British Post Office Philatelic Bureau, 21 South Gyle Crescent, Edinburgh EH12 9PB

£1 Booklets

All booklets were sold at the cover price of £1 although some contain stamps to a greater value

Type FH1

(Des N. Battershill)

1979 (3 Oct). *Industrial Archaeology Series. Red and green cover as Type FH1 (90 × 49 mm). Containing ten 10p. (No. X887).* A. *Selvedge at left.* B. *Selvedge at right.*

		A	B
FH1	Design No. 1, Ironbridge, Telford, Salop	4·50	4·50

No. FH1 is inscribed "August 1979".

1980 (4 Feb–24 Sept). *Military Aircraft Series continued. Blue and grey covers as Type FE1 (90 × 49 mm). Containing ten 10p. (No. X888).* A. *Selvedge at left.* B. *Selvedge at right.*

		A	B
FH2	Design No. 2, Sopwith Camel & Vickers Vimy ..	4·50	4·50
FH3	Design No. 3, Hawker Hart* & Handley Page Heyford (25.6.80)	6·00	6·00
FH4	Design No. 4, Hurricane & Wellington (24.9.80) ..	4·50	4·50

No FH2 is inscribed "January 1980", No. FH3 "May 1980" and No. FH4 "July 1980".

*On the booklet cover the aircraft is wrongly identified as a Hawker Fury.

Type FH5

(Des M. Newton and S. Paine)

1986 (29 July)–**87**. *Musical Instruments Series. Scarlet and black covers as Type FH5. Containing six 17p. (X952).*

FH5	Design No 1, Violin	5·00

No. FH5 is inscribed "November 1985".

Contents changed. Containing No. X901n.

FH6	Design No. 2, French horn (20.10.86)	5·00
FH7	Design No. 3, Bass clarinet (27.1.87)	5·00

No. FH7 is inscribed "October 1986".

Type FH8

(Des A. Davidson)

1987 (14 Apr)–**88**. *Sherlock Holmes Series. Bright scarlet and grey-black covers as Type FH8. Containing booklet pane No. X901n (FH8/9) or X901na (FH10/11).*

FH 8	Design No. 1, *A Study in Scarlet*	5·00
FH 9	Design No. 2, *The Hound of the Baskervilles* (14.7.87) ...	5·00
FH10	Design No. 3, *The Adventure of the Speckled Band* (29.9.87)	5·00
FH11	Design No. 4, *The Final Problem* (26.1.88)	5·00

Nos. FH8/11 are inscribed "October 1986".
The panes from Nos. FH10/11 have imperforate vertical sides.

1988 (12 Apr). *London Zoo. Children's Drawings Series. Cover as Type FB47 in black and brown. Containing booklet pane No. X901na.*

FH12	Bears design	5·00

No. FH12 is inscribed "October 1986" and has the vertical sides of the pane imperforate.

Type FH13

(Des Liz Moyes)

1988 (5 July)–**89**. *Charles Dickens Series. Orange-red and maroon covers as Type FH13.*

FH13	Designs No. 1, *Oliver Twist*, containing booklet pane No. X901na	6·50
FH14	Design No. 2, *Nicholas Nickleby*, containing booklet pane No. X904m (5.9.88)	6·50
FH15	Design No. 3, *David Copperfield*, containing booklet pane No. X904m (24.1.89)	6·50
FH16	Design No. 4, *Great Expectations*, containing booklet pane No. X1051l (25.4.89)	9·50

No. FH13 is inscribed "October 1986" and No. FH16 "September 1988", Nos. FH13/16 have the vertical sides of the pane imperforate.

1989 (18 July). *Marine Life Series continued. Cover as Type FB50 in turquoise-green and scarlet. Containing booklet pane No. X904m.*

FH17	Design No. 3, Edible Sea Urchin, Common Starfish and Common Shore Crab	6·00

No. FH17 has the vertical edges of the pane imperforate.

Type FH18

(Des J. Sancha)

1989 (2 Oct)–**90**. *Mills Series. Grey-black and grey-green matt card cover as Type FH18.*
FH18 Design No. 1, Wicken Fen, Ely containing booklet pane
No. X960I .... 7·00

As Type FH18 but glossy card cover containing Penny Black Anniversary booklet pane No. 1476I printed in litho by Walsall.
FH19 Design No. 1 (cover in bottle-green and pale green),
Wicken Fen, Ely (30.1.90) .... 9·50
No. FH19 was an experimental printing to test a new cover material. This appears glossy when compared with Nos. FH18 and FH20.

As Type FH18 but changed to matt card cover containing Penny Black Anniversary booklet pane No. 1469I printed in photo by Harrison.
FH20 Design No. 2 (cover in grey-black and bright green),
Click Mill, Dounby, Orkney (30.1.90) .... 7·50

1990 (4 Sept)–**91**. *Mills Series continued. Covers as Type FH18. Containing booklet pane No. X911m.*
FH21 Design No. 3, (cover printed in light blue and buff) Jack
and Jill Mills, Clayton, Sussex .... 5·00
FH22 Design No. 4, (cover printed in dull blue and bright
yellow-green). Howell Mill, Llanddeusant, Anglesey
(25.6.91) .... 5·00
Nos. FH18/22 have the vertical edges of the pane imperforate.

Type FH23

(Des J. Gibbs)

1991 (10 Sept)–**92**. *150th Anniv of Punch Magazine. Magenta and grey-black covers as Type FH23 containing booklet pane No. X927I.*
FH23 Design No. 1, Illustrations by Richard Doyle and
Hoffnung .... 3·50
   a. Corrected rate (10.91) .... 3·50
FH24 Design No. 2, Illustrations by Sir John Tenniel and Eric
Burgin (21.1.92) .... 3·50
FH25 Design No. 3, Illustrations by Sir John Tenniel and Anton
(28.4.92) .... 3·50
FH26 Design No. 4, Illustrations by Sir John Tenniel and
Hewison (28.7.92) .... 3·50
Nos. FH23/6 have the vertical edges of the pane imperforate.
No. FH23a has corrected letter rates as No. FB59a.

(Des J. Matthews)

1992 (22 Sept).   *1000th Anniv of Appointment of Sheriffs. Scarlet and dull blue cover as Type FB63 containing booklet pane No. X927I.*
FH27 Design as Type FB63 but elements in reverse order ... 3·50
No. FH27 has the vertical edges of the pane imperforate.

Type FH28

(Des J. Lawrence)

1993 (9 Feb–6 July).   *Educational Institutions Series. Covers as Type FH28 containing booklet pane No. X1050I printed in litho by Walsall.*
FH28 Design No. 1 (cover in lake-brown and light blue),
University of Wales .... 7·25
FH29 Design No. 2 (cover in deep dull green and lemon), St.
Hilda's College, Oxford (6.4.93) .... 7·25
FH30 Design No. 3 (cover in purple-brown and flesh),
Marlborough College, Wiltshire (6.7.93) .... 7·25

1993 (1 Nov).   *Educational Institutions Series continued. Deep bluish green and lilac cover as Type FH28 containing four 25p. (No. Y1752) printed in litho by Walsall.*
FH31 Design No. 4, Free Church of Scotland College,
Edinburgh .... 7·00

Type FH32

(Des H. Brockway)

1994 (25 Jan). *20th-century Prime Ministers Series. Brown and pale brown cover as Type FH32 containing four 25p. (No. Y1752) printed in litho by Walsall.*
FH32 Design No. 1, Herbert Asquith .... 3·00

(Des H. Brockway)

1994 (26 Apr–6 Sept).   *20th-century Prime Ministers Series continued. Covers as Type FH32. Containing four 25p. (No. Y1681) printed in photo by Harrison.*
FH33 Design No. 2, (cover in sepia and buff) David Lloyd-
George .... 3·00
FH34 Design No. 3 (cover in greenish blue and pale blue),
Winston Churchill (6.6.94) .... 3·00
FH35 Design No. 4 (cover in black and yellow-olive), Clement
Attlee (6.9.94) .... 3·00

Type FH36

(Des L. Thomas)

1995 (7 Feb–4 Apr). *50th Anniv of End of Second World War. Covers as Type* FH36 *containing four 25p. (No. Y1681) printed in photo by Harrison.*

FH36   Design No. 1 (cover in brown-olive and brownish black),
     Violette Szabo (S.O.E. agent) .... 3·00
FH37   Design No. 2 (cover in red-brown and black), Dame
     Vera Lynn (entertainer) (4.4.95) .... 3·00

1995 (16 May–4 Sept). *50th Anniv of End of Second World War Series continued. Covers as Type* FH36 *containing four 25p. (No. Y1682) printed in photo by Harrison.*

FH38   Design No. 3 (cover in black and steel-blue), R. J.
     Mitchell (designer of Spitfire) .... 3·00
FH39   Design No. 4 (cover in grey-green and black), Archibald
     Mcindoe (plastic surgeon) (4.9.95) .... 3·50

Type FH40

1996 (16 Jan). *Multicoloured laminated cover as Type* FH40. *Stamps printed in litho by Questa.*

FH40   Containing four 25p. stamps (No. Y1752) .... 7·00
    For an initial test period No. FH40 was only available from machines at twelve post offices, five in London and seven in Scotland, in addition to philatelic outlets. Stocks were distributed nationally from May 1996.

1996 (8 July)–**97**. *Multicoloured laminated cover as Type* FH40. *Stamps printed in litho by Questa.*

FH41   Containing booklet pane of 1p. × 2, 20p., 26p. × 3 and
     2 labels (No. Y1743l) .... 6·00
    a. Corrected rate (4.2.97) .... 5·25
    No. FH41 was reissued on 4 February 1997 showing the 200g second class rate on the inside cover altered from 47p. to 45p. A further printing issued 5 May 1998 was without the overseas postage rate table.

1998 (1 Dec). *Multicoloured laminated cover as Type* FH40. *Stamps printed in photo by Questa.*

FH42   Containing booklet pane of 1p. × 2, 20p., 26p. × 3 and
     2 labels (No. Y1667l) .... 30·00

1999 (26 Apr). *Multicoloured laminated cover as Type* FH40. *Stamps printed in photo by Questa.*

FH43   Containing booklet pane of 1p., 2p., 19p., 26p. × 3 and
     2 labels (No. Y1667m) .... 6·00

2000 (27 Apr)–**01**. *Multicoloured laminated cover as Type* FH40. *Stamps printed in photo by Questa.*

FH44   Containing booklet pane of 2nd, 1st × 3 and 4 labels
     (No. 1663al) .... 5·00
    a. Containing booklet pane No. 1663ala (17.4.01) ... 5·00

£1.15 Booklets

1981 (26 Jan–18 Mar). *Military Aircraft Series continued. Blue and grey covers as Type* FE1 (90 × 49 *mm). Containing ten* 11½p. *(No. X893). A. Selvedge at left. B. Selvedge at right.*

	A	B
FI1 Design No. 5, Spitfire & Lancaster	5·00	5·00
FI2 Design No. 6, Lightning & Vulcan (18.3.81)	5·00	5·00

Nos. FI1/2 are inscribed "January 1981".

Type FI3

(Des R. Maddox)

1981 (6 May–30 Sept). *Museums Series. Blue and turquoise-green covers as Type* FI3 (90 × 49 *mm). Containing ten* 11½p. *(No. X893). A. Selvedge at left. B. Selvedge at right.*

	A	B
FI3 Design No. 1, Natural History Museum (British		
Museum), London	5·00	5·00
FI4 Design No. 2, National Museum of Antiquities of		
Scotland (30.9.81)	5·00	5·00

Nos. FI3/4 are inscribed "January 1981".

£1.20 Booklets

1980 (4 Feb–24 Sept). *Industrial Archaeology Series continued. Red and green covers as Type* FH1 (90 × 49 *mm). Containing ten* 12p. *(No. X943). A. Selvedge at left. B. Selvedge at right.*

	A	B
FJ1 Design No. 2, Beetle Mill, Ireland	5·00	5·00
FJ2 Design No. 3, Tin Mines, Cornwall (25.6.80)	5·00	6·50
FJ3 Design No. 4, Bottle Kilns, Gladstone, Stoke-on-		
Trent (24.9.80)	5·00	5·50

No. FJ1 is inscribed "January 1980", No. FJ2 "May 1980" and No. FJ3 "July 1980".

1986 (14 Jan).   *Pillar box "Write Now" cover as Type FB31 (90 × 49 mm), printed in yellow-green and pale red. Containing ten 12p. (No. X896).*
A. *Selvedge at left.* B. *Selvedge at right.*

		A	B
FJ4	"Write Now" (Pillar box design) (no imprint date)	7·00	7·00

Type FJ5

(Des R. Maddox)

1986 (29 Apr).   *National Gallery cover as Type FJ5 (90 × 49 mm), printed in magenta and blue-green. Containing ten 12p. (No. X896).* A. *Selvedge at left.* B. *Selvedge at right.*

		A	B
FJ5	National Gallery design	6·50	6·50

No. FJ5 is inscribed "November 1985".

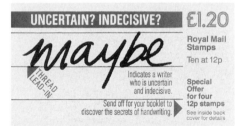

Type FJ6

(Des Trickett and Webb Ltd)

1986 (29 July).   *Handwriting cover as Type FJ6 (90 × 49 mm), printed in bright orange and bright blue. Containing ten 12p. (No. X896).* A. *Selvedge at left.* B. *Selvedge at right.*

		A	B
FJ6	"Maybe"	6·50	6·50

No. FJ6 is inscribed "November 1985".

£1.25 Booklets

1982 (1 Feb–6 Oct).   *Museums Series continued. Blue and turquoise-green covers as Type FJ3 (90 × 49 mm). Containing ten 12½p. (No. X898)* A. *Selvedge at left.* B. *Selvedge at right.*

		A	B
FK1	Design No. 3, Ashmolean Museum, Oxford	5·50	5·50
FK2	Design No. 4, National Museum of Wales, Cardiff (6.5.82)	5·50	5·50
FK3	Design No. 5, Ulster Museum, Belfast (11.8.82)	5·50	5·50
FK4	Design No. 6, Castle Museum, York (6.10.82)	5·50	5·50

Nos. FK1/4 are inscribed "February 1982".

Type FK5

(Des S. Paine)

1983 (16 Feb–26 Oct).   *Railway Engines Series. Red and blue-green covers as Type FK5 (90 × 49 mm). Containing ten 12½p. (No. X898).* A. *Selvedge at left.* B. *Selvedge at right.*

		A	B
FK5	Design No. 1, GWR *Isambard Kingdom Brunel*	7·00	7·00
FK6	Design No. 2, LMS Class 4P Passenger Tank Engine (5.4.83)	8·50	8·50
	a. Corrected rate	75·00	£120
FK7	Design No. 3, LNER *Mallard* (27.7.83)	7·00	7·00
FK8	Design No. 4, SR/BR *Clan Line* (26.10.83)	7·00	7·00

No. FK5 is inscribed "February 1982" and Nos. FK6/8 "April 1983".
The corrected rate reads, "36p. for 200g" instead of "37p. for 200g".

£1.30 Booklets

Type FL1

(Des J. Gibbs)

1981 (6 May–30 Sept).   *Postal History Series. Covers as Type FL1 (90 × 49 mm). Containing No. X894l.* A. *Selvedge at left.* B. *Selvedge at right.*

		A	B
FL1	Design No. 1, Penny Black (red & black cover)	7·00	5·50
FL2	Design No. 2, The Downey Head, 1911 (red & green cover) (20.9.81)	9·50	30·00

No. FL1 is inscribed "April 1981" and No. FL2 "September 1981".

Type FL3

(Des J. Thirsk)

1984 (3 Sept)–**85**. *Trams Series. Yellow-orange and purple covers as Type FL3 (90 × 49 mm). Containing ten 13p. (No. X900). A. Selvedge at left. B. Selvedge at right.*

		A	B
FL3	Design No. 1, Swansea/Mumbles Railway Car No. 3	5·50	5·50
FL4	Design No. 2, Glasgow Car No. 927 & Car No. 1194 (15.1.85)	6·25	6·25
FL5	Design No. 3, Car No. 717, Blackpool (23.4.85)	6·25	6·25
FL6	Design No. 4, Car No. 120 & "D" Class Car, London (23.7.85)	5·50	5·50

Nos. FL3/6 are inscribed "September 1984".

Type FL7

(Des Anne Morrow)

1986 (20 Oct). *Books for Children. Cover as Type FL7 (90 × 49 mm) printed in rose-red and lemon. Containing ten 13p. (No. X900). A. Selvedge at left. B. Selvedge at right.*

		A	B
FL7	Teddy bears design	5·50	5·50

Type FL8

(Des Trickett and Webb Ltd)

1987 (27 Jan). *"Keep in Touch" cover as Type FL8 (90 × 49 mm), printed in light green and bright blue. Containing ten 13p. (No. X900). A. Selvedge at left. B. Selvedge at right.*

		A	B
FL8	Handclasp and envelope design	5·50	5·50

No. FL8 is inscribed "October 1986".

Type FL9

(Des Hannah Firmin)

1987 (14 Apr). *"Ideas for your Garden". Cover as Type FL9 (90 × 49 mm) printed in bistre and orange-brown. Containing ten 13p. stamps (No. X900). A. Selvedge at left. B. Selvedge at right.*

		A	B
FL9	Conservatory design	5·50	5·50

No. FL9 is inscribed "October 1986".

Type FL10

(Des Trickett and Webb Ltd)

1987 (4 July). *"Brighter Writer". Cover as Type FL10 (90 × 49 mm) printed in orange and bright reddish violet. Containing ten 13p. stamps (No. X900). A. Selvedge at left. B. Selvedge at right.*

		A	B
FL10	Flower design	5·50	5·50

No. FL10 is inscribed "October 1986".

Type FL11

(Des E. Stemp)

1987 (29 Sept). *"Jolly Postman". Cover as Type FL11 (90 × 49 mm) printed in pale blue and deep blue. Containing ten 13p. stamps (No. X900). A. Selvedge at left. B. Selvedge at right.*

		A	B
FL11	Boy drawing design	5·75	5·75

No. FL11 is inscribed "October 1986".

Type FL12

(Des E. Hughes)

1988 (26 Jan). *Bicentenary of Linnean Society. Cover as Type FL12 (90 × 49 mm) printed in blue and claret. Containing ten 13p. stamps (No. X900). A. Selvedge at left. B. Selvedge at right.*

		A	B
FL12	Mermaid, fish and insect (from "Hortus Sanibatis", 1497)	6·75	6·75

No. FL12 is inscribed "October 1986".

Type FL13

(Des Hannah Firmin)

1988 (12 Apr). *Recipe Cards. Cover as Type FL13 (90 × 49 mm) printed in brown and green. Containing ten 13p. stamps (No. X900). A. Selvedge at left. B. Selvedge at right.*

		A	B
FL13	Vegetables design	5·50	5·50

No. FL13 is inscribed "October 1986".

Type FL14

(Des Trickett and Webb Ltd)

1988 (5 July). *"Children's Parties". Cover as Type FL14 (90 × 49 mm) printed in blue-green and bright purple. Containing ten 13p. stamps (No. X900). A. Selvedge at left. B. Selvedge at right.*

		A	B
FL14	Balloons and streamers design	5·50	5·50

No. FL14 is inscribed "October 1986".

£1.40 Booklets

1981 (26 Jan–18 Mar). *Industrial Archaeology Series continued. Red and green covers as Type FH1 (90 × 49 mm). Containing ten 14p. (No. X946). A. Selvedge at left. B. Selvedge at right.*

		A	B
FM1	Design No. 5, Preston Mill, Scotland	5·50	5·50
FM2	Design No. 6, Talyllyn Railway, Tywyn (18.3.81)	5·50	5·50

Nos. FM1/2 are inscribed "January 1981".

Type FM3

(Des E. Stemp)

1981 (6 May–30 Sept). *19th-century Women's Costume Series. Claret and blue covers as Type FM3 (90 × 49 mm). Containing ten 14p. (No. X946). A. Selvedge at left. B. Selvedge at right.*

		A	B
FM3	Design No. 1, Costume, 1800-15	5·50	5·50
FM4	Design No. 2, Costume, 1815–30 (30.9.81)	5·50	5·50

Nos. FM3/4 are inscribed "January 1981".

Type FM5

(Des A. Drummond)

1988 (5 Sept). *"Pocket Planner". Cover as Type FM5 (90 × 49 mm) printed in grey-black and yellow. Containing ten 14p. stamps (No. X903). A. Selvedge at left. B. Selvedge at right.*

	A	B
FM5 "Legal Charge" design	5·50	5·50

Type FM6

(Des Debbie Cook)

1989 (24 Jan). *150th Anniv of Fox Talbot's Report on the Photographic Process to Royal Society. Cover as Type FM6 (90 × 49 mm) printed in reddish orange and black. Containing ten 14p. stamps (No. X903). A. Selvedge at left. B. Selvedge at right.*

	A	B
FM6 Photographs and darkroom equipment	5·75	5·75

No. FM6 is inscribed "September 1988".

£1.43 Booklets

1982 (1 Feb–6 May). *Postal History Series continued. Covers as Type FL1 (90 × 49 mm). Containing No. X899l. A. Selvedge at left. B. Selvedge at right.*

	A	B
FN1 Design No. 3, James Chalmers (postal reformer) (orange & turquoise-blue cover)	6·00	6·00
FN2 Design No. 4, Edmund Dulac (stamp designer) (brown & red cover) (6.5.82)	6·00	6·00

Type FN3

(Des J. Gardner)

1982 (12 July). *"Holiday Postcard Stamp Book". Purple and turquoise-blue cover as Type FN3 (90 × 49 mm). Containing No. X899l. A. Selvedge at left. B. Selvedge at right.*

	A	B
FN3 Golden Hinde on front, postcard voucher on back	6·00	6·00

1982 (21 July)–83. *Postal History Series continued. Covers as Type FL1 (90 × 49 mm). Containing No. X899l. A. Selvedge at left. B. Selvedge at right.*

	A	B
FN4 Design No. 5, "Forces Postal Service" (grey & violet cover)	6·00	6·00
FN5 Design No. 6, The £5 Orange (orange & black cover) (6.10.82)	6·00	6·00
FN6 Design No. 7, Postmark History (brt scarlet & dp dull blue cover) (16.2.83)	6·00	6·00

No. FN1 is inscribed "February 1982". FN2/3 "May 1982", FN4 "July 1982", FN5 "October 1982", FN6 "November 1982".

For booklet No. FS2 with cover price of £1.45, see £1.60 booklets.

£1.46 Booklets

1983 (5 Apr–26 Oct). *Postal History Series continued. Covers as Type FL1 (90 × 49 mm). A. Containing No. X899n. B. Containing No. X899na.*

	A	B
FO1 Design No. 8, Seahorse High Values (blue & green cover)	11·00	11·00
a. Corrected rate	48·00	24·00
FO2 Design No. 9, Parcel Post Centenary (turquoise-blue & carmine cover) (27.7.83)	9·50	9·50
FO3 Design No. 10, Silver Jubilee of Regional Stamps (dull green & reddish violet cover) (26.10.83).	9·50	9·50

No. FO1 is inscribed "March 1983", No. FO2 "May 1983" and No. FO3 "June 1983".

The corrected rate reads, "36p. for 200g" instead of "37p. for 200g".

£1.50 Booklets

1986 (14 Jan). *Pillar box "Write Now" cover as Type FB31 (90 × 49 mm), printed in ultramarine and red. A. Containing No. X897l. B. Containing No. X897la.*

	A	B
FP1 "Write Now" (Pillar box design)	7·00	7·00

No. FP1 shows no imprint date.

1986 (29 Apr). *National Gallery cover as Type FJ5 (90 × 49 mm), printed in violet and vermilion. A. Containing No. X897l. B. Containing No. X897la.*

	A	B
FP2 National Gallery design	7·00	7·00

No. FP2 is inscribed "November 1985".

1986 (29 July). *Handwriting cover as Type FJ6 (90 × 49 mm), printed in blue-green and bright blue. A. Containing No. X897l. B. Containing No. X897la.*

	A	B
FP3 "No"	7·00	7·00

No. FP3 is inscribed "November 1985".

£1.54 Booklets

1984 (3 Sept)–85. *Postal History Series continued. Covers as Type FL1 (90 × 49 mm). A. Containing No. X901l. B. Containing No. X901la.*

	A	B
FQ1 Design No. 11, Old & new Postage Dues (reddish purple and pale blue cover)	6·00	6·00
FQ2 Design No. 12, Queen Victoria embossed stamps (yellow-green & blue-cover) (15.1.85)	6·00	6·00

	A	B
FQ3	Design No. 13, Queen Victoria surface-printed stamps (blue-green & carmine cover) (23.4.85)	6·00	6·00
FQ4	Design No. 14, 17th-century mounted & foot messengers (dp brown & orange-red cover) (23.7.85)	6·00	6·00

No. FQ1 is inscribed "July 1984" and Nos. FQ2/4 are inscribed "September 1984".

£1.55 Booklets

1982 (1 Feb–6 Oct). *19th-century Women's Costume Series continued. Claret and blue covers as Type FM3 (90 × 49 mm). Containing ten 15½p. (No. X948). A. Selvedge at left. B. Selvedge at right.*

		A	B
FR1	Design No. 3, Costume, 1830–50	5·75	5·75
FR2	Design No. 4, Costume, 1850–60 (6.5.82)	5·75	5·75
FR3	Design No. 5, Costume, 1860–80 (11.8.82)	5·75	5·75
FR4	Design No. 6, Costume, 1880–1900 (6.10.82)	5·75	5·75

Nos. FR1/4 are inscribed "February 1982".

£1.60 Booklets

Type FS1

(Des Carol Walklin)

1983 (5 Apr). *"Birthday Box" Design. Magenta and red-orange cover as Type FS1 (90 × 49 mm). Depicting birthday cake and associated items. A. Selvedge at left. B. Selvedge at right.*

		A	B
FS1	Containing ten 16p. stamps (No. X949) (no imprint date)	7·00	7·00
	a. Rates altered and "February 1983" imprint date	70·00	£120

(Des R. Maddox)

1983 (10 Aug). *British Countryside Series. Special Discount Booklet (sold at £1.45). Greenish blue and ultramarine cover as Type FS2 (90 × 49 mm). Containing ten 16p. stamps (No. X949Eu). A. Selvedge at left. B. Selvedge at right.*

		A	B
FS2	Design No. 1, Lyme Regis, Dorset	9·00	9·00

Stamps from No. FS2 show a double-lined "D" printed in blue on the reverse over the gum.

No. FS2 is inscribed "April 1983".

1983 (21 Sept). *British Countryside Series continued. Dull green on violet cover as Type FS2 (90 × 49 mm). Containing ten 16p. stamps (No. X949). A. Selvedge at left. B. Selvedge at right.*

		A	B
FS3	Design No. 2, Arlington Row, Bibury, Gloucestershire	6·00	6·00

No. FS3 is inscribed "April 1983".

Type FS4

(Des M. Newton)

1984 (14 Feb). *"Write it" Design. Vermilion and ultramarine cover as Type FS4 (90 × 49 mm). Containing ten 16p. stamps (No. X949). A. Selvedge at left. B. Selvedge at right.*

		A	B
FS4	Fountain pen	7·00	7·00

No. FS4 is inscribed "April 1983".

£1.70 Booklets

Type FS2

Type FT1

(Des G. Hardie)

1984 (3 Sept). *Social Letter Writing Series. Rose and deep claret cover as Type FT1 (90 × 49 mm). Containing ten 17p. (No. X952). A. Selvedge at left. B. Selvedge at right.*

		A	B
FT1	Design No. 1, "Love Letters"	7·00	7·00

No. FT1 is inscribed "September 1984".

1985 (5 Mar). *Social Letter Writing Series continued. Special Discount Booklet (sold at £1.55). Turquoise-blue and deep claret cover as Type FT1 (90 × 49 mm). Containing ten 17p. (No. X952Eu). A. Selvedge at left. B. Selvedge at right.*

		A	B
FT2	Design No. 2, "Letters abroad"	7·00	7·00

Stamps from No. FT2 show a double-lined "D" printed in blue on the reverse over the gum.

No. FT2 is inscribed "September 1984".

1985 (9 Apr). *Social Letter Writing Series continued. Bright blue and deep claret cover as Type FT1 (90 × 49 mm). Containing ten 17p. (No. X952). A. Selvedge at left. B. Selvedge at right.*

		A	B
FT3	Design No. 3, "Fan letters"	6·50	6·50

No. FT3 is inscribed "September 1984".

Type FT4

(Des B. Smith)

1985 (30 July). *350 Years of Royal Mail Public Postal Service. Special Discount Booklet (sold at £1.53). Cover Type FS4 (90 × 60 mm), printed in rosine and bright blue. Containing ten 17p. (No. 1290Eu) with selvedge at top.*

FT4	Datapost Service design		7·00

The stamps from this booklet show double-lined letters "D" printed on the reverse over the gum.

No. FT4 is inscribed "September 1984".

1985 (8 Oct)–**86**. *Social Letter Writing Series continued. Black and bright scarlet cover as Type FT1 (90 × 49 mm). Containing ten 17p. (No. X952). A. Selvedge at left. B. Selvedge at right.*

		A	B
FT5	Design No. 4, "Write Now" (Pillar box)	6·50	6·50
	a. Revised rates (2nd class (60g) 12p.) (1.86)	25·00	15·00

1986 (29 Apr). *National Gallery cover as Type FJ5 (90 × 49 mm), printed in blue-green and blue. Containing ten 17p. (No. X952). A. Selvedge at left. B. Selvedge at right.*

		A	B
FT6	National Gallery design	7·00	7·00

No. FT6 is inscribed "November 1985".

1986 (29 July). *Handwriting cover as Type FJ6 (90 × 49 mm) printed in red and bright blue. Containing ten 17p. (No. X952). A. Selvedge at left. B. Selvedge at right.*

		A	B
FT7	"Yes"	7·00	7·00

No. FT7 is inscribed "November 1985".

£1.80 Booklets

1986 (20 Oct). *Books for Children. New blue and orange-brown cover as Type FL7. Containing ten 18p. (No. X955). A. Selvedge at left. B. Selvedge at right.*

		A	B
FU1	Rabbits design	7·00	7·00

1987 (27 Jan). *"Keep in Touch" cover as Type FL8 printed in magenta and bright blue. Containing ten 18p. (No. X955). A. Selvedge at left. B. Selvedge at right.*

		A	B
FU2	Handclasp and envelope design	7·00	7·00

No. FU2 is inscribed "October 1986".

1987 (14 Apr). *"Ideas for your Garden". Claret and brown-olive cover as Type FL9 (90 × 49 mm). Containing ten 18p. stamps (No. X955). A. Selvedge at left. B. Selvedge at right.*

		A	B
FU3	Garden path design	7·00	7·00

No. FU3 is inscribed "October 1986".

1987 (14 July). *"Brighter Writer". Turquoise-green and reddish orange cover as Type FL10 (90 × 49 mm). Containing ten 18p. stamps (No. X955). A. Selvedge at left. B. Selvedge at right.*

		A	B
FU4	Berries and leaves design	7·00	7·00

No. FU4 is inscribed "October 1986".

1987 (29 Sept). *"Jolly Postman". Cover as Type FL11 (90 × 49 mm) printed in deep blue and claret. Containing ten 18p. stamps (No. X955). A. Selvedge at left. B. Selvedge at right.*

		A	B
FU5	Girl drawing design	7·00	7·00

No. FU5 is inscribed "October 1986".

1988 (26 Jan). *Bicentenary of Linnean Society. Cover as Type FL12 (90 × 49 mm) printed in dull yellow-green and dull claret. Containing ten 18p. stamps (No. X955). A. Selvedge at left. B. Selvedge at right.*

		A	B
FU6	Wolf and birds (from "Hortus Sanitatis", 1497)	7·00	7·00

1988 (12 Apr). *Recipe Cards. Cover as Type FL13 (90 × 49 mm) printed in claret and Indian red. Containing ten 18p. stamps (No. X955). A. Selvedge at left. B. Selvedge at right.*

		A	B
FU7	Fruits, pudding and jam design	7·00	7·00

No. FU7 is inscribed "October 1986".

1988 (5 July). *"Children's Parties". Cover as Type FL14 (90 × 49 mm) printed in violet and rosine. Containing ten 18p. stamps (No. X955). A. Selvedge at left. B. Selvedge at right.*

		A	B
FU8	Balloons and party hats design	7·00	7·00

No. FU8 is inscribed "October 1986".

£1.90 Booklets

1988 (5 Sept). *"Pocket Planner". Cover as Type FM5 (90 × 49 mm) printed in yellow-green and magenta. Containing ten 19p. stamps (No. X956). A. Selvedge at left. B. Selvedge at right.*

		A	B
FV1	"Marriage Act" design	8·75	8·75

1989 (24 Jan).   *150th Anniv of Fox Talbot's Report on the Photographic Process to Royal Society. Cover as Type FM6 (90 × 49 mm) printed in emerald and black. Containing ten 19p. stamps (No. X956). A. Selvedge at left. B. Selvedge at right.*

	A	B
FV2 Fox Talbot with camera and Lacock Abbey	8·75	8·75

No. FV2 is inscribed "September 1988".

£2 Booklets

Type FW1

(Des Debbie Cook)

1993 (1 Nov)–**94.**   *Postal Vehicles Series. Covers as Type FW1. Containing eight 25p. (No. Y1681).*
FW1   Design No. 1 (cover in dull vermilion and deep blue), Motorised cycle-carrier .... 6·50
FW2   Design No. 2 (cover in green and deep violet-blue), Experimental motor-mail van (26.4.94) .... 6·50
FW3   Design No. 3 (cover in red and black), Experimental electric mail van, 1932 (6.9.94) .... 6·50

Type FW3

(Des The Four Hundred)

1995 (7 Feb–4 Apr)   *Birth Bicentenary of Sir Rowland Hill. Covers as Type FW3. Containing eight 25p. (No. Y1681).*
FW4   Design No. 1 (cover in purple and new blue), Rowland Hill as director of London and Brighton Railway Company   6·50
FW5   Design No. 2 (cover in deep mauve and greenish blue), Rowland Hill and Hazlewood School (4.4.95) .... 6·50

1995 (6 June–4 Sept)   *Birth Bicentenary of Sir Rowland Hill Series continued. Covers as Type FW3. Containing eight 25p. (No. Y1682).*
FW6   Design No. 3 (cover in deep blue-green and dull orange), Rowland Hill as Secretary to the Post Office. .... 7·00
FW7   Design No. 4 (cover in red-brown and orange), Uniform Penny Postage petition and Mulready envelope (4.9.95) .... 7·00

1996 (16 Jan)   *Multicoloured laminated cover as Type FH40. Stamps printed in litho by Questa.*
FW8   Containing eight 25p. stamps (No. Y1752) .... 7·00
For an initial test period No. FW8 was only available from machines at twelve post offices, five in London and seven in Scotland, in addition to philatelic outlets. Stocks were distributed nationally from May 1996.

1996 (8 July)–**97.**   *Multicoloured laminated cover as Type FH40. Stamps printed in litho by Questa.*
FW9   Containing booklet pane of 20p. and 26p. × 7 (No. Y1751l) .... 8·00
          a. Corrected rate (4.2.97) .... 8·00
No. FW9 was reissued on 4 February 1997 showing the 200g second class rate on the inside cover altered from 47p. to 45p. A further printing issued 5 May 1998 was without the overseas postage rate table.

1998 (1 Dec).   *Multicoloured laminated cover as Type FH40. Stamps printed in photo by Questa.*
FW10   Containing booklet pane of 20p. and 26p. × 7 (No. Y1678l) .... 35·00

1999 (26 Apr).   *Multicoloured laminated cover as Type FH40. Stamps printed in photo by Questa.*
FW11   Containing booklet pane of 19p. and 26p. × 7 (No. Y1675l) .... 7·00

2000 (27 Apr).   *Multicoloured laminated cover as Type FH40. Stamps printed in photo by Questa.*
FW12   Containing booklet pane of 2nd × 2 and 1st × 6 (No. 1663am) .... 7·00

Christmas Booklets

Type FX1

(Des J. Matthews)

1978 (15 Nov).   *"Christmas Greetings". Cover Type FX1 (90 × 49 mm). Printed in rose-red and sage-green.*
FX1   £1.60, containing booklet pane No. X875l .... 5·00
No. FX1 is inscribed "August 1978".

Type FX2

(Des P. Sharland)

1979 (14 Nov). *"Christmas Greetings". Red and green cover as Type FX2 (90 × 49 mm), showing Christmas cracker.*
FX2 £1.80, containing booklet pane No. X879l .... 6·00
No. FX2 is inscribed "October 1979".

Type FX3

(Des E. Fraser)

1980 (12 Nov). *Christmas. Red and blue cover as Type FX3 (90 × 49 mm), showing Nativity scene.*
FX3 £2.20, containing booklet pane No. X888m .... 6·50
No. FX3 is inscribed "September 1980".

Type FX4

(Des W. Sanderson)

1981 (11 Nov). *Christmas. Red and blue cover as Type FX4, (90 × 49 mm), showing skating scene.*
FX4 £2.55, containing booklet pane No. X893l .... 8·50
No. FX4 is inscribed "January 1981".

Type FX5

(Des A. Davidson)

1982 (10 Nov). *Christmas. Red and green cover as Type FX5 (90 × 49 mm), showing Christmas Mummers.*
FX5 £2.50, containing booklet pane No. X898l .... 9·50

No. FX5 is inscribed "February 1982" and was sold at a discount of 30p. off the face value of the stamps.
Each stamp in the pane has a blue star printed on the reverse over the gum.

Type FX6

(Des Barbara Brown)

1983 (9 Nov). *Christmas. Brown-lilac and yellow cover as Type FX6 (90 × 49 mm), showing pantomime scenes.*
FX6 £2.20, containing twenty 12½p. (No. X898Ev) .... 8·50
No. FX6 is inscribed "April 1983" and was sold at a discount of 30p. off the face value of the stamps.
Each stamp in the pane has a double-lined blue star printed on the reverse over the gum.

Type FX7

(Des Yvonne Gilbert)

1984 (20 Nov). *Christmas. Light brown and red-orange cover as Type FX7 (90 × 60 mm), showing Nativity scene.*
FX7 £2.30, containing twenty 13p. (No. 1267Eu) .... 9·50
No. FX7 is inscribed "September 1984" and was sold at a discount of 30p. off the face value of the stamps.
The stamps from this booklet show double-lined blue stars printed on the reverse over the gum.

GIBBONS STAMP MONTHLY
– finest and most informative magazine for all collectors. Obtainable from your newsagent or by postal subscription – details on request.

Type FX8

(Des A. George)

1985 (19 Nov). *Christmas. Bright blue and rose cover as Type FX8 (90 × 60 mm), showing The Pantomime.*
FX8 £2.40, containing twenty 12p. (No. 1303Eu) . . . .   9·00
The stamps from this booklet show double-lined blue stars printed on the reverse over the gum.

Type FX9

(Des Lynda Gray)

1986 (2 Dec). *Christmas. Red and dull blue-green cover as Type FX9 (90 × 49 mm), showing Shetland Yule cakes. A. Selvedge at left. B. Selvedge at right.*

	A	B
FX9 £1.20, containing ten 13p. (No. X900Eu)	8·50	9·00

No. FX9 is inscribed "October 1986" and was sold at a discount of 10p. off the face value of the stamps.
Each stamps in the pane has a blue star printed on the reverse over the gum.
For 1990 and later Christmas stamps, see Barcode Booklets Section G.

Type FX10

(Des L. Moberly)

1989 (31 Jan). *Greetings Stamps. Multicoloured cover as Type FX10 (89 × 60 mm). Containing booklet pane No. 1423a, including twelve special greetings labels in a block (3 × 4) at right, attached by the selvedge.*
FX10 Greetings design . . . .   50·00
No. FX10 is inscribed "September 1988".
The cover of No. FX10 shows an overall pattern of elements taken from the stamp designs. Due to the method of production the position of these elements varies from cover to cover.
For Greetings stamps in Barcode booklets, see Barcode Booklets Section F.

These booklets are listed in eight sections.

SECTION C. G numbers containing Machin stamps with face values

SECTION D. H numbers containing Machin NVI stamps

SECTION E. J numbers containing Machin Penny Black Anniversary stamps

SECTION F. KX numbers containing Greetings stamps

SECTION G. LX numbers containing Christmas stamps

SECTION H. M numbers containing self-adhesive NVI definitive stamps

SECTION I. N numbers containing self-adhesive definitive stamps with face values

SECTION J. PM numbers containing both special and definitive self-adhesive NVI stamps

These are produced for sale in both post offices and commercial outlets.

NOTE: All panes are attached to the covers by the selvedge.

Barcode booklet covers are illustrated at two-thirds linear size *unless otherwise stated.*

C. Barcode Booklets containing Machin stamps with values shown as Type **367**.

COVERS. These are all printed in scarlet, lemon and black with the barcode on the reverse. Type GA1 has a clear "window" to view the contents. Type GB3 is shorter and has a stamp illustration printed on the cover to replace the "window". These illustrations show an oblique white line across the bottom right-hand corner of the "stamp". Unless otherwise stated all covers were printed by Harrison.
From early 1997 the printer of each booklet is identified by a small capital letter below the barcode on the outside back cover.

52p. Booklet

Type GA1

1987 (4 Aug). *Laminated cover Type GA1 (75 × 60 mm).*
GA1 Containing booklet pane No. X900n .... 4·00
    No. GA1 is inscribed "20 October 1986".

56p. Booklets

1988 (23 Aug). *Laminated cover as Type GA1 (75 × 56 mm).*
GB1 Containing booklet pane No. X903l .... 6·00

1988 (11 Oct). *Laminated cover as Type GA1 (75 × 56 mm) printed by Walsall.*
GB2 Containing booklet pane No. X903l .... 9·50

Type GB3
Large Crown

1988 (11 Oct). *Laminated cover as Type GB3 (75 × 48 mm) with stamp printed on the cover in deep blue.*
GB3 Containing booklet pane No. X903n .... 7·75
    No. GB3 is inscribed "5 September 1988" and has the horizontal edges of the pane imperforate.

1989 (24 Jan). *Laminated cover as Type GB3 (75 × 48 mm) with stamp printed on the cover in deep blue by Walsall.*
GB4 Containing booklet pane No. X903q .... 40·00
    No. GB4 is inscribed "5 September 1988" and has the three edges of the pane imperforate.

72p. Booklet

1987 (4 Aug). *Laminated cover as Type GA1 (75 × 60 mm).*
GC1 Containing booklet pane No. X955m .... 4·00
    No. GC1 is inscribed "20 October 1986".

76p. Booklets

1988 (23 Aug). *Laminated cover as Type GA1 (75 × 56 mm).*
GD1 Containing booklet pane No. X956l .... 7·75

1988 (11 Oct). *Laminated cover as Type GA1 (75 × 56 mm) printed by Walsall.*
GD2 Containing booklet pane No. X956l .... 8·00

1988 (11 Oct). *Laminated cover as Type GB3 (75 × 48 mm) with stamp printed on the cover in bright orange-red.*
GD3 Containing booklet pane No. X956n .... 9·50
    No. GD3 is inscribed "5 September 1988" and has the horizontal edges of the pane imperforate.

1989 (24 Jan). *Laminated cover as Type GB3 (75 × 48 mm) with stamp printed on the cover in bright orange-red by Walsall.*
GD4 Containing booklet pane No. X956q .... 40·00
    No. GD4 is inscribed "5 September 1988" and has the three edges of the pane imperforate.

78p. Booklet

GD4a (As Type GL1 but, without "4")

1992 (28 July). *Multicoloured laminated cover as Type GD4a (75 × 49 mm) with stamp printed on the cover in bright mauve by Walsall.*
GD4a   Containing two 39p. stamps (No. X1058) (pane No. X1058l with right-hand vert pair removed) and pane of 4 air mail labels .... 3·50
Stamps in No. GD4a have top or bottom edge imperforate.
Booklet No. GD4a was produced in connection with a Kellogg's Bran Flakes promotion.

£1.04 Booklet

1987 (4 Aug). *Laminated cover as Type GA1 (75 × 60 mm).*
GE1   Containing booklet pane No. X971bl .... 20·00
No. GE1 is inscribed "20 October 1986".

£1.08 Booklets

1988 (23 Aug). *Laminated cover as Type GA1 (75 × 56 mm).*
GF1   Containing booklet pane No. X973l .... 14·00

1988 (11 Oct). *Laminated cover as Type GB3 (75 × 48 mm) with stamp printed on the cover in chestnut.*
GF2   Containing booklet pane No. X973m .... 35·00
No. GF2 is inscribed "5 September 1988" and has the horizontal edges of the pane imperforate.

£1.16 Booklets

Type GG1
Redrawn Crown

1989 (2 Oct). *Laminated cover as Type GG1 (75 × 48 mm) with stamp printed on the cover in deep mauve by Walsall.*
GG1   Containing booklet pane No. X1054l .... 17·00
No. GG1 has three edges of the pane imperforate.

1990 (17 Apr). *Laminated cover as Type GG1 (75 × 48 mm) with stamp printed on the cover in deep mauve by Walsall.*
GG2   Containing booklet pane No. X1055l .... 20·00
No. GG2 has three edges of the pane imperforate.

£1.20 Booklets

Type GGA1 ("BY AIR MAIL *par avion*"
at bottom left)

1998 (5 May). *Multicoloured laminated cover as Type GGA1 (75 × 50 mm) with stamps printed on cover in olive-grey by Walsall. Inscr "For items up to 20g" on yellow tab at right..*
GGA1   Containing four 30p. (photo) (No. Y1685) and a pane of 4 air mail labels .... 4·25

Type GGA2 "Create a card Design"

1998 (3 Aug). *Multicoloured laminated cover as Type GGA2 (75 × 50 mm) printed by Walsall. Inscr "See inside for offer details" on yellow tab at right..*
GGA2   Containing four 30p. (photo) (No. Y1685) and a pane of 4 air mail labels .... 4·25
This booklet was not placed on philatelic sale until 7 September 1998.

£1.24 Booklet

Type GH1
Crown on White

1990 (17 Sept). *Multicoloured laminated cover as Type GH1 (75 × 49 mm) with stamp printed on the cover in ultramarine by Walsall.*
GH1   Containing booklet pane No. X1056l .... 7·00
No. GH1 has the horizontal edges of the pane imperforate.

£1.30 Booklet

1987 (4 Aug). *Laminated cover as Type GA1 (98 × 60 mm).*
GJ1   Containing booklet pane No. X900o .... 6·00
No. GJ1 is inscribed "20 October 1986".

£1.32 Booklet

Type GJ1

1991 (16 Sept)–**92**. *Multicoloured laminated cover as Type GJ1 (75 × 49 mm) with stamp printed on the cover in light emerald by Walsall. Inscr "For letters up to 10g" on yellow strip at right.*
GJ1   Containing booklet pane No. X1057I and a pane of 4 air mail labels .... 6·50
  a. Inscr "For Worldwide Postcards" on yellow strip (8.9.92) .... 12·00
Nos. GJ1/a have the horizontal edges of the pane imperforate.

£1.40 Booklets

1988 (23 Aug). *Laminated cover as Type GA1 (97 × 56 mm).*
GK1   Containing booklet pane No. X903m .... 18·00

1988 (11 Oct). *Laminated cover as Type GA1 (97 × 56 mm) printed by Questa.*
GK2   Containing ten 14p. (No. X1007) .... 18·00

1988 (11 Oct). *Laminated cover as Type GB3 (75 × 48 mm) with stamp printed on the cover in deep blue.*
GK3   Containing booklet pane No. X903p .... 10·00
No. GK3 is inscribed "5 September 1988" and has horizontal edges of the pane imperforate.

1988 (11 Oct). *Laminated cover as Type GB3 (75 × 48 mm) with stamp printed on the cover in deep blue by Questa.*
GK4   Containing ten 14p. (No. X1007) .... 18·00

1993 (1 Nov). *Laminated cover as Type GJ1 (76 × 50 mm) with stamp printed on the cover in yellow by Walsall.*
GK5   Containing four 35p. (No. Y1755) and a pane of 4 air mail labels .... 6·25

Type GK6 (without diagonal white line
across corners of stamps)

1995 (16 May). *Multicoloured laminated cover as Type GK6 (75 × 48 mm) with stamps printed on the cover in yellow by Walsall.*
GK6   Containing four 35p. (No. Y1755) and a pane of 4 air mail labels .... 6·25

1996 (19 Mar). *Multicoloured laminated cover as Type GK6 (75 × 48 mm) without "International" and showing Olympic symbols on the back. Stamps printed on the cover in yellow by Walsall.*
GK7   Containing four 35p. (No. Y1755) and a pane of 4 air mail labels .... 6·50

£1.48 Booklets

Type GL1
("Worldwide Postcard Stamps" ranged left)
(without diagonal white lines across corner of stamps)

1996 (8 July). *Multicoloured laminated cover as Type GL1 (75 × 48 mm) showing Olympic symbols on the back. Stamps printed on the cover in bright mauve by Walsall. Inscribed "For Worldwide Postcards" on yellow tab at right.*
GL1   Containing four 37p. (No. Y1756) and a pane of 4 air mail labels .... 10·00

1997 (4 Feb). *Multicoloured laminated cover as Type GL1 (75 × 48 mm) without Olympic symbols on the back. Stamps printed on the cover in bright mauve by Walsall. Inscribed "For Worldwide Postcards" on yellow tab at right.*
GL2   Containing four 37p. (No. Y1756) and a pane of 4 air mail labels .... 10·00

Type GL3

1997 (26 Aug)–**98**. *Multicoloured laminated cover as Type GL3 (75 × 48 mm) printed by Walsall. Inscribed "For Worldwide Postcards" on yellow tab at right.*
GL3   Containing four 37p. (photo) (No. Y1691) and a pane of 4 new design air mail labels .... 5·50
  a. Showing validity notice on inside back cover (5.5.98) .... 4·50
No. GL3 has the postage rate table on the inside back cover.

1998 (3 Aug). *Multicoloured laminated cover as Type GGA2 ("Create a card" design) (75 × 50 mm) printed by Walsall.*
GL4   Containing four 37p. (photo) (No. Y1691) and a pane of 4 air mail labels . . . .   4·50
This booklet was not placed on philatelic sale until 7 September 1998.

£1.52 Booklets

1999 (26 Apr). *Multicoloured laminated cover as Type GGA1 (76 × 50 mm) with stamps printed on cover in ultramarine by Walsall. Inscr "For Worldwide Postcards" on yellow tab at right.*
GLA1 Containing four 38p. (photo) (No. Y1693) and a pane of 4 air mail labels . . . .   5·00

£1.56 Booklet

Type GM1

1991 (16 Sept).   *Multicoloured laminated cover as Type GM1 (75 × 49 mm) with stamp printed on the cover in bright mauve by Walsall.*
GM1   Containing booklet pane No. X1058l and a pane of 4 air mail labels . . . .   11·00
No. GM1 has the horizontal edges of the pane imperforate.

£1.60 Booklet

2000 (27 Apr). *Multicoloured laminated cover as Type GGA1 (76 × 50 mm) with stamps printed on cover in deep azure by Walsall. Inscr "For Worldwide Postcards" on yellow tab at right.*
GMA1 Containing four 40p. (photo) (No. Y1695) and a pane of 4 air mail labels . . . .   7·50

£1.64 Booklets

1993 (1 Nov).   *Laminated cover as Type GM1 (76 × 50 mm) with stamp printed on the cover in drab by Walsall.*
GN1   Containing four 41p. (No. Y1757) and a pane of 4 air mail labels . . . .   7·00

1995 (16 May). *Multicoloured laminated cover as Type GK6 (75 × 48 mm) with stamps printed on the cover in drab by Walsall.*
GN2   Containing four 41p. (No. Y1757) and a pane of 4 air mail labels . . . .   7·00

1996 (19 Mar). *Multicoloured laminated cover as Type GK6 (75 × 48 mm) without "International" and showing Olympic symbols on the back. Stamps printed on the cover in drab by Walsall.*
GN3   Containing four 41p. (No. Y1757) and a pane of 4 air mail labels . . . .   7·00

£1.80 Booklet

1987 (4 Aug).   *Laminated cover as Type GA1 (98 × 60 mm).*
GO1   Containing booklet pane No. X955n . . . .   9·00
No. GO1 is inscribed "20 October 1986".

£1.90 Booklets

1988 (23 Aug).   *Laminated cover as Type GA1 (97 × 56 mm).*
GP1   Containing booklet pane No. X956m . . . .   12·00

1988 (11 Oct).   *Laminated cover as Type GA1 (97 × 56 mm) printed by Questa.*
GP2   Containing ten 19p. (No. X1013) . . . .   24·00

1988 (11 Oct).   *Laminated cover as Type GB3 (75 × 48 mm) with stamp printed on the cover in bright orange-red.*
GP3   Containing booklet pane No. X956o . . . .   12·00
No. GP3 is inscribed "5 September 1988" and has the horizontal edges of the pane imperforate.

1988 (11 Oct).   *Laminated cover as Type GB3 (75 × 48 mm) with stamp printed on the cover in bright orange-red by Questa.*
GP4   Containing ten 19p. (No. X1013) . . . .   24·00

£2.40 Booklets

1994 (9 Aug).   *Laminated cover as Type GM1 (75 × 49 mm) with stamp printed on the cover in dull blue-grey by Walsall.*
GQ1   Containing four 60p. (No. Y1758) and a pane of 4 air mail labels . . . .   8·00

Type GQ2

1994 (4 Oct).   *Laminated cover as Type GQ2 (75 × 49 mm) with stamp printed on the cover in dull blue-grey by Walsall.*
GQ2   Containing four 60p. (No. Y1758) and a pane of 4 air mail plus 4 "Seasons Greetings" labels . . . .   8·00

1995 (16 May). *Laminated cover as Type GK6 (75 × 48 mm) with stamps printed on the cover in dull blue-grey by Walsall.*
GQ3   Containing four 60p. (No. Y1758) and a pane of 4 air mail labels . . . .   8·00

1996 (19 Mar). *Multicoloured laminated cover as Type GK6 (75 × 48 mm) without "International" and showing Olympic symbols on the back. Stamps printed on the cover in dull grey-blue by Walsall.*
GQ4   Containing four 60p. (No. Y1758) and a pane of 4 air mail labels . . . .   8·00

£2.52 Booklets

1996 (8 July). *Multicoloured laminated cover as Type GL1 (75 × 48 mm) showing Olympic symbols on the back. Stamps printed on the cover in light emerald by Walsall. Inscribed "For items up to 20g" on yellow tab at right.*
GR1   Containing four 63p. (No. Y1759) and a pane of 4 air mail labels . . . .   12·00

1997 (4 Feb). *Multicoloured laminated cover as Type GL1 (75 × 48 mm) without Olympic symbols on the back. Stamps printed on the cover in light emerald by Walsall. Inscribed "For items up to 20g" on yellow tab at right.*
GR2   Containing four 63p. (No. Y1759) and a pane of 4 air mail labels . . . .   12·00

1997 (26 Aug). *Multicoloured laminated cover as Type GL1 (75 × 48 mm), but inscr "Worldwide Airmail Stamps". Stamps printed on the cover in light emerald by Walsall. Inscribed "For items up to 20g" on yellow tab at right.*

GR3 Containing four 63p. (photo) (No. Y1704) and a pane of 4
        air mail labels .... 7·25
    No. GR3 shows a "W" on the outside back cover below the barcode.

1998 (5 May). *Multicoloured laminated cover as Type GGA1 (75 × 50 mm). Stamps printed on cover in light emerald by Walsall. Inscr "For items up to 20g" on yellow tab at right.*

GR4 Containing four 63p. (photo) (No. Y1704) and a pane of 4
        new design air mail labels .... 7·25

£2.56 Booklets

1999 (26 Apr). *Multicoloured laminated cover as Type GGA1 (75 × 50 mm). Stamps printed on cover in turquoise-green by Walsall. Inscr "For items up to 20g" on yellow tab at right.*

GS1 Containing four 64p. (photo) (No. Y1705) and a pane of 4
        air mail labels .... 8·00

£2.60 Booklet

2000 (27 Apr). *Multicoloured laminated cover as Type GGA1 (76 × 50 mm) with stamps printed on cover in greenish blue by Walsall. Inscr "For items up to 20g" on yellow tab at right.*

GT1 Containing four 65p. (photo) (No. Y1706) and a pane of 4
        air mail labels .... 9·50

D. Barcode Booklets containing No Value Indicated stamps with barcodes on the back cover.

Panes of 4 2nd Class stamps

Type HA1
Redrawn Crown (small)

1989 (22 Aug). *Laminated cover as Type HA1 (75 × 48 mm) with stamp printed on the cover in bright blue by Walsall.*

HA1 Containing booklet pane No. 1449b .... 7·00
    No. HA1 has three edges of the pane imperforate.
    No. HA1 was initially sold at 56p., which was increased to 60p. from 2.10.89.

1989 (28 Nov). *Laminated cover as Type HA1 (75 × 48 mm) with stamp printed on the cover in bright blue by Walsall containing stamps printed in photo by Harrison.*

HA2 Containing booklet pane No. 1445b .... 22·00
    No. HA2 has three edges of the pane imperforate and was sold at 60p.

Type HA3
Crown on white

1990 (7 Aug). *Multicoloured laminated cover as Type HA3 (75 × 48 mm) with stamp printed on the cover in deep blue by Walsall.*

HA3 Containing booklet pane No. 1515a .... 3·75
    No. HA3 has the horizontal edges of the pane imperforate.
    No. HA3 was initially sold at 60p., which was increased to 68p. from 17.9.90 and to 72p. from 16.9.91.

1991 (6 Aug). *Multicoloured laminated cover as Type HA3 (75 × 48 mm) with stamp printed on the cover in bright blue by Walsall.*

HA4 Containing booklet pane No. 1449c .... 3·50
    No. HA4 has the horizontal edges of the pane imperforate.
    No. HA4 was initially sold at 68p., which was increased to 72p. from 16.9.91.

Type HA5
Olympic Symbols

1992 (21 Jan). *Multicoloured laminated cover as Type HA5 (75 × 48 mm) with stamp printed on the cover in bright blue by Walsall.*

HA5 Containing booklet pane No. 1449bc .... 7·00
    No. HA5 has the horizontal edges of the pane imperforate and was sold at 72p.

PERFORATIONS. Booklets from No. HA6 show perforations on all edges of the pane.

1993 (6 Apr). *Multicoloured laminated cover as Type HA3 (75 × 48 mm) with stamp printed on the cover in bright blue by Walsall.*

HA6 Containing four 2nd Class stamps (No. 1665) .... 4·00
    No. HA6 was initially sold at 72p., which was increased to 76p. from 1.11.93.
    No. HA6 was re-issued on 6 December 1994 showing the inscriptions on the inside of the cover re-arranged.

1993 (7 Sept). *Multicoloured laminated cover as Type HA3 (75 × 48 mm) with stamp printed on the cover in bright blue by Harrison.*

HA7 Containing four 2nd Class stamps (No. 1663a) .... 4·00
    No. HA7 was initially sold at 72p., which was increased to 76p. from 1.11.93.

Type HA8 ("Second Class Stamps" centred)
(with diagonal white line across corners of stamps)

1995 (10 Jan). *Multicoloured laminated cover as Type HA8 (75 × 48 mm) with stamps printed on the cover in bright blue by Harrison.*
HA8   Containing four 2nd Class stamps (No. 1663a) ....   4·00
No. HA8 was initially sold at 76p, which was increased to 80p. from 8.7.96.

1995 (12 Dec). *Multicoloured laminated cover as Type HA8 (75 × 48 mm) with stamps printed on the cover in bright blue by Walsall.*
HA9   Containing four 2nd Class stamps (No. 1665) ....   4·00
No. HA9 was initially sold at 76p, which was increased to 80p. from 8.7.96.

1996 (6 Feb). *Multicoloured laminated cover as Type HA8 (75 × 48 mm) showing Olympic symbols on the back. Stamps printed on the cover in bright blue by Walsall.*
HA10   Containing four 2nd Class stamps (No. 1665) ....   4·00
No. HA10 was initially sold at 76p, which was increased to 80p. from 8.7.96.

NOTE: From No. HA11 onwards, the printer of each booklet is identified by a small capital letter below the barcode on the outside back cover.

Type HA11 ("Second Class Stamps" ranged left)
(without diagonal white line across corners of stamps)

1997 (4 Feb). *Multicoloured laminated cover as Type HA11 (75 × 48 mm). Stamps printed on the cover in bright blue by Walsall.*
HA11   Containing four 2nd Class stamps (No. 1665) ....   4·00
No. HA11 was sold at 80p.

1997 (26 Aug). *Multicoloured laminated cover as Type HA11 (75 × 48 mm). Stamps printed on the cover in bright blue by Walsall.*
HA12   Containing four 2nd class stamps (photo) (No. 1663a) .   3·75
No. HA12 was initially sold at 80p. It was re-issued on 5 May 1998 showing the positions of the imprint and the post code notice transposed, and again on 14 March 2000 with changed telephone number and added website address. The booklet was sold at 76p. from 26.4.99.

Panes of 4 1st Class stamps

1989 (22 Aug). *Laminated cover as Type HA1 (75 × 48 mm) with stamp printed on the cover in brownish black by Walsall.*
HB1   Containing booklet pane No. 1450a ....   8·50
No. HB1 has three edges of the pane imperforate.
No. HB1 was initially sold at 76p., which was increased to 80p. from 2.10.89.

1989 (5 Dec). *Laminated cover as Type HA1 (75 × 48 mm) with stamp printed on the cover in brownish black by Walsall containing stamps printed in photo by Harrison.*
HB2   Containing booklet pane No. 1447b ....   40·00
No. HB2 has three edges of the pane imperforate and was sold at 80p.

1990 (7 Aug). *Multicoloured laminated cover as Type HA3 (75 × 48 mm) with stamp printed on the cover in bright orange-red by Walsall.*
HB3   Containing booklet pane No. 1516a ....   4·00
a. Containing pane No. 1516ca ....   12·00
No. HB3 has the horizontal edges of the pane imperforate.
No. HB3 was initially sold at 80p., which was increased to 88p. from 17.9.90 and to 96p. from 16.9.91.

1992 (21 Jan). *Multicoloured laminated cover as Type HA5 (75 × 48 mm) with stamp printed on the cover in bright orange-red by Walsall.*
HB4   Containing booklet pane No. 1516a ....   4·00
No. HB4 has the horizontal edges of the pane imperforate and was initially sold at 96p., which was increased to £1 from 1.11.93.

PERFORATIONS. Booklets from No. HB5 show perforations on all edges of the pane.

1993 (6 Apr). *Multicoloured laminated cover as Type HA3 (75 × 48 mm) with stamp printed on the cover in bright orange-red by Harrison*
HB5   Containing four 1st Class stamps (No. 1664) ....   5·50
No. HB5 was initially sold at 96p., which was increased to £1 from 1.11.93.

1993 (17 Aug). *Multicoloured laminated cover as Type HA3 (76 × 50 mm) with stamp printed on the cover in bright orange-red by Walsall.*
HB6   Containing four 1st Class stamps (No. 1666) ....   4·00
No. HB6 was initially sold at 96p., which was increased to £1 from 1.11.93.

1994 (27 July). *Multicoloured laminated cover as Type HA3 (76 × 50 mm) with stamp printed on the cover in bright orange-red by Questa.*
HB7   Containing booklet pane No. 1666l which includes a label commemorating the 300th anniv of the Bank of England ....   9·50
No. HB7 was sold at £1.

1995 (10 Jan). *Multicoloured laminated cover as Type HA8 (75 × 48 mm) with stamps printed on the cover in bright orange-red by Walsall.*
HB8   Containing four 1st Class stamps (No. 1666) ....   4·00
No. HB8 was initially sold at £1, which was increased to £1.04 from 8.7.96.

1995 (16 May). *Multicoloured laminated cover as Type HA8 (75 × 48 mm) with stamps printed on the cover in bright orange-red by Walsall.*
HB9   Containing booklet pane No. 1666la which includes a label commemorating the birth centenary of R. J. Mitchell (designer of Spitfire) ....   6·00
No. HB9 was sold at £1.

1996 (6 Feb–Aug). *Multicoloured laminated cover as Type HA8 (75 × 48 mm) showing Olympic symbols on the back. Stamps printed on the cover in bright orange-red by Walsall.*

HB10 Containing four 1st Class stamps (No. 1666) .... 6·00
    a. Without diagonal white line across corners of
       stamps (Aug) .... 75·00
No. HB10 was initially sold at £1, which was increased to £1.04 from 8.7.96.

1996 (16 Apr). *Multicoloured laminated cover as Type HA11 (75 × 48 mm) with stamps printed on the cover in bright orange-red by Walsall. Inscribed "Commemorative Label Inside" on yellow tab at right.*

HB11 Containing booklet pane No. 1666la (includes label
    commemorating the 70th birthday of Queen
    Elizabeth II) .... 6·00
No. HB11 was initially sold at £1, which was increased to £1.04 from 8.7.96.

NOTE: From No. HB12 onwards, the printer of each booklet (with the exception of No. HB19) is identified by a small capital letter below the barcode on the outside back cover.

1997 (4 Feb). *Multicoloured laminated cover as Type HA11 (75 × 48 mm). Stamps printed on the cover in bright orange-red by Walsall.*

HB12 Containing four 1st Class stamps (No. 1666) .... 3·50
No. HB12 was sold at £1.04.

1997 (12 Feb). *Multicoloured laminated cover as Type HA11 (75 × 48 mm). Stamps printed on the cover in bright orange-red by Walsall. Inscribed "Special Label Inside" on yellow tab at right.*

HB13 Containing booklet pane No. 1666la (includes label
    commemorating "Hong Kong '97" international
    stamp exhibition) .... 6·00
No. HB13 was sold at £1.04.

1997 (26 Aug). *Multicoloured laminated cover as Type HA11 (75 × 48 mm). Stamps printed on the cover in bright orange-red by Walsall.*

HB14 Containing four 1st Class stamps (photo) (No. 1664a) .. 4·00
No. HB14 was sold at £1.04. It was re-issued on 5 May 1998 showing the positions of the imprint and the post code notice transposed, on 16 March 1999 with "Please note that the First Class rate is no longer valid to Europe" added to inside back cover and again on 14 March 2000 with changed telephone number and added website address.

1997 (21 Oct). *Multicoloured laminated cover as Type HA11 (75 × 48 mm). Stamps printed on the cover in bright orange-red by Walsall. Inscribed "Commemorative Label Inside" on yellow tab at right.*

HB15 Containing booklet pane No. 1666la (litho) (includes
    label commemorating Commonwealth Heads of
    Government Meeting, Edinburgh) .... 9·50
No. HB15 was sold at £1.04.

1998 (14 Nov). *Multicoloured laminated cover as Type HA11 (75 × 48 mm). Stamps printed on the cover in bright orange-red by Walsall. Inscribed "Commemorative Label Inside" on yellow tab at right.*

HB16 Containing booklet pane No. 1666la (litho) (includes
    label commemorating 50th birthday of the Prince of
    Wales) .... 7·00
No. HB16 was sold at £1.04.

1999 (12 May). *Multicoloured laminated cover as Type HA11 (75 × 48 mm). Stamps printed on the cover in bright orange-red by Walsall. Inscribed "Commemorative Label Inside" on yellow tab at right.*

HB17 Containing booklet pane No. 1664am (photo) (includes
    label commemorating 50th anniv of Berlin Airlift) ... 8·00
No. HB17 was sold for £1.04.

1999 (1 Oct). *Multicoloured laminated cover as Type HA11 (76 × 50 mm). Stamps printed on the cover in bright orange-red by Walsall. Inscribed "Commemorative Label Inside" on yellow tab at right.*

HB18 Containing booklet pane No. 1664am (photo) (includes
    label commemorating Rugby World Cup) .... 4·50
No. HB18 was sold at £1.04.

2000 (21 Mar). *Multicoloured laminated cover as Type HA11 (75 × 48 mm). Stamps printed on the cover in olive-brown by Walsall with Postman Pat. Inscribed "Postman Pat Label Inside" on yellow tab at right.*

HB19 Containing booklet pane No. 2124bl (photo) (includes
    label commemorating "Stamp Show 2000", Earls
    Court) .... 6·00
No. HB19 was initially sold at £1.04, which was increased to £1.08 from 27.4.2000.

2000 (4 Apr). *Opening of National Botanic Garden of Wales. Multicoloured laminated cover as Type HA11 (75 × 48 mm). Stamps printed on the cover in olive-brown by Walsall. Inscribed "Botanic Garden Label Inside" on yellow tab at right.*

HB20 Containing booklet pane No. 2124bl .... 5·00
No. HB20 was initially sold at £1.04, which was increased to £1.08 from 27.4.2000.

Panes of 8 1st Class Stamps plus pane of 2 Millennium commemoratives

Type HBA1

1999 (12 May). *Multicoloured laminated cover as Type HBA1 (76 × 50 mm) showing Millennium and Machin stamps printed by Walsall.*

HBA1 Containing booklet pane No. 2085a and eight 1st Class
    stamps (photo) (No. 1664a) .... 8·00
No. HBA1 was sold at £2.60.

1999 (21 Sept). *Multicoloured laminated cover as Type HBA1 (76 × 50 mm) showing Millennium and Machin stamps printed by Walsall.*

HBA2 Containing booklet pane No. 2108a and eight 1st Class
    stamps (photo) (No. 1664a) .... 8·00
No. HBA2 was sold at £2.60.

2000 (26 May). *Multicoloured laminated cover as Type HBA1 (76 × 50 mm) showing Millennium and Machin stamps printed by Walsall.*

HBA3 Containing booklet pane No. 2126ab and eight 1st Class
    stamps (photo) (No. 2124) .... 10·00
No. HBA3 was sold at £2.70.

2000 (5 Sept). *Multicoloured laminated cover as Type HBA1 (76 × 50 mm) showing Millennium and Machin stamps printed by Walsall.*

HBA4 Containing booklet pane No. 2153a and eight 1st Class
    stamps (photo) (No. 2124) .... 11·00
No. HBA4 was sold at £2.70.

Panes of 10 2nd Class stamps

1989 (22 Aug–2 Oct).   *Laminated cover as Type HA1 (75 × 48 mm) with stamp printed on the cover in bright blue by Harrison.*
HC1   Containing booklet pane No. 1445a .... 11·00
   a. Inside cover with new rates (2 Oct) .... 12·00
   Nos. HC1/a have the horizontal edges of the pane imperforate. No. HC1 was initially sold at £1.40, which was increased to £1.50 from 2.10.89. No. HC1a was sold at £1.50.

1989 (19 Sept).   *Laminated cover as Type HA1 (75 × 48 mm) with stamp printed on the cover in bright blue by Questa.*
HC2   Containing ten 2nd Class stamps (No. 1451) .... 9·50
   No. HC2 has perforations on all edges of the pane and was initially sold at £1.40, which was increased to £1.50 from 2.10.89.

1990 (7 Aug).   *Multicoloured laminated cover as Type HA3 (75 × 48 mm) with stamp printed on the cover in deep blue by Harrison.*
HC3   Containing booklet pane No. 1511a .... 12·00
   No. HC3 has the horizontal edges of the pane imperforate. No. HC3 was initially sold at £1.50, which was increased to £1.70 from 17.9.90.

1990 (7 Aug).   *Multicoloured laminated cover as Type HA3 (75 × 48 mm) with stamp printed on the cover in deep blue by Questa.*
HC4   Containing ten 2nd Class stamps (No. 1513) .... 15·00
   No. HC4 has perforations on all edges of the pane and was initially sold at £1.50, which was increased to £1.70 from 17.9.90.

1990 (7 Aug).   *Multicoloured laminated cover as Type HA3 (75 × 48 mm) with stamp printed on the cover in deep blue by Walsall.*
HC5   Containing booklet pane No. 1515b .... 8·50
   No. HC5 has the horizontal edges of the pane imperforate. No. HC5 was initially sold at £1.50, which was increased to £1.70 from 17.9.90. and to £1.80 from 16.9.91.

1991 (6 Aug).   *Multicoloured laminated cover as Type HA3 (75 × 48 mm) with stamp printed on the cover in bright blue by Questa.*
HC6   Containing ten 2nd class stamps (No. 1451) .... 8·00
   No. HC6 has perforations on all edges of the pane and was initially sold at £1.70, which was increased to £1.80 from 16.9.91.

1991 (6 Aug).   *Multicoloured laminated cover as Type HA3 (75 × 48 mm) with stamp printed on the cover in bright blue by Walsall.*
HC7   Containing booklet pane No. 1449d .... 7·50
   No. HC7 has the horizontal edges of the pane imperforate. No. HC7 was initially sold at £1.70, which was increased to £1.80 from 16.9.91.

1992 (21 Jan).   *Multicoloured laminated cover as Type HA5 (75 × 48 mm) with stamp printed on the cover in bright blue by Walsall.*
HC8   Containing booklet pane No. 1449d .... 6·00
   No HC8 has the horizontal edges of the pane imperforate and was initially sold at £1.80, which was increased to £1.84 from 1.11.93.

1992 (31 Mar).   *Multicoloured laminated cover as Type HA5 (75 × 48 mm) with stamp printed on the cover in bright blue by Questa.*
HC9   Containing ten 2nd Class stamps (No. 1451) .... 8·50
   No. HC9 has perforations on all edges of the pane and was sold at £1.80.

1992 (22 Sept).   *Multicoloured laminated cover as Type HA3 (75 × 48 mm) with stamp printed on the cover in bright blue by Harrison.*
HC10   Containing booklet pane No. 1445a .... 8·00
   No. HC10 has the horizontal edges of the pane imperforate and was sold at £1.80.

PERFORATIONS. Booklets from No. HC11 show perforations on all edges of the pane.

1993 (6 Apr).   *Multicoloured laminated cover as Type HA3 (75 × 48 mm) with stamp printed on the cover in bright blue by Questa.*
HC11   Containing ten 2nd Class stamps (No. 1665) .... 7·75
   No. HC11 was initially sold at £1.80, which was increased to £1.90 from 1.11.93.
   No. HC11 was re-issued on 17 August 1993 showing changes to the text on the inside of the cover and again on 6 September 1994 showing further changes.

1993 (1 Nov).   *Multicoloured laminated cover as Type HA3 (75 × 48 mm) with stamp printed on the cover in bright blue by Walsall.*
HC12   Containing ten 2nd Class stamps (No. 1665) .... 7·75
   No. HC12 was sold at £1.90.

1995 (10 Jan).   *Multicoloured laminated cover as Type HA8 (75 × 48 mm) with stamps printed on the cover in bright blue by Questa.*
HC13   Containing ten 2nd Class stamps (No. 1665) .... 7·75
   No. HC13 was initially sold at £1.90, which was increased to £2 from 8.7.96.

1995 (12 Dec). *Multicoloured laminated cover as Type HA8 (75 × 48 mm) with stamps printed on cover in bright blue by Harrison.*
HC14   Containing ten 2nd Class stamps (No. 1663a) .... 6·00
   No. HC14 was initially sold at £1.90, which was increased to £2 from 8.7.96.

1996 (6 Feb). *Multicoloured laminated cover as Type HA8 (75 × 48 mm) showing Olympic symbols on the back. Stamps printed on the cover in bright blue by Harrison.*
HC15   Containing ten 2nd Class stamps (No. 1663a) .... 6·50
   No. HC15 was initially sold at £1.90, which was increased to £2 from 8.7.96.

1996 (6 Feb). *Multicoloured laminated cover as Type HA8 (75 × 48 mm) showing Olympic symbols on the back. Stamps printed on the cover in bright blue by Questa.*
HC16   Containing ten 2nd Class stamps (No. 1665) .... 9·00
   No. HC16 was initially sold at £1.90, which was increased to £2 from 8.7.96.

NOTE: From No. HC17 onwards, the printer of each booklet is identified by a small capital letter below the barcode on the outside back cover.

1996 (6 Aug). *Multicoloured laminated cover as Type HA11 (75 × 48 mm) but with diagonal white lines across corners of stamps, showing Olympic symbols on the back. Stamps printed on the cover in bright blue by Harrison.*
HC17   Containing ten 2nd Class stamps (No. 1663a) .... 6·50
   No. HC17 was sold at £2.

1996 (6 Aug). *Multicoloured laminated cover as Type HA11 (75 × 48 mm) showing Olympic symbols on the back. Stamps printed on the cover in bright blue by Questa.*
HC18   Containing ten 2nd Class stamps (No. 1665) .... 8·75
   No. HC18 was sold at £2.

1997 (4 Feb). *Multicoloured laminated cover as Type HA11 (75 × 48 mm). Stamps printed on the cover in bright blue by Harrison.*
HC19   Containing ten 2nd Class stamps (No. 1663a) .... 6·50
   No. HC19 was sold at £2.

1997 (4 Feb). *Multicoloured laminated cover as Type HA11 (75 × 48 mm). Stamps printed on the cover in bright blue by Questa.*
HC20   Containing ten 2nd Class stamps (No. 1665) .... 7·00
   No. HC20 was initially sold at £2. It was re-issued on 5 May 1998 showing the positions of the imprint and the post code notice transposed. The booklet was sold at £1.90 from 26.4.99.

1998 (5 May). *Multicoloured laminated cover as Type HA11 (75 × 48 mm). Stamps printed on the cover in bright blue by De La Rue.*
HC21   Containing ten 2nd Class stamps (No. 1663a) .... 6·00
   No. HC21 was initially sold at £2 which was decreased to £1.90 from 26.4.99.

1998 (1 Dec). *Multicoloured laminated cover as Type HA11 (75 × 48 mm). Stamps printed on the cover in bright blue by Questa.*
HC22   Containing ten 2nd Class stamps (No. 1663ab) (photo) 8·75
   No. HC22 was initially sold at £2 which was decreased to £1.90 from 26.4.99. It was re-issued on 14 March 2000 with changed telephone number and added website address.

Panes of 10 1st Class stamps

1989 (22 Aug–2 Oct). *Laminated cover as Type HA1 (75 × 48 mm) with stamp printed on the cover in brownish black by Harrison.*
HD1   Containing booklet pane No. 1447a .... 15·00
   a. Inside cover with new rates (2 Oct) .... 13·00
   Nos. HD1/a have the horizontal edges of the pane imperforate.
   No. HD1 was initially sold at £1.90 which was increased to £2 from 2.10.89. No. HD1a was sold at £2.

1989 (19 Sept). *Laminated cover as Type HA1 (75 × 48 mm) with stamp printed on the cover in brownish black by Questa.*
HD2   Containing ten 1st Class stamps (No. 1452) .... 20·00
   No. HD2 has perforations on all edges of the pane and was initially sold at £1.90, which was increased to £2 from 2.10.89.

1990 (7 Aug). *Multicoloured laminated cover as Type HA3 (75 × 48 mm) with stamp printed on the cover in bright orange-red by Harrison.*
HD3   Containing booklet pane No. 1512a .... 10·00
   No. HD3 has the horizontal edges of the pane imperforate.
   No. HD3 was initially sold at £2, which was increased to £2.20 from 17.9.90 and to £2.40 from 16.9.91.

1990 (7 Aug). *Multicoloured laminated cover as Type HA3 (75 × 48 mm) with stamp printed on the cover in bright orange-red by Questa.*
HD4   Containing ten 1st Class stamps (No. 1514) .... 8·50
   No. HD4 has perforations on all edges of the pane and was initially sold at £2, which was increased to £2.20 from 17.9.90 and to £2.40 from 16.9.91.

1990 (7 Aug). *Multicoloured laminated cover as Type HA3 (75 × 48 mm) with stamp printed on the cover in bright orange-red by Walsall.*
HD5   Containing booklet pane No. 1516b .... 8·75
   No. HD5 has the horizontal edges of the pane imperforate and was initally sold at £2, which was increased to £2.20 from 17.9.90 and to £2.40 from 16.9.91.

1992 (21 Jan). *Multicoloured laminated cover as Type HA5 (75 × 48 mm) with stamp printed on the cover in bright orange-red by Harrison.*
HD6   Containing booklet pane No. 1512a. .... 10·00
   No. HD6 has the horizontal edges of the pane imperforate and was sold at £2.40.

1992 (21 Jan). *Multicoloured laminated cover as Type HA5 (75 × 48 mm) with stamp printed on the cover in bright orange-red by Walsall.*
HD7   Containing booklet pane No. 1516b. .... 7·75
   No. HD7 has the horizontal edges of the pane imperforate and was sold at £2.40.

1993 (9 Feb). *Multicoloured laminated cover as Type HA3 (77 × 44 mm) with advertisement for Greetings Booklet on reverse showing Rupert Bear as in Type KX5. Stamp printed on the cover in bright orange-red by Walsall.*
HD8   Containing booklet pane No. 1516b .... 7·75
   No. HD8 has the horizontal edges of the pane imperforate and was sold at £2.40.

PERFORATIONS. Booklets from No. HD9 show perforations on all edges of the pane.

1993 (6 Apr). *Multicoloured laminated cover as Type HA3 (75 × 48 mm) with stamp printed on the cover in bright orange-red by Harrison.*
HD9   Containing ten 1st Class stamps (No. 1664) .... 12·00
   No. HD9 was initially sold at £2.40., which was increased to £2.50 from 1.11.93.
   No. HD9 was re-issued on 17 August 1993 showing changes to the text on the inside of the covers.

1993 (6 Apr). *Multicoloured laminated cover as Type HA3 (75 × 48 mm) with stamp printed on the cover in bright orange-red by Walsall.*
HD10   Containing ten 1st Class stamps (No. 1666) .... 7·75
   No. HD10 was initially sold at £2.40., which was increased to £2.50 from 1.11.93.
   No. HD10 was re-issued on 17 August 1993 showing changes to the text on the inside of the covers.

1993 (1 Nov). *Laminated cover as Type HA3 (75 × 50 mm) with stamp printed on the cover in bright orange-red by Questa.*
HD11   Containing ten 1st Class stamps (No. 1666) .... 7·75
   No. HD11 was sold at £2.50.
   No. HD11 was re-issued on 4 October 1994 showing changes to the text on the inside of the cover.

1993 (1 Nov). *Laminated cover as Type HA3 (75 × 50 mm) with advertisement for Greetings Booklet on reverse showing Rupert Bear as in Type KX5. Stamp printed on the cover in bright orange-red by Walsall.*
HD12   Containing ten 1st Class stamps (No. 1666) .... 8·75

1994 (22 Feb). *Multicoloured laminated cover as Type HA3 (75 × 48 mm) with stamp printed on the cover in bright orange-red by Walsall. Inscribed "FREE POSTCARDS" on yellow tab at right.*
HD13   Containing ten 1st Class stamps (No. 1666) and additional page giving details of Greetings Stamps postcard offer .... 7·75
   No. HD13 was sold at £2.50.

1994 (1 July). *Multicoloured laminated covers as Type HA3 (76 × 50 mm) with advertisement for Greetings Booklet on reverse showing Rupert Bear as in Type KX5. Stamp printed on the cover in bright orange-red by Walsall. Inscribed "OPEN NOW Chance to win a kite" on yellow tab at right.*
HD14   Containing ten 1st Class stamps (No. 1666) with "Better luck next time." etc on inside back cover .... 8·00
HD15   Containing ten 1st Class stamps (No. 1666) with "You've Won!" etc on inside back cover .... 8·00
   Nos. HD14/15 sold at £2.50 each and were initially only available from branches of W.H. Smith and Son. They were issued in connection with a competition in which the prizes were Paddington Bear kites. The booklets were not available from Royal Mail philatelic outlets until 4 October 1994.

Type HD16

1994 (20 Sept). *Multicoloured laminated covers as Type HD16 (76 × 50 mm) printed by Walsall. Inscribed "ORDER YOURS INSIDE" on yellow tab at right.*

HD16 Containing ten 1st Class stamps (No. 1666) with "DO NOT OPEN UNTIL....." on front cover .... 8·00

HD17 Containing ten 1st Class stamps (No. 1666) with "KEEP IN TOUCH" on front cover .... 8·00

HD18 Containing ten 1st Class stamps (No. 1666) with "HAPPY BIRTHDAY" on front cover .... 8·00

HD19 Containing ten 1st Class stamps (No. 1666) with "What's Happenin'?" on front cover .... 8·00

Nos. HD16/19 were sold at £2.50 each.

1995 (10 Jan). *Multicoloured laminated cover as Type HA8 (75 × 48 mm) with stamps printed on the cover in bright orange-red by Harrison.*

HD20 Containing ten 1st Class stamps (No. 1664) .... 12·00

1995 (10 Jan). *Multicoloured laminated cover as Type HA8 (75 × 48 mm) with stamps printed on the cover in bright orange-red by Questa.*

HD21 Containing ten 1st Class stamps (No. 1666) .... 7·75

1995 (10 Jan). *Multicoloured laminated cover as Type HA8 (75 × 48 mm) with stamps printed on the cover in bright orange-red by Walsall.*

HD22 Containing ten 1st Class stamps (No. 1666) .... 7·75

Nos. HD20/2 were initially sold at £2.50 each, which was increased to £2.60 from 8.7.96.

Type HD23

1995 (14 Feb). *Multicoloured laminated cover as Type HD23 (76 × 50 mm) showing card, Thorntons chocolates and box, printed by Walsall. Inscribed "DETAILS INSIDE" on yellow tab at right.*

HD23 Containing ten 1st Class stamps (No. 1666) .... 7·75

No. HD23 was sold at £2.50.

1995 (4 Apr). *Multicoloured laminated cover as Type HA8 (76 × 48 mm) with stamps printed on cover in bright orange-red by Harrison.*

HD24 Containing ten 1st Class stamps (No. 1664a) .... 7·75

No. HD24 was sold at £2.50.

1995 (24 Apr). *Multicoloured laminated cover as Type HA8 (75 × 48 mm) with stamps printed on cover in bright orange-red by Walsall. Inscribed "W H Smith Special Offer" on yellow tab at right.*

HD25 Containing ten 1st Class stamps (No. 1666) .... 7·75

No. HD25 was sold at £2.50 and was initially only available from W. H. Smith branches and offered 50p. off the purchase of own brand stationery. The booklet was not placed on philatelic sale until 3 October 1995. Its price was increased to £2.60 on 8.7.96.

1995 (26 June). *Multicoloured laminated cover as Type HA8 (76 × 48 mm) with stamps printed on the cover in bright orange-red by Questa. Inscribed "Sainsbury's Promotion" on yellow tab at right.*

HD26 Containing ten 1st Class stamps (No. 1666) .... 7·75

No. HD26 was sold at £2.50 and was initially only available from Sainsbury's branches and offered the chance to win a year's free shopping. The booklet was not placed on philatelic sale until 5 September 1995. Its price was increased to £2.60 on 8.7.96.

1995 (4 Sept). *Multicoloured laminated cover as Type HD23 (76 × 48 mm) showing ceramic figures of Benjy Bear and Harry Hedgehog, printed by Harrison.*

HD27 Containing ten 1st Class stamps (No. 1664a) .... 7·75

No. HD27 was initially sold at £2.50, which was increased to £2.60 from 8.7.96.

1996 (6 Feb). *Multicoloured laminated cover as Type HA8 (76 × 48 mm) showing Olympic symbols on the back. Stamps printed on the cover in bright orange-red by Walsall.*

HD28 Containing ten 1st Class stamps (No. 1666) .... 7·75

No. HD28 was initially sold at £2.50, which was increased to £2.60 from 8.7.96.

1996 (19 Feb). *Multicoloured laminated cover as Type HD23 (76 × 48 mm) showing Walt Disney World, printed by Harrison.*

HD29 Containing ten 1st Class stamps (No. 1664a) .... 7·75

No. HD29 was initially sold at £2.50, which was increased to £2.60 from 8.7.96.

1996 (19 Mar). *Multicoloured laminated cover as Type HA8 (76 × 48 mm) showing Olympic symbols on the back, printed by Harrison.*

HD30 Containing ten 1st Class stamps (No. 1664a) .... 8·75

No. HD30 was initially sold at £2.50, which was increased to £2.60 from 8.7.96.

Type HD31

1996 (13 May). *Multicoloured laminated covers as Type HD31 (76 × 48 mm) showing woman lighting Olympic torch, printed by Harrison, with each booklet showing a scratchcard on the reverse based on different Olympic events.*

HD31 Containing ten 1st Class stamps (No. 1664a) (Shot Put) .   7·75

HD32 Containing ten 1st Class stamps (No. 1664a) (Hurdles) ..   7·75

HD33 Containing ten 1st Class stamps (No. 1664a) (Archery) .   7·75

Nos. HD31/3 were initially each sold at £2.50, which was increased to £2.60 from 8.7.96.

NOTE: From No. HD34 onwards, the printer of each booklet is identified by a small capital letter below the barcode on the outside back cover.

1996 (15 July). *Multicoloured laminated cover as Type HA11 (76 × 48 mm) showing Olympic symbols on the back. Stamps printed on the cover in bright orange-red by Walsall. Inscribed "WH Smith Offer Inside" on yellow tab at right.*

HD34 Containing ten 1st Class stamps (No. 1666) .... 7·75

No. HD34 was sold at £2.60 and was initially only available from branches of W. H. Smith and Sons. It was issued in connection with a special offer of AA/OS Leisure Guides. The booklets were not available from Royal Mail philatelic outlets until 17 September 1996.

1996 (16 Aug). *Multicoloured laminated cover as Type HA11 (76 × 48 mm), but with diagonal white line across corners of stamps and showing Olympic symbols on the back. Stamps printed on the cover in bright orange-red by Harrison.*
HD35 Containing ten 1st Class stamps (No. 1664a) . . . . 8·75
No. HD35 was sold at £2.60.

1996 (16 Aug). *Multicoloured laminated cover as Type HA11 (76 × 48 mm) showing Olympic symbols on the back. Stamps printed on the cover in bright orange-red by Walsall.*
HD36 Containing ten 1st Class stamps (No. 1666) . . . . 7·75
No. HD36 was sold at £2.60.

1996 (9 Sept). *Multicoloured laminated cover as Type HD31 (76 × 48 mm) showing iced cakes on front and back, printed by Walsall. Inscribed "OPEN FOR DETAILS" on yellow tab at right.*
HD37 Containing ten 1st Class stamps (No. 1666) . . . . 7·75
No. HD37 was sold at £2.60.

1996 (7 Oct). *Multicoloured laminated cover as Type HA11 (76 × 48 mm) showing Olympic symbols on the back. Stamps printed on cover in bright orange-red by Walsall. Inscribed "Offer Inside" on yellow tab at right.*
HD38 Containing ten 1st Class stamps (No. 1666) . . . . 7·75
No. HD38 was sold at £2.60 and was initially only available from ASDA stores and offered £1 off greetings cards. The booklet was not placed on philatelic sale until 13 January 1997.

1997 (4 Feb). *Multicoloured laminated cover as Type HA11 (76 × 48 mm). Stamps printed on the cover in bright orange-red by Harrison.*
HD39 Containing ten 1st Class stamps (No. 1664a) . . . . 7·75
No. HD39 was sold at £2.60.

1997 (4 Feb). *Multicoloured laminated cover as Type HA11 (76 × 48 mm). Stamps printed on the cover in bright orange-red by Walsall.*
HD40 Containing ten 1st Class stamps (No. 1666) . . . . 7·00
No. HD40 was sold at £2.60.

1997 (21 Apr). *Royal Golden Wedding. Multicoloured laminated cover as Type HA11 (76 × 48 mm). Stamps printed on the cover in gold by Harrison.*
HD41 Containing ten 1st Class stamps (No. 1664b) . . . . 8·50
No. HD41 was sold at £2.60.

1997 (21 Apr). *Royal Golden Wedding. Multicoloured laminated cover as Type HA11 (76 × 48 mm). Stamps printed on the cover in gold by Walsall.*
HD42 Containing ten 1st Class stamps (No. 1664b) . . . . 8·50
No. HD42 was sold at £2.60.

1997 (15 Sept). *Multicoloured laminated cover as Type HD31 (76 × 48 mm) showing a tropical beach scene printed by Harrison. Inscr "FIRST CLASS TRAVEL" on front, and "OPEN FOR DETAILS" on yellow tab at right.*
HD43 Containing ten 1st Class stamps (No. 1664b) . . . . 8·00
No. HD43 was sold at £2.60.

1997 (8 Nov). *Multicoloured laminated cover as Type HA11 (76 × 48 mm). Stamps printed on the cover in bright orange-red by Walsall.*
HD44 Containing ten 1st Class stamps (photo) (No. 1664a) . . . 7·75
No. HD44 was sold at £2.60. It was re-issued on 5 May 1998 showing the positions of the imprint, which was now vertical, and the post code notice transposed and again on 16 March 1999 with "Please note that the First Class rate is no longer valid to Europe" added to inside back cover.

Type HD45

1998 (2 Feb). *Multicoloured laminated cover as Type HD45 (76 × 48 mm) showing Disney illustration printed by De la Rue, with a scratch card on the reverse. Inscr "See reverse for Scratch and Win" on yellow tab at right.*
HD45 Containing ten 1st Class stamps (photo) (No. 1664a) . . . 7·75
No. HD45 was sold at £2.60

Type HD46

1998 (27 Apr). *Multicoloured laminated cover as Type HD46 (76 × 48 mm) showing Peugeot 106 printed by De La Rue. Inscr "WIN A PEUGEOT 106" on yellow tab at right.*
HD46 Containing ten 1st Class stamps (photo) (No. 1664a) . . . 7·75
No. HD46 was sold at £2.60. This booklet was not placed on philatelic sale until 23 June 1998.

1998 (5 May). *Multicoloured laminated cover as Type HA11 (76 × 48 mm). Stamps printed on the cover in bright orange-red by De La Rue.*
HD47 Containing ten 1st Class stamps (photo) (No. 1664a) . . . 7·75
No. HD47 was initially sold at £2.60, which was increased to £2.70 from 27.4.2000.

1998 (1 July). *Multicoloured laminated cover as Type HD46 (76 × 48 mm) showing JVC Camcorder printed by De La Rue. Inscr "WIN A JVC CAMCORDER" on yellow tab at right.*
HD48 Containing ten 1st Class stamps (photo) (No. 1664a) . . . 7·75
No. HD48 was sold at £2.60. This booklet was not placed on philatelic sale until 27 August 1998.

1998 (3 Aug). *Multicoloured laminated cover as Type GGA2 ("Create a card design") (76 × 48 mm), printed by De La Rue.*
HD49 Containing ten 1st Class stamps (No. 1664a) . . . . 7·75
No. HD49 was sold at £2.60. This booklet was not placed on philatelic sale until 7 September 1998.

1998 (7 Sept). *Multicoloured laminated cover as Type HA11 (75 × 49 mm), with stamps printed on the cover in bright orange-red by Questa.*
HD50 Containing ten 1st Class stamps (litho) (No. 1666) . . . . . 7·75
No. HD50 was sold at £2·60.

1998 (1 Dec). *Multicoloured laminated cover as Type HA11 (75 × 48 mm). Stamps printed on the cover in bright orange-red by Questa.*
HD51 Containing ten 1st Class stamps (photo) (No. 1664ab) . 14·00
     No. HD51 was sold at £2.60. It was re-issued on 16 March 1999 with "Please note that the First Class rate is no longer valid to Europe" added to inside back cover.

2000 (6 Jan). *Multicoloured laminated cover as Type HA11 (75 × 48 mm). Millennium definitives printed on the cover in olive-brown by Questa.*
HD52 Containing ten 1st Class stamps (photo) (No. 2124d) . 7·75
     No. HD52 was initially sold at £2.60, which was increased to £2.70 from 27 April 2000. It was re-issued on 14 March 2000 with a changed telephone number on the inside back cover.

2000 (6 Jan). *Multicoloured laminated cover as Type HA11 (75 × 48 mm). Millennium definitives printed on the cover in olive-brown by Walsall.*
HD53 Containing ten 1st Class stamps (photo) (No. 2124) .... 7·75
     No. HD53 was initially sold at £2.60, which was increased to £2.70 from 27 April 2000. It was re-issued on 14 March 2000 with a changed telephone number on the inside back cover.

Panes of 4 European Air Mail Stamps

Type HF1

1999 (19 Jan). *Multicoloured laminated cover as Type HF1 (75 × 50 mm). Stamps printed on the cover in deep blue by Walsall. Inscr "For items up to 20g" on yellow tab at right.*
HF1 Containing four European Air Mail stamps (No. 1664c) and pane of four air mail labels .... 4·50
     No. HF1 was initially sold at £1.20 which was increased to £1.36 from 25.10.99 and £1.44 from 27.4.2000.
     It was re-issued on 27 April 2000 showing an amended Customer Services telephone number on the inside back cover.

E. Barcode Booklets containing Penny Black Anniversary stamps with barcodes on back cover.

60p. Booklet

Type JA1

1990 (30 Jan). *Laminated cover as Type JA1 (75 × 48 mm) showing Penny Black Anniversary stamp in bright blue. Containing booklet pane. No. 1475l, printed in litho by Walsall.*
JA1 Containing booklet pane No. 1475l .... 7·00
     No. JA1 has three edges of the pane imperforate.

80p. Booklets

1990 (30 Jan). *Laminated cover as Type JA1 (75 × 48 mm) showing Penny Black Anniversary stamp in brownish black and cream. Containing booklet pane No. 1476m, printed in litho by Walsall.*
JB1 Containing booklet pane No. 1476m .... 10·00
     No. JB1 has three edges of the pane imperforate.

1990 (17 Apr). *Laminated cover as Type JA1 (75 × 48 mm) showing Penny Black Anniversary stamp printed on the cover in brownish black by Walsall containing stamps printed in photo by Harrison.*
JB2 Containing booklet pane No. 1469r .... 8·00
     No. JB2 has three edges of the pane imperforate.

£1.50 Booklets

1990 (30 Jan). *Laminated cover as Type JA1 (75 × 48 mm) showing Penny Black Anniversary stamp in bright blue. Containing booklet pane No. 1467l printed by photo by Harrison.*
JC1 Containing booklet pane No. 1467l .... 10·00
     No. JC1 hs the horizontal edges of the pane imperforate.

1990 (17 Apr). *Laminated cover as Type JA1 (75 × 48 mm) showing Penny Black Anniversary stamp printed on the cover in bright blue by Questa.*
JC2 Containing ten 15p. (No. 1477) .... 20·00

1990 (12 June). *Laminated cover as Type JA1 (75 × 48 mm) showing Penny Black Anniversary stamp in bright blue. Containing booklet pane No. 1475m, printed in litho by Walsall.*
JC3 Containing booklet pane No. 1475m .... 12·00
     No. JC3 has three edges of the pane imperforate.

£2 Booklets

1990 (30 Jan). *Laminated cover as Type JA1 (75 × 48 mm) showing Penny Black Anniversary stamp in brownish black and cream. Containing booklet pane. No. 1469m, printed in photo by Harrison.*
JD1 Containing booklet pane No. 1469m .... 11·00
     No. JD1 has the horizontal edges of the pane imperforate.

1990 (17 Apr). *Laminated cover as Type JA1 (75 × 48 mm) showing Penny Black Anniversary stamp printed on the cover in brownish black by Questa.*
JD2 Containing ten 20p. (No. 1478) .... 22·00

1990 (12 June). *Laminated cover as Type JA1 (75 × 48 mm) showing Penny Black Anniversary stamp in brownish black and cream. Containing booklet pane No. 1476n, printed in litho by Walsall.*
JD3 Containing booklet pane No. 1476n .... 16·00
     No. JD3 has three edges of the pane imperforate.

F. Barcode Booklets containing Greetings stamps with barcodes on the back cover.

£2 Greetings Booklet

Type KX1
(Illustration reduced. Actual size 135 × 85 mm)

(Des Michael Peters and Partners)

1990 (6 Feb). *Greetings Stamps. Cover printed in scarlet, lemon and black as Type KX1 (135 × 85 mm). Containing booklet pane No. 1483a, and a separate sheet of 12 greetings labels.*
KX1 "Smile" design cut-out showing stamps inside .... 30·00

Greetings Booklets containing No Value Indicated stamps

Type KX2

(Des T. Meeuwissen)

1991 (5 Feb). *Greetings Stamps. Multicoloured laminated cover as Type KX2 (95 × 69 mm). Containing booklet pane No. 1536a, including twelve special greetings labels in a block (3 × 4) at right, attached by the selvedge.*
KX2 "Good Luck" charms design .... 17·00
No. KX2 was initially sold at £2.20, which was increased to £2.40 from 16.9.91.

Type KX3

(Des Michael Peters and Partners)

1991 (26 Mar). *Greetings Stamps. Multicoloured laminated cover as Type KX3 (95 × 69 mm). Containing booklet pane No. 1550a, including twelve special greetings labels in a block (3 × 4) at right, attached by the selvedge.*
KX3 Laughing pillar box design .... 11·00
No. KX3 was initially sold at £2.20, which was increased to £2.40 from 16.9.91 and to £2.50 from 1.11.93.

Type KX4

(Des Trickett and Webb)

1992 (28 Jan). *Greetings Stamps. Multicoloured laminated cover as Type KX4 (95 × 69 mm). Containing booklet pane No. 1592a, including twelve special greetings labels in a block (3 × 4) at right, attached by selvedge.*
KX4 Pressed Flowers design .... 11·00
No. KX4 was initially sold at £2.40, which was increased to £2.50 from 1.11.93 and to £2.60 from 8.7.96.

Type KX5

(Des Newell and Sorrell)

1993 (2 Feb). *Greetings Stamps. Multicoloured laminated cover as Type KX5 (96 × 60 mm). Containing booklet pane No. 1644a and pane of twenty special greetings labels in a block (5 × 4), both panes attached by a common gutter margin.*
KX5   Children's Characters design . . . .   11·00
No. KX5 was initially sold at £2.40, which was increased to £2.50 from 1.11.93.

Type KX6

(Des Newell and Sorrell)

1994 (1 Feb). *Greetings Stamps. Multicoloured cover as Type KX6 (96 × 60 mm). Containing booklet pane No. 1800a and pane of twenty special greetings labels in a block (5 × 4), both panes attached by a common gutter margin.*
KX6   Children's Characters design . . . .   11·00
No. KX6 was initially sold at £2.50, which was increased to £2.60 from 8.7.96.

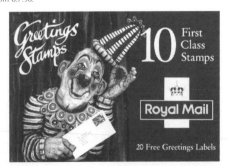

Type KX7

(Des Newell and Sorrell)

1995 (21 Mar)–**96**. *Greetings Stamps. Multicoloured cover as Type KX7 (96 × 60 mm). Containing booklet pane No. 1858a and pane of twenty special greetings labels in a block (5 × 4), both panes attached by a common gutter margin. Inscr "Pull Open" on yellow strip at right.*
KX7   Clown design . . . .   11·00
      a. No inscr on yellow strip (5.2.96) . . . .   12·00
Nos. KX7/a were initially sold at £2.50, which was increased to £2.60 from 8.7.96.

Type KX8

(Des M. Wolf)

1996 (26 Feb–11 Nov). *Greetings Stamps. Multicoloured cover as Type KX8 (96 × 60 mm). Containing booklet pane No. 1905a and pane of twenty special greetings labels in a block (5 × 4), both panes attached by a common gutter margin.*
KX8   "MORE! LOVE" design . . . .   10·00
      a. Containing pane No. 1905pa (11 Nov) . . . .   17·00
No. KX8 was initially sold at £2.50, which was increased to £2.60 from 8.7.96.
No. KX8a shows a redesigned inside front cover which omits references to 1996 dates.

Type KX9

(Des Tutssels)

1997 (6 Jan). *Greetings Stamps. 19th-century Flower Paintings. Multicoloured cover as Type KX9 (96 × 61 mm). Containing booklet pane No. 1955a and pane of twenty special greetings labels in a block (5 × 4), both panes attached by a common gutter margin.*
KX9   Gentiana acaulis design . . . .   10·00

No. KX9 was sold at £2.60. It was re-issued on 16 March 1999 with "Please note that the First Class rate is no longer valid to Europe" added to inside front cover.

1997 (3 Feb). *Greetings Stamps. 19th-century Flower Paintings. Multicoloured cover as Type* KX9 (96 × 61 mm) *but with box inscribed "WIN A BEAUTIFUL BOUQUET INSTANTLY?" printed in yellow on red over the flower on the front and with a scratch card on the inside back cover. Inscribed "Open now – See if you've won" on yellow tab at right. Containing booklet pane No. 1955a and pane of twenty special greetings labels in a block (5 × 4), both panes attached by a common gutter margin.*
KX10 *Gentiana acaulis* design .... 12·00
No. KX10 was sold at £2.60.

Type KX11

1998 (5 Jan). *Greetings Stamps. 19th-century Flower Paintings. Multicoloured cover as Type* KX11 (96 × 61 mm). *Inscribed "See reverse for special offer" on yellow tab at right. Containing booklet pane No. 1955a and pane of twenty special greetings labels in a block (5 × 4), both attached by a common gutter margin.*
KX11 Chocolate design .... 12·00
No. KX11 was sold at £2.60.

1998 (3 Aug). *Greetings Stamps. 19th-century Flower Paintings. Multicoloured cover as Type* GGA2 (88 × 61 mm) *printed by Walsall. Containing booklet pane No. 1955a and pane of twenty special greetings labels in a block (5 × 4), both attached by a common gutter margin.*
KX12 "Create a card" design .... 12·00
No. KX12 was sold at £2.60. This booklet was not placed on philatelic sale until 7 September 1998.

G. Barcode Booklets containing Christmas stamps with barcode on the back

Type LX1

(Des A. Davidson)

1990 (13 Nov). *Christmas. Multicoloured laminated cover as Type* LX1 (96 × 60 mm). *Containing booklet pane No. 1526a, attached by the selvedge.*
LX1 £3.40, Snowman design .... 11·00

1991 (12 Nov). *Multicoloured laminated cover as Type* LX1, *but* 95 × 70 mm. *Containing booklet pane No. 1582b attached by the selvedge.*
LX2 £3.60, Holly design .... 11·00

Type LX3

(Des Karen Murray)

1992 (10 Nov). *Multicoloured laminated cover as Type* LX3 (95 × 70 mm). *Containing booklet pane No. 1634a attached by the selvedge.*
LX3 £3.60, Santa Claus and Reindeer design .... 11·00

1993 (9 Nov). *Multicoloured laminated covers as Type* LX3, *but* 95 × 60 mm, *each showing Santa Claus and Reindeer. Panes attached by the selvedge.*
LX4 £2.50, containing ten 25p. stamps (No. 1791) .... 10·00
LX5 £3.80, containing twenty 19p. stamps (No. 1790) .... 12·00
No. LX4 was only available from Post Offices in the Central T.V. area and from philatelic outlets.

Type LX6

351

(Des Yvonne Gilbert)

1994 (1 Nov). *Multicoloured laminated covers as Type* LX6 *(95 × 60 mm), showing different Nativity Play props. Panes attached by selvedge.*
LX6 £2.50, containing ten 25p. stamps (No. 1844) .... 7·75
LX7 £3.80, containing twenty 19p. stamps (No. 1843) .... 11·00

Type LX8

(Des K. Lilly)

1995 (30 Oct). *Multicoloured laminated covers as Type* LX8 *(95 × 60 mm), showing Robins as depicted on the contents. Panes attached by selvedge.*
LX8 £2.40, containing four 60p. stamps (No. 1900) plus 4 air
      mail labels .... 7·50
LX9 £2.50, containing ten 25p. stamps (No. 1897) .... 7·50
LX10 £3.80, containing twenty 19p. stamps (No. 1896) .... 12·00

Type LX11

1996 (28 Oct). *Multicoloured laminated covers as Type* LX11 *(95 × 60 mm), showing scenes from the Nativity as depicted on the contents. Panes attached by selvedge.*
LX11 Containing ten 1st class stamps (No. 1951) .... 8·50
LX12 Containing twenty 2nd class stamps (No. 1950) .... 11·00
      No. LX11 was sold at £2.60 and No. LX12 at £4.

HAVE YOU READ THE NOTES AT THE
BEGINNING OF THIS CATALOGUE?
These often provide answers to the enquiries we receive.

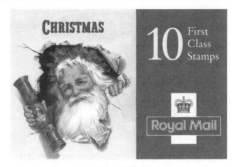

Type LX13

1997 (27 Oct). *Multicoloured laminated covers as Type* LX13 *(95 × 60 mm), showing Father Christmas and crackers as depicted on the contents. Panes attached by selvedge.*
LX13 Containing ten 1st class stamps (No. 2007) .... 8·75
LX14 Containing twenty 2nd class stamps (No. 2006) .... 12·00
      No. LX13 was sold at £2.60 and No. LX14 at £4.

Type LX15

1998 (2 Nov). *Multicoloured laminated covers as Type* LX15 *(95 × 60 mm), showing angels as depicted on the contents. Panes attached by selvedge.*
LX15 £2.60 booklet containing ten 26p. stamps (No. 2065) ... 7·75
LX16 £4 booklet containing twenty 20p. stamps (No. 2064) ... 12·00

Type LX17

1999 (2 Nov). *Multicoloured laminated covers as Type* LX17 (95 × 70 mm), *showing designs as depicted on the contents. Panes attached by selvedge.*
LX17 £2.60 booklet containing ten 26p. stamps (No. 2116) ... 8·50
LX18 £3.90 booklet containing twenty 19p. stamps (No. 2115) 12·00

Type LX19

2000 (7 Nov). *Multicoloured laminated covers as Type* LX19 (96 × 70 mm), *showing designs as depicted on the contents. Inscribed "Season's Greetings" on yellow tab at right. Panes attached by selvedge.*
LX19 £2.70, containing ten 1st class stamps (No. 2171) .... 8·50
LX20 £3.80, containing twenty 2nd class stamps (No. 2170) .. 11·50

2001 (6 Nov). *Self-adhesive booklet panes Nos. 2238a and 2239a, each with a multicoloured header label showing barcode and Royal Mail emblem and further label at foot with telephone numbers, folded to form booklets 119 × 81 mm.*
LX21 £3.24, booklet containing pane of twelve 1st class stamps
(No. 2239a) .... 9·00
LX22 £4.56, booklet containing pane of twenty-four 2nd class
stamps (No. 2238a) .... 13·50
Nos. LX21/2 show the surplus self-adhesive paper around each stamp retained.

2002 (5 Nov). *Self-adhesive booklet panes Nos. 2238a and 2239a, each with a multicoloured header label showing barcode and Royal Mail emblem and further label at foot with telephone numbers, folded to form booklets 105 × 72 mm.*
LX23 £3.24, booklet containing twelve 1st class stamps (No.
2322a) .... 8·00
LX24 £4.56, booklet containing twenty-four 2nd class stamps
(No. 2321a) .... 10·00
No. LX23 was sealed into a cellophane packet which also contained a Lord of the Rings game card.
Nos. LX23/4 show the surplus self-adhesive paper around each stamp retained.

2003 (4 Nov). *Self-adhesive booklet panes Nos. 2410a and 2411a, each with a multicoloured header label showing barcode and Royal Mail emblem and further label at foot with telephone numbers, folded to form booklets 106 × 71 mm.*
LX25 £3.36, booklet containing twelve 1st class stamps (No.
2411a) .... 5·00
LX26 £4.80, booklet containing twenty-four 2nd class stamps
(No. 2410a) .... 7·25
Nos. LX25/6 have the surplus self-adhesive paper around each stamp removed.

H. Self-adhesive Barcode Booklets containing No Value Indicated stamps.

NOTE. All booklets in this section show the surplus self-adhesive paper around each stamp retained, *unless otherwise stated.*

Type MA1

2001 (29 Jan). *Multicoloured laminated cover as Type MA1 (74 × 56 mm).*
Stamps printed on the cover in bright blue by Walsall.
MA1 Containing six 2nd Class self-adhesive stamps (No. 2039)   4·00
No. MA1 was sold at £1.14. It was re-issued on 1 August 2001 showing "Cod Post" added to the "Ffôn Testun" inscription on the back cover.

Panes of 6 1st Class stamps

2001 (29 Jan). *Multicoloured laminated cover as Type MA1 (74 × 56 mm).*
Stamps printed on the cover in bright orange-red by Walsall.
MB1 Containing six 1st Class self-adhesive stamps (No. 2040)   5·50
No. MB1 was sold at £1.62. It was re-issued on 1 August 2001 showing "Cod Post" added to the "Ffôn Testun" inscription on the back cover.

Type MB2

2001 (29 Jan). *Multicoloured laminated cover as Type MB2 (74 × 56 mm).*
Stamps printed on the cover in bright orange-red with portrait of Queen Victoria by Walsall.
MB2 Containing booklet pane No. 2040l (includes label commemorating death centenary of Queen Victoria)   7·50
No. MB2 was sold at £1.62.

Type MB3

2002 (5 June). *Gold laminated cover as Type MB3 (74 × 56 mm) by Questa.*
MB3 Containing six 1st Class self-adhesive stamps (No. 2295)   5·00
No. MB3 was sold at £1.62. It shows the surplus self-adhesive paper around each stamp removed and a single notch at the top right hand edge to facilitate identification by the blind.

2002 (5 June). *Gold laminated cover as Type MB3 (74 × 56 mm) by Walsall.*
MB4 Containing six 1st Class self-adhesive stamps (No. 2295)   5·00
No. MB4 was sold at £1.62. It shows the surplus self-adhesive paper around each stamp removed and a single notch at the top right hand edge to facilitate identification by the blind.

2002 (4 July). *Multicoloured laminated cover as Type MA1 (74 × 56 mm) with stamps printed on the cover in bright orange-red by Questa.*
MB5 Containing six 1st Class self-adhesive stamps (No. 2040)   5·00
No. MB5 was sold at £1.62.

Type MB6
("The Real Network" added below logo)

2003 (27 Mar). *Gold cover with multicoloured emblem as Type MB6 (74 × 56 mm) by Walsall.*
MB6 Containing six 1st Class self-adhesive stamps (No. 2295)   2·40
No. MB6 was initially sold at £1.62. It shows the surplus self-adhesive paper around each stamp removed and has a single notch at top right.

Panes of 10 2nd Class stamps

2001 (29 Jan). *Multicoloured laminated cover as Type MA1 (74 × 56 mm).*
Stamps printed on the cover in bright blue by Questa.
MC1 Containing ten 2nd Class self-adhesive stamps (No. 2039)   6·00
No. MC1 was sold at £1.90 and was intended for use in stamp machines.

Panes of 10 1st Class stamps

2001 (29 Jan). *Multicoloured laminated cover as Type MA1 (74 × 56 mm). Stamps printed on the cover in bright orange-red by Questa.*
MD1 Containing ten 1st Class self-adhesive stamps (No. 2040) 8·50
    No. MD1 was sold at £2.70 and was intended for use in stamp machines.

Panes of 12 2nd Class stamps

2001 (29 Jan). *Multicoloured laminated cover as Type MA1 (74 × 56 mm). Stamps printed on the cover in bright blue by Questa.*
ME1 Containing twelve 2nd Class self-adhesive stamps (No. 2039) . . . . 7·00
    No. ME1 was sold at £2.28. It was re-issued on 1 August 2001 showing "Cod Post" added to the "Ffôn Testun" inscription on the back cover.

Type ME2

2002 (4 July). *Multicoloured laminated cover as Type ME2 (74 × 57 mm) printed by Questa with the surplus self-adhesive paper around each stamp removed.*
ME2 Containing twelve 2nd Class self-adhesive stamps (No. 2039) . . . . 7·00
    No. ME2 was sold at £2.28. It shows the surplus self-adhesive paper around each stamp removed and two notches at the top right hand edge to facilitate identification by the blind.

Type ME3
("The Real Network" added below logo)

2003 (27 Mar). *Blue cover with multicoloured emblem as Type ME3 (74 × 57 mm) by Walsall.*
ME3 Containing twelve 2nd Class self-adhesive stamps (No. 2039) . . . . 3·50
    No. ME3 was initially sold for £2.28. It shows the surplus self-adhesive paper around each stamp removed and has two notches at top right.

Panes of 12 1st Class stamps

2001 (29 Jan). *Multicoloured laminated covers as Type MA1 (74 × 56 mm). Stamps printed on the covers in bright orange-red by Questa (No. MF1) or Walsall (No. MF2).*
MF1 Containing twelve 1st Class self-adhesive stamps (No. 2040) (Questa) . . . . 10·00
MF2 Containing twelve 1st Class self-adhesive stamps (No. 2040) (Walsall) . . . . 10·00
    Nos. MF1/2 were each sold at £3.24. They were re-issued on 1 August 2001 showing "Cod Post" added to the "Ffôn Testun" inscription on the back covers.

2002 (5 June). *Gold laminated cover as Type MB3 (74 × 56 mm) by Walsall.*
MF3 Containing twelve 1st Class self-adhesive stamps (No. 2295) . . . . 10·00
    No. MF3 was sold at £3.24. It shows the surplus self-adhesive paper around each stamp removed and a single notch at the top right hand edge to facilitate identification by the blind.

2003 (27 Mar). *Gold cover with multicoloured emblem as Type ME3 (74 × 57 mm) by Walsall.*
MF4 Containing twelve 1st Class self-adhesive stamps (No. 2295) . . . . 4·75
    No. MF4 was initially sold at £3.24. It shows the surplus self-adhesive paper around each stamp removed and has a single notch at top right.

Panes of 20 1st Class stamps

Type MG1

1993 (19 Oct). *Multicoloured cover as Type MG1 (91 × 77 mm).*
MG1 Containing booklet pane No. 1789a . . . . 18·00
    No. MG1 was initially sold at £4.80 which was increased to £5 from 1.11.93.

Panes of 6 E stamps

2002 (4 July). *Multicoloured laminated cover as Type ME2 (74 × 57 mm) printed by Walsall with the surplus self-adhesive paper around each stamp removed.*
MH1   Containing six E stamps (No. 2296) and six Air Mail labels   6·50
No. MH1 was sold at £2.22. It shows the surplus self-adhesive paper around each stamp removed.

2003 (28 May). *Multicoloured cover as Type MB6 (74 × 57 mm with "The Real Network" added below logo) printed by Walsall with the surplus self-adhesive paper around each stamp removed.*
MH2   Containing six E stamps (No. 2296) and six Air Mail labels   3·50
No. MH2 was sold at £2.28.

Panes of 4 Europe stamps

All booklets in this section show the surplus self-adhesive paper around each stamp removed.

Type MI1

2003 (27 Mar). *Red cover with multicoloured emblem as Type MI1 (74 × 57 mm) by Walsall.*
MI1   Containing four Europe self-adhesive stamps (No. 2358) and four Air Mail labels .... 3·00

Panes of 4 Worldwide stamps

All booklets in this section show the surplus self-adhesive paper around each stamp removed.

2003 (27 Mar). *Ultramarine cover with multicoloured emblem as Type MI1 (74 × 57 mm) by Walsall.*
MJ1   Containing four Worldwide self-adhesive stamps (No. 2359) and four Air Mail labels .... 6·75

I. Self-adhesive. Barcode Booklets containing stamps with face values.

NOTE. All booklets in this section show the surplus self-adhesive paper around each stamp removed.

£2.52 Booklet

2002 (4 July). *Multicoloured laminated cover as Type ME2 (74 × 57 mm) printed by Walsall with the surplus self-adhesive paper around each stamp removed.*
NA1   Containing six 42p. stamps (No. 2297) and six Air Mail labels .... 7·25

2003 (28 May). *Multicoloured cover as Type MB6 (74 × 57 mm with "The Real Network" added below logo) printed by Walsall.*
NA2   Containing six 42p. stamps (No. 2297) and six Air Mail labels .... 3·75

£4.08 Booklet

2002 (4 July). *Multicoloured laminated cover as Type ME2 (74 × 57 mm) printed by Walsall with the surplus self-adhesive paper around each stamp removed.*
NB1   Containing six 68p. stamps (No. 2298) and six Air Mail labels .... 11·00

2003 (28 May). *Multicoloured cover as Type MB6 (74 × 57 mm with "The Real Network" added below logo) printed by Walsall.*
NB2   Containing six 68p. stamps (No. 2298) and six Air Mail labels .... 6·00

J. Self-adhesive Barcode Booklets containing No Value Indicated Special or Occasions issues, with Definitive stamps.

NOTE. All booklets in this section show the surplus self-adhesive paper around each stamp retained, *unless otherwise stated.*

Type PM1

2001 (13 Feb). *Cats and Dogs. Multicoloured cover as Type* PM1 *(84 × 64 mm). Printed by Walsall.*
PM1 (£3.24) booklet containing pane of twelve 1st stamps
(No. 2187b) .... 15·00

Type PM2

2001 (17 Apr). *Centenary of Royal Navy Submarine Service. Multicoloured cover as Type* PM2 *(75 × 57 mm). Printed by Questa.*
PM2 (£1.62) booklet containing pane No. 2207a .... 75·00

2001 (4 Sept). *Punch and Judy Show Puppets. Multicoloured cover as Type* PM2 *(74 × 57 mm). Printed by Questa.*
PM3 (£1.62) booklet containing pane No. 2230a .... 16·00

2001 (22 Oct). *Flags and Ensigns. Multicoloured cover as Type* PM2 *(74 × 57 mm). Printed by Questa.*
PM4 (£1.62) booklet containing pane No. 2208a .... 17·00

2002 (2 May). *50th Anniv of Passenger Jet Aviation. Airliners. Multicoloured cover as Type* PM2 *(74 × 57 mm). Printed by Questa.*
PM5 (£1.62) booklet containing pane No. 2290a .... 3·50

2002 (21 May). *World Cup Football Championship, Japan and Korea. Multicoloured cover as Type* PM2 *(74 × 57 mm). Printed by Walsall.*
PM6 (£1.62) booklet containing pane No. 2293a .... 3·50

Type PM7

2002 (10 Sept). *Bridges of London. Gold cover with multicoloured emblem and stamp illustration as Type* PM7 *(74 × 57 mm). Printed by Questa.*
PM7 (£1.62) booklet containing pane No. 2314a .... 4·00
No. PM7 shows the surplus self-adhesive paper around each stamp removed and a single notch at the top right hand edge to facilitate identification by the blind.

2003 (4 Mar). *"Occasions" Greetings Stamps. Gold cover with multicoloured emblem and stamp illustration as Type* PM7 *(74 × 57 mm). Printed by Questa.*
PM8 (£1.62) booklet containing pane No. 2264ab .... 2·50
No. PM8 shows the surplus self-adhesive paper around each stamp removed and a single notch at the top right hand edge to facilitate identification by the blind.

PM9
("The Real Network" added below logo)

2003 (29 Apr). *Extreme Endeavours. Gold cover with multicoloured emblem and stamp illustration as Type* PM9 *(74 × 57 mm). Printed by De La Rue.*
PM9 (£1.62) booklet containing pane No. 2366a .... 2·40
No. PM9 shows the surplus self-adhesive paper around each stamp removed and has a single notch at top right.

2003 (15 July). *A British Journey: Scotland. Gold cover with multicoloured emblem and stamp illustration as Type* PM9 *(74 × 57 mm). Printed by De La Rue.*
PM10 (£1.68) booklet containing pane No. 2391a .... 2·50
No. PM10 shows the surplus self-adhesive paper around each stamp removed and has a single notch at top right.

2003 (18 Sept). *Classic Transport Toys. Gold cover with multicoloured emblem and stamp illustration as Type* PM7 *(74 × 57 mm). Printed by De La Rue.*
PM11 (£1.68) booklet containing pane No. 2403a .... 2·50
No. PM11 shows the surplus self-adhesive paper around each stamp removed and has a single notch at top right.

2004 (16 Mar). *A British Journey: Northern Ireland. Gold cover with multicoloured emblem and stamp illustration as Type* PM7 *(74 × 57 mm). Printed by De La Rue.*
PM12 (£1.68) booklet containing pane No. 2445a .... 2·50
No. PM12 shows the surplus self-adhesive paper around each stamp removed and has a single notch at top right.

POST OFFICE LABEL SHEETS

At the Stamp Show 2000 International Stamp Exhibition visitors could purchase sheets of 10 × 1st class stamps in the "Smiles" designs (as Nos. 1550/9), each stamp having a *se-tenant* label on which the exhibition visitor's picture was printed, the photographs being taken in a booth at the exhibition.

For those unable to visit the exhibition, the same sheet could be purchased from the Philatelic Bureau and from Post Office philatelic outlets with a "Stamp Show 2000" label in place of the photograph.

For Christmas 2000, sheets of 20 × 19p stamps in the "Robin in Pillar Box" design (as No. 1896) or 10 × 1st class "Father Christmas with Cracker" design (as No. 2007) were available through the Philatelic Bureau, with *se-tenant* labels as part of a "customised" service, purchasers supplying their own photographs for reproduction on the *se-tenant* label.

This service has continued under the name "Smilers", after the initial set of stamp designs employed, and was also made available at photo-booths at selected post offices. Corporate label panes, allowing commercial and charitable organisations to have their logo or message reproduced on the *se-tenant* labels were made available through the Bureau from 2000.

Label sheets have continued to be offered with a standard greeting or message. These "Generic Smilers" have been available from the Philatelic Bureau or from philatelic outlets.

As "personalised", "corporate" and "generic" label sheets could only be purchased at a premium over the face value of the stamps within them, they are not given full listing in this catalogue; neither are individual stamps (with or without their *se-tenant* label), some of which are identifiable as having come from Label Sheets, due to perforation, phosphor or printing differences.

The list which follows comprises the "generic" sheets only. Differences between the stamp in the Label Sheets and those of the standard issues are given under the respective listings in this catalogue.

Type LS1

2000 (22 May). *The Stamp Show 2000. Type* LS1. *Photo Questa. Original selling price £2.95.*
LS1 10 × (1st) "Smiles" stamps, as Nos. 1550/9 and attached labels. .... 50·00

Type LS2

Type LS3

2000 (3 Oct)–**2001**. *Christmas. Types* LS2 *and* LS3. *Photo Questa. Original selling price £3.99* (LS2/2a) *and £2.95* (LS3/a).
LS2 20 × 19p "Robin in Pillar Box" stamps, as No. 1896 and attached labels (Imprint "Post Office 2000") £190
   a. Imprint "Consignia 2001" (9.10.01) ....
LS3 10 × (1st) "Father Christmas with Cracker" stamps, as No. 2007 and attached labels (Imprint "Post Office 2000") . £190
   a. Imprint "Consignia 2001" (9.10.01) ....

Type LS4

2001 (5 June). *"Occasions". Type* LS4. *Litho Questa. Original selling price £5.95.*
LS4 20 × (1st) "Occasions" stamps as Nos. 2182/6 in four vertical columns of five with attached labels .... 85·00

2001 (3 July). *"Smiles". As Type* LS1 *but with greetings shown in attached labels. Litho Questa. Original selling price £2.95.*
LS5 10 × (1st) "Smiles" stamps, as Nos. 1550/9 and attached labels £125

Type LS6

2001 (18 Dec). *"Greetings Cartoons"*. Type LS6. *Litho Questa. Original selling price £2.95.*
LS6 10 × (1st) Greetings Cartoons, as Nos. 1905p/14p and attached labels .... 70·00

Type LS7

2002 (23 Apr). *"Occasions" Stamps*. Type LS7. *Litho Questa. Original selling price £5·95.*
LS7 20 × (1st) "Occasions" stamps as Nos. 2260/4 in four vertical columns of five with attached labels .... 40·00

Type LS8

2002 (21 May). *Football World Cup*. Type LS8. *Litho Questa. Original selling price £5·95.*
LS8 20 × (1st) as bottom right quarter of flag stamp in **MS**2292 and attached labels .... 35·00

Type LS9

2002 (1 Oct). *"Smiles"*. Type LS9. *Litho Questa. Original selling price £5.95.*
LS9 10 × (1st) "Teddy Bear" and 10 × (1st) Dennis the Menace, as Nos. 1550/1, each with attached labels .... 35·00

Type LS10

2002 (1 Oct). *Christmas*. Type LS10. *Litho Questa. Original selling price £5.95.*
LS10 20 × (1st) "Father Christmas with Cracker", as No. 2007, with attached greetings labels .... 35·00

Type LS11

2003 (21 Jan). *Flower Paintings*. Type LS11. *Litho Questa. Original selling price £5.95.*
LS11 20 × (1st) Flowers Greetings Stamps, as Nos. 1955/64 (two of each design) with floral labels attached .... 30·00

Type LS12

2003 (4 Feb). *"Occasions". Type LS12. Litho Questa. Original selling price* £5.95.
LS12 20 × (1st) "Tick box" Occasions stamps, as Nos. 2337/42
(four of Nos. 2338 and 2340 and 3 each of the others)
with attached labels .... 30·00

Type LS13

2003 (29 July). *Crossword Cartoons. Type LS13. Litho Questa. Original selling price* £6.15.
LS13 20 × (1st) Cartoons as Nos. 1905/14 with "Crossword"
labels attached .... 30·00

Type LS14

2003 (30 Sept). *Christmas. "Winter Robins". Type LS14. Litho De La Rue. Original selling price* £6.15.
LS14 20 × (1st) Winter Robins, self-adhesive, as No. 2239 with
labels alongside .... 30·00

Type LS15

Type LS16

2003 (4 Nov). *Christmas. Types LS15 and LS16. Litho De La Rue. Original selling prices* £4.20 (2nd) *and* £6.15 (1st).
LS15 20 × (2nd) Ice Sculptures, self-adhesive, as No. 2410 with
labels showing ice sculptures of polar fauna alongside 14·50
LS16 20 × (1st) Ice Sculptures, self-adhesive, as No. 2411 with
labels showing photographs of polar fauna alongside 30·00

2004 (30 Jan). *Hong Kong Stamp Expo. Litho Walsall. Original selling price* £6.15.
LS17 20 × (1st) "Hello" greetings stamps, as No. 2262 with
attached labels .... 14·50

Type LS18

2004 (3 Feb). *Occasions "Entertaining Envelopes". Type LS18. Litho De La Rue. Original selling price* £6·15.
LS18 20 × (1st) "Entertaining Envelopes" greetings stamps, as
Nos. 2424/8 (four of each design) with attached labels 14·50

COLLECT G.B. STAMPS

Priority order form
Four easy ways to order

Phone:
020 7836 8444

Fax:
020 7557 4499

Email:
stampsales@stanleygibbons.co.uk

Post:
Stamp Mail Order Department
Stanley Gibbons Ltd, 399 Strand
London, WC2R 0LX

Customer details

Account Number ....

Name..

Address ....

.... Postcode...

Country .... Email...

Tel no .... Fax no...

Payment details

Registered Postage & Packaging   £3.60

I enclose my cheque/postal order for £...................
in full payment. Please make cheques/postal orders
payable to Stanley Gibbons Ltd.

Please debit my credit card for £...................in full
payment. I have completed the Credit Card section
below.

Card Number:

☐ ☐ ☐ ☐ ☐ ☐ ☐ ☐ ☐ ☐ ☐ ☐ ☐ ☐ ☐ ☐

Start Date (Switch & Amex)   Expiry Date   Issue No (Switch)

☐ ☐ ☐   ☐ ☐ ☐ ☐   ☐ ☐

Signature .... Date ....

COLLECT G.B. STAMPS

Condition	Country	SG No.	Description	Price
			SUB TOTAL	£
			POSTAGE & PACKAGING	£3.60
			GRAND TOTAL	£

Please complete payment, name and address details overleaf